Developing Essbase Applications

Advanced Techniques for Finance and IT Professionals

Developing Essbase Applications

Advanced Techniques for Finance and IT Professionals

Edited by
Cameron Lackpour

With: Dave Anderson, Joe Aultman, John Booth, Gary Crisci, Natalie Delemar, Dave Farnsworth, Michael Nader, Dan Pressman, Robb Salzmann, Tim Tow, Jake Turrell, and Angela Wilcox

CRC Press
Taylor & Francis Group
Boca Raton London New York

CRC Press is an imprint of the
Taylor & Francis Group, an **informa** business
AN AUERBACH BOOK

CRC Press
Taylor & Francis Group
6000 Broken Sound Parkway NW, Suite 300
Boca Raton, FL 33487-2742

Printed in the United States of America on acid-free paper
Version Date: 20120306

International Standard Book Number: 978-1-4665-5330-9 (Hardback)

Library of Congress Cataloging-in-Publication Data

Developing Essbase applications : advanced techniques for finance and IT professionals / editor, Cameron Lackpour.
p. cm.
Includes bibliographical references and index.
ISBN 978-1-4665-5330-9
1. Database design--Computer programs. 2. Finance--Computer programs. 3. Essbase (Computer file) 4. Application software--Development. I. Lackpour, Cameron.

QA76.9.D26D495 2012
005.1--dc23 2012008169

Visit the Taylor & Francis Web site at
http://www.taylorandfrancis.com

and the CRC Press Web site at
http://www.crcpress.com

CONTENTS

FOREWORD

I must admit, when I was first asked to write the foreword for this book I was deeply honored. However, a glimpse at the list of authors quickly replaced most of the feeling of honor with intimidation, cold sweat, and involuntary shaking. Do not get me wrong, I have been working with multidimensional databases and technologies for 15 years now, doing everything from implementing solutions to innovating new products, but writing a foreword to an Essbase book by 12 hard-core Essbase professionals that are either acknowledged Essbase gurus or certified Oracle ACEs? I'm probably in over my head this time.

A promise is a promise, so with shaking hands I started reading the book (there was not much of an actual book at the time, just a collection of very large PDF files). To be honest, I own many technical books; I actually started reading most of them and even finished a couple. I always found people's ability to read a technical book cover to cover amazing. For me, I just get to the point that I have sufficient (false) confidence to start playing with the product and then Google the gaps as I go. So, the first thing I found intriguing was the Table of Contents. I can describe it in one of two ways, half empty (it is all over the place), or half full (it has everything in it). Whichever way you want to look at it, one thing should be very obvious—this is not a cover-to-cover book. Not that you cannot or should not read it cover-to-cover, just do not expect much of a flow. The book is not a step-by-step guide; each chapter is self-standing and focused on a different key area. The common thread between them is that it is all about being successful with Essbase. Unfortunately, for me, it meant there was no quitting in the middle because mastering Chapter 5 meant nothing to the content in Chapter 6.

And, then it hit me, having me write the foreword actually made perfect sense (at least for me). I am not here to put an expert stamp on it, I'm here as a reader. Albert Einstein once said, "Technological progress is like an axe in the hands of a pathological criminal," and software is no different. Learning facts, features, and tools cannot replace experience. This book will not teach you what Essbase is or how to create a sample database, instead it shares the experience of some of the most skilled Essbase professionals with a collective experience of about 150 years. The book is not necessarily about teaching the science of Essbase as much as it is about understanding the art of it. In many cases, the chapters address topics that can be the difference between a failed implementation and a successful one.

That brings me to the last topic, so why an Essbase book? Why now? In the years after the Oracle acquisition of Hyperion, the Essbase community had to wave off rumors about the end of Essbase or other doomsday predictions fueled by misinformation, translation of ancient Mayan scripts, and fear, uncertainty, and doubt (FUD). In 2010, with the introduction of Oracle Business Intelligence Foundation Suite, Oracle made a clear statement that Essbase is not only an EPM platform and standalone product, but it belongs in the hands of every Business Intelligence user. A year later, this message was cast in iron with the announcement of Exalytics. If you follow Oracle, you would know that there are not many things that are more strategic than the Exa line of servers and Fusion Apps—both which include Essbase. This broadened use of Essbase comes on top of it being the platform for many EPM applications and a successful standalone product of many years. It should be very obvious, in my opinion, that these are exciting days for the Essbase product and for the community because Essbase skills have never been more relevant.

I enjoyed reading this book; the interesting mix of authors and topics kept it fresh and interesting. While there are not many Essbase books out there, this one stands out as targeting those who are already familiar with Essbase. It is clearly not an introductory book, but a book for Essbase users. I can only hope you will find it useful and as valuable as I did.

Gabby Rubin
Senior Director, Oracle
Essbase Product Management

PREFACE

I initiated this project secure in the knowledge that a book, especially a group-authored book, would be easy to produce. The pitch I used to convince my co-authors to sign up for this project was: "You only have to write one chapter. It's like a white paper. How hard could it be?"

How hard indeed. That kind of confidence can only come from complete and utter cluelessness, a personality trait in which I seem to excel. Writing an advanced Essbase book was far, far harder than I anticipated. Setting the vision of the book, defining the content areas, and recruiting and herding the cats known as my esteemed co-authors has been exhausting and exhilarating. It also has been incredibly educational (I will spare you my moments of personal growth) both in managing a large group of writers and with Essbase itself.

When I first considered writing *Developing Essbase Applications: Advanced Techniques for Finance and IT Professionals,* I realized that my Essbase knowledge, which in my modest way I think of as at least adequate, simply would not do the subject justice. So, I contacted almost every talented name in the Essbase space I knew and through more salesmanship than I realized I had, managed to convince them to come together to produce what you are holding in your hands: A unique collection of truly advanced authors, topics, and real world experiences and not merely a rewriting of the documentation.

Essbase as a subject of study is broad; consequently, there are many writers with diverse voices. Think of this book as the proceedings of the most advanced and detailed Essbase conference there ever could be. Just as sessions at a technical conference necessarily differ in style and tone because of the difference in subject, audience, and presenter, so, too, you will find corresponding differences in the chapters.

Developing Essbase Applications: Advanced Techniques for Finance and IT Professionals is structured so that each chapter stands on its own. Of course, all of them relate to the same great subject—Essbase. This means that you can read this book from cover to cover or by individual chapter. I encourage you to read this entire book, even the bits you think you know. I will admit without shame that I learned a *lot* by reading, closely, every chapter during the review and editing process. A common refrain by all of the authors during the writing of this book was: "I thought I knew Essbase, and I didn't know that."

I hope reading this book makes you love Essbase more and better.

Cameron Lackpour
Philadelphia, Pennsylvania

DOWNLOADING THE CODE

Our publisher has generously made the code samples available on their Web site at http://www.developingessbasebook.com.

A QUICK NOTE

The World Wide Web is a fluid ecosystem and, as time passes, links referenced in this text will become outdated. Use your favorite search engine and/or contact the author(s) regarding the resource in question.

CONTACTING US

You can contact the authors at various conferences, the Essbase message boards, our blogs, and at authors@developingessbasebook.com.

ACKNOWLEDGMENTS

THE TEAM

As you may have gathered from the front cover, what you are holding in your hands is the output of many talented people who discussed, argued, reviewed, edited, and generally poked and prodded this book into what you now have in your hands. The whole is most definitely greater than sum of our individual parts. In strict alphabetical order, I would like to thank my fellow co-authors Dave Anderson, Joe Aultman, John Booth, Gary Crisci, Natalie Delemar, Dave Farnsworth, Michael Nader, Dan Pressman, Robb Salzmann, Tim Tow, and Angela Wilcox. Thanks also must be given to my co-editor, Jake Turrell. Our group weekly conference calls were fascinating, freewheeling, and educational—it was lightning in a bottle and I shall never forget them. Further thanks must go to Natalie Delemar, Dan Pressman, and Angie Wilcox who went above and beyond and pitched in during the editing process. To all of you: I knew before we started this book that I could never write this alone and having done it with you as my collaborators, I see how right I was. The fact that this book exists is a tremendous achievement in the face of the demands of our real jobs, family, and life in general. You should all be extremely proud of your accomplishment. I am obliged to you all.

THE GUILTY

Special notice must be made of Dave Farnsworth. Dave, in his understated way, was the one who planted the germ of this idea in my head. He, John Booth, and I put together the book proposal. I am happy and still somewhat astonished that this has all come off. Dave, it would never have started save for you.

TAYLOR & FRANCIS GROUP

John Wyzalek of Taylor & Francis Group believed in the concept of a truly advanced book about Essbase. Thanks, John. I will now go drive someone else insane with a never-ending series of questions.

Joselyn Banks-Kyle and Jay Margolis shepherded the book through its production in the face of our myriad examples of being completely unable to follow simple formatting instructions or even basic English grammar.

ORACLE

This book is one long love letter to Oracle Essbase. Lillian Buziak, Oracle ACE wrangler; Sheila Cepero, manager of the Oracle Publishers Program; and Steve Liebermensch, director of Business Intelligence, Enterprise Solutions Group, all helped make it possible.

ODTUG

I met over 70% of my co-authors through the Oracle Development Tools User Group. If a user group can ever be said to be responsible for a book, ODTUG is it.

PART OF, BUT APART

Beyond the normal support of our families, William Booth, Jennifer Crisci, Kathy Lessa, Kathy Pressman, Elaine Reidich, and Eric Tu all contributed to this book with their support and reasoned critiques.

The Great and Good John Goodwin helped both through answering myriad questions and through his always-excellent blog.

THE ONES THAT GOT AWAY

Both Tim German and Glenn Schwartzberg helped immeasurably with their reviews, edits, comments, and general brainstorming. Only my colossal lack of foresight prevented their participation as authors; the book is poorer for their absence.

MY PERSONAL SUPPORT

As editor-in-chief, I claim the space to thank my wife, Hatsz, and son, Jamie, the Wee Laird, for their forbearance with me while this project absolutely consumed my life. I would never have surfaced from the deep, deep dive into authorship that this book entailed without your patience, understanding, and love. Thanks mum and dad for letting your son go off on one of his even crazier than usual journeys without reeling me in.

WHAT IS THIS BOOK?

This book is the proceedings of the best technical Essbase (**E**xtended **S**pread **S**heet data**BASE**) conference there ever could be with unparalleled investigation and explanation of Essbase theory and good practices.

This book is a team of seasoned consultants who teach proven Essbase implementation practices through practical solutions that do more than show how, but explain why.

This book is a good value for the money—conferences and consultants cost a pretty penny, this book is cheap. Besides, try hiring all of us at the same time.

This book, *Developing Essbase Applications: Advanced Techniques for Finance and IT Professionals*, is all of the above and more—it is the greatest advanced Essbase book that has ever been written.

WHY SHOULD YOU BUY THIS BOOK?

Three properties of *Developing Essbase Applications: Advanced Techniques for Finance and IT Professionals* make this book unique: the deep experience of the contributing authors, real-world solutions, and an examples/theory structure.

This book is a group effort of some of the best and most experienced Essbase practitioners in the world. Crucial subjects like infrastructure, data sourcing and transformation, database design, calculations, automation, application programming interfaces (APIs), reporting, and actual project implementation skills are covered by people who specialize in the tools and techniques on a day-to-day basis. Readers get the benefit of authors with an average of 12 years of Essbase experience; some of the authors have been using Essbase for over 17 years. These deeply seasoned professionals communicate what they know today via blogs, conferences, white papers, Oracle forum posts, and book chapters.

The practical cases in this book stem from the authors' real-world experience. These examples deliver immediate value to the reader because they solve his problems.

Akin to a consultant brought on to solve a specific issue, the tutorials solve common Essbase implementation issues. However, a good Essbase consultant doesn't just build a system, he educates. A client with a strong theoretical understanding of what makes a successful Essbase system goes on to maintain the delivered system and build further successful systems. This book is that seasoned Essbase consultant's skill and knowledge transfer captured on paper.

INSIDE THE COVERS

This book covers every area of advanced Essbase practice there is:

- Essbase infrastructure
- Data quality
- Essbase Studio
- BSO (block storage option) in depth
- BSO to ASO (aggregate storage option) conversions
- Designing ASO for performance
- Practical MDX (multidimensional expressions)
- Essbase Java API
- Automating with Groovy
- Advanced Smart View
- Managing Essbase

WHY SHOULD YOU READ IT?

Essbase is a powerful and intuitive tool used to build highly useful analytical models, reporting systems, and forecasting applications. The ease of use and power of Essbase provide for a rapid development cycle. This highly productive environment does not eliminate the need for good design. Proper design results in an elegant solution with high data quality. Poor design results in one-off solutions and difficult to maintain applications with poor data quality.

We **love** Essbase and **hate** to see Essbase done wrong.

Developing Essbase Applications: Advanced Techniques for Finance and IT Professionals will cover both the **how** and the **why** of successful Essbase implementations. Readers will buy this book because it helps them with their immediate needs and because it gives them the theoretical knowledge to go on to the next level with Essbase.

CONTRIBUTORS

David Anderson (Chapter 11) is a Financial Systems Manager at Pinnacle Foods Group, LLC. From implementations to maintaining systems, he has worked directly and indirectly with Oracle Essbase at several industry-leading corporations since 2004. With his background in both finance and technology, he brings the customer's perspective to managing Essbase environments.

Joe Aultman (Chapter 9) has messed around with computers his entire life and is currently a Senior Application Engineer at AutoTrader.com in Atlanta, GA. His father, an electrical engineer, brought his toys home often (the ones that would fit in the car). The handheld calculator with the red numbers was a favorite. Aultman started his programming career on a TRS-80 from Radio Shack and enjoyed writing amusing BASIC programs on the Atari computers on display at Sears. The Commodore 64 his mother bought him still works.

Essbase boot camp was a revelation, partially because of the enthusiasm it excited in the instructor. Aultman was intrigued that a mere database application could be so inspiring. That was the year 2000. Now an Essbase professional, Aultman has seen that same excitement in the eyes and voices of many friends and associates. He considers himself lucky to do what he does. He can often be heard to say, even when not asked, "Essbase is the coolest tech there is."

John Booth (Chapter 1) is the Infrastructure Practice manager for the OBIEE and Hyperion technologies at Emerging Solutions. He is a contributor to the Oracle Technology Network and Network 54 Hyperion forums. Booth has over 20 years of experience with Information Technology. He specializes in infrastructure and these Oracle EPM products: Planning, Essbase, and Financial Data Quality Management.

Emerging Solutions (Chicago) is a professional services firm helping global and midmarket firms maximize the benefits of business applications by using leading edge technology.

Gary Crisci (Chapter 6) is a Business Intelligence professional with over 17 years of finance, accounting, and information systems experience. He has held various positions throughout his career in credit and cash management, financial planning and analysis, and as an EPM Solutions consultant. Currently Crisci is a vice president, Data Architect at a large commercial bank.

Crisci specializes in Oracle EPM/BI product solutions, with advanced expertise in Oracle Essbase. He was certified in Essbase in 2004, and in 2008 was granted an Oracle ACE Award. In 2010, while serving as president of the Oracle Developer Tools User Group–Hyperion Special Interest Group, he and his fellow board members were awarded the 2010 Oracle Development Tools User Group (ODTUG) Volunteer Award.

Crisci has been a frequent contributor to Oracle/Hyperion online communities like the Oracle Technology Network and Network54 Essbase forum. He believes in being an ambassador of information sharing and frequently speaks in public forums regarding Oracle technology, including the annual ODTUG Kaleidoscope conference. Crisci lives in New Fairfield, Connecticut, and is presently working toward his MBA at Iona College/Hagan School of Business.

Natalie Delemar (Chapter 11) is a manager/consultant with Ernst & Young in Atlanta and has worked with Essbase since 1999. Prior to becoming a consultant in 2010, she held various roles including Essbase developer, Hyperion administrator, and Hyperion systems manager in a number of industries. In addition to her beloved Essbase, she also specializes in the development of Hyperion Planning applications. She is very active in the EPM/BI user community and has served as the EPM/BI content chair of the Kaleidoscope conference for the past two years.

Dave Farnsworth (Chapter 4) is vice president of Solutions Experts, Inc., a systems integrator and software development company specializing in Oracle Essbase and Planning. Trained as a COBOL programmer, he was introduced to Essbase in 1994. He brings many years of experience creating financial, budgeting, accounting, and reporting analysis for corporate users.

Cameron Lackpour (Chapter 2 and editor) is president and chief bottle washer of CL Solve, an Oracle EPM consulting company. He first worked with OLAP technology in the dinosaur days of mainframe multidimensional databases and saw the Essbase light in 1993. He has been in the consulting business since 1996, creating solutions for customers using Essbase, Planning, and anything else that ties to those two products. Lackpour is active on OTN's and Network54's Essbase message boards, the ODTUG Hyperion Special Interest Group, the ODTUG Board of Directors, and his Essbase Hackers blog—sharing knowledge makes his day interesting. An Oracle ACE since 2011, Lackpour thought that writing this book would be "fun." He hopes you enjoy it.

Mike Nader (Chapter 3) has more than 13 years advisory and operational experience in the areas of Enterprise Performance Management and BI (EPM/BI). He has substantial technical and business experience in the areas of data modeling, governance, and OLAP design. Nader started as a curriculum developer (writing course manuals) and technical instructor with Hyperion Solutions in the late 1990s. Since then, he has moved through a series of roles in the EPM/BI space including:

- Manager Essbase Curriculum Team (Hyperion Solutions)
- Principal product manager for Essbase and Smart View (Hyperion Solutions and Oracle Development)

- Global Domain Lead for Essbase and Analytics (Oracle)
- Senior manager Ernst & Young–Advisory Services

Nader was also a lead author of the book *Oracle Essbase & Oracle OLAP: The Guide to Oracle's Multidimensional Solution* (Oracle Press, 2009).

Dan Pressman (Chapter 7) is president of nTuple, LLC, a development company specializing in Oracle EPM, Essbase, and Planning. His experience encompasses the full suite of EPM products, and he is an expert at cube/database tuning and the development of large, complex systems, particularly ASO.

Pressman has a BS in EE/computer science and an MBA in finance from Columbia University. He learned programming first in FORTRAN and Assembler on the IBM 360, and mastered many other languages including his all-time favorite, SNOBOL. He has worked in many industries, eventually becoming a director of Financial Planning and Analysis. After being introduced to Essbase in 1993, he found it to be an ideal vehicle for his combination of technical and financial training and experience. His work has been focused on Essbase and Oracle EPM in the almost 18 years since that introduction.

Robb Salzmann (Chapter 10) has over 20 years of software development and consulting leadership experience; the past 13 years focused specifically on Oracle Hyperion EPM. Currently, he is the Essbase Domain lead at Accelatis, LLC (Wilton, Connecticut). Accelatis produces Ascension Suite, a software product that provides infrastructure management, fault remediation, system optimization, and automation of EPM Systems.

Salzmann also heads an EPM consulting group, ePerformance Path. EPP's work is concentrated in the area of Oracle Hyperion Enterprise Performance Management implementations with an additional focus on software development. It provides EPM solution providers and businesses with creative, flexible solutions through design leadership and EPM product-based solutions by leveraging various technologies and product APIs.

He actively contributes to the EPM community by volunteering with ODTUG, participating as a subject matter expert in forums and on OTN, and provides a regularly updated blog that focuses on EPM technology.

Tim Tow (Chapter 8) is the founder and president of Applied OLAP and the visionary for the Dodeca user interface. He has been an Essbase developer for over 15 years and his frequent contributions to the Essbase community earned him the honor of being the first ever Oracle ACE director in the Hyperion world. Tow has presented dozens of sessions at Microsoft TechEd, Arbor Dimensions, Hyperion Solutions, and ODTUG Kaleidoscope conferences.

Jake Turrell (co-editor) is a senior solution architect and project manager with over 18 years experience specializing in the implementation of Hyperion Planning, Essbase, and related technologies. His technology career began in the early 1990s as a Financial Systems intern at Dell in Austin, Texas, administering IMRS Micro Control (the DOS-based predecessor to Hyperion Enterprise). After working at Dell, Turrell joined Ernst & Young's Management Consulting practice where he worked with a variety of technologies before returning to the Hyperion world and joining a boutique Hyperion partner consulting firm in Dallas, Texas.

Turrell has spent the past 14 years implementing Essbase and Hyperion Planning solutions for a variety of clients ranging from large, international financial institutions to midmarket biotech firms. Certified in both Hyperion Planning and Essbase, he holds a BBA from the University of Texas at Austin. In 2010, he was awarded the ODTUG Kaleidoscope Best First Time Speaker Award for his presentation on "Introduction to Custom JavaScript within Hyperion Planning."

Angela Wilcox (Chapter 5) is currently employed as a BI architect at MedAssets. Prior to JCPenney (retail), she worked for The Principal (insurance), and Brintech (banking). Previous to those positions, she was a career consultant working for AWilcox Consulting, Canutes Consulting, Beacon Consulting, and ShowCase Corporation.

Wilcox has had an active role in the ODTUG community acting as the president of the Hyperion SIG (2010–2011) and secretary (2009–2010). She has presented at many technical conferences in the past 10 years. Loving education and knowledge sharing, and committed to ongoing mentoring, Wilcox is very active on the Network 54 and OTN Essbase message boards.

1

BUILDING THE FOUNDATION: ESSBASE INFRASTRUCTURE

John Booth

CONTENTS

1.1 INTRODUCTION

Essbase is a dynamic product that has evolved and expanded continuously since its initial release by Arbor Software in 1992. Oracle's ownership, starting in 2007, has accelerated its development and growth. One side effect of this evolution is that the deployment of Essbase has gradually become more complex. In Essbase's infancy, a finance user could install Essbase from a few floppy disks in a matter of minutes onto a server under his desk. Today an Essbase installation can take half a day to a week. What has changed? A whole lot of speed, scalability, and, most especially, functionality have been added to the core Essbase goodness and that has meant relational databases, Java application servers, and Web server complexity. Essbase now lives in corporate datacenters with 24/7 uptimes for a global user community. No longer a departmental point solution, Essbase is now an enterprise level tool with a concomitant enterprise level of infrastructure requirements.

A recent major change is a hardware appliance featuring Essbase called Exalytics, which Oracle announced at OpenWorld 2011 in San Francisco. The product is so new there is little hands-on experience. Exalytics is an integrated software and hardware platform featuring in-memory Business Intelligence Foundation Suite (of which Essbase is one component). The product brief reads like a piece of dream hardware for any infrastructure geek. A side benefit is that an appliance like this is as close to "plug it in and go" as you can get. It is built such that it can deal with extremely rich data sets and/or thousands of users. Due to the anticipated price, only large corporations have deep enough pockets to purchase the equipment. As time goes on, perhaps they will turn this into a scalable (lowering entry cost) solution rather than the one size fits all appliance it is today.

1.1.1 Who Should Read This Chapter?

This chapter is aimed at anyone who cares what goes on "under the hood." This chapter gives a broad overview of then infrastructure secrets I've learned over the span of two decades.

1.1.2 What Will Not Be Covered

This chapter is not intended to be a replacement for Oracle installation guides and product information. In my 20 years of experience with the information technology industry, I believe Oracle as a vendor has some of the most robust documentation of any software vendor and I encourage you to read these documents very closely.

Additionally, these specific topics are outside of the scope of this chapter:

- IBM's AS/400 and OS/390 Essbase (which are now obsolete)
- Exalytics (very new and minimal need for infrastructure expertise)

- Operating system installation
- Hardware installation
- Essbase clustering

1.1.3 What Will Be Covered

- Skills
- Hardware/software tips and tricks
- Essbase architecture and sizing
- System maintenance
- Troubleshooting
- Deployment considerations

1.2 INFRASTRUCTURE SKILL SETS

When thinking about an Oracle EPM (Enterprise Performance Management) implementation, I break skill sets up into two major areas:

1. Functional
2. Infrastructure

A functional person handles everything from collection of requirements to writing calculations. Every *other* chapter in this book deals with a functional developer's interaction with Essbase.

This chapter is different, just like infrastructure resources (we are somewhat "different" but nice, honest). An infrastructure resource handles everything from racking a server through installing the base software. The skill sets are different enough that it is rare to find an individual who excels at both. Figure 1.1 is an overview of the different areas an infrastructure person must cover.

1.2.1 Typical Infrastructure Organization

A good Oracle EPM infrastructure person must be able to navigate the maze of corporate information technology (IT). These organizations run the gamut from a single IT person at a $25 million company to a $50 billion company having an IT organization containing thousands of people.

Typical departments within a very large organization are broken out into major categories including:

- Windows®
- Unix™
- Middleware/Web
- Storage
- Database
- Network/Firewall/Load Balancing

The Hyperion infrastructure role may be a separate role or bundled into one of the above areas (usually not Storage or Network). There are formal processes to engage the proper resources from each team as well as formal change processes to approve the work to be performed. Understanding both the processes and delivery timelines for

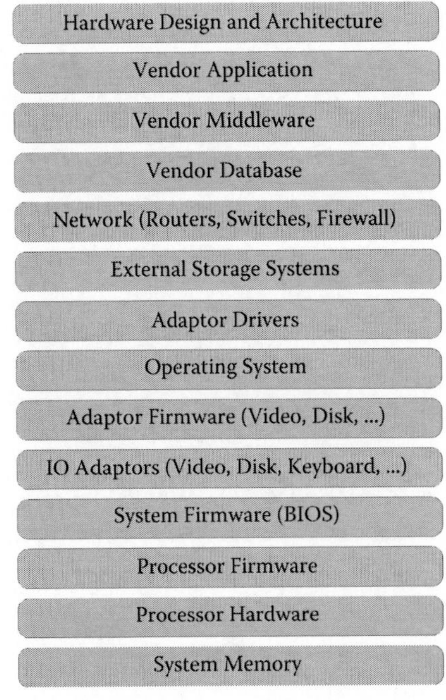

Figure 1.1 Role view.

these roles and tasks will ensure everyone is tracking to a common schedule and set of expectations.

1.3 FOUNDATIONAL HARDWARE AND SOFTWARE TIPS AND TRICKS

The scope of hardware and software to support a production IT system can be mind-boggling. This section describes hardware and software and conveys the practices and knowledge you need to master to be successful in the infrastructure field.

1.3.1 Hardware Tips and Tricks

See Table 1.1.

1.3.2 Software Tips and Tricks

See Table 1.2.

1.3.3 Deployment Considerations

When choosing your operating system and database for the Hyperion stack, I recommend using whatever your IT teams know. In my experience, the majority of Hyperion installations are hosted on Windows Server and Microsoft SQL Server. When scaling to the high hundreds or over 1000 users, most customers tend to use a flavor of Unix; modern Microsoft® server operating systems also scale well, so choice of one or the other is more a preference than a requirement when scaling.

Table 1.1 Hardware

Category	Note
Firmware	• Most modern hardware is a mixture of hardware and software. That software is called firmware or microcode. You will find firmware in everything from processors to host bus adaptors to network switches. Firmware defects can cause very interesting issues, which are more likely to manifest in newly released products. Your infrastructure teams should ensure the firmware is up to date in the systems they support and patch the hardware as necessary before installation and on an on-going basis.
Server Hardware	• Having a basic understanding of server hardware will help you speak intelligently to the teams that support the server infrastructure and hopefully speed resolution time for hardware issues. • The Windows Blue Screen of Death or a Unix Kernel Panic can usually be traced to faulty components, such as memory, internal hard disk, or poorly written device drivers (video and printers in the case of Windows operating systems). • Experience handling hardware components using the proper techniques, such as use of an antistatic wrist strap is critical. Static damage to components can occur very easily when the incorrect procedures are used to install memory, hard disks, video cards, or even replacement motherboards. Damaged components may not immediately cause issues and/or cause intermittent, hard to diagnose issues.
Storage Subsystems: • Internal • Direct Attached • Network Attached • Storage Area Network	• The most common issue with storage systems is performance-related. You should be able to run benchmarking on the storage systems and discuss times of high utilization and ask probing questions about the storage architecture. • Troubleshooting tools include: IOZone (All), iostat (Unix), ATTO's Diskbenchmark (Windows), and Perfmon (Windows).
Network • Load Balancers • Firewall • Routers • Switches	• Firewall issues are generally encountered during the installation phase. Avoid basic architecture issues caused by your Hyperion relational server being distant (> 10 miles) from your other Hyperion application servers for a given environment. • Troubleshooting tools include: Telnet, Ping, and Wireshark.

Linux on Intel® hardware is becoming more and more accepted in corporate IT organizations.

Based on surveys on my blog and data, I have gathered over the past four years the percentage basis of Hyperion installations is depicted in Table 1.3

1.3.4 Number of Environments

A good practice is to maintain at least two separate environments: Development and Production. A Fortune 500 Essbase implementation almost always has at least three environments: Development, Quality, and Production. Why do we have multiple environments? Multiple environments support proper management of an

Table 1.2 Software

Category	Note
Operating Systems: • Windows • Unix	• An infrastructure person worth his salt should be conversant with the command lines of both Windows and Unix and application of operating system patches. • Know how to access Windows event logs and Unix system logs and make sure you have access to them.
Device Drivers	• Device drivers are the glue between an Operating System (OS) and internal server hardware, such as video cards, host bus adaptors, and printers. Ensure these adaptors are up to date as defective drivers can cause performance and/or stability issues.
Virtual Machines (VMs): • VMware ESX • Microsoft Hyper-V • Oracle VM Server	• Be aware of issues like overcommitted resources and fully formatted disks. Administrators of virtual machines have a tendency to grant less than the requested resources as well as run a great deal more virtual servers than are efficient for Essbase. Many virtualization technologies support a thin disk provisioning that formats the disk on the fly. Formatting the disk on the fly will result in very poor server performance; always ensure the disk allocated to the Essbase virtual machines is fully formatted.
Java Application Servers: • Apache Tomcat (Obsolete) • Oracle WebLogic • IBM WebSphere	• A Java application server is a middleware component in which key portions of the Oracle delivered Hyperion applications execute. In current and future releases the typical installation automatically deploys the Java application server. In more complex deployments there are manual steps that can complicate the installation. In larger organizations these are often administered by different groups in an organization than the OS or database. Make sure you get everyone on the same page before implementation begins.
Web Servers: • Microsoft IIS • Oracle HTTP Server/ Apache HTTP Server	• Know how to troubleshoot basic Web server issues, use of secure socket layer certificates, and location of and access to log files.
Relational Databases: • Oracle DB • Microsoft SQL Server • IBM DB2	• Use of basic SQL commands and the willingness to dive in to the Oracle delivered tables (especially Shared Services in later versions) is important. Know what you can change directly in the database safely and what to avoid. • Oracle has documented many of the Hyperion relational schemas in their Enterprise Performance Management Web resources.

Table 1.3 Operating Systems and Database Demographics

Operating System	Windows Server	80%
	Unix (Linux, Solaris, HPUX, AIX)	20%
Database Software	Microsoft SQL Server	55%
	Oracle DB	40%
	IBM DB2	5%

application. This management includes the vital processes of development, testing, and patching.

Why is testing critical? Essbase is a very powerful tool and, as such, testing calculations and outline changes are critical. As an example, if you create a Calc Script and do not focus (FIX) on a specific dataset, it refers to all data in the cube.

Imagine the Essbase Calc Script below:

```
Sales = 0;
```

If there were no FIX statements around this code or if certain members were omitted, Essbase will affect a much larger dataset than intended. This kind of potential disaster (users who have seen all of their precious numbers turn to zero tend not to accept: "We're too poor for multiple environments," as an excuse) means that it is critical to both perform proper testing and also have good backups.

1.3.5 Which Essbase Release?

A question I often hear is: "What version should I choose?" The underlying question is: Will my system be stable? I will make a blanket statement: Every nontrivial software program contains defects. You may treat nontrivial as anything containing greater than 1000 lines of code.

Typical code bases for commercial software have hundreds of thousands of lines of code and can run into the millions of lines of code. There is intensive effort in software quality assurance in order to reduce, locate, categorize, and resolve defects. When releasing software, vendors weigh the severity of known defects to their potential impact. If there are no "show stopper" defects and the product passes their quality tests within acceptable parameters, it will go to a generally available status. In the case of the Oracle Hyperion suite of products, the known defects are communicated to end users in the product README documentation.

At the time of this writing there are two main supported Essbase code lines: 11.1.1.4 and 11.1.2.1; both versions are "dot" releases from the 11.1.1 and 11.1.2 major versions.

Since both releases have been on the market for over three months, either are very good selections. Given an equal level of maturity, I will always choose the higher release version due to its longevity, additional features, and better architecture (Table 1.4).

1.3.6 When an Upgrade Is Not an Upgrade

When selecting the target hardware, you must think about it in terms relative to the older hardware. The expectation of an upgrade is that the system will work better than before. Better usually means faster, more features, and more reliable. A client decides to "upgrade" his system and selects an existing virtualized platform to migrate from a physical server. If the old physical server is faster in terms of clock speed than the clock speed of the physical server the virtualized host resides on, you will see a net decrease in performance and a net increase in unhappy users.

1.3.7 Core Essbase Processes

This section describes the major processes for any Essbase environment. It is not a replacement for formal Oracle documentation nor an attempt to be exhaustive (Table 1.5).

Table 1.4 Release Recommendations

Installation Type	Recommendation
Patch	Individual patch applications usually take less than an hour and the system can be tested in less than a day. Only apply patches that have been released for longer than one month. Always apply patches to your nonproduction environment and allow it to burn in for two weeks.
New install	Select the most recent version when you are implementing Essbase for the first time and your timeline is greater than three months. This will provide the best feature set, support the most recent client software, support the most recent server software, and provide more longevity over older releases.
Service pack	A service pack is a mini in-place upgrade. Wait at least one month before applying a service pack. Perform full regression testing in your nonproduction environment and attain formal sign-off to install in production.
Major upgrade (migration)	Select the most recent version that has over three months of release time. Major upgrades can run from a few weeks for a very small user base with a minimal number of applications to several months for a large global user base with hundreds of applications. A few upgrade good practices: • Enact a change freeze • Do not upgrade in-place; use new environments • Perform full regression test using a POC environment

1.4 ESSBASE ARCHITECTURE AND SIZING

The basic architecture for modern Essbase consists of a Web server, application server, and relational database server (Figure 1.2). When scaling the system up, place print services on dedicated servers, continue to locate Web and Java services on like servers, and continue to keep application servers on dedicated servers.

The logical view in Figure 1.3 shows Essbase's software dependencies. For instance, if either Essbase or the supporting relational database is down, most components in the system will not function. If Reporting and Analysis framework malfunctioned, then Financial Reporting would be impacted; however, Essbase access via Smart View would be unaffected.

1.4.1 A Few essbase.cfg File Settings

Review the Essbase Technical Reference for in-depth descriptions of the essbase.cfg settings below.

Essbase is, in general, a multithreaded application. You will see single-thread behavior with cube restructures and management of the Essbase security file. The single-threaded behavior (at least through version 11.1.2) for management of the security file will cause new logins to the ESSBASE process to queue until the current action affecting the security files is completed. Some other actions that can cause the queuing behavior include: creation of filters (noticeably seen in Planning Filter refresh), copy of application, and copy of database. Cube restructures do not cause the queuing behavior, but are notable as you will note only one processor is used during a restructure operation.

Each thread will take up a certain amount of memory on a given operating system. For instance, one thread on Windows uses one megabyte. This means if you have the

Table 1.5 Ports and Their Use

Major Version	Process	Default Port	Notes
ALL	ESSBASE	1423	• Port must be opened on firewall in order for Essbase add-in to connect.
ALL	ESSSVR	32768–33768	• One process for each application. Databases within applications all share the same application process memory space. • Port must be opened on firewall in order for Essbase add-in to connect. • Two consecutive ports will be used for each application. You may change the default starting and ending ports with the essbase.cfg SERVERPORTBEGIN and SERVERPORTEND parameters.
6+	olapisrv	3388	• Essbase Integration Services is commonly used to build cubes from star schemas and/or provide drill-back to relational tables.
11.1+	startServer	5300, 9080	• Beginning in 11.1.2 EPMA deployments of cubes make use of Studio. 11.1.2.0 Studio used Sun JVM, 11.1.2.1 Studio begins using JROCKIT.
9.2–11.1.1	openldap	58089 (9.X) 28089 (11.X)	• Open LDAP databases can become corrupt if machine is not shutdown properly or the process is terminated. Recovery procedures are documented in Oracle EPM guides. Corruption will prevent Shared Services from starting.
11.1.2+	opmn	6711, 6712	• Starting in 11.1.2 Oracle Process Manager monitors and starts Essbase • Review the file console~Essbase1~EssbaseAgent~AGENT~1.log in cases where Essbase will not start. • This log file resides at: <EPMSYSTEM>/diagnostics/logs/OPMN/opmn

SERVERTHREADS setting list below, 60 Mb of memory will be used for threads on each ESSSVR process.

I treat the below configuration file (essbase.cfg) values as starting points. SERVERTRHEADS should be the only value you need to increase on very large busy applications.

```
; Number of threads each ESSSVR process is allocated.
SERVERTHREADS  100
; Number of threads ESSBASE is allocated
AGENTTHREADS  25
; Number of login requests - this value should never be above 10
AGTSVRCONNECTIONS  10
```

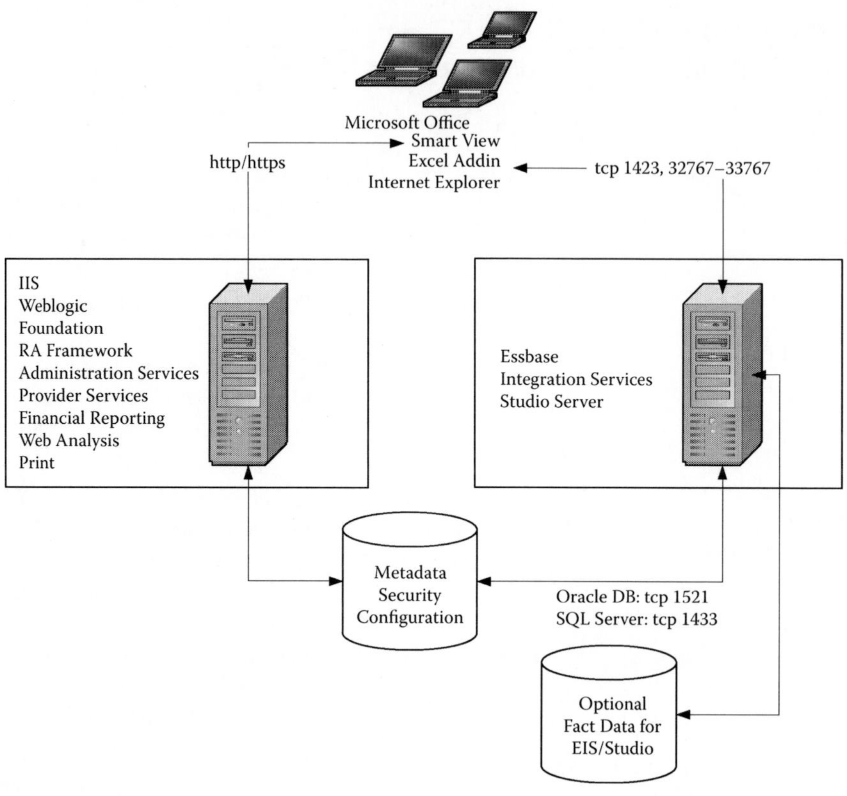

Figure 1.2 Essbase architecture: Physical view.

Note: If you have sufficient processor cores and you wish to optimize data load or data export then review the options: DLSINGLETHREADPERSTAGE, DLTHREADSPREPARE, DLTHREADWRITE, and EXPORTTHREADS.

1.4.2 Sizing

Undersized systems in any environment, be it development, test, or production, have ramifications both on project finances and project schedule. The tendency of IT administrators to undersize development where the bulk of all new work occurs is a very poor trade-off. IT believes they are saving money (on servers). Finance or operations spends money (a lot more than IT saved) on consultants and employees who are waiting on the slower, but less expensive, hardware.

I have seen Essbase installations that range from tens of users through thousands and a handful of applications through hundreds. When you mix and match the number of users with the number of applications and then add the third dimension of reporting versus planning it can make sizing the system daunting.

The hardware is usually installed before the implementation consultants have even started the design. This means the hardware sizing must account for a level of flexibility whether through over-sizing physical servers or through use of virtual servers that can have their resourcing changed relatively easily.

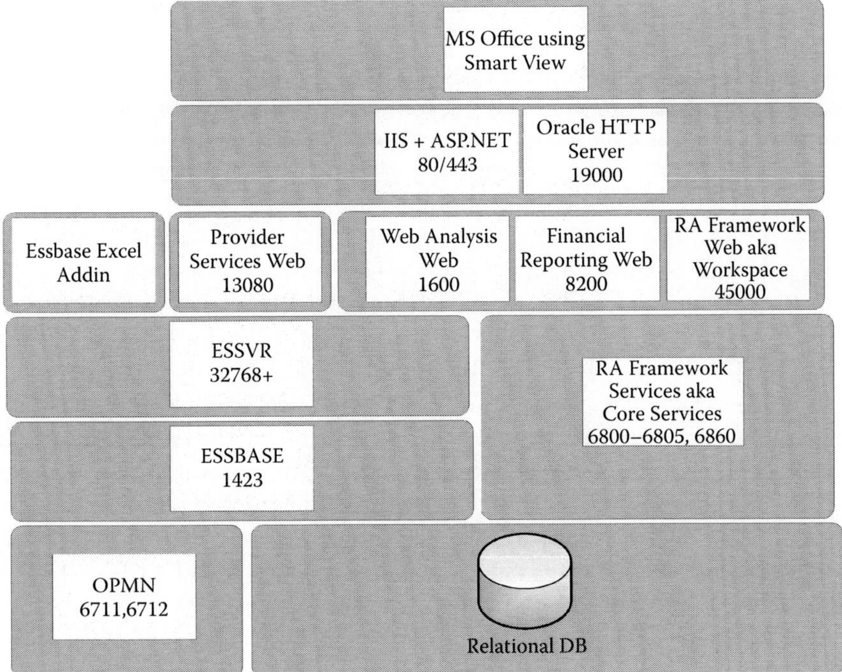

Figure 1.3 Essbase architecture: Logical view.

An environment with plenty of hardware resources does not guarantee excellent performance. Yes, hardware is the foundation and the main component, but there is also a very important factor and that is application design.

Developers should not underestimate the importance of a good application design. A poorly designed application along with poorly designed calculations can cause a bottleneck in the application. When this situation arises, you may hear comments from your IT resources like: "Server utilization is less than 30%," "I don't know, everything looks good from my end," etc. This is something that is out of the hands of an infrastructure resource that tends to have little knowledge of how Essbase works. Spending a good amount of time in design sessions will help avoid situations like this. Providing your development team with access to the nonproduction Essbase server also will help them tune the system properly. Engage performance testing and infrastructure resources in tuning activities to ensure the hardware is fully utilized. In regard to Oracle's assumptions on their sizing, these evolve over time. For instance, the Web server requirements have grown steadily over time. A recently released standard deployment guide simplifies sizing and recommends four physical cores on every machine, 32 Gb on the Foundation Server and 16 Gb on all other servers. While this is an approach that works, it is a one size fits all approach.

You will find more specialized sizing guidelines placed at the end of this section. I suggest you continue reading this section to understand the drivers of load and what rationale went into the sizing guidelines.

Essbase is Memory, CPU (central processing unit), and Input/Output (I/O) intensive—all these needs grow to some extent as you add concurrent users and more applications.

Reporting applications usually have more concurrent retrieve/query operations that cause higher I/O and to a lesser extent CPU usage.

Planning applications have more concurrent calculation operations driving high CPU and I/O; one of the Oracle tuning guides states they have benchmarked a planning system with 2000 users to work with 8 cores (this had to be a very simple planning system), in reality, planning systems tend to be driven by the finance or operations organizations and tend toward being more complex.

The following sections show general sizing rules. In specific instances, these will not meet either performance goals or scaling goals; generally the more resources you throw at the hardware the better performance you can expect. That being said, hardware is not a replacement for proper design and application tuning. Once the hardware is up and going, you then need to count on the functional team to tune the specific application settings to fit the server size. As an example, if you have limited server memory, you may decide to make the caches smaller than would be optimal. Overly large caches also will not provide any additional benefit and can stress the system resources as well. For instance, consider a small server having 2 Gb of free memory where a developer added an additional 2 Gb of data cache to a block storage option (BSO) cube. This type of action could tip the server over the edge and begin constantly using the disk for virtual memory, which is a very bad situation.

1.4.3 Essbase and CPU Cores

Intel is constantly increasing the core count of its processors. When I started out with servers in the 1990s, a server meant one CPU and the server's main jobs were to provide shared file storage and print services, such as NetWare and early Windows Server platforms. Application tasks were relegated to the desktops, minicomputers, and mainframes. As commodity servers became more and more complex, they began being used for tasks more complex than file and print services.

Essbase calculations are bound by processor speed, number of cores, or maximum disk throughput. When money is not an object, you want the fastest clock-speed CPU with the most number of cores to provide the highest performance. When using Intel-compatible CPUs, I recommend at least a 3-GHz clock-speed.

The rule of thumb for number of physical cores for Essbase is 1 core per every 30 users; start out with 4 cores. Try to limit maximum licensed users to 1000 per server and maximum concurrent users to 250.

1.4.4 Web/Java Server CPUs

When focusing only on Essbase, the Java application servers are mainly used for Provider Services, Financial Reporting, and Web Analysis. A routine configuration step is tuning the maximum heap size for the Java Virtual Machine (JVM). Allocate at least one four core server per every 250 users. For very large-scale configurations, double the core count and memory rather than doubling server count.

1.4.5 Memory

Memory is cheaper than ever before; in 1995, I had a machine using FreeBSD Unix on the Internet as a shared server and "invested" nearly $900 in 24 Mb of RAM. In 2011, I purchased 24 Gb of ram for $1000. Over 15 years later, I purchased 1000 times the RAM for less money when accounting for inflation. Skimping on memory can and will affect your application's performance. When a server runs out of memory, it begins using virtual memory, such as the Windows page file or the Unix swap file, which are stored on hard disk drives. Memory speed is measured in nanoseconds and disk speed is measured in milliseconds—virtual memory is a thousand times slower than RAM.

Essbase server memory rule of thumb: 1 Gb per BSO application puts you in a safe zone; you will note the sizing table is more conservative at 1.5 GB per application. For aggregate storage option (ASO) applications, use 2 Gb per application as the rule of thumb. Note that once the RAM is allocated to an active application, Essbase does not release it back to the OS until that application is stopped. A highly complex application may require up to 2 Gb for that given application. For instance, one of my clients has 90 applications, 700 users, and their sizing on the Essbase server was 128 Gb RAM and 24 cores. I have observed older Essbase version installations that have 10 applications and 2 Gb of total RAM—today's typical applications are more complex, have more data, and would not function on a total of 2 Gb.

1.4.6 Storage

As with memory, disk space is cheap. Running out of disk space at least once will cause a system outage and sometimes can corrupt cubes and/or the security file. Keep at least 25% disk space free on your Essbase data drive and expand it as needed and/or archive old data to retain that percentage of free space.

The number of options for your storage is very wide: internal, direct attached, network attached storage (NAS), and storage area network (SAN). When using internal disks or direct attached disks, use RAID 10 (redundant array of inexpensive disks). RAID facilitates both data integrity in the form of redundancy as well as speed in the form of multiple disks used for read and write operations. Never use software RAID; software RAID relies on server CPU resources and will provide suboptimal performance.

When using external storage systems such as NAS or SAN, you want as many spindles (disk drives) as possible while using a RAID mechanism, which supports both reads and writes equally well. Solid state disks (NAND Memory) are becoming fashionable; however, the limited number of write cycles the drives are capable of mean there will be a failure. My belief is due to the amount of data churn in an Essbase application and/or due to how some may have been implemented it could cause a solid state drive failure more quickly than other types of applications. My test setup has a direct attached disk array with a hardware RAID controller and it provides over 1 Gb/sec throughput when using an eight-disk RAID 10 configuration. I have also performed testing with memory file systems and found no discernible speed increase between my direct attached storage and RAM; this means a fast physical disk subsystem will provide sufficient bandwidth and not be a bottleneck. This also means use of solid state disks and/or memory file systems provide no performance boost over a fast physical disk through Essbase version 11.1.2.1; the future may bring us an Essbase version where a memory file system or solid state disk does help performance.

A rule of thumb for number of drives in your RAID/SAN supporting Essbase; generally I start with at least four drives (spindles) in the array that will hold your Essbase data stores. For every 50 users above 100, add another drive. Consider that, for some specific Essbase applications, it may be good to dedicate a set of drives to that app only.

Be aware of complexities involved in NAS, SAN, and/or storage for virtual machines. These are shared storage models where basic design of that storage and/or systems outside the scope of your Essbase server can affect your performance. SAN topologies specifically can be very complex and may have upwards of 50 servers using one physical frame. Use of disk benchmarking tools can assist troubleshooting issues caused by nondirect storage systems.

1.4.7 Installation Planning and Preparation

In preparation for an installation it is critical to review the below reference documents and understand the information contained therein.

- Version-specific Hyperion Installation and Configuration Guide
- Version-specific Hyperion Installation Start Here
- Version-specific Hyperion README documents for each module (Known Issues)
- Version-specific Hyperion product patch sets from "My Oracle Support"

1.4.8 Procure and Install Hardware per Sizing

Ensure the hardware is set up per your requirements. One common issue with virtual environments is that the server administrators do not provide the resources requested. Lack of proper resources will cause the installation to take additional time and also not support real world user loads. The operating system the Hyperion software is installed on must see multiple cores to take advantage of Essbase's multithreaded design. Some administrators may tell you one core is sufficient, this is not correct. Testing the application with a nontrivial amount of data and proper tuning will show this one core is far out performed by many cores. Ensure at least four cores are allocated.

1.4.9 Firewalls and Load Balancers

If your environment will involve firewalls or load balancers, contact the appropriate team weeks in advance of the installation to ensure the settings have been appropriately modified to support your installation.

1.4.10 Sizing Guidelines

Table 1.6 through Table 1.10 are intended to help you to size a system quickly based on a given number of users and set of applications. Performance testing using realistic user cases is the best way to prove the system is working well. This being said, you can almost always count on users to surprise you, especially when they all decide they need to use the system on the last day of a financial cycle.

Table 1.6 Reporting (only) Essbase Server Sizing Guideline

Named Users (Assumes 50% Load)	Cores	RAM/PAGE and Number of Cubes	Data Drives	Supporting Servers
100 Users	4	24 GB/12 GB; up to 10 cubes	4–RAID 10	Single Server configuration. Note a single server configuration limits your growth
250 Users	8	48/24 GB; up to 32 cubes	8–RAID 10	Dedicated Web server(s)
750 Users	12	192/48 GB; up to 128 cubes	12–RAID 10	Dedicated DB server

Table 1.7 Planning (only) Essbase Server Sizing Guideline; Higher CPU and I/O

Named Users (Assumes 50% Load)	Cores	RAM/PAGE and Number of Cubes	Data Drives	Supporting Servers
100 Users	4	24 GB/12 GB; up to 10 cubes	4–RAID 10	Single server configuration. Note a single server configuration limits your growth.
250 Users	12	48/24 GB; up to 32 cubes	8–RAID 10	Dedicated Web server(s)
750 Users	16	192/48 GB; up to 128 cubes	16–RAID 10	Dedicated DB server

Table 1.8 Mixed (Reporting and Planning) Essbase Server Sizing Guideline

Named Users (Assumes 50% Load)	Cores	RAM/PAGE and Number of Cubes	Data Drives	Supporting Servers
100 Users	8	24 GB/12 GB; up to 10 cubes	6–RAID 10	Single server configuration. Note a single server configuration limits your growth.
250 Users	12	48/24 GB; up to 32 cubes	8–RAID 10	Dedicated Web server(s)
750 Users	24	192/48 GB; up to 128 cubes	16–RAID 10	Dedicated DB server

Table 1.9 Web/Java Application Server Guideline

Named Users (Assumes 50% Load)	Servers	Cores	RAM/PAGE	Data Drives
100 Users	1	8	24 GB/12 GB; up to 10 cubes	4–RAID 10
250 Users	1	4	16/8 GB	RAID 1
500 Users	2	4	16/8 GB	RAID 1
750 Users	3	4	16/8 GB	RAID 1

Note: Foundation and BIPLUS require shared disk (CIFS/NFS) for multiple instances.

Table 1.10 Print Server/EPMA Dimension Server Guideline

Named Users (Assumes 50% Load)	Servers	Cores	RAM/PAGE	Data Drives
100 Users	1	8	24 GB/12 GB; up to 10 cubes	4–RAID 10
250 Users	1	4	8 GB/4 GB	RAID 1
500 Users	2	4	8 GB/4 GB	RAID 1
750 Users	3	4	8 GB/4 GB	RAID 1

Note: Dimension server requires clustered disk for multiple instances.

1.5 AN APPLE A DAY

Prepare and *prevent* are two very good verbs in the infrastructure vocabulary. Prepare for the possibility of data issues with tested backups. Prevent issues with system monitoring.

As an example, one early afternoon the day before a holiday break a long-time client reached out after he clicked a wrong button during routine maintenance and then answered a question improperly after that click. The result was his Essbase databases were recreated and his data was dropped. We were able to work around this moment of panic because the system had a tested backup process. Some people have not been as fortunate as you may read on the technical forums where they are asking what they can do to restore their data when they have no backup; at that time it's too late to make things better. The moral of both of these stories is you better have a good backup if you do not want to ruin your holiday, vacation, weekend, or continued paid employment.

Table 1.11 shows a minimum set of recommended maintenance activities for your Essbase environment.

We monitor systems in order to reduce system down time and, for those of us in any type of customer support role, to preserve our sanity. Table 1.12 below outlines the most important items I recommend that you focus on when monitoring your environment.

Table 1.11 System Maintenance

Maintenance Activity	Notes
Essbase data backup	• Cold backups of Essbase must be performed with the Essbase services fully shut down. • A warm backup operation can be made with level-0 export scripts.
Application server backup	• The Oracle Hyperion applications store key information in the system registry, temporary directories, user profile directories, and the application file system. • Ensure the full backup captures the system registry, temporary directories, and user profile directories, and the application file system. • Note: In order to ensure the system backups have integrity, all services should be shut down while the system is being backed up. • The Framework Services Repository Directory must be backed up at the same time as the BIPLUS relational database.
Relational database backup	• Setup procedures to have the transaction logs cleared after they have been backed up. • If the BIPLUS database is restored, it must be restored in conjunction with the Framework Services Repository. Failure to keep the BIPLUS database and Framework Services Repository synchronized will cause issues with Financial Reports and Financial Report database connections.
Archive logs	• Maintenance archives of log files and remove old archives. Log files older than one month are usually not valuable.
Defragment	• Over the period of several days or weeks cubes that have changing data can become fragmented. Fragmentation can increase the size of database files on disk and also reduce performance. Enact a scheduled process to load and calculated data or restructure the cube.

1.5.1 Evolving Location of Logs

As Essbase has evolved so has the location and number of log files. The basic log files are the Essbase.log and the individual application logs. Table 1.13 shows how these files have changed. I have hopes that going forward with 11.1.2 the log files will continue to be in a consistent area.

Table 1.12 System Monitoring

Monitoring Activities	Recommendations
Application	• Setup monitoring of the services, system daemons, and TCP ports for the applications and database.
Application and database backups	• Confirm both your application and database backups are scheduled and monitored. When you need a backup, it is critical the process is working.
CPU	• CPU spikes for periods of several minutes can be normal when calculation and system design is optimized or during periods of heavy load. Full use of all CPUs for over 30 minutes is cause for concern.
Memory	• Ensure at least 10% of system memory is free. In situations where you are below this, consider increasing system memory or reducing Essbase caches.
Disk space	• Both operating system and application disk space should be monitored and automated alerts for drives that are within 25% of their established maximum.
Disk queues and wait times	• If you notice the system is always waiting on resources investigate memory, CPU, and disk.
SAN monitoring	• Storage Area Network (SAN) devices are now a standard infrastructure component. They tend to be shared by many servers and can act as a performance bottleneck if not properly configured, low on internal caches, or many servers are using the same SAN port.

Table 1.13 Essbase Logs

Major Version	Path from Installation Drive/Directory
IBM DB2 OLAP Server	• IBM/db2olap/app/<APPNAME>/<APPNAME>.log
6/7	• Hyperion/Essbase/ESSBASE.log • Hyperion/Essbase/<APPNAME>/<APPNAME>.log
9	• Hyperion/AnalyticServices/Essbase.log • Hyperion/AnalyticServices/<APPNAME>/<APPNAME>.log
11.1.1	• Hyperion/logs/essbase/Essbase.log • Hyperion/logs/essbase/<APPNAME>/<APPNAME>.log
11.1.2	• <ESSBASELOGS>/Essbase.log • <ESSBASELOGS>/app/<APPNAME>/<APPNAME>.log • <OPMNLOGS>/OPMN/opmn/*.log • <ESSBASELOGS> path: • Oracle/Middleware/user_projects/epmsystemX/diagnostics/logs/essbase/essbase/essbase_0 • <OPMNLOGS> path: • Oracle/Middleware/user_projects/epmsystemX/diagnostics/logs

Note: Beginning in 11.X Essbase log files are separate from other Essbase application files, e.g., *.otl, *.ind, *.pag, etc.

1.6 WHEN IT ALL GOES WRONG

Over the life of complex systems or during times of large change, such as an upgrade, you may find you need help diagnosing issues. This section highlights several very useful tools that may be used in a variety of problem analysis situations (Table 1.14). When diagnosing a problem, I suggest: reviewing the log files, using any tools that seem to make sense for the given situation, and, after you have exhausted your knowledge and/or patience, logging a support case with the appropriate vendor.

1.6.1 Troubleshooting Tools and Tuning Documents

If you are in any type of infrastructure role, I hope the below utilities are familiar to you (Table 1.15). If not, check them out and, hopefully, you find them as useful as I do.

The resources in Table 1.16 provide further information on specific platforms and/or tuning.

1.7 ADDITIONAL DEPLOYMENT CONSIDERATIONS

1.7.1 Supported Software

In order to qualify for support from your software vendors, you must use a supported operating system. Oracle maintains a certification matrix that documents the operating systems and other supporting software both on server and client.

Table 1.14 Troubleshooting Steps

Major Version	Symptom	Recommended Action
ALL	Essbase does not start	1. Check disk space on application and data drives 2. Review Hyperion log files 3. Review operating system log files and/or windows event viewer 4. Versions 9–11.1.1 Confirm Shared Services and OpenLDAP are started; assumes you are using Shared Services security
ALL	Application does not start	1. Check disk space on application and data drives 2. Review Hyperion log files 3. Confirm no other ESSSVR processes are running for specific application name 4. Confirm that no third-party backup process has application files locked 5. Cycle machine if 3 and 4 are not issues 6. If cycling machine does not work, you likely have a corrupted database 7. Confirm you have a good backup before proceeding with this step. Remove the following type of files from your database directories: *.ind, *.pag, *.esm, *.tct. Next start the database, then restore and calculate your data
ALL	Corrupt security file	1. Essbase.log file says your security file is corrupted 2. Locate last backup of the file (ideally from previous night), restore and restart Essbase

Table 1.15 Troubleshooting Tools

Platform	Tool and Notes
Windows/Unix	• Wireshark • Web site: http://wireshark.org • Network packet capture and tracing software that was formerly called Ethereal
Windows/Unix	• Netstat, Ping, and Telnet • tracert (Windows)/traceroute (Unix) • Basic utilities to troubleshoot networking and ports
Windows	• Fiddler • Web site: http://www.fiddler2.com • Web debugging proxy software. When installed, sits between your windows Web browser and the Internet; useful for debugging sessions
Windows/Unix	• IOZone • Web site: http://www.iozone.org • Disk benchmarking tool
Windows	• ATTO's GUI Disk benchmarking tool • Web site: http://www.attotech.com/products/product.php?sku=Disk_Benchmark
Windows	• Perfmon • Windows internal performance monitor
Firefox Browser	• Firebug • Web site: http://getfirebug.com • Debug and monitor CSS, HTML, and JavaScript
Windows	• Process monitor and process explorer • Web site: http://technet.microsoft.com/en-us/sysinternals Process Monitor monitors file system, registry, and process/thread activity in real time. • The main reason I like Process Explorer is you can see the full path of the command and, therefore, when looking at ESSSVR you know which process ID is associated with a given application; of course, you may review the log files grab the process ID out and review that column in task manager as well.
Unix	• ps, iostat, vmstat, grep
Linux	• NMON • Web site: http://nmon.sourceforge.net • Console GUI that allows you to monitor key performance information in one location

Table 1.16 Tuning Guides

Document Title	Document Location	Authoring Company
Linux Performance and Tuning Guidelines	www.redbooks.ibm.com	IBM
Performance Tuning Guidelines for Windows Server 2008 R2	msdn.microsoft.com	Microsoft
AIX 5L Practical Performance Tools and Tuning Guide	www.redbooks.ibm.com	IBM
EPM – OBI Product Assurance Engineering Blog	blogs.oracle.com/pa	Oracle
HP-UX Performance Cookbook	Perform a Web search	Hewlett Packard
Oracle Database Support for Server Virtualization	oracle.com	Oracle
ISV Licensing in Virtualized Environments	vmware.com	VMware

1.7.2 Antivirus

Essbase is a multidimensional database that stores data and key security information in binary files. Like other database software antivirus scans of the database, files can cause performance issues. Oracle recommends excluding antivirus real-time scanning of the Hyperion installation directories and/or a scheduled scan with the Hyperion suite shutdown.

1.7.3 Hyperthreading

Intel released a technology called Hyperthreading in 2003. This technology makes one core appear as two cores to the operating system. Some applications have a performance gain with Hyperthreading and some have a net loss. Essbase experiences a net loss in performance with Hyperthreading and every server that runs the ESSBASE/ESSVR processes should have Hyperthreading disabled. The performance loss to Essbase from Hyperthreading is between 15 and 20%. Conversely, the Java application servers do have a performance gain.

1.7.4 Virtual versus Physical

Installation on a physical machine is straightforward. Essbase will have all the performance characteristics of that machine.

Virtualization for Intel x86 servers went mainstream in 2001 with the introduction of VMware's server virtualization. In the decade since, virtualization has become a normal tool in IT datacenters.

Virtualization apportions the physical machine into logical segments or virtual machines (VMs) that run independently of one another. VM performance depends on the competing requirements of the other VMs running on the physical machine plus some virtualization overhead. Virtualization can offer many benefits when used properly with flexible scalability and fault tolerance as the two main strengths.

I have seen virtualization work well as well as work poorly. In the cases where it works poorly, the issues are a combination of age of the physical hardware, lack of resources (CPU/memory) on physical hardware, overcommitted virtual machines, and poor performance of the storage subsystems. Consider physical machines or large-scale Unix implementations for more than 500 users.

When using virtualization, I recommend VMware as I feel they have a focused concentration and vested interest in the technology compared to other vendors who spread their focus on more products. See Table 1.17 for a listing of virtualization products.

1.7.5 Ensure File Systems Are Fully Formatted

IBM's AIX has a hard drive partitioning it brands as LPAR (Logical Partition). LPARs may host IBM operating systems other than AIX as well; however, AIX is the only operating system on the IBM POWER platform that supports the Hyperion stack.

HP's HPUX nPar technology is their hard partitioning technology.

The Solaris equivalent hard partitioning technology has been branded OracleVM Server, which was previously named LDOM (Logical Domains). Oracle also has made OracleVM Server available in their Oracle Enterprise Linux (a Redhat Linux variant).

1.7.6 Named User versus Processor Licensing

Oracle has two main user licensing schemes: Named User and Processor Licensing. Processor licensing allows for an unlimited number of users, but limits performance

Table 1.17 Virtualization Software

Vendor	Product	Notes
VMware	ESXi	• When used with Oracle Processor licenses, you must ensure that you have enough processor licenses for every CPU on the physical machine that are in the resource pool. For instance, if you have 3 Physical Servers with a total of 30 cores, then you would need to have a processor license supporting 15 CPUs (using the current CPU factor of .5). This is regardless of how many virtual CPUs your given Essbase server may have allocated.
Microsoft	Hyper-V	• Microsoft acquired the underlying technology in 2003 with the purchase of Connectix's Virtual PC. • When used with Oracle Processor licenses you must ensure that you have enough processor licenses for every CPU on the physical machine that is in the resource pool. For instance, if you have 3 Physical Servers with a total of 30 cores, then you would need to have a processor license supporting 15 CPUs (using the current CPU factor of .5). This is regardless of how many virtual CPUs your given Essbase server may have allocated.
IBM	AIX LPAR	• IBM's AIX has a hard partitioning they brand as LPAR (Logical Partitions). LPARs may host IBM operating systems other than AIX as well; however, AIX is the only operating system on the IBM POWER platform the supports the Hyperion stack. LPARS are fully compatible with Oracle Processor Licensing.
Hewlett Packard	HPUX nPar and vPar	• HP's HPUX has a technology called nPar that is their hard partitioning technology. The virtual partitioning technology is called vPar. Both nPar and vPar are fully compatible with Oracle Processor licensing.
Xen.org	Xen	• An open source virtualization platform with contributions to its code base from many industry heavyweights, such as Amazon, IBM, Citrix, and Oracle. To ensure full compatibility with Oracle Processor licensing, a configuration setting to pin CPUs to limit those for specific virtual machines must be used.
Oracle	Oracle VM Server for x86	• The x86 Oracle VM Server is based on Xen virtualization platform. To ensure full compatibility with Oracle Processor licensing, a configuration setting to pin CPUs to limit those for specific virtual machines must be used.
Oracle	Sun Dynamic System Domain	• Dynamic System Domains are fully compatible with Oracle Processor licensing.

based on number of cores. When using Processor Licensing with virtualization, Oracle requires either a hard partitioning capable virtualization to be used or specifies the physical number of cores in the hardware hosting the VMs. This latter requirement usually has architectural implications for systems using soft partitioning, e.g., VMware and Hyper-V.

1.8 CONCLUSION

In closing this chapter, I hope you found this information valuable or at least entertaining for those of you of the geek persuasion.

1.8.1 Parting Shots

- Essbase thrives on CPU, memory, and I/O.
- Skimping on your hardware costs time, money, and effort in the end.
- Always have a nonproduction environment.
- Failure to maintain proper backups will give you or at least your users a headache.
- Do not mix upgrades and redesigns and expect to have both go live at the same time.
- Test, test, test.
- Always read the documentation.

2

SLAY BAD DATA IN ESSBASE

Cameron Lackpour

CONTENTS

2.1 INTRODUCTION

It seems self-evident that an Essbase data must be complete and correct every time it is loaded, for what is the purpose of an inaccurate analytical tool—bad analysis? Without good data, Essbase is just a collection of metadata and reports, of little worth, except possibly to the consulting company that was paid to develop it. With good data, Essbase is a powerful tool that empowers users to analyze reliable, accurate, and validated data to make informed decisions.

And yet, most Essbase databases are at least temporarily incorrect after data is loaded. Why this bad data is tolerated is a mystery; perhaps it is insufficient budget, or the belief that figuring out how to eliminate bad data is difficult, or maybe just that no one has tried. Regardless of cause, the mission of this chapter is to give you the tools to Slay Bad Data with minimal manual intervention.

2.1.1 Assumptions about You, Dear Reader

Who are you? What, you don't know your own name? This sounds like a case for a psychiatrist and a strong dose of … whoops, wrong book, you need to go to the self-help section and put this one back where it belongs.

Are you still here? If so, you are likely an Essbase developer who has experienced the pain of bad data, knows all too well the consequences, and does not ever want to repeat the experience. If you have somehow blissfully skated through your professional Essbase life *not* experiencing the pain that is bad data, you have been lucky. Since you are reading this chapter, you are to be commended for realizing that you have been dodging fate. Regardless of experience, you are searching for a way to slay the bad data that is storming the beautiful design of your Essbase outline.

2.1.1.1 Scope One of the many great aspects about Essbase is that it is not tied to any single data source; universality and adaptability have been key ingredients to success with Essbase. Given the wide variety of data sources, be it a general ledger, sales forecasting system, or a series of spreadsheets, it is beyond the scope of this chapter to cover data *extraction*. You or your Information Technology (IT) Department must master that, not inconsiderable, challenge. In the end, however, the user never sees that part of the process, it is you and your cube who will be blamed if there are data errors. The concepts and techniques in this chapter will help guarantee that the load of this extracted data to Essbase is complete and internally consistent, with bad data if not actually slain then highlighted, and the effects measureable and mitigated and not simply hidden in an error file somewhere.

While every effort to fully explain this chapter's theories and processes will be made, space considerations require that you have some familiarity with data-loading techniques. Table 2.1 lists the concepts you should be familiar with before you read this chapter. The table is grouped by technology type.

Each technology type will have advanced content beyond these prerequisites, which will be fully explained in this chapter.

Table 2.1 Technology Prerequisites

Technology	Prerequisites
Essbase	• Familiarity with ASOsamp.Sample • Data load rules • Dimension load rules • Report scripts
MaxL	• Data loads • Dimension loads • Parameter variables
SQL	• Simple INSERT and SELECT statements
ODI	• Interfaces • Packages • Data models • Designer • Operator

2.1.2 A Note about the Examples

2.1.2.1 Too Hot, Too Cold, Just Right When building the technical examples for this chapter, I struggled quite a bit with the completeness of the solutions. Should a given example provide the most bulletproof, fully featured, chrome-laden solution to a problem or should it instead provide an answer that is purposely simple to clearly illustrate the concept, even if it is missing some of the completeness needed in the real world? I went with the latter approach. My hope is that you will read this chapter, look at the code, and think: "Yeah, that's interesting, but he should have done X to show Y." That will mean that the concept has hit home and your brain is already absorbed in making it better. If that is the result then great, I have done my job.

2.1.2.2 SQL Is Integral I also will note that you will see a fair bit of my child-like SQL (Structured Query Language). An Essbase developer writing SQL code is akin to a carpenter performing neurosurgery: He might be able to get the skull open with a compass saw, but that Yankee screwdriver might not be the best tool for closing it all back up. As for the patient's long-term prognosis … perhaps it is best not to dwell overmuch on that subject. All I can say is that the code works and that you are more than welcome to improve upon it. Again, if you do, it means that this chapter has succeeded in engaging you.

2.1.2.3 ASOsamp.Sample The solution in this chapter uses the same ASOsamp.Sample Essbase database that has come with every copy of Essbase since version 7.1. ASOsamp (as I shall refer to it henceforth) is the source and the target of all code examples and solutions.

2.1.2.4 Sample.Basic Sample.Basic, aka "Cameron's Very Favorite Essbase Database in the Whole Wide World," was regrettably not chosen for this chapter because it is *too* simple. However, it is rich with Load Rule examples that have been used to illustrate Load Rule concepts.

2.1.3 Where's the Code?

This chapter describes a complete solution to bad data in Essbase. While code samples, of course, are interspersed throughout the text, the full code stream is separated into an Appendix at the end of the chapter to keep the narrative cohesive.

2.2 BAD DATA KILLS ESSBASE DATABASES

Users love Essbase databases they trust and run away as fast as their feet will carry them from all others. There is a qualitative difference between a database incomplete via omission and one that is inaccurate through the commission of bad data. The former are candidates for improvement, the latter are practically radioactive, except instead of deadly gamma and beta waves, they radiate unemployment.

Unlike SQL databases that operate top-down, Essbase databases are effectively bottom-up. In SQL, when a user queries for "Total Sales by Department," it will not matter if on some invoice somewhere a bad SKU (stock-keeping unit) was typed. The total sales will be correct. The error will only be apparent when it is noticed that the query for "Total Sales by SKU" is run and it does not tie with the department total. In Essbase, the data for the bad SKU will be rejected when the cube is loaded and both queries will be wrong. You and your cube will be blamed for their failure to maintain "referential integrity." Therefore, this bad data ***must be slain***.

2.2.1 What Is Bad Data?

Bad data has four characteristics:

1. It is inconsistent in its process and sources.
2. Exceptions are handled on an ad hoc basis.
3. The effort required to load it is manual and time consuming.
4. It cannot be fully validated against its source.

If you recognize any of the above characteristics in your Essbase databases read on, and read quickly.

2.2.2 What Is Good Data?

Given the above, good data has an opposite set of characteristics:

1. Processes and sources are consistent from load to load.
2. Exception handling is in-built.
3. Loading is automatic and quick.
4. Data at both a load and reporting level is fully validated.

Does it not feel great to know that all of your systems are just like the above? They are, right?

2.2.3 Trust Is Essential and Easily Lost

The implementation of an Essbase database means many things to many people:

- Software sales revenue to Oracle
- Revenue to server manufacturers
- Commitment of IT capital
- A purchase order for consulting (hopefully some of it for your authors)
- A lot of time and effort for all concerned

Perhaps most importantly, from the business owner's perspective, it represents an extension of trust that the implementers of the system get it all right so that the owner can use Essbase to make better decisions.

That business owner is convinced of Essbase's technical capabilities; otherwise, he would be going down some other path. However, he is taking a chance on the implementation. Whether you are internal finance staff, internal IT staff, an outside consultant, the system administrator, or the senior power user, he is taking a chance on *you*.

That risk is twofold: (1) can the database reflect the analytical needs through the outline, calculations, and reports (this is where your Essbase genius shines through, right?), and (2) is the data you are loading (oh, Essbase genius) to this ultra-super-awesome Essbase database correct?

2.2.4 Good Data Drives Business Decisions

With good data in Essbase, the fancy formulas, dimensions, calculations, and reports you create help the business make informed decisions. This is why the business/client/customer went through the trouble and expense of bringing Essbase in the door. In the simplest of terms, with good data *Essbase is awesome.*

2.2.5 In Good Data We Trust

Your business application owner, whether he be your boss, your peer, or your client, knows that good data is a requirement for a successful Essbase implementation even if he can barely spell Essbase. He knows that bad numbers beget bad decisions and, hence, even more bad numbers. *You* know that there are no guardian angels for data.

That business owner does not believe in data fairy godmothers, either, but he does believe that you can get the data right. Yes, you are the Essbase expert and good data management is just one of the many skills you are expected to have.

It can all seem a bit unfair—you do not own the data, nor do you use it on a daily basis, nor are you likely have any control over it. Yet, you are expected get it right in Essbase. Welcome to the world of Essbase development; this is why you (hopefully) earn the big bucks/pounds/Euros.

2.2.6 What Happens When Data Goes Bad

If the business owner and his users think the data is bad, the database will be effectively *abandoned* (nobody would dare turn it off, then they would have to admit it was a money-wasting error). That capital (economic, reputational, political, and maybe even spiritual) that the business has invested in that shiny new Essbase database (*and you*) is considerable. Despite this, if the system has bad data, watch everyone, including the business owner, jump ship at the first opportunity. And, then the "bad things" start to happen.

2.2.6.1 Bad Things Come in Threes Once the trust in the Essbase database has been lost, some but not all of the users will go back to the source system or to the spreadsheets or relational data sources or chicken bones or whatever they used in the past for their numbers. Guess what? This makes any data integrity issue that, in theory, Essbase solved even worse. Essbase is now just one more dodgy data source in a sea of unreliable data.

Another casualty will be credibility, and three actors are going to take the hit: the Essbase database, the business owner/sponsor, and you. Yes, it is important that the numbers are right in every detail, and professional integrity requires that you never let down a project sponsor, but consider about how this bad data will impact you directly.

Do you know what happens to developers who have no credibility because they built bad Essbase databases? The most common euphemism is: "Spending more time with his family," aka "You're fired." Bad data results in unpleasant consequences for all involved and so from a self-preservation perspective alone, **bad data must be slain**.

2.2.7 Three Tales of Data Error, Terror, and Learning

Presented for your rueful consideration are three semigruesome, real-world, as I saw or heard them examples of data errors causing deep financial pain. These stories are completely true yet are obfuscated and declarified enough so that the guilty can escape the shame and contempt that is surely their due and, of course, so that "the author" does not get sued. Read on to learn the lesson that lies within each Geek Tragedy.

2.2.7.1 The Error of Complexity A customer (of someone, somewhere) had a SQL-based budgeting system. Said system was the personification of scope creep—it did many, many things, some of which were clearly defined. The options, code blocks, and launching processes were so multifarious and complicated that aggregate data values were inconsistent, i.e., the system never reported the same number twice.

I was summoned and analyzed this system with an eye toward replacing it with an Essbase database and found over 800 (yes, really) separate code streams and over 300 tables (yes, really, again). Given the complexity of the system, I wondered how a correct number ever came out. It probably never did.

What was the eventual outcome (the Stones of Data Justice ground slowly, but exceedingly finely) of this overly complex financial reporting system? The outcome was termination with cause for the employee who built it. Never let it be said that poor data quality cannot directly impact the size of a developer's paycheck. And what was the eventual outcome for me and my paycheck/fee? Joy, happiness, and significant billable hours as I fully implemented a reporting system in Essbase.

2.2.7.2 The Error of Hubris This next story concerns a consultant, one that the author is intimately acquainted with, and one who is willing to publicize his stupidity so that others may not share his fate. Who is this dope? Yup, it is I. At least it was a long time ago, so memory has softened the edges of my failure.

The client was new to Essbase with Finance absolutely sold on the power of Essbase and IT much more in the wait-and-see camp. Particularly when I rather publicly proved that a $25,000 Windows® server performed Essbase calculations 11% faster than the $250,000 Unix™ box IT had specified. Proving that the IT department was the Naked Emperor might not have been the best approach when it came to asking for their help in data sourcing. Sometimes I only learn through pain.

I Am Not an Infrastructure Consultant

Now I am not saying Essbase runs better on Windows than on Unix. In fact, I have since seen and learned much about Unix installations. I am just saying that the way this particular client had this particular Unix server specified and configured was suboptimal. Perhaps it was too complex for them. But, this is all another matter and not germane to my story, I just want to make sure you did not think I was dumping on Unix and you Unix lovers can tamp down your indignation. Okay, back to the tale of your intrepid Not An Infrastructure Consultant.

The data issue was twofold:

1. The data quality was bad and the dataset was very large. This made diagnosing and correcting errors through dataload.err difficult because of the slow fix iteration, the inflexibility of Load Rules, and the sheer number of fixes required. Think of multiple 100+ megabyte text files (when that was an impressive size) across a slow LAN to a server that your current smartphone could likely outrun. It was painful.
2. The IT department was disinclined to help the outside consultant who had shown them the error of their ways. Hubris, as per the title of this section, really is a fatal flaw, but, hey, really man, I was right! Not that it did me any good, which I suppose is the whole point of the word.

And, what tool did I use to scrub the data? Essbase data Load Rules is what.

Question: Why did I write this chapter?
Answer: The horror of actually trying to do Extract Transform and Load (ETL) in a Load Rule scarred my soul. Hence, I must travel the Earth warning all who would attempt my folly lest they share my fate.

I never did get the data right thanks to an ever-changing set of data requirements and a tool ill-suited to do more than the simplest of transformations. The data quality issues eventually killed my "fix" opportunity and ended one of the shortest commutes (door-to-door, 20 minutes) I've ever had.

2.2.7.3 The Error of Secrecy Imagine a data warehouse that feeds a multidimensional database with full data integrity checks. This was considered pretty fancy stuff in the late 1980s. The term *data warehouse* did not even exist, nor did our beloved Essbase.

However, good data practices, relational data stores, and mainframe-based multidimensional databases did exist and these combined at a large heavily unionized manufacturer.

This proto-data warehouse was loaded on a nightly basis with manufacturing and sales data. When processing hiccups occurred, the time-consuming data constraints were turned off to allow the numbers to roll in, with the understanding that data would be fixed the next night.

Imagine one of these something-went-wrong-with-the-data nights with the constraining routines set to OFF. The next morning, the hero (?) of this story arrives at work at his usual 7 a.m. time and takes a look at his cube only to discover that the plant dimension has a newly constructed factory for a total of five instead of yesterday's four. As the processes to make this company's products are long, involved, and very, very big, this is a puzzler.

Our hero embarks on a quest through the known IT and Finance world asking all who will listen about this new plant. No one knows anything about it because bringing a new plant online would be a huge multibillion dollar capital expense that everyone would know about for literally years before it happened—and no one did. What was going on? Surely, this was some kind of error. Our conscientious consultant was determined to run it down.

Growing increasingly alarmed as he questioned the quality of the data, our hero reexamined the base tables for Factory Five; yup, there it was. As this simply could not be, he was tireless in his questioning of various business stakeholders. By midmorning, everyone and his brother knew that somehow the company had sprouted a new plant overnight.

All was confusion until a vice president came out of the corner office and confronted our questing consultant with a stern (but whispered), "Shut up with the questions!"

It seems that the company had surreptitiously set up a foreign factory to which they shipped partially finished work in unmarked railcars for final processing. Said factory's production data was spread across the four factories via secret nightly processing routines. Through a distinct lack of foresight, this allocation process was tied to the nightly data constraints and when those routines were turned off, the plant identifier manifested itself in the data.

This rather convoluted subterfuge was because the fifth plant was union-free in a company that was otherwise heavily unionized. Did I mention that the collective bargaining agreement included the right to organize all new plants and that a breach of the agreement was cause for industrial action? Whoops. I wonder what it is like to have your very own case history with the National Labor Relations Board.

No, this unique professional footnote did not make our sadder but wiser protagonist happy. Nor did it give his consulting manager a toothsome smile. Nor, for that matter, did it make the owner of the consulting firm particularly cheery. In fact, it made them all very, very sad because they were dragged into a lengthy and costly legal controversy that was not of their making simply for doing their good data duty. I told you that bad data is not fair. In conclusion, I pose this question: Was this really bad data or was it simply data used badly? This was a matter to be settled in litigation.

2.2.7.4 What Have We Learned from These Amusing/Instructive/Disturbing Anecdotes? The first lesson is easy: bad data kills everything it touches, regardless of cause, be that complexity, consultant hubris, or secrecy. There are real consequences to getting data wrong and as you are the responsible Essbase developer, that means *your* job, *your* engagement, and *your* business are all vulnerable.

The second lesson is that you, the Essbase developer, must create systems with *good* data that eschew complexity and use tools fit for purpose. As you may have noticed in the above, I do not consider Essbase Load Rules a proper place to do ETL and they are certainly not fit for that purpose. But, exactly why do I so horribly denigrate doing ETL with Load Rules? Three reasons stand out:

1. Load Rules are slow.
2. Load Rules have limited functionality.
3. ETL should all be done in one place, not partially in the extraction and partially within Essbase, which makes multiple transforms much harder to debug.

That is two out of the three dealt with, what about that last "tale," the one about secrecy? Ironically, that organization actually had the right idea about data quality, although lying to their employees bit them in the you-know-where, and rightfully so, because what everyone thought was good data, really was not. This brings us right back to the quality issue. As all of this book's readers are forthright and honest Essbase developers who only want to do good, they will never fall into that trap. Honesty, in data as in life, is always the right policy. So, the third lesson is that you, the ethical Essbase developer, must understand your data sources so that you validate them correctly. In the end remember that you were the last one to touch it, so whatever is in the cube is your responsibility.

2.3 QUALITY DATA EQUALS A QUALITY ESSBASE DATABASE

As I hope my artfully disguised, yet all too real, Essbase horror stories showed, an Essbase database worth its salt is built on the foundation of good data; anything else is suitable for the trash bin and should be tossed there before *you* end up alongside it. Now that I have scared you witless, it is time to build you back up with an approach to data quality that ensures you never end up with a *Tale of Terror* of your own.

2.3.1 How Not to Solve the Problem of Bad Data

2.3.1.1 Where Is the Worst Place to Pretend That Essbase Is Really an ETL Tool? Alas, it is included with each and every copy of Essbase and has been there since approximately the year dot, which just goes to show that a bad idea can gain adoption through repetition despite its manifold shortcomings. Bad tool I name thee: "Essbase Load Rules." I speak heresy given its almost universal usage. Regardless, I am the Essbase Load Rule apostate and I shall explain why you should be one as well in the most restrained manner I can manage.

Lest you think I have well and truly gone off the deep end of Load Rule hate, I am not suggesting that you take up manual dimension building or loading data through free form text files in an effort to become ideologically pure. While Load Rules are a good way to load data and create dimensions, they are very much the wrong way to do the transformations that are the "T" in true ETL. Load Rules are simply a maintenance black hole if they are filled with transformations.

2.3.1.2 Historical Context When Essbase was new, circa 1993, Essbase databases tended to have ad hoc data sources and the tool itself was the ward of the Finance department. Less than rock-solid data sources and a lack of IT involvement meant that Essbase developers had only their wits and Load Rules to rely on for data manipulation; Arbor and then Hyperion charged a pretty penny for the SQL option and few purchased it. I was not lucky enough to often come across clients who owned it.

Time has moved on, anyone still involved with Essbase is older and hopefully wiser, the IT department is now is at least a co-owner of Essbase, and yet Load Rules remain largely unchanged with the huge exception that the SQL interface is now standard and available without additional cost.

2.3.1.3 A Tool Not Fit for Purpose I have related how I relied on Load Rules on a project and was badly burnt. Much of this was my fault for not pushing back harder to the client when inadequate metadata and data was dropped in my lap. But, I was young, foolish, and convinced that Load Rules could do anything. They could not then and cannot now. In retrospect, it is not hard to understand why—heavy-duty ETL is not what Load Rules were designed to do. Let my transgression of relying on Load Rules be an isolated one.

2.3.1.4 The Load Rules ETL Diatribe Space considerations have precluded me from including my well-rehearsed lecture on why Essbase Load Rules are a really bad place to do anything but the most simple forms of ETL.

I, however, have been given room to note that there are over 45 possible settings in a given Load Rule (remember that a Load Rule can do both data and dimension loading) and, depending on your definition, at least 20 possible transformations including these 10 most common ones:

1. SELECT statement if a SQL data Load Rule
2. Field moves, splits, joins, creates with joins, creates with text
3. Case changes
4. Prefixes
5. Suffixes
6. Scaling
7. AND/OR operators at a field and global rule level
8. Reject/Select
9. Sign flip
10. Sorting

I will illustrate the danger of a Load Rule by showing Sample.Basic's Data Load Rule in Figure 2.1. Can you see the nine field edits? No? Me neither.

A few, very simple transformations within a Load Rule are perfectly acceptable. Indeed, there are some actions that are best done in a Load Rule or at least when done in a Load Rule provide enormous flexibility. For instance, later in this chapter, I will illustrate how to dynamically define a dimension via a SQL-driven header; this simply cannot be done elsewhere. Nevertheless, performing extensive transformations in a Load Rule is a maintenance nightmare because the changes can be in so many different places and because the Load Rule interface does not expose any transformations except through examination of all of the transformation options both at a global rule level and in each column.

2.3.2 The Data Challenge Remains, Even If Essbase Cannot Resolve It

Essbase excels in data analysis and has an excellent (no, amazing) calculation engine. Essbase is not a data manipulation tool, despite the pretensions of foolish young consultants to the contrary. And, yet, somehow data that is complete and accurate has to get

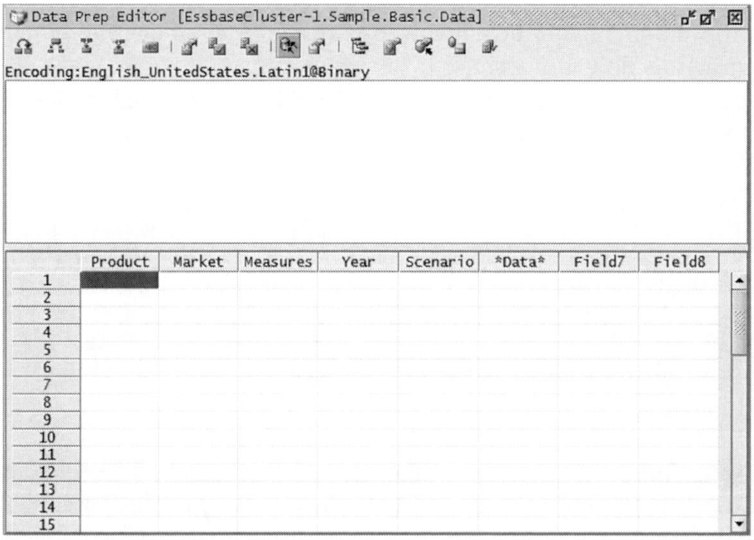

Figure 2.1 Sample.Basic's Data Load Rule.

into Essbase so those cool calculations and amazing we-never-even-considered-doing-it-in-Essbase analyses can occur.

2.3.3 *Unique, Just Like You*

Your Essbase database has one-of-a-kind data quality issues given your unique business environment. Given that Essbase Load Rules are not the place to fix them, the approaches and techniques used to guarantee that only good fact data and metadata are loaded to Essbase depend upon your database's requirements. This chapter cannot specifically address those circumstances because they are unknown to the author.

What this chapter *can* and *will* cover is the single most common data quality issue: unloaded data. By this I mean data that exists in a fact source and should be loaded to Essbase, but is instead rejected during the load because Essbase dimension metadata is missing. Loading *all* of the data, *every* time, is the bedrock requirement for data validation and quality.

2.3.4 *Constraints on Everything*

Does Essbase know that there is data in a data source for which there is no home in the target database? Surprisingly, yes. Essbase can figure this out, but only on data load when it rejects records with unknown members and pipes them to dataload.err. At that point it is too late; the data load process is finished, but incomplete and, hence, incorrect. There is no universal or foolproof way to undo that incorrect data load within Essbase.

BSO (block storage option) calc scripts and the ASO (aggregate storage option) MaxL "clear data in region" command can clear selected data, but those techniques presume that you know where the bad data resides unless you are clearing *all* of the data. You could load dataload.err back to Essbase, but what happens if you have more errors than dataload.err traps? Both of these mitigation approaches and others that let incomplete data get loaded in the first place are imperfect at best and, thus, will result in data that is still most likely to be bad.

The answer to the above problem of not knowing what and where the bad data exists is to somehow have a process that compares what metadata is in Essbase and what data is in the data source *before* the data load starts. I think of it as checking that there is a home for every piece of data and, if not, creating one before the load. Alas, we know that Essbase cannot do this.

2.3.5 *Good Data Is Spelled E-T-L*

What is needed is a tool that is more robust than Essbase Load Rules. This tool must be able to source any data be it relational, file-based, or otherwise. It must have a robust transforming functionality that can apply Essbase conforming logic. Finally it must be able to load that data to Essbase and validate against Essbase.

To guarantee that this data is good *before* it is loaded into Essbase, referential integrity between the fact data and the Essbase metadata must be imposed. Referential integrity is a relational database concept that declares and enforces a dependency relationship between tables. An example of referential integrity can be illustrated with two relational objects: a Product dimension and fact table. The Product dimension table contains the full Product hierarchy with a primary key on level-0 Products. The fact table has a Product field that contains level-0 Products with a foreign key assigned to the Product dimension lookup table. Once the relationship is defined, referential integrity can now be enforced. A Product cannot be added to the fact table unless it first exists in the Product dimension table. The Product dimension table could have more level-0 Products than the fact table, but never the converse.

If Essbase's data and metadata always resided in a relational data store, you could use this SQL concept of referential integrity to guarantee that bad data loads that result from missing dimension metadata never occur. If all the sourcing systems were perfectly designed this way and all of the data came from the same system and not a little bit from here and more from there, etc., then you would not need this chapter. Your clients will guarantee, and promise and swear, that this will be true. However, remember they will only be looking at your cube and you were the last one to touch the data, so *you* will be blamed if the data is bad. The notion of referential integrity seems like a blind alley. Or is it?

An extract, transform, and load (ETL) package has the power and flexibility to stage data and metadata from source systems and Essbase itself. It can enforce fact data to dimension metadata referential integrity regardless of the quality or composition of the source, and, finally, transfer that fully constrained data and metadata to Essbase in a fully automated manner. ETL then is the mechanism to Slay Bad Data.

Referential Integrity by Other Means

One important point to note: This chapter's path to referential integrity between fact data and dimension metadata is accomplished not through foreign keys, but via routines that identify missing dimension metadata and programmatically add those members to Essbase. This enforces metadata referential integrity by creating homes for the homeless. The reasons for not using an approach involving the use of primary and foreign keys are threefold:

1. True referential integrity cannot be enforced between the fact data and Essbase dimension metadata because Essbase is not a relational data source.
2. The timing of the values in fact data and the dimensional metadata are often likely to be dissimilar. Using the example of Product, think of new Products that might be in a fact table before they are loaded to the Essbase Product dimension.
3. Shared members or duplicate member hierarchies would break the primary key requirements on the dimension metadata table. These primary keys could be expanded to multiple fields, but then the fact table would need to carry corresponding extra fields to match as a foreign key.

2.3.5.1 Four Steps to Data Quality The following four steps create referential integrity between the fact data and Essbase.

1. Extract Essbase dimension metadata to a table to ensure the most current values. This is done after you run any of your existing metadata build rules. You know, the ones that are supposed to have been supplying you perfect data.
2. Identify and load missing dimension metadata.
   a. Compare each dimension's extracted metadata to the data source(s) via SQL.
   b. Load the metadata difference between the extracted Essbase dimensions and those found in the fact data creating unassigned or suspense hierarchies in each dimension (dimensional orphanages).
   c. Note that attribute dimensions are not considered as they are not needed to find orphan data. Attributes are properties of dimension metadata and thus are related, but not directly tied to the data.
3. Load the fact data
   a. Load the data, letting Essbase test for bad records knowing that they cannot happen.
   b. Feel awfully clever as you now have bulletproof data loading.

4. Validate to load source.
    a. Extract total values from Essbase
    b. Sum data in SQL fact table
    c. Compare Essbase data to SQL

Why this last step? Because sometimes even you make a mistake (you are only human) and sometimes even your code fails to correctly identify or plan for or fix bad data. Just an example: Essbase member names and aliases cannot begin with a space or an open parentheses and cannot contain certain nonprintable characters (such as a <ctrl> Z). If a homeless dimensional member like this is found in your fact data and you try to build a home for this orphan, it will be rejected. Do you know every one of these possible gotchas? And, even if you did, you would have to fix it, not just by creating an acceptable metadata member, but you also would have to fix the fact data file. Another reason validation is critical is complexity. It is possible that the data is there, but something else is amiss in the design, such as a partition definition.

To paraphrase President Ronald Reagan, "Trust in your data, but verify."

2.3.6 Tool Selection, or Why There Aren't Any Perfect Solutions

As in real life, there are a variety of ways to accomplish these four steps with each demonstrating a different approach to *Slaying Bad Data* in Essbase via ETL. Here is a partial list by category:

Custom Scripting
- Some combination of scripting languages, e.g., VBScript, PowerShell, Perl, SQL and/or, MaxL

Metadata Management
- Oracle Hyperion Data Relationship Management, Fusion Edition (DRM)

Data Loading
- Oracle Hyperion Financial Data Quality Management, Fusion Edition (FDM)

Warehouse-Based Builders
- Oracle Essbase Integration Studio (EIS)
- Oracle Essbase Studio

Data Quality
- FDM (arguably)
- Oracle Data Quality for Data Integrator (ODQ)
- Oracle Data Profiling (ODP)

Extract, Transform, and Load
- Hyperion Data Integration Management (DIM) aka Informatica
- IBM DataSphere
- The late, not so great, Hyperion Application Link (HAL)
- Oracle Data Integrator (ODI)

2.3.7 Why You Need ODI

Although these are all worthy products, many of them deal with only part of the ETL puzzle and require combination with other technologies, e.g., DRM addresses metadata only, FDM tackles data only, Studio can solve data quality issues, but only when sourcing from a data warehouse with full referential integrity.

The tools that *do* cover the gamut of the ETL process are the data integration packages. They can extract from a myriad of data sources, use a variety of technologies to transform the data, and load directly to Essbase. Within that subclass of full data integration tools, DIM is deprecated except for Informatica shops, DataSphere is unknown outside of IBM-centric organizations, and HAL is so obsolete it is (thankfully) literally impossible to purchase. That leaves one product: ODI.

2.3.8 ODI Is Super

ODI isn't just the choice by a process of elimination, it has compelling features:

- Universality: ODI reads and writes to practically every data source under the sun via its Knowledge Modules (KMs); these KMs can be customized to communicate with nonstandard technologies.
- Prebuilt functionality: ODI has a slew of objects such as Data Capture, Event Detection, File handling, the Internet, and miscellaneous Utilities. When these are combined in a Package for automation, they make a developer *very* productive.
- Execution: ODI's Operator module monitors job execution, logs success and failure by step with full integration to the source artifacts, and has an in-built scheduler.
- Abstraction: The physical and logical layers are split to aid reuse and migration.
- Migration: ODI has in-built functionality for migrating across environments.
- Direction: ODI is Oracle's stated direction for ETL and is embedded in the heart of Oracle's product line.

In short, ODI is a powerful tool with data manipulation and deep Essbase functionality at its core; there's nothing to touch it when fixing Essbase data quality.

2.3.9 SQL

ODI implicitly uses SQL to perform its data transformations. This chapter's examples sometimes explicitly use SQL code (albeit within an ODI shell) in place of native ODI functions for two reasons:

1. When variable-driven, the SQL approach can be more flexible and reusable than the pure ODI-object approach.
2. SQL code can be easily ported to other approaches such as other ETL tools and scripting.

This is not cheating. It is just the recognition that sometimes there are advantages to explicitly writing abstracted, variable-based SQL versus the purist way of using the less flexible ODI native functions, which implicitly use SQL anyway. Whichever way it is done, we get the advantages of ODI's built-in functionality of the type noted above.

2.4 FOUR STEPS TO DATA QUALITY AND SUCCESS

This section will demonstrate the four steps to data quality as implemented through ODI Interfaces, Procedures, Packages, Scenarios, and Load Plans. Space considerations dictate that I must assume the user has basic familiarity with building an ODI package. If you are not conversant with ODI, some of the terminology might be confusing, but if you follow along you will see the pieces of a real implementation. You will be able to fill in the details as you become more adept with ODI. In any case, we will follow the all-important four steps. I am sure you remember them, but just in case:

1. Extract dimension metadata to a table.
2. Identify and load missing dimension metadata.
3. Load the fact data.
4. Validate the data in Essbase to the fact data.

A Note about ODI Project Organization

SubfFolders

A folder hierarchy within an ODI Project is not mandatory, but it can help logically organize code modules. Numbering the folders, as in Figure 2.2, will sort them in logical process order and, yes, these are the four steps to data quality realized in ODI.

Location of Objects

To get around ODI's default unorganized lists of objects, I match the location of objects with their scope, such as Procedures that are local to a subfolder within that folder. Project global objects are stored in the default location in the Project's First Folder. As an example, the Procedure PROC_DataNotInMetaData is only used in the Packages within the subfolder 2—LoadMissing, and consequently is stored there per Figure 2.3.

Naming Conventions

Although categorizing objects through subfolders aids organization, it is easy (at least for me) in an even moderately complex project to get very confused as to what a given object does. Looking at Figure 2.4, is it obvious what each object does?

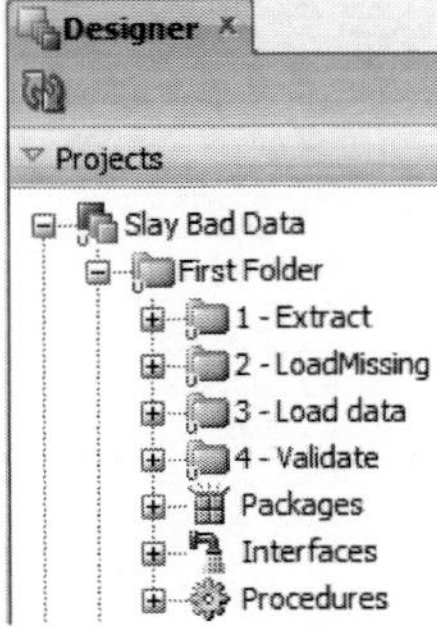

Figure 2.2 Designer folders.

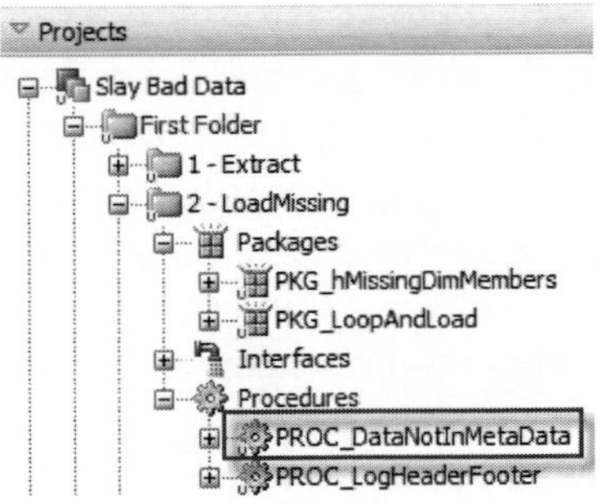

Figure 2.3 Object organization.

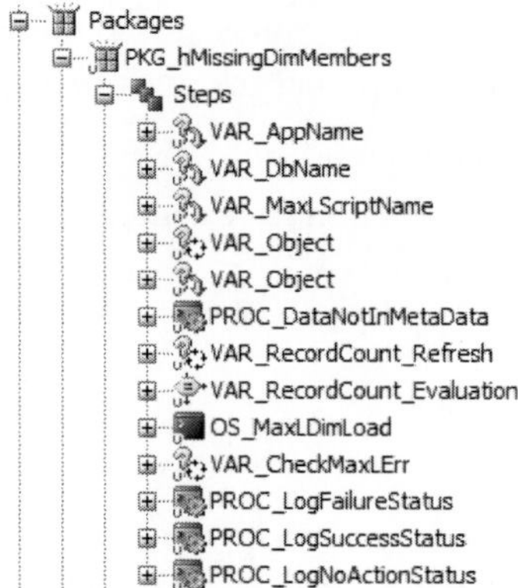

Figure 2.4 Mnemonic naming convention in Designer.

Table 2.2

Object Type	Icon	Prefix	Sample
Interface		INT	INT_Years
OS Command		OS	OS_MaxLDimLoad
Load Plan		PLAN	PLAN_ASOsamp
Procedure		PROC	PROC_LogSuccessStatus
Scenarios		SCN	SCN_PKG_HMISSINGMEMBERS
Variable		VAR	VAR_Object

Hopefully, the mnemonic names aid in describing their object's function. Did you notice the VAR_, OS_, PROC_, and PKG_ prefixes? I use a kind of modified Hungarian notation, but instead of making the prefix lower case, I made the descriptive prefix upper case because ODI desperately wants to create all names in upper case anyway. This naming convention is not a requirement, but I find it much easier to read, particularly in the ODI Designer Navigator as shown in Figure 2.3 and Figure 2.4. Table 2.2 shows the object types, their icons prefixes, and sample object names from this chapter's solution.

2.4.1 Extract Essbase Dimensionality to a Table

If ASOsamp was fully built from known dimension sources that, in turn, were constrained against the fact data, there would be no need to test that the data matches the database metadata; it could not be any other way. This absolute match of data and metadata achieved through referential integrity is the hallmark of a data warehouse. As I have noted, however, many Essbase databases are *not* built from data warehouses. Frequently, Essbase databases are built from multiple data sources, some of which are more reliable than others. Some are downright *un*reliable. I am talking about spreadsheets and text files that are "always right," except when they are not, which is often.

Moreover, dimension maintenance of some but not all dimensions is often manual. What happens when part of a data source does not match dimensionality or an administrator erroneously renames a member? We both know the answer: KABOOM! Insert the mental image of a bad data mushroom cloud rising ominously over your Essbase database.

A process that reverses out the dimensions to a SQL table so that constraints in the form of INNER JOINs can occur is the first step in guaranteeing that the fact data can be successfully loaded into the database.

2.4.1.1 Extracting Dimensions While this step could be done through one of the several freeware outline extractors (Applied Olap's OutlineExtractor and Sebastién Roux's outlinereader are the two most common) or via Essbase 11.1.2.x's MaxL "export outline" command, ODI was used for this part because it can write directly to a SQL table. The freeware products only write to flat files and MaxL outputs only to XML.

Before ASOsamp's dimensions are extracted to the Dimensions table through a series of dimension-specific Interfaces, Data Models for Essbase and the Dimensions table target and their concomitant Physical and Logical schemas must be defined first in Topology Manager. Your environment will dictate the specific schema and other definitions. After you reverse the objects, the Essbase ASOsamp and SQL table Dimension Data Models will look like Table 2.3.

The Dimensions Data Model contains some fields that are for the dimension tagged as "Accounts" only, e.g., TimeBalance, VarReporting, etc. These properties are ignored for non-Accounts dimensions on reversal and are set to NULL. ODI will automatically map Essbase and SQL field names in Interfaces if the names are identical. The Essbase Data Model names are defined by ODI so it is up to you to define your SQL target fields in the same way. The alternative is to manually map fields, but why would anyone want to create manual, error-prone Interface mapping requirements?

Table 2.3

Essbase ASOSamp.Sample Used in Diagrams Hierarchy Age ASOSamp_SampleData (ASOSamp_Sample) Geography Income Level Measures Payment Type Products Promotions Stores Time Transaction Type Years Hidden Datastores	SQL ASOSamp Used in Diagrams Hierarchy DataNotInMetadata Dimensions Columns DimName sortID ParentName MemberName Alias DataStorage TwoPassCalc Consolidation UDA Formula Comment TimeBalance TimeBalanceSkip VarReporting CurrConv CurrConvCategory
ASOsamp.Sample Essbase data model	ASOsamp.dbo.Dimensions SQL data model

Staging Areas and Work Tables

ODI uses a concept called Extract, Load, and Transform (E-LT), which means that it performs data processing on the target using the target's own internal language. This target orientation can lead to a smaller footprint memory/disk footprint, fewer servers, and better performance than a traditional ETL tool, which does its processes in a separate staging area using its own processing engine. In ODI, E-LT's target orientation means that any temporary work tables are dynamically created and used solely in the target environment.

By default, these temporary tables are deleted to clean up the data target. However, this automatic deletion can be undesirable as the work tables can be a rich source of debugging information if something goes wrong. It is nice to be able to see what the last successful (or otherwise) pull of information was in an n-step process beyond what the ODI Operator scheduler and job console shows.

To keep those temporary tables from being deleted, go to the Flow tab in a given Interface, select the Source Set object (that's what you're reading from) and, as in Figure 2.5, set the DELETE_TEMPORARY_OBJECTS option from the default TRUE to FALSE. ODI will automatically drop and recreate the tables on the next run.

However, Figure 2.6 illustrates the problem when E-LT processing is used as these temporary tables appear in the database/schema list as below.

This is a minor annoyance with one work table; when extended to multiple work tables, it can clutter the table list and make navigation difficult. Moreover, it is highly likely that the SQL username ODI is using will have table write access, but will not have table create rights in the target environment, resulting in execution errors when ODI tries to create those tables. Can ODI's temporary work tables exist in an E-LT paradigm?

Yes, by using a different data store for its processing than the target. While this can be done in the ODI server's memory, using either the MEMORY_ENGINE or the SUNOPSIS_MEMORY_ENGINE as defined in the Interface Definition

LKM Selector: LKM Hyperion Essbase METADATA to SQL

Options:

Name	Value
LOG_ERRORS	<default>:true
ERROR_LOG_FILENAME	c:\tempdir\ODI\logs\ExtractAge.err
ERR_COL_DELIMITER	<default>:,
ERR_ROW_DELIMITER	<default>:\r\n
ERR_TEXT_DELIMITER	<default>:
ERR_LOG_HEADER_ROW	<default>:true
DELETE_TEMPORARY_OBJECTS	false
ALIAS_TABLE	<default>:

Figure 2.5 DELETE_TEMPORARY_OBJECTS ODI Interface Flow Dialog Box.

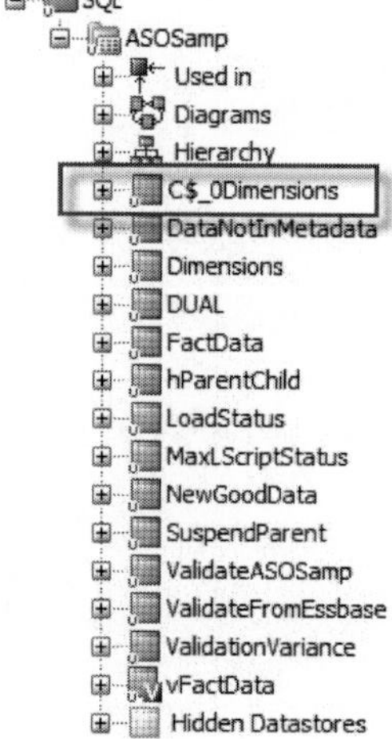

Figure 2.6 ODI Data Model of target SQL databases.

tab, the ephemeral nature of these RAM-based processing areas makes debugging impossible as once the process is finished, any temporary tables are destroyed. Additionally, while the in-memory engines are fast, they do not scale well as they are limited by available memory.

A better approach is to use a separate SQL data store that has already been defined as an ODI Data Model. That means that there are three data stores in a given process: the source, the staging area, and the target. "What," you gasp as you fight for air, "break the E-LT architecture after Oracle went through all that trouble to make it faster/better/smarter?" You bet, because with Essbase the concept of E-LT has already struck out:

- There are no tables at the Essbase target as Essbase is not relational, so tables cannot be created there, only in some third area. Strike one against E-LT for Essbase.
- There is no data manipulation language at the Essbase target. Essbase has MDX formulas and external ASO Calc Scripts, BSO Calc Scripts, MaxL, Esscmd, and the various APIs, but nothing that acts as a data manipulation language. Strike two against E-LT for Essbase.
- The lack of target tables and data manipulation functionality means something has to perform Extract, Transform, and Load processing. Essbase thus requires an ODI server agent and engine. Note: the ODI server and agent can coexist with many other products on a given physical server; it need not truly be a separate box. Strike three against E-LT for Essbase.
- No change on your part is required; the default processing within the in-memory engine using implicit SQL puts paid to the notion of Essbase E-LT: Essbase with ODI is not E-LT. For your purposes, this is great because you can take advantage of the traditional ETL architecture by picking a separate relational data store to cleanly store those temporary work tables, as shown in Figure 2.7. Choosing this relational data store is as easy as ticking the "Staging Area Different From Target" box on the Interface Overview tab and then selecting the relational staging Data Model, in this example named ODISTAGE.

This selection results in temporary tables written to the separate staging area, thus providing the best of both worlds: supplemental debugging information and an uncluttered, easy to read target data store.

Each extracted dimension requires its own Interface. There are only a few things to note in Figure 2.8's Interface:

- The DimName field is hard coded with the dimension name.
- Identical field names map automatically.
- MemberName is the primary key for the Dimensions table.
- All mapping takes place in the Staging Area.

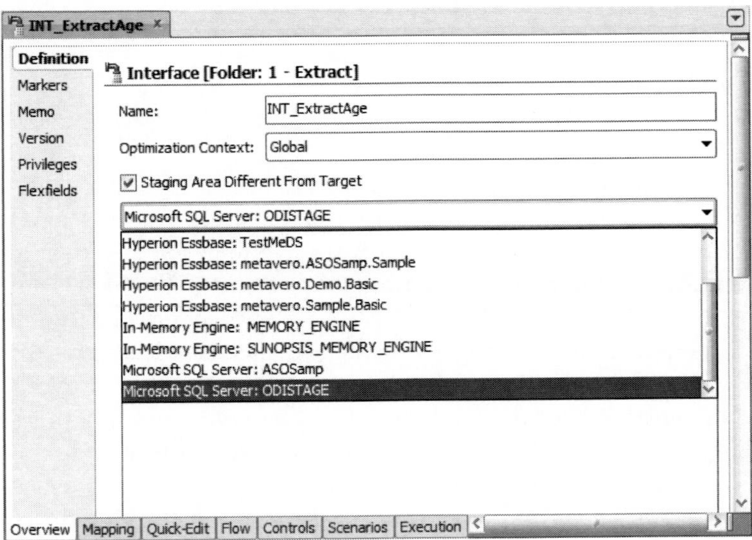

Figure 2.7 Selecting a different staging area.

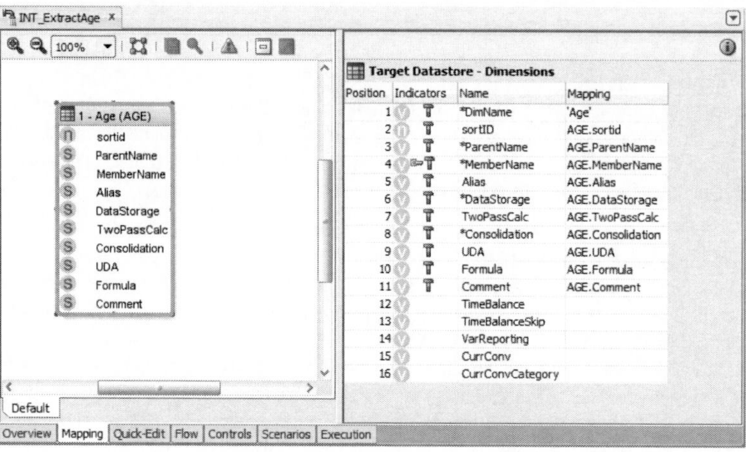

Figure 2.8 INT_ExtractAge Interface.

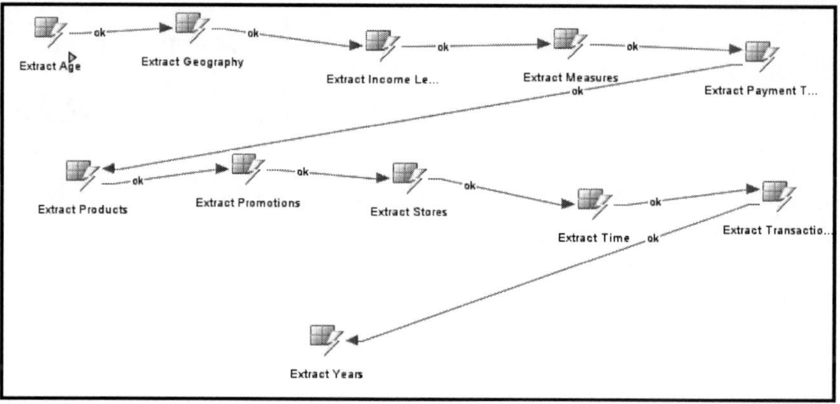

Figure 2.9 Package PKG_Extract_ASOsamp.

If you got excited by the dimension name constant in the target, e.g., Age, Geography, etc., do not bother; you are stuck with setting up each dimension separately as each Interface is inextricably linked to a physical Essbase dimension as shown in the source pane on the left. After something as important (and permanent) as that is put into play, a mere string constant is not material. Alas, this is how ODI works when it comes to reversing Essbase dimensions short of programmatically generating Interfaces through code. This is an advanced book, but not that advanced. This object-based approach is used for reversing dimensions because of its ease; the other components of this solution use more flexible approaches. And, if you can figure out a way to generalize this extraction portion, please let me know (contact information is on page x).

Compiling the individual Interfaces to Scenarios and then linking them together in a Package, as shown in Figure 2.9, allows all of the dimensions to be extracted to the Dimensions table.

2.4.2 *Comparing Dimensionality*

With ASOsamp's dimensions in a table, SQL can be used to compare the extracted dimensionality to the data to be loaded *before* the fact data is loaded, so there are *no* data load errors. This is the referential integrity discussed previously with after-the-fact enforcement. If the fact data contains members that are not in Essbase, special suspense or unassigned members can act as a temporary load location so that at least the data gets counted at the total dimension level. It would be nice to know if this occurred, on a dimension-by-dimension basis, and when, so an administrator can identify which dimensions need attention (there really is a proper place for those missing members, somewhere) and how often this unassigned load occurs.

2.4.2.1 Typical ODI Approach In order to implement the discovery, repair, and report tasks discussed above, the typical process would be to build a series of Interfaces to perform the "are all of the data's members in Essbase" test and then load the difference to suspense parents. Each Interface would be hard coded to the Essbase application and database and indeed to each dimension. This requires lots of dragging and dropping and general GUI-ness (graphical user interface), repeated 10 times, once for each dimension.

Moving this functionality to another database would require recreating all of the hard coded Interfaces (and that really frosts my cookies). I will not even touch the whole spaces-in-dimension-names-make-ODI-throw-a-rod issue.

2.4.2.2 The Better Way Do not misunderstand me, ODI, despite its quirks, is a powerful and flexible tool that can do almost anything. That flexibility is manifested in ODI's step-based Packages. They can accommodate the standard GUI way as outlined above or combine Interfaces, Variables, OS objects, and especially SQL-rich Procedures into a portable and powerful combination that loops a database's dimensions, loads missing dimensionality, and logs process status. This approach is just a little more complicated to set up than a series of Interfaces, but, oh so much more flexible.

The above paragraph's promotion of Procedures is likely to send ODI purists into an architectural tizzy because:

1. Procedures use code.
2. Objects within Procedures are not dynamically updated.

There can be no question that Procedures use code, which is antithetical to the spirit of GUI ETL tools. However, in the context of the solution this chapter provides, and when used with restraint, Procedures within Packages are far more flexible and reusable than Interfaces. Moreover, if you do not plan on using ODI, you can take the SQL in the Procedures and script it in the language of your choosing. That flexibility of reuse and transferability would be hard to duplicate in object-based Interfaces.

I will cop to the charge that Procedures are not dynamically updated the way Interfaces are, with columns added or removed as the logical schema changes, although Variable name changes do propagate through. More importantly, we will mitigate this lack of dynamic updating within procedures by using variables to parameterize the SQL in the procedures in the next section.

2.4.2.3 Code, Variables, Procedures, and MaxL Again, the GUI in ODI is great, except when it is not. When a graphical representation of an ETL process is simple and direct, it is the way to do things, such as the reversing of Essbase dimensions to SQL. However,

Table 2.4 Variable Types

Type	Purpose
Set Variable	Assign a value at design time
Declare Variable	Receive a value from another process as a parameter
Evaluate Variable	Test a variable value
Refresh Variable	Value a variable from code within the variable itself via SQL or other code

there are many use-cases that show the purely graphical approach to be too rigid; this is where code comes into play. Happily, ODI anticipates this need by providing Refresh Variables, Procedures, and OS Command objects, all of which support code.

Variables are just that, variables, but there are four different kinds, all of which are used in this chapter's Packages per Table 2.4.

A given variable can have multiple types within a Package. A variable can start out as a Refresh Variable to get a value via an SQL query and then become an Evaluate Variable so that the result can be tested. This polymorphism can be confusing, but is a very powerful concept. All that it takes is dragging and dropping the variable into the Package twice or more and then setting the variable type. Refresh Variables typically, but not always, use SQL to provide single numeric or alphanumeric values.

Procedures are a set of commands (just like variables, many different languages are supported although this example only uses SQL) that perform extracts and transformations and return sets of values. As a bonus, within the context of Essbase and ODI, they can be considerably more flexible than Interfaces as we shall see.

Alas, there is no MaxL Knowledge Module for ODI. However, that is not an issue as MaxL scripts can be launched through ODI's OS Command object. Make that MaxL script just as parameterized as you need; I have stopped short of the full treatment to make it somewhat more readable.

2.4.3 Load Missing Dimensionality to Essbase

2.4.3.1 Compare the Fact Data to the Dimension Just to be clear, we are comparing the metadata references in the fact data to the metadata in the dimension (again checking that all data has a home) and loading the missing dimensionality (creating homes for the homeless).

The package, PKG_hMissingDimMembers, in Figure 2.10, loads missing dimensionality through the following objects and steps:

1. VAR_AppName, VAR_DbName, and VAR_MaxLScriptName are Declare Variables that receive their values through the calling Package PKG_LoopAndLoad.
2. VAR_Object queries the dimension list in the vDimList relational view to get the dimension name based on the value of #VAR_Kounter (not visible in this Package, but in the PKG_LoopAndLoad calling code).
3. PROC_DataNotInMetaData compares the extracted Essbase level-0 dimension members for a single dimension against the fact table FactData and writes the results to the table hParentChild.
4. If hParentChild has only the default two records, a "No Action" message is piped to the LoadStatus table.
5. If hParentChild is more than two records long (these header records are always created), the MaxL script LoadDim.msh is launched.

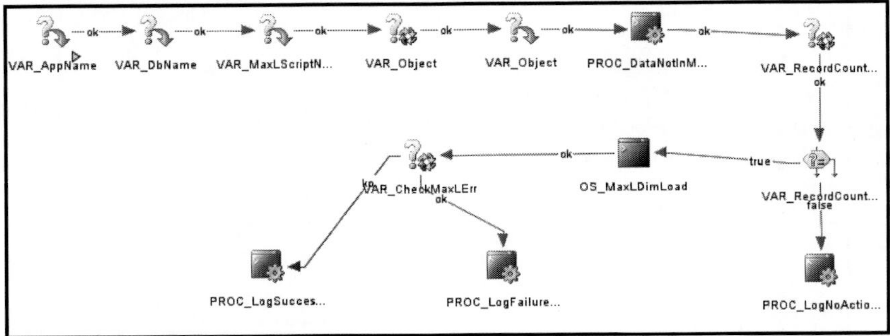

Figure 2.10 Package PKG_hMissingDimMembers.

6. If LoadDim.msh's STDERR produces a LoadDim.err file with a file length greater than zero bytes (the file is always generated regardless of error condition), a failure notice is written to the LoadStatus table, else a success message is written.

2.4.3.2 Loop the Dimensions Every dimension represented in the fact data can potentially have orphan members not represented in the target Essbase database ASOsamp. While the above Package is suitable for one dimension, this is no more functional than a single dimension Interface and, in fact, is quite a bit more complicated. Going through this much trouble only makes sense if the Package's logic can be encapsulated and called as a subroutine. Compiling the Package to the Scenario SCN_PKG_HMISSINGDIMMEMBERS makes PKG_hMissingDimMembers an object that can referenced as needed and driven through a simple dimension loop for *n* dimensions instead of creating multiple Interfaces. That has been done in PKG_LoopAndLoad. And, for you ODI purists out there, please note that this reuse is exactly what would not have been possible without the use of parameterized SQL procedures.

PKG_LoopAndLoad in Figure 2.11 loops the dimensions in the view vDimList and loads missing dimension members through the following objects and steps:

1. The Set Variable counter VAR_Kounter is set to 1. Note: Variables can be Set at design time and then Refresh their value through code as shown in this Package.
2. VAR_AppName and VAR_DbName are Declare Variables set by the calling Load Plan PLAN_ASOsamp. They pass their values to the compiled PKG_hMissing-DimMembers through the Scenario SCN_PKG_HMISSINGDIMMEMBERS.
3. VAR_Status is set to an initial value of "Start" for writing to the LoadStatus table.
4. PROC_LogHeaderFooter writes a start status message to the table LoadStatus.
5. The Refresh Variable VAR_MaxDimCount performs and stores a row count of the view vDimList.
6. The Refresh Variable VAR_LoopDimName gets the dimension name based on VAR_Kounter's value.
7. SCN_PKG_HMISSINGDIMMEMBERS tests the dimension value of VAR_LoopDimName and loads missing metadata if necessary.

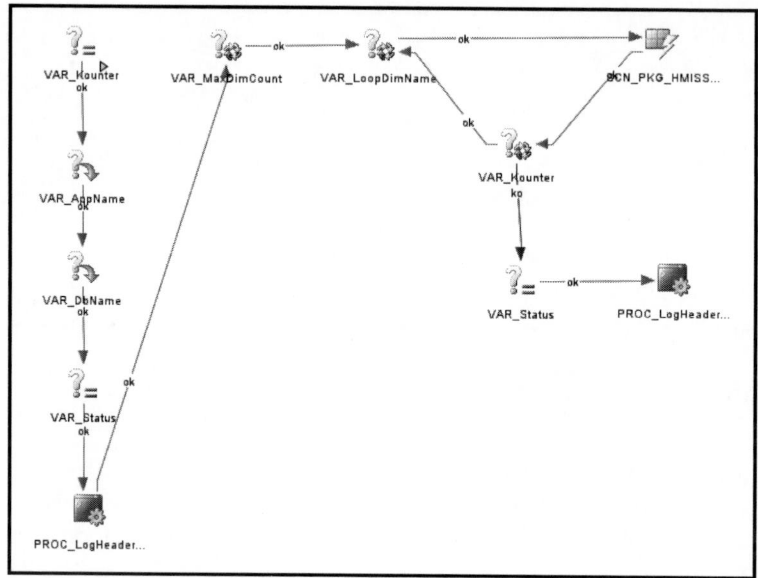

Figure 2.11 Package PKG_LoopAndLoad.

```
Years
 ├─Curr Year (+) (Alias: Current Year)
 ├─Prev Year (~) (Alias: Previous Year)
 ├─Variance (~)
 └─Variance % (~)
```

Figure 2.12 Years dimension before PKG_LoopAndLoad.

```
⊟-Years
   ├─Curr Year (+) (Alias: Current Year)
   ├─Prev Year (~) (Alias: Previous Year)
   ├─Variance (~)
   ├─Variance % (~)
   ⊟-SuspendYears (+) (Alias: Suspend Years)
      ├─1911 (+)
      └─Next Year (+)
```

Figure 2.13 Years dimension after PKG_LoopAndLoad.

8. VAR_Kounter increments itself by 1, and tests to see if it is equal to VAR_MaxDimCount. If the values match, the flow branches to VAR_Status, if not, VAR_LoopDimName refreshes again.
9. When all of the dimensions in vDimList have been looped, PROC_LogHeaderFooter writes an end message to LoadStatus.

Using the examples of data orphans in the Years dimension, Figure 2.12 shows the Years dimension before PKG_LoopAndLoad is run.

Figure 2.13 shows the Years dimension after PKG_LoopAndLoad is executed with orphan members loaded under the parent SuspendYears, thus ensuring that the fact data rows that contain Years 1911 and Next Year can be loaded to ASOsamp.

The Building Blocks

The second step in slaying bad data is "Identify and load missing dimension data." The ODI Packages PKG_hMissingDimMembers and PKG_LoopAndLoad are the structure for performing that discovery and dynamic dimension building. Within that framework, three key components must be created and executed:

1. Finding the missing members.
2. Building a parent/child table to load those missing members to a suspense parent.
3. Creating an Essbase Load rule to read the parent/child table.

Finding Those Missing Members

A simple SQL query can test the fact data against the extracted Dimensions table for the Years dimension as shown below. In parameterized form, this code is the "Find Non Matching Members" step of PKG_hMissingDimMember's Procedure PROC_DataNotInMetaData.

```
--      Purpose:        Write to DataNotInMetaData all members in the fact table
--                      not in the Dimensions table
--      Modified:       11 November 2011, initial write
--      Written by:     Cameron Lackpour
--      Notes:          This sample code is for the Years dimension only.
--                      The LEFT OUTER JOIN of FactData to Dimensions where the
--                      Dimensions result set is Null gives us ALL of the records
--                      in FactData that don't match Dimensions.
--      Clear out the target table
TRUNCATE TABLE DataNotInMetadata
--      Find those missing members
INSERT
        INTO DataNotInMetadata
SELECT DISTINCT
        'Years' AS Dimension,
        F.Years AS 'Years'
FROM FactData F
LEFT OUTER JOIN Dimensions D
        ON F.Years = D.MemberName
WHERE D.MemberName IS NULL
```

Given that there are rows in the fact data that have in the [Years] column "1911" and "Next Year" in addition to the expected [Curr Year] and [Prev Year] Years dimension members, the query output looks like Table 2.5.

This SELECT result describes the members that are not in Essbase, but are in the data. This is a start, but not enough to load the dimension to Essbase. While 1911 and Next Year could be loaded to the Years dimension as is without specifying a parent, they would automatically go in at generation one. In a dimension like Years, that is fine. But, it is clearer to put them under a parent that highlights that they have been added, such as [Suspend]. Furthermore, if the dimension had alternate hierarchies, then Suspend would simply be the top of a new alternate hierarchy. Therefore, we must give as a grandparent of [Suspend] either the dimension name (if no alternates) or the name of the Primary hierarchy. Taking care of this detail would require a hard coded value for each dimension. But, that is easily accomplished and it is suggested to the reader as an exercise.

For now, just focus on the base case where there is only a primary hierarchy in each dimension. What is needed is a query that creates a complete parent/child or recursive table with a predetermined parent.

Build That Parent/Child Table

There are three parts to this query: the header, the parent record, and finally those missing members found above. To get this requires only a little string manipulation and a sort order field to get everything in the right order as shown in the segment of code below.

```
--      Purpose:        Create the content of a dimension load rule from
--                      missing metadata
```

Table 2.5 Missing Members

Dimension	MemberName
Years	1911
Years	Next Year

```
--      Modified:       11 November 2011, initial write
--      Written by:     Cameron Lackpour
--      Notes:          This sample code is for the Years dimension only.
SELECT
        A.Parent,
        A.Member,
        A.Alias
FROM
        (
        -- Header record
        --      PARENT0, CHILD0, and ALIAS0 are hardcoded
        --      The concatenated dimension name completes the header
        SELECT
                '900' AS 'Order',
                'PARENT0,' + P.DimName AS 'Parent',
                'CHILD0,' + P.DimName AS 'Member',
                'ALIAS0,' + P.DimName AS 'Alias'
        FROM SuspendParent P
        WHERE P.DimName = 'Years'
        -- Join header and body
        UNION
        -- Parent record
        -- The dimension name, member name, and alias are all
        -- in the SuspendParent table
        SELECT
                '800' AS 'Order',
                P.DimName AS 'Parent',
                P.SuspendParent AS 'Member',
                P.SuspendAlias AS 'Alias'
        FROM SuspendParent P
        WHERE P.DimName = 'Years'
        UNION
        -- Missing members, the result of an INSERT SELECT statement
        SELECT
                '700' AS 'Order',
                S.SuspendParent AS 'Parent',
                D.MemberName AS 'Member',
                '' AS Alias
        FROM
                DataNotInMetadata D
        INNER JOIN SuspendParent S
                ON D.Dimension = S.DimName
        ) AS A
ORDER BY [Order] DESC
```

Given the above output from the table DataNotInMetadata, Table 2.6 reflects this query's output.

The above is a dimension source ready for loading in every detail and completely data-driven. In parameterized form, this SQL code is the "Create ParentChildLoadFormat" step in PROC_DataNotInMetaData.

Note that the [Suspend] member name is actually generated as "Suspend" + DimensionName with DimensionName coming from the SuspendParent table in the middle SELECT. If I had not done that then there would be duplicate members if more than one dimension needed "Suspend" members. In some cases, the users may want the suspend members to be at a specific place in the outline. That can be handled when you enhance this solution with the "Suspend Grandparent" needed to deal with Alternate hierarchies as mentioned above.

Table 2.6 Missing Members with Dimension and Suspense Parent

Parent	Child	Alias
PARENT0,Years	CHILD0,Years	ALIAS0,Years
Years	SuspendYears	Suspend Years
SuspendYears	1911	
SuspendYears	Next Year	

A Really Dynamic Essbase Dimension Load rule

It also would be nice if this dimension build table could be used with a single dimension Load rule; lazy programmers hate to build more Load Rules than absolutely required and if there is one thing I am, deep in my heart of hearts, it is that I am lazy. As an example, I think I am still working on mowing the back yard from my list of chores, circa 11th grade. As that was during the Reagan administration, you begin to understand my powers of procrastination.

A Really Dynamic Essbase Dimension Load rule

The standard way to build a Load rule is to assign it to a specific dimension and then assign the columns to the parent, child, alias, property, formula, UDA, etc. In a 10-dimension database like ASOsamp, with 10 possibly nonmatching dimensions in the fact data, many Load rules would have to be built and tested; 10 of them, actually.

Figure 2.14 is an example from Sample.Basic's Parchil dimension Load rule. Note the header strings as there will be a quiz later on their significance:

- PARENT0, Product
- CHILD0, Product
- ALIAS0, Product

The standard way to build a dimension Load rule, be it Parent/Child, Generation, or whatever, is to assign via the Dimension Build Settings dialog box the dimension name and build method.

That is the standard way; the lazy programmer selects the Data Source Properties dialog box in the Load rule editor per Figure 2.15 and sets the "Record containing dimension building field name" Header property to 1.

With this set, all that is needed is a header record that looks just like a Parent/Child Load rule; this header record must include the dimension name. If the data source can supply that dimension information within the header, only one Load rule is required for *all* dimensions. One caveat, you must manually associate the Dimension Build Settings as Parent/Child for each one of the dimensions.

The Procedure PROC_DataNotInMetaData populates the table hParentChild with all of the information needed to load a suspense hierarchy and does it dynamically for each dimension. A simple SELECT statement in the Load rule (SELECT * FROM hParentChild) gives Dynamic dimension building for all dimensions with one Load rule. Figure 2.16 illustrates the Year dimension suspense member dimension Load rule after it loads from the hParentChild table. It still is not much to look at. Oddly, the header records in the lower pane do *not* show the expected field type and generation information as per Figure 2.14; if this were sourced from a text file it would. One of the "mysteries" of at least my install of Essbase 11.1.2.1, but nothing to worry about.

What *is* important is that invisible record. Yes, I know, it cannot be seen in the Load rule, so take a look at row 1 of Figure 2.17. In the below query output, the first row contains PARENT0, Years, CHILD0,Years, and ALIAS0,Years. Those field values are the information Essbase needs to identify the dimension and the field properties, just as if they had been manually defined in the Load rule.

Putting It All Together

PROC_DataNotInMetaData finds orphaned members in fact data and dynmically creates parent/child hierarchies that the Load rule hDynSQL can use for all dimensions. This combination, when called by ODI Packages, reduces 20 potential

Data Prep Editor [EssbaseCluster-1.Sample.Basic.Parchil]

Encoding:English_UnitedStates.Latin1@Binary

```
1    200    200-10  Old Fashioned
2    200    200-20  Diet Root Beer
3    200    200-30  Sasparilla
4    200    200-40  Birch Beer
5    200    200-50  With Caffeine
```

	PARENT0,Product	CHILD0,Product	ALIAS0,Product
1	200	200-10	Old Fashioned
2	200	200-20	Diet Root Beer
3	200	200-30	Sasparilla
4	200	200-40	Birch Beer
5	200	200-50	With Caffeine

Figure 2.14 Sample.Basic's Parchil Dimension Load rule.

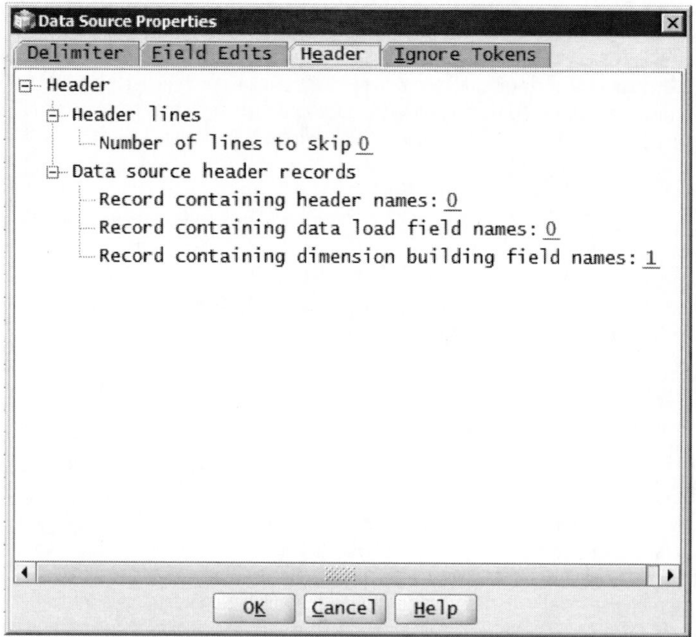

Figure 2.15 Load rule Header properties.

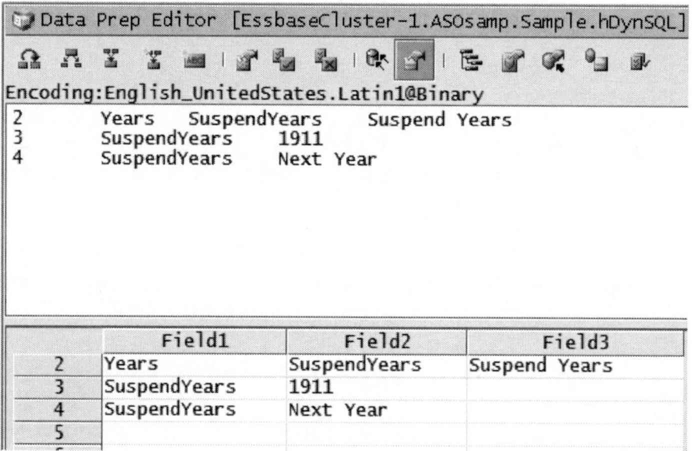

Figure 2.16 Years suspense hierarchy in Load rule hDynSQL.

objects in ODI (10 Interfaces) and Essbase (10 Load rules) to two overall. It has been my experience that the fewer the objects, the less there is to go wrong, Additionally, the Procedure and Load rule (the Load rule will need a one-time dimension assignment per database) can be used across multiple Essbase databases. This flexibility and reuse underscores the flexibility and power of both ODI and Essbase, They really are that awesome.

2.4.4 Loading Data

Now that every dimension that could have orphaned metadata has been dealt with, a simple data load to Essbase must occur. Note that like the dimension building Packages, this step does not use the standard ODI GUI approach for two reasons:

hParentChild

	Parent	Child	Alias
1	PARENT0,Years	CHILD0,Years	ALIAS0,Years
2	Years	SuspendYears	Suspend Years
3	SuspendYears	1911	
4	SuspendYears	Next Year	

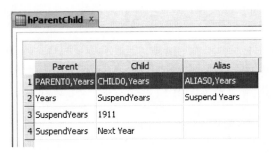

Figure 2.17 Years suspense SQL output.

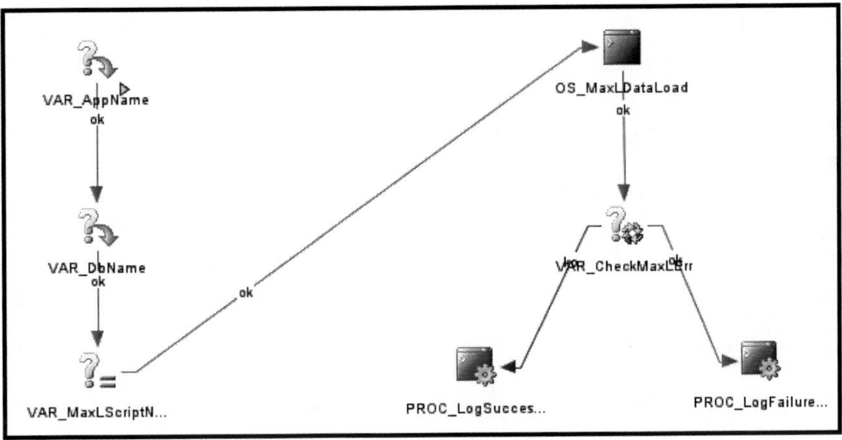

Figure 2.18 Package PKG_dLoadData.

1. A data loading Interface is inextricably tied to the target Essbase database, thus preventing reuse.
2. Essbase dimension names with spaces create a failure in the data loading Interface. Three of ASOsamp's dimensions, [Transaction Type], [Payment Type], and [Income Level] have spaces in their names.

PKG_dLoadData in Figure 2.18 loads the current year and month data from the fact source through the following objects and steps:

1. The Declare Variables VAR_AppName and VAR_DbName are passed from the calling Load Plan PLAN_ASOsamp.
2. The Set Variable VAR_MaxLScriptName is set in this Package to LoadData.
3. The VAR_AppName, VAR_DbName, and VAR_MaxLScriptName are passed to the OS_MaxLDataLoad object that runs the script LoadData.msh.
4. If LoadData.msh's STDERR produces a LoadData.err file with a file length greater than zero bytes, a failure notice is written to the LoadStatus table or else a success message is written.

2.4.5 Validating Data

"Wait," you say, "how can the data not be good?" (You are at least thinking this, right?) What about all of those many, many steps that guarantee that all members in the source fact data have a home in Essbase? How can data not have been loaded? I have two good reasons why data might not be correct:

1. As I previously related, data can still fall through the cracks through illegal characters. Per President Reagan, "Trust in your data, but verify."
2. There is this guy named Murphy, and he has a law "If anything can go wrong, it will."

I do not live my life by hoary old maxims, but these are two sayings that any cautious/continually employed Essbase developer should take to heart. I have, hence these validation steps.

1. PKG_ExtractValidateReport in Figure 2.19 runs an Essbase Report Script to disk, imports it to a table, and then compares the Essbase data to the summed fact data through the following objects and steps. The Set Variable VAR_MaxLScriptName value is set to Validate.
2. The Declare Variables VAR_AppName and VAR_DbName are passed from the calling Load Plan PLAN_ASOsamp.
3. The Set Variable VAR_MaxLReportName is set to Validate.
4. The OS Command object OS_MaxLReportRun is passed the parameters for the Essbase application, database, MaxL script, and Report Script name, which it then runs. The Report Script Validate.rep produces a report for the current year and month at a total dimension level for Original Price, Price Paid, Returns, Units, and Transactions.

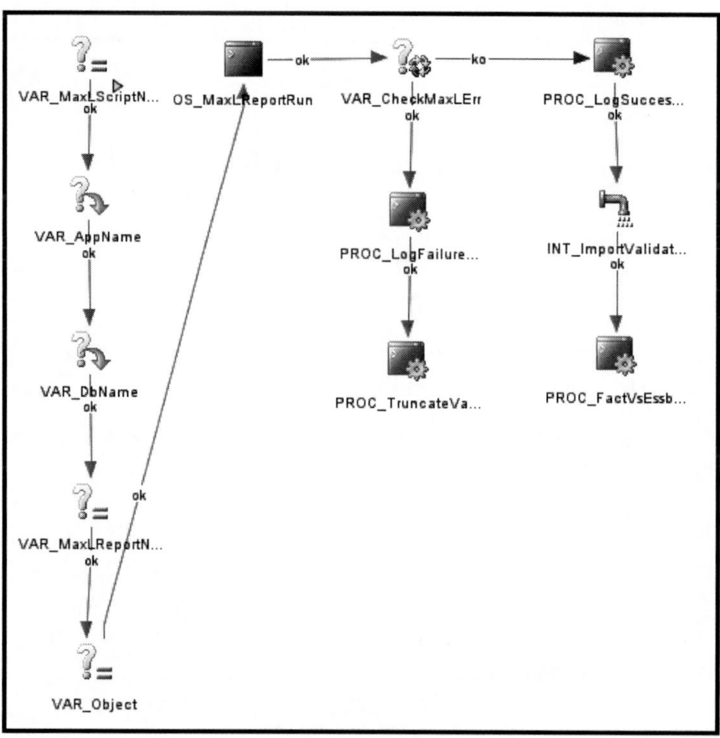

Figure 2.19 Package PKG_ExtractValidateExport.

5. The Refresh Variable VAR_CheckMaxLErr tests Validate.msh's STDERR output. If a Validate.err file with a file length greater than zero bytes is found, a failure notice is written to the LoadStatus table through the Procedure PROC_LogFailureStatus and the ValidateVariance table is truncated via the Procedure PROC_TruncateVariance.
6. If Validate.err has a zero length, the flat file output from Report Script Validate.rep is imported to the table ValidateASOsamp through the Interface INT_ImportValidateReport.
7. The Procedure PROC_FactVsEssbase compares the data values from Essbase to a SQL-consolidated result set from the fact data. The difference is written to the table ValidationVariance. With luck and clean living the variance should (must) always be zero for all members.

Three Notes about Validation

1. The SQL aggregation in PROC_FactVsEssbase sums full totals for all dimensions. If desired, multiple levels of aggregation by dimension in SQL with similar Essbase extracts could be created to make the variance test more granular.
2. This validation process does not guard against incomplete attribute dimension association. If ASOsamp's Square Footage attribute dimension is part of the retrieval and all level-0 Stores are *not* associated with Square Footage, then the retrieved data results will be wrong, A separate base dimension to attribute dimension validation must occur.
3. The process in PKG_ExtractValidateReport validates that all data sent to Essbase actually made it into the cube. Beware, however, if the original extraction process from the true source to the FactData table failed to pick up some data, that error will not be flagged.

One thing that you could do to help trap this kind of data extraction error is to have the users create a top-level query directly from the source system. Then, write a procedure to add a check against that value as well as the one we developed here from the extracted data. Completing this process will make your IT auditors very happy. While this is yet another challenge, you should balance it against the serenity that happy auditors bestow on their victims versus the sheer terror they invoke when system totals do not balance. Such are the troubles and travails of the valiant Essbase developer.

2.4.6 Really Tying It All Together

So, now that we have a four-part solution to data quality in Essbase that:

- Extracts dimension metadata to a table
- Identifies and loads missing dimension metadata
- Loads the fact data
- Validates the data in Essbase to the fact data,

the question arises: How does all of this get put together in a single process?

2.4.6.1 Packages I have used Packages to tie together steps within the ODI Project; that is the traditional way to *package* ODI objects into a flow. The graphical linking metaphor of drawing arrows from one object to another in Packages to denote process steps is perfectly satisfactory for simple program flows. This approach breaks down when the level of complexity becomes even moderately high.

To reduce complexity within Package diagrams, logical Packages can be compiled into Scenarios that can contain their own Packages-compiled-to-Scenarios, but this process of encapsulation gets difficult to manage as steps are added. At some point it all becomes a bit like Ouroboros, the snake of Greek mythology that eats its tail, except in ODI's case, it is not a metaphor for the circle of life, but is just a mess instead.

2.4.6.2 Load Plans to the Rescue ODI 11.1.1.5 introduced a new way to link together steps in a global sequence: Load Plans. Think of Load Plans as ODI's list-based way of addressing multistep complex processes with hierarchical steps, in-built parallelism (think of the scripting pain of kicking off parallel loads to an ASO load buffer—all auto-magic in a Load Plan), ability to restart, and exception handling. Additionally, there is a unified Operator execution reporting view.

Load Plans are exclusively based on Scenarios, the compiled output of Variables, Interfaces, Procedures, and Packages. The act of dragging any one of those uncompiled objects into a Load Plan forces compilation on the fly removes the manual design-time step.

Alas, Load Plans do not support looping like the Package PKG_LoopAndLoad does. This seems an insurmountable issue. This chapter's solution explicitly rejects linked Interfaces in favor of a code-based Package. What to do?

As you have likely noticed, ODI is flexible, almost to a fault. That flexibility and resultant plasticity extends to Load Plans. With that in mind, use Load Plans where hierarchy, parallelism, and in-built exception handling is important, i.e., practically always. When a process requires looping, such as in PKG_LoopAndLoad, or other functionality a Load Plan does not support, continue to use Packages.

The Load Plan PLAN_ASOsamp in Figure 2.20 shows the steps that correspond to the four Slay Bad Data steps in the Project.

1. "Extract Essbase to SQL" links the individual dimension extraction Interfaces and extracts ASOsamp's metadata to the Dimensions table.
2. "Load missing hierarchy" executes the Package PKG_LoopAndLoad (remember, this is the looping process that cannot be translated to a Load Plan) to identify and load missing dimension data.

PLAN_ASOSamp

Definition
Steps
Exceptions
Variables
Privileges
Version
Flexfields

#	Steps Hierarchy	Enab...	Scenario/Variable	Restart	Context	Logical Agent
0	Extract, find and load missing hierarchy,	✓		Restart from failure		
1	Extract Essbase to SQL	✓		Restart from failure		
2	SCN_INT_EXTRACTAGE	✓	SCN_INT_EXTRACTAGE Version ...	Restart from new session	Global	OracleDIAgent
3	SCN_INT_EXTRACTGEOGRAPHY	✓	SCN_INT_EXTRACTGEOGRAPHY...	Restart from new session	Global	OracleDIAgent
4	SCN_INT_EXTRACTINCOMELEVEI	✓	SCN_INT_EXTRACTINCOMELEVE...	Restart from new session	Global	OracleDIAgent
5	SCN_INT_EXTRACTMEASURES	✓	SCN_INT_EXTRACTMEASURES V...	Restart from new session	Global	OracleDIAgent
6	SCN_INT_EXTRACTPAYMENTTYP	✓	SCN_INT_EXTRACTPAYMENTTY...	Restart from new session	Global	OracleDIAgent
7	SCN_INT_EXTRACTPRODUCTS	✓	SCN_INT_EXTRACTPRODUCTS V...	Restart from new session	Global	OracleDIAgent
8	SCN_INT_EXTRACTPROMOTION:	✓	SCN_INT_EXTRACTPROMOTION...	Restart from new session	Global	OracleDIAgent
9	SCN_INT_EXTRACTSTORES	✓	SCN_INT_EXTRACTSTORES Vers...	Restart from new session	Global	OracleDIAgent
10	SCN_INT_EXTRACTTIME	✓	SCN_INT_EXTRACTTIME Version...	Restart from new session	Global	OracleDIAgent
11	SCN_INT_EXTRACTTRANSACTIO	✓	SCN_INT_EXTRACTTRANSACTI...	Restart from new session	Global	OracleDIAgent
12	SCN_INT_EXTRACTYEARS	✓	SCN_INT_EXTRACTYEARS Versi...	Restart from new session	Global	OracleDIAgent
13	Load missing hierarchy	✓		Restart from failure		
14	SCN_PKG_LOOPANDLOAD	✓	SCN_PKG_LOOPANDLOAD Versi...	Restart from new session		
15	Load data	✓		Restart from failure		
16	SCN_PKG_DLOADDATA	✓	SCN_PKG_DLOADDATA Version ...	Restart from new session		
17	Validate	✓		Restart from failure		
18	PKG_EXTRACTVALIDATEREPORT	✓	PKG_EXTRACTVALIDATEREPOR...	Restart from new session	Global	OracleDIAgent

Figure 2.20 Load Plan PLAN_ASOsamp.

3. "Load data" loads fact data to Essbase.
4. "Validate" validates the fact data totals to Essbase totals.

Why Continue Using Packages if Load Plans Are So Great?

As previously noted, sometimes Load Plans are not a good replacement for Packages as in PKG_LoopAndLoad because of missing Load Plan functionality.

Relevant Examples

If you examine the steps "Load data" and "Validate," you will see that these are also Packages. I purposely did not convert these to Load Plan steps because Load Plans are so new and the solutions I have provided are not the standard ODI Interface approach. I wanted to reach the majority of ODI installations today that are using older versions of the product as of the writing of this book. However, the sequential steps in these Packages could easily be converted to a Load Plan (another challenge to the reader).

2.5 CONCLUSION

And, so we come to the end of an epic data quality quest. Do your feet hurt? Or maybe your head? No matter, together we have Slain the Beast called Bad Data. May it never stain your Essbase database's honor.

Was the journey worth the cost? What *you* need to decide is, was this chapter's long trip to data quality worthwhile? Of course I am ever so slightly biased, but consider this:

- The case for the dangers of bad data has been made by real world examples. Recall that these examples mostly ended in unemployment. If you do not have this issue licked, begin trembling in terror.
- The where (and the where never) and how to ensure data quality is laid out in a heavily annotated form over the four steps of metadata extraction, missing metadata identification, metadata and data loading, and Essbase to source data validation. You can use this approach and much of the code in your databases, even if you never use ODI.
- Following on that last point, a slew of advanced ODI, MaxL, and SQL techniques are demonstrated and documented in this chapter's appendix. The concepts behind the code can be used in nondata validation tasks.

Just as I channeled and then paraphrased President Reagan about trusting, but verifying data, you must channel President Kennedy and hold that: "Let every business owner know that you shall pay any price, bear any burden, meet any hardship, support any friend, oppose any foe, in order to guarantee good data in Essbase and assure continued employment."

Bad data in Essbase means pain for all concerned, yet it occurs all the time. We Essbase developers all know this and if we have any imagination about its impact on our livelihoods, we fear it. That this evil persists when the tools to combat it fall readily to hand makes its propagation all the more difficult to understand.

This chapter cannot explain why we Essbase practitioners tend to honor data quality more in the breach than in the observance, especially given the direct professional and personal consequences. Perhaps this chapter *is* a kind of pop psychology guide that will make you more strongly consider including a data quality step in your current and upcoming Essbase projects. Or, maybe you can use it as a lever on a tight-fisted project sponsor who does not want to pony up the cash to get his data right from the start.

The weapon to Slay Bad Data is in your hands in the form of this chapter. Use these harrowing, but true, stories of the malignant impact of bad data, a conceptual argument for good data, how not to mend data, and, finally, a fully documented solution that illustrates how to ensure good data ends up in your database.

I look forward to a world where no one ever worries about the foundation of a sound Essbase database. May universal referential integrity rule. Go forth and not only do good data, but do good data well.

2.6 APPENDIX: THE CODE

The following sections list the ODI, Essbase, and relational objects used to build the Slay Bad Data solution described in this chapter. The full code stream is here; you can copy the code in the Variables, Procedures, and MaxL scripts to use in your own projects or simply download the code from the book Web site.

2.6.1 ODI Objects

2.6.1.1 ODI Objects

2.6.1.1.1 Subfolder 1: Extract

Type	Name	Purpose
Package	PKG_Extract_ASOsamp	Extract all dimensions of ASOsamp.Sample to the table Dimensions using compiled Scenarios of extract Interfaces. This Package is not used as the Load Plan PLAN_ASOsamp executes the Interfaces.
Interface	INT_ExtractAge INT_ExtractGeography INT_ExtractIncomeLevel INT_ExtractMeaures INT_ExtractPaymentType INT_ExtractProducts INT_ExtractPromotions INT_ExtractStores INT_ExtractTime INT_ExtractTransactionType INT_ExtractYears	Each Interface reverses a single Essbase dimension.
Scenario	SCN_INT_ExtractAge SCN_INT_ExtractGeography SCN_INT_ExtractIncomeLevel SCN_INT_ExtractMeaures SCN_INT_ExtractPaymentType SCN_INT_ExtractProducts SCN_INT_ExtractPromotions SCN_INT_ExtractStores SCN_INT_ExtractTime SCN_INT_ExtractTransactionType SCN_INT_ExtractYears	Compiled Interfaces for use in Package and Load Plan.
	SCN_PKG_EXTRACT_ASOSAMP	Compiled Package called by the Load Plan PLAN_ASOsamp.
Procedure	N/A	

2.6.1.1.2 *Subfolder 2: LoadMissing*

Type	Name	Purpose
Package	PKG_hMissingDimMembers	Identify orphan members in fact data and load them to a single Essbase dimension.
	PKG_LoopAndLoad	Loop all dimensions in the view vDimList and call Scenario SCN_PKG_HMISSINGDIMMEMBERS.
Interface	N/A	
Scenario	SCN_PKG_ HMISSINGDIMMEMBERS	
SCN_PKG_ LOOPANDLOAD	Execute PKG_ hMissingDimMember and PKG_LoopAndLoad from Load Plan PLAN_ASOsamp.	
Procedure	PROC_DataNotInMetaData	Identify orphaned fact data and create table for dimension load.
	PROC_LogHeaderFooter	Write process success/failure to the Status table.

2.6.1.1.3 *Subfolder 3: Load Data*

Type	Name	Purpose
Package	PKG_dLoadData	Load data from the fact data source to Essbase.
Interface	N/A	
Scenario	SCN_PKG_DLOADDATA	Execute PKG_dLoadData from Load Plan PLAN_ASOsamp.
Procedure	N/A	

2.6.1.1.4 *Subfolder 4: Validate*

Type	Name	Purpose
Package	PKG_ExtractValidateReport	Extract Essbase totals and sum SQL totals, compare, and write the difference, if any, to the table ValidateASOsamp.
Interface	INT_ImportValidateReport	Import the Essbase Report Script output to the table ValidateASOSamp.
Scenario	SCN_PKG_ EXTRACTVALIDATEREPORT	Execute PKG_ExtractValidateReport from Load Plan PLAN_ASOsamp.
Procedure	PROC_FactVsEssbase	Compare the data values in the Fact table to the upper-level Essbase export and write the variance to the table ValidationVariance.
	PROC_TruncateVariance	Truncate the table ValidationVariance.

2.6.1.1.5 Folder First Folder

Type	Name	Purpose
Package	N/A	
Interface	N/A	
Scenario	N/A	
Procedure	PROC_LogFailureStatus	Write time/date stamped failure message to the LoadStatus table.
	PROC_LogNoActionStatus	Write time/date stamped no action message to the LoadStatus table.
	PROC_LogSuccessStatus	Write time/date stamped success message to the LoadStatus table.

2.6.1.1.6 Load Plan PLAN_ASOsamp PLAN_ASOsamp executes ODI Interfaces and Packages to perform the four steps of quality data via its Load Plan task hierarchy.

Extract, find and load missing hierarchy—This is the overall master step for all ODI processing. All of the following steps reside under and are controlled by this master step.

Extract Essbase to SQL—Execute all of the Interfaces in subfolder 1: Extract.

Load missing hierarchy—Execute the Scenario SCN_PKG_LOOPANDLOAD to find and load orphan metadata to ASOsamp.

Load data—Execute the Scenario SCN_PKG_DLOADDATA to load data to Essbase.

Validate—Execute the Scenario SCN_PKG_EXTRACTVALIDATEDATAREPORT to compare the data in Essbase versus the data in SQL.

2.6.1.2 Knowledge Modules Knowledge Modules (KMs) are the adapters ODI uses to interface with different technologies.

2.6.1.2.1 Subfolder 1: Extract

Type	Name	Purpose
Reverse-Engineering (RKM)	RKM Hyperion Essbase	Used to reverse engineer the Essbase database to a Data Model. This reversal process is only done once unless dimensions are added or removed.
Loading (LKM)	LKM Hyperion Essbase METADATA to SQL	Extract dimensional metadata from the Essbase Data Model to a temporary SQL data store based on mappings in Interfaces.
Integration (IKM)	IKM SQL to SQL Control Append	Write Essbase dimensional metadata from the temporary tables to the permanent Dimensions table.

2.6.1.2.2 Subfolder 2: LoadMissing and Subfolder 3: Load Data As no Interfaces are used, there are no KMs.

2.6.1.2.3 Subfolder 4: Validate

Type	Name	Purpose
Loading (LKM)	LKM SQL to SQL	Extract data from the ValidateASOSamp flat file.
Integration (IKM)	IKM SQL to SQL Control Append	Load the mapped flat file data to the table ValidateASOSamp.

2.6.1.3 Variables The Variables VAR_AppName, VAR_DbName, VAR_MaxLReportName, VAR_MaxLScriptName, and VAR_Status are either Set or Declare variables without Refreshing code.

VAR_CheckMaxLErr, VAR_Kounter, VAR_MaxDimCount, VAR_Object, and VAR_RecordCount all have Refreshing code of either Jython or SQL and are documented below.

2.6.1.3.1 VAR_CheckMaxLErr **Purpose**—MaxL creates a STDERR file even when there is no error; STDERR in this case has a zero length. This code (courtesy of John Goodwin's "More To Life Than This Blog") tests to see if the file has any content. If the code errors out, the file is empty, so there is no error; if the file has a length greater than zero, there is an error.

Note: This Jython code uses the ODI variable VAR_MaxLScriptName to define the error file; the error file must match the script name.

Code

```
select C1
from TABLE
/*$$SNPS_START_KEYSNP$CRDWG_TABLE
SNP$CRTABLE_NAME=ERROR_LOG
SNP$CRLOAD_FILE=<%=odiRef.getSchemaName("D")%>\#VAR_MaxLScriptName.
err
SNP$CRFILE_FORMAT=DSNP$CRFILE_SEP_FIELD=09
SNP$CRFILE_SEP_LINE=0D0A
SNP$CRFILE_FIRST_ROW=0SNP$CRFILE_ENC_FIELD=
SNP$CRFILE_DEC_SEP=SNP$CRSNP$CRDWG_COLSNP$CRCOL_NAME=C1
SNP$CRTYPE_NAME=STRINGSNP$CRORDER=1SNP$CRLENGTH=1000
SNP$CRPRECISION=1000SNP$CR$$SNPS_END_KEY*/
```

2.6.1.3.2 VAR_Kounter **Purpose**—Increment VAR_Kounter by 1, except where VAR_Kounter <= VAR_MaxDimCount using SQL.

Note: The Jython code <%=odiRef.getObjectName("*TableName*")%> resolves to a fully qualified database (or schema), owner, and table name; this is common ODI practice to produce context independent code.

Code

```
--      Increment the VAR_Kounter variable by one so long as
--      VAR_Kounter + 1 is <= the row count of vDimList.
--      When VAR_Kounter = vDimList's row count, branch
--      to Package stop.
SELECT
        #VAR_Kounter+1
FROM
        <%=odiRef.getObjectName("DUAL")%>
WHERE #VAR_Kounter + 1 <= #VAR_MaxDimCount
```

2.6.1.3.3 VAR_MaxDimCount **Purpose**—Get the row count of the table SuspendParent for use in the Package PKG_LoopAndLoad.

Code

```
--      Get the row count of the table SuspendParent
SELECT COUNT(*) FROM <%=odiRef.getObjectName("SuspendParent")%>
```

2.6.1.3.4 VAR_Object **Purpose**—Get the dimension name from the vDimList view based on VAR_Kounter value.

Code

```
--     Get the dimension name from the vDimList view based on the
--     Counter field (which is really a row counter).
--     Use the ODI Refresh Variable #VAR_Kounter which is
--     incremented for each dimension in the vDimList view
SELECT
       DimName,
       Counter
FROM
       <%=odiRef.getObjectName("vDimList")%>
WHERE
       COUNTER=#VAR_Kounter
```

2.6.1.3.5 VAR_RecordCount **Purpose**—Get the record count of the dimension parent/child hierarchy in the hParentChild table. If the count is greater than two, the dimension load can start.

Code

```
--     Record count must be greater than two to fire off dimension
load
-- Record1: PARENT0,Years CHILD0,Years ALIAS0,Years
-- Record2: DimNames SuspendDimName Suspend Dimname
-- Set this to an Evaluate Variable in the package and ODI will
test the
--     Record count to see if it's greater than two
SELECT COUNT(*) FROM <%=odiRef.getObjectName("hParentChild")%>
```

2.6.1.4 Procedures

2.6.1.4.1 Proc_DataNotInMetaData **Purpose**—Find members in fact data that are not in metadata.

Note: This Procedure uses multiple Detail steps to allow more detailed Operator logs; this code could have been combined into a single stream (and, in fact, was prototyped in SQL that way). Each Detail step has a Command on Source and a Command on Target split, which are noted as used.

Code Steps

Truncate

Command on Target

```
TRUNCATE TABLE <%=odiRef.getObjectName("#VAR_Table")%>
```

Find Nonmatching Members

Command on Source

```
SELECT DISTINCT
       '#VAR_Object' AS 'DimensionName',
       N."#VAR_Object" AS 'Member'
FROM <%=odiRef.getObjectName("FactData")%> N
LEFT OUTER JOIN Dimensions D
```

```
      ON N."#VAR_Object" = D.MemberName
WHERE D.MemberName IS NULL
```

Command on Target

```
INSERT INTO <%=odiRef.getObjectName("DataNotInMetadata")%>
VALUES(:DimensionName, :Member)
```

Truncate hParentChild

Command on Target

```
TRUNCATE TABLE <%=odiRef.getObjectName("hParentChild")%>
```

Create ParentChild load format

Command on Source

```
SELECT
      A.Parent,
      A.Member,
      A.Alias
FROM
      (
      -- Header record
      SELECT
            '900' AS 'Order',
            'PARENT0,' + P.DimName AS 'Parent',
            'CHILD0,' + P.DimName AS 'Member',
            'ALIAS0,' + P.DimName AS 'Alias'
      FROM <%=odiRef.getObjectName("SuspendParent")%> P
      WHERE P.DimName = '#VAR_Object'

      -- Join header and body
      UNION

      -- Parent record
      SELECT
            '800' AS 'Order',
            P.DimName AS 'Parent',
            P.SuspendParent AS 'Member',
            P.SuspendAlias AS 'Alias'
      FROM <%=odiRef.getObjectName("SuspendParent")%> P
      WHERE P.DimName = '#VAR_Object'

      UNION

      -- Missing members
      SELECT
            '700' AS 'Order',
            S.SuspendParent AS 'Parent',
            D.MemberName AS 'Member',
            '' AS Alias
      FROM
            <%=odiRef.getObjectName("DataNotInMetadata")%> D
      INNER JOIN <%=odiRef.getObjectName("SuspendParent")%> S
            ON D.Dimension = S.DimName
      ) AS A
ORDER BY [Order] DESC
```

Command on Target

```
INSERT INTO <%=odiRef.getObjectName("hParentChild")%>
VALUES(:Parent, :Member, :Alias)
```

2.6.1.4.2 PROC_LogHeaderFooter **Purpose**—Write "Start" and "End" to the LoadStatus table.

Code Steps

Write Status

Command on Target

```
INSERT INTO <%=odiRef.getObjectName("LoadStatus")%> VALUES('#VAR_
AppName.#VAR_DbName', 'LoadDim','N/A','#VAR_Status', SYSDATETIME() )
```

2.6.1.4.3 PROC_FactVsEssbase **Purpose**—Compare the data values in Essbase via a Report Script output and the summed fact data.

Code Steps

Compare data in Fact versus data from Essbase

Command on Target

```
--     Purpose:     Compare the data values in the Fact table to the
--                  upper level Essbase export
--     Modified:    11 November 2011, initial write
--     Written by: Cameron Lackpour
--     Notes:

-- Declare temporary table to hold results of SUMmed Fact
-- and Essbase extract
DECLARE @Validate TABLE(
        Years NVARCHAR(80),
       [Time] NVARCHAR(80),
       ID INT,
       [Original Price] MONEY,
       [Price Paid] MONEY,
       [Returns] MONEY,
       [Units] MONEY,
       [Transactions] MONEY
)

-- Aggregate the Fact table
INSERT INTO @Validate
SELECT
      Years,
      [Time],
      1,
      SUM([Original_Price]) AS 'Original Price',
      SUM([Price_Paid]) AS 'Price Paid',
      SUM([Rtns]) AS 'Returns',
      SUM([Units]) AS 'Units',
      SUM([Transactions]) AS 'Transactions'
FROM
      <%=odiRef.getObjectName("FactData")%>
WHERE
-- I leave it to the reader the simple ODI exercise of adding and
-- valuing variables to drive Year and Time.
```

```
      Years = 'Curr Year' AND
      [Time] = 'Jul'
GROUP BY Years, [Time]
--Retrieve the values exported from Essbase
INSERT INTO @Validate
SELECT
      Years,
      TimePeriod AS 'Time',
      2,
      OriginalPrice AS 'Original Price',
      PricePaid AS 'Price Paid',
      Rtns AS 'Returns',
      Units,
      Transactions
FROM <%=odiRef.getObjectName("ValidateASOsamp")%>
--Do the variance
TRUNCATE TABLE <%=odiRef.getObjectName("ValidationVariance")%>
INSERT INTO <%=odiRef.getObjectName("ValidationVariance")%>
SELECT
      F.Years,
      F.[Time],
      F.[Original Price] - E.[Original Price] AS 'Fact vs. Essbase
        OP Var',
      F.[Price Paid] - E.[Price Paid] AS 'Fact vs. Essbase PP Var',
      F.[Returns] - E.[Returns] AS 'Fact vs. Essbase Rtns Var',
      F.Units - E.Units AS 'Fact vs. Essbase Units Var',
      F.Transactions - E.Transactions AS 'Fact vs. Essbase Trans Var'
FROM
      @Validate F
INNER JOIN @Validate E
      ON F.ID != E.ID AND F.Years = E.Years AND F.[Time] = E.[Time]
WHERE F.ID = 1
```

2.6.1.4.4 PROC_TruncateVariance **Purpose**—Clear out the table ValidationVariance when the MaxL script Validate.msh fails.

Code Steps

Truncate variance table ValidationVariance

Command on Target

```
TRUNCATE TABLE <%=odiRef.getObjectName("ValidationVariance")%>
```

2.6.1.4.5 PROC_LogFailureStatus **Purpose**—Write out Essbase application and database, MaxL script name, Dimension, Failure flag, and date and time to the LoadStatus table.

Code Steps

Write Status

Command on Target

```
INSERT INTO <%=odiRef.getObjectName("LoadStatus")%> VALUES('#VAR_
AppName.#VAR_DbName', '#VAR_MaxLScriptName','#VAR_
Object','Failure', SYSDATETIME() )
```

2.6.1.4.6 PROC_LogNoActionStatus **Purpose**—Write out Essbase application and database, MaxL script name, Dimension, No Action flag, and date and time to the LoadStatus table.

Code Steps
Write Status
Command on Target

```
INSERT INTO <%=odiRef.getObjectName("LoadStatus")%> VALUES('#VAR_
AppName.#VAR_DbName', '#VAR_MaxLScriptName','#VAR_Object','No
Action', SYSDATETIME() )
```

2.6.1.4.7 PROC_LogSuccessStatus **Purpose**—Write out Essbase application and database, MaxL script name, Dimension, Success flag, and date and time to the LoadStatus table.

Code Steps
Write Status
Command on Target

```
INSERT INTO <%=odiRef.getObjectName("LoadStatus")%> VALUES('#VAR_
AppName.#VAR_DbName', '#VAR_MaxLScriptName','#VAR_
Object','Success', SYSDATETIME() )
```

2.6.2 Essbase

2.6.2.1 Essbase Objects

Type	Name	Purpose
Report Script	Validate	Export the current year and month's Original Price, Price Paid, Returns, Units, and Transactions at the total level for all dimensions.
Rules Files	dData	Load all data from the table FactTable.
	hDynSQL	Load unassigned members from the table hParentChild.
MaxL Scripts	LoadDim.msh	Load a single dimension using the Load Rule hDynSQL.
	LoadData.msh	Load data using the Load Rule dCurMth.
	Validate.msh	Run the Report Script Validate and write the contents to a file.

2.6.2.2 MaxL

2.6.2.2.1 LoadDim.msh **OS_MaxLDimLoad Command line**

```
cmd /c C:\Oracle\Middleware\EPMSystem11R1\products\Essbase\
EssbaseClient\bin\startMaxl.cmd c:\tempdir\MaxL\scripts\#VAR_
MaxLScriptName.msh #VAR_MaxLScriptName #VAR_AppName #VAR_DbName
```

Purpose—Load missing dimension members through the SQL Load Rule hDynSQL.
Code

```
/*
        Purpose:     Load Dimension
        Written by:  Cameron Lackpour
        Modified:    11 November 2011, initial write
        Notes:       Parameter variables:
                     -- $1 = Script name
                     -- $2 = Application name
                     -- $3 = Database name
*/
        /* Turn on timestamping */
```

```
set timestamp on ;
/*    Define STDOUT and STDERR outputs */
spool stdout on to "c:\\\\Tempdir\\\\MaxL\\\\Logs\\\\$1.log" ;
iferror "BadLogFile" ;
spool stderr on to "c:\\\\Tempdir\\\\MaxL\\\\Logs\\\\$1.err" ;
iferror "BadErrorFile" ;
/*    Log in to Essbase  */
login admin epmtestdrive on metavero ;
iferror 'BadLogin' ;
/*    only supervisors and developers may connect */
alter application $2 disable connects ;
iferror "CouldNotDisable" ;
/*    Load dimension */
import database $2.$3 dimensions connect as 'hypsql' identified by
'hypsql' using server rules_file 'hDynSQL' on error write to
"c:\\\\Tempdir\\\\MaxL\\\\Logs\\\\hDynSQL.err" ;
iferror "DimLoadFailed" ;
/*    Quit MaxL without a predefined error code */
exit ;
/*    Create label for login errors */
define label "BadLogin" ;
/*    Quit MaxL with a 10 error code */
exit 10 ;
/*    Create label for log file errors */
define label "BadLogFile" ;
/*    Quit MaxL with a 20 error code */
exit 20 ;
/*    Create label for error file errors */
define label "BadErrorFile" ;
/*    Quit MaxL with a 30 error code */
exit 30 ;
/*    Create label for disable connects errors */
define label "CouldNotDisable" ;
/*    Quit MaxL with a 40 error code */
exit 40 ;
/*    Create label for dimension load errors */
define label "DimLoadFailed" ;
/*    Make sure that connections are enabled */
alter application Sample enable connects ;
/*    Quit MaxL with a 50 error code */
exit 50 ;
/*    Create label for enable connects errors */
define label "CouldNotEnable" ;
/*    Quit MaxL with a 60 error code */
exit 60 ;
```

2.6.2.2.2 LoadData.msh OS_MaxLDimLoad Command line

```
cmd /c C:\Oracle\Middleware\EPMSystem11R1\products\Essbase\
EssbaseClient\bin\startMaxl.cmd c:\tempdir\MaxL\scripts\#VAR_
MaxLScriptName.msh #VAR_MaxLScriptName #VAR_AppName #VAR_DbName
```

Purpose—Load the current month's data to ASOsamp.Sample.
Code

```
/*
      Purpose:     Load Data
      Written by:  Cameron Lackpour
      Modified:    11 November 2011, initial write
      Notes:       Parameter variables:
                   -- $1 = Script name
                   -- $2 = Application name
                   -- $3 = Database name
                   hDynSQL uses the following artifacts:
                   -- Essbase substitution variables:
&ASOsamp_CurYear and
&ASOsamp_CurMonth
*/
/*    Turn on timestamping */
set timestamp on ;

/*    Define STDOUT and STDERR outputs */
spool stdout on to "c:\\\\Tempdir\\\\MaxL\\\\Logs\\\\$1.log" ;
iferror "LogFile" ;
spool stderr on to "c:\\\\Tempdir\\\\MaxL\\\\Logs\\\\$1.err" ;
iferror "ErrorFile" ;

/*    Log in to Essbase  */
login admin epmtestdrive on metavero ;
iferror 'Login' ;

/*    Clear out the current month's data using logical clear */
alter database $2.$3 clear data in region '{([&ASOsamp_CurMonth],
[&ASOsamp_CurYear])}' ;
iferror 'Clear' ;

/*    Create a load buffer for data */
alter database $2.$3 initialize load_buffer with buffer_id 1
resource_usage .5 property ignore_missing_values, ignore_zero_
values, aggregate_sum ;
iferror 'CreateBuffer' ;

/*    Load data to buffer
NB -- Even though this is a single source, use the load buffer to
sort and preagg duplicate records. */
import database $2.$3 data connect as 'hypsql' identified by 'hypsql'
using server rules_file 'dCurMth' to load_buffer with buffer_id 1 on
error write to "c:\\\\Tempdir\\\\MaxL\\\\Logs\\\\dCurMth.err" ;
iferror "DataLoadToBUffer" ;

/*    Commit load buffer to Essbase */
import database $2.$3 data from load_buffer with buffer_id 1 add
values create slice ;
iferror 'LoadFromBuffer' ;

/*    Quit MaxL without a predefined error code */
exit ;

/*    Create label for login errors */
define label "Login" ;
/*    Quit MaxL with a 10 error code */
exit 10 ;

/*    Create label for log file errors */
```

```
define label "LogFile" ;
/*    Quit MaxL with a 20 error code */
exit 20 ;

/*    Create label for error file errors */
define label "ErrorFile" ;
/*    Quit MaxL with a 30 error code */
exit 30 ;

/*    Create label for data clear error */
define label "Clear" ;
/*    Quit MaxL with a 40 error code */
exit 40 ;

/*    Create label for create buffer error */
define label "CreateBuffer" ;
/*    Just in case it actually got created, destroy the load buffer
*/
alter database $2.$3 destroy load_buffer with buffer_id 1 ;
/*    Quit MaxL with a 50 error code */
exit 50 ;
/*    Create label for data load to buffer error */
define label "DataLoadToBuffer" ;
/*    Just in case it actually got created, destroy the load buffer
*/
alter database $2.$3 destroy load_buffer with buffer_id 1 ;
/*    Quit MaxL with a 60 error code */
exit 60 ;

/*    Create label for load from buffer error */
define label "LoadFromBuffer" ;
/*    Just in case it actually got created, destroy the load buffer
*/
alter database $2.$3 destroy load_buffer with buffer_id 1 ;
/*    Quit MaxL with a 70 error code */
exit 70 ;
```

2.6.2.2.3 Validate.msh **OS_MaxLReportRun Command line**

```
cmd /c C:\Oracle\Middleware\EPMSystem11R1\products\Essbase\
EssbaseClient\bin\startMaxl.cmd c:\tempdir\MaxL\scripts\#VAR_
MaxLScriptName.msh #VAR_MaxLScriptName #VAR_AppName #VAR_DbName
#VAR_MaxLReportName
```

Purpose—Run the Report Script Validate.rep to a local text file. This upper-level data will be pulled into SQL via ODI and compared to a relationally summed table.

Code

```
/*
      Purpose:      Export current top level data for validation
      Written by:   Cameron Lackpour
      Modified:     11 November 2011, initial write
      Notes:        Parameter variables:
                    -- $1 = Script name
                    -- $2 = Application name
```

```
                    -- $3 = Database name
                    -- $4 = Report name
                    Uses the following artifacts:
                    -- Report script: Validate.rep
                    -- Essbase substitution variables:
&ASOsamp_CurYear and
&ASOsamp_CurMonth
*/
/*     Turn on timestamping */
set timestamp on ;

/*     Define STDOUT and STDERR outputs */
spool stdout on to "c:\\\\Tempdir\\\\MaxL\\\\Logs\\\\$1.log" ;
iferror "BadLogFile" ;
spool stderr on to "c:\\\\Tempdir\\\\MaxL\\\\Logs\\\\$1.err" ;
iferror "BadErrorFile" ;

/*     Log in to Essbase  */
login admin epmtestdrive on metavero ;
iferror 'BadLogin' ;

/*     Run report */
export database $2.$3 using server report_file "$4" to data_file
"c:\\\\tempdir\\\\MaxL\\\\Data\\\\$4.txt" ;
iferror "RunReportFailed" ;

/*     Quit MaxL without a predefined error code */
exit ;

/*     Create label for login errors */
define label "BadLogin" ;
/*     Quit MaxL with a 10 error code */
exit 10 ;

/*     Create label for log file errors */
define label "BadLogFile" ;
/*     Quit MaxL with a 20 error code */
exit 20 ;

/*     Create label for error file errors */
define label "BadErrorFile" ;
/*     Quit MaxL with a 30 error code */
exit 30 ;

/*     Create label for disable connects errors */
define label "CouldNotDisable" ;
/*     Quit MaxL with a 40 error code */
exit 40 ;

/*     Create label for dimension load errors */
define label "RunReportFailed" ;
/*     Quit MaxL with a 50 error code */
exit 50 ;
```

2.6.3 *SQL Objects*

Table Name	Purpose	Fields
DataNotInMetadata	Store a single dimension's unassigned members. Programmatically written and loaded to Essbase.	• Dimension • MemberName
Dimensions	Database members by dimension	• DimName • SortID • ParentName • MemberName • Alias • DataStorage • Consolidation • UDA • Formula • Comment • TimeBalance • TimeBalanceSkip • VarReporting • CurrConv • CurrConvCategory
FactData	Data loaded to ASOsamp.Sample. This is the same data set as the dataload.txt that comes with ASOsamp.Sample.	• DimName • sortID • ParentName • MemberName • Alias • DataStorage • TwoPassCalc • Consolidation • UDA • Formula • Comment • TimeBalance • TimeBalanceSkip • VarReporting • CurrConv
hParentChild	Dimension load-ready table of a single dimension's unassigned members, programmatically populated.	• Parent • Child • Alias
LoadStatus	Dimension load process status.	• Application • ProcName • Action • Condition • DateTime
MaxLScriptStatus	MaxL script process status.	• ScriptName • Status • DateTime

SuspendParent	Default unassigned parents by dimension.	• DimName • SuspendParent • SuspendAlias
ValidateASOsamp	Upper-level Measures data extracted from ASOsamp.Sample.	• Years • TimePeriod • OriginalPrice • PricePaid • Rtns • Units • Transactions
ValidationVariance	Difference between SQL aggregation of FactData and ValidateASOsamp	• Years • Time • Fact vs. Essbase OP Var • Fact vs. Essbase PP Var • Fact vs. Essbase Rtns Var • Fact vs. Essbase Units Var • Fact vs. Essbase Trans Var

3

FINDING THE DIRT: TRICKS FOR RAPID PROTOTYPING WITH ESSBASE STUDIO

Mike Nader

CONTENTS

3.1 INTRODUCTION

Every other Wednesday in my house is cleaning day. This would, on the surface, not seem to be a significant occasion. However, at least it my home, it brings out an age-old argument. You see, we prepare the house for the cleaning by cleaning it. The term, I believe, is universally referred to as *precleaning*. The concept has often escaped me. Why do I need to clean for the cleaner? I pay her. She is excellent. I can guarantee that she is more than capable of cutting through the clutter and focusing on the salient details. Nonetheless, I am compelled by unnatural force to acquiesce and "preclean."

The unnatural force I am referring to is marital pressure. The entire discussion around "precleaning" highlights a natural mental division between my wife and me. We both have the same goal in mind—we want a clean house. However, to assume that my wife and I approach the world of cleaning with a similar perspective is like stating a duck and an otter have similar perspectives on the world because both get their butts wet. Add to this two teenage/preteen boys and now the duck and the otter are joined by a Beagle and a Labrador. All are interested in the water, but exist in completely different universes.

Before I get in too much trouble, let me state (for the record) that I see the value of precleaning. If you can cut through the clutter up front, you can more easily focus on the real dirt. That it is not to say that my techniques do not work. If there is a stain on the carpet, you can simply move the clutter and clean it. You can do that because you know it is there. Conversely, if you do not know where the stains are, they never get cleaned until the clutter is out of the way. Further, if you have ever dealt with boys, you know that they are very good at hiding stains.

If you think about it, this concept is not dissimilar from creating an EPM (Enterprise Performance Management)/BI (Business Intelligence) system. You can approach the solution from just the business requirements, focus on the reports, dig through the clutter, and build the dimensions. The problem, of course, is that when someone else tries to understand what you have done (no matter how good your documentation), they often get lost in the clutter of data and metadata. Also, the clutter can often derail even the most elegant solution.

The alternative to the focused approach is to remove the clutter and start with a clean space. Both methods often yield the same final result. The important differences are time, money, and the feasibility of actually cleaning things up. Take my word for it, the residue from sticky hands never comes off of the ceiling (at least not without paint).

The question we then must answer is how do you decide your approach? Do you insist on the clean data and metadata before proceeding on a deployment or do you start, knowing you have at least fixed it during the build in other projects and hope to will meaning out of chaos on this one? It might seem like that statement lends itself to a particular point on view, far from it.

In any implementation you have to balance available resources (time, money, people, etc.) with an ideal situation. At the risk of using a generality, available resources and ideal situations are perfectly asymptotic lines. They might get close, but they really do not intersect.

What does all of this, you might ask, have to do with Essbase Studio? The short answer is: Everything. Understanding a client's data is about iteration. We often overlook one important aspect of Essbase deployments in tool selection, and actually in development and consulting in general—the aspect of prototyping. You may never fully understand all the nuances or complexities until you hit roadblocks in the build process. Studio is a great tool for the prototyping phase (if used for nothing else).

It may seem strange that a book focused on application deployment should dedicate thoughts and pages to a potential nonproduction activity. However, there is often no more important phase in a deployment than developing the skeleton models, calculations, rules, and data files in an effort to more fully understand both the user requirements and the availability of the data to meet those needs. In short, prototyping *is* good development, and Studio is a great tool to help with this phase of an Essbase implementation.

3.2 UNDERSTANDING THIS CHAPTER

Before we progress, it is important to understand something of the nature of this chapter. It is focused tips and tricks for leveraging Studio for rapid prototype development. That is not to say that the advice in the following pages is not useful from a production deployment perspective (it is often equally so), only that final production decisions are a combination of factors that, in many cases, are driven by considerations beyond the best technical practices of a single component.

The assumption in this chapter (and much of this book) is that the reader is already (to some degree) familiar with Essbase and Essbase Studio. Instead of focusing on creating a flowing narrative that goes step-by-step from data source to cube, this chapter highlights key areas of the modeling process in an effort to provide guidance for effective use of the tool.

3.2.1 Understanding the Studio Process

While this chapter relies on the reader's knowledge of Studio, it is also important to build a framework we can use to discuss the content. To that end, we should start with a baseline understanding of what it takes to move from data source to cube. In short, there are five general steps:

1. Map data sources (relational, text, OBIEE)
2. Model the data source (create required joins, understand the data)
3. Build hierarchies and custom members
4. Model the cube (create the cube model and schema)
5. Deploy to Essbase

The sections that follow directly relate to the five phases listed above. While it is not the intention of this chapter to provide a step-by-step workflow through Studio, the tips and tricks are organized to follow a logical progression.

3.3 MAPPING THE DATA SOURCES

One of the more interesting aspects of Studio, compared to EIS (Essbase Integration Services) and other building methodologies, is that it abstracts the complexity of data access and treats both relational and text-based sources in much the same manner. Note that I did not state that it treats them in the same manner, it does not. Studio provides a much more robust set of capabilities when leveraging relational sources. However, when first exploring data during prototyping for a deployment, it is important to simply get the data. To that end, it is just as advantageous to get access to data in a flat file as it is in a relational connection.

3.3.1 You Do Not Need 39 Dimensions: Working with Text Sources

It is worth repeating, Studio does not provide the same breath of capability when working with text sources as it does when working with relational. For example, when working with text sources, you do not have the ability to create joins and, thereby, create dimensions by combining multiple text files. The only exception is performing a recursive join on a text file to enable a parent/child build. Nonetheless, Studio does provide a robust means of both introspecting and modeling with text.

A question often asked is whether or not it is worth using Studio if you are leveraging flat files? As an experienced Essbase developer, there is no doubt that you are adept at working with Load Rules (whether in prototyping or production). However, depending on the nature of the file and the dimensional requirements of the business, Studio can be significantly easier. This is easily illustrated by telling a story about the 39 dimensions.

"We would like 39 dimensions," the client said with great confidence. Their current BI deployment had 39 dimensions, so they felt that they Essbase model should have 39 dimensions as well. It is important to note, at this point that they were talking about base dimensions, not attributes. They were convinced that Essbase was the proper solution, but they also were convinced that they needed to see what 39 dimensions with their data would look like. The sample source data was provided in one 3-Gb file with 70 columns as seen in Table 3.1.

Looking at the names of the columns in the file, it is obvious to a true online analytical processing (OLAP) person that much of this information is either not relevant to the solution or can be leveraged in other ways (such as with an attribute or UDA [user-defined attribute]). The client, being newer to Essbase had to be convinced. In this situation, you can either sit through multiple meetings explaining the dimensional options or you can build the prototype the client is asking for along with a prototype of your own design. In leveraging Studio, our team was able to build the 39 dimensions in a single day from the test file and a "more proper" prototype in another day. To have done the same thing with the Data Prep Editor would have taken the better part of a week (barring major error). To have retrofitted the file into a relational model would have involved three days of IT (Information Technology) requests and another few days of setting of the system. Studio's flat file functionality allowed for quick conversations and modeling that cut through the clutter and came up with a good business solution for long-term deployment. In short, you should absolutely consider leveraging Studio for flat files.

3.3.1.1 Importance of Server.Properties While it may seem remedial, it is important to remember that all text sources for Studio need to reside in a single root directory. This directory is determined by the Studio server.properties file. This master directory can contain subdirectories, and it need not be on the same physical volume as Studio. It simply denotes a consistent location for data file location (not dissimilar from a system DSN (data source name) pointing to and setting properties for a relational source). Within the file, the specific property line denoting the data file location is **server.datafile.dir** as shown in Figure 3.1.

Table 3.1 Source Columns

• Ord_Dt	• Channel
• Actvt_Dat	• CDMA2
• Hwd_Type1	• Fullfillment
• Hdw_Type2	• Lead
• Pgm1	• ID
• Pgm2	• SDMA
• Fee_Required	• Property
• Cus_DMA	• MDU_Type
• Reason_Code	• M_State_Code
• Reason_Actn	• M_State_Name
• Work_Ord_R	• to_Cancellation
• Install_Orig	• Resched_Reason
• Install_Latest	• Cycle_Status
• Install_Actual	• Email_Captured
• Act_Actual	• Pkg_Cat1
• OTS_Cancellation	• Pkg_Cat2
• Disconnect_Ten_Mn	• Score1
• Impact_of_Resched	• Score2
• Aging_for_Unsched	• Email_Captured
• Mkt_Desc	• Incentive
• Sub_Mkt_Desc	• Pay_Method
• Acct_Type_Code	• Cr_Card_Type_Name
• Acct_Type_Desc	• O_Count
• Acct_Type_Desc_wCode	• Act_Count
• Payment	• 6m_Cnt
• DNIS	• Cancelled
• Key_Code	• Pending
• Keycode_Desc	• Unsched
• State_Code	• Resched
• State_Name	• Sales_Cancelled
• Stat_Desc	• Modified_Order
• Cat_at_Act	• LC_Pending
• Cat_at_Ord	• Acct_Cnt
• Reason_Cat	• Box1
• Cancel_Reason	• Box2

In the more recent releases of the Oracle EPM System, this file can be found in the following directory:

...`Middleware\user_projects\epmsystem1\BPMS\bpms1\bin`

Note: Any change to this file requires restart of the Studio service.

3.3.1.2 Text Options Ultimately, the selections you make when setting up a text file connection are similar to setting up your data source properties in the Data Prep Editor (in Essbase Administration Services [EAS]). What is often confusing about setting up a text connection in Studio (aside from the file location) is the multiple means of setting

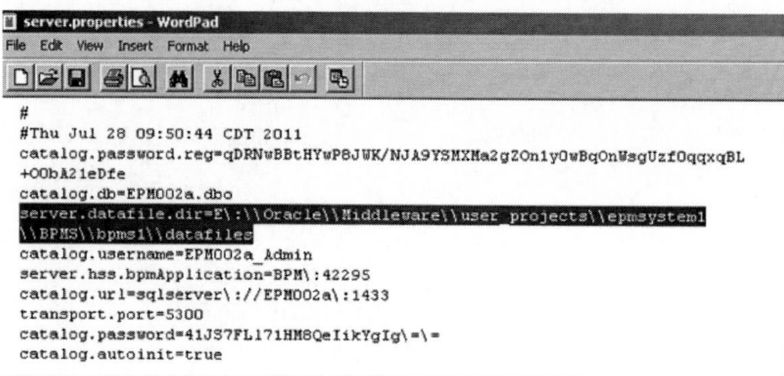

```
#
#Thu Jul 28 09:50:44 CDT 2011
catalog.password.reg=qDRNwBBtHYwP8JWK/NJA9YSMXMa2gZOn1yOwBqOnWsgUzfOqqxqBL
+OObA21eDfe
catalog.db=EPM002a.dbo
server.datafile.dir=E\:\\Oracle\\Middleware\\user_projects\\epmsystem1
\\BPMS\\bpms1\\datafiles
catalog.username=EPM002a_Admin
server.hss.bpmApplication=BPM\:42295
catalog.url=sqlserver\://EPM002a\:1433
transport.port=5300
catalog.password=41JS7FL171HM8QeIikYgIg\=\=
catalog.autoinit=true
```

Figure 3.1 Server.properties.

Figure 3.2 Connection wizard.

up the properties. When you first initiate the data source connection, you have the option of specifying standard properties (such as delimiter, header lines to skip, etc.) as shown in Figure 3.2.

However, after selecting these options and clicking **Next**, you are presented with both the list of data files and the same options. The options on the first screen are simply a set of default options. These become a starting point for the options on the second screen. You can, on the second screen, set individual properties per data file. It is important to remember that once you select the data source options and create the data source you cannot change these options for a file. Although you have the option of incrementally updating a text data source (as shown in Figure 3.3), the options to commit data source changes on incremental update are disabled. In short, if you forget to

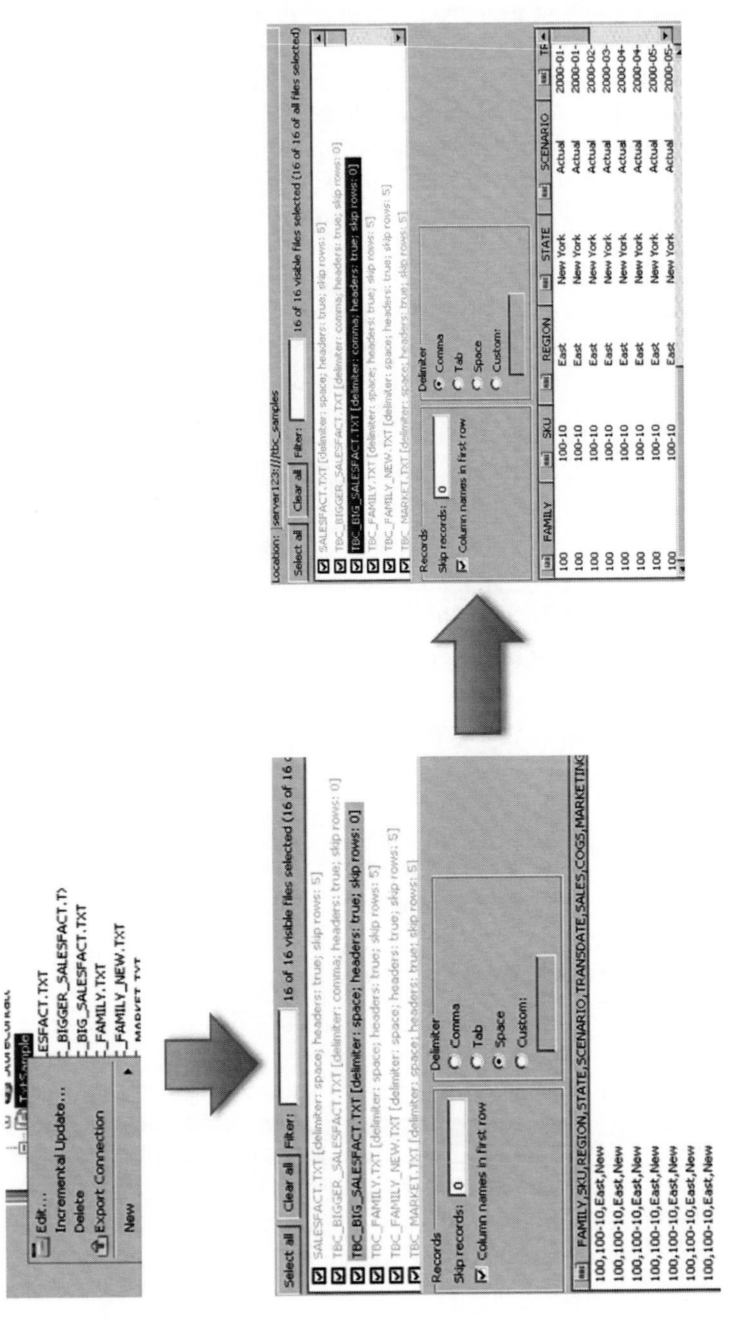

Figure 3.3 Incremental property setting.

specify the properties for a file, you need to delete the text file from the data source and incrementally add it back in with the proper settings.

3.3.1.3 Think Ahead; Select a Number Just as it is easier to think ahead and specify the file properties correctly the first time, you also should consider the eventual creation of the cube schema. A cube schema *requires* the existence of a numeric field in your data source. If you do not have a numeric field, you can define one when creating the data source. The question then arises: Why you would have a source without a numeric field? The answer is quite simple. Depending on the nature of the data you are given, there may or may not be a numeric field present. Take for example our 39 dimension, 70-column example. While there are columns in the text file that are most definitely relational, the client extracted that data in a hurry and wrote the 3-Gb file as all text.

Later in this chapter, I will discuss a trick for deploying a cube from Studio leveraging metadata only, but the most common approach is to ensure you have a numeric field up front. When setting most file properties if you do not initially select a given property, you can delete the file and incrementally update the data source, add the file back, and specify the desired settings. However, this is not true for changing column properties.

If you neglect to specify the desired data type you cannot change this within the data source. In order to read the text file with the new column properties, you need to add a completely new text data source, select the desired file, and then set the properties.

3.3.2 To Change Column Data Type

To change the column data type in either text or relational sources, perform the following steps:

1. On the data source wizard, define the data source connection, click **Next**.
2. On the Model tab (of the data source wizard in Figure 3.4), click **Edit Column Properties**.
3. Click **Next** to get to the desired column, specify the data type, and click **OK**.

Note: You also can get to the properties screen by right clicking on the column header.

3.3.3 Effectively Leveraging Relational Connections

Direct relational connections are where Studio excels. When connecting to a relational source the breadth of available capabilities ranges from cross table joins to the full scope of Common Platform Language (CPL is Studio's command line language functions). From a connection perspective, however, earlier versions of Studio left quite a bit to be desired. For example, pre-11.1.2.x versions of Studio did not allow for the incremental updating of a relational source once it had been brought into the Studio metadata catalog. Instead, you had to add the new tables in a second data source. As can be seen in Figure 3.5, the more recent versions of Studio allow for the addition of tables to a data source via the incremental update capability.

Note: When possible it is more stable (from a maintenance perspective) to base Studio connections on views. Any change to column names, data types, or existence of a given column in a table can have an impact on the hierarchical and cube schema objects based on the data source. While view changes can have an impact as well, you (as a database

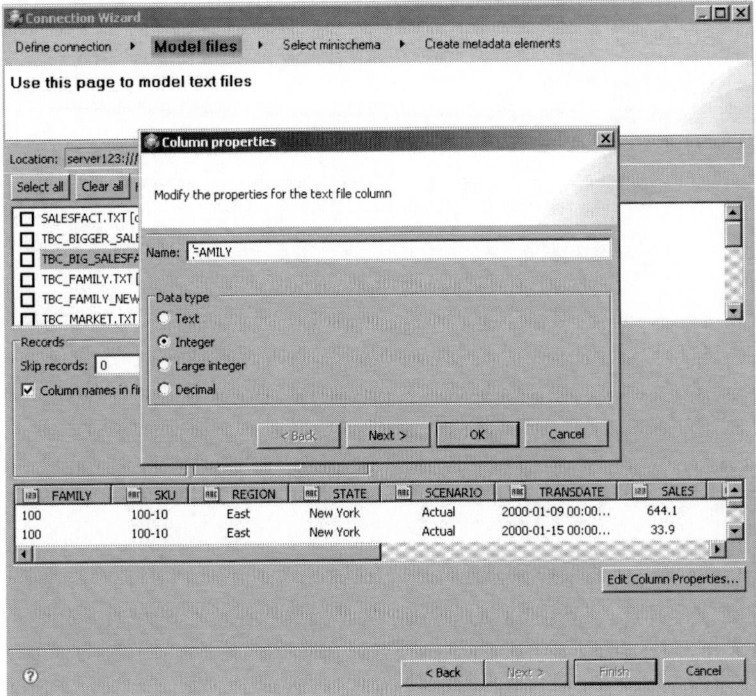

Figure 3.4 Data source wizard model tab.

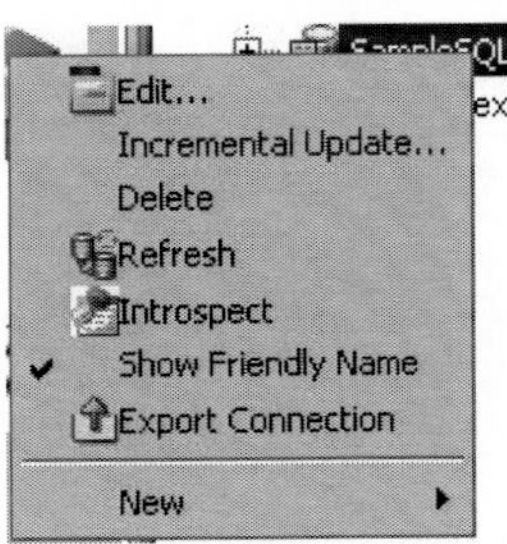

Figure 3.5 Incremental update capability.

consumer) often have a greater level of control with database views in respect to column names and long-term persistence.

3.3.4 Working with User-Defined Tables

One element of the connection process that is specific to relational connections is the ability to create user-defined tables. The user-defined table is useful in situations where you need an additional view created in the data source and are waiting for the database owner to complete the process. They also are useful when you need to create data source joins for a hierarchical object. Essentially, any SQL (Structured Query Language) query that can be issued directly against a source can be used to define a table directly within Studio. This table (and columns) then can be used to create custom member nodes and hierarchy objects.

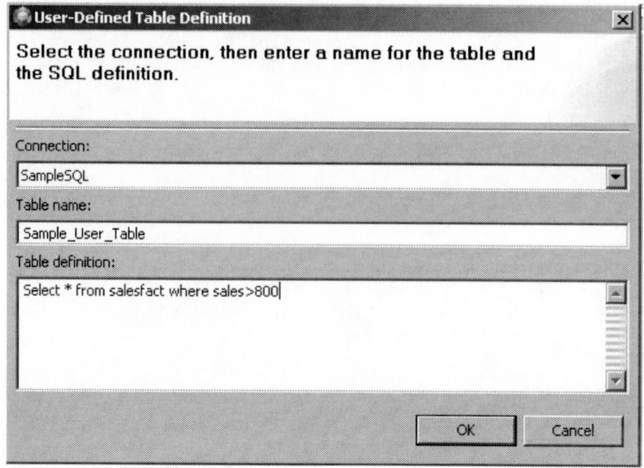

Figure 3.6 User-defined table definition.

It is important to note that queries through user-defined tables are extremely slow and should be used primarily as temporary objects while a proper view is being created within the relational source. They are most useful in validating the SQL that will ultimately be used in a proper view, prior to making the formal request from the database team.

3.3.4.1 Creating a User-Defined Table

1. Right-click on the desired data source.
2. Select **New->User-Defined Table ...**
3. In Figure 3.6's dialog box, enter a Table Name and type/paste the Table definition SQL.
4. Click **OK.**
   a. If the SQL validates without error, the table is created.
   b. If there is an error, it displays in the UI (user interface).

3.4 MODELING THE DATA SOURCE

After creating the initial connections, the next step prior to actually creating hierarchies is to determine whether or not modeling need be applied to the tables or files. Modeling, quite simply, is the creation of joins and the creation of mini-schema for the data source. Studio *does not* require that you create a mini-schema to build dimensionality (Figure 3.7).

The only times you must have a mini-schema in place are when you are doing the following:

1. Creating hierarchies across multiple tables (only available for relational sources)
2. Loading relational data from within Studio
3. Creating a hierarchy from a single table/file using parent and child columns

Just a brief word about item 2. It may sound strange to think of loading of data without using Studio. It is often assumed that because you are using Studio to model a data source and build a prototype you would also leverage Studio to load data. We will touch

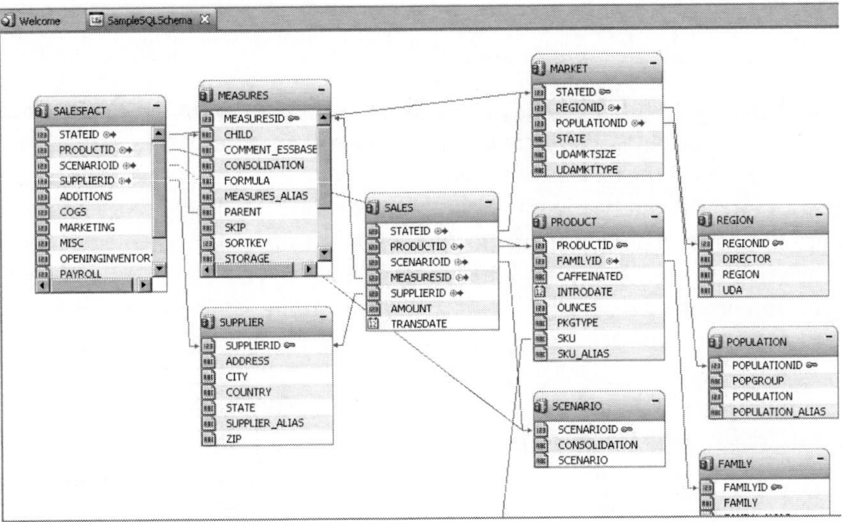

Figure 3.7 Sample mini-schema.

on this topic later in the chapter; however, in respect to data I often recommend the modeling of dimensionality with Studio, but loading data directly with the Data Prep Editor. To take that sentiment one step farther, I often recommend that you model your dimensionality with Studio, but perform the dimension build processes manually leveraging the Load Rules Studio generates.

At its core, Essbase Studio tool is a graphical Load Rule generator whose output need not be a cube. In fact, there is an overt option to simply generate Load Rules, which can then be used in standard batch process or leveraged manually to build the dimensionality and load the data as you see fit.

If you do end up creating a mini-schema, there are a number of options to consider when selecting and joining tables within the mini-schema. In general, you should only add those tables to the mini-schema that are necessary for the following purposes:

- To derive the required hierarchies (either cross-table or within table)
- To load data from the primary or alternate fact table (assuming data is being loaded via Studio)

Adding nonjoined tables simply clutters the user interface. Furthermore, adding additional (optional) tables to the join process unnecessarily complicates the SQL issued by Studio.

3.4.1 Mini-Schema versus View/Tables

From a prototype perspective, leveraging the mini-schema to handle to cross-table dimension builds and complex data loads is fine. However, for longer-term scalability, it is preferable to build tables or views directly in the relational source and minimize the required joins and cross-table builds within the mini-schema. Placing the tables or views directly in the source allows Studio to go after a single database object per dimension.

This has advantages from two perspectives. First, the SQL issued for dimension builds is far less complex. Second, the relational DBAs (database administrators) can write more efficient SQL to define the table or view. While you have the option of writing custom SQL for data loads, Studio does not allow custom SQL for dimensional/hierarchical objects. As such, the SQL optimization opportunities are limited.

3.4.1.1 Adding Joins and Adding Joins by Inspection When working with mini-schemas, you have the option of either creating joins manually from table to table or add views by inspection. In general, regardless of whether you are prototyping with Studio or leveraging the tool for a production deployment, adding joins by inspection is not a recommended practice. Please note that Studio adds joins automatically when adding tables to a mini-schema. Tables with key fields are joined where the column names match.

When adding joins by inspection, Studio tends to add both too many joins and joins in a less optimal direction. For example, Figure 3.8 shows optimal joins between dimension tables and a fact table.

Notice that there is a single join between the dimension tables and the fact table in this image. Further, the joins go from the fact table out to the dimension tables. Creating your joins from the fact table out allows Studio to generate more optimal SQL. If you must create a dimension from multiple tables (in more of a snowflake fashion), the joins are more optimal moving from the fact table out. The join should move from the fact table out to the most immediately connected dimension table and then out to the secondary dimension table (as shown in Figure 3.9).

Figure 3.10 illustrates the same relational source after adding joins by inspection.

Notice in this instance that the Studio engine pattern-matched field names and created all possible joins to ensure you can create dimensionality across tables and link everything back to the fact table. In this simple example, there are only a few additional joins added. However, the more complex the underlying structure, the more complex the join population becomes. While this may result in the same dimensionality and overall end product, the SQL generated will be significantly more complex and slower. If you run into issues or inconsistent results during the dimension build or data load stages, having the extended set of joins makes this much more difficult to troubleshoot.

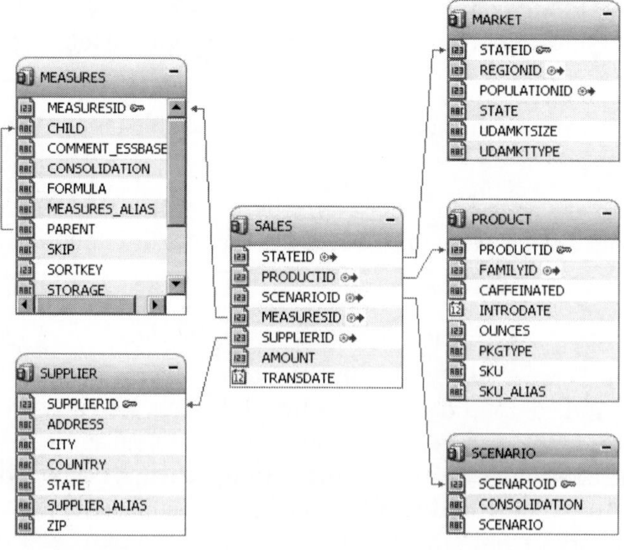

Figure 3.8 Fact table star schema joins.

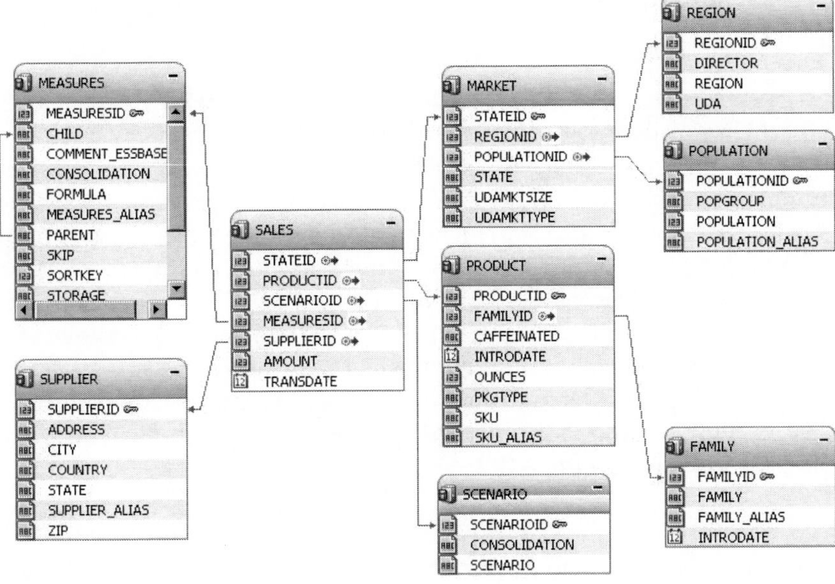

Figure 3.9 Fact table snowflake joins.

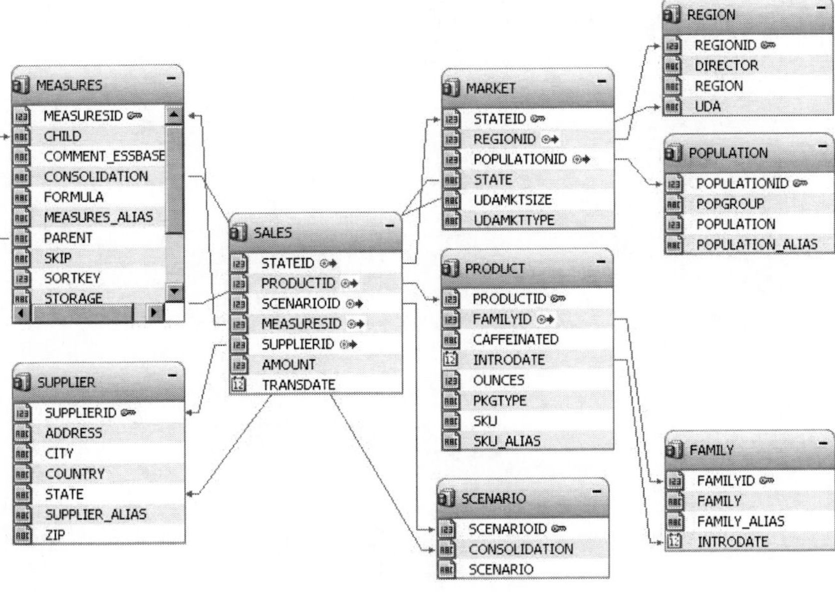

Figure 3.10 Snowflake joins through inspection.

Proper prototyping (not unlike proper production work) is about getting the job done as simply as possible. Simplicity is elegance.

To add Joins by Inspection:

1. Open a mini-schema diagram.
2. Right-click on the open space in the mini-schema area.

3. Select **Add joins by inspection ...**
4. Click **OK**.

3.4.2 Recursive Joins for Parent/Child Hierarchies

One area in which you always need to add joins (regardless of whether you are leveraging a relational or flat file connection) is when creating a parent/child (or recursive) build. To accommodate this type of build, you need to add the table/file to an existing mini-schema (if one exists for the data source) or create a new one. Once the table is in place you simply add the join from the parent column to the child, as shown in Figure 3.11.

In this example, a flat file was used. The recursive, or self, join is the only type of join available for a flat files within Studio. Once the join is in place, the hierarchy is created by adding both the parent and the child to the hierarchy definition.

The preceding image is different from how this would have been done in EIS. In EIS, you would only add the child to the hierarchy. If you do this in Studio, you get very different results (as shown in Figure 3.12).

3.4.3 Automatic Introspection for Full Modeling and Hierarchies

The concept of mini-schema in Studio (while not overly stimulating) is important because it represents a foundation step for ensuring you get the desired results in both data and metadata builds. The discussion on mini-schema is incomplete without an overview on the topic of full introspection.

Studio provides the capability of taking a relational data source and performing a full introspection to determine both the joins and potential hierarchies. For example,

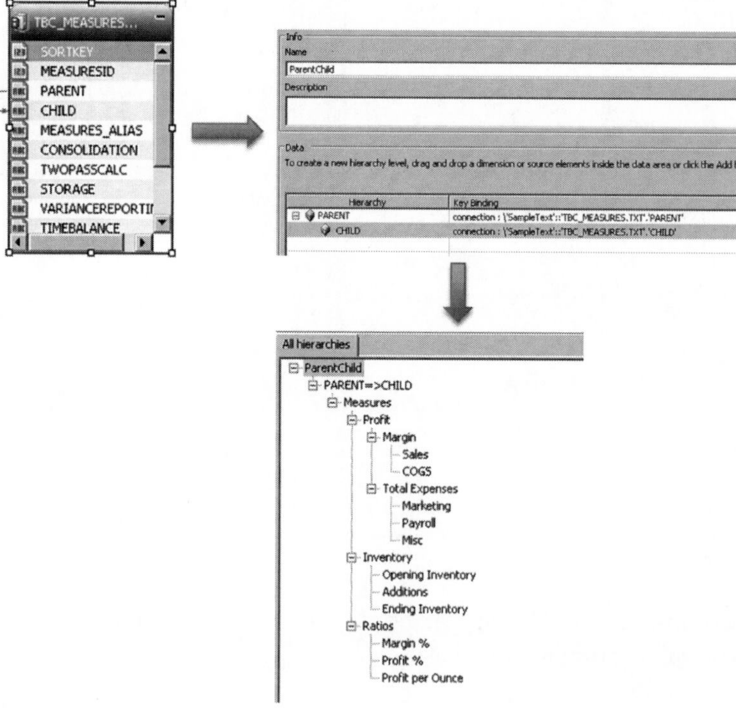

Figure 3.11 Parent/child joins.

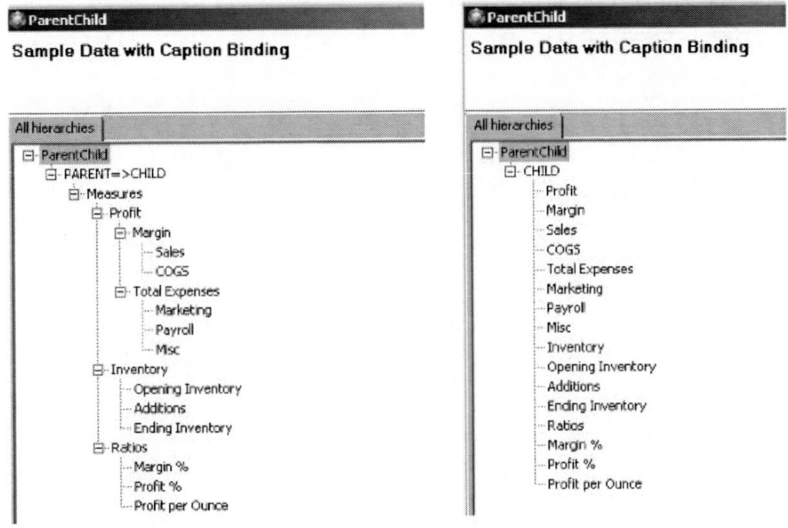

Figure 3.12 Studio versus EIS child add to hierarchy.

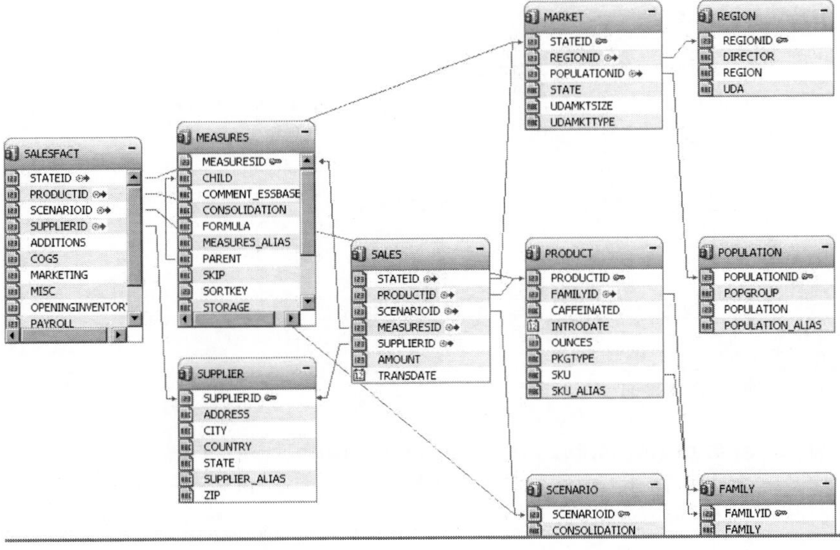

Figure 3.13 Introspection-based mini-schema.

performing a full introspection on the sample model (specifying the desired tables up front) creates Figure 3.13's mini-schema, as well as Figure 3.14's sample hierarchies.

In this example, while the mini-schema is reasonable, the resultant hierarchies are (to say the least) silly. It is easy enough to resolve issues in hierarchies in a source as simple as the Sample.Basic sample (provided with Studio). The column names are explicit and the data is contrived for Essbase modeling. In a real world system, however, with realistic complexity, it is not likely to be as simple.

In short, use introspection for quick modeling and exploration. It provides some level of automated inspection into data relationships. However, it does not always provide

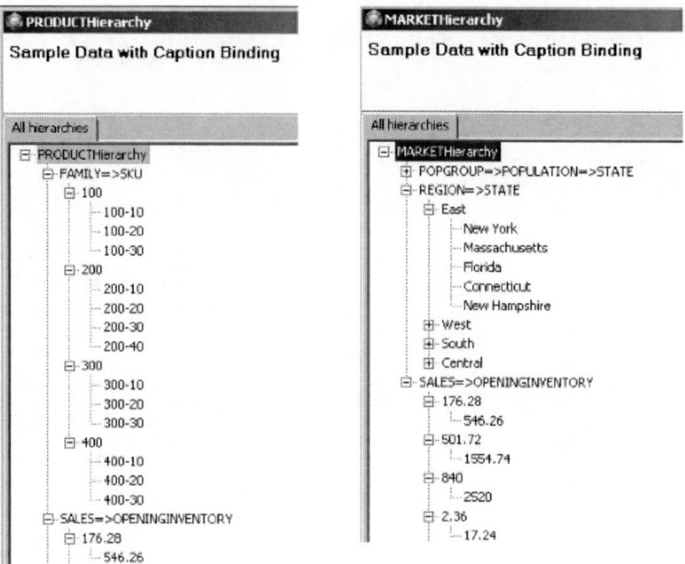

Figure 3.14 Sample hierarchies from introspection.

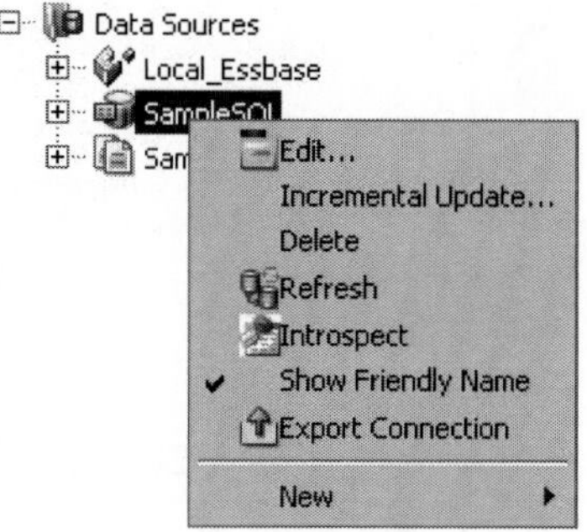

Figure 3.15 Selecting introspection.

deployable hierarchies (for either prototyping or production). You need to review both the hierarchies and mini-schema and correct them in the Introspection wizard prior to completion.

Note: If you limit the selection to the most appropriate fact table and specify a tight set of dimension tables, introspection can produce reasonable initial hierarchies. The mini-schema and hierarchies can be corrected after completing the introspection wizard.

3.4.3.1 Introspecting a Data Source

1. In the data source panel, right-click on a data source.
2. Select **Introspect** (Figure 3.15).
3. Select **Create a new schema diagram**, and click **Next**.
4. Select the desired fact table or tables and click **Next**.
   Studio preselects what it believes to be the fact tables. You can either keep these selections or select new tables.

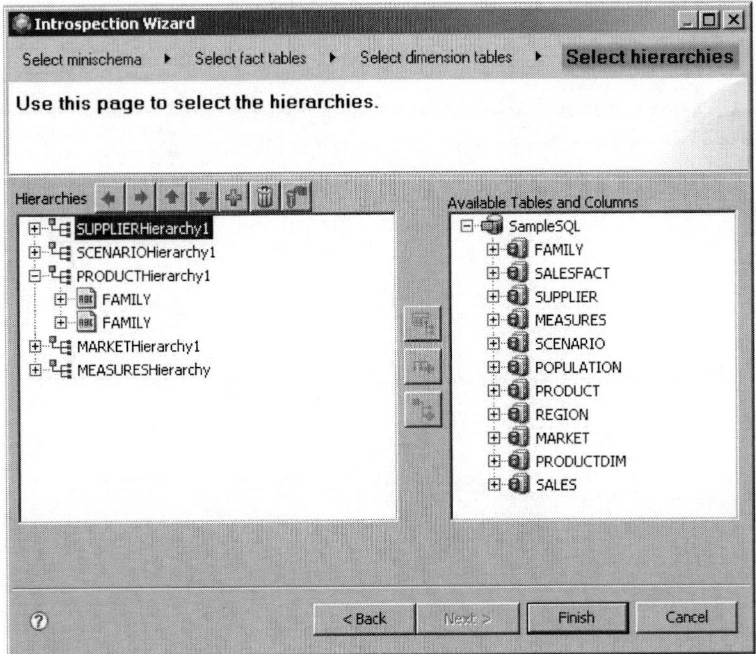

Figure 3.16 Final introspection step.

5. Select the desired dimension tables and click **Next**. Studio preselects what it believes to be the dimension tables based on the keys/joins to the fact table. You can either keep these selections or select new tables.
6. Accept, add, or edit the hierarchies and click **Finish** (Figure 3.16).

3.5 BUILDING HIERARCHIES AND CUSTOM NODES

Once you have the data sources completely defined, the next step is to create dimension elements and hierarchies. In general, the process of setting up both types of objects is simple. Dimension objects at their core are simply columns from tables or text files. Hierarchies are simply combinations of those elements. The most interesting tips and tricks when working with Studio center on the creation and use of elements and hierarchies.

3.5.1 Capabilities of Functions

One of the least used capabilities of Studio is Common Platform Language (CPL) functions. CPL functions enable a host of features within Studio around creation unique and dynamic hierarchies.

The simplest CPL functions are evident when extracting date–time elements from a column with a relational date–time stamp that should not be confused with a date–time hierarchy type. Figure 3.17 shows how right clicking on a date–time column allows the selection of the option **Create Date Elements.**

Once the date elements are created, the resultant nodes are essentially custom nodes created with CPL functions. For instance, Figure 3.18 is an example of the Quarter dimension element created using the right-click shortcut.

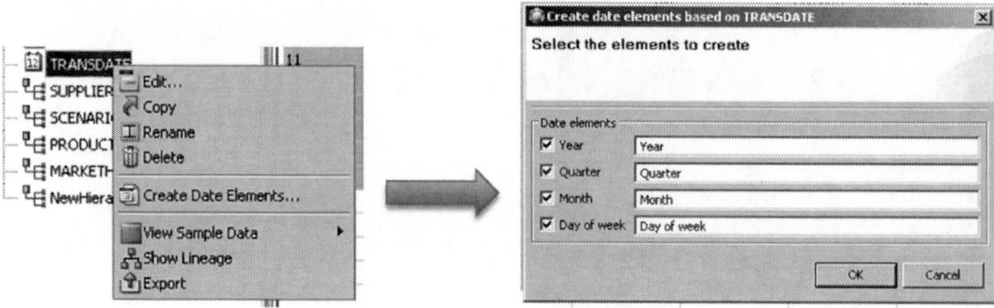

Figure 3.17 Create date elements.

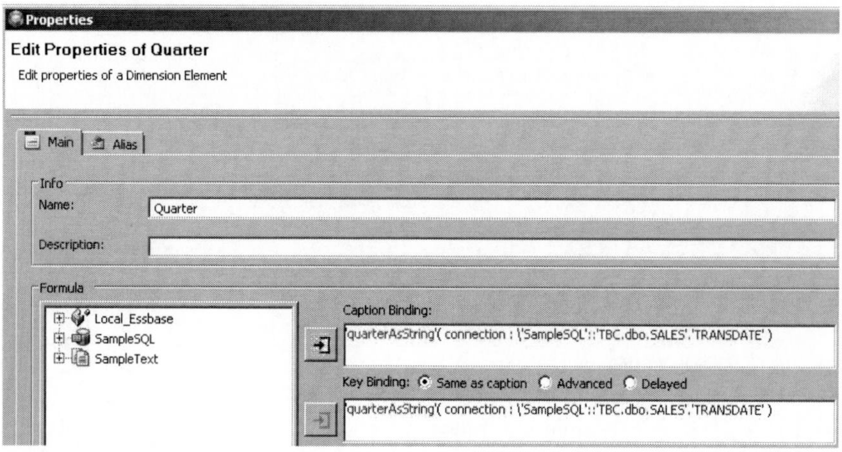

Figure 3.18 Month.

Notice that in this example the "quarterAsString" function extracts the quarter from the date–time stamped column. You can create the same result by creating a new Dimension Element and using the "quarterAsString" function in the Caption Binding area. The right-click option is a timesaving shortcut provided in the Studio UI.

Aside from the various date–time options there are a series of functions that are useful for crafting dimension elements. The string functions, for example, are particularly useful in crafting elements. For instance, you can substring the contents of a column and concatenate the contents to another column to create a unique set of member names. This code concatenates the product code to the first four characters of the product vendor code:

```
'substr'( connection : \'SampleSQL'::'TBC.dbo.SUPPLIER'.'SUPPLIER_
ALIAS', 0, 5 ) || "-" || connection :
\'SampleSQL'::'TBC.dbo.PRODUCT'.'SKU'
```

There are a few things to note about this example:

1. The substring function starts at the first character in the input column (denoted by 0) and then proceeds to the fifth character, exclusive.
2. The || character denotes concatenation in PL/SQL; T-SQL uses the + character.
3. The TBC.dbo.PRODUCT.SKU field comes from a different table. As such, this combined function example leverages the mini-schema and a join from one dimension table, across the fact table and into another dimension table.

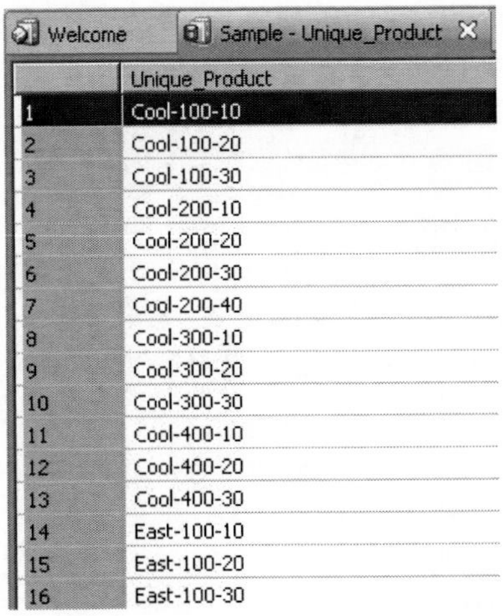

Welcome | Sample - Unique_Product

	Unique_Product
1	Cool-100-10
2	Cool-100-20
3	Cool-100-30
4	Cool-200-10
5	Cool-200-20
6	Cool-200-30
7	Cool-200-40
8	Cool-300-10
9	Cool-300-20
10	Cool-300-30
11	Cool-400-10
12	Cool-400-20
13	Cool-400-30
14	East-100-10
15	East-100-20
16	East-100-30

Figure 3.19 Unique member names.

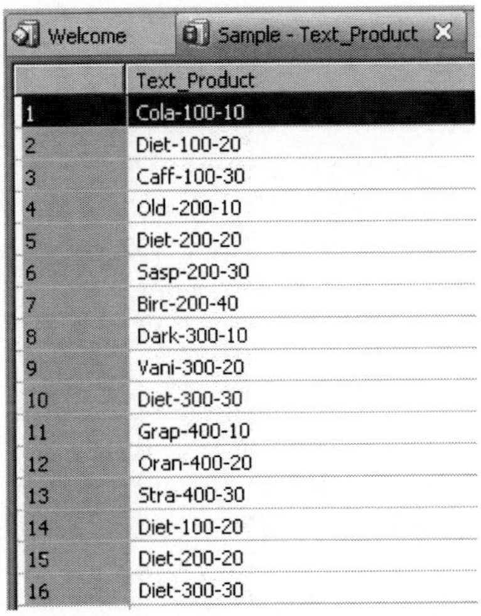

Welcome | Sample - Text_Product

	Text_Product
1	Cola-100-10
2	Diet-100-20
3	Caff-100-30
4	Old -200-10
5	Diet-200-20
6	Sasp-200-30
7	Birc-200-40
8	Dark-300-10
9	Vani-300-20
10	Diet-300-30
11	Grap-400-10
12	Oran-400-20
13	Stra-400-30
14	Diet-100-20
15	Diet-200-20
16	Diet-300-30

Figure 3.20 Text-derived unique member names.

The resulting member set (when sampled) looks like Figure 3.19.

While the preceding example leverages a relational connection, it is important to note that many functions (especially the string manipulation functions) also work with text files. For example, this function performs a similar substring and concatenation on a text file source:

```
'substr'( connection : \'SampleText'::'TBC_PRODUCTDIM.TXT'.'SKU_
ALIAS', 1, 4 ) || "-" || connection : \'SampleText'::'TBC_
PRODUCTDIM.TXT'.'SKU'
```

The resulting sample can be seen in Figure 3.20.

Note: Since this is a text source, you cannot leverage functions to work across tables because the text mini-schema does not allow for joins across flat files.

3.5.2 *Creating Custom/Filtered Sets*

While functions on the surface are generally straightforward, when you start combining functions with Boolean logic filtering, you can create powerful dynamic selection tools. For instance, consider the following requirements for creating the product hierarchy:

- Product SKU (stock-keeping unit) grouped into product families (leveraging the same concatenation and substring requirements from the previous example)
- Alternate hierarchies for all package types
- Alternate hierarchy for caffeinated products with sales greater than $800

The first two requirements are easily handled as standard hierarchies or subhierarchies. In fact, the second requirement could be easily handled as an attribute dimension. The third requirement, unfortunately, is a little more complex. You need to create a hierarchy that changes dynamically based on both the attributes of a given product as well as the numeric sales of that product. All three requirements can be handled with the application of various CPL functions and the Studio filtering capabilities. To create this specific hierarchy leveraging the Sample.Basic sample SQL source, you use multiple tables (SUPPLIER, SALESFACT, PRODUCT, PRODUCTDIM):

1. Create a dimension element using the following CPL code in the **Caption Binding** area:
   ```
   'substr'( connection : \'SampleSQL'::'TBC.dbo.
   SUPPLIER'.'SUPPLIER_ALIAS', 0, 5 ) || "-" || connection :
   \'SampleSQL'::'TBC.dbo.PRODUCT'.'SKU'
   ```
2. In the Filter area, type the following CPL code:
   ```
   connection : \'SampleSQL'::'TBC.dbo.SALESFACT'.'SALES' >= 800
   and connection : \'SampleSQL'::'TBC.dbo.PRODUCT'.'CAFFEINATED'
   == "True"
   ```
   In this case, notice that the AND clause combines both the test for CAFFEINATED attribute as well as filtering the result set where SALES from the SALESFACT table is greater than or equal to $800.
3. Create two additional dimension elements for the package types of can and bottle using the same caption binding listed in step 1 and filtering for bottle and can (use the filtering code in step 2 as an example). For example:
   Caption Binding
   ```
   'substr'( connection : \'SampleSQL'::'TBC.dbo.
   SUPPLIER'.'SUPPLIER_ALIAS', 0, 5 ) || "-" || connection :
   \'SampleSQL'::'TBC.dbo.PRODUCT'.'SKU'
   ```
   Filter
   ```
   connection : \'SampleSQL'::'TBC.dbo.PRODUCT'.'PKGTYPE' ==
   "BOTTLE"
   ```
4. Create a new hierarchy object and leverage the dimension elements created in the previous step (Figure 3.21).

The preview of this hierarchy can be seen in Figure 3.22.

Note: This hierarchy contains a series of user-defined members (UDMs) to separate the hierarchies and act as totals ("All Products," "Product by Package Type," etc.). Further, when performing actions on existing dimension elements, it is recommended that you make copies and perform all actions on the copies. This allows you to revert to the original element to make additional custom nodes as required.

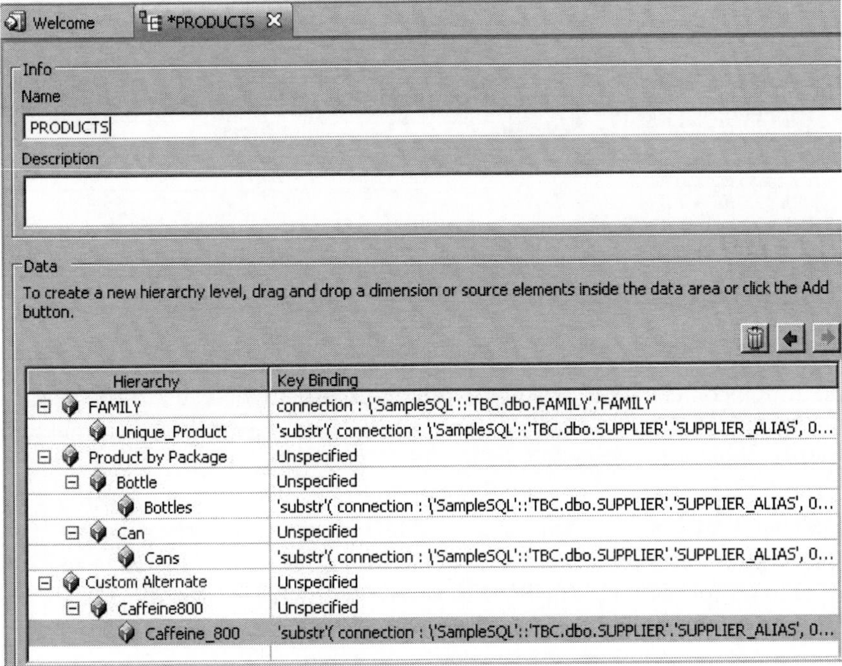

Figure 3.21 Products hierarchy.

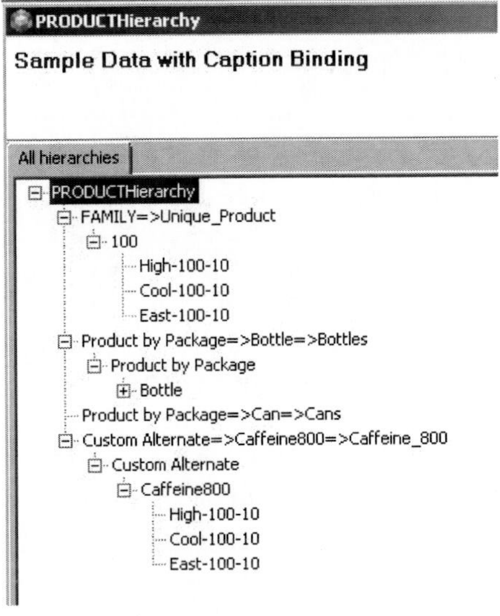

Figure 3.22 Product hierarchy preview.

3.5.3 Node Properties versus Deployment Properties

One of the hidden values of performing concatenations, substrings, and other actions on dimension elements is that these changes automatically flow through into the final cube definition (also known as a cube schema). Moreover, because these settings are made in objects outside of the cube schema, every schema that leverages a specific dimension

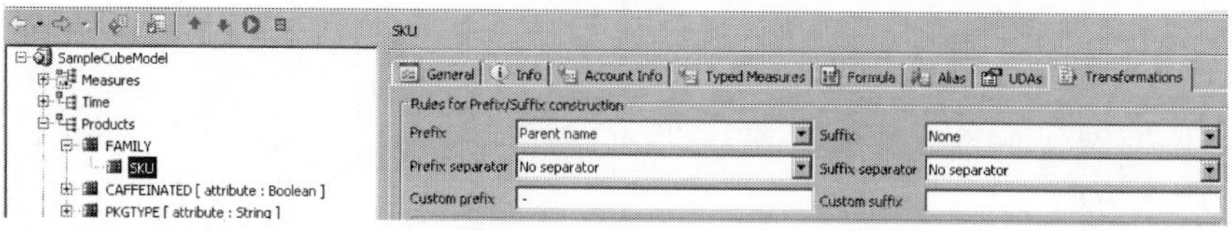

Figure 3.23 Prefix/suffix setting.

element inherit the properties. This inheritance is a marked difference from deployment properties.

It is important to understand the difference between the cube schema Essbase properties and dimension elements settings. In short, where possible, use dimension element properties for any settings you want universally applied. Leverage cube schema properties to further refine settings prior to a specific cube deployment.

For example, for general concatenations of product codes, you can use the dimension element properties to ensure consistency of SKU-level names regardless of hierarchy in a specific cube. You might, however, decide for a given cube that the product family name needs to be appended to the SKU as you drill down the hierarchy. In this particular case, you can leverage the prefix capabilities of the cube schema's Essbase properties to ensure that the name is appended as desired for that specific cube (Figure 3.23).

3.5.4 *Simple Hierarchy Types*

Before we get into detail on specific techniques for creating dimension or hierarchical elements, we should discuss the fundamental hierarchy types within Studio. While this may seem an obvious topic, there is often confusion around the three Studio hierarchy types:

1. Standard Hierarchy: This basic Studio hierarchy type is most often used. Hierarchies of this type can represent ANY base dimension type in Essbase (including accounts/measures, and time). The only exception to this is the Date–Time dimension type.
2. Measure: This is a specialized measure/accounts hierarchy. Whether you use this hierarchy type or a standard hierarchy type depends on the nature of table you are leveraging for the build (more on this topic in a moment).
3. Calendar: This is a specialized hierarchy type specifically for the creation of an Essbase Date–Time calendar dimension. The Date–Time dimension type was introduced in version 9.x of Essbase to allow for more complex Date–Time logic in Essbase. The assumption when using a Date–Time dimension is that your model only requires a single time dimension representing a true date continuum. This hierarchy type is not commonly used in both Studio and Essbase in general.

3.5.5 *When to Use the "Measures" Dimension*

One of the most common questions when working with hierarchies in Studio pertains to the use of standard hierarchy versus "Measures" hierarchies for the creation of an Essbase accounts dimension. The answer to this question is that it depends on the structure of the table(s) you use to build the dimension.

If you use a dimension table that enumerates the accounts in a level/generation fashion, or if you are using a fact table with multiple fact columns, then you can leverage a "Measures" hierarchy type. For example, look at the table in Figure 3.24.

Welcome | Sample - SALESFACT

	STATEID	PRODUCTID	SCENARIOID	SUPPLIERID	TRANSDATE	SALES	COGS	MARKETING	PAYROLL	MISC
1	6	1	1	2	Sun Jan 23 00:...	176.28	70.46	24.44	13.26	0.0
2	6	1	1	2	Sun Jan 09 00:...	501.72	200.54	69.56	37.74	0.0
3	6	1	2	1	Fri Jan 07 00:0...	840.0	340.0	90.0	40.0	0.0
4	6	2	1	1	Sat Jan 08 00:0...	2.36	2.88	0.94	0.86	0.02
5	6	2	1	3	Sun Jan 02 00:...	29.5	36.0	11.75	10.75	0.25
6	6	2	2	3	Wed Jan 19 00:...	37.8	48.6	10.8	10.8	0.0
7	6	2	1	1	Sun Jan 09 00:...	86.14	105.12	34.31	31.39	0.73
8	6	2	2	3	Thu Jan 20 00:...	102.2	131.4	29.2	29.2	0.0
9	6	3	1	2	Fri Jan 14 00:0...	1.45	0.95	0.3	0.22	0.0
10	6	3	2	3	Wed Jan 05 00:...	14.4	8.8	1.6	1.6	0.0
11	6	3	1	2	Mon Jan 24 00:...	15.95	10.45	3.3	2.42	0.0
12	6	3	1	3	Wed Jan 05 00:...	18.85	12.35	3.9	2.86	0.0
13	6	3	1	3	Tue Jan 04 00:...	108.75	71.25	22.5	16.5	0.0
14	6	3	2	3	Wed Jan 05 00:...	165.6	101.2	18.4	18.4	0.0

Figure 3.24 Multiple fact column table.

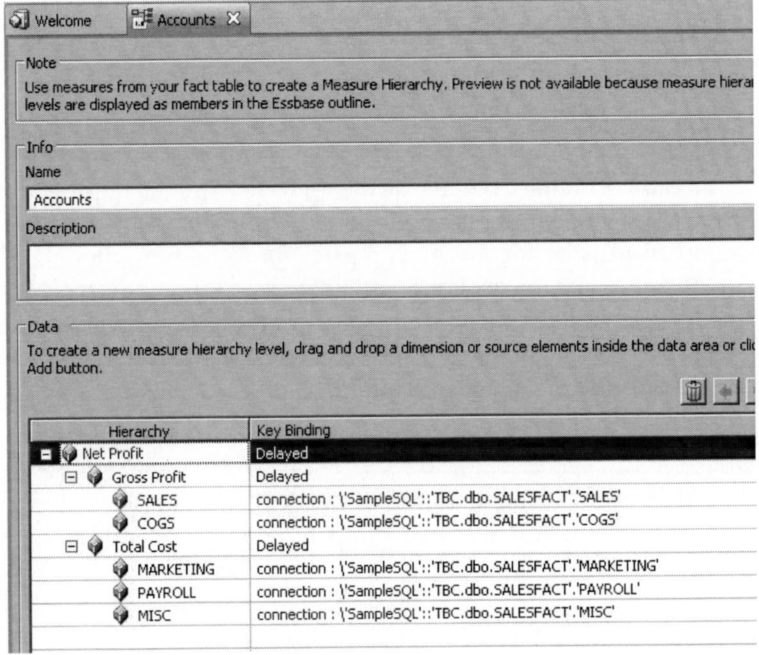

Figure 3.25 Accounts hierarchy.

In this example, the individual measures (such as "payroll," "sales," and "cogs") are column headers. Each column represents a distinct fact that can be loaded to Essbase at deployment. If you use this table to build the Accounts hierarchy, it is easier to use the "Measures" hierarchy type.

By adding a number of user-defined children/siblings, you can build an effective accounts dimension hierarchy. In the following images, "Net Profit," "Gross Profit," and "Total Cost" are user-defined members that represent totals or subtotals in the final Essbase model. The table columns (dimension elements) are nested under each user-defined member and represent locations where Studio loads data during deployment.

Trying to user a standard dimension type with this table results in the structure seen in Figure 3.25.

You will notice in this instance that you can derive the same structure using either hierarchy type. The primary difference (in this example) is that leveraging the

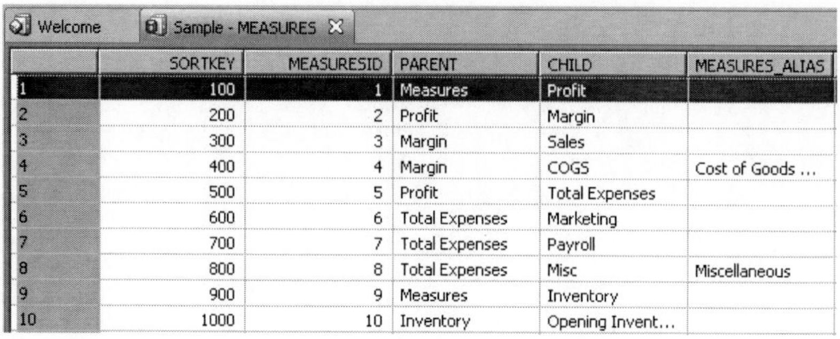

Welcome | Sample - MEASURES

	SORTKEY	MEASURESID	PARENT	CHILD	MEASURES_ALIAS
1	100	1	Measures	Profit	
2	200	2	Profit	Margin	
3	300	3	Margin	Sales	
4	400	4	Margin	COGS	Cost of Goods ...
5	500	5	Profit	Total Expenses	
6	600	6	Total Expenses	Marketing	
7	700	7	Total Expenses	Payroll	
8	800	8	Total Expenses	Misc	Miscellaneous
9	900	9	Measures	Inventory	
10	1000	10	Inventory	Opening Invent...	

Figure 3.26 Recursive Measures table.

"Measures" type explicitly tells Studio that this is the fact dimension. When this dimension is deployed to Essbase it becomes "Accounts."

Note: In this example, the use of the user-defined members is optional. Your dimension table may already contain the totals, or the totals may not be required for the overall analytical solution. Further, it also is important to understand the implications of using an accounts dimension for ASO (aggregate storage option) models. The dimension tagged as Accounts for an ASO model is dynamic (and compressed by default). When building an ASO model, there are many circumstances where you do not want the classical measures dimension tagged as "Accounts" and instead want to use another dimension where member formulae are required.

Figure 3.26 shows a very different path to the same hierarchy, but through a recursive dimension table.

When your table represents the Measures dimension through two recursive columns, do not use the "Measures" hierarchy type, but instead create a standard dimension and let Studio leverage the self-join in the mini-schema (discussed earlier in this chapter) to build the dimensionality.

In summary, if you have a table or fact table that fully enumerates the members of the measures dimension, use the "Measures" hierarchy type. If you have a recursive table to build the measures dimension, use the standard hierarchy type.

3.6 MODELING AND DEPLOYING THE CUBE

The final phase in moving from data source to Essbase cube involves modeling and deploying the cube. When I talk about modeling in this phase, I am referring to the process of selecting hierarchies for a given cube and specifying the desired deployment properties. While on the surface, this phase of working with Studio appears generally straightforward, there are a number of tricks you can utilize to more effectively deploy your Essbase database.

3.6.1 Creating a Cube Schema without Metrics

The first step in the deployment phase is selecting the desired hierarchies for the Essbase cube. When selecting the hierarchies you must specify the standard dimensions as well as the Measures dimension or column.

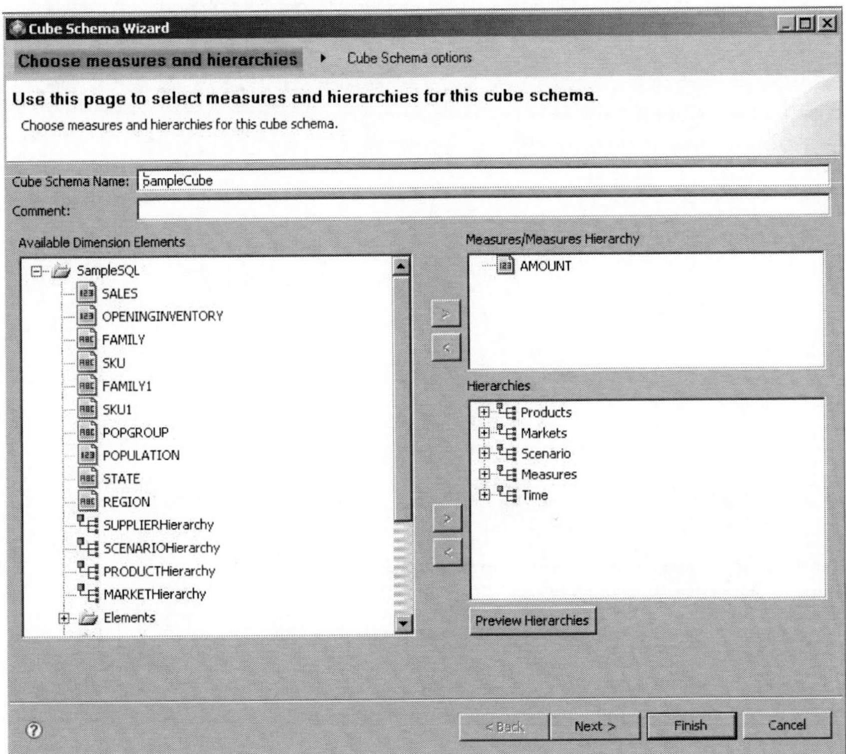

Figure 3.27 Specifying dimensions.

Figure 3.27 shows a single column as the Measures. This is done because, in the specific model, the Measures dimension was built from a recursive table as a standard hierarchy type leveraging the parent/child relationship. The fact table used for this build contains a single data column ("AMOUNT").

What do you do, however, if you are simply creating a prototype with Studio and either do not have a data file or want to load the data from a process external to Studio? In either case, you can trick Studio into believing you have a measures column. Instead of adding a true data column to the Cube Schema wizard, you can add any column with a numeric data type to this portion of the UI to simply move forward. For example, in Figure 3.28, PRODUCTID from the Product table is added to the Measures area of the Cube Schema Wizard. Once in place, the UI lets you move forward to the next step as in Figure 3.29.

If you plan to employ this trick during the deployment phase, make sure you think ahead when adding a data source to Studio and confirm that it has a numeric column in one of tables or text files.

Note: This trick only works if you use a standard hierarchy as your Accounts/Measures dimension. This hierarchy is added to the standard dimension area like products, time, or any other hierarchy. If you have a "Measures" type hierarchy and you want to add it to your Essbase cube, this definition must be added to the Measures Hierarchy area on the cube schema wizard (Figure 3.30).

PRODUCTID	SCENARIOID	MEASURESID	SUPPLIERID	TRANSDATE	AMOUNT
1	2	3	1	Wed Jan 05 00:...	38.4
1	2	3	1	Fri Jan 07 00:0...	544.0
1	1	3	1	Sun Jan 09 00:...	644.1
1	2	3	1	Fri Jan 14 00:0...	6.4
1	1	3	1	Sat Jan 15 00:0...	33.9
1	2	3	1	Sun Jan 16 00:...	51.2
1	2	3	1	Thu Feb 10 00:...	18.3
1	2	3	1	Tue Feb 15 00:...	213.5
1	2	3	1	Fri Feb 25 00:0...	378.2
1	1	3	1	Fri Feb 25 00:0...	645.0
1	1	3	1	Sun Mar 12 00:...	675.0

Figure 3.28 Faked Measures table.

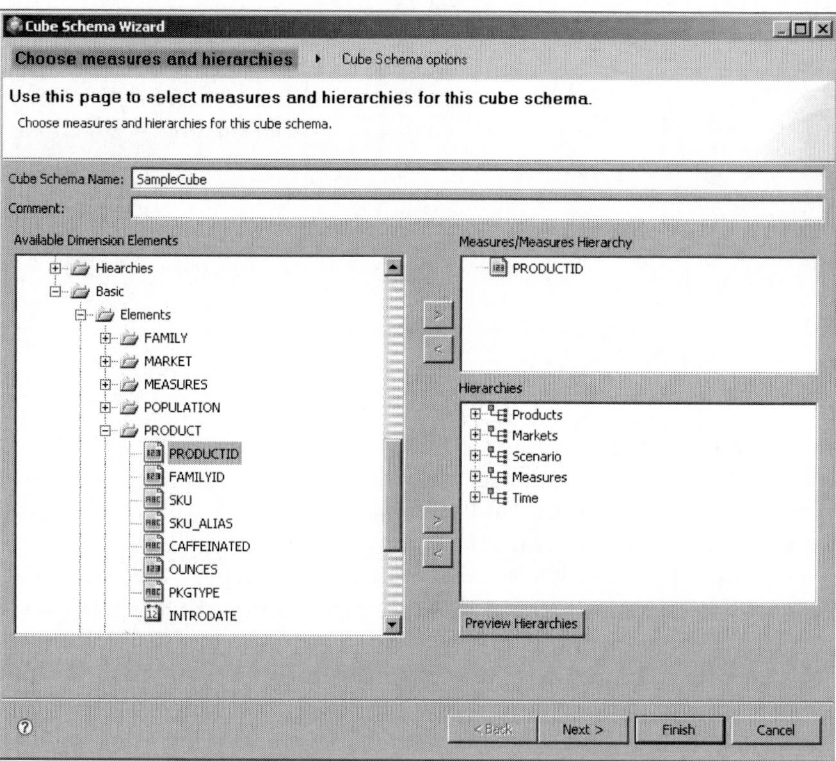

Figure 3.29 Specifying dimensions with a faked Measures table.

3.6.1.1 Loading Data External to Studio After the metadata is in place, your next decision is how to load the data. From a data load perspective, a cube built using Studio via the Cube Deployment Wizard or directly from a numeric data source is like any other Essbase database. It is only natural to question why you would load data external to Studio after leveraging Studio to build the dimensionality. The answer is: Control.

When loading data with Studio you have the option of writing custom data-load SQL. This is good, assuming you are leveraging a relational source, but not always ideal.

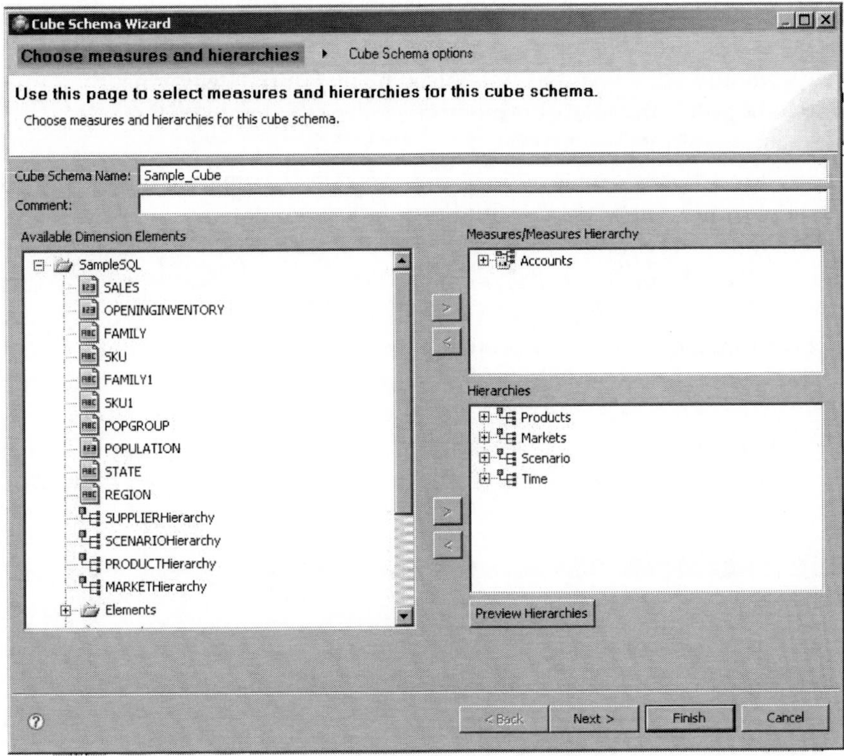

Figure 3.30 Specifying dimensions with "Measures" hierarchy type.

For instance, if you are building an ASO model, you may want to take advantage of multiple load buffers to expedite load process.

From a prototype perspective, it is often easier and quicker to go directly to the data source or use a secondary flat file for the data load. From a production deployment perspective, you should benchmark the load time results from Studio compared to other methods to determine which method yields the most efficient and manageable results.

3.6.2 Leveraging Open Properties to Validate Dimensionality

Everyone believes his or her data is clean. To be blunt, it never really is. This statement is not intended to insult an organization or an individual. People honestly believe that their data is in a good state and ready to build; there are those rare instances when that is the case. The problem, often, is not data—it is people. Data is clean and rules are followed until humans get involved and break the rules. Over time the tightest of systems experience a level of dirty data and metadata. Further, the definition of what represents clean data varies from one person to another.

For instance, a client might find it perfectly acceptable that there are duplicate members in the Markets dimension when you intend to follow Essbase best practice and create a unique member model. Inevitably the understanding and discovery of data inconsistencies comes out during the load and build process. These can often be very difficult to scrub. However, you can leverage open settings and incremental build options in Studio to help find and resolve these inconsistencies.

The recommended practice for Essbase is to (when possible) create unique member names in the cubes. It is also a recommended practice, when creating ASO models, to have as few dynamic dimensions as possible. On your initial deployment of dimensionality from Studio, you can violate both of these rules to validate the metadata being sent to Essbase, as shown in Figure 3.31.

When Studio validates dimension settings and the schema prior to deployment, it literally validates only those things. Studio does not validate the metadata being sent to Essbase. If you select unique member names and then try to deploy to Essbase with duplicate metadata, the deployment fails at the Essbase side, and you need to then start trouble-shooting to understand why. If you instead allow duplicate members, you can build all of the dimensionality and validate dimension by dimension in EAS.

Figure 3.32 shows turning off duplicates on a dimension-by-dimension basis after the duplicate member name enabled cube is deployed.

As long as the outline validates, you know that you do not have a duplicate issue (for instance) in a given dimension. If you do run into duplicate issues in a dimension, then

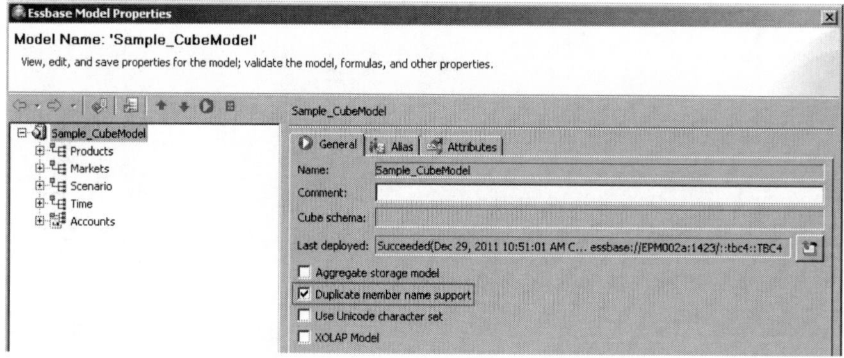

Figure 3.31 Duplicate Members enabled.

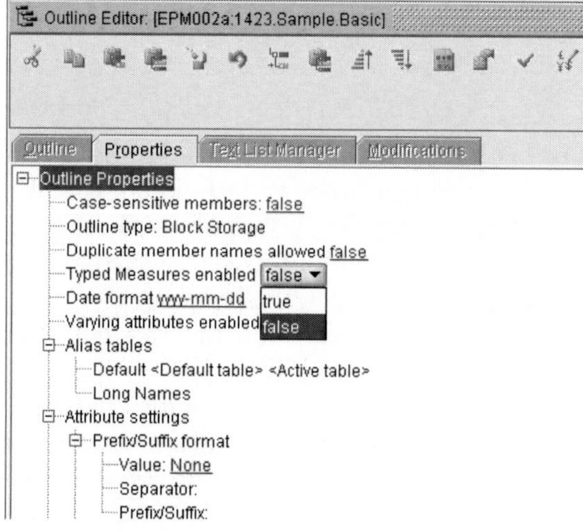

Figure 3.32 EAS duplicate Member setting.

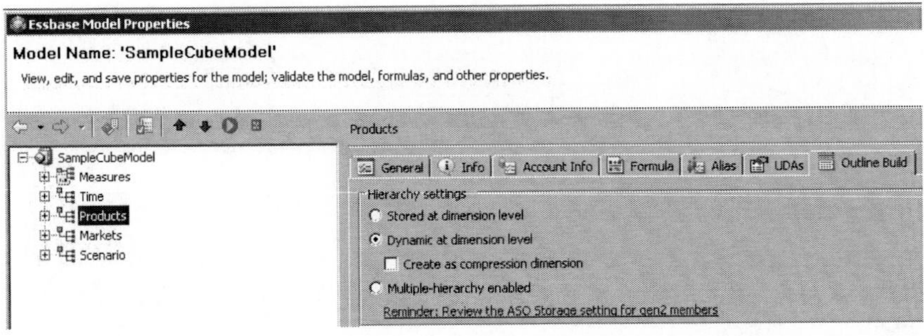

Figure 3.33 Defining hierarchy as Dynamic.

you can turn off duplicates on a level-by-level basis in that dimension and continue to validate the outline until you focus in on the specific members that are causing the issue. Along the same line, when you are dealing with ASO models, you can set the dimension types to all "Dynamic" for initial deployment purposes, as in Figure 3.33.

Even after you have scrubbed duplicate members out of the dataset, you might end up in a situation where multiple shared members appear in a dimension hierarchy. Like unexpected duplicates, this causes the cube deployment to fail on the Essbase side. Making all dimensions dynamic on the initial deployment, Essbase allows all consolidation operators and multiple shared members to deploy in a dimension or hierarchy. In a similar process to duplicate, you can then go into EAS and toggle each dimension from "dynamic" to "stored" or to "multiple hierarchies enabled" and validate the outline. This lets you see the specific hierarchies and members where you have issues.

3.6.3 Incremental Building to Validate Dimensionality

One final consideration in deploying the cube from Studio is leveraging incremental build options. This makes sense, of course, when adding to an existing cube. It also is quite useful when first deploying a cube.

The deployment process from Studio can take minutes or hours (usually somewhere in between). At any point during the deployment, if a dimension fails the entire deployment is aborted (even if multiple other dimensions have, in theory, built correctly). If you are dealing with large dimensions, such as a "Work Order Tasks" dimension with a million members, a failure can cost you hours of downtime. Instead, you can leverage the incremental build capabilities to deploy the model one dimension at a time and key in on a dimension or set of dimensions that cause a failure.

To leverage incremental building on the initial deployment:

1. Create an empty application and database in using Essbase Administration Services.
2. In Studio, initiate the Cube Deployment Wizard.
3. Fill in the **Application** and **Database** name with the application and database you created in step 1, and click **Next**.
4. Select the option for **Incremental Load** (Figure 3.34).
5. In the Scheduling Options area, select **Deploy Now** and click **Next**.
6. Select **Update or Build Selected Hierarchies** (Figure 3.35).
7. Select a desired hierarchy or hierarchies and click **Rebuild**.

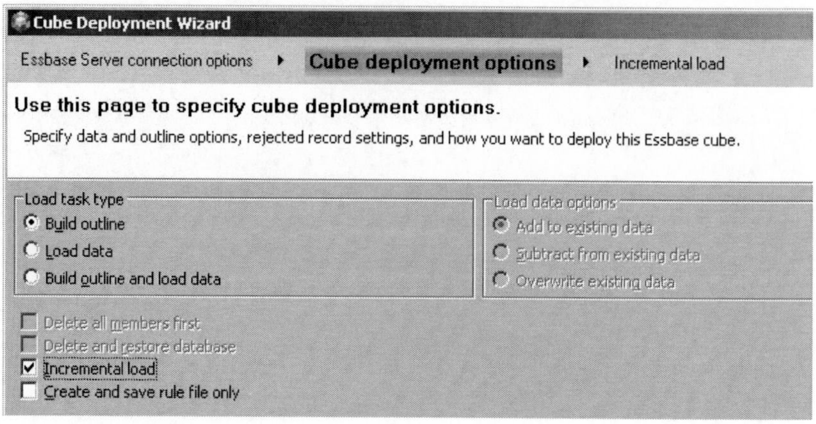

Figure 3.34 Incremental Load.

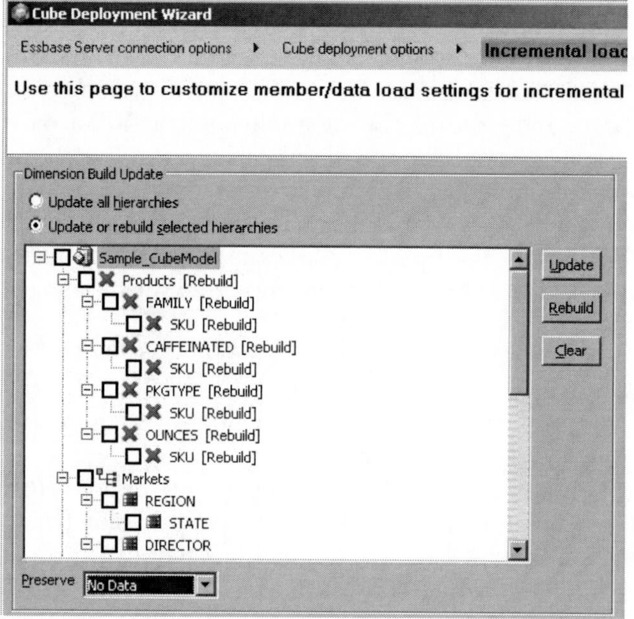

Figure 3.35 Update or rebuild without data.

8. Under **Preserve** select **No Data**.
9. Click **Finish**.
10. Repeat the process for all remaining dimensions.

3.6.4 Understanding Alternate Data Source Mappings

If you do choose to leverage Studio for loading data you have options in respect to how that data load is handled. If you are working with a relational source, Studio uses the fact table for data loads. You, however, can override the data source and leverage an alternate source for data loads.

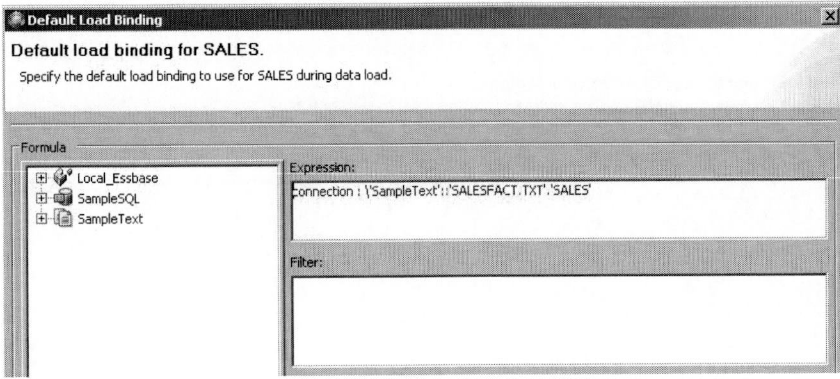

Figure 3.36 Default Load Binding.

An example might be an application with dimensionality from a development environment, but data sourced from a staging or production system for more robust testing. This is accomplished using the alternate data source bindings capability that overrides the fact table and pushes the data load to whichever additional source specified.

To use alternate data source bindings:

1. On the cube schema properties select **Override default data load bindings** (Figure 3.36) and click **Next.**
2. On the Define Data Load Mappings screen go to the base members of the accounts dimension and double-click the empty Data Load Binding field (Figure 3.37). Then click on the ellipses in the field.
3. Using the data sources in the formula area, browse to the desired alternate data source binding and double-click it to add it to the Expression area.
4. Click **OK** and repeat for the additional measures.
5. Deploy the model and load data as normal.

Note: This example shows alternate data source bindings for a relational source. When working with a relational source, this is an option. When using a text data source, you need use the alternate data source bindings to have Studio process the data load.

3.6.5 Generating Load Rules and Integrating with MaxL Automation

A common complaint about Essbase Studio is that there is no built in scheduling mechanism. The lack of a built in scheduler is an overt omission by the development team because **Studio does not need one.** Essbase Studio is a graphical Load Rule generator. The final output of all of your work in Studio is a set of Load Rules that can either be used to deploy a cube from the Studio UI or to build a cube based on your current Essbase automation processes.

If you are simply prototyping with Studio, then you can deploy from the Studio UI. However, if you use Studio in a production environment, there are two capabilities to let you dovetail the Studio output directly into MaxL:

1. Generate and leverage Load Rules from Studio
2. Generate a MaxL script from the deployment process

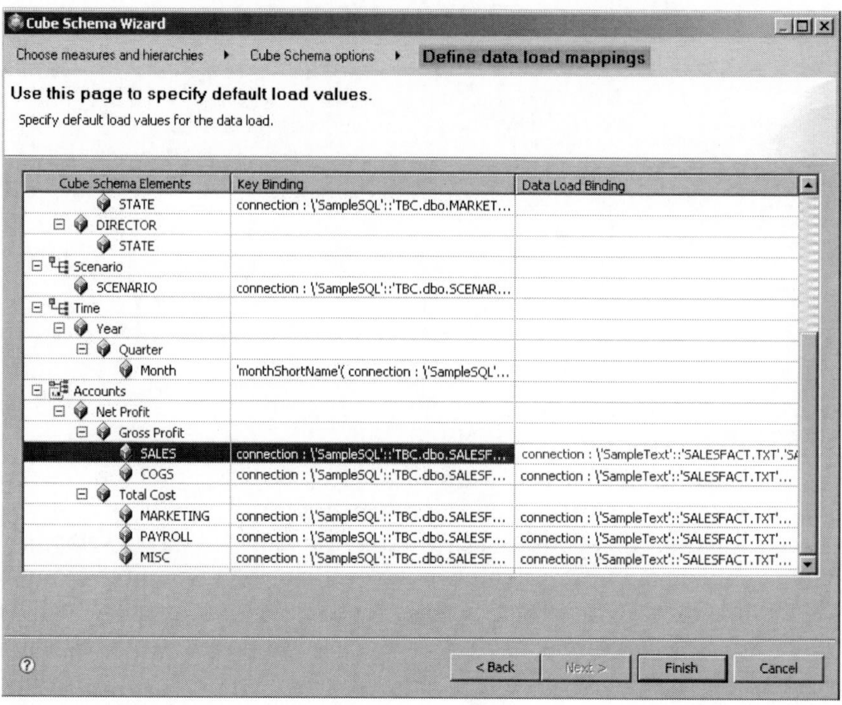

Figure 3.37 Custom Load Bindings.

In respect to the first capability, Studio always generates Load Rules when you perform a dimension build deployment task. What is often missed is that you have the option of not building dimensions or loading data from the Studio UI, but only deploying the Load Rules to the Essbase cube (Figure 3.38).

By selecting this option, Studio ignores the Load Task Type setting (for example, "Build Outline") and performs the following tasks:

- Creates the Essbase application and database (assuming they do not already exist).
- Reviews the hierarchies and Essbase properties and generates Load Rules for each hierarchy and subhierarchy. It is important to note that attribute dimensions and secondary hierarchies often get independent Load Rules from the primary hierarchy in a dimension.
- If using a relational source, it generates a data Load Rule for the cube.

In addition to the generation of Load Rules, newer versions of Studio also provide the capability of generating a MaxL script so you do not have to write the MaxL code yourself. This is an option at the bottom of the final screen of the Cube Deployment Wizard in Figure 3.39.

The MaxL output looks similar to this:

```
deploy all from model 'SampleCubeModel' in cube schema '\SampleSQL\
Basic\Cubes\SampleCube' login $1 identified by $2 on host 'EPM002a'
to application 'tbc6' database 'tbc' add values using connection
'Local_Essbase' keep 200 errors on error ignore dataload write to
default;
```

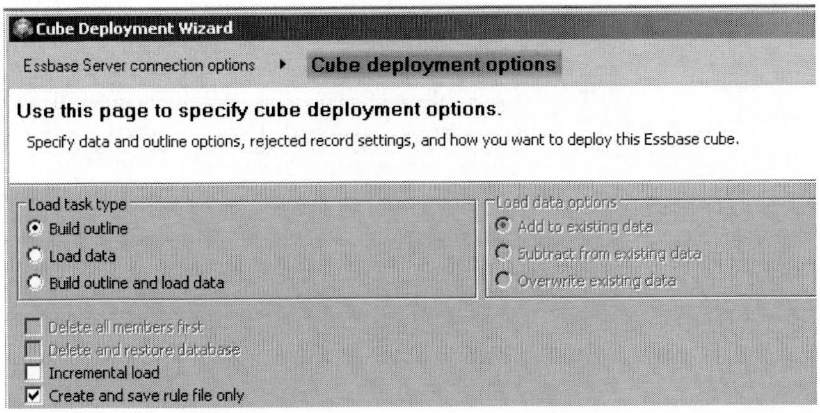

Figure 3.38 Deploying Load Rules only.

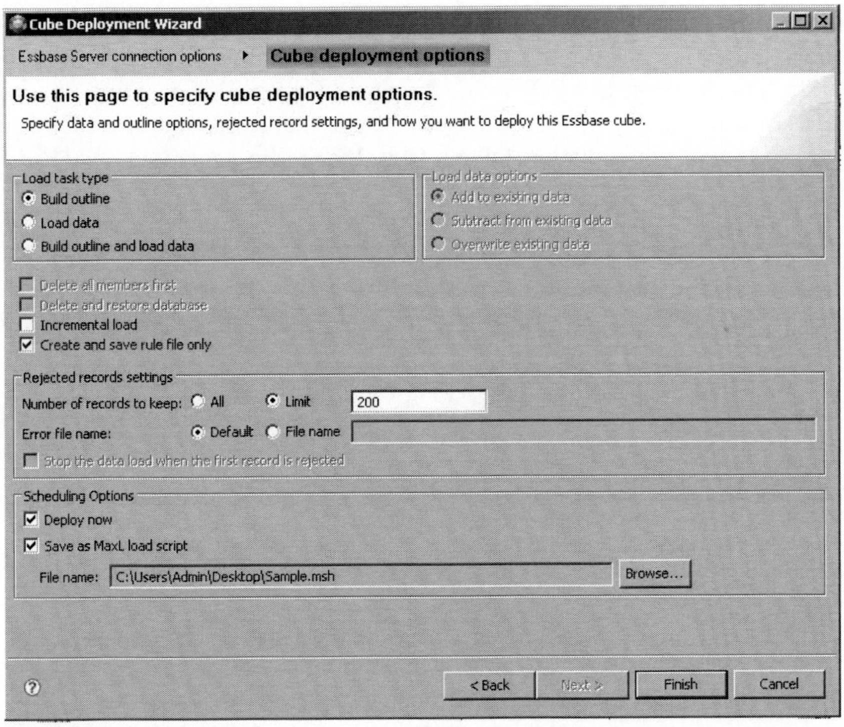

Figure 3.39 Generate MaxL Load script.

Note: The MaxL script generated by Studio contains specific syntax to trigger the Studio generated rules. It does not call out each Load Rule individually as you would do when creating a customary MaxL script. Studio internally tags each load it creates so Essbase can pick up the specific rules generated by Studio and execute them based on the abbreviated script Studio generates. This does not preclude you, however, from writing a more standard MaxL script and using the Studio-generated Load Rules.

3.7 ADDITIONAL THOUGHTS

The reality is that Essbase Studio is a simple tool for modeling and deploying Essbase cubes. While there are a variety of techniques you can use to increase Studio's functionality, in general, what you see is what you get. The real trick is knowing where to look, and this chapter has given you the map. The following sections cover some of the best of the rest.

3.7.1 Stealing SQL

A common request from people working with Essbase Studio is the ability to leverage custom SQL as opposed to the SQL the Studio generates. Studio's programmatically generated SQL is not optimized because it must be universally accepted for a given data source. This means it cannot take into account indexing strategies on the fact table or other optimizations that may have been implemented in SQL Server 2008, for example.

In respect to data loading, this is easy to do. You can select the option in the upper left corner of Figure 3.40 to use custom SQL on the Essbase properties dialog for a given cube schema.

What you cannot do from the Studio UI is leverage custom SQL for dimensions. In fact, while there is a trick for stealing the SQL Studio generates for dimension builds, you cannot force Studio to leverage this SQL for deployment. If you are using Studio to prototype against a relational source and then want to leverage that same SQL in a SQL Interface-Based Load Rule, you can copy the SQL out from the Studio-generated Load Rules.

3.7.1.1 See Studio's Dimension Build SQL Studio

1. Use the Cube Deployment Wizard to deploy the Essbase cubes using the Create and save rule file only option.
2. Once the deployment is completed, browse to the Essbase database directory using the Windows/Linux/Unix file system.
3. Open the Load Rule in a text editor (Figure 3.41).

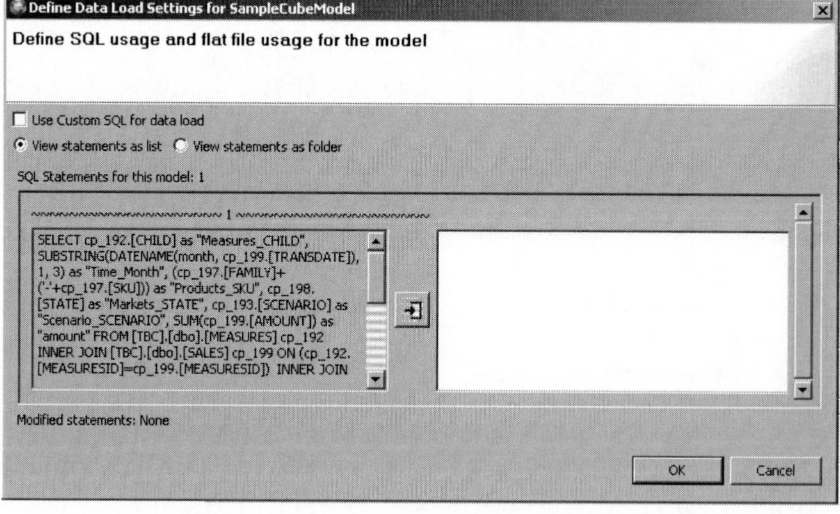

Figure 3.40 Data Load SQL dialog box.

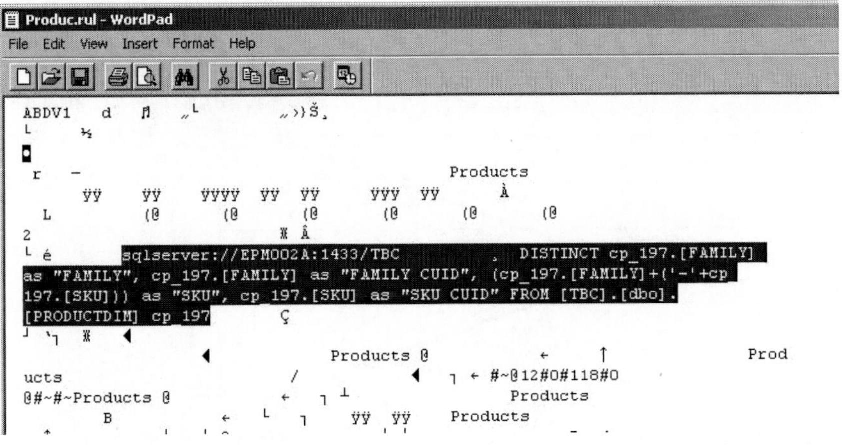

Figure 3.41 Produc.rul opened in a text editor.

4. The clear text in the Load Rule is the SQL generated to build the dimension. This SQL can be copied out and leveraged as the basis for the SQL in the SQL Interface-Based Load Rules.

Note: Making any changes to the SQL in the Load Rule in the text editor is not a supported action. Yes, this is a hack, but a cool and useful one.

3.7.2 To Stream or Not to Stream

One of the often-overlooked capabilities of Studio is data and metadata streaming. Studio performs its modeling tasks using JDBC (Java database connectivity) drivers. However, when you deploy a cube using the Cube Deployment Wizard, that build is handed off to the Essbase SQL Interface and ODBC (open database connectivity) connections. That means that the Essbase server must have the proper drivers installed and ODBC connections setup prior to deployment (Figure 3.42).

If you are running in a stand-alone environment where you have control, ensuring the ODBC connections are in place is easy. However, there is a very good chance that the Studio and Essbase servers are on separate physical boxes. If that is the case, you may not have access to either, then create an ODBC connection on the Essbase box or set up the required ODBC connections.

Studio provides the option to force (or stream) the entire deployment process to run from the Studio server and the JDBC connections. Streaming is controlled in the Studio server.properties file. To enable streaming add the following line to the Studio server.properties file:

```
server.essbase.streamingCubeBuilding=true
```

Note: In general, streaming provides slower build and load times as compared to the Essbase SQL Interface. Also, in newer versions of Studio, you also have the option, as shown in Figure 3.43, of having Essbase dynamically generate the ODBC connections at time of deployment. This uses the built-in drivers on the Essbase server and the connection information in Studio.

Note: When using the Oracle database as a source, you have the option of leveraging an OCI connection to optimize processing.

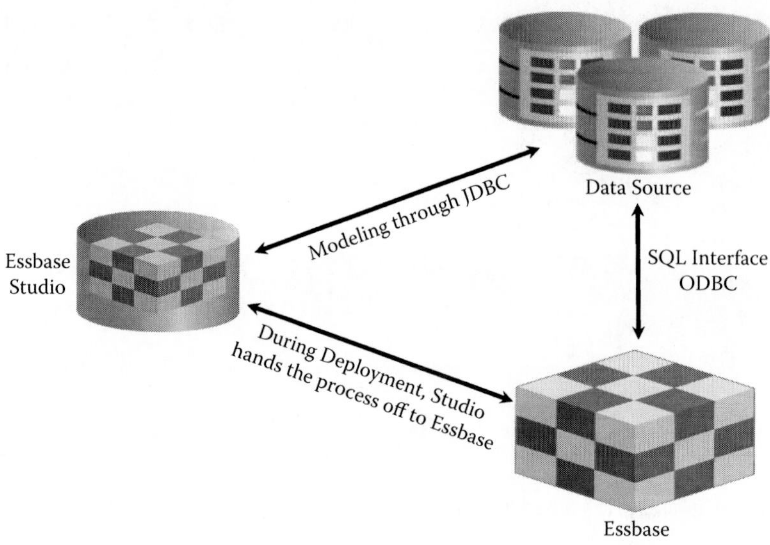

Figure 3.42 Essbase, Studio, and Data Source connections.

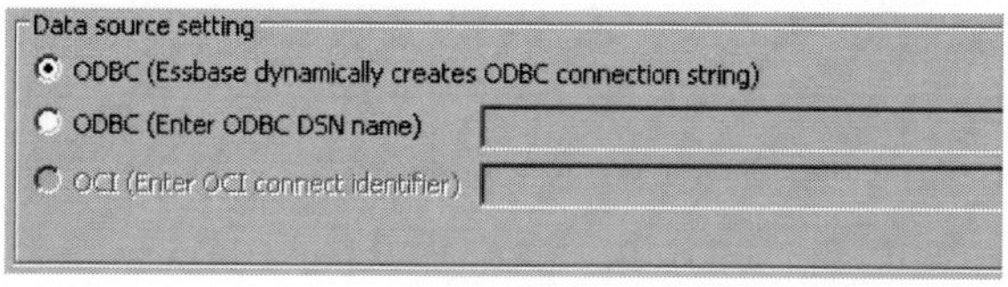

Data source setting
(•) ODBC (Essbase dynamically creates ODBC connection string)
( ) ODBC (Enter ODBC DSN name)
( ) OCI (Enter OCI connect identifier)

Figure 3.43 Dynamic ODBC connection string.

3.7.3 Considering XOLAP

While Studio provides a breadth of capabilities for modeling and deploying Essbase cubes, the majority of those features can be handled by other build methods. The SQL interface and the Data Prep Editor can handle SQL and text file modeling. Essbase Integration Services can create and deploy drill-through reports (and you also can create drill-through reports via MaxL in recent incarnations of Essbase). The one capability where you must use Essbase Studio is in creating and deploying an XOLAP model.

XOLAP is simply leveraging Essbase for metadata navigation and the OLAP ad hoc experience while generating dynamic SQL back to the data source to bring back the numbers; in short, it is the Essbase version of ROLAP.

XOLAP models are ASO cubes modeled into Studio and deployed with a specific set of options and restrictions (more on these in a moment). The value in XOLAP models is in three main areas:

1. Latency: There zero latency between changes in the data source and the values shown in Essbase. If the source data systems change, you see those results as soon as you refresh your report.
2. Navigation: By leveraging Essbase, you still have the OLAP navigation capabilities (zoom-in, zoom-out, keep only, etc.), and you have access to the data through all Essbase reporting front ends and APIs.

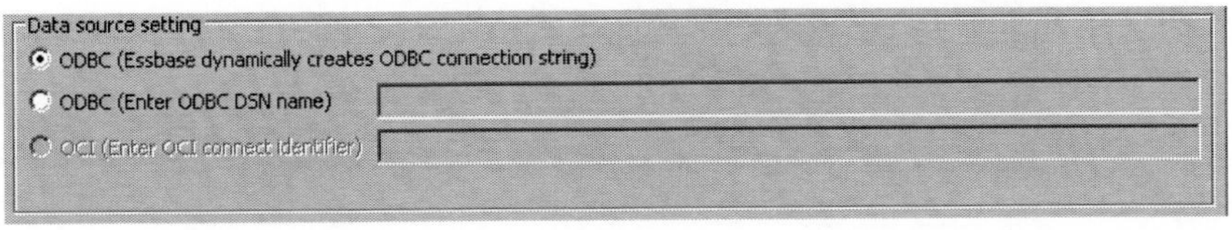

Figure 3.44 Selecting the XOLAP model.

3. Calculation: Calculations (member formulae) in XOLAP models are handled by the Essbase calculation engine. As such, complex calculations that are often more difficult relationally can be handled in the OLAP engine.

The main downside (aside from the design restrictions) is performance. With an XOLAP, model performance is no longer governed by Essbase, but rather the underlying data sources. If the source system is slow to respond, so is Essbase. Further, you cannot generate custom SQL when working with XOLAP, you have to use the generic SQL generated by Studio. In short, XOLAP models are very often significantly slower than full OLAP models.

Although performance concerns must be considered, from a prototyping perspective, XOLAP models provide an excellent vehicle for data exploration in the source systems. Because XOLAP models deployments are metadata only, they are extremely fast (comparatively) to deploy. You can then use an XOLAP model to walk through the dataset with the client or key stakeholders and validate assumptions about the source data.

To build an XOLAP model from Studio, you need to select the following Essbase properties for cube schema:

- Aggregate Storage Model
- Duplicate Member Name Support
- XOLAP Model

Note: When you select XOLAP Model, as in Figure 3.44, the other two options are automatically selected and "grayed out" because they are not optional for XOLAP.

In addition to the Essbase property requirements, there are hierarchy/dimension design restrictions when working with XOLAP:

- Derived text measures cannot be used. No hierarchies allowed in attribute dimensions.
- Recursive tables for hierarchy definition are not allowed.
- Hierarchical measures are not allowed.
- Level 0 user-defined members are not allowed.
- Filters cannot be used on the hierarchies used in the model.

3.7.4 Managing Studio Processes

Given that Studio is a front end for Essbase, it is easy to forget that under the hood, Studio is a server. It is a stand-alone engine that performs modeling tasks directly on data sources and communicates with and deploys models to the Essbase server. As such, the Studio server has a series of settings you can manage and monitor for troubleshooting purposes. These settings center on how Studio handles parallel processes and how the server handles thread usage.

Table 3.2 Studio Console Commands

dumps	Displays information on a current server threads
pconf	Displays state of the Studio server (threads, resources, etc.)
squeue	Displays and lets you set number of tasks waiting to be executed by the Studio server
sthd	Sets the number of threads being used by the Studio server
sres	Sets the number of concurrent tasks being executed by the Studio server (20 is the default)

While much of this chapter talks about ideas on prototyping with Studio, this section is more relevant for those situations when you are using Studio in an ongoing production scenario. The commands in Table 3.2 may never need be changed from their default settings, but it is useful to understand how to monitor and modify how Studio uses threads and other system resources.

All of these commands can be executed directly in the Studio server. For example, you can display the server threads and set concurrent tasks by issuing the following commands in the Studio server window:

```
pconf
sres 250
```

Realistically, however, the Studio server is likely running as a service. As such, you can place these commands in the Studio Server.Properties file. For instance, to set the number of server resources (sres), you include this line in the Server.Properties file:

```
server.resourceCount=250
```

Note: Any commands issued directly in the Studio server temporarily override conflicting commands in the Server.Properties file.

3.7.5 *Retrofitting Existing Models*

Another common question when working with Essbase Studio is the ability (or inability) to leverage an existing Essbase cube. If you want to leverage Studio for an ongoing production deployment, what do you do with your existing Essbase cubes? Can you convert the current models quickly into Studio? Can you simply add drill-through reports to an existing Essbase cube?

The realistic answer is: It depends. Studio is a long-term replacement for EIS. If you have an existing deployment leveraging EIS, then you can use the EIS catalog migration wizard in Figure 3.45 to migrate the mini-schema, hierarchies and other artifacts to the Studio catalog environment. While this does not create a perfect replica of the EIS deployment, it does provide a solid foundation for migrating an existing deployment.

If you are leveraging Load Rules for the current deployment, you cannot import these rules into Studio. The hierarchies they represent, including any transformations, need

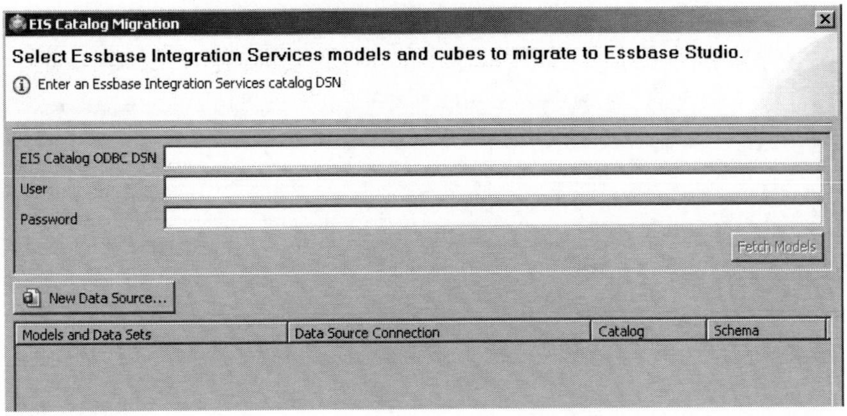

Figure 3.45 EIS catalog migration.

to be rebuilt as Studio hierarchies and deployed to Essbase using the Cube Deployment Wizard.

Often, what people want to do with Studio when they talk of retrofitting existing models is the population of existing cubes (including Hyperion Planning cubes) with Studio drill-through reports. To reliably populate a drill-through report definition into an Essbase cube, Studio must deploy the outline. An additional complexity with Studio drill-through report definitions is that to execute and display reports you need to use Smart View for Office and the Essbase Smart View Provider (Analytic Provider Services). As such, properly deploying the cube via the Studio (even if just deploying the application and database definition with Load Rule) through the cube deployment wizard is the best way to ensure your drill through definitions work as designed.

Instead of concentrating on retrofitting an existing Essbase or Planning model to contain drill-through definitions, you should consider building a secondary reporting model (likely in ASO) to leverage for both larger user reporting and drill-through. Many Planning deployments, for example, contain an ASO component for either quicker reporting or to combine the Planning data with other required data for complete reporting. You can use Studio to build and deploy this reporting model using the same dimensionality as the Planning or custom Essbase cubes, and embed the desired drill-through reports.

In addition to directly connecting to the source relational or flat-file sources, when working to mimic an existing Planning model, there are a number of options to keep the dimensionality synchronized between the source Planning model and the Studio generated cube:

- Use shared EPMA dimensions (Figure 3.46): Studio can connect to EMPA as a data source (Dimension Server) and use "shared" dimensions to build a cube.
- Data Relationship Management (DRM) exports: Studio can use flat file exports from DRM to build the reporting cube.
- Financial Quality Data Management (FDM): Studio can use either flat file exports from FDM or can connect directly to the FDM relational table to source hierarchies.

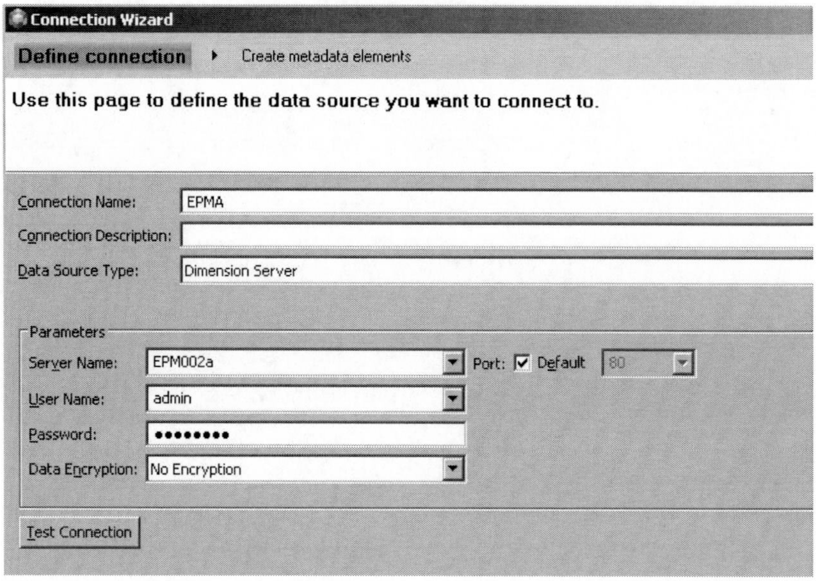

Figure 3.46 EPMA dimensions.

3.8 SWEEPING AWAY THE DIRT

One of the prevailing questions about Studio is why would you use Studio to build and deploy Essbase cubes? That is a fair question. Oracle (and partners) have provided multiple ways to build an Essbase model:

1. Load rules (data prep editor)
2. Essbase Integration Services
3. Essbase Studio
4. Enterprise Performance Management Architect
5. Essbase Analytics Link (specialized for HFM Reporting)
6. Informatica/ODI adapters
7. Direct, persisted cubes from OBIEE (for query optimization, planned)

There are undoubtedly other methods missing from the list. The point is that Oracle, as the software vendor, does not provide a consistent message or methodology for building models. It is no surprise that there is confusion in the market. Given all the alternatives, why would you use Studio to build a model?

The prevailing wisdom holds that you should use Studio when:

- You need drill-through capabilities (especially to OBIEE).
- You have a star or snowflake schema as the underlying data source.
- Your current deployment uses Essbase Integration Services (EIS).
- You have a “greenfield” (or new) deployment.
- You want to leverage XOLAP.
- The development team is IT-oriented and Studio can bridge the understanding gap between relational and OLAP.

All of these scenarios need to be considered within the context of your project. Drill-through from Studio only works for Smart View, and Oracle provides at least three other methods for drill-through possibilities (MaxL, ERPi, and EIS, for instance). A snowflake or star schema can be easily accessed using Load Rules (and the SQL interface), and a new deployment may be better served with Load Rules and ODI automation. The most compelling reason on paper is the replacement of EIS. Oracle has publically stated that the EIS component is being sunsetted in favor of Studio.

I use and recommend Studio because its flexibility and power gives it the ability to bridge all data gaps. When you are trying to get things cleaned up, you often have to compromise. You clean some rooms because you have time for it. In other places, you focus on the known issues. What Studio provides is a tool that allows you to quickly and iteratively transform a completely unsuitable data source to one that is just clean enough. To repeat a statement from earlier in the chapter: *Understanding a client's data is about iteration. You may never fully understand all the nuances or complexities until you hit roadblocks in the build process.*

Studio is that ideal component for cutting through the clutter so you can quickly provide value to the user community. To take that a step farther, from my perspective, Essbase Studio is key to prototyping in Essbase. If for no other reason, that powerful and flexible prototyping functionality is why Studio should be included in your development process.

4

BSO WILL NEVER DIE AND HERE IS WHY

Dave Farnsworth

CONTENTS

4.1 WHO SHOULD READ THIS CHAPTER?

Writing a chapter about the block storage option (BSO) within Essbase comes with a substantial amount of risk. No matter how carefully the topic is researched, there will always be exceptions to database behavior. Use the ideas presented here as guidelines and not absolutes. This chapter is aimed squarely at the BSO developer or administrator who knows the basics, but does not have a solid understanding of the underlying technology; this is not a chapter for the novice BSO developer or administrator. BSO is almost 20 years old and there are already numerous books, whitepapers, and online resources that are terrific when it comes to the basics. The chapter will appeal to:

- Those who want to understand the elements that impact database performance.
- Anyone who is confused with the plethora of BSO cache settings.
- Those who want to take advantage of the log messages while tuning calculations scripts.
- Anyone needing to efficiently create data blocks in a calculation script.
- Administrators or developers seeking the "choke point" of a calculation script.

This chapter is full of ideas and examples that will encourage you to create efficient and robust Essbase databases and inspire you to improve your existing calculation scripts.

4.2 PREREQUISITES

It is absolutely critical that the reader have at least moderate administration experience with Essbase and, in particular, with BSO. In addition, it will be helpful to be very familiar with Essbase Administration Services (EAS) and how to view application logs and database statistics.

4.3 WHY BSO, INDEED

With apologies to Mark Twain, reports of the death of Essbase block storage are greatly exaggerated. We have heard all of the reasoning for the demise of block storage: BSO has limitations on the number of practical dimensions, sparse/dense configuration is confusing, dense block has size limitations, and, finally, the calculations are too slow. Oh, and let us not forget data explosion. Okay, I understand the issues, but tell me this: Name another tool that offers in-place write back along with scores of functions for manipulating data. These are the features that separate Essbase block storage from every other tool and reasons why BSO will be around for some time.

What about the performance-related concerns, you ask? Admittedly, there can be issues. One only needs to look on the Oracle Technology Network (OTN) message boards to view performance difficulties that others have experienced. Like any technology, there is a time and place when BSO is the correct choice. No good discussion of BSO can begin without identifying where BSO is not a good fit. Before the advent of aggregate storage options (ASO), block storage Essbase was used for every type of application imaginable. Today, BSO is best used for read/write applications and databases that use complex allocations and calculations. I am not saying that BSO cannot be used for large reporting applications, it certainly can. I am asserting that because of scaling constraints that is not its best application. Regardless of use, I am going to show you how to use the power of Essbase block storage to build databases that perform to the best of their ability.

Certainly you have all heard that Essbase design is more art than science. Truer words have never been spoken. What works with one database might not work as well with another. I will help you understand the variables that affect performance. After that, it is your responsibility to try various options and then test, test, and test some more.

4.3.1 Need for Speed

Without exception, the most important ingredient of every successful Essbase application is speed. If you scan OTN, a substantial portion of threads are performance-related. The typical scenario is a company that has an application that they like, but is just too slow and they are looking for that magic setting that will resolve the performance issues. Sadly, as in almost everything else in life, there are no quick fixes. Without a solid design, your database is doomed. Author Dan Neil said it best, "The problem with making a silk purse out of a sow's ear is that your purse will still smell faintly of bacon." The moral here is to design the database correctly from the onset with performance in mind. There is no hidden switch that will make a poorly designed database run faster.

4.4 WHAT IS "GOOD" PERFORMANCE?

Performance with regards to databases can mean different things depending on the application. For applications that are primarily used for reporting and analysis, calculation performance is probably not a big issue. On the other hand, for a budgeting application, where end users enter data, execute calculations, and then wait for a response, calculation performance is paramount. There might not be a single design that is best in both situations. When designing an application, the first step is to decide what defines acceptable performance for this particular application. Will it be based on calculations, reporting speed, data load times, or something else? How many users will be simultaneously hitting the database?

4.4.1 Know the Basics for Good Performance

The Essbase Database Administrator's Guide (DBAG) has at least 100 pages devoted to application tuning. There are also numerous white papers and presentations on the Internet covering the same subject. The fact is that many of the suggestions offered by these documents are beneficial while others have little impact on overall performance. The sheer number of factors makes it impossible to test every scenario. Even when we have the will to perform comprehensive performance testing, we just do not have the resources to test everything. To simplify matters, I am going to discuss the top three things that impact performance the most: dimensionality design, system caches, and configuration file settings and calculations.

4.4.2 Dimensionality

The process of defining the dimensionality of the database is beyond the scope of this chapter, but the organization and content of the dimensions have a major impact on performance. One of the best and also worst things about Essbase is that there is a multitude of ways that a database can be designed. Some designs will work and there are others that just will not work. Actually, they will work, but they will make your life miserable. Here are a few that come to mind:

- Databases having more than 10 real (nonattribute) dimensions.
- Too many dynamic or dynamic calc and store sparse dimensions.
- Dense blocks without any dynamic calculations.
- Two or more large flat sparse dimensions.
- Databases with many attribute dimensions based on large sparse dimensions.
- Databases having more than six or seven levels in a very large sparse dimension.

Keep in mind the bullets above reflect guidelines. We have all built BSO databases that go against the rules and they work, kind of. The point is that for read/write databases, where performance is critical, know the pitfalls. Do not handicap yourself if you can avoid it.

4.4.2.1 Databases Having More Than 10 Real (Nonattribute) Dimensions Not only are databases having 10 or more dimensions slow, they are usually cumbersome for the end user. BSO databases are usually designed with 10 or more dimensions for one of two reasons. The most common reason is dimensional irrelevance. This occurs when a database is used for multiple purposes. For example, sales and marketing and balance sheet functionality should not be combined into a single database. Sales and marketing applications typically have large product and customer dimensions that have no significance for a balance sheet. Likewise, the hundreds or even thousands of balance sheet accounts are irrelevant for sales and marketing. The better option is to create separate databases.

The second contributor to an overly high dimension count is dimensions that should be combined, but are left to stand alone. This situation is most often seen with year and month, or state, city, and zip code. In the relational world, it is common to see these as separate dimensions. Essbase works best for both performance and usability when city, state, and zip code are combined into a single hierarchy. If you absolutely must include more than 10 dimensions, the majority should have few members and you should pay close attention to the dimension order.

4.4.2.2 Dynamic or Dynamic Calc and Store Sparse Dimensions This one seems to be pretty obvious, but I included it because I recently encountered a client's database where almost every parent of the sparse dimensions was dynamic calc and store. Sure, there were no batch calculation time, but retrievals were painful. To make matters worse, there were no dynamically calculated members in the dense block because Essbase could not lock enough blocks in 32 bit. This database was an extreme case. More commonly, you will encounter only three or four members in a sparse dimension that are candidates for the dynamic tag. Even still, be careful here and watch the order of calculation. Often times, your quarter time period results will not be what you expect.

4.4.2.3 Dense Blocks without Any Dynamic Calculations This is another tip that seems pretty obvious, but never fails to surprise me as often I see it: nonaggregating dimensions in the dense block. Dynamic calculations in the dense block are the best way to reduce the stored data footprint. In plain English, the PAG file will be smaller. Dynamic calculations also take advantage of the modern multiprocessor environment, so why waste a perfectly good dense block by having dimensions that do not need calculations? It should be noted that the official Oracle Essbase documentation warns that having too many dynamic calculations can have a negative impact on performance. Frankly, I have never seen a case where in memory calculations are slower than data retrieval.

4.4.2.4 Two or More Large, Flat Sparse Dimensions Flat dimensions are those that have few parents with many children. BSO will issue warnings when the number of children exceeds 100. Do not worry too much about 100 children, but when there are thousands, expect trouble. The best solution is to create additional levels. Let us consider an employee budgeting database as an example. The employee dimension has 15,000 employees and has no natural hierarchy. If the employees are listed alphabetically, then create a level of the alphabet. Keep splitting the letters into subletter groups until the calculation performance is reasonable.

4.4.2.5 Databases with Many Attribute Dimensions Based on Large Sparse Dimensions Attribute dimensions are glorified sparse dynamic calculations. Reporting on one or two attribute dimensions might seem fast, but do not assume that there is not a limit. Not that many years ago, I was involved with a project that had a sparse dimension that had 25,000 level-0 members. Oh, the joy! Associated with the dimension were 32 attributes dimension. More joy! Sure, we knew that the design was suspect, but we just could not convince the client that reporting could get pretty slow. Besides, how many attributes could an analyst specify on a single report? We did not need to wait long to find out that the favorite report had all 32 attributes specified. Not only was reporting slow, Essbase crashed and Planning died. The moral of the story is that there is a practical limit for the number of attribute dimensions depending on the number of members in the associated dimensions and the number of concurrent users. For this particular database, we found the limit to be about four attributes.

4.4.3 Block Size Mysteries

The number one issue that determines whether a BSO database is fast or slow is disk Input/Output (I/O). Reads and writes of data are the limiter of performance. The best way to create fewer blocks is to place as much data as possible into each block. That sounds pretty simple does it not? Actually, it is a little more complicated, but the goal is still the same, reduce the number of blocks.

First, let us talk about the physical size limitations of the block. The administrators guide for 11.1.2 states that the size should be between 8 and 100 kb. For clarity, the block size is determined by multiplying the number of stored members of the dense dimensions. That product is then multiplied by 8 bytes. As an example, assume the dense dimensions are Measures, Year, and Scenario, which have 8, 14, 3 stored members, respectively. The block size would be 8 × 14 × 3 × 8 bytes or 2688 bytes.

Now, do not get hung up on the size too much. This 8–100 k is just a guideline and exceptions are common. I have seen databases with blocks of 250 k bytes that work just fine. In this scenario, a balance sheet database had 250 departments and 1500 cost centers. Even though the blocks were large there were not very many of them. Aggregations were quick, but reporting could be slow if the report listed all of the cost centers on the row axis. By slow, I mean 5 to 10 second retrievals instead of 2 to 3 seconds. For large blocks, it is important to adjust the database caches so that Essbase can load a sufficient number in memory. I will cover that in depth later in the chapter.

When it comes to choosing the dense dimensions, I have seen all kinds of methods. One method is to try every combination of dimensions until the smallest PAG file is achieved. That seems like a lot of work and the end result might be the densest database, but not necessarily the fastest. This approach is less tedious. Following are the guidelines for determining whether a dimension should be dense or not:

1. Choose dimensions that aggregate dynamically. The best way to save data space is to not store the data in the first place. Dynamic calculations are in-memory calculations and are very fast. They will utilize additional processors if they are

available. As I mentioned, the DBAG cautions that too many dynamic members can negatively impact performance. The processor penalty may be desirable over disk IO.

2. Eliminate large dimensions from consideration for inclusion in the dense block. The objective in selecting dimensions is to pack the block as tightly with data as possible. Density decreases as the size of the dimension increases. The measures dimension is the exception to this rule.
3. Consider the measures and time period dimensions. Because many BSO databases are financially oriented, measures and time periods are probably good candidates for the dense block. These two dimensions when used in combination are naturally packed with data. If one measure has data, the odds are that many will be populated.
4. Eliminate dimensions that will grow significantly over time. The block size should stay relatively the same size over the life of the database.
5. Consider whether the data in the dimension will provide opportunities to restrict the amount to be processed. This is particularly true for budgeting applications where the calculation is restricted to a single year. Set dimensions that will to be used to subset the data as sparse.
6. Reject dimensions that are or will be partitioned. A common approach to improve performance is to partition large databases. Partitioning on a dense dimension is more processor intensive than using one that is sparse by causing multiple retrieves across the partition to pull one partitioned block. For this reason it is not a good idea to make the partitioned dimension dense.

4.4.4 Dimension Order

Does the dimension order really make a difference? The answer is sometimes, but there can be unintended consequences. There are two schools of thought with regards to the dimension order in the outline file. The hourglass format was adopted during the early days of Essbase. I think that I first heard about it with version 5. One of the advantages of this format is that the last dimension in the outline is used as the anchor dimension when calculating the calculator cache. The calculator cache is used by BSO to keep track of the level-0 member that has data during aggregations. There is not much public information about this process other than it is in bitmap form. All of the sparse dimensions other than the very last one are represented in the bitmap. In relation to calculator cache, the last sparse dimension that is not represented in the bitmap is called the anchor. Making the largest dimension last reduces the bitmap size, increasing the chance that there will be enough room in the cache for multiple bitmaps. When there is enough memory for multiple bitmaps, the parents *and* children are in the bitmap, not just children. The order is:

- Time (if dense)
- Account (if dense)
- The remaining dense dimension ordered largest to smallest
- The sparse dimension ordered smallest to largest

Figure 4.1 shows Sample.Basic in the hourglass arrangement. In this and all subsequent examples assume a sparse Scenario dimension; by default it is dense in Sample.Basic.

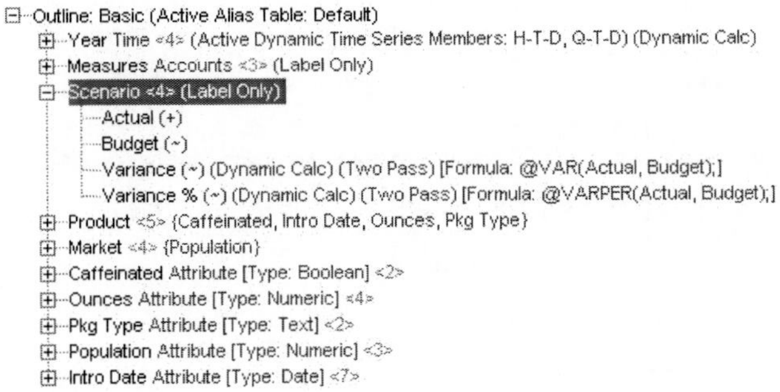

```
Outline: Basic (Active Alias Table: Default)
  Year Time <4> (Active Dynamic Time Series Members: H-T-D, Q-T-D) (Dynamic Calc)
  Measures Accounts <3> (Label Only)
  Scenario <4> (Label Only)
    Actual (+)
    Budget (~)
    Variance (~) (Dynamic Calc) (Two Pass) [Formula: @VAR(Actual, Budget);]
    Variance % (~) (Dynamic Calc) (Two Pass) [Formula: @VARPER(Actual, Budget);]
  Product <5> {Caffeinated, Intro Date, Ounces, Pkg Type}
  Market <4> {Population}
  Caffeinated Attribute [Type: Boolean] <2>
  Ounces Attribute [Type: Numeric] <4>
  Pkg Type Attribute [Type: Text] <2>
  Population Attribute [Type: Numeric] <3>
  Intro Date Attribute [Type: Date] <7>
```

Figure 4.1 Sample.Basic in an hourglass arrangement. (From Oracle Essbase Administration Services. With permission.)

```
Maximum Number of Lock Blocks: [1820] Blocks
Completion Notice Messages: [Disabled]
Calculations On Updated Blocks Only: [Disabled]
Clear Update Status After Calculations: [Enabled]
Calculator Cache With Multiple Bitmaps For: [Market]

[Fri Jan  6 13:47:26 2012]Local/Sample/Basic/dfarnsworth@Native Directory/1
Calculating in serial

[Fri Jan  6 13:47:26 2012]Local/Sample/Basic/dfarnsworth@Native Directory/1
Calculator Information Message:

Total Block Created: [3.9400e+02] Blocks
Sparse Calculations: [3.9400e+02] Writes and [1.5740e+03] Reads
Dense Calculations: [3.5400e+02] Writes and [3.5400e+02] Reads
Sparse Calculations: [4.2552e+04] Cells
Dense Calculations: [4.2480e+03] Cells

[Fri Jan  6 13:47:26 2012]Local/Sample/Basic/dfarnsworth@Native Directory/1
Total Calc Elapsed Time for [all.csc] : [0.16] seconds
```

Figure 4.2 Hourglass calc all application log.

Figure 4.2 is the application log output of a Calc All. It tells us that the anchor dimension for the calculator cache is Market. The calculation generated 394 writes and 1574 reads of the sparse dimensions.

The other common outline format is called the hourglass on a stick and also is known as the lollipop, as shown in Figure 4.3. With this arrangement, the nonaggregating sparse dimensions are moved to the end of the outline file following the largest dimensions.

Moving the nonaggregating dimensions accomplishes two things. First, it reduces the number of reads and writes during the calculation possibly reducing calculation time. Secondly, the anchor dimension changes to the last dimension allowing the larger dimension to be included in the calculator cache bitmap. In theory, this should result in faster aggregations. The downside is that placing the large dimension in the bitmap eliminates any chance of using multiple bitmaps. In most cases, the database will be too large for multiple bitmaps, anyway. With hourglass on a stick format, there were 242 and 1220 sparse dimensions writes and reads, respectively, as shown in Figure 4.4.

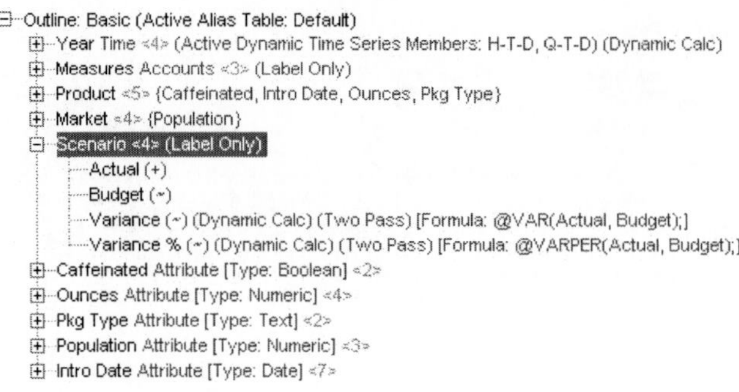

Figure 4.3 Hourglass on a stick. (From Oracle Essbase Administration Services. With permission.)

```
Maximum Number of Lock Blocks: [1820] Blocks
Completion Notice Messages: [Disabled]
Calculations On Updated Blocks Only: [Disabled]
Clear Update Status After Calculations: [Enabled]
Calculator Cache With Multiple Bitmaps For: [Scenario]

[Fri Jan  6 13:39:36 2012]Local/Sample/Basic/dfarnsworth@Native Directory/.
Calculating in serial

[Fri Jan  6 13:39:36 2012]Local/Sample/Basic/dfarnsworth@Native Directory/.
Calculator Information Message:

Total Block Created: [2.4200e+02] Blocks
Sparse Calculations: [2.4200e+02] Writes and [1.2200e+03] Reads
Dense Calculations: [3.5400e+02] Writes and [3.5400e+02] Reads
Sparse Calculations: [2.6136e+04] Cells
Dense Calculations: [4.2480e+03] Cells

[Fri Jan  6 13:39:36 2012]Local/Sample/Basic/dfarnsworth@Native Directory/.
Total Calc Elapsed Time for [all.csc] : [0.16] seconds
```

Figure 4.4 Hourglass on a stick—calc all application log.

That is substantially fewer reads and writes than the standard hourglass design. Fewer reads and writes often translate to better performance. However, all is not rosy with the hourglass on a stick format. When switching to the hourglass on a stick design, there are a few concerns. First, the calculator cache needs to be tuned again. In the second example, the cache anchor is now Scenario where it was Market before the change. Instead of being the anchor dimension, Market is now in the bitmap. BSO will now be able to track the Market dimension members during aggregations using the calculator cache.

Secondly, using the hourglass on a stick design approach causes Essbase to use the last dimension to distribute data to the individual file when using parallel exports. When the final dimension is large, the data is distributed fairly evenly across all of the output files. If the last dimension has few members, there is an increased chance of an imbalance. For example, assume that the last dimension is YEAR with members FY11, FY12, FY13, and FY14. Also assume that FY11 is the only member with data. A parallel data export that specifies four output files will have data in the first file, but only header information in files two, three, and four. To compound the felony, should the total output exceed 2 Gb, all data beyond 2 Gb will be written to files, but not those defined by the parallel export.

Finally, moving the nonaggregating dimensions to the end of the outline file requires changes to the CALCTASKDIMS setting if parallel calculations are being used. Review the next section for an explanation of task dimensions.

4.5 GETTING THE MOST FROM MULTIPLE PROCESSORS

Using parallelism can have huge benefits, but the relationship between CALCPARALLEL and CALCTASKDIMS is not always obvious. The first thing that needs to be understood is that you cannot have one without the other. There can be no parallelism without a CALCTASKDIMS setting. In order for Essbase to utilize multiple processors, the outline must be evaluated to determine which sections of the outline can be processed in parallel. The output of the evaluation is called the task list. The CALCTASKDIMS statement tells Essbase how many dimensions to consider when developing the task list. The key concept here is how BSO determines the dimensions to consider when building the task list. The largest aggregating dimensions offer the best opportunities for parallelism. Reviewing the statement CALCTASKDIMS X, Essbase uses the last X dimensions in the outline to determine the task list. If a database having two large aggregating dimensions uses the hourglass organization, then CALCTASKDIMS 2 is a good starting point for testing. On the other hand, if the hourglass on a stick format is used and the last two dimensions are nonaggregating, CALCTASKDIMS must be increased until the largest dimensions are included in the scope. In the example, testing should start at three or four to ensure that the large dimensions are evaluated.

4.6 CACHE IS KING; KNOW THE BASICS

Caches in BSO are a powerful yet poorly understood subject. Let me relay a story that sums up the state of cache tuning. A few years ago, I visited a customer as a member of a team that was tasked with addressing a BSO calculation issue. The customer had a calculation script or, more accurately, a Planning business rule that was taking three minutes to complete. This was their primary rule that would get executed extensively during the forecasting period. The rule needed to complete in no more than 10 seconds. My associate, whom I had never met, was a self described Essbase tuning expert. I will call him Bill for the sake of the story. Bill immediately viewed the contents of the Essbase.cfg file. With much confidence Bill declared that he had found the problem. There were missing entries in the configuration file. The customer was thrilled and I could not wait to see how he was going to reduce the calculation time from three minutes to a hand full of seconds. Just when I thought that it could not get stranger, Bill opened the configuration file in the editor. Striking a pose reminiscent of Joey Tribbiani's (TV's *Friends*) smell-the-fart act, Bill added the following to the file:

```
CALCLOCKBLOCKHIGH 2000
CALCLOCKBLOCKDEFAULT 1000
CALCLOCKBLOCKLOW 500
CALCCACHE TRUE
CALCCACHEHIGH 199000000
CALCCACHEDEFAULT 100000000
CALCCACHELOW 50000000
```

In the calculation script header, Bill inserted the following:

```
SET LOCKBLOCK HIGH;
SET AGGMISSG ON;
SET CACHE HIGH;
SET CALCPARALLEL 4;
SET UPDATECALC OFF;
```

Bill did not ask anything about the server memory or processors, the number of concurrent users, or what the calculation was supposed to do. For Bill, testing was not a priority. In any event, the customer just stared. They were mesmerized. You would have thought Bill was Rain Man. Did it decrease the calculation time? Of course not. Sadly, this story defines the state of BSO tuning today. Somehow the bigger-is-better philosophy became the rule. The simple truth is that there is no one size fits all when it comes to BSO tuning.

To illustrate my point, let us start the tuning discussion by describing the caches that can make a difference. Consider this a quickie discussion for setting caches for those who do not have three weeks to dedicate to benchmarking. The object here is to make the system as fast as possible in a reasonable time frame, rather than make it worse. Keep in mind that improving calculation time may slow user reporting and vice versa; the optimum configuration is likely to be a compromise. Finally, when the operating system is 32 bit, there is a hard limit of 4 Gb of memory. Exceed this limit and bad things will happen. Whether the server is 64 or 32 bit, never allocate more resources than are available on the server.

Most often, caches are tuned in a vacuum rather than real world conditions. Unfortunately, the data, data file, index, and operating system caches are shared by everyone using the database. Each request competes for resources. Testing processes in isolation might pinpoint best case performance, but probably not real-world results. For simplicity, I suggest that initial tests be done individually for expediency.

For final testing, it is important to determine that the test simulates the production environment complete with activity. Are calculations scripts and reports both to be tested? Is the purpose the test to determine best, average, or worse case performance? How many concurrent calculations? Are the calculations batch or interactive? How many concurrent calculations and reports will be tested? If there is no stress testing software available, execute multiple MaxL processes from a command file.

4.6.1 Index Cache

This is the easiest cache to set particularly in 64 bit. Place the entire index in memory. For those in 32 bit or, in a tight memory situation where the index is really large, test with 50 or 75% of the index in memory. For testing, aggregate the sparse dimensions increasing the index cache size with each test. Start the testing with the upper blocks calculated or not, but be consistent. If the upper blocks are cleared prior to the test, I have seen situations where a dense restructure will shrink the PAG file and speed the aggregation. Stopping and starting the database will flush the caches. Under no circumstances set the cache larger than the index because Essbase will allocate everything that is specified. Figure 4.5 captures the physical index size for Sample.Basic is 8,216,576 bytes as shown in EAS.

Figure 4.6 shows that the index cache setting is 1,024,000 and the current value is also 1,024,000. As an experiment, I increased the index cache from 1024 kb to double the physical index size of 16,433 kb. Be certain to stop/start the database after changing the cache settings and then execute a calculation. Figure 4.7 shows the results.

Database: EssbaseCluster-1.Sample.Basic

General | Dimensions | Statistics | Caches | Transactions

Current I/O access mode: Buffered I/O

Pending I/O access mode: Buffered I/O

Data compression: Bitmap encoding

Disk Volume	Partition Size
Click here to add	
/data	Unlimited

Data/Index File Type	
Index	8216576
Data	1146706

Figure 4.5 Sample.Basic index size. (From Oracle Essbase Administration Services. With permission.)

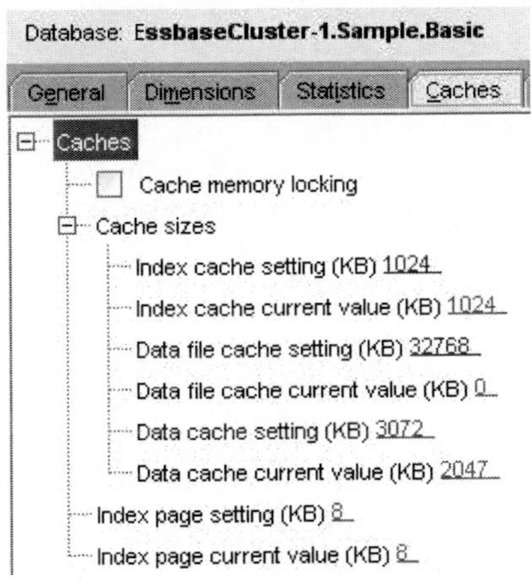

Figure 4.6 Sample.Basic cache statistics. (From Oracle Essbase Administration Services. With permission.)

Notice that the current index cache value is now twice as large as the physical index size. BSO will claim whatever is specified up to the limit of 4,294,967,295 bytes. If MEMSCALING is specified in the configuration file, the limit is extended for 64 bit. Periodically review the index cache size and update the cache accordingly.

4.6.2 Data Cache

Before discussing the data cache, it is important to understand compression and how it relates to the cache. Physical data blocks are stored in the ESS*. PAG file(s) in compressed form assuming that some lunatic has not turned off compression. There are three types of compression in BSO: bitmap, RLE, and ZLib. ZLib is primarily a zipped format that is slow relative to the other two. ZLib is used when disk space is an issue. Bitmap, as the name implies, places a bitmap in the header of each block. The bitmap is used to tell BSO which cells have data and which have missing values. As the block size increases, so does the bitmap size increasing the block header overhead. RLE stands

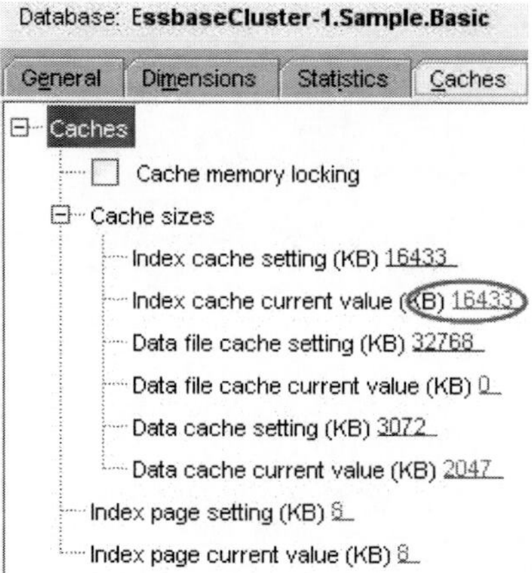

Figure 4.7 New Sample.Basic cache statistics. (From Oracle Essbase Administration Services. With permission.)

for run length encoded. The header for RLE is fixed at approximately 72 bytes. RLE compression type stores the value and then a count indicating the consecutive blocks that have the value. RLE works best when there are many missing values or values that repeat in the data block. According to the documentation, if RLE is specified, Essbase will analyze the data and choose the appropriate compression. I tried very hard to prove the documentation correct or otherwise, but I did not see this behavior. There is no substitute for testing. In general, larger blocks will probably produce smaller PAG files using RLE than Bitmap and vice versa.

Now back to cache settings. As BSO writes a data block, the uncompressed block (stored cells × 8 bytes) is compressed and moved to the operating system cache. The block is then written to the PAG file by the operating system. If using direct I/O, the data is written to the PAG file directly from the Essbase data file cache bypassing the operating system cache altogether. The data and data file caches give BSO a place to save blocks in case it needs them again, saving a fetch from the relatively slow PAG disk file. The Essbase kernel will continue writing blocks to the cache until it is full. Once the cache is full, older blocks are replaced by more recently retrieved data blocks. The object of sizing the caches is to increase the likelihood that the data block will be in the cache. The BSO data cache default size is 3072 kb. Dividing 3,072,000 by the block size gives the number of blocks that fit in the data cache. In most cases, the default is too low. To size the cache, double it for test, stopping and starting the database after the change. Then run a full aggregate and note the time. When aggregations times stop improving or improve only slightly, the cache is too large. The correct value is somewhere between the data cache setting of the last two tests. Perform several tests adjusting the cache between the two values until the optimum value is found.

4.6.3 Data File Cache

This cache is only used with Direct I/O. As stated earlier, for Direct I/O, the data cache and the operating system cache are not used. Direct I/O is better suited to 64-bit operating systems because they are able to address larger amounts of memory. The data blocks stored in the data file cache are compressed. Let me say that again. The key concept to understand about Direct I/O is that the data file cache blocks are the same size as the compressed blocks in the PAG file. It is feasible to place the entire database into memory by setting the data file cache to the PAG size. Should you choose this route, Oracle recommends:

1. Direct I/O should be set at the server level.
2. The Essbase server should be on a dedicated box and not be in a shared resources environment.
3. Memory must be carefully monitored.
4. Restart the server regularly. Do not exceed server memory.

4.6.4 *Calculator Cache*

Calculator cache is used to track the children of parent members during calculations. If the database is small enough and multiple bitmaps are possible, the cache also tracks the parents. In short, the cache is used most commonly during aggregations. The DBAG has an excellent write up that covers calculator cache, so I am not going to repeat it here. What the documentation does not say is that calculation cache operates differently than index and data caches. While the index and data caches are shared by all of the users of a given database, calculator cache is not shared. In fact each calculation creates its own calculator cache for each processor thread. Please go back and read that last sentence again. It means if CALCCACHE = 199M and a single calculation script logs the message "Calculating in parallel with [5] threads," then the Essbase kernel could use as much as 1 Gb of memory for the calculator cache alone. Considering that each script has its own calculator cache, memory can be an issue during periods of high concurrency.

Hence, if 199M is not the right answer, what is? That is easy, we test. For starters, when the database is small, use the guidelines in the documentation and try to achieve multiple bitmaps. An hourglass organization may be required for multiple bitmaps. When the database is large, as mine always seem to be, only single bitmap is available. In this situation, Oracle offers one suggestion: Do not set the calculator cache higher than 50 Mb. This is because the calculator cache has no index. The search method is sequential. The thinking is that at some point it takes longer to search than to retrieve. Somewhere there must be a database that needs 199M calculator cache, but I have never seen one.

Optimize calculator cache after the index and data caches have been tuned. Set the calculator cache in the Essbase.cfg file to 20M, 50M, and 100M for Low, Default, and High, respectively. Recycle the Essbase server to reset the values. Clear the upper blocks of the database and then run a script that aggregates the sparse dimensions first with CALCCACHE set to Low. Repeat the test for 50M and 100M. If there is not a measureable improvement of say 5 to 10%, then stay with the lower value. Only set the calculator cache to 199M if there is a provable performance benefit. In general, scripts that aggregate large dimensions require larger calculator caches. Scripts that utilize multiple processors have smaller calculator cache needs because each thread has its own cache.

4.6.5 *Dynamic Calc Cache*

This cache is used for reporting. The formula is pretty straight forward, so do the math, but do not exceed your operating system resources. DYNCALCCACHEMAXSIZE is the name of the Essbase.cfg file setting and the default value is 20 Mb. The calculation using the variables in Table 4.1 would be:

```
Dynamic Calc Cache in bytes = C * S * U
```

Table 4.1 Calc Cache Variables

Variable	Description
C	Lock block value
S	Expanded block size
U	Estimated number of concurrent users

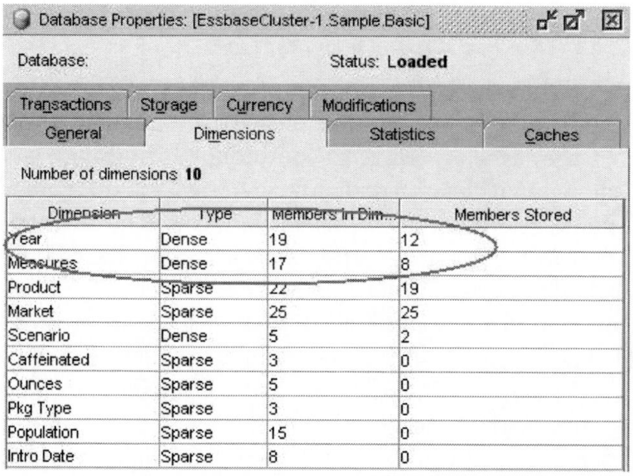

Database Properties: [EssbaseCluster-1.Sample.Basic]

Database: Status: **Loaded**

Transactions | Storage | Currency | Modifications
General | Dimensions | Statistics | Caches

Number of dimensions **10**

Dimension	Type	Members in Dim...	Members Stored
Year	Dense	19	12
Measures	Dense	17	8
Product	Sparse	22	19
Market	Sparse	25	25
Scenario	Dense	5	2
Caffeinated	Sparse	3	0
Ounces	Sparse	5	0
Pkg Type	Sparse	3	0
Population	Sparse	15	0
Intro Date	Sparse	8	0

Figure 4.8 Members in dense dimensions. (From Oracle Essbase Administration Services. With permission.)

The lock block value is displayed in the log if the calc script contains “Set Msg Summary” or “Set Msg Detail.” The message looks as follows:

```
Maximum Number of Lock Blocks: [5000] Blocks
```

To calculate the expanded block, the total members in the dense dimension are used instead of stored members, as shown in Figure 4.8. Using Sample.Basic as an example, the expanded block size is 19 * 17 = 323 cells or 2584 bytes (8 bytes per cell).

In this pretend world, 15 simultaneous users are expected; the Dynamic Calc Cache should be set to 5000 * 2584 * 15 or 193,800,000 bytes. A Dynamic Calc Cache of this size can hold 75,000 blocks.

Going forward, the dynamic calc cache can be monitored using the application log. As reports are executed, the kernel writes informational messages showing the number of blocks inserted into the cache.

```
Extractor Big Blocks Allocs -- Dyn.Calc.Cache:[9504] non-Dyn.Calc.
Cache:[0]
```

The first half of the message indicates that this report needed 9504 blocks and they all fit in the cache. If the non-Dyn.Calc.Cache value is consistently greater that zero, consider raising the size using the DYNCALCCACHEMAXSIZE in the Essbase.cfg.

4.7 CHECK YOUR WORK

So far we have covered two of the three factors that impact performance the most: dimensionality and cache settings. Before discussing calculations, it is important to establish a testing strategy. There is some value in tuning processes individually. It certainly is faster, but is it realistic? Let me give you an example. Consider a test database that has a block size of 32,832 and two large sparse dimensions: Customer (2,000 members) and Products (20,000 members). The database has 615 k blocks and a block density of 1.6%. The server is a 64-bit Linux with six processors.

Figure 4.9 shows the basic script used to aggregate the database.

It is pretty obvious that with the server capacity and database dimensionality, parallel calculations should have a positive effect. The question is how much? The Essbase documentation says that the ratio of the task schedule to the empty task schedule provides a good indication as to whether parallel calculations will have a positive influence. A ratio greater than 50% means that parallelism may not help. Task values can be obtained from the log, shown in Figure 4.10, after a calculation is run.

This particular database has 54,000 tasks followed by 3,620, and so on. According to the documentation, the benefit of parallelism decreases after the first few steps. Looking at the empty tasks line, we see that 41,000 level-0 tasks are empty. If 41,000/54,000 is greater than 50%, then parallelism may not provide any improvement. The value of 75% is way above 50%. This should make for an interesting test case.

The test will be run for one, two, three, four, and six processors. CALCTASKDIMS will be set to two for all but the single processor because a setting of greater than two made no difference in the task schedule or timed performance. The testing scenario is:

1. Clear the upper blocks prior to each test.
2. Stop the database prior to each test.
3. The calculation times were the logged times.
4. Each test was executed four times.
5. The longest and shortest times where thrown out. The remaining times were averaged.

```
FIX(@Relative(Account,0),@Relative(Periods,0),@Relative(Channel,0),
    @Relative(Years,0),@Relative(Scenario,0))
Agg(Customer,Product);
ENDFIX
```

Figure 4.9 Essbase calc script to aggregate database.

```
Calculating in parallel with [2] threads

[Thu Dec  1 14:37:54 2011]Local/apb_c/Apb20/dfarnsworth(
Calculation task schedule [54000,3630,1800,450,90,27,3]

[Thu Dec  1 14:37:54 2011]Local/apb_c/Apb20/dfarnsworth(
Parallelizing using [2] task dimensions.

[Thu Dec  1 14:39:12 2011]Local/apb_c/Apb20/dfarnsworth(
Empty tasks [41000,2759,1369,342,68,20,2]
```

Figure 4.10 Application log messages after a calculation.

Table 4.2 Calc Time by Number of Processors

Processors per Calculation Script	1 Processor	2 Processor	3 Processor	5 Processor	6 Processor
Total Elapsed Time	133 seconds	79 seconds	68 seconds	42 seconds	62 seconds

Table 4.3 Calculation Speed by Processor

Processors per Calculation Script	1 Processor	2 Processor	3 Processor	5 Processor
Total Elapsed Time	653 seconds	663 seconds	698 seconds	773 seconds

So, what do the test times in Table 4.2 tell us? Clearly this database likes processors. In this case, the clock seems more accurate than the task ratio calculation. Take special note to compare the times between five and six processors. This is not an anomaly. This single aggregation continued to respond favorable to additional processors. Once the number of processors specified in the script equaled the number available on the server, performance dropped. The conclusion is that it is important to leave a processor for the operating system.

Can this test be considered real world? Certainly, if this calculation is run in batch mode where it is the only calculation running. What happens if there are multiple calculations? Will parallelism still be faster? Oracle suggests that if the database must support highly concurrent calculations, such as in a Planning application, CALCPARALLEL should be used with great care. The theory is that when there are multiple calculations executed concurrently, the number of processors on the server can be exceeded when multiple processors are specified in the script. To prove this out, I created four identical databases so that block locking would not be an issue. Four MaxL scripts were launched simultaneously from a single CMD Windows batch file. None of the scripts share cache resources other than the operating system file cache. There will be disk contention because the storage is common to all. The calculation is the previous aggregation script that showed improvement as the number of processors increased (Table 4.3).

The results are interesting. The first test reserved four processors, one for each of the MaxL scripts. The second test occupied eight processors and so on. The tests clearly show that requesting more processors than are available on the server degrades the performance.

If this were a real world test where this script was run concurrently, what is the correct number of processors? That all depends on whether we are tuning for worst case, best case, or average. Worst case, the number of processors should be one; best case, we might assume that it is unlikely that multiple scripts would ever be run, so the number of processors would be set to five. For the average case, two processors show the largest performance boost when the script is run stand alone, but only suffers slightly with four competing calculations. A specification of two processors takes advantage of parallel processing when fewer calculations are in the mix, but does not suffer the huge hit that is seen with greater than two processors.

4.7.1 Block Count as a Speedometer

When trying to quantify calculation scripts overall, time is the metric that counts, but I also like to use data blocks. The log file captures information about reads and writes of the databases that are invaluable. Not only can I/O information help with tuning a script, it also can provide information about the data distribution within the database. Recently,

I had a conversation with a client concerning the size of a particularly large Planning application. The application is three years old and the client periodically copies a forecast to a new scenario to be used later for reporting. The continual growth of the database is becoming an issue. The administrator asked me to help him quantify the overhead of each scenario. Looking at the statistics that are available for each database in EAS, we can see the total number of blocks: level-0 blocks and upper-level blocks. What is not available is any information about how the data is distributed. It would be great if there was a way to tell how many blocks were in a specific scenario. Well, actually there is, and here is how.

My example uses Sample/Basic, which has dense dimensions Year, Accounts, and sparse dimensions Product, Market, and Scenario. The database has 704 blocks with 354 at level-0 and 350 upper-level blocks. The calculation script uses "Set Msg Summary" that places read/write statistics in the application log. The statistics are for the entire script so sometimes it is necessary to break the code into multiple scripts. The message looks like:

```
Total Block Created: [2.4200e+02] Blocks
Sparse Calculations: [2.4200e+02] Writes and [1.2200e+03] Reads
Dense Calculations: [3.5400e+02] Writes and [3.5400e+02] Reads
Sparse Calculations: [2.3232e+04] Cells
Dense Calculations: [4.2480e+03] Cells
```

The second line that details sparse calculations block writes and reads is the one that we are interested in. For those not familiar with scientific notation, 2.4200e+02 equals to 242. 1.2200e+3 equals 1220 block reads.

For this example, I have changed Sample.Basic making Scenario sparse so that the Actual and Budget scenarios are in different blocks. The entire database has 748 blocks. How many of the blocks are in the budget scenario? To decipher this, we need a calculation script that fixes on the Budget scenario. Including Jan in the fix is not required, but the script runs a little faster. If there is no statement between the FIX and ENDFIX, Essbase is smart enough not to loop through the blocks. The statement "Sales = Sales;" sets the member value to itself, which does not do anything other than cause the script to execute. If this were a production database, I would have added a dummy account to the database and referenced that instead of live data. The script follows:

```
Set UPDATECALC OFF;
Set Msg Summary;
FIX (Jan, Budget)
Sales(
Sales=Sales;
)
ENDFIX
```

The application log message is "Sparse Calculations: [0.0000e+00] Writes and [3.7400e+02] Reads" indicating that 374 Budget blocks were read. Running the script for the Actual scenario also returns 374 blocks, which confirms that the total blocks in the database is 748 blocks. Do not expect every database to reconcile as nicely as Sample. Basic. Scientific notation becomes less precise as the numbers get larger. Percentage wise, the results are still meaningful.

Variants of the script also can be used to find the level-0 blocks:

```
"FIX (Jan, Budget, @LEVMBRS (Product,0), @LEVMBRS (Market,0))"
```

Or, the blocks in a slice of multiple sparse selections:

```
"FIX (Jan, Budget, @IDESCENDANTS (Product), @IDESCENDANTS (East))"
```

4.7.2 Whoa! My Script Is Slow

One of the fun things about being a consultant is being called in when things are really bad. Really bad usually translates to "we have this calculation script that absolutely must run in fewer than 10 seconds, but it is taking 10 minutes instead." If I want to have the client throw me out the door, I can always suggest starting with a database design session. In most cases, unless the database design is total junk, the best approach is to try and tweak the script. The mistake that most make is to start rewriting the script before understanding the database design, the goal of the script, and the bottlenecks. Here is my approach:

1. Review the outline. Make note of the dense dimensions and the block size. Overly large block sizes need special analysis.
2. Gain a complete understanding of the goal of the script in business terms. Often times a less experienced developer takes the long way to achieve the intended results. There may be an easier, faster way.
3. Review the script, but do not start coding just yet. BSO calculation performance is highly dependent on database design, block size, the number of data blocks, and the distribution of the data. I have yet to meet the person who can consistently identify the bottleneck in most scripts. There is no worse feeling than spending 20 minutes rewriting a chunk of code only to find out that it ran in 1 second before the changes anyway.
4. Add "Set Msg Summary" to the script and run it. Make note of the elapsed time and the sparse blocks read and written. Do not worry about the dense calculations for now.
5. Break the script into pieces that can execute individually. I like to create four scripts if possible. Do not focus on the number of lines in each script. In most cases, there is no relationship between the number of lines and the execution elapsed time.
6. Run each script. Do not be too concerned that the calculations are correct. The purpose is to find the bottlenecks in the code and not the calculated totals. Capture the total time of each script and the block reads and writes.
7. It is not uncommon for one or two of the scripts to consume the bulk of the run time. If so, then this is where the tuning efforts should be focused.
8. Break the long running scripts into even smaller scripts. Sometimes an individual function is the culprit.

Let us work through an example. This is a nonsensical calculation script and the dimensionality is irrelevant for our analysis.

--- beginning of script #1 ---

```
FIX(@DESCENDANTS("Segment 1"), "Budget", "Version_1", "FY12", "New
  Product 1")
    ("Volume"="Volume"*1.10;
    "Price"="Price"*1.10;
    "Other Revenue"="Other Revenue"*1.10;
    "COGS Rate"="COGS Rate"*1.10;
```

```
    "COGS Assembly"="COGS Assembly"*1.10;
ENDFIX
FIX(@DESCENDANTS("Segment 1"), "Budget", "Version_1", "FY12", "New
  Product 1")
    "Mth End Bal" = (@MDSHIFT( "Payments" ,11,"period", ,
      -1,"Years",)
        + @MDSHIFT( "UnLiquidated Payments" ,11,"period", ,
          -1,"Years",) -
        "Billings" + ("Sales" - "Shipment Billing")); )
ENDFIX
```

--- end of script #1 ---

--- beginning of script #2 ---

```
FIX("Ac_6004", "Actual", "Cur Est", "FY12")
   CALC DIM ("Version", "Location", "Entity", "Discretionary");
ENDFIX
```

--- end of script #2 ---

--- beginning of script #3 ---

```
FIX(@LEVMBRS("Location", 0), "FY12")
    FIX(@LEVMBRS("Entity", 0), @LEVMBRS("Discretionary", 0),
     @LEVMBRS("Version", 0))
        FIX("Jan":"DEC")
            CLEARDATA "Cur Est";
        ENDFIX
    ENDFIX
```

--- end of script #3. Note add an ENDFIX so the script validates. ---

--- beginning of script #4 ---

Note: Prefix with: `FIX(@LEVMBRS("Location", 0), "FY12")`

```
       FIX("D_00", "Load")
           FIX("Jan":"DEC")
               FIX(@ATTRIBUTE("Budget Self"), @ATTRIBUTE("Prior
                History"))
                   "Cur Est" = "Plan 2011"->"Dept_JX"->"Final";
               ENDFIX
               FIX(@ATTRIBUTE("Budget at Parent 4JX"))
                   "Cur Est" = "Plan 2011"->"Dept_JX"->"4JX"
                   ->"Final" ;
               ENDFIX
               FIX(@ATTRIBUTE("Budget Self at Parent"),
               @ATTRIBUTE("Prior History"))
                   "Cur Est" = @PARENTVAL("Entity", "Plan
                   2011"->"Dept_JX"->"Final") ;
               ENDFIX
           ENDFIX
       ENDFIX
ENDFIX
```

--- end of script #4 ---

Once execution times and block counts are available from each script, address the slowest sections first. This is where creativity comes into play. For example, in the first script consider making the accounts dynamic. In-line formulas are faster than formulas in script. Include the calculation for "Mth End Bal" in the first FIX. Can @DESCENDANTS ("Segment 1") be changed to process only level-0 blocks. In the second script make sure that all of the dimensions truly need the CALC DIM, otherwise use AGG if there are nondynamic upper-level members to be calculated. Is it feasible to clear the upper blocks prior to the calc dim? It might make sense to combine #3 and #4 if it is possible to clear and calculate "Cur Est" in a single pass. Often times I find that certain calculation functions are culprits. Consider eliminating the function and writing the code long hand. Make use of the block counts during the tuning. Reducing the number of blocks almost always results in better performance. Do not be afraid to experiment.

Give this method a try. It is truly eye opening.

4.7.3 Script Variables: Are They Useful?

Those new to calculation scripts attempt to use variables because they have used them in procedural languages. They usually are not successful because they do not understand how Essbase loops through the dense array. I use variables more than most because I do not like to add members to the database if they provide no multidimensional value. Variables are particularly useful as switches to control execution within a script, collect running totals, and store data values used in calculations. As an introduction, this first script uses variables to illustrate the Essbase order of operation within a dense block. The database is Sample.Basic and the dense block has Measures and Year in that order.

```
set updatecalc off;
set Msg Summary;
VAR vcount = 0;
FIX("100-10",Florida)
    Actual (
    IF (@ISMBR(@IDESCENDANTS ("Year")))
        vcnt=vcnt + 1;
        Actual = vCnt;
    ENDIF;)
ENDFIX
```

The script defines a variable named "vcount" which is initialized as zero. Here are the rules for variables.

- Variables persist for the life of the script.
- Variables store only numeric data.
- Variables must be referenced within a member calculation block.

The script above processes on a single block of data that is Product = "100-10," Market = "Florida," and Scenario = "Actual." As each member of the dense block is processed, the variable "vcount" is incremented. The new "vcount" value is written to the current member.

Figure 4.11 illustrates the block that was modified by the variable calc script. The cells in column B were processed first starting with B3. Cell B5 looks odd because Margin is a dynamically calculated as Sales–COGS. A value of 3 was written to B5, but it was trumped by the formula.

In this exercise, the months are processed in order and all accounts are processed before moving to the next month. Is that always the case? Currently the dense order is Measures and Year. Let us flip the dimension order to Year first and Measures second in the outline order and rerun the calculation, viewing the results in Figure 4.12.

	A	B	C	D	E	F	G	H
1		100-10	Florida	Actual				
2		Jan	Feb	Mar	Qtr1	Apr	May	Jun
3	Sales	1	11	21	33	31	41	51
4	COGS	2	12	22	36	32	42	52
5	Margin	-1	-1	-1	-3	-1	-1	-1
6	Marketing	4	14	24	42	34	44	54
7	Payroll	5	15	25	45	35	45	55
8	Misc	6	16	26	48	36	46	56
9	Total Expenses	15	45	75	135	105	135	165

Figure 4.11 Dense block modification example.

	A	B	C	D	E	F	G	H
1		Cola	Florida	Actual				
2		Jan	Feb	Mar	Qtr1	Apr	May	Jun
3	Sales	1	2	3	6	4	5	6
4	COGS	15	16	17	48	18	19	20
5	Margin	-14	-14	-14	-42	-14	-14	-14
6	Marketing	29	30	31	90	32	33	34
7	Payroll	43	44	45	132	46	47	48
8	Misc	57	58	59	174	60	61	62
9	Total Expenses	129	132	135	396	138	141	144

Figure 4.12 Results after flipping order of time and measures.

The order changed. I should not be surprised because the order of processing is clearly explained in the DBAG. However, the test demonstrates the importance of dimension order if we are expecting all of the accounts to be calculated for a month before moving on to the next month.

4.7.4 Reduce Processing and Simplify Code

Variables are also handy when it is necessary to control the processing of a calculation script. Let us assume that we have an employee forecasting application and there is a need to calculate benefits for each of our 50,000 employees based on a blended rate. The application has many rates and rather than clog up the Employee database, the benefit rate is stored in a BSO database called Emp_Rates. The benefit rate is pulled from the EMP_Rates database using the @XREF.

```
Benefits = Salary * @XREF("_RateCube_", "Emp_Rates", "Blended Rate" )
```

Certainly the code will work, but it takes a lot of processing and network traffic to do this 50,000 times. The rate could be pulled once and stored in an account for use by the formula, but that defeats the purpose of the rate database. A better solution is to use a variable in a calculation script.

```
VAR vInitialize = 0;
VAR vBlendedRate = 0;
FIX(OUTLOOK, BUDGET, FY12,@RELATIVE(EMPLOYEES,0))
    Benefits(
    IF(vInitialize ==0) /*execute first time only */
        vBlendedRate = @XREF("_RateCube_","Emp_Rates", "Blended
          Rate";
        vInitialize = 100;
    ENDIF
```

```
    :: -- additional code
    :: -- additional code
    Benefits = Salary * vBlendedRate;
    :: -- additional code )
ENDFIX
```

There are quite a few interesting things going on with this script. First, a rate database is used instead of co-mingling the rates with the other accounts in the Employee database. In most cases, rates are not multidimensional and only bloat the dense block needlessly. Secondly, a variable is used to control when the rate is retrieved from the Emp_Rate database. Variable vInitialize is set to zero when it is defined. It is still zero when the first employee is processed so the blended rate is retrieved and saved in variable vBlendedRate. Variable vInitialize is set to any value other than zero so that the Blended Rate will not be fetched again for the life of the script. Variable vBlendedRate can now be used like any other member, but with much less processing overhead than @XREF. It is worth noting that the scope of a variable is the entire script. If there were additional FIX statements in this script, the value of vBlendedRate persists.

Another handy feature of variables is the array variable. In the spirit of honesty, I never used array variables and, in fact, did not know how they worked until I started researching this chapter. The array documentation is pretty weak. After much experimentation, I got arrays to work and I must say that they are pretty slick. Arrays are defined in the first part of a script much like single dimensional variables.

What makes the variable an array is the association with a dimension. For example, the Scenario dimension in Sample.Basic has four members. If the application called for there to be a different blended rate for both Actual and Budget, an array works perfectly. Array variables can be defined in a number of ways.

```
ARRAY vaBlendedRate[Scenario];
```

This defines an array named vaBlendedRate that has four occurrences (Actual, Budget, Variance, Variance %). The array can be initialized at definition by any of the following:

```
ARRAY vaBlendedRate[Scenario] = {.3,.35,0,0};
ARRAY vaBlendedRate[Scenario] = {.3,.35};
```

Both statements are the same. They evaluate as Actual = .3, Budget = .35. Variance = 0, Variance % = 0. Providing values for the Variance and Variance % make little sense as they are dynamic.

Arrays values also can be set in code. Fix on a single cell to set the value for better performance. To set the value, arrays need to be in a member calculation block. Here are examples of setting the Actual and Budget occurrences:

```
ARRAY vaBlendedRate[Scenario];
FIX (Jan,Sales)
    Actual (
        vaBlendedRate = .3;
    )
ENFIX
FIX (Jan,Sales)
```

```
    Budget (
        vaBlendedRate = .35;
    )
ENFIX
```

Occurrence #1 or Actual is now set to equal .3 and #2 or Budget to equal .35. A new member named Benefits was added to the Measures dimension of Sample.Basic. This member will be used to store the new benefit calculation.

```
FIX (Actual, Budget)
    Benefits (
        Benefits = Payroll * vBlendedRate;
    )
ENDFIX
```

Unlike most languages, it is not necessary to explicitly specify vBlendedRate(1) when we want to reference the Actual blended rate. Essbase will use the appropriate blended rate value to calculate Benefits depending on the scenario being processed. In the example above, if the current scenario is actual, Benefits = Payroll * .3. When the current member is Budget, Benefits = Payroll * .35.

4.7.5 Aggregate Only What Is Needed

Database aggregations are some of the most time-consuming functions that calculation scripts perform. When running in batch mode, it is not so bad, but having end users wait for aggregation is undesirable. This issue prompted this book's editor, Cameron Lackpour (Chapter 2), to create a technique for aggregating databases that reduces the overall time dramatically. He has presented this technique at an ODTUG (Oracle Development Tools User Group) Kaleidoscope Conference and has written about it on his blog, but it bears repeating.

The premise behind the technique is that when changes occur in a single data block, it is faster to update (aggregate) just the data blocks that need to be changed to derive the correct total. Much the way that the intelligent calculation feature works, the outline structure identifies the blocks that need to be updated. It sounds so simple. I do not understand why it took Lackpour 10 years to figure it out?

Here is how the technique is used. Assume that while building a budget, the end user selects a product and market so that sales estimates can be entered. Once the data entry is finished, the numbers must be aggregated into the totals. Aggregations could be performed on the entire database, but it is preferable to update as few blocks as possible. Here is the test calculation script.

```
Set UpdateCalc off;
Set Msg Detail;
FIX (Jan:Dec, Budget,"Oregon","100-10")
    Sales=50;
ENDFIX
FIX ("Jan":"Dec", "Budget")
    FIX ("Oregon")
        @IALLANCESTORS("100-10") ;
    ENDFIX
    FIX (@IALLANCESTORS("100-10"))
```

```
        @IALLANCESTORS("Oregon") ;
    ENDFIX
ENDFIX
```

This script is officially dubbed as "Cameron's Aggregation Trick." The script fixes on the market and product that will be updated. If this were a Planning application, Oregon and 100-10 would be user selections via Run Time Prompts. Once the changes are made, the ancestors for product 100-10 are aggregated followed by the ancestors of the Oregon market. A separate fix block is required for each dimension that must be aggregated. I do not expect anyone to take my word that this script arrives at the correct answer. Instead I will prove it out.

The first part of the script simulates a user changing Sales = 50 for Oregon and product "100-10." This command slows the script by about 15%, so never use it in production. Following the script execution, we could verify that the aggregation worked by running a few reports, but there is another way. The calculation statement "Set Msg detail;" sends a message to the log showing the sparse member combination for every block that is updated. Thankfully, Sample.Basic is pretty small making it easy to identify the blocks that needed to be updated. Look at the application log output below.

Output from @IALLANCESTORS("100-10")

```
Calculator Information Message: Executing Block - [100], [Oregon],
[Budget]
Calculator Information Message: Executing Block - [Product],
[Oregon], [Budget]
Total Block Created: [0.0000e+00] Blocks
Sparse Calculations: [2.0000e+00] Writes and [9.0000e+00] Reads
Dense Calculations: [0.0000e+00] Writes and [0.0000e+00] Reads
Sparse Calculations: [2.1600e+02] Cells
Dense Calculations: [0.0000e+00] Cells
Calculating in serial
```

Output of from @IALLANCESTORS("Oregon")

```
Calculator Information Message: Executing Block - [100-10], [West],
[Budget]
Calculator Information Message: Executing Block - [100], [West],
[Budget]
Calculator Information Message: Executing Block - [Product],
[West], [Budget]
Calculator Information Message: Executing Block - [100-10],
[Market], [Budget]
Calculator Information Message: Executing Block - [100], [Market],
[Budget]
Calculator Information Message: Executing Block - [Product],
[Market], [Budget]
Calculator Information Message:
Total Block Created: [0.0000e+00] Blocks
Sparse Calculations: [6.0000e+00] Writes and [3.3000e+01] Reads
Dense Calculations: [0.0000e+00] Writes and [0.0000e+00] Reads
Sparse Calculations: [6.4800e+02] Cells
Dense Calculations: [0.0000e+00] Cells
```

In the first section, we see that nine data blocks were read and two written. The written blocks were 100->Oregon->Budget and Product->Oregon->Budget. The next section rolls up market updating six blocks. This section performed 33 reads and six writes. Using the log output, there are two ways to determine if all of the appropriate blocks have been aggregated. First, the outline can be compared to the blocks outputted to the log file. A second and easier method is to change the sales number for "100-10" and Oregon, followed by "Calc All" with intelligent calculation turned on. The log will show every block that Essbase thinks it needs to change. Note that the read and write counts may differ slightly because Essbase processes the blocks a little more efficiently.

4.7.6 Create Blocks Explained

Missing data blocks in BSO can be perplexing. For anyone new to Essbase, the concept of missing blocks is hard to grasp. Even experienced developers and administrators find block creation confusing. I expect that most of the readers have experienced situations when blocks must be explicitly created. For those who have not, this section might not make a lot of sense, but eventually you will need these tips.

The most important thing to remember when creating blocks is that the goal is to create the appropriate block without creating extra blocks. As mentioned repeatedly in this chapter, the more blocks that are processed, the slower the database. It is for this reason that the more experienced developer's tend to shy away from the statements CREATEBLOCKONEQ and CREATENONMISSINGBLK. While these statements are powerful, they can needlessly increase the number of blocks if not used correctly.

The commands CREATEBLOCKONEQ and CREATENONMISSINGBLK have not always been available in Essbase. Prior to their introduction, blocks were created by rearranging the formula so that the result is placed into a sparse member. The following script will not create a block because Sales is a member of a dense dimension.

This script assumes that the block for Cola->Nevada->Actual did not exist prior to running the script, as shown in Table 4.4.

```
FIX (Cola, Nevada, Actual)
    SET CREATEBLOCKONEQ OFF;
    Sales = "NEW YORK" + 100;
ENDFIX
```

Rewriting the formula so that the result is placed in Nevada, which is sparse, creates the necessary block, as shown in Table 4.5.

Table 4.4 Data Results

		Sales	Jan
		Actual	**Budget**
Cola	Nevada	#Mi	#Mi
	New York	25	#Mi

Table 4.5 Data Results after Change

		Sales	Jan
		Actual	**Budget**
Cola	Nevada	125	#Mi
	New York	25	#Mi

```
FIX (Cola, Sales, Actual)
    SET CREATEBLOCKONEQ OFF;
    Nevada = NEW YORK" + 100;
ENDFIX
```

Placing a sparse member on the left side of the formula is not without its dangers. Consider the following script:

```
FIX (Cola)
    SET CREATEBLOCKONEQ OFF;
    Budget = actual->Sales->"NEW YORK" + 100;
ENDFIX
```

Budget is a member of a sparse dimension and the formula readily creates blocks. In fact, as shown in Figure 4.6, it might create more blocks than expected.

Because the Market dimension was not restricted in the FIX, Cola blocks were created for every market. When working with formulas that have a sparse member on the left of the equal sign, it is a good idea to monitor the number of blocks that get created. Once blocks are created, they are difficult to remove.

4.7.6.1 Data Copy There are two advantages to using DATACOPY to create blocks. First, the number of blocks that will be created is known. The chances of exploding the database with unneeded blocks are greatly reduced. Secondly, DATACOPY is probably faster than using either CREATEBLOCKONEQ or CREATENONMISSINGBLK.

Creating blocks using DATACOPY works best when there is another dimension to use as a model. One example would be to use the Budget Scenario to create the blocks for the Forecast Scenario. When using the DATACOPY, consider this trick. Instead of fixing on a dense block cell that has live data, set the FIX on a dummy member that is either #Missing or has meaningless data. Even if the dense member being copied is empty, Essbase will create the block. Often times I see calculations that copy meaningful data and then another pass to zero it out. This technique saves the second pass. The caveat when creating completely empty blocks is that a dense restructure will delete them. In many cases, this might not be a bad thing.

4.7.6.2 Using the CREATEBLOCKONEQ Statement For those times when blocks cannot be created by formulas on the sparse dimension or using data copies, Essbase has special commands. These are very powerful commands, so use them with great care. It is far too easy to create many more blocks than are needed. Of the two commands, CREATEBLOCKONEQ runs much faster, but it is a little tricky to get working.

Table 4.6 Block Explosion

		Sales	Jan
		Actual	**Budget**
Cola	Connecticut	#Mi	101.1
	California	#Mi	101.1
	Oregon	#Mi	101.1
	Nevada	#Mi	101.1
	California	#Mi	101.1
	New York	1.1	101.1

The first warning is to make sure that the FIX tightly controls the number of blocks that will be processed. I have already shown what happens when a large dimension is not included in the fix.

The rules for CREATEBLOCKONEQ include:

- The result of the formula must be a member of a sparse dimension.
- Do not use cross-dimensional formulas.
- CREATEBLOCKONEQ statement forces a top-down calculation.

Below is an example of a cross-dimensional formula. Measures and Year are dense. All other dimensions are sparse. The database is completely empty except for Cola->New York->Actual->Sales->Jan.

```
FIX ("Cola")
    SET CREATEBLOCKONEQ OFF;
    "Nevada" = "Actual"->"New York" + 100;
ENDFIX
```

Note that CREATEBLOCKONEQ is OFF. Table 4.7 shows the results of this adjusted formula.

Even though CREATEBLOCKONEQ is OFF, the budget block for Nevada is created. When there is a cross-dimensional formula, CREATEBLOCKONEQ does not influence the result.

The next script is exactly the same as the prior script except that the cross-dimension reference has been removed. CREATEBLOCKONEQ is still set to OFF.

```
FIX ("Cola")
    SET CREATEBLOCKONEQ OFF;
    Nevada = "NEW YORK" + 100;
ENDFIX
```

As can be seen in Table 4.8, blocks were created for Actual, but not Budget for Nevada.

In this next example, CREATEBLOCKONEQ is ON and the cross-dimensional formula has been removed.

```
FIX ("Cola")
    SET CREATEBLOCKONEQ OFF;
    Nevada = "NEW YORK" + 100;
ENDFIX
```

Table 4.7 Block Explosion Eliminated

		Sales	Jan
		Actual	**Budget**
Cola	Connecticut	#Mi	#Mi
	California	#Mi	#Mi
	Oregon	#Mi	#Mi
	Nevada	101.1	101.1
	California	#Mi	#Mi
	New York	1.1	#Mi

Table 4.8 Without Cross-Dimensional Formula

		Sales	Jan
		Actual	**Budget**
Cola	Connecticut	#Mi	#Mi
	California	#Mi	#Mi
	Oregon	#Mi	#Mi
	Nevada	101.1	#Mi
	California	#Mi	#Mi
	New York	1.1	#Mi

Table 4.9 Final Block Creation Results

		Sales	Jan
		Actual	**Budget**
Cola	Connecticut	#Mi	#Mi
	California	#Mi	#Mi
	Oregon	#Mi	#Mi
	Nevada	101.1	100
	California	#Mi	#Mi
	New York	1.1	#Mi

The blocks for Nevada were created for Actual and Budget as shown in Table 4.9. This example is how CREATEBLOCKONEQ should work.

4.7.6.3 CREATENONMISSINGBLK When Nothing Else Works The CREATENON MISSINGBLK statement is the "last resort" option. Not only can this statement create more blocks than you need, it also creates them slowly. This command follows the outline processing the "potential" blocks according to the FIX statement. Each potential block is loaded into memory. When all of the blocks have been consumed by the fix, Essbase then writes any block that has a value. Blocks that are entirely empty are discarded, hence, the name CREATENONMISSINGBLK. Essbase will then log a message specifying the number of missing blocks that were *not* written back. Use this feature only in FIX statements that tightly control the number of blocks being processed.

One might ask why use a command that has so many negative side effects? The answer is that sometime there is no other way. Table 4.10 shows the results of the script below. Note that the formula result is a dense member and the formula itself has cross-dimensional references.

```
FIX (Budget);
     SET CREATENONMISSINGBLK ON;
     (Sales=Sales->Actual * 1.1;
     Misc = Misc->Actual * .95 ;)
ENDFIX
```

Budget data blocks were created where actual data existed. Blocks where the formula resolved to #Missing did not get created. The following log message specified the number of blocks that were calculated in memory, but were not written.

```
Total #Missing Blocks Not Written Back: [4.5000e+002] Blocks
```

Table 4.10 Results of Dense Cross-Dimensional Calc

	Cola	Sales				
	Actual	Actual	Actual	Budget	Budget	Budget
	Jan	Feb	Mar	Jan	Feb	Mar
New York	678	645	675	745.8	709.5	742.5
Massachusetts	494	470	492	543.4	517	541.2
California	#Mi	#Mi	#Mi	#Mi	#Mi	#Mi
Oregon	#Mi	#Mi	#Mi	#Mi	#Mi	#Mi

4.7.7 What Do They Mean, Why Do I Care?

The terms CELL, BLOCK, TOPDOWN, and BOTTOMUP are the final mechanisms we will address. CELL and BLOCK modes are mutually exclusive calc modes as are TOPDOWN and BOTTOMUP. They all identify how Essbase processes the data. BLOCK and BOTTOMUP calc modes are the default and they definitely calculate the fastest. Under certain conditions, Essbase will revert to CELL or TOPDOWN modes to ensure that calculations work correctly. When this happens, Essbase will write a message to the log file. In most cases, it is possible to override the processing mode by specifying @CALCMODE (CELL|BLOCK|TOPDOWN|BOTTOMUP) in the calculation script. Before overriding the mode, it is important to understand the impact.

To understand block mode, let us consider Sample.Basic, which has Measures and Year as dense dimensions. With block mode, Essbase will group the dense formulas in the most efficient way and process them as a block. Under block calculation mode, Jan might not calculate before Feb and so on. Essbase does this for performance. When executing certain functions, particularly time-based functions, Essbase will switch to CELL mode just in case there are dependencies. Some of the functions that trigger cell mode are @ISMBR, @PRIOR, @NEXT, @CURRMBR, etc. These are commonly referred to as expensive commands because cell mode slows the calculation. Below is a sample script that requires cell mode. The @CALCMODE (CELL) statement is for documentation purposes only. Essbase switches to cell mode automatically. Before executing the script below, Jan:Mar are missing, but the block exists.

```
FIX (Cola, Nevada, Budget)
    Sales (
    @CALCMODE (CELL);
    IF (@ISMBR (Feb))
        Sales = Jan + Feb;
    ELSEIF (@ISMBR (Mar))
        Sales = Jan + Feb + Mar;
    ELSEIF (@ISMBR (Jan))
        Sales = 10;
    ENDIF)
ENDFIX
```

Essbase declares that it is using cell mode with the following log message:

```
Formula for member [Sales] will be executed in [CELL] mode
```

Table 4.11 Correct Values with Cell Mode

	Cola	Sales		
	Jan	Feb	Mar	Qtr1
	Budget	Budget	Budget	Budget
Nevada	10	10	20	40

Table 4.12 Incorrect Values with Block Mode

	Cola	Sales		
	Jan	Feb	Mar	Qtr1
	Budget	Budget	Budget	Budget
Nevada	10	#Mi	#Mi	10

Table 4.11 shows the correct values. First Jan is set to 10, Feb = 10 + #missing, and Mar = 10, 10. After clearing Jan:Mar and changing @CALCMODE (CELL) to @ CALCMODE (BLOCK), the script is rerun.

In this case, the values in Table 4.12 are incorrect. It looks as though Jan was calculated after Feb and Mar when block mode is used. When Essbase encounters certain functions, it does not know that there is a dependency. It errs on the side of caution just in case. If the developer knows that there is no dependency, it is permissible to override the mode taking advantage of the performance benefit.

4.8 BSO MATTERS AND THEN SOME

Despite BSO Essbase being almost old enough to buy a drink, there are still misunderstandings, misconceptions, and plain misuse of the tool. I hope that this chapter has helped clear up some of the common and maybe not so common areas of BSO's sometimes mysterious workings and given you clear guidance on BSO good practices.

BSO Essbase will be with us for some time to come and indeed shows no sign of slowing down within Planning. Where it makes sense, it is an incredibly powerful and useful tool. I hope that this chapter helps you maximize Essbase's original data storage option.

5

BSO IS DEAD. LONG LIVE ASO (CONVERTING BSO TO ASO)

Angela Wilcox

CONTENTS

5.1 WHY WOULD I CONVERT TO USING ASO CUBES?

"If it looks too good to be true, then it probably is." That is the first thing that came to my mind the very first time I saw a demo converting a traditional Essbase cube to this new-fangled ASO storage kernel. "There has to be a catch," I kept thinking. "It simply cannot be this easy." So, for more years than I can justify, I tenaciously held to my traditional cubes, failing to endorse and embrace the new world of ASO. I was wrong. It was that easy.

For many of you, the history of Essbase may be well known, but you may not be as familiar with the timeline with respect to the introduction of the ASO storage kernel. To keep the facts straight, let me provide a little refresher:

- 1992: Arbor Software shipped the first release of Essbase.
- 1998: Arbor was acquired and merged with Hyperion.

- 1998: IBM started shipping Essbase under the name of "DB2 OLAP Server," a porting of the software to their platforms for widespread release with their OS that continued until 2005.
- 2005: ASO was introduced with version 7.
- 2005: Essbase was declared one of the most Influential technologies of the last 10 years by Information Age Magazine.
- 2007: Hyperion (who was in the middle of renaming Essbase for some unknown and undisclosed reason) was acquired by Oracle.
- 2009: Oracle renamed the product officially to "Oracle Essbase" (loss of the Essbase name had not been treated happily in most technical and even business realms and everyone jumped for joy at its return).

That traditional Essbase cube first developed in 1992 and still developed today now has several names. Often, you can tell how long someone has been working with this OLAP (online analytical processing) technology by which names they use when they refer to Essbase. You may see within Oracle materials the references to Essbase BSO (Block Storage Option), BSO cubes, or Essbase Analytics. It is one of the two storage kernel options now available to the developer when creating a cube from scratch. Selecting this option allows you to create cubes as they have been created for the past 20 years, taking considerable time to determine (among other things) which dimensions should be Dense versus Sparse. Time also will be spent considering whether the resulting block size will be optimal, or if the system will run out of memory because the block size is too big. On and on goes the list of worries and angst that exist when we build traditional Essbase BSO cubes. The entire debate becomes so complex that it has always been essential to have a good consultant at your beck and call to help you determine how to best configure your cube.

This is contrasted to the newer technology option that also has several names in the literature and marketing materials. Essbase ASO (Aggregate Storage Option), ASO cubes, and Enterprise Analytics are all references that can be found and are valid. With ASO cubes, many of the things we worry about with regard to BSO cubes are gone. You can just build your dimensions, add member calcs using MDX (multidimensional expressions), load your data, and you are ready to go. No more Dense versus Sparse debates. No more spreadsheets to evaluate optimal block size. The dimensionality can increase in ways you never dreamed (depth and breadth). You also can store a much greater volume of data with ASO. The disk footprint is incredibly smaller, and many times the batch load and calc times drop so dramatically that it seems like magic. Little did anyone realize that the simplicity this brought to many cube designs would be a trait as well, which caused many developers (including myself) to shun it for years. The belief that "it just cannot be this easy" was pervasive and rampant among my peers. I was not alone.

Erring on the side of caution, I built BSO cube after BSO cube, despite the growing amount of white papers and conference presentations on how great ASO cubes were. I would listen to talk after talk on how they could be built faster, loaded faster, aggregated faster, and how you could have dozens of dimensions and millions of members in a dimension if you wanted it. That was unheard of and I continued to savor my own skepticism, knowing that some undefined pitfall was lurking nearby that would surely catch the ASO cube users unaware and I alone would be saved.

The turning point for me was the day I was asked to reduce the amount of disk space my 80 BSO cubes were taking up. Since these were well built, streamlined, fully optimized BSO cubes, this was not a simple directive to fulfill. I could not just go chop off some fluff inside the cube and provide the requested disk reduction. "Well," I said to myself, "I guess I have no choice except to try this ASO thing. It probably will not work, and my terrifically designed cubes will really not run well, but I need to be able to tell them I tried and to go ahead and just purchase more disk space; after all, disk is cheap." So, I set off and started converting cube after cube. The results were staggering. Hours on hours were knocked off of our load and calc each night and weekend. Our disk footprint was reduced to a mere 20% of the original amount of disk. In most instances, although not all, the users' reports were faster. From that day forward, I was a convert and I have never looked back or regretted that move. I only wish I had jumped on the band wagon sooner and begun embracing the ASO technology immediately instead of waiting so long. To quote an old idiom—better late than never. At least I had not missed the entire party, and now neither will you.

One of the simpler methods to learn what an ASO cube does is to compare it to something you are intimately familiar with: the BSO cube. The easiest way to review a summary of the functionality or capabilities available in an ASO cube versus a BSO cube is in a table format. Drawn together from a great many sources, the following is a high-level summary comparison to assist you in working through your decision process. Not every BSO cube is an appropriate candidate to become an ASO cube. The decision on whether to convert it or not should be a purposeful move. Table 5.1 is not considered to be an all-inclusive table of every function or capability available within the two complementary technologies. Some of these facts may surprise even seasoned developers.

This type of list was first produced by consultants in the early adoption of ASO technology. I wish I had some of my earliest comparison papers and lists; the comments I wrote in the margins would be very interesting to read (and laugh about) now. Typically, a new version of the software would be released. We would download and install it and then take it for a test run with our favorite "difficult" application (because everyone knew that all releases look good when you run Sample or Demo Basic) and our favorite front-end tool. After we had it properly installed and fully loaded, we would do our checkbox comparison. With each new release what we found to be happening is that there were fewer blanks or negatives on the ASO column, and more blanks or negatives on the BSO column. Slowly but surely, ASO started having a greater number of advantages than disadvantages. Finally, I think we can openly declare that there is a new development standard. The "new norm" among many respected developers is that you always design using ASO cubes, falling back to BSO cubes only when absolutely necessary (and mostly in context with Planning Applications as well as homegrown budgeting/forecasting applications).

"Should I immediately start converting all my BSO cubes to ASO cubes?" No, definitely not. There are some key questions and considerations to think about before launching on a large or small conversion project. Determining if your BSO cubes are good candidates for conversion is not necessarily a straightforward task and there are a lot of things to consider. Hopefully, the next few pages will help with that task. Approaching it analytically with an open mind will allow you to accurately determine the best course of action for existing cubes. Just as important in this process, though, is the need to start thinking through which technology should be used for new implementations, and why. Don't be like I was and stay with BSO cubes only because it is what you know, and more importantly, what makes you comfortable. Use this resource guide to empower you to

Table 5.1 Functional Comparison of Essbase Storage Kernels

BSO	ASO	Functionality Description/Notes
Y	Y	Supports user queries with OLAP enabled reporting tools
Y	Y	Supports write-back applications (ASO can only write back to level-0)
Y	Y	Supports partitioning (ASO has no outline synchronization)
Y	Y	Supports Development of Member Specific Calculations
Y	Y	Supports Creation of Calculations at all member levels (ASO has some limitations)
Y	N	Supports data loads at all levels of the cube
N	Y	Allows the developer to determine the order in which a member calculation occurs (BSO can only control scripted calculations, not member calculations that follow native rules)
Y	Y	Supports use of Calc Scripts in batch processing (new ASO feature and there are significant limitations to functionality)
N	Y	Supports greater than 12 dimensions in a design with ease
N	Y	Supports dimensions with hundreds of thousands to millions of members
Y	N	Supports Multiple Databases per Application (while supported, it is not recommended anymore for BSO)
Y	Y	Supports use of Attribute Dimensions and Attribute Calculations (ASO: Sum only)
Y	N	Supports Association of Attribute Dimensions with the Dimension tagged Accounts
Y	Y	Supports Ragged Hierarchies
Y	Y	Supports Alternate Hierarchies
Y	Y	Supports User Defined Attributes (UDA)
N	Y	Supports multiple slices of data that can be merged on request
N	Y	Supports replacement of the entire contents of a database, or just an incremental slice
N	Y	Supports automatic update of aggregations after a load (ASO: If aggregates exist, they are updated; BSO all required calc scripts must be run)
Y	Y	Supports variance reporting
Y	Y	Supports Y-T-D Reporting
Y	N	Supports all four unary types (+, –, /, *)
N	Y	Supports Date/Time Dimension Type (Text Metrics)
Y	Y	Supports Report Writer Functionality
Y	Y	Supports Spreadsheet add-in
Y	Y	Supports Export Functionality (ASO Level-0 Only)
Y	Y	Supports API
Y	Y	Supports MDX Queries
Y	Y	Supports use of alternate Alias Tables
Y	N	Supports Currency Conversion Module
Y	N	Supports Data Mining Module
Y	N	Supports Linked Reporting Objects (LRO)
Y	Y	Supports Hybrid Analysis (ASO some exceptions)
Y	Y	Supports Time Balance Accounting and Reporting (ASO some exceptions)

learn and stretch your skills and start utilizing the full OLAP platform and both storage kernels available to you. Having options and knowing you have options is a key turning point in your education.

5.2 WHEN SHOULD I NOT TRY TO USE ASO CUBES?

While ASO cubes have really come a long way since the initial release in version 7 and are definitely a great tool in the Essbase arsenal, there are still some times when you may want to stick with the traditional BSO cube for your ultimate solution. In my opinion, there are two significant differentiators that have to be fully considered, and then a number of more minor ones. The single most important differentiator is write-back, followed closely by calculations and calc functions. Although an ASO cube can facilitate write-back now (it could not in the version 7 release), it is still only available at level-0 of the dimensional hierarchy. There are many instances where I may have design reasons to create an application where I am writing back to an intersection that is not at level-0 of every dimension. That is a design decision, and if I decide that is indeed what I want or need to do, then a BSO cube is still my storage option and design choice. In view of the fact that ASO cubes allow for an increased breadth of dimensionality (more dimensions), as well as a greater depth of dimensionality (more children members), writing back to level-0 of all dimensions can get very complex indeed.

Another thing to consider is the calculations or prebuilt calc functions that I want to use in my cubes. I do not endorse the attitude to always use BSO cubes if you have any complex calculations. I did this originally and now believe it was a mistake. MDX as a calculation language is very robust. While the learning curve is often very steep for "old school" Essbase developers, if you work with people who are good with MDX, you will soon realize that you can do some very complex calculation sequences in Essbase. I believe the more appropriate consideration is whether you want to use some prebuilt functionality provided within Essbase. A secondary consideration is whether this functionality can readily and accurately be reproduced in MDX. Sometimes, we do things because we can, not because it is the correct or most appropriate choice for the circumstance at hand. Why would I want to spend 200 hours coding a function in an ASO cube using MDX and creating a maintenance headache for the cube administrator, when I can just use a prebuilt function in a BSO cube to do the same thing? If there is nothing else preventing me from using a BSO cube, then the answer would be that I would not want to do that. I should take the path that will provide the greatest amount of flexibility with the least amount of ongoing maintenance.

To help in this decision point, review the calculation functions you are using in the *Essbase Technical Reference*. There is a lot built into a function like @ALLOCATE or @ MDALLOCATE, two of the common functions used to determine where to push/split an expense in the hierarchy based on business rules. To rebuild an MDX sequence to accomplish what these functions automatically do for you would be laborious at best. Admittedly, financial applications are the single most affected group of applications when you start looking at calculations. With functions like @IRR (calculates the internal rate of return on cash flow) and @DECLINE (calculates the depreciation of a member over time), you can only imagine the amount of MDX code that would have to be built to mimic what these calculations do out of the box with no coding. If any of these calculation functions are something you need to utilize in your cube design, and there is not an acceptable (or easily developed) MDX replacement, then you may want to stick with the BSO cube option.

While it is not a calculation function, per se, I will quickly mention Variance Reporting. Variance Reporting (the ability to tag Expense Items in the Accounts Dimension and have the variance between Actual and Budget represented appropriately to the report consumer) is a very desirable feature for a lot of corporations with respect to their financial reporting. This feature cannot be used with ASO cubes.

Another consideration is whether you need or want to utilize Custom-Defined Functions (CDFs) or an equally new function, Custom-Defined Macros (CDMs), in your Essbase cube. The ability to create CDFs was introduced early in Version 9 of Essbase. If you are not familiar with the creation and usage of CDFs, there have been several presentations on them at the last few Oracle Developers Tools User Group Conferences (ODTUG). These presentations are available for download on the ODTUG site and provide a great starter guide. Essbase Developers have developed many of these and provided them free of charge on various Web sites as shareware. In addition, some are available directly through Oracle and are even now provided with the base product installation. Written in Java and then registered with Essbase using MaxL, they are considered an indispensable tool by many developers and administrators. Although this has never been formally documented, I am surmising that because they are an extension of the Essbase Calculator Framework, they are not available for use with ASO cubes (as there is no MDX equivalent of the Essbase Calculator Framework). If using the CDF and/or the CDM functions are important to you, you will need to stick with the BSO cube option.

One Essbase feature that has been used sporadically throughout the years is Linked Reporting Objects (LRO). The LRO allows the cube designer to attach documentation to a cell within the database. This documentation can include a cell note (or series of notes), a linked document (any type), or a URL (uniform resource locator) to a location on the Web or corporate intranet to provide the user additional information. While some developers may not even be aware of the existence of LROs, numerous developers and administrators in finance areas have grown to love this feature. I have seen this feature used to allow cell annotations for budgeting and forecasting applications. I also have seen this feature used by insurance companies (the insured item in the database may have a picture accessed by LRO), and research hospitals (the database may contain a picture that shows what the research statistics pertain to). Functionally, an LRO is stored within the block in a BSO cube. Because that construct does not exist in an ASO cube, these cannot exist. If you already use this feature and are not willing to give it up then stick with your BSO cube as this is not available in ASO cubes.

Another Essbase feature that seems to be either loved or hated is the currency conversion module. Currency conversion is accomplished by adding a second database to the application. Some setup is done and references are created within the outline. This is actually a very nice feature and it works very well. A lot of developers over the years bypassed this feature (especially if the customer had to purchase it), and created their own home-grown calculations and scripts to do currency conversion. If you already own the module, and you want to implement it, you will need to stick with BSO cubes. As you may not yet know, ASO cubes can only have one Database per Application. Therefore, even if you wanted to use it with your ASO cube, you could not because you cannot create the currency database where it needs to be within the application to work correctly. If you are willing to give it up, another solution can be developed to support the database side of currency conversion. Make sure if you go that route you consider whether it will support the reporting side of the currency conversion module (which allows you to report in any currency across the board in your database). This reporting feature sometimes gets overlooked when converting the cube from BSO to ASO and is a big gotcha when you get ready to start converting reports. Often, it is caught by ad hoc report users who can no longer do the same things they used to do when the cube had the currency conversion module sitting behind it.

Just a parting note lest someone ask why partitioning was not included in this section. As of version 11.1.x, almost all of the partitioning types are now fully supported for both ASO and BSO cubes and allow the use of ASO and BSO cubes interchangeably as the Source or the Target. Prior to version 11, ASO cubes as a data source could only be partitioned to BSO cubes as a data target. ASO cubes could not be partitioned to ASO cubes and BSO cubes could not be partitioned to ASO cubes. These were some severe limitations that you had to design around if partitioning was a main part of your design considerations. Today, the only major concern is the limitation when using Replicated Partitioning. Not every combination of the two cube types works. Check the *Essbase Database Administrator's Guide* (DBAG) for detailed information on this topic.

5.3 WHAT IS THE EASIEST WAY TO CONVERT A BSO CUBE TO AN ASO CUBE?

After having thought through the circumstances under which you should not convert a BSO cube to an ASO cube, you are ready to move forward. You have made the decision to convert one of your existing BSO cubes to an ASO cube. Perhaps you want to join in the hoopla and rejoicing around the greatness of ASO cubes. Or maybe you have, as I did, a requirement that was handed to you that can only be met by resignedly endorsing this technology. Possibly, you just want to see how well your BSO cube would work as an ASO cube and explore the differences between the two of them. No matter how or why the decision was made, you are now here and need to know what to do and how to go about this proposal. The next section will walk you through some best practices and tips to remember as you perform this conversion.

5.3.1 Using the Wizard

The first thing to look at is the Aggregate Storage Outline Conversion Wizard. You access this by opening Essbase Administration Services (EAS) and going to File > Wizards > Aggregate Storage Outline Conversion, as shown in Figure 5.1.

Although the Wizard contains the mechanism to convert a flat file outline object that is not set up as a cube on your server (File System Tab), I have found the conversion process to be easier to work with if you have already set up the outline as a BSO cube. An even better situation is to have data loaded so you can do a before-and-after comparison using reports or the data preview option in EAS. While having the loaded cube on a different server will work fine, I like to eliminate potential issues by having my source and target objects co-existing on the same server. As a result, I have fewer unanswered questions and the comparative process (if there is a need to debug something) is much simpler. In some cases, loading data may not be possible, or you may not want to load data for some other reason. That is okay and will not change your experience when using the Wizard.

If you are doing the conversion on a Development Server, and the source cube is on a Production Server, simply copy the application across servers. Again, you do not need data loaded because the conversion process only converts the outline, it does not do anything

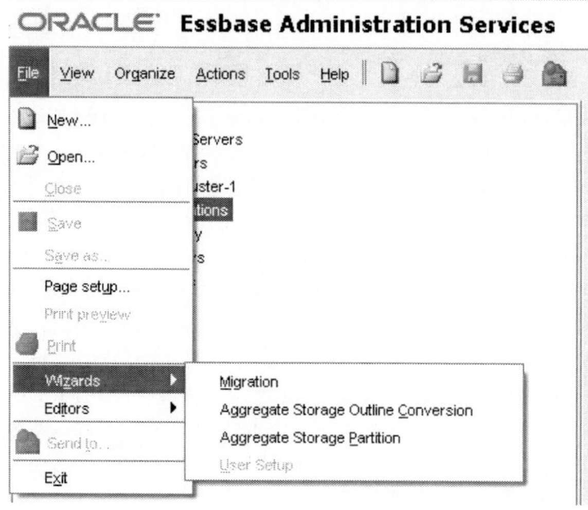

Figure 5.1 File Path to start the ASO Wizard. (From Oracle Essbase Administration Services. With permission.)

at all with the data. It does not discard the data; it ignores the data. The process only works with the outline object and disregards everything else within the application folders, including data. In most cases, you can do an export from the BSO cube and import that file directly into the ASO cube once it is built. The only instance where this would be a problem is if you had dimension members that were removed by the Wizard. You would have to re-create those members to complete the import successfully. Note that the most likely reason the Wizard would remove a member is if the member name violates a naming convention in the ASO cube. For instance, you cannot use the word "log" as a member name in an ASO cube; I am not sure why you would ever actually have a member with that name, but it is my example. In this instance, you would want to rename that member in the BSO cube prior to doing the outline conversion, so that no members are deleted and the members used in the export will match the members used for the import. It is important to point out a nuance in conversions that often creates an issue later on in the process. The Wizard does not do anything with existing rules files (for data loading and dimension building), Report Scripts, or Calculation Scripts. Moving and converting these objects will be subsequent tasks that need to be completed manually.

After opening the Wizard, point to the Essbase Server Tab and select the Essbase outline you want to convert.

Note: If you highlight the application in the application navigation panel prior to opening the Wizard, the proper application and database selection will be made for you.

You can either drill down in the window on the database object to get to the outline object or click Next (and the wizard will drill for you). The outline name will then appear in the File name window as shown in Figure 5.2. Click Next to continue to the Verify Corrections to Outline window.

The Verify Corrections window will address the outline members that the system is unable to change in order to convert the outline member. It picks up things like member labels that do not meet ASO rules, outline member formulas that are not in the dimension tagged as Accounts, and member names that violate ASO naming conventions,

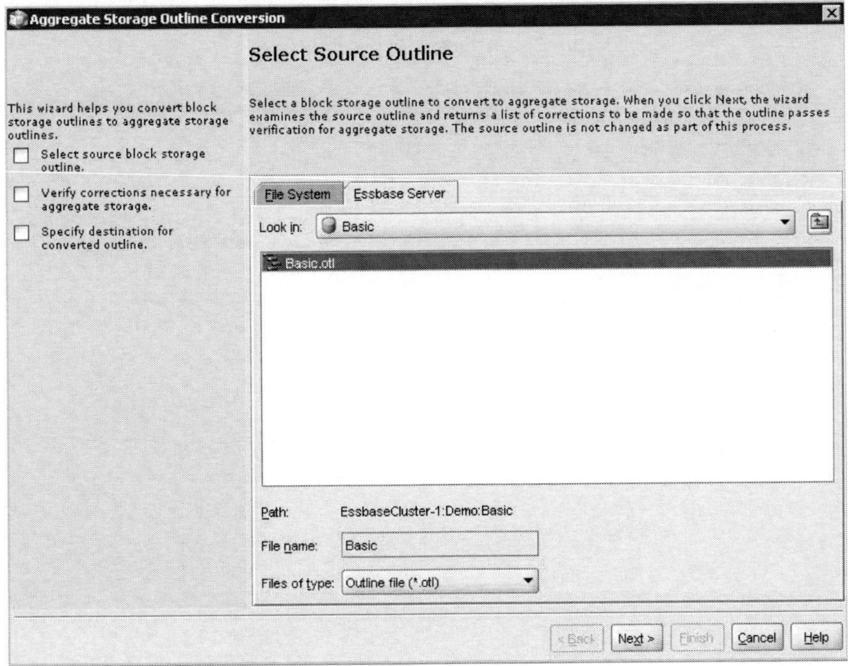

Figure 5.2 Wizard Select Source outline screen. (From Oracle Essbase Administration Services. With permission.)

to name a few issues. Keep in mind that this Wizard does not flag calculations that need to be converted in the dimension tagged as Accounts, neither does it convert your formulas to MDX. That is a separate step you will take in the conversion process. Once you have looked through the items flagged by the Wizard and made note of things you may need to manually update later when the conversion process is finished, look to the bottom of the window and note there is a radio option to allow you to pick whether to automatically correct these or do an interactive correction. Typically, users leave this at the default value of Automatic outline correction, as shown in Figure 5.3.

An interactive outline correction is often not done because it is understood that you will have a great deal of changes you are going to have to make manually. Most of these changes are to deal with member formulas that must be converted to MDX. Hence, the path of least resistance is to go ahead and allow the system to change what it can, knowing you will do the rest of the changes manually after the conversion process is complete. The verification information shown is a redisplay of the same screen that is shown when you are working on an outline inside of EAS and you click the verify outline button. Something to note when you take the Automatic outline correction option: The system can and will delete members if it finds a serious enough conflict that it cannot either ignore or resolve. You will know this happened when you click Next to continue. The next screen you move to inside the Wizard will provide a message on how many members were modified and how many were deleted. The message in Figure 5.4 is an example of what you would see if you converted the Demo Basic BSO cube to an ASO cube. (My examples will revolve around that very conversion to keep the conversation as simple as possible.)

If any members were deleted, this will affect your ability to load in an export file from your BSO cube. If you choose to take the interactive correction, it will open up

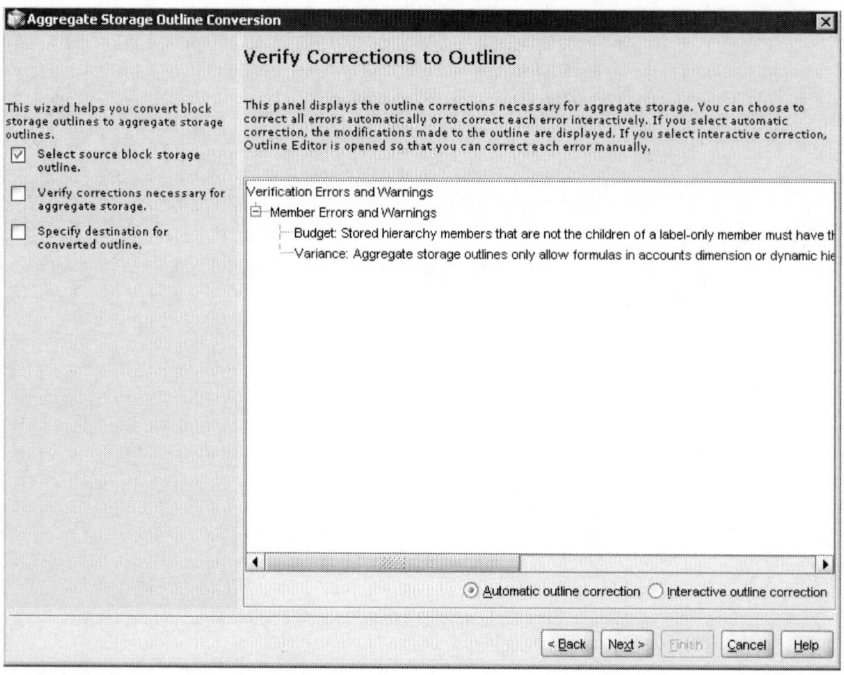

Figure 5.3 Wizard Verify Corrections to Outline Screen. (From Oracle Essbase Administration Services. With permission.)

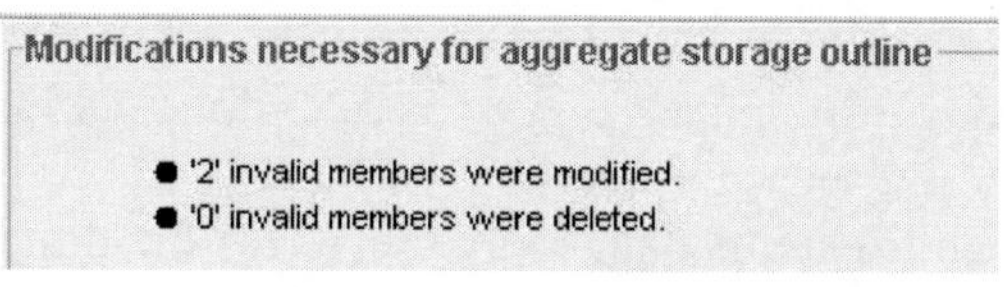

Figure 5.4 Essbase modification error message. (From Oracle Essbase Administration Services. With permission.)

the outline in the outline editor and allow you to make the changes immediately. If you have already forgotten what the errors were from the previous Wizard screen, just click on the verify checkmark and they will be displayed again. You may not be prepared to write new MDX formulas, so you may want to comment out the current formula that is causing the error and continue making corrections until clicking the verify button produces no errors.

After reviewing the summary messages on the necessary modifications the system made to be able to create the ASO cube, click Next to continue. At this point you are ready to provide the destination for your converted outline. You can click on the File System Tab and put the converted outline back onto your file system to be imported at a later time. Conversely, you can click the button near the lower right-hand corner of the screen to "Create Aggregate Storage Application," as shown in Figure 5.5.

Typically, most developers would choose to "Create Aggregate Storage Application" so that they can immediately continue working on the converted ASO cube. After providing the application and database name, click OK and you are done. Click Finish to exit the Wizard unless you have another outline to convert, in which case you can take

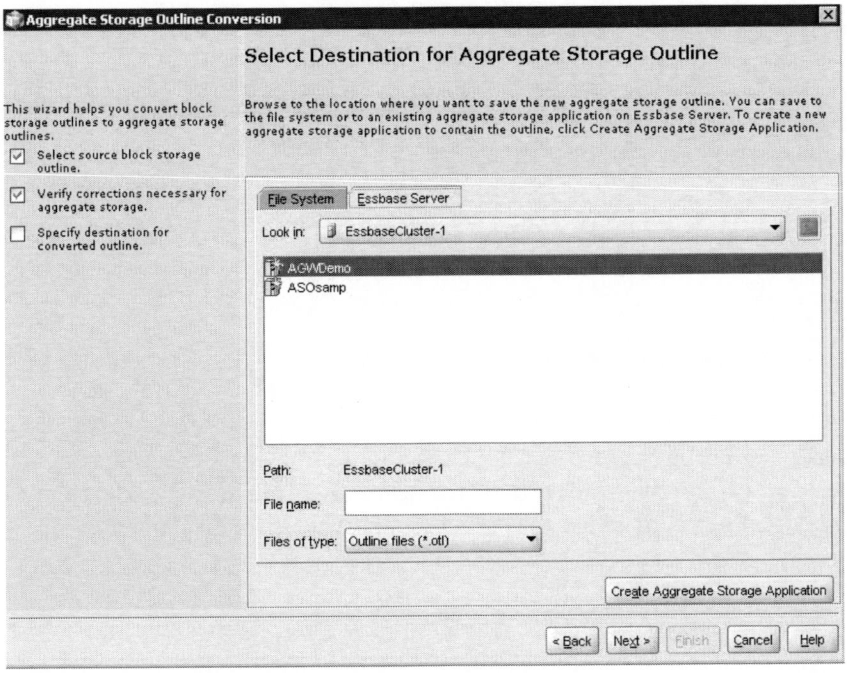

Figure 5.5 Wizard select destination screen. (From Oracle Essbase Administration Services. With permission.)

that option and start the process anew. The most essential part is now complete; you can now begin to work with your ASO cube. However, there are several more tasks to complete before your conversion can be considered finished.

5.3.2 Converting Calculations

Converting Member Calculations is typically the next task you will need to address. This can be a very simple to an extraordinarily complex task. As was discussed earlier in this chapter, this is one of the biggest considerations to determine before you decide to convert a BSO cube to an ASO cube: Can the Business Rules (Member Formulas) be converted to MDX? In most instances, the answer to this is a qualified yes. Qualified because you will either need to learn MDX to do the conversion yourself, or hire a consultant who knows MDX to do the conversion for you. If you choose to do this yourself, as I did, you need to understand that the learning curve can be steep and the path somewhat jagged. In the end, there is a great deal of satisfaction in making a complete conversion on your own.

Typically, the calculation conversion process is going to involve one of two scenarios. You will either be converting calculations in the dimension tagged as Accounts (Scenario 1), or you will be converting calculations found in other dimensions (Scenario 2). When the calculations are in other dimensions than the dimension tagged as Accounts, this generally will force you to complete additional steps. If we used Demo Basic as an example, we can step through both of these scenarios.

Note: I keep referring to the “dimension tagged as Accounts” because the dimension itself may not actually be called that. You may have named the dimension Metrics, or Sales Data, and then given it the Accounts tag. So, I use the “dimension tagged as Accounts” reference to be very clear which dimension I reference.

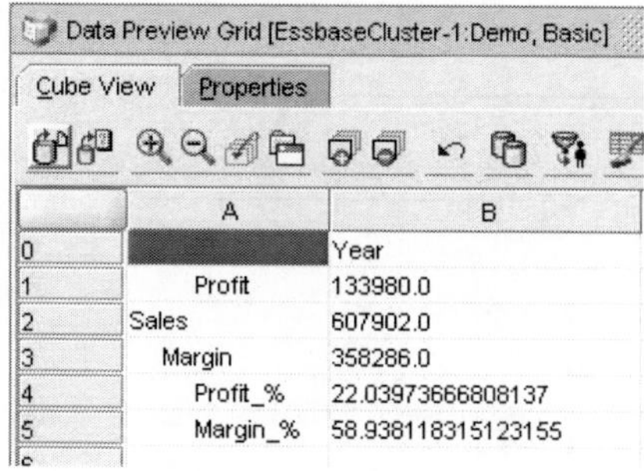

Figure 5.6 Data preview of Demo Basic after a default load. (From Oracle Essbase Administration Services. With permission.)

First, let us examine converting calculations in the dimension tagged as Accounts. In Demo:Basic, we can see that we have two members with formulas in the BSO cube: Profit_% and Margin_%. Both of these use the prebuilt Essbase mathematical operator: "%".

```
Profit_% = "Profit % Sales";
Margin_% = "Margin % Sales";
```

When you open the ASO outline, you can see the formula was converted as is, but if you validate this or try to resave the outline, you will get an MDX error (and it does not tell you what is wrong or how to fix the error). So, how do you fix the calculation? First, you need to know what the calculation is actually doing so you can recode it in MDX. The "%" operator evaluates Member1 as a percentage of Member2. A data preview in EAS of the Demo Basic cube after a default load and calc would reflect the values shown in Figure 5.6.

This would enable us to determine that Profit_% is using this formula:

```
(Profit/Sales) * 100
133,980/607,902 = .220397 * 100 = 22.0397
```

While MDX does not have a % function for us to use, we can certainly recreate the member calculation as:

```
([Accounts].[Profit]/[Accounts].[Sales])*100
```

After we change both formulas and load the same data that was in the original BSO cube (Demo) to the new ASO cube (ASODemo), we can now do a data preview as shown in Figure 5.7 on our converted cube and validate that the data does indeed match and the calculated values are exactly the same.

Thus, for each member calculation you will proceed through three steps:

1. Evaluate the BSO calculation and determine mathematically what it is doing.
2. Convert that information to an MDX formula.
3. Run a report (or data preview) in the original BSO cube as well as the new ASO cube and verify that the values are correct.

Once you have completed this process for each member calculation, the conversions for Scenario 1 would be deemed complete. There is a good chance that all of the calculations will not be this simple, and you will need to complete another task in order to

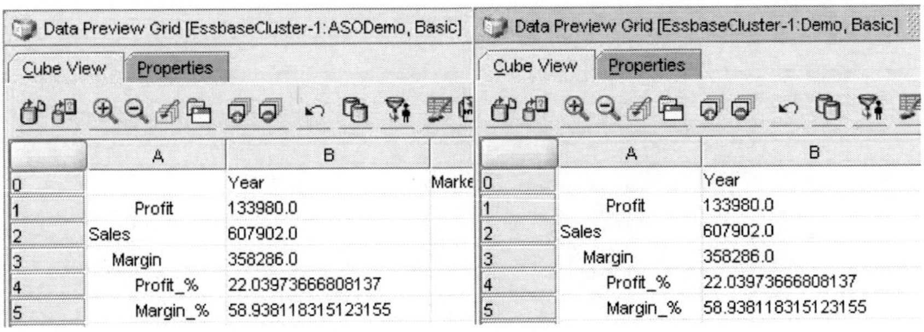

Figure 5.7 Comparative Data Preview before and after calculation change to MDX. (From Oracle Essbase Administration Services. With permission.)

retrieve the correct values. That task involves determining the solve order for the calculation. We will address this in more detail after we discuss Scenario 2—Calculations that are in other dimensions.

When we were using the Wizard, one of the error messages we received for the member Variance was that Aggregate Storage Outlines only allow calculations in the Accounts Dimension or in a dimension with a Dynamic hierarchy. If you examine the converted outline, Variance is a member of the dimension called Scenario. In the Demo cube, the formula on this member was:

```
Actual - Budget;
```

Unlike the Accounts dimension where the formulas were brought into the ASO cube as they existed in the BSO cube, the formula was removed altogether. This is because the definition of the dimension has to be altered to facilitate member calculations; it has to be changed from Stored to Dynamic or Hierarchies Enabled. If the cube does not have a significant amount of data, changing the dimension to be Dynamic should work fine. On the other hand, if the cube has a lot of data, you will want to use Hierarchies Enabled. This will allow you to have multiple hierarchies with a mixture of Stored and Dynamic settings. Using this should improve your report times after the cube is aggregated. The aggregation is similar to completing the default calculation on a BSO cube. It is the activity that provides upper level values for speed of retrieval. The members where the data is loaded can be in a section tagged as Stored and the member with the calculation can be in a section tagged as Dynamic. Once the appropriate hierarchy information has been changed, the calculation formula can be added to the member.

Using the converted Demo cube outline, this change is made by opening the ASODemo outline in EAS and right-clicking on the Scenario member. Select the option to Edit Member Properties and you will be in the Information Tab by default. Approximately three quarters of the way down the page is a section called Hierarchy Information. Click on the area where it currently has the value of Stored and choose the new value. Figure 5.8 shows the original Demo outline, the ASODemo outline using a Dynamic setting, and the ASODemo2 outline using a Hierarchies Enabled setting.

To use the Hierarchies Enabled option, I created some additional parent members to separate the loaded versus the calculated members. For me, the third panel has been the most optimal method for adding member calculations to other dimensions than the dimension tagged as Accounts. With that task complete, we have finished converting

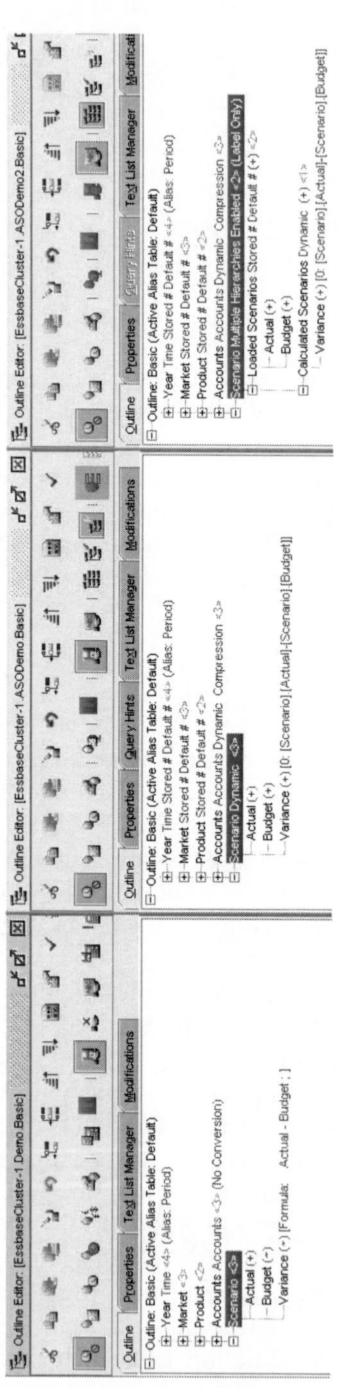

Figure 5.8 Comparison of three outline change methods. (From Oracle Essbase Administration Services. With permission.)

all the member calculations that were in the BSO cube (Demo). Oh, that all of your calculations (and mine) were this easy to convert. I know when I was first learning and writing MDX code, the Network 54 Essbase message board (http://www.network54.com/Forum/58296/) was a priceless tool and kept me sane. I asked a lot of questions on how to convert various BSO calculations to their ASO counterparts. As we continue this chapter, we will assume the calculations are now coded in MDX. Determining Solve Order is the next task we want to focus on as we get close to completing the conversion process.

5.3.3 Determining Solve Order

Simply put, in the context of a member calculation within the outline, the solve order is a mathematical assignment from 0 to 127 that we assign a member in the outline. This assignment determines the order in which the cube will execute the member calculation at report run-time, and takes into account all members involved in the query process. Custom Solve Orders also can be added to MDX queries. This chapter is not addressing that particular usage of Solve Orders. Solve Order was always the feature I wished I had in a BSO cube. As you know, in BSO cubes calculation orders are determined by rules within Essbase—looking at a combination of dimension and member tags, Sparse and Dense Designations, and the order of the outline. You had to watch carefully to make sure you avoided "Forward Calculation References." Understanding it, especially when you had a calculation issue, could become complex. The DBAG dedicates dozens of pages to making sure you understand these rules and complexities. Inevitably, the thing that would make you crazy was the total inability to control it all in a simple manner. Working within the confines of the "rules" to manipulate the outline and members was the best that you could accomplish.

In sharp contrast, this is a very neat and tidy process in an ASO cube. Once you have added the calculation to a member in the outline, right click on the member and go to Edit Member Properties. The last selection under the Type section is to input the desired solve order. The higher the number, the later the calculation occurs during the run-time process of the report. A 1 would happen after all the defaults (0s), then a 2 would execute next, and so on. Typically, developers will add these in increments of 5 so if you need to insert one you do not have to renumber everything to which you have already assigned a solve order in a specific sequence. After typing in the number (let's pretend we assign a 5), click OK and you should now be able to see the assigned solve order in the outline. It will typically look like this:

```
MemberName (+) [5: [Dim].[Member1]-[Dim].[Member2]]
```

You can use this as soon as the outline has been saved. This change will cause a restructure to occur so beware of the fact that a fully loaded and aggregated cube could restructure for a lengthy amount of time. I have a very large ASO cube that this type of change would launch a 60 to 90 minute restructure process. Assuming that your initial changes are made to an empty cube, this should not be an issue at the start.

"When do I need a solve order?" For sure, any member in your BSO cube that was tagged as two-pass will most likely need a solve order added to it. For the most part, you just need to think through your calculations and dependencies. If I had the following scenario:

```
MemberA - Loaded
MemberB - Loaded
MemberC - Loaded
```

```
MemberD - Custom Calculation of A+B
MemberE - Ratio of MemberD to MemberC
```

I would need to define several solve orders. MemberD would need to be calculated after A, B, and C. MemberE would need to be calculated after D. Assigning 5 to D and 10 to E would guarantee that the calculations are executed at run-time in the desired order. This brings us to the next logical question. "Does each calculation need a unique solve order?" No, they definitely do not. The solve orders only matter in relationship to other members in the outline involved in a specific calculation sequence, such as the example I provided above with MembersA to E. If I were to take the same cube where we had the A to E scenario and now add the following scenario:

```
MemberT - Loaded
MemberU - Loaded
MemberV - Loaded
MemberW - Custom Calculation of T+U
MemberX - Ratio of MemberW to MemberV
```

I would assign a solve order of 5 to MemberW and a solve order of 10 to MemberX. Even though this is the same as the assignment I made to D and E above, it would be fine. In relationship to the elements that need to execute at run-time, the correct order will be maintained and the formula will materialize in the correct sequence.

5.3.4 Converting Dimension Build Rules and Dimension Tags

At this point, your outline conversion is nearly complete. The last major task is to go through the dimension build and data Load rules and make sure they have been moved to the new ASO cube and that they still work correctly. Happily, most rules files work effortlessly with an ASO cube that has been converted from a BSO cube. To move them to your ASO cube, you can simply copy them in EAS, or you can open them and do a Save As and save them to the new ASO cube. I tend to just copy them as I have had no negative experiences doing it that way. Once I have them all relocated in the ASO cube, I normally open each one, retrieve data into it, check the settings, and complete a validation check. While this will not catch everything, it should catch most issues, if there are any. The rule will most likely work "as is" to load the data.

Note: The more significant change in the area of loading data will be to change your MaxL automation scripts—converting the scripts to allow the newly created ASO cubes to use data load buffers—a feature that did not exist in BSO cubes. In brief, a data buffer is an object that data is loaded into, and then the buffer has behaviors that can be controlled during the load process as well as doing some optimization (like sorting) as a function of the buffer.

5.3.5 Converting Report Scripts and Calculation Scripts

After copying your Rules files to your new ASO cube, you may have thought you were finally finished with this conversion process. However, there are at least two additional objects that also will need to be manually converted to your new ASO cube. The first object is the Report Script. With some minor exceptions, Report Scripts work the same way with an ASO cube that they did with a BSO cube. If you have Report Scripts that you use, these will need to be copied the same way you copied the Rules files. Open EAS and browse to the original BSO application, drilling down and opening the Report

Scripts folder. Right-click on the Report Script you want to keep and copy it to the new ASO cube. After repeating this for each Report Script, open each one in the ASO cube and validate the script for potential syntax errors that may arise due to changes in the outline during the conversion process.

Note: If you have Report Scripts that are used as part of the validation process, these are great to run after you load the same data in both the BSO and ASO cubes for comparative purposes. This will test the script conversion as well as testing the cube conversion by evaluating whether the results in both executed scripts match.

Calculation Scripts are the last object that you will need to spend time considering how to handle in the conversion process. This is not as simple as converting the Rules files or Report Scripts. Remember that a careful review and assessment of the Calculation Scripts should have been performed prior to starting the conversion process to determine whether the BSO cube was an appropriate candidate to be converted to an ASO cube. When discussing Calculation Scripts, there are several things that need to be clarified right away or you will risk becoming very confused in an extremely short matter of time.

As you know, BSO Calculation Scripts have a .csc extension in the file system and are most commonly stored in the database directory of an Essbase application. In the 11.1.2.x release, Custom Calculations on Aggregate Storage Databases were introduced. This has commonly been referred to in blogs and other media as Calculation Scripts for ASO cubes. In many respects, this is a true statement. These are still in their infancy and they are certainly not as robust as a BSO Calculation Script. They are a start, a beginning point that Oracle will continue to build upon. The DBAG reveals the fact that Custom Calculations were created to "extend the analytic capabilities of Essbase by enabling the execution of recurring calculations on aggregate storage databases." These calculations can only target Level-0 cells and they are written using MDX. Once the file is created, these objects also have the .csc extension. In case you are curious, this .csc object cannot be run like a calculation script in a BSO cube. They can only be executed in one of three ways (none of which is a right-click in EAS):

- Using the aggregate storage version of the MaxL **execute calculation** statement
- Using the Essbase Application Programming Interface (API)
- Using Hyperion Calculation Manager to design and deploy to Enterprise Scheduling Services

See the "Sample Use Case for Custom Calculations" in the DBAG for more detailed information. Hence, while the object extension is familiar and the concept is familiar, Custom Calculations are not like anything you may have previously used. As they exist today, these will take some study and consideration to determine best use cases for them in ASO cubes.

A third object with a .csc extension in Essbase is a stored aggregation file. Later in this chapter we will discuss the process of saving off recommended aggregate views. The file created by this process has a .csc extension and it also is located in the database directory (the same location as the Calculation Script in a BSO cube). Three different objects with the same extension could be confusing if you do not understand ahead of time what you are creating.

Given these facts, what do you do with Calculation Scripts in an ASO conversion? Typically, you would evaluate the contents of the Calculation Script and determine how you will handle the existing process the script provides given the capability of the ASO cube. Calculation Scripts were often created to just aggregate the cube in a specific order. This will no longer be necessary with an ASO cube. Instead, you will have Solve Orders defined in the outline. The same statement can be made for scripts that were designed and used to perform back-calcs (calculations completed after aggregation in order to derive the correct mathematical answer). For any process that remains in the script, I would attempt to map them to member formulas, creating new members and formulas where appropriate. There are a large number of developers who put every single calculation they used in a BSO cube in the Calculation Script. They did not even attempt to create member formulas even when it was appropriate. Their rationale for using this method of coding was that they could better control the calculation outcome if it was in a script. For the few remaining complex tasks, like allocations, you may find the need to create one of the new Custom Calculations we discussed earlier in this section. Read up and carefully study the constraints in the DBAG before attempting to create a Custom Calculation. You may find you suddenly have the desire to make a member calculation (or some other process) work.

The conversion process from a BSO cube to an ASO cube is now essentially complete. (Well done. Now, load data and play with some of the advanced concepts from Chapter 7 by Dan Pressman.) There will still be a few miscellaneous tasks you will have to finish to prepare the cube for use:

- Set up security filters.
- Update provisioning of existing groups to point to the new cube.
- Shut down the old cube if you do not want it to be used (by deleting it or by removing provisioning; renaming it is not enough).
- Update batch processing scripts; many MaxL commands have an ASO version that will need to be used.
- Update user information or training guides if hierarchy structures were changed significantly.
- Update partitioning scripts (if applicable).

All in all, converting a cube from one kernel storage type to another is not such a terrible process, is it? This is a one-way metamorphosis. You can convert BSO to ASO, but you cannot convert ASO to BSO. That being said, if you think you might want to revert back to your old BSO cube at some point, you will want to archive off the contents of the database file prior to deleting the BSO application from the Essbase system.

5.4 WHAT ABOUT REPORTING CUBES?

In the discussion that was just completed regarding the converting of a BSO cube to an ASO cube, the situation was straightforward. I want to make the conversion and then get rid of the BSO cube completely. There are situations that arise, however, where this is not the case. Sometimes, a mechanism to allow faster reporting is what is needed. Nothing is being replaced or deleted. Some sample scenarios might include:

- An ASO calculation is too costly for large scale ad hoc reporting; to speed things up, a temporary BSO cube is used to calculate the data and then the result is extracted and loaded into an ASO reporting cube.
- A specified BSO cube is too slow for widespread ad hoc reporting because the cube is optimized for complex calculations; as with the first scenario, to speed things up, calculated data is extracted and loaded into an ASO reporting cube.

- Hybrid BSO/ASO Reporting (the desired result is a single cube to be used for comparative analysis) is achieved by partitioning a BSO cube with budgeting and forecasting data to an ASO reporting cube that is also partitioned to an ASO cube containing actuals data.

The one solitary fact that should be emerging from the haze is that the combination of these two storage kernels allows you to create a myriad of different design combinations to meet the requirements of your users. Hybrid solutions are becoming more common as developers and architects become more familiar with the strengths of ASO cubes. The decision on which technology should ultimately be used should be based on the requirements. The technology combination that will fulfill the requirements and requested functionality in the least amount of development time is what should be selected. Speed to market is becoming more critical in every reporting solution, especially in vertical industries like retail where the competition is stiff. Due to rapid shifts in market demands, solutions must be developed and implemented quickly. This makes the use of ASO cubes ideal in most designs.

5.5 WHAT GREAT THINGS CAN I ONLY DO WITH ASO CUBES?

5.5.1 Making a Cube Smarter through Use: Training a Cube

During the requirements-gathering phase, one of the areas for extensive consideration and exploration is: "How will this cube be queried?" While the developer does not care how the BSO cube will be queried because everything is aggregated during the default or custom calculations, this is not true of an ASO cube. Unlike a BSO calc script that creates the cube aggregations, ASO aggregations are created through a Wizard that is assisted by any one of many methods described in this chapter. If the developer knows the usage behaviors, the aggregations can be designed and implemented in a very optimal manner. Thus, it is helpful to try to gather hardcore detailed information on usage patterns and expectations. This is most useful if it can be related to hierarchical terms. Will most users (80/20 rule) query the most granular levels (level-0) of the data, or will querying summary information be more common and the querying of details will be the exception? This distinction is important because it affects what kind of work is done initially to determine appropriate aggregate views. It also determines the ongoing strategy recommendations for aggregating the cube (if any). Sometimes, no one seems to know this information. One cause for lack of concrete knowledge may be that the subject area is new, and no one understands exactly how the new information will be used. Another cause for lack of information might be that the correct group of individuals has not been interviewed. Someone knows the answer to these questions , just not the "someone" that has been interviewed up to this point in time.

There are several methods available to optimize query performance in ASO cubes (even if it is not known exactly what needs to be optimized). It is vital to state that these strategies are not an excuse or replacement for poor design. Review Pressman's excellent chapter (Chapter 7) on how ASO works to determine the best usage of these features within your cube design. That being said, utilization of one or more of these methods can assist the developer in achieving required performance Service Level Agreements (SLA) in addition to creating easily maintained high-performing aggregate processes. One of the more significant, but greatly underutilized, features of an ASO cube is its ability to become smarter through use and training. I am, of course, referring to Query

Tracking and the implementation of recommended views based on the collected usage data. To provide one example of how to utilize Query Tracking, this deployment strategy might be used to optimize aggregations for a cube that was reloaded weekly:

1. Create and load the cube, using the default out-of-the-box aggregation.
2. Turn on Query Tracking for Week 1.
3. Prior to updating the cube the next weekend, run the Design Aggregation Wizard to determine and save recommended aggregate views as a script.
4. Save the resulting script with a unique name.
5. Update the cube and aggregate using the saved aggregation script from Week 1.
6. Turn on Query Tracking for Week 2.
7. Repeat Steps 3 and 4.
8. Update the cube and aggregate using the new saved aggregation from Week 2.

Continue repeating this process for 4 to 12 weeks; the goal being to track actual usage for an entire quarter. In most corporations, weekly reports may differ from monthly reports, which are different yet again from quarterly reporting. Remember that one of the reasons to use Query Tracking is because no one could accurately define how the data would be queried. Discuss expectations with users prior to the go-live kick off. The users need to understand that the system may be slow to start (and it might be lightning fast), with a high likelihood that it will grow faster and more efficient at retrieving data with each additional week of usage and training.

If a strategy, such as the one described, above is employed, it is crucial that documentation is carefully kept and that statistics are appropriately gathered each week. The following suggestions may help define a good starting point:

- Save each aggregation script (using dates or week numbers in the name may be helpful).
- Gather statistics on average query times for each completed week; have a target SLA identified for comparison.
- Track aggregate size growth; while the loaded data may not take up much space, the aggregate views can start growing immensely in size.
- Track the total aggregate processing time; there is probably an acceptable limitation on the amount of time that can be spent processing aggregations based on server resource capacity and server resource availability.

There comes a point in ASO cubes where adding additional aggregates may provide diminishing returns. More is not always better. At the end of the 12 weeks of Query Tracking, if it can be determined that the best performance resulted after query tracking for week 8 was implemented, then use that script permanently in the weekly update process. It also might be discovered that while the best performance results occurred after week 12, the total processing time and space utilized exceeded acceptable thresholds. In this instance, go back to a previous week until a script is identified that best meets the performance SLA as well as resource capacity limits. Remember, very little actual work is occurring during this process. Allowing the system to track and determine suggestions is just utilizing a feature that is provided. Allowing this process to continue over an extended amount of time just provides better suggestions based on reality. This can be shortened or eliminated altogether if gathering data is not within defined time constraints.

To turn on Query Tracking follow these steps:

1. Load the cube and perform the default aggregation.
2. Right-click on the database > Select Query Tracking > Select Enable.

Query Tracking is now turned on. One thing to keep in mind is that when Query Tracking is turned on, Essbase will evaluate queries that include attribute dimension data and possibly will include attribute dimensions in the recommended aggregate view selections. This point is mentioned because the thought process regarding attribute dimensions has always been that they are "free" and have no resource cost when used. While this may be mostly true in BSO cubes, it is not true in ASO cubes. Pressman has an excellent conversation regarding this in Chapter 7 on understanding ASO cubes.

While Query tracking is turned on, there are some Essbase activities that will need to be avoided. The query tracking information will be lost if:

- Data is loaded or cleared.
- An aggregation is materialized (the aggregation is actually created, not just defined).
- The option is taken to clear aggregations.
- Query Tracking is turned off.

Leave Query Tracking enabled until after the Aggregation Design Wizard is run. Because this process can materialize an aggregation (if you select that option), the Wizard will turn the Query Tracking off.

Note: Don't prematurely run this just to see what has been gathered "so far" and then cancel out of the process. This will cause the tracking information gathered up to this point to be lost. You must complete the process once you start and materialize the views. If you do that, you can enable Query Tracking again and continue the process because you will have captured what was gathered up to the point in time when you got curious.

The Aggregation Design Wizard is accessed through EAS. To run the Aggregation Design Wizard:

1. Right-click on the database level > Select Design Aggregation.
2. In the Select Aggregation Task window, select the radio option to "Design, Materialize, and Save Aggregation" > Click Next.
3. In the Consider Existing Aggregate Views window, select the radio option to "Add to existing aggregate view selection" > Click Next.
4. In the Specify Stop Criteria for Selection Process window, select the radio option to "Select all recommended aggregate views" > Click Next.
5. In the Select Aggregate Views window, click on the checkbox at the bottom of the window to "Use query tracking data during view selection," then click the Start button.
6. When completed, the window will show the suggested views with an option to deselect any unwanted views if the query cost or database size is determined to be unsuitable (retaining all suggested views is typical but not optimal—see Chapter 7 on how to read the recommendation screen to best choose specific aggregations) > Click Next.

7. In the Save and Materialize Aggregation window, check the "Save Aggregation as" box and input a name. The checkbox to "Materialize aggregation" can also be selected although it is not required (selecting to materialize will update the cube aggregates immediately before exiting the Wizard) > Click Next.
8. A confirmation message that your aggregation was saved will appear > Click Finish.

The Wizard will close and the new aggregation script is saved and can be referenced in batch load and aggregation processes.

Another method for optimizing aggregates is to use User-defined views. When using this method, the user who is doing the defining is the administrator. They define information for each dimension. This information will sway how the views are selected during the aggregate process. To access this feature, open EAS and right-click on the outline to open it in the Outline Editor. Right-click on the dimension name and select the Information tab. Near the bottom of the screen, you will see the section for Hierarchy information. Click in the dropdown next to Level Usage for Aggregation, as shown in Figure 5.9, and select the option that best represents how this dimension should be considered in views. Only one can be selected, so go with the 80/20 rule.

For detailed information on each of these choices, and some interesting nuances of each, see the DBAG.

Query Hints are utilized in the final optimization method. Remembering that even the default aggregation provided within Essbase does not aggregate everything (in contrast to a BSO default Calc), Query Hints are another method to help the system determine what aggregate views will be most helpful when this cube is queried. There is not a great deal of documentation, blogging, or research on how well Query Hints do or do not work. After following them through several releases nonetheless, it can be noted that they continue to change. This speaks to the fact that they must work and that Oracle development sees some degree of value in continuing to provide this feature. Query Hints are created inside of the Outline Editor. Once an outline is opened, the third tab is Query Hints. Using Figure 5.10 as a reference, we can see creating a hint is very simple. Click on the provided space under the dimension name and select any member from the level of the dimension that will be queried (only one member is needed). Leaving an asterisk (*) indicates that any member from that dimension is as likely as any other to be queried.

In the example shown, one Query Hint was added to suggest that monthly data (Jan) at the summary product level-1 (Visual) across any market or account is a likely candidate for a view.

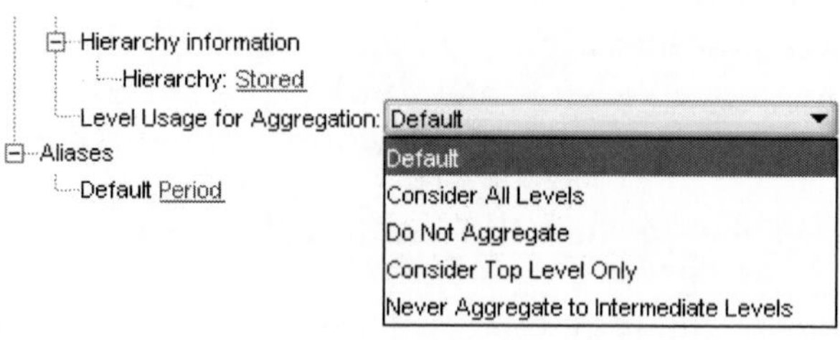

Figure 5.9 Level usage for Aggregation options. (From Oracle Essbase Administration Services. With permission.)

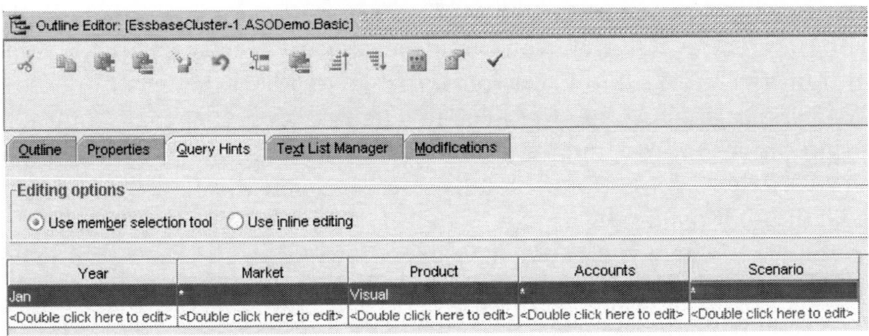

Figure 5.10 Creating a Query Hint. (From Oracle Essbase Administration Services. With permission.)

Note: Dynamic dimensions cannot be included in Query Hints and subsequent view selections. This is another supporting reason to choose Hierarchies Enabled instead of Dynamic.

You can create as many hint combinations as are applicable.

Three different methods have been discussed that can be used for optimizing aggregations. There is a hierarchy of precedence to how each one is considered when views are created, so never use all three:

1. Query Tracking (Usage-defined views) is considered first and overrides the other two.
2. User-defined views created from setting hierarchy properties is considered next and overrides Query Hints.
3. Query Hints is considered last and is not going to accomplish much if either of the previous two methods are employed.

5.5.2 Working with Slices

5.5.2.1 Data versus Aggregations The most exciting advancement to ASO cubes in the past four years without question has got to be the creation of Data Slices, which provides every Essbase developer the ability to do true incremental data loads and true regional data clears. Those two abilities totally change how ASO cubes are currently used, and offer new and exciting possibilities for how they might be used in the future. The reality of real-time or near real-time updates to ASO cubes is now within reach. To understand why this would create such stupefying excitement (it literally makes me giddy to discuss it), you would need to think back first to where ASO cubes have come from. In the first release of ASO cubes, what was the behavior of the cube if you did ANYTHING at all to it? Why, thanks for asking. The database would unceremoniously (and mostly without warning) just dump the data. This was frustrating beyond belief.

Picture yourself completing a benign task that you did all the time in BSO cubes; something simple, such as adding a new member to the metrics dimension. The member would be added, the formula completed, and off to Excel® you went to check the results. You whipped a query right up and it would come back as #MISSING. "Hmmm," you would say, "I must have done something wrong in my MDX statement (since, of course, I am brand new to this)." Accordingly, you would go look at the formula and study its construction, going back and forth with MDX references before finally determining that it was written correctly. "Hmmm," you would pause again, "I must have done something wrong with my query." Back to Excel you would go to adjust the query only to have it return #MISSING again. Off you would go to database properties to do some checking on your aggregations only to find that you have 0 cells loaded and 0 cells aggregated on this cube. "What the ...," you would literally scream, "I hate this tool. It just dumped the data." Yep it did—all the time.

That is the place where ASO cube developers started—with a new technology that carried with it a great deal of excitement, but within a tool that felt very fragile. If you disturbed the cube in almost any way, the data had to be reloaded. Those early days in ASO cube development found developers creating load files that needed no Load rules so that reloads were quick and easy, because they were done over and over and over again. It certainly is no wonder that many shunned this new storage kernel after only a few attempts to use it.

Fast forward to present day ASO cube development. Now, not only can you update dimensionality without disturbing the data, you can incrementally update the database without disturbing the main dataset by using Data Slices. Incremental data load times are proportionate to the size of the data that is being loaded, not to the size of the existing database and this is a very significant differentiation. Just because the database is enormous does not mean adding data to it will take an excessive amount of time. Present day, not only can you incrementally update the data, but you do not have to rerun the aggregations because they update automatically as needed. The system does it for you. How fantastic is that? I feel a bit like I am in a television infomercial right now and want to yell "KABOOM." Seriously, that is how exciting this new development in ASO cube processing is.

This section will walk through a sequential explanation of how Data Slices work, and the steps involved in using them in a summary fashion. Once that is completed, the journey will continue by exploring a week of time and processing in a real-life production set of cubes that are using these specific techniques (this is very fresh, as those cubes went into production while this book was being written). This will allow for complete access to production code, production situations, and production pros and cons. In addition, some assurance can be felt in the knowledge that these strategies and technologies are currently being used successfully and, hopefully, that knowledge will help to alleviate any fears or angst over trying it out.

The usage of Data Slices is a very simple concept. In its most basic form, the steps to use a Data Slice include:

- Data is loaded into the main part of the database and aggregated using normal processes.
- A new load is defined and when the data is loaded from the buffer, the system is told to situate it next to the existing database as a Data Slice, instead of merging it directly into the existing database.
- When the Data Slice is loaded, the system automatically creates the required views for that slice and the system completes this task prior to making the new Data Slice visible to user queries.
- Multiple slices can be added during the same process.
- Eventually, query performance will degrade as the slices pile up; a fact that will be seen in the statistics provided in EAS on the cost of querying the slices.

- Once it is determined that querying the slices is too expensive, there are two options to resolve this issue:
  - Merge together the incremental slices into a single incremental slice; or
  - Merge all of the slices with the existing database to recreate a single unit
- Aggregations will be dropped and the merge process completed (no worries, the system will issue a reminder if the aggregations were not dropped before the process was started).

The decision regarding which of these two options is the best choice is based on numerous factors that might include size of the main database and current management process for the cube as a whole. There are many factors to consider that are unique to each and every installation.

5.5.2.2 Use Case Example This use case example is real and will discuss (demonstrate where appropriate) and provide production code for each of the following tasks:

- Creating the main database
- Creating a Slice
- Updating dimensions
- Merging Slices
- Clearing Slices

Note: I felt it was incredibly important in this section to provide real production code as we found a significant amount of issues with code that we tried to use from various sources when we were first beginning to use Data Slices. I will say that we were in an early release of this feature and the newer documentation (all sources) appears to be much more accurate and complete than the sources that we were using.

This use case example involves a set of five cubes being used in retail for analysis (sorry in advance about having to be so generic in descriptions; it would be a lot more interesting to be able to disclose the details). The requirements for this implementation had some unique characteristics that no previous implementation had:

1. Essbase was to be the database of record; data from 25 disparate sources would be provided. The staging tables would hold one week only and then be cleared. No other database in the corporate data warehouse would contain the complete two years of history plus the one year building.
2. The data would need to exist at a very granular level for one dimension; this would create a dimension that went down six levels and had a million plus members (with potential for growth).
3. Weekly load volumes were estimated at 50 million records to start, growing to approximately 300 million records when the implementation was fully deployed.
4. Most data would be created in the staging area on the weekend, but an additional data load to the staging area would occur on Monday and on Thursday. This data would need to be loaded while the cube was in use, i.e., no downtime for the load and aggregation process; the cubes would need to be up Monday through Friday.

5. Dimensional updates would be on the weekends only (the cubes could be taken offline at that time).
6. Essbase Classic Add-In Templates would be used for reporting; no ad hoc reporting (thank you) and the SLA for report retrievals was less than 30 seconds.

After reviewing these requirements, frankly, I was scared and a little bit leery of whether this could even be done with Essbase. Mind you, I was well past those early skeptical days I discussed at the beginning of this chapter. I knew what could be done with ASO cubes, but this exceeded anything I had ever attempted. I did not want to be cutting edge. The project was too high profile to end up not working. So, what were the concerns? First, being the database of record was very concerning, especially since it looked like it was going to be a very large database. Not having a corporate data warehouse to fall back on to reload all of history, should something go wrong, was very scary. Also, Essbase being the database of record places some additional pressures and responsibilities on me as the architect. For instance, it is the architect's job to design a fail-proof back-up plan so that in every instance the data is safe and can be easily recovered. Another responsibility is to make sure there is a method predetermined for extracting the data if any down-stream systems later determine that they need this data. The second concern was the size of the largest dimension. I had never worked with a million member dimension in a cube; I had only read about them in case studies and white papers. I could not find anyone amongst my peers using something this large in real life. I had no idea what to expect, and no one to ask. The final concern was that, like it or not, I was going to be on the cutting edge (no, bleeding edge) of relatively new technology. I was going to have to take a leap of faith and use these new Data Slices in my design to make this all work. What about volume? No, I had already done cubes with as much volume (or more), so the volume was not a worry. I knew Essbase could handle that. To try and mitigate some of these concerns (and risks), I did two things before I committed to this implementation.

First, I built a Proof of Concept (POC) using a six-dimension model with 10 million members in the largest dimension and 24 metrics. This was pretty close to what I understood was needed. This model was loaded with two years of data. Existing elements in the data warehouse were used to provide real distribution within the ASO cube. We felt this would make the queries (using default aggregations only) as close to the final experience as was possible. The results were simply astounding. The speed with which we could query this cube blew our socks off. No one could actually even believe it. Completing this POC confirmed two critical pieces of information:

1. The existing shared platform could handle this size of a cube (although I would eventually order more memory and disk space).
2. There was a good chance the SLAs being requested could be met (barring anything dramatic changing in the rollout, like 10 dimensions instead of 6, or 200 metrics instead of 24 in the final design).

The second thing I did to try and mitigate my risk was to call my Oracle partners. I asked that they please find me at least one company that had a model this big running in production. Oh, and did I mention I preferred the reference also be running Essbase on AIX? I did not need to talk to them (there can be much political angst when you make that kind of request), I just wanted an outline of their dimensionality (number of members in each dimension) and an assurance that they were running in production.

It took them a few days to come back to me and they found exactly one. This allowed me the freedom to tell my management (with some modicum of honesty) that I was not the first person to do this.

The final solution had five cubes. One cube held the million member dimension; the rest were all significantly smaller. For clarity and ease of reference, this case study will just reference the largest cube—cubel—and just one of the smaller cubes—cube2—because the small ones were all handled in exactly the same manner. For a reference point, Table 5.2 provides the dimensionality and member counts for cubel.

In contrast, Table 5.3 reflects dimensionality and member counts of cube2 (the largest of the four smaller cubes).

The process that was built is fully scripted in shell scripts calling MaxL commands. Running on an AIX LPAR, the server is a dual core 64-bit with three (3) CPU and 28 Gb of memory. None of the processes described are done manually; everything is fully automated, although any of it can be run on demand as needed. Assuming that the first week has occurred already, the weekly process that was put into place is as follows:

- Saturday Morning:
  - Drop aggregations on cubel and cube2.
  - Export Data on cubel and cube2.
  - Merge Slices.
  - Re-aggregate cube2.
- Sunday Morning:
  - Rebuild Dimensions on cubel and cube2.
  - Aggregate cubel.

Table 5.2 Case Study Cubel Dimension Members and Counts

Dimensions of cubel	Total	Stored
Metrics	171	169
Dimension1	215	215
Dimension2	6	6
Dimension3	25	11
Dimension4	228	228
Dimension5	1159	1148
Dimension 6	1039504	843779

Table 5.3 Case Study Cube2 Dimension and Member Counts

Dimensions of cube2	Total	Stored
Metrics	41	40
Dimension1	215	215
Dimension2	6	6
Dimension3	25	11
Dimension4	228	228
Dimension5	1159	1148
Dimension 6	480252	479614

- Sunday Afternoon:
  - Add Current Week Data Slices to cube1 and cube2.
- Monday Morning:
  - Add Data Slice to cube2.
- Thursday Evening:
  - Add Data Slice to cube2.
- Saturday Morning: Start the Process All Over Again.

This is the final process and in its current state, it is not exactly how it existed when it was originally put into production. A few steps had to be altered as discoveries were made on what does and does not work well with slices in real life with production volumes. A review of this information and discovery process is included in the next few pages. In addition, as each component of the process is discussed, the code relevant to that part of the process is also provided.

5.5.2.2.1 The Saturday Morning Process In the original deployment, the starting concept was how very cool it would be to keep the aggregations each week and *not* have to rebuild them. After all, this is an advantage of using Data Slices, and aggregations take up the most time in the ASO cube-building process. In real life, there were two complications with keeping the aggregations. The first complication was that the system required you to drop the aggregations to merge the slices. Because the team had no idea how long you could legitimately go without merging slices before performance was affected, and the process needed to be automated, and there was an entire weekend that could be used for processing, proceeding with caution and merging weekly seemed to be the best solution. The second complication was more practical: dimension builds take forever and a day if you perform them on a large aggregated cube. It is really not the dimension build that takes so long, but the restructure. This was an initial mistake that was made out of ignorance. In the original process, the reaggregation of all the cubes was done on Saturday nights, and the dimension builds were completed on Sunday mornings when the files were available. On cube1 the dimension builds were excessive even when the cube had only one or two weeks of data, and they got worse as data was added. Each week that was added caused the build and restructure process to extend one to two hours more. It was very quickly recognized that it would not take many weeks to blow the timeline right out of the water, and by year's end this step in the weekly update would be taking until Wednesday to finish. Hence, a change was made to the process to accommodate these real life lessons learned. The small cubes are still aggregated on Saturday because the system can handle the time these take from a resource perspective. The servers are much busier on Sundays and getting the small cubes out of the way is one less task that has to be done. The code used to complete the first Saturday task to drop the aggregations is:

```
alter database ${APP_NAME}.${DB_NAME} clear aggregates;
```

The second task on Saturday mornings is to export the data. The export is a critical part of the disaster recovery (DR) plan and it has already been implemented several times. Essentially, if the ETL (extract, transform, and load) folks provide the wrong data and too many steps are processed, there may come a moment that the need to revert back to the starting point is identified. The lesson that was learned the hard way has been that although calculations can be written to clear specific cube regions, on cube1, in particular, it is much faster in some instances to reload the cube to that week's starting point on Saturday morning and reprocess it completely. The exports are also a key part of the DR plan, if the primary backups fail for some reason. If the cube is of any size at all, dropping the aggregates seems to positively affect the export speed. The code used to complete the second Saturday task to export the data is:

```
export database ${APP_NAME}.${DB_NAME} level0 data to data_file
'${APP_NAME}.export.txt';
```

The third task on Saturday morning is to merge the data slices. While the export might be slightly more efficient after the merge, the gains in efficiency did not warrant the assumed risk. Essentially, the export needs to be completed prior to altering the cube in any significant way to avoid risk of any type. The code used to complete the third Saturday task to merge all data slices into the main data slice is:

```
alter database ${APP_NAME}.${DB_NAME} merge all data;
```

It is good to note here that there are options with regards to how data is merged. There is another variant of the command to merge all data slices into the main slice and remove zero values:

```
alter database ${APP_NAME}.${DB_NAME} merge all data remove_zero_
values;
```

In this use case, that variation of the command can never be used because meaningful zeros are loaded into the database. It would be detrimental, to say the least, to remove those zeros programmatically.

There is also a variant of the command to merge the incremental data slices into a single slice:

```
alter database ${APP_NAME}.${DB_NAME} merge incremental data;
```

While this might be useful in other strategies, it is not in this particular use case because the merge was happening every Saturday. To merge and create smaller incremental Data Slices that would later have to be merged again was too many steps, and difficult to script in an automated fashion. Do not forget that merging slices requires the same security privileges that are needed for loading data. This makes sense because the structure of the data is being altered in a significant way. Statistics regarding the slices and incremental data are provided in EAS.

1. Open EAS.
2. Drill down to the database level of the cube.
3. Right-click on the database and select Edit > Properties.
4. Select the Statistics Tab.

Figure 5.11 shows a sampling of the statistics for cube1 after the weekly processing is completed and right before the Saturday morning tasks have started.

This is an excellent place to point out a small curiosity that was discovered while working with Data Slices. One of the things that caused extreme confusion in the

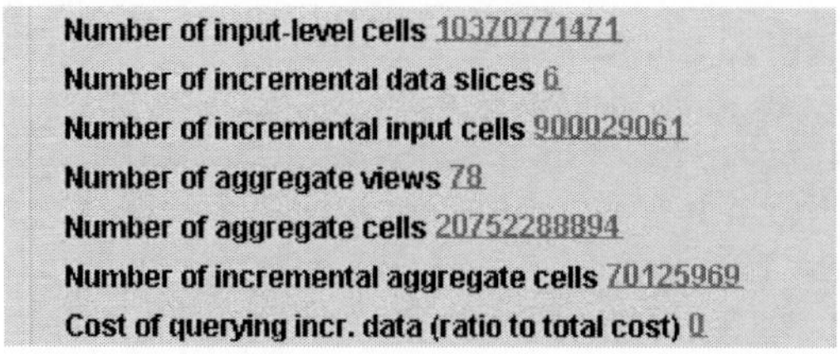

Number of input-level cells 10370771471
Number of incremental data slices 6
Number of incremental input cells 900029061
Number of aggregate views 78
Number of aggregate cells 20752288894
Number of incremental aggregate cells 70125969
Cost of querying incr. data (ratio to total cost) 0

Figure 5.11 Use Case cube1 input and aggregations statistics. (From Oracle Essbase Administration Services. With permission.)

Table 5.4 Example of Data Slice Merging Behavior by Cell Count

Load #	Cell Count	Result
1	75,000	1 Slice with 75,000 cells
2	400,000	1 Slice with 475,00 cells (merged because slice one had less than 100,000 cells)
3	1,000,000	2 Slices; 1 with 1,000,000 cells and 1 with 475,000 cells (nothing was merged because load #3 is greater than two times larger than the existing slice)
4	300,000	2 Slices; 1 with 1,000,000 cells and 1 with 775,000 cells (load 4 is merged with loads 1 and 2 because that slice is less than 2 times the size of the new slice)

beginning was how Essbase counts slices. Ten separate loads would be executed with the expectation that they would result in 10 slices of data. This did not happen. Well, sometimes it happened … . Sometimes there would be eight slices, sometimes nine, and other times seven. This was very perplexing. What was later discovered was that Essbase helps (on its own) to make the system as optimal as possible. When a new data slice is loaded, it scans the incremental Data Slices and makes a decision on whether to automatically merge one or more incremental slices with the new Data Slice. According to the DBAG, "… to qualify for an automatic merge, a slice must be smaller than 100,000 cells or smaller than two times the size of the new slice. Slices larger than 5,000,000 cells are never automatically merged." It was so good to realize this was a built-in feature, and not that basic math had somehow suddenly become elusive. Perhaps the mathematical example in Table 5.4 will help make this concept even more concrete.

In the end, it became an accepted fact that Essbase manages Data Slices the way it needs to in order to be the most efficient. Understanding what it was doing, however, did create an audible sigh of relief in the room.

The final task on Saturday morning is to reaggregate cube2. As was discussed, the four small cubes are still aggregated on Saturdays because there is time and resource availability. Additionally, they are small enough that the dimension build and restructure times are not as grossly affected as they are with cube1. Reaggregating will employ whatever aggregate strategy was developed for the cube. That will typically be either:

- Default aggregation
- Aggregation based on a specified amount of disk space
- Aggregation based on usage-tracking with a specified saved view

The code used to complete the fourth Saturday task to reaggregate the cubes using the default aggregation is:

```
execute aggregate process on database ${APP_NAME}.${DB_NAME};
```

5.5.2.2.2 The Sunday Morning Process Updating the dimensions cannot occur until Sunday morning because that is when the data warehouse updates occur. There is nothing special about building the dimensions. The cube1 process would be considered a normal dimension build process. The cube2 process might be considered abnormal by some because it has aggregations in place already. The code used to complete the first Sunday morning task to build dimensions is:

```
import database ${APP_NAME}.${DB_NAME} dimensions
connect as ${USER}identified by '${PWD}' using server rules_file
'${LD_RULE1}',
connect as ${USER}identified by '${PWD}' using server rules_file
'${LD_RULE2}'
on error append to '${ESS_ERROUT}';
```

The second task for Sunday Morning is reaggregating cube1 after the dimension builds have completed. Cube1 has a custom view script built through the Query Tracking techniques described earlier in Section 6.5.1. The code used to complete the second Sunday morning task to execute this custom aggregation is:

```
execute aggregate build on database ${APP_NAME}.${DB_NAME} using
view_file '${AGG_VIEW}';
```

5.5.2.2.3 The Sunday Afternoon Process The base cubes are now ready to have the new week of data loaded. This data is loaded as one or more Data Slices. As was previously indicated in this use case, there are a significant number of data sources so each cube has at least five data loads. They all use a similar process:

- A load buffer is created.
- One or more loads are imported into that buffer.
- The buffer is loaded as a slice.

The code used to complete the Sunday afternoon task to load data is:

```
alter database ${APP_NAME}.${DB_NAME} initialize load_buffer with
buffer_id 1
      resource_usage 1.0 property ignore_missing_values;
import database ${APP_NAME}.${DB_NAME} data connect as ${USER}
identified by '${PWD}'
      using server rules_file ${LD_RULE} to load_buffer with
      buffer_id 1
      on error write to '${ESS_ERROR_DIR}${JOB_FILE_PREFIX}.${APP_
      NAME}.${LD_RULE}.err';
import database ${APP_NAME}.${DB_NAME} data from load_buffer with
buffer_id 1 create slice;
```

This is a good place to note that there are additional options with the create slice syntax as well. Using the statement "override values create slice" will replace all #MISSING values with zeros. This option can be much slower than using the add values or subtract values options.

5.5.2.2.4 The Monday and Thursday Loads The remainder of the processing includes the Monday and Thursday loads. The methods used to perform these loads are no different than the Sunday afternoon loads, which were described previously. The great thing to mention is that the Monday and Thursday data files are very small (compared to the Sunday files) and they load in very quickly, building the required aggregate views in a flash. This does not disrupt the users at all. Essbase does not allow the data to be used until the aggregate updates are complete, so there are absolutely no worries over users accessing data that is invalid or is only partially complete. All in all, once it was thoroughly understood, this process was fairly easy to implement and deploy.

"So what's the catch?" Yes, there is always something that is not so easy. With Data Slices, the thing that is not so easy is fixing slices if they are wrong. Another challenge is how to go about deleting slices. One of the frustrating things early on was the fact that a slice cannot be identified by a name. Wouldn't it be nice if you could name a slice, e.g., this is my "budget" slice, and then manipulate the slice by name? That is not actually possible (as you may have guessed by now). How are corrections and changes made, especially if these corrections need to be made prior to merging the results into the main database? In the end, several different strategies had to be developed. The strategy that was deployed depended on what specifically was wrong, when it was caught, and what data existed to work with.

In the most extreme case, if the entire week's processing is in question, the safest path is to rebuild the cube from the exports taken the previous Saturday and just rerun the entire process after the staging tables have been fixed using the exports created in the DR process. This assumes that there are staging tables to work with, and that another week has not completely passed. This is a simple solution, easy to implement, and virtually risk free. This solution has already been implemented twice and it works exceptionally well. While it is an annoyance, it is not an issue.

There are two commands built into ASO that can be used to facilitate making corrections. The first command is at the database level and is not one that would be used in this use case because the ability to reload any of the history except for the current week is not an option. The command, for future reference, is:

```
import database ${APP_NAME}.${DB_NAME} data from load_buffer with
buffer_id 1 override all data;
```

This import command would replace the contents of the entire database. The second command is appropriate for this use case. If there are six incremental Data Slices when weekly processing is complete, and they all need to be "deleted" so the process can be started over, then this is the command that would be used. The first load would be prepared, and then the script would be altered for that load as follows:

```
import database ${APP_NAME}.${DB_NAME} data from load_buffer with
buffer_id 1 override incremental data;
```

This import command (using the override statement) will replace all six incremental slices with the new Data Slice. The subsequent loads can all be rerun using the original syntax. Aggregations are adjusted automatically, so this is not an issue that needs to be addressed.

That is a good solution when all six slices need to be replaced. What can be done to fix just one Data Slice? Is there anything built in for that situation? Yes and no. One solution that has been implemented with success is to load the original file with a subtract values statement. This requires that the original data is available for use in the reload (they need to have not already fixed the staging table):

```
import database ${APP_NAME}.${DB_NAME} data from load_buffer with
buffer_id 1 subtract values create slice;
```

While this process does create an additional slice, it reverses out the values and then the reload of the new corrected data creates yet another slice. When the merge is done there could conceivably be a few extra zeros in the database, but in this use case, there are so many zeros already this is probably not an issue.

What about fixing data once the bad data has been merged into the main database? The solution to this problem is no doubt the second greatest addition to ASO cube capabilities in the last few releases. In the documentation, this feature is described as "Clearing Data from Specific Regions of Aggregate Storage Databases." This was a remarkable advancement for ASO cubes and the strength of this feature cannot be touted highly enough. Again, understanding what was originally done may help prove this point. Up until the first release offering this feature, if existing data in a cube needed to be changed, a process similar to this would have to be implemented:

1. Extract the "bad data" using a Report Script.
2. Clear the "bad data" intersections by taking the extract file and reloading it (to get all the proper intersections where the "bad data" lived), replacing the existing data values with #MISSING.
3. Load the new "good data."

I actually have run this process for years because it was the only option available. It works well, but on a large cube, it could take as much as six hours to fully process.

Fast-forward to present day and watch the number of steps go down. Another great thing about this new process for clearing data is that the data is physically removed from the database. Using the old method, intersections were not removed; their values were simply replaced with #MISSING values. In light of what has already been revealed with regard to Data Slices, there are a number of things to keep in mind when working with the clearing process.

To use the clear data region statement, a specific region of the database where the clear is to occur must be identified as an "MDX set expression." It is a good idea to write an MDX Query using the correct set expression to confirm the records it retrieves are the records to be deleted. Once the set expression works in a query, then it can be executed in the clear data region statement.

The second thing to keep in mind is that a number of things will automatically happen if there are multiple slices in the cube when this command is issued. The system will:

- Merge the slices
- Clear the specified region
- Rematerialize all aggregate views

If this command were issued on cube1 from the use case, the total time might be as much as six hours to process completely. Keep this in mind before proceeding and make sure there is a sufficient window and resources to process the request. Because this can be a destructive process, and a disaster if not done correctly, it would be a prudent move to make a copy of the cube and try it on the copy. The physical version of the command would be as follows if the desired result is to clear all of the data for a specific week (in this case week 48):

```
alter database ${APP_NAME}.${DB_NAME} clear data in region
'{2011W48}' physical;
```

The logical version of the "clear data in region" command works a little bit differently. Instead of actually physically clearing the data from database, the input cells are written to a new Data Slice with reversing values (sound familiar?). This results in zeros for the region that is to be cleared. A warning: This could be an issue if you have formulas that are looking for #MISSING values in "empty cells" and an adjustment of the formulas may be required. The code is the same except the physical parameter is removed:

```
alter database ${APP_NAME}.${DB_NAME} clear data in region
'{2011W48}';
```

Additionally, the logical method does not alter any existing data slices (unless the slices are involved in the region to be cleared). It is expected that the administrator will get rid of these zeros when the merge process is run by using the remove zero syntax discussed earlier. As can be seen from the high degree of integration, this new clear data in region command is an integral part of the Data Slices logic. There are some additional rules and warnings in the DBAG, but this is enough to get started on using what I consider to be the most significant improvement in ASO cubes since they first came out. Happy Slicing.

5.6 SO WHAT GREAT THINGS CAN I DO WITH BOTH ASO AND BSO CUBES?

5.6.1 Extreme Partitioning

Within Essbase, there are three types of partitions available. Each type has a specific purpose or task that it helps the developer to achieve. In the order of frequency of use (most to least), the types of partitions (including a summary description) include:

- Transparent Partition: This partition type typically stores no data in the Target cube (although it can) and is used to allow the user seamless access to multiple Source cubes from a single Target cube; the Source cubes may be on one or more servers.
- Replicated Partition: This partition type allows the developer to copy portions of Source cubes to Target cubes; as the name indicates, its sole purpose is to replicate data.
- Linked Partition: This little-used partition type navigates the user from a cell in one Source cube to a cell in a Target cube; dimensionality is typically quite different between the two cubes providing the user with a different point of view for the same data.

Starting with late version 7.x up to the newest releases of 11.1.2.x, how Essbase handles the use of partitioning with ASO cubes has dramatically changed. In the late version 7, if a partitioning source to target table had existed, it would have looked like Table 5.5.

As indicated by the source and target cells in bold, there were not very many combinations of partitioning that included ASO cubes that were valid. The fact is that Oracle did not even bother with a chart in the DBAG (even in version 9.3.1) because what could be done with ASO cubes in partitions had not changed. A lot of time was spent writing up how you could create write-back applications for ASO cubes by creating a transparent partition between a Source ASO cube and a Target BSO cube. They tried, then and now, to sell everyone on how efficient this would be—decreasing calculations and reducing the size of the database. Did anyone actually implement this as a solution for write-back? If it was implemented in this fashion, it certainly was not wide-spread.

Fast-forward to today and the most recent version, and that same partitioning source to target table would now look like Table 5.6.

Table 5.5 Version 7.x Partition Capabilities (4 Options)

Partition Type	Source	Target
Replicated	Block Storage	Block Storage
	Aggregate Storage	Block Storage
	Aggregate Storage	Aggregate Storage
	Block Storage	Aggregate Storage
Transparent	Block Storage	Block Storage
	Aggregate Storage	Block Storage
	Aggregate Storage	Aggregate Storage
	Block Storage	Aggregate Storage
Linked	Block Storage	Block Storage
	Aggregate Storage	Block Storage
	Aggregate Storage	Aggregate Storage
	Block Storage	Aggregate Storage

Table 5.6 Version 11.1.2.x Partitioning Capabilities (10 Options)

Partition Type	Source	Target
Replicated	Block Storage	Block Storage
	Aggregate Storage	Block Storage
	Aggregate Storage	Aggregate Storage
	Block Storage	Aggregate Storage
Transparent	Block Storage	Block Storage
	Aggregate Storage	Block Storage
	Aggregate Storage	Aggregate Storage
	Block Storage	Aggregate Storage
Linked	Block Storage	Block Storage
	Aggregate Storage	Block Storage
	Aggregate Storage	Aggregate Storage
	Block Storage	Aggregate Storage

With the exception of Replicated Partitions, you can now use partitioning in all directions between ASO and BSO cubes. This greatly enhances solution possibilities for ASO cubes. It is imperative to remember that partitioning combinations with ASO cubes do not always work exactly the same as when you use BSO cubes.

The following is an example of behavior I have tested and verified myself. How this works surprised me a bit because, technically, I could not explain why.

- BSO cube A = Actuals Data.
- BSO cube B = Budget Data.
- I create a transparent partition from BSO cube B (Source) to BSO cube A (Target) based on the Scenario of Budget; the partition is created with no errors or warnings.

When I query the BSO cube A I can see both Actuals and Budget Data. This is the expected result. Now I change the Scenario:

- ASO cube A = Actuals Data.
- ASO cube B = Budget Data.
- I create a transparent partition from ASO cube B (Source) to ASO cube A (Target) based on the Scenario of Budget; the partition is created with the warning "The Essbase cube has data, which will not be considered during query time."

When I query the ASO cube A, I can only see Budget Data–Actuals Data returns all #MISSING. This is not an expected result because there is not an overlap of the partition. I have to assume this is not a bug because I was given a warning message that accurately anticipated what would happen if I proceeded with the partition. None of the data in the ASO cube A can be queried. It is as if it is not there. So, I change the Scenario again:

- ASO cube P = Empty Partition cube—No Data.
- ASO cube A = Actuals Data.
- ASO cube B = Budget Data.
- I create a transparent partition from ASO cube B (Source) to ASO cube P (Target) based on the Scenario of Budget; the partition is created with no errors or warnings.
- I create a transparent partition from ASO cube A (Source) to ASO cube P (Target) based on the Scenario of Actual; the partition is created with no errors or warnings.

When I query the ASO cube P, I can see both Actual and Budget Data. This is the expected result. The lesson learned from this is that ASO cubes cannot act as a Target *and* provide data as a Source. When made a Target, the ability to provide data in a query is invalidated. Effectively, this means that ASO Target cubes should always be empty. They should never have data in them. If they do have data, it will not be able to be queried once the partition is created making it a target. Although this behavior is not the same as that of a BSO cube, it is easy enough to work around once you understand it.

If partitioning is something you have never considered in your designs, it should be. I have not built a BI solution in the past 10 years that did not invoke partitioning. Some of my counterparts may scoff at that statement, but when utilized correctly, transparent partitioning, in particular, is an extremely powerful tool. This tool is something that can often help you achieve:

- Smaller databases (which translates to faster databases in most cases).
- Faster loads (with subject areas broken up you can simultaneously load more).
- Shared data between subject areas (same database can be partitioned to multiple targets).
- Improved scalability (databases can be split across processors, or even servers).

On the other hand, you will not want to use partitioning when:

- There are identified network constraints in your organization; partitioning just worsens these even if the partitions are on the same server.
- Complex calculations exist that require knowledge of the total (at top of the house); a workaround can be developed for this issue, but you will need to do something to assist Essbase.
- Databases are not in the same Unicode mode or language; while I have never had this occur, I assume in a multinational corporation the circumstance certainly could exist.

A real life example might be of interest. In my current work place, I have a subject area for Retail Analytics. The users required a 19-dimension model that had 8 Scenarios. The four largest dimensions have 8500, 1500, 750, and 450 members with the remaining dimensions each having less than 50 and 9 of those having less than 10 members each. Some of the data is reloaded weekly, and some of the data is updated nightly. ASO cubes were used to meet the requirements of the 19 dimensions. The resulting cube distribution is as follows:

- Six ASO cubes hold actuals scenario data with a custom cube to provide it with top of the house totals (this is my work-around cube needed due to the weakness indicated previously of handling top of the house calculations).
- Six ASO cubes hold other scenarios: one scenario per cube to reflect varying refresh rates (I found it is easier to control refreshes and updates if they are segregated).
- Four ASO cubes hold custom calculations; one metric per cube due to their complexity and required refresh rates.
- One BSO cube ties it all together; the other 16 cubes are partitioned to this one; this cube holds a minimal amount of data as well and performs as few calculations as necessary to fulfill all requirements.

This was created after another group had tried unsuccessfully to build just a portion of this as a single cube. Performance was awful and the refresh time was exceeding the weekend window. Nightly refreshes of required data were completely out of consideration. By simply breaking things up in logical places that could be easily partitioned back together for the user, the whole solution fell into place. If a scenario needs updates or repairs, it can be removed from the partition so the rest of the solution is still usable, while this segment of the solution is being addressed. When the system needs to be down for maintenance, it is simple to pull the 1 BSO partition out of the group provisioning so that no one can access the cubes while they are under maintenance. I am obviously a huge fan of partitioning. Contrary to popular belief, it does not slow down user queries, unless it is built improperly. An improperly constructed partition can absolutely destroy performance; knowledge and experience are always helpful as you work with this tool. Do not be afraid to think out of the box with designs. There are enough tools within Essbase to construct very elegant solutions without jamming square pegs in round holes.

5.6.2 Typed Measures: Text and Date Measures

The introduction of Typed Measures in version 11.1.1.1 of Essbase was met with a great deal of excitement amongst cube developers. Although this functionality is available to both ASO and BSO cubes, it is included in this chapter section because I think it is one the great things you can do with an ASO cube. An effort will be made to make distinction where appropriate of features that are only ASO or BSO capable. The term *Typed Measures* actually refers to a collection of new functionality, which is sometimes confusing in the literature as only parts of this collection are presented. There are three distinct features within Typed Measures:

1. Cell contents of numeric type measures can be associated with format strings (this one is often left out when typed measures are discussed).
2. Text Measures can be created (also called Text Metrics in various places).
3. Date Measures can be created (also referred to as Date Metrics).

This section will walk through examples of how to use each of these Typed Measures with the cubes discussed earlier in this chapter.

In the past, Attribute Dimensions would have been used to accomplish what seems like the same thing. So, why not just use Attribute Dimensions? The biggest reason is because an attribute dimension cannot deliver a cell value that is textual or is a date. It can only deliver a number and associate it with an outline member. It is somewhat of an understatement to say how cool it is to run a report and have dates appear in the retrieval cells. Maybe fantastic is a more accurate term. For years, cubes have been manipulated to death to do Human Resources (HR) analytics. The need to store the hire date, the termination date, the anniversary date, etc., was just downright painful to manipulate and force a cube to do. If the dates needed to be smart and do math (length of employment as of today, for instance), it went from painful to excruciating. It could be done, but it was not easy. In the end, it was often decided that perhaps that HR cube ought to just be a relational database and use some sort of SQL (structured query language) front-end to deliver the reporting and analytics. Typed Measures changes all of that.

To use any of the three features available in Typed Measures, the first step is to activate the outline to enable Typed Measures. In EAS, open the outline in Outline Editor. On the Properties Tab, change the Typed Measures Enabled to true (it is false by default). Once this is done, the three different features available with Typed Measures can be used. Remember that once the outline has this feature enabled, it cannot be set back to false (turned off). The drop down that was used to set the value to true will no longer be available.

The first feature allows the developer to present strings of information (based on the numeric values) instead of numeric values, to the report consumer. These have to be created using an MdxFormat statement. For example, create a member called "Sales Range." If using a BSO cube, make the member dynamic and input the simple formula:

```
"Sales";
```

Right-click on the created member and in the Associate format string input the following:

```
MdxFormat(IIF(CellValue()<0, "Sales Need to Increase", "Sales are
Great!"))
```

When a query is run, if the Sales value is less than zero then the message "Sales Need to Increase" will be displayed. Otherwise, "Sales are Great!" will be displayed. While this is a trivial example, it is easy to see what an easy to use and powerful analytic feature this can be. Instead of displaying a number, the report can display a more meaningful textual string in its place (without altering the original number; this is just a format of the number). Let's imagine that satisfaction rankings for customers are captured with a rank value of 1 to 10, with 1 being low and 10 being high. Instead of displaying these as values, we could convert the values to three ranges: Highly Satisfied (8–10), Neutral (4–7), and Dissatisfied (1–3). Now instead of the report displaying a series of numeric values, it can display their textual equivalents. These can be tied to conditional formatting, and, *voila*, I created a stoplight report in seconds. In this instance, in a BSO cube, the satisfaction ranking could be averaged as it was aggregated and these formatted values will appear at every level. Because an ASO cube cannot do anything but sum the values (no custom aggregations), this is not as helpful and is something to be considered when using them. The upper level results may not be what is desired and are difficult to control.

While format strings have great potential, there are some limitations to keep in mind:

- Format strings cannot be used across partitions.
- Shared members (including implied shared members) have the same format string as the member they are based on.
- Essbase ignores invalid format strings and outlines can be saved with invalid strings.

These apply to any member in the dimension marked as accounts as well as any member in any other dimension that has a formula associated with it.

For those who have built Planning cubes, the idea of Text Measures is very similar to functionality that already existed for years in the Planning Product in the form of Smart Lists. At their essence, the Text Measure is nothing more than a metric value that is converted to a mapped list value at query run-time. Once the outline is enabled to use Typed Measures, then Text Measures can be set up by following these steps:

1. In EAS, open the outline in Outline Editor.
2. Select the third tab—Text List Manager.
3. Click New then double-click the entry in the text lists panel to give the list a name. **Note:** Once a list is created with a name, the name cannot be changed. To change the name of the list, the list must be deleted and recreated.
4. On the right-side panel, click the plus sign to add new members to the list.
5. Input the Name (text that will display) and the ID (numeric value that Essbase will store).
6. Save the list and restructure.
7. Create a member in the dimension tagged as accounts that the list will be associated to.
8. Right-click on the new member from Step #7 select Edit Member Properties.

9. On the Information Tab, change the Type from Numeric to Text.
10. Underneath that select the list created in Step #3.
11. Click OK and Save.

Note that the aggregation symbol for the member will automatically be changed to a caret, which means "Never Consolidate Member."

Using Date Measures is the simplest of the three functions to implement. Once a Date Measure is set up, there are a number of formulas that work with regards to this member. Some examples of calculations you could perform in BSO cubes:

- @TODAY: For instance, calculate the time between the data in the field and today. Useful if you were to store something like a hire date and want to know length of employment as of today.
- @DATEDIFF: Could be used to calculate the difference between two different Date Measures that have been captured. Maybe you captured Date of Purchase and Date of Warranty Expiration and want to calculate the amount of time left on Warranties.

MDX versions of both of these examples exist for ASO cubes as well. Of interest is the fact that there are three more functions available to ASO cubes than are available to BSO cubes with Date Measure Calculations.

Once the outline is enabled to use Typed Measures, then Date Measures can be set up by following these steps:

1. In EAS, open the outline in Outline Editor.
2. Create a member in the dimension tagged as accounts that the Date data will be loaded to.
3. Right-click on the new member and select Edit Member Properties.
4. On the Information Tab, change the Type from Numeric to Date.
5. In the outline properties, set a date format; All Date Measures will use this same format.
   Note: You cannot use the Associate Format String for a Date Measure.
6. Click OK and Save.

Before you go crazy, though, and start adding Typed Measures to all of your cubes, understand that there are some functional and practical limitations to their use.

- In BSO cubes: Text and Date Measures can be loaded at any level in contrast to ASO cubes where they can only be loaded at level-0.
- Once Typed Measures are enabled for an outline, this cannot be reversed (reminder).
- With Text Measures, your list can only be 1024 values in length (using a list that even comes close to approaching this length will have detrimental effects on query times).
- Custom aggregations of Text Measures can only be done in BSO cubes; it is not recommended to aggregate even a Typed Measures in ASO cubes.
- Typed Measures are not supported when using partitions.
- Text lists are not restructured when an outline restructure is performed, so add new members to the bottom of the list to avoid altering the mapping of existing items in the list.
- Exports that contain Text Measures and Date Measures cannot be reimported; these cause the import to fail.

I hope this chapter has caught your attention and imagination. The things that can be done with ASO cubes, in particular, and in combination solutions are limited only by the boundaries we place on our own imaginations. If you have the ability to free your mind and step outside of the box, outside of your personal comfort zones, and outside of the things you have previously learned and know to be true, tried, and tested, your imagination will take you to places you never dreamed you could reach. I wish you happy explorations. Let me know how your journey goes.

REFERENCES

http://www.cubegeek.com/2007/05/aso_vs_bso.tml.
https://forums.oracle.com.
http://www.network54.com/Forum/58296.
http://looksmarterthanyouare2.blogspot.com/2008/12/aso-vs-bso.html.
http://en.wikipedia.org/wiki/Essbase.
http://dssresources.com/papers/features/pendse10062002.html.
http://mindstreamanalytics.com/content/Essbase%20Today%20OAUG%20Presentation%201-20-11.pdf.
Oracle Essbase Database Administrator's Guide Release 11.1.2.1, © 1996, 2011.
Oracle Essbase Technical Reference Release 11.1.2.1, © 1996, 2011.

6

PRACTICAL MDX FOR ESSBASE DEVELOPERS

Gary Crisci

CONTENTS

6.1 INTRODUCTION

Multidimensional Expressions (MDX) is a query language written for retrieving data from multidimensional databases. Similar in some ways to Structured Query Language (SQL) for relational databases, it is a flexible language that allows the user to not only retrieve data, but also to manipulate the data and perform numerous other functions. MDX should not be considered a robust reporting language, due to its limited formatting capabilities, but instead is best used behind the scenes of reporting tools that will retrieve data from a database and then apply formatting within the reporting application. Although presentation quality reporting is not its strength, MDX can be used for simple reporting requirements where formatting is not particularly important.

While MDX's primary purpose is to retrieve data from multidimensional databases using structured queries, it also serves another purpose for Essbase developers: MDX is the mechanism used to define member formulas for aggregate storage option (ASO) databases. Leveraging the functionality of a subportion of an MDX query known as the WITH MEMBER specification, MDX is used within an Essbase ASO outline to define calculations that range from simple equations to very complex formulas.

Essbase developers should note the difference from block storage option (BSO) applications in that BSO cubes use the proprietary Essbase calculation script language to perform functions in calculation scripts and outline member formulas. Beyond member formulas, MDX also can be a useful tool for Essbase administrators to understand and manage their applications. Administrators can leverage the MDX language to query information about the Essbase outline. Using simple queries, the administrator can derive information that is useful for outline maintenance as well as tuning and optimization. Keep in mind that while MDX can only be used in member formulas in an aggregate storage database, the use of MDX to run a query applies to both aggregate storage *and* block storage applications.

MDX's query operations, ASO member formula language use, and metadata management functionality make MDX a very powerful tool that every Essbase developer and administrator should experience and utilize.

6.2 OBJECTIVES

The goal of this chapter is to convey useful information, and my personal experience, to other developers. This work is not meant to read like a computer science textbook, and, as such, more technical definitions may be found in other literature. My objective is to explain concepts in layman's terms using examples that should be familiar to both novice and seasoned professionals. The chapter will be broken into various subsections to allow the reader to use the chapter as a reference guide in the future. It is not necessary to have previous experience with MDX; however, the reader should have a general understanding of multidimensional database technology. Experience with other query languages, such as SQL, would be helpful.

6.3 HOUSEKEEPING

For starters, the first thing needed to run an MDX query against an ASO database is an MDX client. Essbase Administration Services (EAS) and MaxL are the default MDX clients for Essbase. These tools are basically the same since EAS leverages many MaxL commands behind the scenes. Note that there are also third-party MDX clients that can be utilized to run queries. My personal preference when running MDX queries is to use MaxL. Typically MaxL is thought of as the language for automating administrative tasks, like loading data or executing an aggregation. While this is accurate, MaxL also allows users to execute MDX queries within MaxL scripts. Although MDX is not a reporting language, there are a few settings that can be altered to manipulate the way the results look when Essbase returns them via MaxL. Furthermore, MaxL has a little known command set that applies to MDX output. Using the ALTER SESSION command in MaxL, the user has the ability to "set dml_output," where dml stands for Data Manipulation Language (in other words, MDX). Setting the dml output allows the user to toggle on/off various settings like alias, metadata only, cell status, numerical display, and precision. Note that Oracle chose to make member name aliases the default instead of member names, so you will often want to set alias OFF. You also can leverage a couple of the MaxL shell settings to set the column width and include timestamps to help you track performance on how long your queries take to run. Here's an example of what you might put in your MaxL statement before your MDX query:

```
alter session set dml_output alias off;
alter session set dml_output numerical_display fixed_decimal;
alter session set dml_output precision 2;
set column_width 50;
set timestamp on;
```

For complete details on the commands and options look at the "Alter session" syntax in the MaxL section of the Technical Reference.

6.4 MDX BASICS

6.4.1 Terms and Syntax

An MDX developer should be familiar with a number of terms.

6.4.1.1 Cube A cube is a common term used for a multidimensional database.

6.4.1.2 Dimension Dimensions are a logical grouping of members that share a relationship with each other. They are usually structured in some type of organized taxonomy, and each dimension represents a consistent subject matter theme. Examples of dimensions are Time, Geography, Products, Measures, and Scenarios.

6.4.1.3 Member A member defines an object in a dimension. Jan, Feb, Mar, and Qtr1 are examples of members of a Time dimension. Note that there are rules regarding when it is necessary to enclose member names in brackets, such as when the name has embedded blank space. As a general best practice, I recommend that member names should always be enclosed in square brackets in queries and member formulas (i.e., [Jan], [Feb], [Mar], [Qtr1]).

6.4.1.4 Tuple Sometimes people argue about how to properly pronounce Tuple. Some pronounce it like "pupil," while others pronounce it like "couple," It really doesn't matter how you pronounce it, but it is important to understand what it is and how it works because it is a fundamental concept.

For those familiar with the classic Essbase calculation language, a Tuple is very similar to a cross-dimensional operator.

The purpose of the Tuple is to focus or restrict the scope to a specific intersection or cell in the cube. To clarify, a cell should be envisioned as an intersection of all the base dimensions in the cube. As an example, let us look at the Sample.Basic database, which has five base dimensions (Year, Measures, Product, Market, and Scenario). A single data cell where a data value is stored could be ([Jan], [Sales], [100-10], [New York], [Actual]). This cell is a Tuple.

A Tuple is the way we identify a single data cell in a multidimensional database. It is the combination of one member from every base dimension. Now, if you have some basic experience working with Tuples, you might find that last statement a little confusing. Someone might say "([Jan], [Sales]) is a Tuple" and they would be correct. This might seem puzzling because I just said a Tuple was the intersection of a member from *every* base dimension and this example only has two members from the Time and Measures dimension. This is due to the fact that MDX uses implied dimension members for dimensions that are not explicitly referenced when running a query. In Essbase, the default members of a dimension are the dimension root members. Therefore, the Tuple ([Jan], [Sales]), when interpreted by Essbase, is actually "([Jan], [Sales], *[Product], [Market], [Scenario]*). Jan and Sales are explicit while Product, Market, and Scenario are implied. We can take this a step farther and apply it to a single member. [Sales] is a member, but ([Sales]) is also a Tuple when enclosed in parenthesis. A Tuple can be specified by a single member because, as we saw above, even though we have only explicitly defined ([Sales]) in our Tuple, we know that Essbase will automatically add the default members of all the other base dimensions not explicitly defined in the query to derive the fully qualified Tuple.

Tuples are very important in MDX, not just for defining multidimensional members to retrieve in a query, but particularly for driving the correct results of a calculation. Let's say you have a requirement to calculate some figures in a "What If" scenario. You have a simple cube with three dimensions: Measures, Period, and Scenario. The manager states she wants to see [Actual] increased by ten percent in the "What If" scenario. This is fairly simple. From an Essbase perspective, you would create a [What If] member in your Scenario dimension and then apply a member formula. At first thought, you might say the calculation is ([Sales]) * 1.1. You need to be extremely careful when doing this. As we discussed before, Essbase will complete the Tuple in the formula based on the context of the query for dimensions that are not defined. Please refer to the example in Figure 6.1.

The [What If] member has the formula ([Sales]) * 1.1 and the result for all periods is NULL or 0. This is the result of not properly scoping my Tuple. I have not defined the member of the Scenario dimension on which the calculation should be based. To properly execute this function, I need to modify it to ([Sales], [Actual]) * 1.1. This results in the correct values as seen in Figure 6.2.

Note: Be aware of implied shares, particularly in flat dimensions where the first member rolls to the dimension root. When you first test this, many of you may have an outline structure that will result in ([Sales]) * 1.1 returning the correct results. This can be caused by a few different issues, such as the Scenario dimension structured with [Actual] as the first child member and Scenario structured as label only. In that case, the Scenario member will have an implied share that returns the value of Actual. This

	A	B	C
1		Sales	
2		Actual	What If
3	Jan	1000	0
4	Feb	2000	0
5	Mar	3000	0
6			

Figure 6.1 The result of an improperly scoped Tuple.

	A	B	C
1		Sales	
2		Actual	What If
3	Jan	1000	1100
4	Feb	2000	2200
5	Mar	3000	3300

Figure 6.2 The result of a properly scoped Tuple.

will result in the first formula working correctly, even though it is using the implied [Scenario] member rather than the explicit [Actual] member.

It is a better practice to scope the formulas properly using a more fully defined Tuple rather than relying on default behaviors. Relying on default behaviors can result in formulas returning an incorrect value in the future when an outline change may happen. In the example provided, assume six months from now someone decides to add a [Budget] member to the outline and sets it as the first child of [Scenario]. If the formula for [What If] is ([Sales]) * 1.1, the results for [What If] will now be based on [Budget] rather than [Actual]. This behavior should not be overlooked. Once you understand this concept, you will see how it can apply later to much more complex formulas.

6.4.1.5 Sets In its simplest form, a Set is a collection of Tuples. Similar to the rules for a Tuple, a Set can be made of one Tuple, and since a Tuple can consist of one Member, a Set can simply be a single Member. Most Sets contain more than one Member/Tuple. However, it should be noted that a Set can be empty. I will demonstrate the use of empty Sets in a query later in the chapter. A common example of a Set is a member range. A member range can be defined using a function like MemberRange([Jan], [Dec]) or an alternate syntax like [Jan] : [Dec]. Other common Set functions are Children(), Descendants(), and Members().

Sets have some basic rules. If you have multiple Tuples in a Set, they must have the same dimensional cardinality and they must adhere to the same dimensional order. {([Actual], [Jan]), ([Budget], [Feb])} is a valid set.

{([Actual], [Jan]), ([Feb], [Budget])} and {([Jan]), ([Feb], [Budget])} are invalid sets because the first set has a mixed dimension order and the second set has unbalanced cardinality.

Note that unless the set is being returned by a function, it must be enclosed in curly braces { }. Additionally, a Set also can be made up of other Sets.

6.4.1.6 Member Specification and Fully Qualified Member Names A member name can be specified in a few different ways. The most common method is to solely use the member name (or alias) by itself. A member name only requires brackets [ ] if the name contains spaces. For BSO developers, these are the same rules that apply with double quotation marks in the calc script language. However, as a best practice for better readability, I suggest always putting members in brackets. For further clarity, a member also can be defined not only by its name but by identifying its dimension or any one ancestor member name and attaching it to the member name as a prefix. While it is acceptable to use a member name alone like [Jan], [Period].[Jan] or [Qtr1].[Jan] provides more clarity. This is particularly useful when scoping shared members from an alternate hierarchy.

Fully qualified member names become even more important when your database has duplicate member names enabled. When duplicate member names are enabled, it becomes necessary to distinguish between two members with the same name. For example, you may have a Geography dimension with ambiguous city names, such as Portland: [Geography].[USA].[Maine].[Portland] and [Geography].[USA].[Oregon].[Portland]. Again, you do not have to use all levels when qualifying, just enough to clarify any ambiguities, such as [Maine].[Portland] and [Oregon].[Portland], while [New York City] is probably unique and does not require [New York].[New York City].

As a general rule, I do not advocate enabling duplicate member names. While there are times where it can be useful, I stay away from it for various reasons, such as difficulty with hierarchy maintenance, potential for confusion with end users, and potential misinterpretation of information in reports. If you are using duplicate member names, I suggest reading the Member Specification section of the Essbase Technical Reference for a detailed explanation of the best utilization of fully qualified member names.

6.5 PROPERTIES

It is hard to get into details about MDX properties without rewriting the section in the Technical Reference. Because the Technical Reference does a very good job at explaining this, I am going to limit this section to briefly explaining what properties are. This will demonstrate why you should research them further and, more importantly, why you might use them and how they may not be as useful as hoped.

There are two types of properties that are exposed in MDX: intrinsic and custom. The custom properties include MEMBER_NAME, MEMBER_ALIAS, LEVEL_NUMBER, and GEN_NUMBER. How the results are returned and what you can do with them is a different story. Generally, this information when returned via a query is not in a format that is very useful. Instead the information returned is likely of more use when pushing through to another reporting type of system, perhaps through the application programming interfaces (APIs) where that reporting system can better interpret the results.

Of more use to most MDX developers are custom properties. Custom properties in Essbase are defined by Attributes, User Defined Attributes (UDAs), and alias table names. Later in Section 6.10 (Tips and Tricks), I will explore ways to use custom properties in your queries. Additionally, you can review some of the sample queries to see examples where custom properties like DIMENSION PROPERTIES are used.

6.6 FUNCTIONS

Functions are used to make writing MDX queries easier and expand the robustness of the analytics. Functions can return metadata (i.e., member sets, member properties, etc.) or they can return numerical results. Functions eliminate the need to explicitly define what you are looking for in a query. For instance, if you wanted all Cola product codes in your query from Sample.Basic, you could explicitly state the set {[100-10], [100-20], [100-30]}. Using a function can simplify what needs to be specified. Instead of spelling out each member, you could use a member set function like Children(). For example, note that the style conventions Children([Colas]) or [Colas].children are interchangeable, although you may find one is more readable depending on your preference. Be careful when using a function that you understand the nature of dynamically generated results. In the example I have provided, it is easier to use Children([Colas]) than it is to type out the individual members. Some sets could contain hundreds of members, in which case the only practical solution is to use a function. However, be clear on the requirement. If the requirement is children of Colas, then by all means use the function, but if the requirement is specifically {[100-10], [100-20], [100-30]}, be careful using the Children() function as a short cut because if a new product member were to be added to the database under Colas, the Children() function will return the new member as part of the set. In many ways this is another benefit of using functions because it keeps the set definitions in sync with the outline. Be aware, however, of what you are doing because, if your requirement was to pull back those three products specifically, then using a set function when a new member is added would return incorrect results.

Data value functions are helpful when looking for mathematical results in a query. Sticking with the example above, assume you are looking for the Average Sales for the children of Colas. You could leverage the Avg() function.

```
Avg([Colas].children, [Measures].[Sales], INCLUDEEMPTY)
```

Note that the INCLUDEEMPTY keyword enhances the power of the Avg() function by including null members in the denominator count. If you leave this key word out, you will get a weighted average where the denominator will be based on the count of members with nonnull values.

Essbase has a robust list of functions for MDX that span the following categories: Members, Sets, Tuples, Numbers, Dimensions, Layers, Booleans, Dates, and Strings. Once again, I will suggest reviewing the Technical Reference for specific function definitions and examples of how to utilize them in queries and member formulas.

6.6.1 Crossjoin

One function that deserves special mention is the Crossjoin. The Crossjoin is used to return the cross product of two sets from different dimensions. Note that I said two and only two. If you want to Crossjoin more than two sets, you will need to nest Crossjoins.

I like to think of the Crossjoin function as a way of generating dynamic Tuples. For instance, assume you wanted to have on your rows both the children of [East] and the children of [Colas]. You could long-hand it like {([Cola], [New York]), ([Cola], [Florida]),,,([Diet Cola], [New York), ([Diet Cola], [Florida]),,,ETC}, or you could use a Crossjoin().

```
SELECT
{} ON AXIS(0),
Crossjoin([Colas].children, [East].children) ON AXIS(1)
FROM [Sample.Basic];

Axis-1
+-----------------------------------------------
 (Cola, New York)
 (Cola, Massachusetts)
 (Cola, Florida)
 (Cola, Connecticut)
 (Cola, New Hampshire)
 (Diet Cola, New York)
 (Diet Cola, Massachusetts)
 (Diet Cola, Florida)
```

```
(Diet Cola, Connecticut)
(Diet Cola, New Hampshire)
(Caffeine Free Cola, New York)
(Caffeine Free Cola, Massachusetts)
(Caffeine Free Cola, Florida)
(Caffeine Free Cola, Connecticut)
(Caffeine Free Cola, New Hampshire)
```

The Crossjoin makes things much easier, particularly when working with large sets, where it would not be practical to hard code every member combination.

It is important to understand the order in which the Crossjoin will return member sets:

```
Crossjoin({[Jan], [Feb], [Mar]}, {[Sales], [COGS], [Margin]})
```

will return:

```
([Jan], [Sales]), ([Feb], [Sales]), ([Mar], [Sales]), ([Jan],
[COGS]), ([Feb], [COGS]), ([Mar], [COGS]), ([Jan], [Margin]),
([Feb], [Margin]), ([Mar], [Margin]).
```

This is important to be aware of particularly when using other functions that are sensitive to order, like Head() or Tail(). The Head() and Tail() functions allow you to grab a particular Tuple from a set based on its position from the beginning or end of the set. Therefore, it is crucial to understand the result set order to return the correct results.

6.7 QUERY STRUCTURE

6.7.1 Axis

Now that we understand all the pieces that make up an MDX query, let's start to put them together to actually create an MDX query. In multidimensional terminology, an axis represents how a Set is presented in the results of a query. An axis can be thought of as a column or a row on a spreadsheet. Multiple axes are used to present data where Sets are nested. While you can specify up to 64 axes in a query, only the first five axes are defined by keywords. The axes are COLUMNS, ROWS, PAGES, CHAPTERS, and SECTIONS. In general, I find it easier to just use the Axis ordinal (i.e., AXIS(0), AXIS(1), AXIS(2), etc). You cannot skip an axis; you must start with 0 or COLUMNS and proceed in order. It is possible to place an empty Set { } on an AXIS. I will demonstrate later in the chapter how this might be useful when talking about metadata queries where you are querying outline information, but not looking to return actual data.

An example of a simple MDX query is:

```
SELECT
{[Sales], [COGS], [Margin]} ON AXIS(0),
{[Year].Children} ON AXIS(1)
FROM [Sample.Basic];
Results in:

Axis-1   (Sales)     (COGS)     (Margin)
+--------+----------+---------+--------
 (Qtr1)   96820.00  42877.00  53943.00
 (Qtr2)  101679.00  45362.00  56317.00
```

```
 (Qtr3)   105215.00   47343.00   57872.00
 (Qtr4)    98141.00   43754.00   54387.00
```

Note that on AXIS(1), I enclosed [Year]. Children in curly braces { }. As mentioned above, if the set is being returned via a function, the braces are not necessary. However, as a best practice you should always enclose Sets in curly braces, which will reduce syntax errors. I will briefly mention that Essbase is not great at explaining MDX errors, so it can be challenging sometimes trying to determine the origin of the syntax issue. By using best practices and standards, such as always using brackets, qualifying the member names with an ancestor member, etc., you can more easily weed out the problem.

6.7.2 *Where Slicer*

The Where Slicer is very useful in MDX queries for limiting the scope of the query. However, I have also found it is one of the more misunderstood aspects of the MDX language, particularly for users of the SQL language. In a SQL query, the Where clause is used to filter results. For example you might have a SQL query that looks like the following:

```
SELECT Year, Product, Market, Scenario, Measures
FROM Fact_Table
WHERE Year = 'Jan'
```

This query will return all records from the Fact_Table for the month of January. In MDX, it is tempting to think the use of the WHERE clause is similar to SQL, and it is, with one major exception, you cannot specify a dimension in the WHERE slicer that has been placed on an axis. You might expect to be able to do something like the following, but it would be invalid:

```
SELECT
{[Sales]} ON COLUMNS,
{[Year].members} ON ROWS
FROM Sample.Basic
WHERE [Year].CurrentMember IS [Jan]
```

This is invalid because the Year dimension was already placed on the ROWS axis. A valid way to write this would be:

```
SELECT
{[Sales]} ON COLUMNS,
{[Jan]} ON ROWS
FROM Sample.Basic
```

Note there is no need for the WHERE slicer in this case. You would only use the WHERE slicer if Year was not on an axis. Let's change the query to show members of the Market dimension on the ROWS axis.

```
SELECT
{[Sales]} ON COLUMNS,
{[Market].[East].children} ON ROWS
FROM Sample.Basic
WHERE ([Year].[Jan])
```

```
Axis-1                    (Sales)
+-------------------+--------
 (New York)                3479.00
 (Massachusetts)           1251.00
 (Florida)                 1321.00
 (Connecticut)             1197.00
 (New Hampshire)            532.00
```

Note that we do not use a function with the WHERE slicer, we are only specifying a Tuple. Remember that a Tuple can be a single member and any dimensions not specified in the WHERE slicer or on another axis will resolve with the default member for those dimensions. So, the above query could be written without a WHERE slicer as:

```
SELECT
{[Sales], [Year].[Jan]} ON COLUMNS,
{[Market].[East].children} ON ROWS
FROM Sample.Basic
```

And the only difference would be in the way the column header appears:

```
Axis-1    (Sales, Jan)
```

There also is no logic allowed in the WHERE slicer. You cannot say WHERE [Sales] > 100000.

The easiest way to conceptualize the WHERE slicer is to think of it as the Point Of View (POV) or the spreadsheet header (Figure 6.3).

More often than not, when users are trying to utilize the WHERE slicer, they actually need a Filter() function. The Filter() function allows the user to filter the results returned from a set. Building on the example above, the developer can do the following:

```
SELECT
{[Sales]} ON COLUMNS,
{Filter([Year].members, [Year].CurrentMember IS [Jan])} ON ROWS
                    FROM Sample.Basic
```

```
Axis-1                    (Sales)
+-------------------+------
 (Jan)                     32538
```

WHERE SLICER →		Jan	*Product*	*Scenario*
AXIS(0) →		Sales		
AXIS(1) →	New York	3479		
	Massachusetts	1251		
	Florida	1321		
	Connecticut	1197		
	New Hampshire	532		
	East	7780		

Figure 6.3 Visualizing the WHERE Slicer.

This is obviously more complicated, but as the logic gets more complicated it becomes necessary. Let us say you wanted to filter for periods that begin with the letter "J":

```
SELECT
{[Sales]} ON COLUMNS,
{Filter([Year].members,
Substring([Year].CurrentMember.Member_Name, 1, 1) =
"J")}ON ROWS
FROM Sample.Basic

Axis-1                  (Sales)
+-------------------+-------
 (Jan)                   32538
 (Jun)                   35088
 (Jul)                   36134
```

Or, going back to our issue of only returning Sales that are greater than 100,000:

```
SELECT
{[Sales]} ON COLUMNS,
{Filter([Year].members, [Sales] > 100000)} ON ROWS
FROM Sample.Basic

Axis-1                  (Sales)
+-------------------+-------
 (Year)                 401855
 (Qtr2)                 101679
 (Qtr3)                 105215
```

Note: This is one of the few times when you can make reference to the same dimension on more than one axis.

I will present more ways to use the Filter() function later in the chapter. For now, understand the WHERE slicer is not a filter. It is a dimensional slice most similar to the concept of dimensional headers or POV in a spreadsheet.

6.7.2.1 Creating Calculated Members in a Query Using "With" Specification Essbase developers are very comfortable creating calculated members with member formulas in the Essbase outline. This is partially due to the ease of maintenance a developer has with an Essbase outline using a tool like Essbase Administration Services (EAS). Other OLAP (online analytical processing) products are not as flexible, and even with Essbase, there are times when it is not convenient to add a member to an outline. Adding members can result in database restructures, which can be time-consuming operations. In addition, sometimes the calculation that is needed is only needed by one or a few users, or only for a limited time. MDX queries can help by using something called the "WITH MEMBER" specification. Using WITH MEMBER, a query writer can define a calculated member for use in their query that does not need to exist in the database.

For example, let us assume we have a requirement to calculate Margin Percent and this member does not exist in the database. We have [Sales] and we have [Margin]. We want to create a virtual member to calculate Margin Percent and return the results for all 12 months of the year.

```
WITH MEMBER [Measures].[Margin Per] AS
       '([Measures].[Margin] / [Measures].[Sales]) * 100'
SELECT
{[Measures].[Sales], [Measures].[Margin],
[Measures].[Margin Per]} ON COLUMNS,
{[Year].levels(0).members} ON ROWS
FROM Sample.Basic

Axis-1          (Sales)          (Margin)          (Margin Per)
+-------------+-------------+-------------+-----------
 (Jan)          32538.00         18378.00            56.48
 (Feb)          32069.00         17762.00            55.39
 (Mar)          32213.00         17803.00            55.27
 (Apr)          32917.00         18242.00            55.42
 (May)          33674.00         18618.00            55.29
 (Jun)          35088.00         19457.00            55.45
 (Jul)          36134.00         20012.00            55.38
 (Aug)          36008.00         19736.00            54.81
 (Sep)          33073.00         18124.00            54.80
 (Oct)          32828.00         18186.00            55.40
 (Nov)          31971.00         17766.00            55.57
 (Dec)          33342.00         18435.00            55.29
```

Note that within the WITH MEMBER specification, everything between the single quotes is exactly what you would find in a member formula if you had created the [Margin Per] member in an ASO Essbase outline.

The WITH MEMBER specification can be extremely useful for creating calculated members on the fly for ad hoc or one-time use. Essbase developers also can leverage this functionality to test the results of potential member formulas before adding them to the outline. A formula can be developed and tested without touching the database, which can be very helpful in decentralized environments.

6.7.3 Solve Order

Solve order is an optional property you can add to a calculated member in an MDX query. It is also a property that can be assigned directly to a member through a member formula in an ASO Essbase outline. Solve order allows you to control the order in which calculations are executed when they are simultaneously queried. There are times when the results of one calculation may be dependent upon the results of another calculation. In these cases, it is important to properly define which calculation should execute first. When defining solve order for a calculated member, the calculations will execute in ascending order, so the lowest number will execute first and the highest number will execute last. In the event of a tie where the solve orders are the same, the members execute in outline order, with the members belonging to the dimension that comes later in the outline winning the tie.

Solve order should be considered for performance tuning as well. While I have been unable to find documentation that directly supports this (until the writing of this book), my experience with Essbase ASO databases has been that often I can get better query response time on members that have complex member formulas when I increase the solve order from the default value. I strongly recommend reading Chapter 7 where Dan Pressman speaks extensively on this subject.

6.7.4 ASO Member Formulas

Member formulas are very common in Essbase applications. A member formula can be something as simple as [Sales] – [COGS] or it can be extremely complicated with many lines of code. Developers should remember that member formulas are dynamic and they execute upon query. Unlike BSO applications, you cannot calculate members with formulas at the bottom of a hierarchy, and then roll the results up to the higher levels. This must be done either prior to loading of the data or as of the latest release of Essbase v11.1.2.1 using the ASO calculation script functionality. Developers need to keep this in mind and weigh various optimization strategies when leveraging MDX member formulas.

6.8 ADVANCED MDX

6.8.1 Conditional Logic

A very common requirement when creating MDX calculations is to implement conditional logic. Conditional logic is most commonly thought of as an "IF" statement (i.e., if "A" then "B" otherwise "C"). MDX has an IIF function to perform this type of logic. Note the IIF function has two "Is". In addition to the IIF function, MDX also has a CASE statement. CASE works similar to IIF, but can often be easier to work with, particularly with multiple criteria logic.

Let's start off with a simple IIF and comparable CASE statement. Going back to the beginning of the chapter, the manager has asked to see a "What If" analysis showing Actuals times 10%. As shown in the beginning of the chapter, this was accomplished with the following member formula ([Sales], [Actual]) * 1.1. As a query, it would look like the following:

```
WITH MEMBER [Scenario].[What If] AS
       '([Sales], [Actual]) * 1.1'
SELECT
{[Scenario].[Actual], [Scenario].[What If]} ON COLUMNS,
{[Qtr1].Children} ON ROWS
FROM Sample.Basic
WHERE ([Measures].[Sales])

Axis-1      (Actual)    (What If)
+---------+---------+---------
 (Jan)      32538.00    35791.80
 (Feb)      32069.00    35275.90
 (Mar)      32213.00    35434.30
```

Now, let's assume the manager has changed the criteria a bit and says the "What If" analysis should show an increase of 10% in the first period, but then only 5% for the other periods. Using the IIF function we could do the following:

```
WITH MEMBER [Scenario].[What If] AS
      'IIF([Year].CurrentMember IS [Jan], ([Sales], [Actual]) *
      1.1, ([Sales], [Actual]) * 1.05)'
```

```
SELECT
{[Scenario].[Actual], [Scenario].[What If]} ON COLUMNS,
{[Qtr1].Children} ON ROWS
FROM Sample.Basic
WHERE ([Measures].[Sales])

Axis-1     (Actual)   (What If)
+---------+---------+---------
 (Jan)     32538.00   35791.80
 (Feb)     32069.00   33672.45
 (Mar)     32213.00   33823.65
```

Here is the same example using a CASE statement:

```
WITH MEMBER [Scenario].[What If] AS
'CASE WHEN [Year].CurrentMember IS [Jan] THEN
([Sales], [Actual]) * 1.1
ELSE ([Sales], [Actual]) * 1.05 END'
SELECT
{[Scenario].[Actual], [Scenario].[What If]} ON COLUMNS,
{[Qtr1].Children} ON ROWS
FROM Sample.Basic
WHERE ([Measures].[Sales])

Axis-1     (Actual)   (What If)
+---------+---------+---------
 (Jan)     32538.00   35791.80
 (Feb)     32069.00   33672.45
 (Mar)     32213.00   33823.65
```

I personally find the CASE statement to be easier to read, and, although in this example it results in more lines of code, you can quickly see where it has its advantages. Assume the requirement changes yet again. Is this starting to sound more and more like the real world? The requirement now is to have Jan * 10%, Feb * 5%, and Mar to stay flat. The IIF statement now has to be nested and starts to get a bit ugly.

```
WITH MEMBER [Scenario].[What If] AS
'IIF([Year].CurrentMember IS [Jan],
      ([Sales], [Actual]) * 1.1,
            IIF([Year].CurrentMember IS [Feb],
            ([Sales], [Actual]) * 1.05,
                  IIF([Year].CurrentMember IS [Mar],
                  ([Sales], [Actual]) * 1,
MISSING)))'
SELECT
{[Scenario].[Actual], [Scenario].[What If]} ON COLUMNS,
{[Qtr1].Children} ON ROWS
FROM Sample.Basic
WHERE ([Measures].[Sales])

Axis-1     (Actual)   (What If)
+---------+---------+---------
 (Jan)     32538.00   35791.80
 (Feb)     32069.00   33672.45
 (Mar)     32213.00   32213.00
```

Keeping track of the parenthesis with nested IIF statements can be a bit difficult. By comparison, the CASE statement now looks nicer.

```
WITH MEMBER [Scenario].[What If] AS
'CASE
WHEN [Year].CurrentMember IS [Jan] THEN
([Sales], [Actual]) * 1.1
WHEN [Year].CurrentMember IS [Feb] THEN
([Sales], [Actual]) * 1.05
WHEN [Year].CurrentMember IS [Mar] THEN
([Sales], [Actual]) * 1
ELSE MISSING
END'
SELECT
{[Scenario].[Actual], [Scenario].[What If]} ON COLUMNS,
{[Qtr1].Children} ON ROWS
FROM Sample.Basic
WHERE ([Measures].[Sales])

Axis-1     (Actual)   (What If)
+---------+---------+---------
 (Jan)     32538.00   35791.80
 (Feb)     32069.00   33672.45
 (Mar)     32213.00   32213.00
```

Note that when in a member formula you want to return a NULL value, you use the string MISSING with no quotes, no brackets, and no punctuation marks. And, for all of you who learned on Essbase BSO, it is just Missing, not #Missing.

6.8.1.1 Nesting versus AND When performing conditional logic, the developer has the ability to use additional logic terms like "AND" or "OR." While there are many applications of these logical constructs, one particular issue that I would like to share has to do with optimization. An extremely common request is when someone says they want to do one thing if all the members are level-0, but something else when any of the members are nonlevel-0. Consider the following example and note that I have already explained my preference toward CASE opposed to IIF and will be using CASE in the examples.

```
WITH MEMBER [Measures].[Test1] AS
'CASE WHEN IsLevel([Time].CurrentMember, 0)
AND IsLevel([Years].CurrentMember, 0)
AND IsLevel([Transaction Type].CurrentMember, 0)
AND IsLevel([Payment Type].CurrentMember, 0)
AND IsLevel([Promotions].CurrentMember, 0)
AND IsLevel([Age].CurrentMember, 0)
AND IsLevel([Income Level].CurrentMember, 0)
AND IsLevel([Products].CurrentMember, 0)
AND IsLevel([Stores].CurrentMember, 0)
AND IsLevel([Geography].CurrentMember, 0)
THEN SUM([Geography].members, [Transactions]) ELSE MISSING END'
SELECT
{[Measures].[Units], [Measures].[Transactions], [Measures].[Test1]}
ON AXIS(0),
{[Jan]} ON AXIS(1),
```

```
{[Curr Year]} ON AXIS(2),
{[Sale]} ON AXIS(3),
{[Cash]} ON AXIS(4),
{[No Promotion]} ON AXIS(5),
{[1 to 13 Years]} ON AXIS(6),
{[Under 20,000]} ON AXIS(7),
{[Memory]} ON AXIS(8),
{[05351]} ON AXIS(9),
{[Stores].levels(0).members} ON AXIS(10)
FROM ASOsamp.Sample

Versus

WITH MEMBER [Measures].[Test1] AS
'CASE WHEN IsLevel([Time].CurrentMember, 0) THEN
CASE WHEN IsLevel([Years].CurrentMember, 0) THEN
CASE WHEN IsLevel([Transaction Type].CurrentMember, 0) THEN
CASE WHEN IsLevel([Payment Type].CurrentMember, 0) THEN
CASE WHEN IsLevel([Promotions].CurrentMember, 0) THEN
CASE WHEN IsLevel([Age].CurrentMember, 0) THEN
CASE WHEN IsLevel([Income Level].CurrentMember, 0) THEN
CASE WHEN IsLevel([Products].CurrentMember, 0) THEN
CASE WHEN IsLevel([Stores].CurrentMember, 0) THEN
CASE WHEN IsLevel([Geography].CurrentMember, 0) THEN
SUM([Geography].members, [Transactions])
ELSE MISSING END
ELSE MISSING END
ELSE MISSING END
ELSE MISSING END
ELSE MISSING END
ELSE MISSING END
ELSE MISSING END
ELSE MISSING END
ELSE MISSING END
ELSE MISSING END'
SELECT
{[Measures].[Units], [Measures].[Transactions], [Measures].[Test1]}
ON AXIS(0),
{[Time]} ON AXIS(1),
{[Curr Year]} ON AXIS(2),
{[Sale]} ON AXIS(3),
{[Cash]} ON AXIS(4),
{[No Promotion]} ON AXIS(5),
{[1 to 13 Years]} ON AXIS(6),
{[Under 20,000]} ON AXIS(7),
{[Memory]} ON AXIS(8),
{[05351]} ON AXIS(9),
{[Stores].levels(0).members} ON AXIS(10)
FROM ASOsamp.Sample
```

Both of these examples will yield the same results. The second example has more lines of code, but depending on the size of the database and what you are trying to execute, in many cases the second example will return faster. For instance, if I run the first query against ASOsamp, it returns in approximately seven seconds. The second query resolves the same results in approximately six seconds. Now that is not much of an argument for one against the other; however, in both cases, we are returning all level-0 members and, therefore, allowing the calculation to execute. What if we change [Jan] to the nonlevel-0 member [Time]? The second query returns in approximately four seconds.

It is hard for me to draw any definitive conclusions from such a simple test, particularly on what is a relatively small ASO database. However, my experience with larger databases leans toward this theory: Nested case statements resolve quicker than multiple AND logic statements. I have seen considerable improvement in some cases that has led me to this belief. My speculation is that it takes considerably more resources to resolve a large array that would be created by multiple AND statements than it would to evaluate the case statements line by line. While I will not state this is a hard rule that will yield better results in all situations, I feel it is worthy of mention and that developers should explore and test in their own environments to see if they can improve performance when working with calculations such as this one.

6.9 TIME FUNCTIONALITY

Without a doubt, the primary use for MDX in Essbase ASO applications is to implement Time calculations. When talking about "Time Calculations," I am primarily referring to Period-to-Date calculations and, secondly, to Time Balancing. Other uses for time calculations might involve trending and rolling calculations.

Let's begin with Period-to-Date functionality. This is one of the areas where BSO developers get stuck when setting up their first ASO applications. Block Storage has an incredibly useful feature known as dynamic-time-series (DTS). DTS allows BSO developers to easily implement Period-to-Date functionality without any customization. It is an "out of the box" feature that works extremely well. Another advantage in BSO databases is that the Time dimension is very often set as a dense dimension. Without getting into differences between dense and sparse dimensions (see other chapters in this book), time period calculations that are calculated within the same block when it is in memory are exceptionally efficient.

In the ASO world, where dimensionality is inherently sparse and all non-Stored, non-Additive calculations are dynamic, time calculations can run into some serious performance lags. As with most cases, it comes down to the complexity of the application, how large the dimensions are, Dynamic versus Stored hierarchies, etc. For smaller ASO applications (note that a small ASO app can still be pretty large), MDX can be a quick and easy way to perform time calculations. For larger, more complex applications, more thought will need to be put into the outline design. Most solutions will require some MDX.

6.9.1 Period-to-Date

Let us discuss some of the various ways you can achieve Period-to-Date (PTD) functionality. Keep in mind that this chapter is about MDX, so I am not going to get into too many details about the non-MDX ways of performing time calculations. However, we cannot have this conversation without speaking briefly about these other options.

The first method of generating PTD calculations in an ASO database is to utilize multiple hierarchies in the Time dimension. A review of the ASOsamp application that ships with Essbase shows this approach. Using this method involves building out the time dimension with a primary Stored hierarchy and then creating secondary Dynamic hierarchies with members like [YTD(Aug)] or [QTD(Mar)]. Because these members are part of a Dynamic hierarchy, the developer is able to add MDX member formulas to these members to calculate the needed results. For example [YTD(Aug)] has the MDX member formula [1st Half]+[Jul]+[Aug]. This is somewhat better than what some developers may do, which is to just hard code [Jan]+[Feb]+[Mar]+[Apr]+[May]+[Jun]+[Jul]+[Aug] or to use the Sum() function as Sum([Jan]:[Aug]). While these are all simple, they are more dynamic in nature. At least the ASOsamp version tries to make use of the [1st Half] member from the Stored hierarchy.

In reality, a developer does not even need to use MDX to do simple period-to-date functionality like this. Instead of using MDX, the developer could just use shared members and create alternate rollups where [YTD(Feb)] has two children [Jan] and [Feb], which are shared from the primary hierarchy. To expand upon this approach, the developer could move the [YTD(Feb)] member to Generation-2 of the Time dimension and switch it to a Stored hierarchy instead of a Dynamic hierarchy. Then, during aggregations, the developer can enable alternate rollups to be considered for aggregate views. This will yield very good performance and works well on smaller ASO applications.

There are two factors with the above approach that make it less than desirable. The first is that it requires the developer to create many new members in the alternate Rollups. Whether using MDX or shared members, the developer has to create 12 new YTD members, potentially 12 QTD members, and perhaps a few others depending on requirements. While that may be acceptable in a monthly model, what happens when building a daily model or a fiscal year crossover model where years and months are in the same dimension? The developer could be in a situation to create hundreds of PTD members.

The second problem with this approach is that it decouples the relationship between similar time members. [Jun] and [Jun_YTD] are now two different members in the database. If a user has a report with 12 period members in the header column and they want to see YTD values, they must replace all 12 members with different YTD members. This is inconvenient and does not exemplify ease of use. [Jun] and [Jun_YTD] are not unique content; the difference between them is a matter of context. To alleviate this discontinuity and reduce hierarchy complexity, a developer needs to consider a View dimension, or what I like to call an Analytic dimension.

6.9.2 *Analytic Dimensions*

The premise of an analytic dimension, in general terms, is a dimension added to a data model with one default stored member. All other members in the outline are calculated members, or label only members that are only used to help group-related calculated members. Generally, the analytic dimension is not related to the subject data in the model. To this end, you will find there are some general categories for analytic dimensions and you will be able to reuse the same code in multiple models. Analytic dimensions work by leveraging the power of Tuples. The default member of the analytic dimension joins with the members of other dimensions to create multidimensional members against which you can execute functions.

Assume you are working with the ASOsamp database and you add a new dimension [View] and set it to be a Dynamic hierarchy. Beneath the dimension root member [View], add a member [Periodic]. Update any Load rules you may have to add [Periodic]

View Dynamic <2> (Label Only)
Periodic (~)
YTD (~)

Figure 6.4 An example of View dimension. (From Oracle Essbase Administration Services. With permission.)

as a Load rule header; you will now be able to load data to the database and everything will look the same with the exception of this new dimension. Any query of [Periodic] (or [View] for that matter) will return the same results you would have gotten before the View dimension was added. Now add a new member [YTD] as a sibling of [Periodic] (Figure 6.4).

Now add the following member formula to YTD.

```
SUM(PeriodsToDate([Time].Generations(2), [Time].CurrentMember),
[View].[Periodic])
```

Looking closer at this formula, you will first see that we are using the PeriodsToDate() function. The PeriodsToDate() function is a very useful member set function. The name is a little misleading as it is not restricted to working with time. It is simply a variation of the MemberRange() function; note that it can be used with nontime-related dimensions. It is obviously very helpful with time calculations and, in this case, it will return the member range we are looking for, dynamically based on the generation layer we specify. In many cases, Generation-2 will be appropriate for YTD, but depending on how your time dimension is structured, it may be necessary to change the ordinal to a different generation layer. The next thing to notice is the use of the Sum() function. A lot of people miss this and assume PeriodToDate() will return the number they are looking for. It is important to distinguish between functions that return numbers and functions that return members. PeriodToDate() is a set function and returns members. Therefore, it is necessary to wrap PeriodToDate() in a Sum() function to get the summation value. The next and most important piece is where we specify [View].[Periodic] as the numeric value expression parameter of the Sum() function. When the function evaluates, every member of the Time dimension that is returned from the PeriodToDate() function will be summed against [View].[Periodic] and because all data is loaded to [View].[Periodic] we are able to get the results we are seeking.

```
SELECT [View].children ON AXIS(0),
Hierarchize({[Time].members}, POST) ON AXIS(1)
FROM ASOsamp.Sample
WHERE ([Measures].[Original Price], [Years].[Curr Year])

Axis-1                (Periodic)           (YTD)
+-------------------+-------------------+------------
 (Jan)                  7498269.25          7498269.25
 (Feb)                  3543554.00         11041823.25
 (Mar)                  5625366.50         16667189.75
 (Qtr1)                16667189.75         16667189.75
 (Apr)                  3678482.25         20345672.00
 (May)                  7394460.00         27740132.00
 (Jun)                  5400841.00         33140973.00
```

```
(Qtr2)                16473783.25          33140973.00
(1st Half)            33140973.00          33140973.00
(Jul)                  4879566.25          38020539.25
(Aug)                    #Missing          38020539.25
(Sep)                    #Missing          38020539.25
(Qtr3)                 4879566.25          38020539.25
(Oct)                    #Missing          38020539.25
(Nov)                    #Missing          38020539.25
(Dec)                    #Missing          38020539.25
(Qtr4)                   #Missing          38020539.25
(2nd Half)             4879566.25          38020539.25
(MTD)                 38020539.25          38020539.25
(Time)                38020539.25          38020539.25
```

Note: Take notice of the use of Hierarchize() function with the keyword POST. By default MDX returns results with parents before children. Use Hierarchize(,POST) to return results in the familiar Excel add-in format.

It is now easy to create some other members like quarter to date (QTD) and simply tweak the member formula. Add member [View].[QTD] and add the following member formula.

```
SUM(PeriodsToDate([Time].Generations(3), [Time].CurrentMember),
[View].[Periodic])
```

If this is a daily model, you can add a [View].[MTD] for month to date and simply change the Generations layer level to (4) (or whatever is appropriate for your application).

At this point, I am going to say that while the preceding example is an effective way to implement period-to-date functionality, it is actually not my preference in many situations. In fact, Because it uses Dynamic calculation, it has the same performance problems that we found when we first started discussing Time-Functionality.

Dan Pressman discusses in Chapter 7 (How ASO Works and How to Design For Performance) an even more effective way to structure the primary hierarchy in the Time dimension to optimize Stored hierarchies (see Section 7.6.2.1, Time Spans (YTD, QTD) Using Stored Hierarchies).

If you decide not to use the approach Pressman suggests, the basic rule of thumb when writing MDX in an ASO database is to **leverage nonlevel-0 members of Stored hierarchies whenever possible**. This is because there is a good chance that many of those members will have been preaggregated in a view during the aggregation process. So, if you have a choice when setting up [YTD(Mar)] to sum [Jan] through [Mar] or point to Qtr1, which is the parent of [Jan], [Feb], and [Mar] in the primary Stored hierarchy, reference Qtr1 if possible rather than forcing a pure dynamic calc of the level-0 members. In fact, you should use this rule of thumb whenever you write MDX not just when writing it for the Time dimension.

Returning to Pressman's solution in Chapter 7, the trick is how you make what might look ugly and unusable to a user more palatable using a view dimension that is clearly explained in that chapter. One other thing you will need to know for his chapter is how to do some string concatenation in MDX. Pressman's approach requires a consistent naming convention and, by doing so, allows us to use MDX text functions to dynamically generate the name of the nonlevel-0 member we want to capture in our formula.

For his method, you will need to understand and leverage an MDX formula like the following:

```
StrToMbr(ConCat([Time].CurrentMember.MEMBER_NAME, "_YTD"))
```

This function takes the member name of the current member and concatenates it with the text string "_YTD." The StrToMbr() function converts the newly concatenated string that is being returned to an Essbase member name. The result of this formula will point to a nonlevel-0 member of the primary Stored hierarchy in Pressman's examples. Finally, you do have to make it a Tuple with the [Periodic] member of the View dimension:

```
(StrToMbr(ConCat([Time].CurrentMember.MEMBER_NAME, "_YTD")),
[Periodic]).
```

In my opinion, Pressman's method is the most efficient way of calculating period to date results for ASO cubes with large time dimensions; if your time dimension is not very large, then some of the other approaches discussed above may be easier to implement and maintain.

6.9.3 Time Balancing

Time balancing is another feature BSO developers enjoyed that was missing from ASO when it was first released. Time Balancing has since been added to ASO as an option; however, it is often not practical to utilize ASO's native time balancing functionality because it limits the developer in a number of other areas.

First, it is important to understand what Time Balancing is and why it is necessary. In many applications, there are certain measures that do not aggregate over time, such as balance sheet accounts. Many applications load the monthly closing balance to the balance sheet account and not the monthly activity. In this case, it is not accurate to aggregate balances period over period. Instead, the proper result for upper level, subtotal members, is to reflect the last balance. Sometimes it may be necessary to capture a starting balance. This issue also can be applied to other measures, such as head counts and inventory measures.

If the application design is simple, it is possible to use the native time balancing functionality. However, very often this is not optimal. For starters, in order to use Time Balancing in ASO, you must tag a dimension as Account. While an Account dimension was central to BSO applications because of its unique functionality, the term carried over to ASO without any of the benefits. In fact, setting a dimension as the account dimension can often be very bad for performance because tagging a dimension as an Account dimension sets a dimension storage type to a Dynamic hierarchy. If the account dimension is large, this can be very bad for performance. Secondly, in order to leverage Time Balancing in ASO you can only have Stored hierarchies in your Time dimension, which may be an issue for you depending on your requirements.

Fortunately, through the use of MDX, you can achieve Time Balancing results. One example may be that you only have one or two members that need to be Time Balanced. If so, depending on if you already have a View dimension or not, you may just opt to create a member in the measures dimension to deal with Time Balancing.

As an example, determining headcount may clarify this technique. Create a member called Load_Headcount and, in the data Load rules, load headcount data to this member. Then create a member of a Dynamic hierarchy with a member formula called [Headcount] with the following formula:

```
IIF(IsLeaf([Time].CurrentMember), [Measures].[Load_Headcount],
(ClosingPeriod ([Time].Levels(0), [Time].CurrentMember),
[Measures].[Load_Headcount]))
```

Here we are saying if the member is level-0, go ahead and grab the level-0 member value of the load member, but if it is a nonlevel-0 member, then using the ClosingPeriod() function find the value of the last level-0 descendant of the member being queried. You could just as easily use the OpeningPeriod() function if your need is to get the starting balance.

One complication to this is when users want to skip missing values. I'm not a big fan of this, even when it was easy in BSO, but there are certainly use cases for it. This can be accomplished using MDX, but admittedly it is a bit more complicated.

```
IIF(IsLeaf([Time].CurrentMember), [Measures].[Load_Headcount],
IIF(NonEmptyCount ([Time].CurrentMember.Children, [Measures].[Load_
Headcount]) > 0,
([Measures].[Load_Headcount], Tail(Filter(DESCENDANTS([Time].
CurrentMember,10,LEAVES),
Not IsEmpty ([Measures].[Load_Headcount]))).Item(0).Item(0)),
MISSING))
```

Here we are using some conditional logic to seek out the last member with a value and skip over the missing cells. First we evaluate if the current member of time dimension is level-0. If it is, then we just return the loaded value. If it is a nonleaf member (leaf is another way of saying level-0), then we first do an evaluation by doing a nonempty count of the children. This tells us if there is a value to be found. If there is, then we use a filter function to find the nonempty members of the set and use the Tail() function to grab the last one.

Another approach to this is to go back to our method of using a View dimension. To accomplish this, we use UDAs, which as mentioned earlier are exposed to MDX through custom properties. Very simply, you choose the members in your outline that need to be Time Balanced and you add a UDA like 'TB_LAST'.

Using the same example with [HeadCount], you can add the following formula to your existing [View].[YTD] member:

```
CASE WHEN IsUDA([Measures].CurrentMember, "TB_Last") THEN
IIF(IsLeaf([Time].CurrentMember), [View].[Per],
IIF(NonEmptyCount ([Time].CurrentMember.Children, [View].[Per]) > 0,
([View].[Per], Tail(Filter(DESCENDANTS([Time].
CurrentMember,10,LEAVES),
Not IsEmpty ([View].[Per]))).Item(0).Item(0)), MISSING))
ELSE SUM(PeriodsToDate([Time].Generations(2), [Time].
CurrentMember), [View].[Per]) END
```

Similar to what we did above, we are still seeking out the last nonempty member, but this time we are using the IsUDA() function to determine to which members the logic should be applied. Also note in the ELSE clause that we are inserting our YTD logic. Hence, now we have logic for our YTD member that crosses all members, knows which need to be time balanced and which need to be summed up. This gives the end users a very simple POV option in their reports to toggle on and off Time functionality.

6.10 TIPS AND TRICKS

There are numerous tips and tricks that could be included in this section. The following pages will review some of my favorite tricks for querying metadata including:

- Returning all Members of a Dimension
- Querying for Descendants
- Querying for Ancestors
- Querying Level-0 Members
- What Level/Generation?
- Counts
- Filter Counts
- Filters
- Querying Properties
- Filtering on Attributes
- Filtering on UDAs
- Counts with UDAs and Attributes
- Query for Shared Members
- Calculating Optimal Sparse Dimension Order

6.10.1 Querying Metadata

One of the more useful purposes I have found for MDX is to query the outline to find out things about my metadata. As an administrator, I often have questions about the outline that I need to know in order to answer a user request or perhaps leverage for optimization. Below are a number of examples that I have used. Because I have already explained the basics of queries, we can just run through these with a brief explanation and a code example. I encourage readers to work with these examples and tweak them for your own applications.

Note that in most examples I am not looking to return data, I just want a list of members that meet certain criteria. For these samples, I am going to use an empty set, defined by curly braces with nothing in them { }, on my COLUMN axis.

6.10.1.1 Returning All Members of a Dimension Using the Members() function with any dimension will return a set with all members of the dimension. It is also possible to specify a particular layer to limit the members returned to a single layer. A layer is another way of saying a Generation or a Level.

```
SELECT {} ON AXIS(0),
[Year].Members ON AXIS(1)
FROM [Sample.Basic];

Axis-1
+------------------
 (Year)
 (Qtr1)
 (Jan)
 (Feb)
```

```
 (Mar)
 (Qtr2)
 (Apr)
 (May)
 (Jun)
 (Qtr3)
 (Jul)
 (Aug)
 (Sep)
 (Qtr4)
 (Oct)
 (Nov)
 (Dec)
```

6.10.1.2 Querying for Children Members Many functions have the option of being written in traditional format, such as Children([Time]) or a type of MDX shorthand [Time].children.

```
SELECT {} ON AXIS(0),
{[Year].[Qtr1].Children} ON AXIS(1)
FROM [Sample.Basic];

Axis-1
+-------------------
 (Jan)
 (Feb)
 (Mar)
```

Sometimes a user may want to join two sets together. Note that this is different from a Crossjoin() that combines sets from different dimensions. In this example, we are simply combining two sets to make one larger set.

```
SELECT {} ON AXIS(0),
{[Qtr1].Children, [Qtr2].Children} ON AXIS(1)
FROM [Sample.Basic];

Axis-1
+-------------------
 (Jan)
 (Feb)
 (Mar)
 (Apr)
 (May)
 (Jun)
```

When combining two sets, it is possible to return the same member twice if the member is in both sets as shown in the example below. It is up to the user to remove duplicates by using other functions, such as the Union() function and the Distinct() function.

```
SELECT {} ON AXIS(0),
{[Year].Members, [Year].Children} ON AXIS(1)
```

```
FROM [Sample.Basic];

Axis-1
+-------------------
 (Year)
 (Qtr1)
 (Jan)
 (Feb)
 (Mar)
 (Qtr2)
 (Apr)
 (May)
 (Jun)
 (Qtr3)
 (Jul)
 (Aug)
 (Sep)
 (Qtr4)
 (Oct)
 (Nov)
 (Dec)
 (Qtr1)
 (Qtr2)
 (Qtr3)
 (Qtr4)

SELECT {} ON AXIS(0),
Distinct({[Year].Members, [Year].Children}) ON AXIS(1)
FROM [Sample.Basic];

OR

SELECT {} ON AXIS(0),
Union({[Year].Members}, {[Year].Children}) ON AXIS(1)
FROM [Sample.Basic];

Axis-1
+-------------------
 (Year)
 (Qtr1)
 (Jan)
 (Feb)
 (Mar)
 (Qtr2)
 (Apr)
 (May)
 (Jun)
 (Qtr3)
 (Jul)
 (Aug)
 (Sep)
 (Qtr4)
 (Oct)
 (Nov)
 (Dec)
```

Note that with the Union() function, using the ALL keyword will retain duplicates.

```
Union({[Year].Members}, {[Year].Children}, ALL)
```

6.10.1.3 Querying for Descendants These examples show how to query descendants. To save some trees, I will not output all the results because the results should be pretty self-explanatory.

This query will return descendants, including the query member. Note that this function works with any member, not just the dimension root, so you could use a member that is in the middle of the hierarchy and return all descendants from that member down.

```
SELECT {} ON AXIS(0),
{Descendants([Year])} ON AXIS(1)
FROM [Sample.Basic];
```

This query returns descendants, excluding the query member.

```
SELECT {} ON AXIS(0),
Except({Descendants([Year])}, {[Year]}) ON AXIS(1)
FROM [Sample.Basic];
```

This query will only return level-1 descendants of the query member.

```
SELECT {} ON AXIS(0),
{Descendants([Year], 1)} ON AXIS(1)
FROM [Sample.Basic];
```

This query will only return level-0 descendants of the query member.

```
SELECT {} ON AXIS(0),
{Descendants([Year], Levels([Year],0))} ON AXIS(1)
FROM [Sample.Basic];
```

6.10.1.4 Querying for Ancestors This query allows you to query for ancestor members of the query member, searching up two levels. Take note that while the function requires a layer or index, it is not necessary to know exactly how many levels are in the dimension. There is no upper level on the index, so if you simply want to return all ancestors, you could use a number like 1000 instead of 2 in the index and still get the same results.

```
SELECT {} ON AXIS(0),
{Ancestors([Jan], 2)} ON AXIS(1)
FROM [Sample.Basic];

Axis-1
+-------------------
 (Year)
 (Qtr1)
 (Jan)
```

This query searches for ancestor members of the specified member, up to one level.

```
SELECT {} ON AXIS(0),
{Ancestors([Jan], 1)} ON AXIS(1)
FROM [Sample.Basic];

Axis-1
+-------------------
 (Qtr1)
 (Jan)
```

This query will return ancestors that are 0 levels up, essentially returning the query member. Note that while this is not usually practical, it is valid.

```
SELECT {} ON AXIS(0),
{Ancestors([Jan], 0)} ON AXIS(1)
FROM [Sample.Basic];
```

6.10.1.5 Querying Level-0 Members The query below returns all level-0 members of the dimension. Note the use of the Order() function in this example. Typically, Order() leverages a numeric value expression for sorting. Think of a case where you want to sort members in descending order by sales. In this case, we are looking to sort the member set alphabetically based on the member name overriding the default hierarchy order.

```
SELECT {} ON AXIS(0),
ORDER({[Year].levels(0).members}, [Year].CurrentMember.MEMBER_NAME)
ON AXIS(1)
FROM [Sample.Basic];

Axis-1
+-----------------------------
 (Apr)
 (Aug)
 (Dec)
 (Feb)
 (Jan)
 (Jul)
 (Jun)
 (Mar)
 (May)
 (Nov)
 (Oct)
 (Sep)
```

As mentioned above, sorting by [Sales] would be accomplished by:

```
SELECT {[Sales]} ON AXIS(0),
ORDER({[Year].levels(0).members}, [Measures].[Sales], BDESC) ON
AXIS(1)
FROM [Sample.Basic];

Axis-1              (Sales)
+-------------------+----------
 (Jul)              36134.0000
 (Aug)              36008.0000
 (Jun)              35088.0000
```

```
 (May)                   33674.0000
 (Dec)                   33342.0000
 (Sep)                   33073.0000
 (Apr)                   32917.0000
 (Oct)                   32828.0000
 (Jan)                   32538.0000
 (Mar)                   32213.0000
 (Feb)                   32069.0000
 (Nov)                   31971.0000
```

Notice the use of the key word BDESC in this case to sort the results in descending order.

This next query returns all level-0 members of the queried member. This is a little trickier, requiring us to use the full functionality of the Descendants() function.

```
SELECT {} ON AXIS(0),
{Descendants([Time].[1st Half], [Time].levels(0), SELF)} ON AXIS(1)
FROM [ASOSamp.Sample];
```

OR

```
SELECT {} ON AXIS(0),
{Descendants([Time].[1st Half], 100, LEAVES)} ON AXIS(1)
FROM [ASOSamp.Sample];
```

6.10.1.6 What Level/Generation? Sometimes an administrator may require certain information about their database. This query returns a list of all members and their level by using the intrinsic DIMENSION PROPERTIES.

```
SELECT {} ON AXIS(0),
[Time].members DIMENSION PROPERTIES [Time].[LEVEL_NUMBER] ON AXIS(1)
FROM [ASOsamp.Sample];

Axis-1                  Axis-1.properties
+-------------------+------------------
 (Time)                 (LEVEL_NUMBER = 4,
 (MTD)                  (LEVEL_NUMBER = 3,
 (1st Half)             (LEVEL_NUMBER = 2,
 (Qtr1)                 (LEVEL_NUMBER = 1,
 (Jan)                  (LEVEL_NUMBER = 0,
 (Feb)                  (LEVEL_NUMBER = 0,
 (Mar)                  (LEVEL_NUMBER = 0,
 (Qtr2)                 (LEVEL_NUMBER = 1,
 (Apr)                  (LEVEL_NUMBER = 0,
 (May)                  (LEVEL_NUMBER = 0,
 (Jun)                  (LEVEL_NUMBER = 0,
 (2nd Half)             (LEVEL_NUMBER = 2,
 (Qtr3)                 (LEVEL_NUMBER = 1,
 (Jul)                  (LEVEL_NUMBER = 0,
 (Aug)                  (LEVEL_NUMBER = 0,
 (Sep)                  (LEVEL_NUMBER = 0,
 (Qtr4)                 (LEVEL_NUMBER = 1,
 (Oct)                  (LEVEL_NUMBER = 0,
 (Nov)                  (LEVEL_NUMBER = 0,
 (Dec)                  (LEVEL_NUMBER = 0,
```

Use this query to return all members on the same level as the queried member.

```
SELECT {} ON AXIS(0),
{[Time].[Qtr1].Level.members} ON AXIS(1)
FROM [ASOsamp.Sample];

Axis-1
+--------------------
 (Qtr1)
 (Qtr2)
 (Qtr3)
 (Qtr4)
```

The following queries are the same as the queries above except they are based on Generation instead of Level.

```
SELECT {} ON AXIS(0),
{[Qtr1]} DIMENSION PROPERTIES [Time].[GEN_NUMBER] ON AXIS(1)
FROM [ASOsamp.Sample];

SELECT {} ON AXIS(0),
{[Time].[Qtr1].Generation.members} ON AXIS(1)
FROM [ASOsamp.Sample];
```

6.10.1.7 Counts Some very useful information can be derived using the Count() function. For instance, a developer or administrator may be interested in knowing how many level-0 members are in a particular dimension. Note that because we are now generating a numerical result instead of just a list of members, we cannot use an empty set on the column axis.

```
WITH
MEMBER
      [Year].[YearMemberCount] AS
             'Count([Year].Levels(0).members)'
SELECT {[Measures]} ON AXIS(0),
       {[Year].[YearMemberCount]} on AXIS(1)
FROM Sample.Basic;

Axis-1                (Measures)
+-------------------+-------------------
 (YearMemberCount)    12.00
```

This query will count the number of children for the specified member.

```
WITH
MEMBER
      [Year].[YearChildrenCount] AS
             'Count([Year].Children)'
SELECT {[Measures]} ON AXIS(0),
       {[Year].[YearChildrenCount]} on AXIS(1)
FROM Sample.Basic;
```

```
Axis-1                 (Measures)
+------------------+------------------
 (YearChildrenCount) 4.0000
```

This query will count the number of descendants for the specified member.

```
WITH
MEMBER
      [Year].[YearDescCount] AS
             'Count(Descendants([Year]))'
SELECT {[Measures]} ON AXIS(0),
       {[Year].[YearDescCount]} on AXIS(1)
FROM Sample.Basic;
```

```
Axis-1                 (Measures)
+------------------+------------------
 (YearDescCount)      17.00
```

6.10.1.8 Filter Counts Filters with counts can be very useful in scoping the set to certain criteria. Use this query to search for members that have only one child member. This can be useful when trying to understand your implied shares:

```
SELECT {} ON AXIS(0),
{FILTER({[Stores].members},
COUNT({[Stores].CurrentMember.Children}, IncludeEmpty) = 1)} ON
AXIS(1)
FROM [ASOsamp.Sample];
```

```
Axis-1
+---------------------------
 (Electronic Essentials)
 (Club Electronics)
```

This next query can be used to search for members that have more than 100 children. This is another query that can be used to help optimize an outline.

```
SELECT {} ON AXIS(0),
{FILTER({[Geography].members},
COUNT({[Geography].CurrentMember.Children}, IncludeEmpty) > 100)}
ON AXIS(1)
FROM [ASOsamp.Sample];
```

```
Axis-1
+---------------------------
 (CO)
 (KS)
 (NE)
 (IA)
 (IL)
 (IN)
 ...
```

6.10.1.9 Filters This next query uses the Filter() function and a text function to find members that begin with a particular text string; "801".

```
SELECT {} ON AXIS(0),
{FILTER({[Geography].members},
Substring([Geography].CurrentMember.Member_Name, 1, 3) = "801")} ON
AXIS(1)
FROM [ASOsamp.Sample];

Axis-1
+-----------------------------
 (80101)
 (80107)
 (80154)
 (80116)
...
```

Similar to the query above, this query will search for members that end with a particular text string, "25":

```
SELECT {} ON AXIS(0),
{FILTER({[Area Code].levels(0).members},
       Substring([Area Code].CurrentMember.Member_Name,
              Len([Area Code].CurrentMember.Member_Name ) - 1) =
              "25")} ON AXIS(1)
FROM [ASOsamp.Sample];

Axis-1
+-----------------------------
 (225)
 (425)
 (925)
```

In a similar manner to the two queries above, this query will search for members that contain a particular text string ("Digital") acting as the equivalent of a wildcard.

```
SELECT {} ON AXIS(0),
{FILTER({[Products].members},
       InStr(1, [Products].CurrentMember.Member_Name,
              "Digital", 1) > 0)} ON AXIS(1)
FROM [ASOsamp.Sample];

Axis-1
+-----------------------------
 (Digital Cameras/Camcorders)
 (Digital Cameras)
 (Digital Recorders)
 (Digital Recorders)
```

Take note that using Distinct() will not eliminate duplicates in this situation because shared members are not considered duplicates.

```
SELECT {} ON AXIS(0),
Distinct({FILTER({[Products].members},
       InStr(1, [Products].CurrentMember.Member_Name,
             "Digital", 1) > 0)}) ON AXIS(1)
FROM [ASOsamp.Sample];
```

This query is an example where Distinct() works. In the first query, we create a compound set of all level-0 members of the Time dimension and the children of [Qtrl]. Because children of [Qtrl] are level-0 members of the time dimension, this will intentionally result in a set with duplicate members. In the second query, the use of the Distinct() function eliminates the duplicate members from the compound set.

```
SELECT {} ON AXIS(0),
       {[Time].levels(0).members, [Qtr1].Children} ON AXIS(1)
FROM [ASOsamp.Sample];

/*vs*/

SELECT {} ON AXIS(0),
       Distinct({[Time].levels(0).members, [Qtr1].Children}) ON
AXIS(1)
FROM [ASOsamp.Sample];
```

6.10.1.10 Querying Properties These are codes used by Essbase for member-type properties. Note that in this context a "Measure" will be any member in the dimension tagged "Account," which does not have a member formula and is not the dimension root member.

```
0 = Member (Non-Measure)
1 = Dimension Root member
2 = Member with Formula
3 = Measure
```

This query returns a list of members with the member type property displayed.

```
SELECT {} ON AXIS(0),
[Measures].members DIMENSION PROPERTIES MEMBER_TYPE ON AXIS(1)
FROM Sample.Basic;

Axis-1              Axis-1.properties
+-------------------+-------------------
 (Measures)          (MEMBER_TYPE = 1, t
 (Profit)            (MEMBER_TYPE = 3, t
 (Margin)            (MEMBER_TYPE = 3, t
 (Sales)             (MEMBER_TYPE = 3, t
 (COGS)              (MEMBER_TYPE = 3, t
 (Total Expenses)    (MEMBER_TYPE = 3, t
 (Marketing)         (MEMBER_TYPE = 3, t
 (Payroll)           (MEMBER_TYPE = 3, t
 (Misc)              (MEMBER_TYPE = 3, t
 (Inventory)         (MEMBER_TYPE = 3, t
 (Opening Inventory) (MEMBER_TYPE = 2, t
```

```
 (Additions)            (MEMBER_TYPE = 3, t
 (Ending Inventory)     (MEMBER_TYPE = 3, t
 (Ratios)               (MEMBER_TYPE = 3, t
 (Margin %)             (MEMBER_TYPE = 2, t
 (Profit %)             (MEMBER_TYPE = 2, t
 (Profit per Ounce)     (MEMBER_TYPE = 2, t
```

Use this query to find only members that have member formulas.

```
SELECT {} ON AXIS(0),
       {FILTER([Measures].levels(0).members,
              [Measures].CurrentMember.MEMBER_TYPE = 2)} ON AXIS(1)
FROM Sample.Basic;

Axis-1
+-------------------
 (Opening Inventory)
 (Margin %)
 (Profit %)
 (Profit per Ounce)
```

Use one of these queries to find members tagged as Expense. Note that this will only apply to BSO because ASO databases do not support expense members.

```
SELECT {} ON AXIS(0),
       [Measures].members DIMENSION PROPERTIES [Measures].[IS_
EXPENSE] ON AXIS(1)
FROM Sample.Basic;

OR

SELECT {} ON AXIS(0),
       {FILTER([Measures].members,
              IsAccType([Measures].CurrentMember, Expense))} ON
AXIS(1)
FROM Sample.Basic;

Axis-1
+-------------------
 (COGS)
 (Total Expenses)
 (Marketing)
 (Payroll)
 (Misc)
 (Opening Inventory)
 (Additions)
 (Ending Inventory)
```

6.10.1.11 Filtering on Attributes Utilize one of these queries to find members with a particular text attribute.

```
SELECT {} ON AXIS(0),
Attribute([Bottle]) ON AXIS(1)
FROM [Sample.Basic];
```

```
OR

SELECT {} ON AXIS(0),
Withattr([Pkg Type], "==", "Bottle") ON AXIS(1)
FROM [Sample.Basic];

Axis-1
+-------------------
 (100-30)
 (200-10)
 (200-20)
 (200-30)
 (200-40)
 (300-10)
 (300-20)
 (400-10)
 (400-20)
 (400-30)
```

Utilize one of these queries to find members with a specific Boolean attribute set to true.

```
SELECT {} ON AXIS(0),
{FILTER({[Product].members},
       [Product].CurrentMember.[Caffeinated])} ON AXIS(1)
FROM [Sample.Basic];

OR

SELECT {} ON AXIS(0),
Withattr([Caffeinated], "==", "TRUE") ON AXIS(1)
FROM [Sample.Basic];

Axis-1
+-------------------
 (100-10)
 (100-20)
 (200-10)
 (200-20)
 (300-10)
 (300-20)
 (300-30)

OR to look for the opposite

SELECT {} ON AXIS(0),
Withattr([Caffeinated], "==", "FALSE") ON AXIS(1)
FROM [Sample.Basic];
```

Note that the following two examples will not work because "TRUE" is not a member of an attribute dimension in this database. "TRUE" is a property of a Boolean Type Attribute Dimension. Do not get confused with Text Attribute types where in another database a developer may have created members in the attribute dimension with the names "TRUE" and "FALSE."

```
SELECT {} ON AXIS(0),
Attribute([True]) ON AXIS(1)
FROM [Sample.Basic];

AND

SELECT {} ON AXIS(0),
Attribute([Caffeinated].[True]) ON AXIS(1)
FROM [Sample.Basic];
```

When using Date attributes, the following will not work.

```
SELECT {} ON AXIS(0),
Withattr([Intro Date], "==", "04-01-1996") ON AXIS(1)
FROM [Sample.Basic];
```

The correct way to query date attributes is to leverage the Todate() function as in the following example:

```
SELECT {} ON AXIS(0),
Withattr([Intro Date], "==", Todate("mm-dd-yyyy", "04-01-1996"))
ON AXIS(1)
FROM [Sample.Basic];
```

Lastly, to demonstrate using a numeric attribute, we use the following:

```
SELECT {} ON AXIS(0),
Withattr([Population], ">=", 12000000) ON AXIS(1)
FROM [Sample.Basic];

Axis-1
+-------------------
 (New York)
 (Florida)
 (California)
 (Texas)
 (Illinois)
 (Ohio)
```

6.10.1.12 Filtering on UDAs These queries allow the user to query members based on a User Defined Attribute.

```
SELECT {} ON AXIS(0),
{Uda([Market], "Major Market")} ON AXIS(1)
FROM [Sample.Basic];

OR

SELECT {} ON AXIS(0),
{FILTER({[Market].members},
       IsUda([Market].CurrentMember, "Major Market"))} ON AXIS(1)
FROM [Sample.Basic];
```

```
Axis-1
+-------------------
 (East)
 (New York)
 (Massachusetts)
 (Florida)
 (California)
 (Texas)
 (Central)
 (Illinois)
 (Ohio)
 (Colorado)
```

This is an example of how to combine functions to further scope the query.

```
SELECT {} ON AXIS(0),
{FILTER({Uda([Market], "Major Market")},
       Substring([Market].CurrentMember.Member_Name, 1, 3) =
"New")} ON AXIS(1)
FROM [Sample.Basic];

Axis-1
+-------------------
 (New York)
```

6.10.1.13 Counts with UDAs and Attributes Again, using counts can yield useful information about the database outline. This query returns the count of members with a particular attribute.

```
WITH
MEMBER
      [Geography].[AreaCode719Count] AS
             'Count(Withattr([Area Code], "==", "719"))'
SELECT {[Measures]} ON AXIS(0),
       {[Geography].[AreaCode719Count]} on AXIS(1)
FROM ASOSamp.Sample;

Axis-1                  (Measures)
+-------------------+---------
 (AreaCode719Count)     50.0000
```

Use this next query to compare counts of members with and without an attribute. This can be very helpful in resolving data that does not tie out due to a member not being properly tagged with an attribute. Problems are often caused by improper outline maintenance such as when a new SKU (stock-keeping unit) is added and the person adding it forgets to associate a color for the SKU; now the sum of all colors will not equal all SKUs in the base dimension.

```
WITH
MEMBER
       [Geography].[NoAttribute] AS
              'Count(Filter( [Geography].levels(0).members, NOT
              IsValid([Geography].CurrentMember.[Area Code])))'
```

```
MEMBER
       [Geography].[HasAttribute] AS
             'Count(Filter( [Geography].levels(0).members,
             IsValid([Geography].CurrentMember.[Area Code])))'
MEMBER
       [Geography].[Lev0Count] AS
             'Count([Geography].Levels(0).members)'
SELECT {[Measures]} ON AXIS(0),
       {[Geography].[NoAttribute], [Geography].[HasAttribute],
       [Geography].[Lev0Count]} on AXIS(1)
FROM ASOSamp.Sample;

Axis-1                (Measures)
+--------------------+----------
 (NoAttribute)            0.0000
 (HasAttribute)        9398.0000
 (Lev0Count)           9398.0000
```

Notice that the ASOSamp application has all attributes associated properly. However, if I edit the outline and remove the attribute from member [Geography].[80101] and rerun the query, I get the following results:

```
Axis-1                (Measures)
+--------------------+----------
 (NoAttribute)            1.0000
 (HasAttribute)        9397.0000
 (Lev0Count)           9398.0000
```

I can now run the next query to identify the member that does not have an attribute associated with it.

```
SELECT {} ON AXIS(0),
{Filter( [Geography].levels(0).members, NOT
 IsValid([Geography].CurrentMember.[Area Code]))} on AXIS(1)
FROM ASOSamp.Sample;

Axis-1
+--------------------
 (80101)
```

The next query is written to count the number of members tagged with the “Major Market” UDA.

```
WITH
MEMBER
       [Market].[MajorMarketCount] AS
             'Count(UDA([Market], "Major Market"))'
SELECT {[Measures]} ON AXIS(0),
       {[Market].[MajorMarketCount]} on AXIS(1)
FROM Sample.Basic;

Axis-1                (Measures)
+--------------------+----------
 (MajorMarketCount)      10.0000
```

6.10.1.14 Query for Shared Members Identifying shared members is a bit more complicated and requires the use of the Generate() function. This query will return all members of a dimension and flag which ones are shared members or duplicate members.

```
WITH MEMBER [Measures].[Products_SharedMembers] AS
        'Count(
        Generate({[Products].CurrentMember} AS [var1],
        Generate(Filter([Products].Levels(0).Members,
        [Products].CurrentMember.[MEMBER_NAME] =
        [var1].Item(0).Item(0).[MEMBER_NAME]),
        Filter ({[Products].CurrentMember},
        IsAncestor( [Products], [Products].CurrentMember )))))'
SELECT
{[Measures].[Products_SharedMembers]} ON AXIS(0),
[Products].Levels(0).Members ON AXIS(1)
FROM [ASOSamp.Sample];
```

Use this query to refine the query above and only return the shared members or duplicate members.

```
WITH MEMBER [Measures].[Products_SharedMembers] AS
'Count(
Generate({[Products].CurrentMember} AS [var1],
Generate(Filter([Products].Levels(0).Members,
[Products].CurrentMember.[MEMBER_NAME] =
[var1].Item(0).Item(0).[MEMBER_NAME]),
Filter({[Products].CurrentMember},
IsAncestor([Products], [Products].CurrentMember)))))'
SELECT {} ON AXIS(0),
Filter(
Except([Products].Levels(0).Members,
Descendants([All Merchandise])),
[Measures].[Products_SharedMembers] > 1) ON AXIS(1)
FROM [ASOSamp.Sample];

Axis-1
+-------------------
 (Flat Panel)
 (HDTV)
 (Digital Recorders)
 (Notebooks)
```

6.10.2 Calculating Optimal Sparse Dimension Order

It has long been believed that the hourglass model of largest dense to smallest dense and then smallest sparse to largest sparse would yield the best outline order for a BSO application. In many cases, this is true, but it is not based on the dimensions with largest or smallest member counts, but rather the largest and smallest parent to child ratios. Because this has been generally difficult to calculate, most developers have used member count as the starting point for assessing outline dimension order. Using the query below, an administrator can quickly calculate a dimension's parent/child ratio and compare with other dimensions to determine optimal outline order. Run the queries below and then match up against the member counts for the dimensions. I think you will be surprised with what you find and may reconsider the dimension order for the outline. I acknowledge that Sample.Basic is too small to notice a performance difference, but you can build on this and use it with your larger BSO applications for potential improvements in aggregation time.

```
WITH
MEMBER [Measures].[Market Ratio] AS
'(COUNT([Market].members) - COUNT([Market].levels(0).members)) /
(COUNT([Market].members) - 1)'

MEMBER [Measures].[Product Ratio] AS
'(COUNT(Except([Product].members, Descendants([Diet]))) -
       COUNT(Except([Product].levels(0).members,
       Descendants([Diet])))) /
       (COUNT(Except([Product].members, Descendants([Diet]))) - 1)'
SELECT {[Year]} ON AXIS(0),
{ [Measures].[Market Ratio], [Measures].[Product Ratio] } ON AXIS(1)
FROM [Sample.Basic];

Axis-1                (Year)
+-------------------+------
 (Market Ratio)       0.2083
 (Product Ratio)      0.2941
```

A review of the Dimensions tab for Sample.Basic in EAS shows that the Product dimension has fewer stored members compared to the Market dimension and, therefore, the designer set the Product dimension to precede the Market dimension in the outline order. Based on the calculations above, there is a good argument to have the Market dimension precede the Product dimension based on the smaller parent/child ratio. As with most concepts pertaining to Essbase, it is hard to put an absolute rule that will always present optimal results. Nonetheless, I encourage developers to run this calculation and consider testing alternate outline to see if BSO calculation performance can be enhanced.

6.11 CLOSING

My hope in writing this chapter is that the reader comes away from it with a better understanding of not only how to make MDX work, but, more importantly, some creative ways to use MDX. My experience has been that very few Essbase users use MDX for anything other than member formulas in an ASO database. While admittedly that is a required skill for ASO developers, I believe MDX can enhance the user experience beyond member formulas. One of the reasons I think it is difficult to get users to invest time in learning MDX is because in many ways it goes against the ease of use that Essbase offers. Why should someone learn how to write complex MDX scripts when they can simply use the Office Add-In or SmartView to easily retrieve a lot of the same content without the use of scripts? Hopefully, I have done a good job of demonstrating some use cases where it would be difficult to obtain the same results using anything other than MDX. My expectation is that the reader of this book is not the everyday Essbase end user and, therefore, will have an appreciation for the nuances that MDX offers. I also believe that a thorough understanding of these concepts will enable any Essbase developer to write more advanced member formulas when the requirement arises. Best of luck in your coding journeys.

7

HOW ASO WORKS AND HOW TO DESIGN FOR PERFORMANCE

Dan Pressman

CONTENTS

7.1 INTRODUCTION

Like everyone else, when I first saw ASO (aggregate storage option) I was amazed how fast it was; it could return results without the long "cooking" time required by BSO (block storage option) cubes. All of that Dense/Sparse stuff was no longer important, and I no longer had to worry when blocks were created or about database size explosion, etc. Initially, I learned to write the simple MDX (multidimensional expressions) needed to convert BSO member formulae for use in ASO and then I gradually learned to write MDX and used it to add some of the features not available when ASO first came out, such as time balance and nonpositive consolidation tags in the Accounts dimension. While this added needed functionality, soon I noticed my cube load time was slowing down and the queries were getting pokey.

With much reading and experimenting, I learned to design cubes that would load, aggregate, and retrieve with all the speed of my first, simple cubes. This chapter lists a number of design rules I have developed and now use to optimize performance, along with the reasons behind those rules. It is my hope that you the reader will be able to not only use these rules, but also gain an understanding of the reasons in order to make informed decisions. The implications of not following the rules can be major, but if you decide to relax them, then you will be able to understand and accept the consequences.

Let me state clearly that the purpose of this chapter is to design a cube that performs maximally, ***minimizing the need for extensive aggregations by maximizing the opportunities for powerful, highly leveraged aggregations that work over the widest number of queries.*** This will reduce the trap that I fell into in the beginning, an overdependence on aggregations. I will show that aggregations have a cost, not only in the time to compute them, but in the all-important footprint your cube occupies in memory. Aggregated Views are an incredibly powerful tool, albeit, potentially costly; by optimizing your design, you will maximize their benefit.

7.1.1 Who Should Read This Chapter

This chapter is recommended for those who have built at least a few ASO cubes and have already fought with the wizard as it converts your nice old BSO cube to an ASO cube that really should have been faster. You probably have already built an alternate hierarchy or two, and fought your way through at least a couple of conversions from BSO member formulae to MDX (you certainly do not need to be anywhere near an expert).

Most important, your situation might be one of these:

- Your cube is slow to query.
- Your cube requires extensive aggregation to make it usable.
- You are getting ready to build a really big cube.

7.1.2 What Will and Will Not Be Covered

It will be assumed that you either know how to or can find out how to build dimensions with either EAS or MaxL. The same holds for performing aggregations and querying the cube by retrieving from the Excel® Add-in or SmartView™.

7.2 SUMMARY: RULES OF ASO DESIGNING FOR PERFORMANCE

As I said in the introduction, I have developed design rules that I use in my work. In the belief that sometimes it is easier to start with conclusions, I have listed them as **Rules of ASO Designing for Performance**. The balance of this chapter will explain how Essbase ASO works and the underlying reasons for my rules. In fact, if you find some of the details presented more than you wish to follow, you can skim, focusing on the rules only, and spend time on Section 7.6.2 (Alternative Design Options: Designing to Maximize Use of Stored Hierarchies), which provides examples of designs that make use of these rules. I hope that you will return to the explanatory text later to gain an understanding of ASO design and the reasons behind the rules.

R1: The Input-level and Aggregation-data for all loaded ASO cubes should fit into memory (or it ain't really ASO).

R2: Wherever possible, data should be calculated from Stored nonformula Members.

R3: All queries against the same aggregation level take the same time.

R4: Do not depend on aggregation or other "Maintenance" to make up for bad design.

R5: Alternate hierarchies, whether Dynamic or Stored or Attribute, are almost always cheap … give the user what they want.

R6: Label-Only members have no cost—use them to enhance your cube's readability.

R7: Changes to hierarchy order are cheap or free, so design for user convenience.

R8: Designs requiring queries of multiple Attributes of the same base dimension may suffer performance degradation; evaluate and consider alternatives.

R9: The use of a Compression dimension is not a given; consider and test alternatives including not having a Compression dimension.

R10: The use of the Accounts dimension tag has substantial costs; alternatives should be considered strongly.

R11: Analysis dimensions are cheap or free; use them.

R12: A query will be run against the smallest View whose aggregation level on each dimension is less than or equal to the aggregation level of the query (for the same hierarchy), so you do not have to create Aggregated Views on all dimensions.

And, One More Rule:

Pop's Rule: "Computers do arithmetic very fast, but they don't like to run errands."

7.3 ASO QUERIES: HOW THEY WORK

In order to understand how ASO queries work, we first have to understand how ASO cubes store data. Essbase is all about hierarchies, whether we are talking ASO or BSO. Some people have described Essbase as essentially an SQL (Structured Query Language) database with automatic materialized views at each level of the combined dimensional hierarchies. (*Note:* "Materialized view" is the Oracle term, "materialized query tables" is used in DB2, "indexed views" is used in Microsoft® SQL Server.) This is close, but it is an oversimplification. With BSO cubes, the cube calculation process materializes an aggregated, dense block for every nondynamic, upper-level sparse member combination. Then, within each of those aggregated dense blocks, it calculates any nondynamic upper-level dense members. An SQL materialized view is dynamic and changes when the underlying data changes. In contrast, in BSO, the values in all of the aggregated, calculated dense blocks are not dynamic and are valid only for the level-0 data at the time of running the calculation. One must rerun the calculation to update them.

ASO cubes work differently. Instead of materializing the view and adding up all of the data values for each hierarchy combination (as BSO does), ASO essentially materializes an index (which I will call a bitmap) and attaches it to the input-level data. This bitmap index is designed to allow every level of the hierarchy to be rapidly calculated dynamically at the time of the query.

Then, if that still is not fast enough, ASO allows the creation of materialized views of this bitmap enhanced input data. These are known as Aggregations or Aggregated Views.

7.3.1 What Does a Cube Look Like?

Before I go into the details of how ASO creates this multilevel index and the performance insights we can learn from those details, let us first look at a physical analog of an ASO cube.

7.3.1.1 A Cube You Can Hold in Your Hand How many readers have actually seen an ASO cube? Really, are you sure? Could you describe what you saw? In reality, I think you will admit that you have seen how an ASO cube can be *used*, but have not seen an actual cube (can you look into your server's memory and see how all of those transistors lithographed on the memory chips form a cube-like structure?).

Once upon a time, over 40 years ago, people would do data analysis using physical data cards that may or may not have been generated from a computer database. Here is a physical "cube" that was first produced in 1961 (Figure 7.1) (similar guides were available for gardeners and bird watchers).

I recently discovered that this mineral sort guide is still manufactured and available for sale today. Can you imagine someone sitting down and patiently punching out these cards? I am told that users like the portability and visualization of the query process they get when using this system. In Figure 7.2, you can see a close-up of what a portion of an ASOsamp data card would look like.

When using these cards:

- Punched holes represent the absence of metadata.
- Notches represent metadata.
- Holes & Notches were used for both:
  - Level-0 metadata
  - Upper-level metadata
- Fact data was printed on the card body.

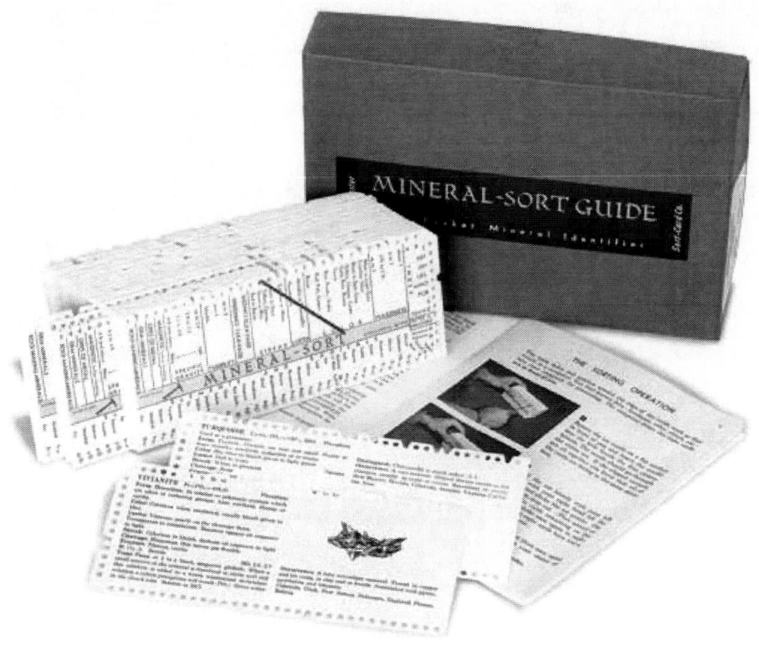

Figure 7.1 Physical data cube.

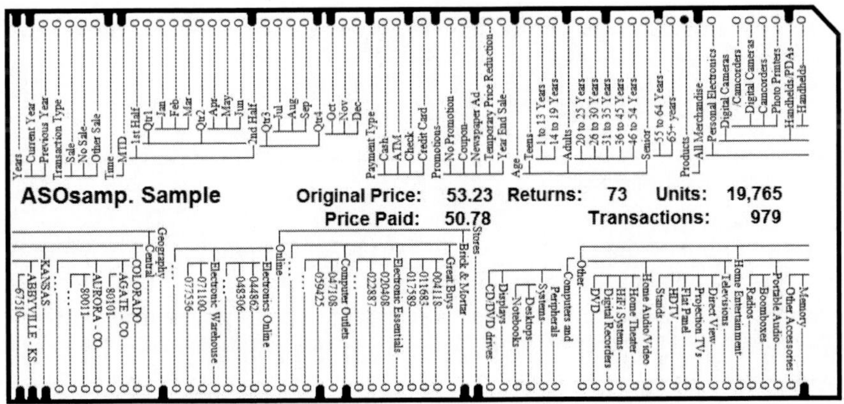

Figure 7.2 Close-up of a portion of an ASOsamp data card.

So, a query for [Televisions] (a level-1 member in the [Product] dimension) would involve pushing the needle through that spot on the card and lifting the cards up. The cards that *did not lift* would be [Televisions]. Of course, I could only fit a portion of the metadata onto the card; that is why you notice the **...** members in Figure 7.2 above indicating where some members have been left out.

Manual Calculation—There was no way to add up any fact data printed on the card. This system was useful only in querying to find the subset of cards with the specified metadata.

7.3.1.2 The Query Needle The actual query was done by the use of a "Query-Needle" or "Sorting-Needle" (Figure 7.3) that was passed through the deck of cards for each

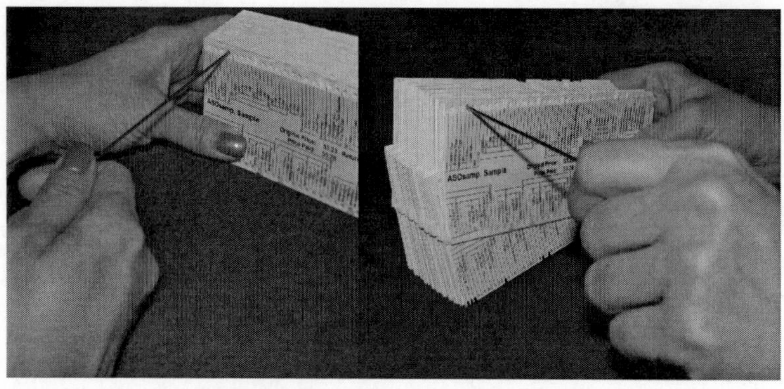

Figure 7.3 Demonstration of the use of the Sorting-Needle.

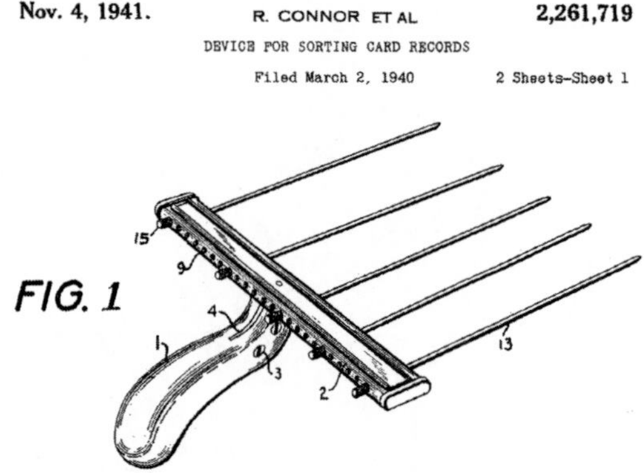

Nov. 4, 1941.
R. CONNOR ET AL
2,261,719
DEVICE FOR SORTING CARD RECORDS
Filed March 2, 1940
2 Sheets-Sheet 1
FIG. 1
15
9
4
1
3
2
13

Figure 7.4 Multiprocessor Sorting-Needle.

metadata element in the query. The needle was passed through for each piece of metadata in the query and then lifted up, bringing with it the subset of cards that had the queried values. "OR" clauses in the query were performed by repeating the process on the original box of cards. "AND" clauses were executed by performing the needle query only on those cards lifted previously:

A major innovation (one worthy of a patent) was the multiprocessor sorting-needle (Figure 7.4).

7.3.2 The Essbase ASO Implementation of the Sorting-Needle, the Holes, and the Notches

ASO cubes work similarly to the deck of punched/notched cards described above. Each piece of numeric fact data stored on the card is represented as an "input-level" cell in Essbase. A binary code representing each piece of level-0 metadata in each dimension is attached to the input-level cell. Additionally, a binary code representing each upper-level classification of metadata in each dimension is attached. The binary code combines to be the equivalent of the holes and notches punched on the card.

I will refer to this binary code in this chapter as the "bitmap." With this bitmap attached to each input-level cell, ASO is able to search for any member, even upper-level

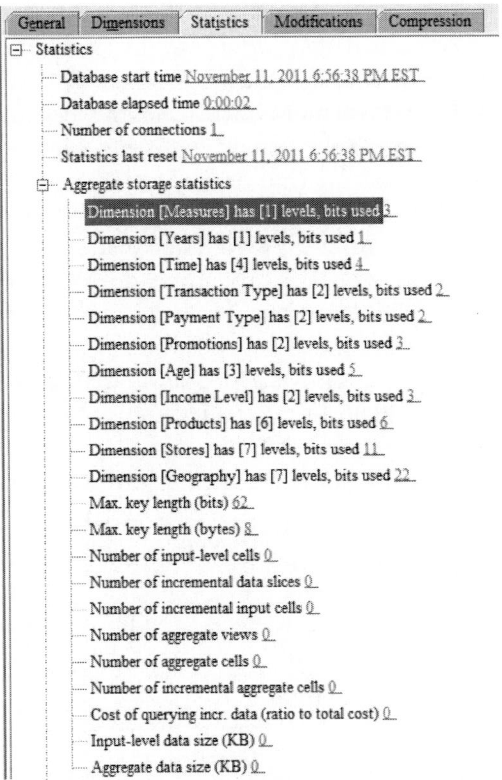

Figure 7.5 ASOsamp.Sample database properties: Statistics. (From Oracle Essbase Administration Services. With permission.)

ones because the input-level cell is uniquely identified in its own right and as a descendant of its ancestors. The structure of this bitmap can be seen on the "Statistics" tab in the "Database Properties" dialog in Essbase Administration Services (EAS) (Figure 7.5).

The fact that the **bitmap identifies each level-0 member directly, without wandering through the hierarchy, is the key to understanding ASO**. As a simple example of this direct identity, consider a cube for my family: A query would find me as one of the descendants of my grandfather Nathan Pressman without having to check the genealogy contained in the outline that indicates I am the son of Abraham Pressman who is, in turn, the son of Nathan.

The role of the sorting-needle is played by a bitmap "mask" that the query engine generates when it translates your query for execution. This mask indicates where there must be a 0 (zero) and where there must be a 1 and can also in some implementations indicate where it could be either, resulting in a bit string that might look something like 00000100??????1010?????????. A query then becomes a simple matter of comparing this mask to the bitmap attached to each input-level cell. As I will show, the bit code attached to each input-level cell is not just a simple hole or punch (bit) for each member, but is instead a multibit code that identifies not only the member name to which the card data applies (let us say their current age), but also a series of bits that allows my card to be identified as belonging to me or to a descendant of my father or to a descendant of my grandfather, all of which I (hopefully) am.

A query that was to find the combination of me (Dan) and my brothers, Norman and Eric, and to compute our combined ages, would (in the simplest technical implementation) have to make three passes through the stack of fact data cards: One to find Dan, another for Eric and a third for Norman. Each time, the age would be grabbed and a running total calculated. Alternatively, a smarter sorting-needle would make one pass, checking each card to see if it was for Dan or Eric or Norman, and again, totaling the age for each card found. Even better, if you knew that the three brothers were the *only* descendants of Abraham, then a single pass could be made.

The computer version of these queries, of course, does not utilize a sorting-needle, but uses the bitmap mask. It should be noted that this comparison of a set of bits to a "mask" is something that computers have been designed to do extremely quickly. In fact, there is often a machine-level hardware operation that allows a range of keys to be evaluated by a mask and the data portion summed.

7.3.3 The Essbase ASO Implementation of the Card Box: The Importance of Memory Space

Of course (returning to the analogy of the physical cards above), all of the cards must be in one "box" and the length of the sorting-needle long enough to pass through the entire box. Otherwise the queries will be slowed down as each of the "boxes" in the database is picked up and the needle passed through. In case you have not guessed already, the size of the box is analogous to the amount of memory available. This brings us to the first **Rule of ASO Designing for Performance:**

R1: The Input-level and Aggregation-data for all loaded ASO cubes should fit into memory (or it ain't really ASO).

In other words, you should have enough RAM available to accommodate the total size of the ASO .dat files for the cubes you plan to run. The .dat file size also can be found on the Statistics tab in the Database Properties dialog in EAS by adding "Input-level data Size" and "Aggregate Data Size" (see Figure 7.5).

Okay, at this point some of you who have already built ASO cubes are going to be quite surprised. You may have already built some large ASO cubes that could not fit into memory or that could not fit after you added a lot of aggregations. But think back, why was Essbase and BSO invented in the first place? Because the analysis of a large SQL database took too long. This was for two reasons: (1) the star schema on which it was most likely based had to be traversed, and (2) because all of the tables of that schema had to be read off the disk. BSO was an answer because it blended what was essentially a normalization of the fact data into two groups (the dense and the sparse) and combined the metadata descriptions into the outline. That took care of the star schema. Then BSO went on to precompute all of the hierarchies' combinations so they would be available quickly without reading all of the input data.

When Essbase version 5 came out, dynamic calculation was added, which was most often used for calculations within the dense block. This recognized that computers were larger and had more memory, thus more data could fit into that memory and be calculated on the fly. Reading the data does not take long if it is already in memory. ASO takes that one step farther and does all of its calculations on the fly. If that data has to be read off the disk drive, you are little better off than with a SQL database. I will return to this topic later when I introduce the last rule (Pop's Rule) and again in Section 7.8 (A Final Word about Rule R1).

In summary, I say "it ain't really ASO" if you have to be reading off the disk drive. By having all of the .dat file information in RAM, ASO Essbase can dynamically do the stored rollups that are the essence of ASO quickly and easily.

Note: I am not referring to the memory in the aggregate storage cache. The total unused memory available on your machine after starting all services (EPM and other programs) and loading all of the BSO and ASO cubes you plan to run should equal the sum of all the ASO .dat files for the cubes you plan to load. In Windows, this memory available may be found on the Resource Monitor's Memory tab. On the bar graph, it would be the sum of the dark (Standby) and light blue (free) areas. The Green In-Use area includes the ASO Caches for your loaded cubes.

7.3.4 The Essbase Implementation of the Data Card

The data on the face of the card is either the numeric fact data itself or simply the metadata description (in Essbase, the alias) of the data punched on the perimeter (effectively, the Member name). Nothing surprising there. But, what is "punched" on the perimeter, i.e., seen in the bitmap? Metadata identifying any level-0 stored data of course, but what about upper-level data? The only upper-level data that can be punched on the perimeter is that from a known hierarchy; one without dynamic calculations (either consolidation or formula based).

What do I mean by that last sentence? With a physical card, if we had a dataset of circular objects (say, buttons), we would most likely have the radius of each button as a data element on the card. We could include the value of that radius in a set of hole punches. If we also wanted to know the surface area of the button, we would have to calculate πr^2. If we wanted that value as a searchable piece of metadata punched on the card, we would have to calculate it in advance and then have a set of punches for the different area measurements. The sorting-needle could not make the calculation for us because it can only sort based on ready-to-go metadata, i.e., data that has been punched on the edge.

An upper-level cube member cube works the same way. In order for the result of a calculation to be found by the bitmap, it would have to be precalculated. An upper-level member that is the result of calculation, such as πr^2, cannot be queried directly by the bitmap mask, just as it could not be queried by the sorting-needle. In ASO terms, πr^2 is dynamic. If you take out your calculator (or have SQL do it before load) and compute it, you could punch the resulting value onto the card and ASO can code it into the bitmap. But, the formula would not really be on the card, would it? The results of applying the formula would be on the card. It certainly would not change dynamically when the value of r (presumably a data element on the card) was changed.

In Essbase terms, the *only* dynamically calculated data that can be found as the equivalent of a hole on the card is the additive sum of predefined sets of lower-level members as organized in the hierarchy. As mentioned earlier, the bitmap identifies data not just by its member name, but also by the upper-level hierarchies to which it belongs. Actually, that last sentence should be modified to read "… the upper-level *Stored* hierarchies to which it belongs." Upper-level membership in Stored hierarchies is the *only* upper-level membership to be found in the bitmap.

7.3.4.1 Stored Dimensions/Hierarchies The punched card description/analogy and bitmap mask comparison (or sorting-needle-like processing) applies *only* to Stored dimensions, and only Stored dimensions take advantage of aggregation. This yields the second **Rule of ASO Designing for Performance:**

R2: Wherever possible, data should be calculated from Stored dimensions.

This is the single most important rule and the one most often overlooked in cube design.

In Essbase terms, the dynamically calculated nonadditive data must be members of a Dynamic hierarchy. In fact, returning to our button example, suppose we had an outline where both the radius r and the area were level-zero members. Because we are not calculating the area πr^2 before the data load, there must be a formula on the area member calculating it as a function of the (stored) member r. When you look in EAS, the area's member property appears as "stored" and, in this case, it also is a level-0 member. It is really level-0 in name only, and only because it has no children below it. In reality, it does have a lower-level member on which it depends for its value: the radius r, which is a level-0 member elsewhere in the dimension. If the area had been precalculated and the result loaded, then it truly would be a stored level-0 member. As we continue to look at Essbase outlines, you will often see this distinction made in references to "Stored level-0 nonformula members." It is these "Stored level-0 nonformula members" that are represented in the bitmap.

Actually, let us take a few moments to discuss the terms "Stored" and "Dynamic," particularly for those who are used to BSO Essbase cubes. In BSO, "Stored" and "Dynamic" refer to members. Stored upper-level BSO members have their values determined when the database is calculated; Dynamic BSO members have their values determined during retrieval. In contrast, both Stored and Dynamic upper-level ASO members have their values determined at retrieval time. This is actually a curiosity that comes from looking at the member level storage properties for upper-level members. They always appear as stored. One might say that all upper-level Stored ASO members are *dynamically calculated* by summation of the lower-level stored members.

The "Stored" term for upper-level Stored hierarchy ASO members refers to the fact that they are *storable using an aggregation* or summation of lower-level Stored members. This "selective" summing is performed by comparison of the data's bitmap or key with a bitmap mask as defined by the query.

For now let me sum up the discussion of Stored dimensions by saying that they are the key to ASO performance and design alternatives are presented in Section 7.6.2 to facilitate the use of Stored dimensions and avoid the use of MDX (which is, of course, a dynamic operation) where possible. The summary in Section 7.9 provides strategies for organizing and thinking about your MDX in ways that leverage Stored hierarchies.

An Exercise for the Reader: Think about how the bitmap mask is used. Why is the addition (+) consolidation operation the only operator that can be used in Stored hierarchies?

You may have noticed that I just switched from using the term "Stored dimension" to "Stored hierarchies." By enabling "Multiple Hierarchies" (Outline: Member Properties at the dimension level "Information" tab "Hierarchy Information"->"Hierarchy"-> "Hierarchies Enabled"), a *dimension* can be both "Stored" and "Dynamic." The individual hierarchies within it are then each either Stored or Dynamic. Please consider the use of the term "Stored dimension" to be interchangeable with "Stored hierarchy" for a "Multiple Hierarchies Enabled" dimension. This is also true for the terms "Dynamic dimension" and "Dynamic hierarchy."

7.3.4.2 Dynamic Hierarchies You may have noticed when modifying an outline that you can add lower-level members to be consolidated or write an MDX formula for a level-0 member of a Dynamic hierarchy. This is true even if the "Data Storage" member property is set to "Store Data."

What then of a Dynamic dimension level-0 member with the "Data Storage" member property set to "Store Data" that does *not* have a member formula? It behaves exactly like a member of a Stored dimension in queries. In fact, we will see that a flat Dynamic dimension with "Label Only" or "No Consolidation" at the dimension level behaves exactly like a Stored dimension. This is really an exception to my emphatic use of *only* when I said above "... the above description/analogy applies *only* to Stored dimensions ..." and leads to a slight technical modification of that rule:

R2: Wherever possible, data should be calculated from Stored nonformula Members.

This rule originally said Stored dimensions. "Stored Members" includes level-0 members of Dynamic dimensions that do not have MDX formulas.

Remember, of course, that a Stored upper-level member of a Dynamic hierarchy cannot take advantage of aggregation ;in other words, it cannot be materialized in an aggregation.

7.3.4.3 Dynamic Query Performance and the Critical Importance of Solve-Order The details of how MDX should be written are discussed in Chapter 6 (Practical MDX for Essbase Developers) by Gary Crisci.

In this chapter, however, I deal only with the performance impact of dynamic operations, be they MDX formulae or dynamic outline consolidation . It is critical to realize that all queries are eventually resolved by the ASO query engine into a combination of queries against Stored hierarchies or stored members. In Chapter 6, Crisci notes that member formulae are seen in the MDX version of queries as "WITH" clauses. It is as if the base part of the MDX (the Select statement) is executed against the Stored members, and then the WITH clause is executed on the result.

Bad design can result in a dynamic query being split into multiple stored queries. Query-based aggregation will then speed up these generated stored queries, but the results will still have to be combined in the ASO cache by the MDX processor. And that adds to query response time.

Understanding that all queries are eventually resolved to a dynamic combination of queries against stored members is important. Also, it is important to remember that aggregations are stored query results with some or all dimensions being at upper-levels. In fact, one could call the input-level data the level-0 aggregation (and because aggregations also are known as Views, this chapter and the literature will often refer to the input-level data as the level-0 View). Knowing this and thinking back to the punched cards in the physical data cube described above, it should be apparent that:

R3: All queries against the same aggregation level take the same time.

With punched cards, it takes the same amount of time to run the sorting-needle through the hole for an upper-level member as for several lower-level members (with the multiprocessor model of the sorting-needle as in Figure 7.4). Similarly, each query of the data at the same level of aggregation requires the same time to query.

7.3.4.4 Compression Dimension The concept and use of dimension tag "Compression" is an important factor in ASO performance and is related to the physical example of how data is stored on the card. Since tagging a dimension as Compression forces it to be Dynamic, let us touch on it briefly and then return to it in Section 7.4.3.3 when we have the tools to delve into it more fully.

The Compression dimension allows multiple pieces of fact data to be grouped together and identified when they have common metadata; essentially placed together on the same card and categorized by a common set of holes and notches. The members grouped together in a dimension tagged as "Compression" may or may not be consolidated in a hierarchy (which would have to be a Dynamic hierarchy), and they may or may not be referenced by MDX. Returning to the analogy of the physical cards, the level-0 members of the Compression dimension operate like multiple pieces of fact data on the face of the same data card. These different pieces of fact data share the same notches and holes (metadata) of the other dimensions, thus avoiding having multiple cards with identical metadata.

In ASO terms, the level-0 members of the Compression dimension share the same bitmap identifying them in the outline. As I will show, the metadata for the small outline ASOsamp requires a bitmap of 8-bytes (the Key Length on the Statistics page). That means 8 bytes of overhead for each set of fact data. ASO requires 8 bytes for each element of fact data in the fact data set. Without Compression, there is only one piece of fact data in the set, so the overhead is 8 bytes of metadata for each 8 bytes of fact data, or 100%. With Compression, the five level-0 members of [Measures] (40 bytes) share the same 8 bytes of metadata, so only a 20% overhead.

Remember that this savings comes at the cost of giving up on any possible Stored hierarchy (i.e., additive) consolidations that might be possible in the dimension. The dimension tagged as Compression *must* not only be Dynamic, but it must be Dynamic in its entirety; i.e., it cannot have "Multiple Hierarchies Enabled."

This tradeoff will be considered in more detail in Section 7.4.3.3. For now, I would ask that you ignore the issue of Compression on performance until the bitmap construction is addressed.

7.3.5 Is It Really That Simple?

With all your experience with computers and databases, etc., I know you realize that there are always more issues, and you probably have already thought of a few of them. Many of the ones I suspect you have thought of, such as alternate hierarchies and attributes, will be addressed. It is important to understand that if the basic rules to be learned from the bitmap are not adopted, no amount of aggregation or slice clean-up will help. In fact, let us make this our fourth rule:

R4: Do not depend on aggregation or other "Maintenance" to make up for bad design.

Okay, on to the bitmap.

7.4 THE BITMAP: ITS ROLE AND FUNCTION

I have discussed the bitmap generically and how it effectively creates an index that allows queries to directly access any level-0 member or all of the level-0 descendants of an upper-level member. Where BSO calculation "precooked" the data at all levels, ASO effectively "precooks" by providing an index at all levels.

Moving from a generic to a more specific analysis, the data found in EAS, on the "Statistics" tab of the "Database Properties" dialog, is crucial to understanding performance implications of your cube design. In Figure 7.5, the "bits used" for each dimension are shown. When combined, they make up the bitmap that is attached to each input-level cell. The "Max. key length (bits)" is the sum of these "bits used." The "Max. key length (bytes)" is the bitmap overhead attached to each input-level cell. It is the "Max. key length (bits)" rounded up to the nearest 8 byte (64 bit) boundary.

7.4.1 Why Should Anyone Care about the Bitmap?

Why indeed? From a high level, the reasons include:

- Increasing the use of Stored hierarchies and attributes can greatly improve performance, but there are costs to be paid in terms of the size of the bitmap.
- It can be worth paying the "cost" of increasing the bitmap and the input-level data size to increase performance without aggregation.
- There are ways to design the hierarchies to minimize the length of the bitmap and, therefore, the input-level database size.
- Dynamic members can be used to make a cube that has been optimized as suggested above to appear to the user as originally designed (see Section 7.6.2.1).

In actuality, all of the above relate to the reducing size of the input-level database and are derived from the prime importance of R1: We need to reduce the footprint of the cube to enable it to fit into memory.

7.4.2 How Is the Bitmap Constructed?

The bitmap is calculated independently for each standard dimension (with attribute dimensions operating effectively as alternate hierarchies). The number of bits will depend on the number of siblings at each level and the number of levels. The number of bits required for each dimension is then summed and rounded up to the nearest multiple of 64 bits. The DBAG (Database Administrators Guide) documentation of this is shown below. Mastering the details of the construction described in the remainder of this section is not strictly required to take advantage of the lessons to be gained from the result of that construction. The reader should feel free to skip ahead and come back for detail later.

The following is reprinted with permission from Oracle Corporation, *Oracle Essbase Administrators Guide Release 11.1.2.1* (Oracle Press, 1996, 2011) Chap. 62, p. 934 (DBAG):

64-Bit Dimension Size Limit For Aggregate Storage Database Outline

An aggregate storage database outline cannot exceed 64-bits per dimension.

The number of bits needed by a dimension is the maximum number of bits used by any level 0 child, including the level 0 children in alternate hierarchies and associated attribute dimensions. For the purposes of member numbering, attribute dimensions are treated as alternate hierarchies of their base dimensions.

In general, the formula to determine the number of bits required for any member in a dimension can be expressed as:

```
# _ bits _ member's _ parent + log(x)
```

where x is the number of children of the parent.[DBAG 1]

For example, if the member's parent is member A, which requires 5 bits, and A has 10 children, the number of bits required by each child is:

```
5 + log(10) = 9 bits
```

The top member of a dimension or hierarchy usually uses 0 bits. However, when one or more top generations consist of label-only members, the label-only members do not receive member numbers (because they are not considered stored members) [DBAG 2]. Therefore, if there are x members in the first nonlabel-only generation[DBAG 3], those members use log(x) bits. The rest of the children below them are numbered normally.

Similarly, if a dimension or hierarchy is dynamic, only the level-0 members that are stored or shared receive member numbers. The number of bits required for those members is log(x), where x is the number of level-0 members that are stored or shared (that is, the number of level-0 members that are not formula members)[DBAG 4].

If, however, any alternate hierarchies have stored (nonshared) level-0 members, each member of every hierarchy in the dimension (including associated attribute dimensions) uses an extra log(x) bit, where x is the total number of hierarchies and associated attribute dimensions for this base dimension[DBAG 5].

The following example uses the Products dimension in the ASOsamp.Sample database (Figure 7.6):

The Products dimension has two hierarchies: All Merchandise and High End Merchandise, which is an alternate hierarchy. High End Merchandise has one stored level-0 member: Stored Member. The Products dimension does not have any associated attribute dimensions.

Members All Merchandise and High End Merchandise use log(2) = 1 bit.

Note: If the alternate hierarchy High End Merchandise did not have any stored level-0 members, the top members of each hierarchy (and associated attribute dimensions) would each use 0 bits.

The calculation of the number of bits required by each level-0 children:

```
All Merchandise = 1 bit
    Personal Electronics, Home Entertainment, Other = 1 + log(3) =
    3 bits
        Digital Cameras/Camcorders, Handhelds/PDAs, Portable
        Audio = 3 + log(3) = 5
```

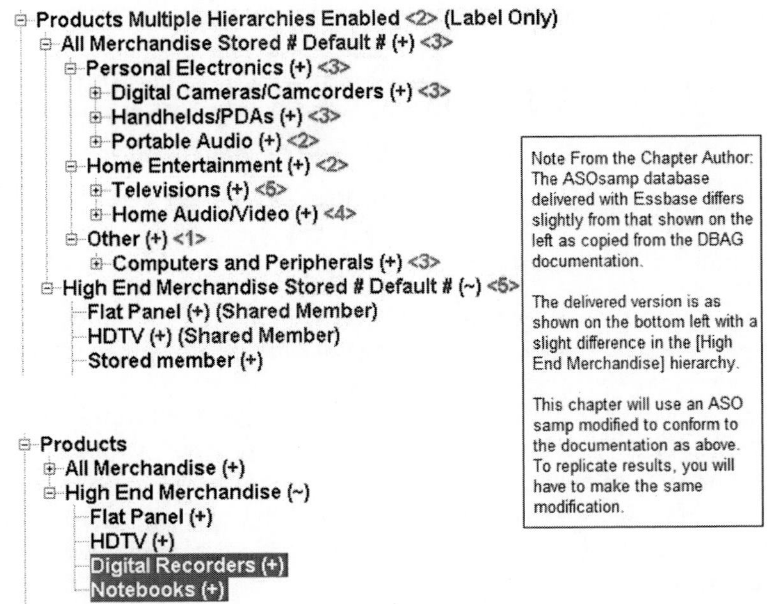

Figure 7.6 DBAG v11.1.2.1, Chap. 62, p. 935. (From Oracle Essbase Administration Services. With permission.)

```
          Children of Digital Cameras/Camcorders = 5 + log(3) = 7
          Children of Handhelds/PDAs = 5 + log(3) = 7
          Children of Portable Audio = 5 + log(2) = 6
      Televisions, Home Audio/Video = 3 + log(2) = 4
          Children of Televisions = 4 + log(5) = 7
          Children of Home Audio/Video = 4 + log(4) = 6
      Computers and Peripherals = 3 + log(1) = 3 **
      Systems, Displays, CD/DVD drives = 3 + log(3) = 5
          Children of Systems = 5 + log(2) = 6
High End Merchandise = 1 bit
    Flat Panel, HDTV, Stored Member = 1 + log(3) = 3 bits
```

Member Computers and Peripherals has the same number of bits (3) as its parent Other[DBAG 6].

The maximum bits used by any level 0 children in the Products dimension is 7 (Children of Digital Cameras and Children of Televisions). Therefore, Products uses 7 bits, which is less than the dimension size limit of 64 bits.

Note: Referencing marks have been added as [DBAG #] for use later in this chapter.

Note: References to the log(x) function should be assumed to mean the log-Base2(x) or log(x,2).

7.4.2.1 Bitmap Construction Summary: For a Dimension with a Single Stored Hierarchy Using the information from the DBAG, we can deconstruct how a bitmap is calculated for a dimension with a single Stored hierarchy. For each set of level-0 siblings in the hierarchy, calculate recursively up the hierarchy the number of bits per sibling family as:

Log(SiblingCount) + Log(SiblingCount(Parent))

Or, using non-recursive notation:

$$\text{\# bits per sibling family} \equiv \sum_{i=\text{level}-0}^{\text{level}-\max} \text{Log SiblingCount}(l(i))$$

and find the maximum number of bits over all sets of sibling families.

$$\text{\# bits per Stored hierarchy} \equiv \max(\text{\# bits per sibling family})^{[\text{DBAG 1}]}$$

This maximum will be the number of bits required for the Stored hierarchy, where:

- Parents with only one child are effectively ignored in the bitmap and level count[DBAG 6] because Log(1) = 0. This behavior is not related to the "Never Share" tag and appears to be unaffected by this tag.
- *level-max* above is the highest level that is not tagged "Label Only"[DBAG 2]. The sentence from the DBAG above: "Therefore, if there are x members in the first nonlabel-only generation …" [DBAG 3] should probably refer instead to the highest level that is not tagged "Label Only." Anyone who has struggled to understand the outline verification message "Label only members must span all of the uppermost levels" has wrestled with the differing definitions. In support of this assertion, it should be noted that the error message refers to *uppermost levels*, not *generations*. This explains why a formerly balanced hierarchy when made ragged by adding new generation(s) results in this message.

7.4.2.2 Bitmap Construction Summary: For a Dimension with a Single Dynamic Hierarchy Once we understand a dimension with a single Stored hierarchy, the single Dynamic hierarchy is simply:

$$\text{\# bits per Dynamic hierarchy} \equiv \text{Log}(\text{Count}(\text{level} - 0, \text{nonformula members}))^{[\text{DBAG 4}]}$$

7.4.2.3 Bitmap Construction Summary: For a Dimension with Multiple Stored and/or Dynamic Hierarchies Bitmap construction for a multiple hierarchies-enabled (combination) dimension is only a little more complex. Calculate the #bits for each of the Stored or Dynamic dimensions separately, as above. Then find the maximum bit length amongst these Alternate hierarchies. In addition to this maximum value, if and only if any of the alternate hierarchies contains a nonformula, non-shared level-0 member, you would add log(Count(hierarchies)) [DBAG 5]. In this case, the bitmaps for each of the nonmaximum length hierarchies essentially lay "on top" of the bitmap for the largest hierarchy and is differentiated by the hierarchy number.

Remember that Attribute dimensions are *considered* alternate hierarchies of the dimension on which they are based. Therefore, their bitmaps must be computed and considered when calculating the hierarchy with the longest bitmap.

Also, beware that in cases where Multiple Hierarchies are not enabled but an attribute dimension has been associated, Multiple Hierarchies, in fact, are implicitly enabled. It is easy to miss this situation when calculating the bitmap length, so watch for it.

7.4.3 Primary Lessons from the Bitmap

7.4.3.1 Alternate Hierarchies Because the bitmaps for alternate hierarchies are shorter and effectively overlay that of the bitmap of the hierarchy requiring the longest bitmap (the primary), cube designers should feel free to add alternate hierarchies. There is little cost in terms of impact on the length of the bitmap and, therefore, database size and/or performance. Stated as our fifth rule:

R5: Alternate hierarchies, whether Dynamic or Stored or Attribute, are almost always cheap … give the user what they want.

At most, the cost of adding an alternate hierarchy is the addition of log(# of hierarchies) bits. This cost occurs only if any of the secondary hierarchies have a nonshared level-0 member as noted at [DBAG 5]. Stated another way, if the set of secondary level-0 members is a subset of the set of primary level-0 members, then the addition of log(# of hierarchies) bits is not required.

Note: The hierarchy with the longest bitmap (whether it is listed first or not) is known as the primary hierarchy, and the remainder are the secondary hierarchies.

Unless you have an alternate hierarchy with a very expensive design, add alternates without fear. I have had a number of clients who have asked for dictionary-style hierarchies that listed all of their members alphabetically by member name or by description, or even, ordered by a secondary alias table. By doing this with a Dynamic hierarchy with label-only section headings, there was no cost to the length of the bitmap, only in build time for the outline. In fact, let us include a rule about "Label Only" members:

R6: Label-Only members have no cost; use them to enhance your cube's readability.

Because the number of alternate hierarchies in a single dimension typically does not exceed 8 or, in some cases, 16, then only 3 or 4 bits would be added. Even in the extreme case where the number of hierarchies reached the maximum of 256 (requiring 8 bits), we would have to assume that the count of level-0 members would be so high that these 8 bits would not be material. Next, note that because the bitmaps of the shorter hierarchies overlay the longest and that it is only in the special situation found in [DBAG 5], which is dependent on hierarchy order, that performance will be little affected by changing the hierarchy order. Thus, our next Rule:

R7: Changes to hierarchy order are cheap or free, so design for user convenience.

Just to make things clear, changes are cheap in terms of cube performance because the bitmap length is nominally impacted, if at all. There may be a one-time cost in terms of reorganization if you make the change with data already loaded.

A caveat to R7: In a somewhat cryptic conversation with developers (cryptic due to the subject's encroachment on "trade secrets"), it was noted that situations wherein some of the level-0 members were *not* shared (i.e., did not appear in the first, primary hierarchy), alternate hierarchies can result in difficult (longer) run times when the outline must be restructured. This situation is similar to that shown in Figure 7.6

where the member [Stored member] makes its first (and only) appearance in the outline in the hierarchy [High End Merchandise]. If you do reorganizations with the data still in the cube and find your restructures either failing or running inordinately long, you should test to measure the impact and consider alternatives, such as clearing and reloading the data, or rethinking your hierarchies to see if the [DBAG 5] situation can be eliminated.

By the way, the [DBAG 5] issue can come up when not expected. Suppose you had a first hierarchy that had 100% of the level-0 members in it and all of the alternates had a subset of those level-0 members appearing as shared. I have seen cases where the longest hierarchy (the primary, i.e., the one that determines the bitmap length) is not this first 100% hierarchy. This type of a situation would occur if an alternate hierarchy had many more levels than the first. Now, if it also has 100% of the level-0 members *and no additional new (nonshared)* members, then there would be no issue. It would simply become the primary and there would be no nonshared members in any of the alternates. If it had, say, only 90% of the level-0 members found in the first hierarchy and a much more detailed set of levels above them than the first hierarchy, a 90% hierarchy could have a longer bitmap. It would become the primary hierarchy, and the first hierarchy with its now newly identified 10% would become the secondary. Thus, you may expectantly end up with the situation described in the preceding paragraph.

7.4.3.2 Attribute Dimensions Attribute dimensions are a powerful tool to use in your design. Unlike a standard alternate hierarchy, they can be used to create a cross-tab query. Using ASOsamp as an example, you could generate a report of unit sales by size, with the products on the rows and the sizes as column headings. If size was instead modeled as an alternate hierarchy, there would be a [Size] Stored hierarchy added to the [Product] dimension with the different size classifications appearing as children of [Size] and the level-0 product members appearing as shared members under the appropriate size classification. However, this design would not allow a cross-tab report of the type described above because it would require members of the same dimension, [Products], to appear as both row headings and as column headings.

Therefore, designing your cube with [Size] as an attribute seems the way to go. Of course, you also could make [Size] its own Stored dimension, but then you would have to add size information to your data load and you would have an increase in the size of the bitmap. Unlike BSO, Attribute dimensions are *not* always calculated dynamically and, therefore do not have the performance penalties they had in BSO. It is not explicitly stated anywhere, but all *Attribute dimensions are Stored hierarchies.* In fact, it is stated that *Attribute dimensions are regarded as alternate hierarchies of the base hierarchy.* Now this seems confusing. In the above paragraph, I described alternative cube designs for [Size], modeling it first as an alternate hierarchy and then as an Attribute dimension. I then showed that there were advantages to designing [Size] as an Attribute dimension. But, now I state that Attribute dimensions are regarded as alternate hierarchies anyway. This confusion stems from the use of the word *regarded.* From the point of view of the bitmap, they are alternates and as alternates are represented in the bitmap within the same set of bits reserved for the base dimension. It is a confusing description. Maybe Attribute dimensions should be described as "internally de facto alternate hierarchies," but that is not a distinction the documentation makes, so we will have to live with the confusion, drawing some comfort from knowing how they behave in reality.

At first look, Attribute dimensions being Stored are fast to calculate and can be aggregated, and because there is no net effect on the bitmap length, they should be cheap to incorporate in your cube and have no special implications to the query performance of your cube. Unfortunately, that might not always be the case. In the DBAG, we find the following, which is reprinted with permission from Oracle Corporation, *Oracle Essbase Administrators Guide Release 11.1.2.1* (Oracle Press, 1996, 2011) Chap. 62, p. 933, with my highlighting in italics on the most important parts:

Design Considerations for Attribute Queries

When selecting and building views based on attribute query data, some queries on attribute data are always dynamically calculated at the time of retrieval, which may affect query performance.

Every query involving attribute dimension members also must include at least one member from the base dimension. If the query involves a single attribute dimension and a sum-of-all dimension member, Essbase aggregates the query data, potentially improving query performance. *In other cases, Essbase must calculate the query at the time of retrieval.* (Table 200 describes attribute query types and how Essbase calculates the query.)

Table 200 Attribute Queries and Calculation Performance

Attribute Query Type	Query Calculation Type
Query involves a sum-of-all base dimension member and members from one attribute dimension.	Essbase can aggregate query data, potentially improving query performance.
Query involves any member of the base dimension and members from multiple attribute dimensions.	*Essbase calculates the query at the time of retrieval based on the level 0 input data.*
Query involves any child member of the base dimension member (or dimension member that is tagged as label-only) and members from one attribute dimension.	Essbase calculates the query at the time of retrieval based on the level 0 input data, or on data from aggregations on the base dimension.

The first Query type can take advantage of aggregations on the Attribute dimension and is no problem (assuming that Attribute aggregation has been enabled using "Consider Alternate Hierarchies" and aggregations have been materialized). The third type of query is also not a problem. While queries of the third type are not as easily improved as the first type, they can take advantage of base dimension aggregations. It is the highlighted second type of query that presents a problem. This is a very common situation. Queries are often run on multiple Attributes of the same dimension and you should carefully consider how your cube will be used.

It should be noted that queries of the second type are not totally out of the realm of improvement from aggregations: It would simply have to be an aggregation in another dimension. Aggregations are not required for all cases (e.g., upper-level members of all dimensions) to be useful; if they were, then we essentially would have a BSO cube. Instead, they are like stepping stones, different ones can be used to cross the river without getting your feet wet (i.e., querying the input-level data). In this case, the query engine simply would be restricted to choosing an Aggregation with level-0 for the [Products] dimension.

This could be expressed by a slight rewrite of the Query Calculation Type for the second type of query: Essbase calculates the query at the time of retrieval based on a View that retains the level-0 input data for the base dimension.

Why does ASO have this limitation anyway? We actually can see why by returning to the construction of the bitmap. The algorithm selects the hierarchy with the longest required bitmap for any dimension. Remember that within the set number of bits, the actual encoding on the record on disk and in memory can reflect only *one hierarchy at a time*. A member, even if it has one or more alternate incarnations as a shared member in other hierarchies, cannot be simultaneously in two places at once. In ASOsamp terms, at least while looking at the bitmap encoding, [HDTV] cannot be described as a descendant of both [All Merchandise] and [High End Merchandise] simultaneously. Similarly, a store cannot be represented in the bitmap as both [Brick & Mortar] and [10000] square feet. The bitmap cannot simultaneously represent both the base member name and the Attribute name (in a sense, the Attribute name is effectively an alias); the combination of the two does not exist and, therefore, cannot be Aggregated.

If the bitmap does not show the intersection of [Brick & Mortar] and [10000], there is no way that an Aggregated View could.

The solution, in extreme cases, would be to load the Attribute dimension as a Standard dimension. With separate bits reserved in the bitmap for the now separate dimensions, a query can find the fact data rows that are both [Brick & Mortar] and [10000]. This solution does have its costs, however. The Attribute-to-base relationship is no longer supplied at the time of outline building. Instead, it will be added to every row of fact data to be loaded. Additionally, it may result in exceeding the ASO limit on the number of Views.

ASO cubes are limited to having a maximum of 2**52 Views or "Stored dimension level combinations" (see DBAG v11.1.2.1 Appendix A Table 239). This number can be calculated by taking the product of the levels as seen in Figure 7.5. The product of these levels 1 * 1 * 4 * 2 * 2 * 2 * 3 * 2 * 6 * 7 * 7 equals 56,448. If the [Square Footage] Attribute dimension is converted to a standard dimension, its 2 levels are removed from the original 7 of the [Stores] dimension and become their own member of the calculated product of the levels: 1 * 1 * 4 * 2 * 2 * 2 * 3 * 2 * 6 * 5 * 2 * 7 equals 80,640 Views.

This issue is an important enough design consideration to warrant a rule:

R8: Designs requiring queries of multiple Attributes of the same base dimension may suffer performance degradation; evaluate and consider alternatives.

Another alternative, particularly for small Attribute dimensions, would be to build a compound attribute dimension. There is no logical candidate for this in ASOsamp, but if an auto manufacturer were to have a cube of its SKUs (stock-keeping units) as well as have two attribute dimensions of [Make] and [Color], and these were to be queried frequently together, there could be performance issues. Instead of converting one or both of these to standard dimensions, it might make sense to combine the [Make] and [Color] attributes into a compound attribute dimension. This technique is shown in Section 7.6.2.5.

It also should be noted that the "Varying Attributes" feature appears to effectively implement this compound Attribute in a more easily maintained manner. There is no guidance in the documentation for the effect of this feature on performance and as of this writing, I have not tested it.

Finally, before I leave the topic of Attributes, pay close attention to the issue of the Implied Share of the top level of an attribute dimension. Most cubes are designed such that every base member is *supposed* to be given an attribute association. When this is not done, it is often because of a failure in the metadata build process. For instance, returning to our auto manufacturer example, a new color option was added, but was not included in the metadata, so the new SKUs that were created were not able to associate to this new color and, therefore, have no color. Two problems result from this situation: (1) queries against [All Colors] will yield the wrong results (as they do not have a color), and (2) queries against [All Colors] and some other Attribute will be slow. This second situation arises because in the original case (before the addition of the "bad" unassociated SKU) where every level-0 member of the base dimension is in the primary hierarchy and every one of those level-0 members has an association to the [All Colors] dimension, [All Colors] becomes an implied shared alias of the top member of the base dimension primary hierarchy. As such, a query against [All Colors] and any other attribute of the base dimension is not really a query against "Two Attribute Dimensions" and, therefore, performed well.

Now consider the same query against [All Colors] and some other base dimension attribute after the addition of the "bad" (no color attribute) SKU. The member [All Colors] is no longer an implied share, so now the query *really is* a two-attribute query and will perform poorly.

The solution is to make sure that this failure in metadata creation never occurs. I also refer you to Crisci's Chapter 6 where he defines a query to test for this condition. I also suggest that as a backup, care should be exercised when defining partitions or smart slices. If an Attribute dimension is to be hidden from a user, then it *should not be referenced* in the smart slice definition. This will avoid exposing users to incorrect results for an Attribute that they do not even know exists.

Finally, it is a recommended best practice to include in an attribute dimension, such as [All Colors], a member such as [No Color] to be used as a default color when the color is unknown.

7.4.3.3 The Compression Dimension Now that you have left BSO, you thought you were done with Dense and Sparse, but not quite. In BSO, you would tend to group those dimensions that were commonly queried together as Dense dimensions. Then, starting in Version 5, the "Dynamic Calc" tag added the ability to delay the intra-Dense Block calculations until retrieval time. The objective became to find the set of dimensions with the most calculations. As memory became cheaper, the size of the dense block of data in most designs increased—to save more time during the cube calculation phase. This was an example of a rule my father (a hardware designer beginning in the late 1940s) taught me when I was 12 years old:

Pop's Rule: "Computers do arithmetic very fast, but they don't like to run errands."

I might not have understood what that really meant when I was 12, but I understood enough of his explanation to remember the rule (he actually had me write numbers on slips of paper and put them on a table in the next room). He told me that I was allowed to retrieve numbers one at a time. Even at 12, I could add faster than I could run; I learned that lesson quickly. It will always be faster to read two numbers (A and B) from a disk and calculate their sum (A + B) in memory than it will be to read three values (A, B, and the precalculated A + B). That was the guiding principle behind BSO Dense and Sparse. Dynamic calcs within the dense block were essentially the first-level implementation of my father's rule. In fact, you might ask why was Essbase designed to calculate anything in advance? The answer is that computers (i.e., memory) were not large enough to read all of the data in at one time to allow the "arithmetic" to run without interruptions ("errands") to get more data.

Now with larger computers and larger memory spaces, ASO completes the implementation of my father's rule and as a result: **In ASO, nothing is precalculated**. I should qualify that statement with a slight addition: **In ASO, nothing is precalculated in the level-0 View.**

Will there ever be a day when computers are fast enough that we do not need even the precalculations of ASO Aggregated Views? Not with the current design, where main memory is separated from the CPU and transfer is limited to bus speeds. There is still an "errand" to run, to fetch the number from memory. Oh, it is far faster than fetching from disk, but still the errand must be run. Maybe someday a "quantum" computer or some other new design might merge memory and processing, but until the day when "errands" are eliminated, we all will be slaves to their running to some extent.

In ASO, there is an opportunity to make a choice similar to Dense/Sparse by tagging one dimension as the "Compression" dimension. I described some of the workings of the Compression dimension a number of pages back when we discussed the five members of the [Measures] dimension in ASOsamp, but now I will go into the full story.

A dimension tagged as Compression is essentially a one-dimensional "Dense Block." Unlike BSO, where grouping into a dense block was done to avoid precalculation, our motivation in ASO is different because nothing is precalculated. As has been seen, ASO works its magic by attaching a long bitmap with a key length of some multiple of 8 bytes (let us assume 24 bytes for a medium metadata cube, so we are no longer referring to ASOsamp) onto each 8 bytes of fact data. This long key works like the punched cards to allow ASO to work at any level of the Stored members of the cube.

The 24 bytes of metadata for each 8 bytes of fact data work out to a cost overhead of 300% for each data element. What happens with Compression is that groups of up to 16 stored fact data members (in the dimension tagged as Compression) are combined to a total 128 bytes (16 members * 8 bytes) , and that group then has 24 bytes of metadata attached. This results in only 18.75% (24 ÷ 128) cost overhead for the data grouped by compression, a significant reduction.

This reduction from 300% to just 18.75% (a 281.75 point reduction) in the overhead is the best case. ASO groups the data into "bundles" of up to 16, so if there is not some multiple of 16 stored members in the Compression dimension, the last bundle will be only partially filled, thereby reducing the overall gain. The bitmap key now serves the function of the sparse index entry in BSO. Also, if some pieces of fact data do not always exist for each member of your Compression dimension, ASO will have to leave the corresponding "spot" blank.

7.4.3.3.1 Average Bundle Fill (ABF) ASO builds the members of the Compression dimension into the bundles of 16 in the order in which they first appear in the outline (it does not matter if they later appear as shared). If any member of a bundle of 16 exists in the fact data, then a "card" with that full set of 16 members is built. Given a dimension with 48 level-0 members, the bundles will be built (BM = bundle member) with BM1–BM16 on one record, BM17–BM32 on another record, and BM33–BM48 on another record. Now suppose that your fact data is only *populated* for BM3, BM5, and BM7 on the first record, and BM 24 and BM31 on the second record, and there are no instances of data populated that would go onto the third record. Half of your data would then be on records with 3 of the 16 spots occupied, and half would have only 2 of the 16 spots occupied. This would give (assuming that fact data *always* exist for these 5 members) an Average Bundle Fill (ABF) of 2.5. Notice that because no data exist for members of the third bundle, so the third record would never have to be created. This is why the DBAG suggests that you should order your outline so that those level-0 nonformula compression members that are most likely to be populated appear first in your outline.

In reality, you will never have a situation where fact data values either always exist or never exist across dimension members because they will vary with the data (hey, if they never exist, why are they in your outline?). The point is that the best case savings of 281.5% points only happens when you have a multiple of 16 fact data members in your Compression dimension and when all of each bundle of 16 either appear or do not appear. The ABF is a number that can only be calculated by looking at the specifics of your data. The Database Properties -> Compression tab makes this calculation assuming differing Compression dimensions (Figure 7.7).

In addition, ASO Compression does something to help when bundle members are missing. It varies the length of the record ("card") so that it does not always assume that all 16 bundle members will have data. Remember that the record length for a compressed cube would be (according to the description seen above) be equal to the metadata bytes

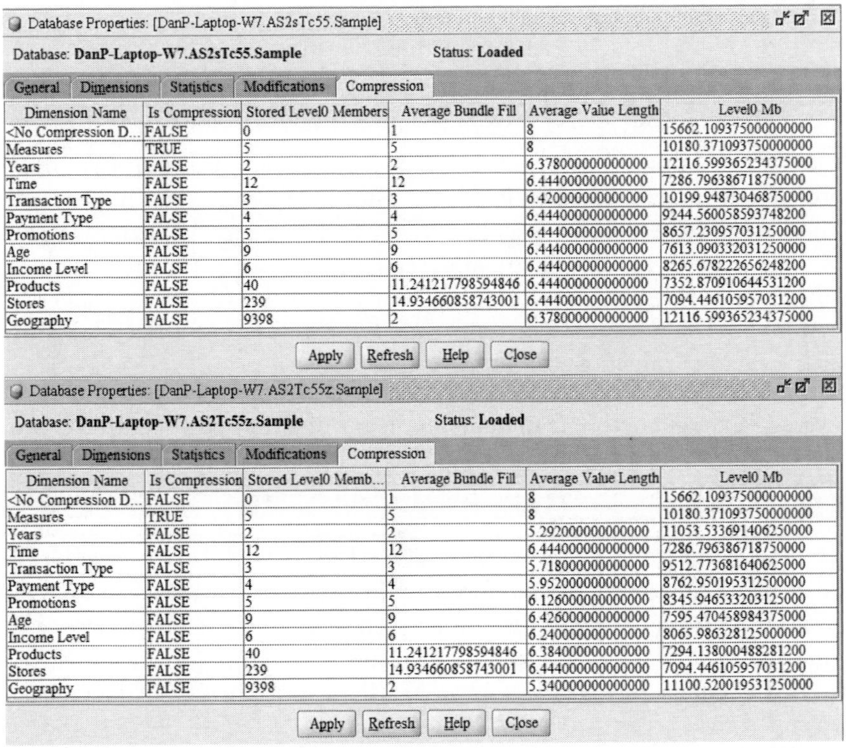

Database Properties: [DanP-Laptop-W7.AS2sTc55.Sample]

Database: **DanP-Laptop-W7.AS2sTc55.Sample** Status: **Loaded**

General | Dimensions | Statistics | Modifications | Compression

Dimension Name	Is Compression	Stored Level0 Members	Average Bundle Fill	Average Value Length	Level0 Mb
<No Compression D...	FALSE	0	1	8	15662.109375000000000
Measures	TRUE	5	5	8	10180.371093750000000
Years	FALSE	2	2	6.378000000000000	12116.599365234375000
Time	FALSE	12	12	6.444000000000000	7286.796386718750000
Transaction Type	FALSE	3	3	6.420000000000000	10199.948730468750000
Payment Type	FALSE	4	4	6.444000000000000	9244.560058593748200
Promotions	FALSE	5	5	6.444000000000000	8657.230957031250000
Age	FALSE	9	9	6.444000000000000	7613.090332031250000
Income Level	FALSE	6	6	6.444000000000000	8265.678222656248200
Products	FALSE	40	11.241217798594846	6.444000000000000	7352.870910644531200
Stores	FALSE	239	14.934660858743001	6.444000000000000	7094.446105957031200
Geography	FALSE	9398	2	6.378000000000000	12116.599365234375000

Apply | Refresh | Help | Close

Database Properties: [DanP-Laptop-W7.AS2Tc55z.Sample]

Database: **DanP-Laptop-W7.AS2Tc55z.Sample** Status: **Loaded**

General | Dimensions | Statistics | Modifications | Compression

Dimension Name	Is Compression	Stored Level0 Memb...	Average Bundle Fill	Average Value Length	Level0 Mb
<No Compression D...	FALSE	0	1	8	15662.109375000000000
Measures	TRUE	5	5	8	10180.371093750000000
Years	FALSE	2	2	5.292000000000000	11053.533691406250000
Time	FALSE	12	12	6.444000000000000	7286.796386718750000
Transaction Type	FALSE	3	3	5.718000000000000	9512.773681640625000
Payment Type	FALSE	4	4	5.952000000000000	8762.950195312500000
Promotions	FALSE	5	5	6.126000000000000	8345.946533203125000
Age	FALSE	9	9	6.426000000000000	7595.470458984375000
Income Level	FALSE	6	6	6.240000000000000	8065.986328125000000
Products	FALSE	40	11.241217798594846	6.384000000000000	7294.138000488281200
Stores	FALSE	239	14.934660858743001	6.444000000000000	7094.446105957031200
Geography	FALSE	9398	2	5.340000000000000	11100.520019531250000

Apply | Refresh | Help | Close

Figure 7.7 Database Properties > Compression Tabs for ASOsamp cubes with 1,026,432,000 cells. (From Oracle Essbase Administration Services. With permission.)

(**K**ey **L**ength **KL**) + data bytes (bundles of 16 * 8 bytes for each data element), or a total of **KL + 128 bytes.** We know that not all cubes have a nice, even multiple of 16 members in the Compression dimension. If the combination of all of the other non-Compression dimensions together are thought of as an ASO Sparse Key (SK), not all SK combinations will necessarily have data values for each of the members of the Compression dimension. (*Note*: SK is a term coined by the author and not normally used in ASO.) To minimize the wasted space, ASO does something additional for dimensions tagged as Compression: It adds 4 bytes to the record, which tells ASO which of the 16 members of the bundle are actually populated for this **SK**. Furthermore, the 32 bits found in these 4 bytes are broken into 16 sets of 2 bits. As we know, 2 bits can hold 4 unique values and ASO utilizes one of the four values to indicate that data exist. ASO goes on to indicate whether each of the 16 potential bundle members requires 2, 4, 6, 8, or 0 bytes to hold the actual fact data.

7.4.3.3.2 Average Value Length (AVL) Wait, less than 8 bytes? Where did that come from? ASO recognizes that not all pieces of fact data require all 8 bytes (the length of a double precision floating point number) to represent the required precision. The exact method of data value storage and its relation to precision are not disclosed. The algorithm is clearly skewed to minimize storage of values requiring no more than two digits after the decimal. This is hinted at in the DBAG where it provides some guidance to getting the most compressible data. The following is reprinted with permission from Oracle Corporation, *Oracle Essbase Administrators Guide Release 11.1.2.1* (Oracle Press, 1996, 2011) Chap. 62, p. 939):

Average Value Length

> The average value length is the average storage size, in bytes, required for the stored values in the cells. It can vary between 2 bytes and 8 bytes with 2 bytes being the best. Without compression, it takes 8 bytes to store a value in a cell. With compression, it can take fewer bytes, depending on the value length. For example, 10.050001 might take 8 bytes to store even when compressed, but 10.05 may only take 2 bytes (4 bytes to store when compressed). Dimensions with a smaller average value length compress the database better.
>
> Rounding the data values to no more than two digits after the decimal point can reduce the average value length, improving compression.

The Average Value Length (AVL) refers to the number of bytes required to store your fact data across all of the data in your cube. This is similar to the analysis that is required to calculate the ABF discussed above. The Database -> Properties -> Compression Tab provides some guidance to the size reduction you gain with use of the Compression dimension. In Figure 7.7, you can see the ABF and AVL. You also can see the effects on AVL of loading nearly identical data into the two cubes. Cube AS2sTc55 (top) has three decimal values for each of two of the compressed members [Original Price] and [Price Paid], while cube AS2Tc55z (bottom) has two decimal values for [Original Price] and [Price Paid]. The cubes are otherwise identical. Figure 7.8 shows the data as loaded for these two cubes:

(Be aware that on a large cube, opening up the Compression Tab could take a considerable amount of time. Be patient and do not ctrl-alt-dlt out of EAS during this process.)

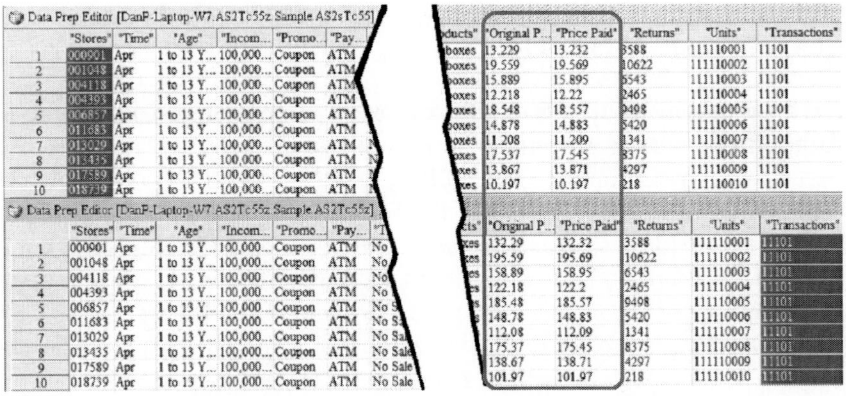

Data Prep Editor [DanP-Laptop-W7.AS2Tc55z.Sample.AS2sTc55]

	"Stores"	"Time"	"Age"	"Incom...	"Promo...	"Pay...
1	000901	Apr	1 to 13 Y...	100,000...	Coupon	ATM
2	001048	Apr	1 to 13 Y...	100,000...	Coupon	ATM
3	004118	Apr	1 to 13 Y...	100,000...	Coupon	ATM
4	004393	Apr	1 to 13 Y...	100,000...	Coupon	ATM
5	006857	Apr	1 to 13 Y...	100,000...	Coupon	ATM
6	011683	Apr	1 to 13 Y...	100,000...	Coupon	ATM
7	013029	Apr	1 to 13 Y...	100,000...	Coupon	ATM
8	013435	Apr	1 to 13 Y...	100,000...	Coupon	ATM
9	017589	Apr	1 to 13 Y...	100,000...	Coupon	ATM
10	018739	Apr	1 to 13 Y...	100,000...	Coupon	ATM

"Original P...	"Price Paid"	"Returns"	"Units"	"Transactions"
13.229	13.232	3588	111110001	11101
19.559	19.569	10622	111110002	11101
15.889	15.895	6543	111110003	11101
12.218	12.22	2465	111110004	11101
18.548	18.557	9498	111110005	11101
14.878	14.883	5420	111110006	11101
11.208	11.209	1341	111110007	11101
17.537	17.545	8375	111110008	11101
13.867	13.871	4297	111110009	11101
10.197	10.197	218	111110010	11101

Data Prep Editor [DanP-Laptop-W7.AS2Tc55z.Sample.AS2Tc55z]

	"Stores"	"Time"	"Age"	"Incom...	"Promo...	"Pay...	"T
1	000901	Apr	1 to 13 Y...	100,000...	Coupon	ATM	No
2	001048	Apr	1 to 13 Y...	100,000...	Coupon	ATM	No
3	004118	Apr	1 to 13 Y...	100,000...	Coupon	ATM	No
4	004393	Apr	1 to 13 Y...	100,000...	Coupon	ATM	No
5	006857	Apr	1 to 13 Y...	100,000...	Coupon	ATM	No S
6	011683	Apr	1 to 13 Y...	100,000...	Coupon	ATM	No S
7	013029	Apr	1 to 13 Y...	100,000...	Coupon	ATM	No Sa
8	013435	Apr	1 to 13 Y...	100,000...	Coupon	ATM	No Sale
9	017589	Apr	1 to 13 Y...	100,000...	Coupon	ATM	No Sale
10	018739	Apr	1 to 13 Y...	100,000...	Coupon	ATM	No Sale

"Original P...	"Price Paid"	"Returns"	"Units"	"Transactions"
132.29	132.32	3588	111110001	11101
195.59	195.69	10622	111110002	11101
158.89	158.95	6543	111110003	11101
122.18	122.2	2465	111110004	11101
185.48	185.57	9498	111110005	11101
148.78	148.83	5420	111110006	11101
112.08	112.09	1341	111110007	11101
175.37	175.45	8375	111110008	11101
138.67	138.71	4297	111110009	11101
101.97	101.97	218	111110010	11101

Figure 7.8 Data loaded for cube AS2sTc55 (top) and AS2Tc55z (bottom). (From Oracle Essbase Administration Services. With permission.)

The estimated cube size in Mb (Level-0 Mb) in Figure 7.7 can be calculated as:

$$\frac{[\text{Compressed Record Count}] * [\text{Avg Compressed Record Size}]}{1024 ** 2 \text{ (Note: this is to convert the result to Mb)}}$$

Where

$$[\text{Compressed Record Count}] \equiv \frac{[\text{Number of Input-Level Cells}]}{[\text{ABF}]}$$

$$[\text{Avg Compressed Record Count}] \equiv ([\text{Max.Key Length(bytes)}]) + [\text{ABF}] * [\text{AVL}] + 4)$$

Note that only two of the five fact data values have been changed. The three unchanged fact data members hide, to some extent, the impact of the change from three to two digits after the decimal point. Other tests (results not shown here) on cubes with only one member [Original Price] loaded in the [Measures] dimension show a reduction from AVL = 7.52 with three decimals data loaded to AVL = 3.83 with two decimals loaded.

To summarize the discussion of AVL, remember it only matters if you are using compression and, as in the results noted just above, not storing unnecessary digits can result in significant reductions to the input-data Size. Remember, a smaller input-data Size means a smaller box of cards and less memory and, therefore, improved performance.

7.4.3.3.3 The Compression Dimension—Will It Help? The description of the Compression dimension certainly was not short or, even with all the help and suggestions I received from the co-authors of this book, easy to understand. In the end, what have we learned and how will those lessons improve performance? So far, we know only that using a Compression dimension will (virtually always) reduce the size of the database on disk and in memory. That will certainly help performance. Counterbalancing this is the requirement that the Compression dimension *must* be a Dynamic dimension.

In the ASOsamp cube the Dynamic [Measures] dimension, as designed, does not have any examples of additive (+) consolidation that could take advantage of a Stored hierarchy. The only calculations within [Measures] are ratios that could not take advantage of Stored consolidation. Thus, there is nothing to be lost in making [Measures] a

Compression and, therefore, Dynamic dimension. In Figure 7.7, the reduction is from 15.662 Gb to 10.180 Gb. Why not have a smaller cube that takes up less space on disk and in memory?

Usually, however, things are not so clear cut. Most dimensions do need some additive consolidation. In particular, the larger dimensions such as [Stores] in Figure 7.7 show the greatest reduction of cube size from 10.180 Gb if [Measures] is chosen down to 7.094 Gb. Do you really want to give up all of the Stored consolidation and aggregation on the 239 members in [Stores]? Because of the extensive additive consolidation in the [Stores] dimension, there is a lot to lose when selecting it for Compression, as opposed to [Measures] where there is nothing to lose and only gains from the smaller size. Besides, [Stores] in ASOsamp has two attribute dimensions associated to it and you cannot associate an attribute dimension to a dimension tagged as Compression.

Stored consolidation is extremely powerful, and only Stored hierarchies with Stored (+) consolidations can be Aggregated. The overriding theme of this chapter has been to encourage the use of designs that leverage Stored hierarchies, and in Section 7.6.2 some alternatives that are not obvious are presented.

The Compression dimension becomes the subject of our next rule:

> R9: The use of a Compression dimension is not a given; consider and test alternatives including not having a Compression dimension.

Finally, did the idea of using a dimension with a single Stored member as found in a typical "Analysis" dimension, such as [Time Span] or [Data View] for the Compression dimension, occur to you as it did to me? Reconsider it. For Compression to work (i.e., to result in a smaller cube) on a single Stored member dimension, the AVL would have to be two bytes. Even then, the [Average Compressed Record Size] would only be reduced from 8 (for an uncompressed cube) to 6. The "+ 4" in the equation for the compression overhead ruins the idea. The ABF would, by definition, be one (one filled member per bundle); the fact data and, therefore, the record itself either exist or does not exist when the Compression dimension has only a single Stored member.

7.4.3.4 The Accounts Dimension Before I introduce any unnecessary confusion, let me distinguish between a dimension tagged as "Accounts" and a dimension tagged as "Compression." Before version 11 there was no distinction. The dimension tagged as "Accounts" was automatically (implicitly) tagged as "Compression." The values of the two tags have now been disassociated and I will refer to the tags independently.

As with the Compression dimension, tagging a dimension "Accounts" requires that the entire dimension be dynamic. The primary advantage of tagging a dimension "Accounts" is that the "Time balance," "Skip," and "Flow" options become available. Generally, only a subset of the members in the Accounts dimension require these options. This must be balanced against the loss of the advantage of stored consolidation and, of course, aggregation of the stored consolidation upper-level members.

At this point, many designers will raise one of these two issues:

- My Accounts dimensions *must* already be dynamic because of the inclusion of pluses (+) and minuses (–) in the hierarchy, typical in accounting applications.

- My data is all or largely balance-sheet related or point-in-time measurements and not transactional in nature and, therefore, heavy use is made of the Time Balance tags.

The accounts dimension is often large, with many levels of consolidation. Making it dynamic will have a major negative impact. There are alternative design options for the two objections raised above that should be given serious consideration. For the first point, I refer the reader to Section 7.6.2.1 (Time Spans (YTD, QTD) Using Stored Hierarchies). For the second, please consider Section 7.6.2.4 (Loading "Balance Data" or "Flow Data").

The typical large size of the Accounts dimension and its many levels make it a good candidate for leveraging the power of stored consolidation and aggregations. Of course, this requires that the dimension be stored. You may find that the cube performance is so much improved by converting the dimension to Stored that the process of designing and materializing aggregations, though now possible, is not really needed.

The discussion of the Accounts dimension is summarized with our next rule:

> R10: The use of the Accounts dimension tag has substantial costs; alternatives should be considered strongly.

The extra emphasis in R10 "alternatives should be considered *strongly*" regarding the Accounts tag versus in rule R9 regarding the Compression tag is intentional. There are really good alternatives and no performance-related benefits to using the Accounts dimension tag that I know of.

7.4.3.5 Implied Sharing and "Never-Share" As introduced earlier (in Section 7.4.2.1), the concepts of Implied Sharing and the "Never-Share" tag are still in use in ASO cubes as they were in BSO. As in the example just referenced, Implied-Share members do not affect the size of the bitmap. However, tagging them as "Never-Share" also does not appear to affect the size of the bitmap. The only impact of setting the "Never-Share" tag appears to be that noted in the DBAG, which is reprinted with permission from Oracle Corporation, *Oracle Essbase Administrators Guide Release 11.1.2.1* (Oracle Press, 1996, 2011) Chap. 62, p. 932:

> **Note:** In an aggregate storage database, a shared member automatically shares any attributes that are associated with its nonshared member. This also applies to an implied shared member (for example, a member that has only one child). See "Understanding Implied Sharing". You can prevent implied sharing by setting the Never Share property; see "Determining How Members Store Data Values". This behavior of shared members and attributes in aggregate storage databases is different from the behavior in block storage databases.

7.4.3.6 Most Efficient Hierarchies You may have noticed the use of the phrase "almost always cheap" back in rule R5:

> R5: Alternate hierarchies, whether Dynamic or Stored or Attribute, are almost always cheap … give the user what they want.

Let us take a minute to think about the bitmap and the most efficient possible design for a hierarchy. Similar-sized families counting from the bottom up would avoid having unused bits. If my parents and most of my uncles had three children, but one uncle had 17, then we would need to use log(17) or 5 bits to be able to list all of my cousins. Three of those five bits would be unused for all families except that of my most prolific uncle. Furthermore, if everyone had the same number of children and that number was a power of 2, then the bits used for each family would be fully used (families of 2, 4, 8, etc., children or "densely packed" families). This is known as a "densely packed" hierarchy.

Next, consider the number of generations. If my great-great grandfather (the progenitor or dimension head of my known family tree) had one line of descendants that all started reproducing at age 15 (and they all lived in [*insert the name of your favorite state here]*), while everyone else waited until age 25, the early-reproducing branch would have more generations. Assuming that I am in the civilized, later-reproducing branch, the last 99 years would have produced 4 generations (I would now be looking frantically for the mother of my first child to be born 12 months from now to maintain the reproduction rate by age 25, and I guess we would have to have twins, quads, or octuplets because we only have time for one birth). The early reproducing branch of the family would have produced 6 generations. Assuming the same-size families of four children each, these two extra generations require a total of 4 additional bits that will be unused by other branches of the family. This is known as the "Ragged hierarchies" issue.

How much should anyone really worry about "densely packed" families or "Ragged hierarchies"? In my opinion, not too much. Unlike my example, typical hierarchies do not tend to be the same size all the way down. The level-0 families tend to be the largest; typical accounting or product hierarchies have two to six members until you get to the bottom of the hierarchy, where there might be 20 or more at level-0. Because the levels overlap each other (and not the generations), the extra generations (or upper levels) found only on some branches (the two earliest generations in my example) tend to be the smallest, adding only a few bits each.

The next issue in defining the most efficient hierarchy concerns the text referenced in [DBAG 5] and discussed in Section 7.4.2.3. This refers to the way most people design cubes: The first hierarchy has all of the primary (nonshared) members, and the remaining hierarchies have either full or subsets of those, with no nonshared, nonformula level-0 members in the secondary hierarchies. The text referenced above details the penalty to be paid when this practice is not followed. Repeating what was said for Rule R7:

R7: Changes to hierarchy order are cheap or free, so design for user convenience.

Yes, if your primary hierarchy has the *entire* set of original nonshared level-0s, and the other hierarchies have only shared level-0 members, then your bitmap will be the shortest. Changing the order would add at most log(# hierarchies).

To summarize the subject of the most efficient hierarchies: Do not worry too much about it. Unless you have an alternate hierarchy that is wildly larger (in required bits) than the now largest (again, in bits) hierarchy in the dimension, adding alternates should not hurt. The simplest way to test this is by changing all of the alternate Stored hierarchies to Dynamic and then switch them back to Stored one at a time and see if one makes the key length jump. Suggestion: Do this on a cube without any data loaded.

7.4.3.7 Analysis or View Dimensions As some people have seen, the addition of analysis dimensions, such as [TimeSpan] or [Time View], [DataType] or [Data View] or [Variance], can make a spreadsheet or report much easier to design, but it may take a bit of training for your users to get used to the new design. These dimensions, which generally have only one stored member and the remainder dynamic with formulas, add nothing to the bitmap. If the MDX is written well, they are very fast. Examples of Analysis or View dimensions:

- TimeSpan: Instead of having Jun, Jun QTD, Jun HTD, and Jun YTD all in one Month dimension, just include the 12 months. Add a second dimension with Month (the only stored member), QTD, HTD, and YTD.
- Variance: What about members such as [Vs Prior Yr], [Prior Mo], [Vs Plan], etc., and [Vs Prior Yr %], [Vs Prior Mo %], [Vs Plan %], etc., where should you put these? In the Year, the Month, or the Scenario dimension? That becomes confusing and soon multiplies the combinations out of control. Instead, a Variance dimension with [NoVar] (the only stored member), [Vs Prior Yr], [Prior Mo], [Vs Plan], will be much easier to use. In fact, as users have sometimes objected to seeing [NoVar] on a column heading next to [Vs Prior Year], I have found that renaming the member [I I] reduces these objections because it appears to be blank.
- DataType: Data (the only stored member), [per case], [per some other unit] [% of acct dimension parent], [% of product dimension parent], etc.

This is important enough to become our next rule:

R11: Analysis dimensions are cheap or free, use them.

An example of an analysis dimension for TimeSpan will be shown in Section 7.6.2 (Designing to Maximize Use of Stored Hierarchies).

7.5 UNDERSTANDING AGGREGATIONS AND SLICES

As I stated in the Introduction, the purpose of this chapter is to design a cube that performs maximally, minimizing the need for extensive aggregations by maximizing the opportunities for powerful, highly leveraged aggregations that work over the widest number of queries. A detailed discussion of aggregations, including Hinting or related options, is beyond the scope of this chapter. For information of this type, the reader is referred to Tim German's excellent presentation at Kaleidoscope 2011, *Essbase ASO: Optimizing Aggregations*, which can be found at http://www.odtug.com/apex/f?p=500:595:1219041880560478::NO::P595_CONTENT_ID:5348.

Nevertheless, a chapter entitled How ASO Works and How to Design for Performance warrants a few remarks about aggregations:

7.5.1 Aggregation and the Bitmap

By now, you might be able to guess at how aggregation and the bitmap interact. Repeating some of what was said above in Section 7.4.3.2: The bitmap algorithm selects the hierarchy with the longest required bitmap for any dimension. Remember that within the set number of bits, the actual encoding on the record on disk and in memory can reflect only *one hierarchy at a time*. In the input-level data, aka the level-0 View, the longest bitmap (primary) hierarchy will be what is seen for each dimension on each record. A member, as represented by the hierarchy on the record can reflect only one hierarchy at a time, even if it has one or more aliases in other hierarchies, cannot simultaneously show (referring to the product dimension as seen in Figure 7.6) [HDTV] as a descendant of both [All Merchandise] and [High End Merchandise]. Similarly, a store cannot be represented in the bitmap as both [Brick & Mortar] and [10000] square feet.

Okay, let me back up a second and mention that an Aggregated View is not one "answer" or one record, but a set of records. An Aggregated View of ASOsamp "at level-1 of the [Age] dimension" would have a set of records for each of the level-1 members of the members [Age] or a set of records for [Teens], [Adult], and [Senior] (Figure 7.9). The set of records for [Teens] would have records with all of the level-0 nonformula *combinations* of the other dimensions. Therefore, to keep the example and notation simple, lets ignore all dimensions other than [Measures], [Year], [Age] members. Now let us assume that the level-0 View has fact data existing for the following [Measures], [Year], [Age] members combinations *only*:

- ([Original Price], [Curr Year], [1 to 13 years])
- ([Original Price], [Curr Year], [14 to 19 years])

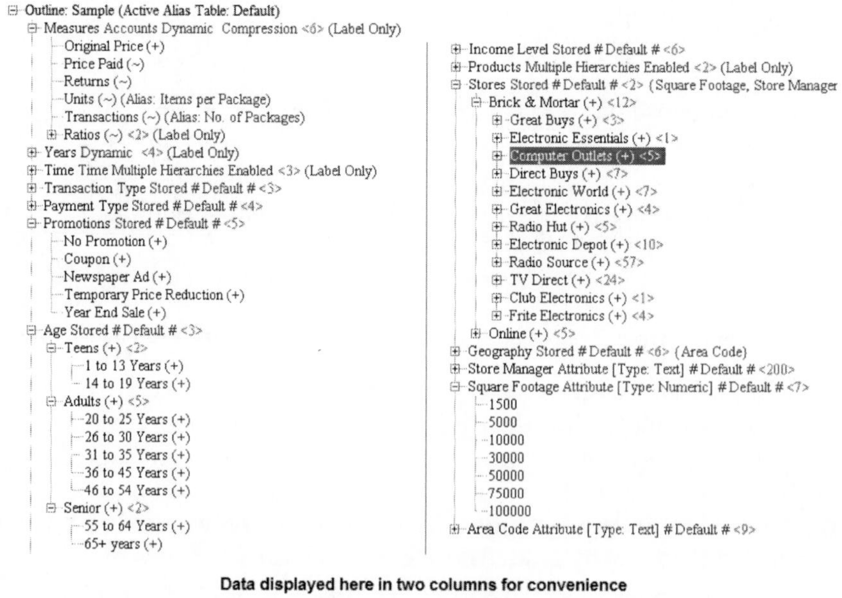

```
Outline: Sample (Active Alias Table: Default)
  Measures Accounts Dynamic  Compression <6> (Label Only)
    Original Price (+)
    Price Paid (~)
    Returns (~)
    Units (~) (Alias: Items per Package)
    Transactions (~) (Alias: No. of Packages)
    Ratios (~) <2> (Label Only)
  Years Dynamic  <4> (Label Only)
  Time Time Multiple Hierarchies Enabled <3> (Label Only)
  Transaction Type Stored # Default # <3>
  Payment Type Stored # Default # <4>
  Promotions Stored # Default # <5>
    No Promotion (+)
    Coupon (+)
    Newspaper Ad (+)
    Temporary Price Reduction (+)
    Year End Sale (+)
  Age Stored # Default # <3>
    Teens (+) <2>
      1 to 13 Years (+)
      14 to 19 Years (+)
    Adults (+) <5>
      20 to 25 Years (+)
      26 to 30 Years (+)
      31 to 35 Years (+)
      36 to 45 Years (+)
      46 to 54 Years (+)
    Senior (+) <2>
      55 to 64 Years (+)
      65+ years (+)
  Income Level Stored # Default # <6>
  Products Multiple Hierarchies Enabled <2> (Label Only)
  Stores Stored # Default # <2> (Square Footage, Store Manager
    Brick & Mortar (+) <12>
      Great Buys (+) <3>
      Electronic Essentials (+) <1>
      Computer Outlets (+) <5>
      Direct Buys (+) <7>
      Electronic World (+) <7>
      Great Electronics (+) <4>
      Radio Hut (+) <5>
      Electronic Depot (+) <10>
      Radio Source (+) <57>
      TV Direct (+) <24>
      Club Electronics (+) <1>
      Frite Electronics (+) <4>
    Online (+) <5>
  Geography Stored # Default # <6> (Area Code)
  Store Manager Attribute [Type: Text] # Default # <200>
  Square Footage Attribute [Type: Numeric] # Default # <7>
    1500
    5000
    10000
    30000
    50000
    75000
    100000
  Area Code Attribute [Type: Text] # Default # <9>
```

Data displayed here in two columns for convenience

Figure 7.9 Selected portions of the ASOsamp outline. (From Oracle Essbase Administration Services. With permission.)

- ([Price Paid], [Prev Year], [1 to 13 years])
- ([Price Paid], [Prev Year], [14 to 19 years])
- ([Price Paid], [Prev Year], [50 to 64 year

A View *aggregated* only at level-1 of the [Age] dimension would have records for:

- ([Original Price], [Curr Year], [Teens])
- ([Price Paid], [Prev Year], [Teens])
- ([Price Paid], [Prev Year], [Senior])

How many records would be in the resulting set overall? That is hard to determine, unless we make a few assumptions: That data had existed for all 9 level-0 members of [Age] and that any combination of the other dimensions that existed, existed equally (i.e., there were the same combinations of all other dimensions) for all 9 members, then we can say that the size of the Aggregated set would have been 3/9 of the size of the original (3 for the three members of level-1 and 9 for the level-0 members). Without these assumptions, there is little we can do to estimate the actual size as measured by the record count.

In this example, I have aggregated only on the [Age] dimension. ASO is not limited to a single dimension at a time. What is important to realize here is that an Aggregated View is really a set of records, essentially a small cube without any of the lower-level detail in the aggregated levels in each dimension.

Next, as mentioned above, the Bitmap can represent only one hierarchy per dimension at a time. Furthermore, assuming that attributes were associated at level-0, an Aggregated View above level-0 loses the association to the attribute. If we were to query in ASOsamp on the [Stores] dimension to get a report of [Computer Outlets] by [Square Footage], the query could not use any Aggregated View of the [Stores] dimension above level-0. Depending on the levels of the other dimensions of the query, it could make use of Aggregated Views of upper levels in those dimensions.

Let us stop and learn about the Aggregated View notation; it might help us to understand.

7.5.2 What Is the Meaning of Those Numbers in the Recommended View?

Ignoring for the moment how ASO determines what are the most advantageous queries to be saved as Aggregated Views, let us look at what is being aggregated. In the ASOsamp cube we have been using (the one seen in Figure 7.6 that notes the slight difference to the delivered ASOsamp) when we run the initial recommended Design Aggregations (after loading the delivered dataload.txt file) we get the results found in Figure 7.10.

Twenty six views are recommended … well, actually, 25 because the first one outlined in the Level Info column is the input-level data also known as the level-0 data view or the level-0 Aggregated View. The database size column shows the cumulative size of the cube including level-0 view and each of the views on that particular row and the rows above it. The size of any one view would be the difference between it and the row immediately above it. We see that the memory requirement for this cube started out at 6.5 Mb, and 30 Mb of aggregations were added in the 26 views, for a total of 36.5 Mb. In fact, two of the views (those circled in the Database Size column), View 15 and View 25 (on the 16th and the 26th rows), are nearly as large as the original level-0 View, remembering that the size of the view is equal to current row less prior row of the Database Size column.

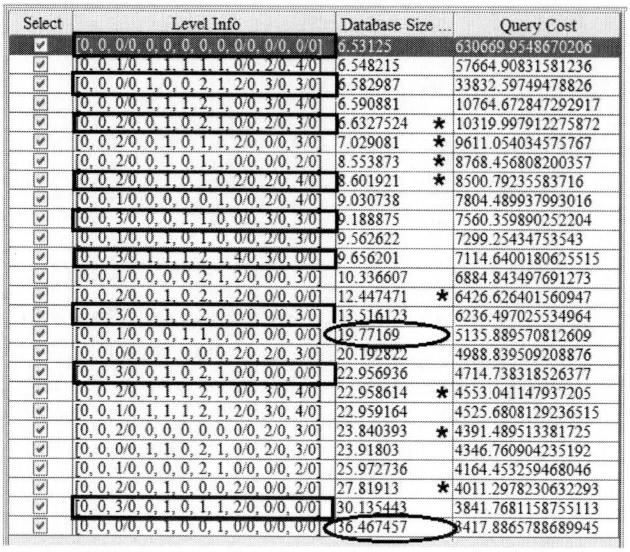

Select	Level Info	Database Size ...	Query Cost
☑	[0, 0, 0/0, 0, 0, 0, 0, 0, 0/0, 0/0, 0/0]	6.53125	630669.9548670206
☑	[0, 0, 1/0, 1, 1, 1, 1, 1, 0/0, 2/0, 4/0]	6.548215	57664.90831581236
☑	[0, 0, 0/0, 1, 0, 0, 2, 1, 2/0, 3/0, 3/0]	6.582987	33832.59749478826
☑	[0, 0, 0/0, 1, 1, 1, 2, 1, 0/0, 3/0, 4/0]	6.590881	10764.672847292917
☑	[0, 0, 2/0, 0, 1, 0, 2, 1, 0/0, 2/0, 3/0]	6.6327524 *	10319.997912275872
☑	[0, 0, 2/0, 0, 1, 0, 1, 1, 2/0, 0/0, 3/0]	7.029081 *	9611.054034575767
☑	[0, 0, 2/0, 0, 1, 0, 1, 1, 0/0, 0/0, 2/0]	8.553873 *	8768.456808200357
☑	[0, 0, 2/0, 0, 1, 0, 1, 0, 2/0, 2/0, 4/0]	8.601921 *	8500.79235583716
☑	[0, 0, 1/0, 0, 0, 0, 0, 1, 0/0, 2/0, 4/0]	9.030738	7804.489937993016
☑	[0, 0, 3/0, 0, 0, 1, 1, 0, 0/0, 3/0, 3/0]	9.188875	7560.359890252204
☑	[0, 0, 1/0, 0, 1, 0, 1, 0, 0/0, 2/0, 3/0]	9.562622	7299.25434753543
☑	[0, 0, 3/0, 1, 1, 1, 2, 1, 4/0, 3/0, 0/0]	9.656201	7114.6400180625515
☑	[0, 0, 1/0, 0, 0, 0, 2, 1, 2/0, 0/0, 3/0]	10.336607	6884.843497691273
☑	[0, 0, 2/0, 0, 1, 0, 2, 1, 2/0, 0/0, 0/0]	12.447471 *	6426.626401560947
☑	[0, 0, 3/0, 0, 1, 0, 2, 0, 0/0, 0/0, 3/0]	13.516123	6236.497025534964
☑	[0, 0, 1/0, 0, 0, 1, 1, 0, 0/0, 0/0, 0/0]	19.77169	5135.889570812609
☑	[0, 0, 0/0, 0, 1, 0, 0, 0, 2/0, 2/0, 3/0]	20.192822	4988.839509208876
☑	[0, 0, 3/0, 0, 1, 0, 2, 1, 0/0, 0/0, 0/0]	22.956936	4714.738318526377
☑	[0, 0, 2/0, 1, 1, 1, 2, 1, 0/0, 3/0, 4/0]	22.958614 *	4553.041147937205
☑	[0, 0, 1/0, 1, 1, 1, 2, 1, 2/0, 3/0, 4/0]	22.959164	4525.6808129236515
☑	[0, 0, 2/0, 0, 0, 0, 0, 0, 0/0, 2/0, 3/0]	23.840393 *	4391.489513381725
☑	[0, 0, 0/0, 1, 1, 0, 2, 1, 0/0, 2/0, 3/0]	23.91803	4346.760904235192
☑	[0, 0, 1/0, 0, 0, 0, 2, 1, 0/0, 0/0, 2/0]	25.972736	4164.453259468046
☑	[0, 0, 2/0, 0, 1, 0, 0, 0, 2/0, 0/0, 2/0]	27.81913 *	4011.2978230632293
☑	[0, 0, 3/0, 0, 1, 0, 1, 1, 2/0, 0/0, 0/0]	30.135443	3841.7681158755113
☑	[0, 0, 0/0, 0, 1, 0, 0, 1, 0/0, 0/0, 0/0]	36.467457	3417.8865788689945

Figure 7.10 ASOsamp Design Aggregation using dataload.txt and all recommended views. (From Oracle Essbase Administration Services. With permission.)

Simple math tells us that these two views are 95.78% and 96.95% of the level-0 view. Now, remember what Rule R3 told us:

R3: All queries against the same aggregation level take the same time.

Just as the sorting-needle had to pass through all of the cards in the box, ASO must compare the bitmap mask (whatever it may be) to all rows of the View. Does it really serve much purpose to have as Aggregated View(s) a set of rows almost as large as the original level-0 View? The percentage saving by using either View 15 or 25 will be small (the size of the card deck to be queried is almost as large as the original). So, in my opinion, no. Remember that to process these two views they have to be in memory, and that is a relatively large percentage of incremental memory for a very small percentage gain. The situation is even worse if you are memory-constrained and have to compromise regarding rule R1:

R1: The Input-level and Aggregation-data for all loaded ASO cubes should fit into memory (or it ain't really ASO).

If these two views are not in memory now, think of all that I/O (input/output) just to get a view that is only a few percentage points faster. Actually having those views in a severely limited memory situation will result in worse performance than if they had never been created. (The exact amount of degradation would depend on the relative speed of your disk to memory transfers and the exact query distribution over time).

Memory is indeed cheap nowadays, but it seems that even if memory is not a constraint in your implementation, the combined 12 Mb of these two queries could be better used for other, more beneficial Aggregated Views. Remember that the dataset loaded into this cube is the demo dataset. It is quite small and might not be representative. This is an important consideration. The selection of the most advantageous views cannot be made except on a live dataset, and it must be reviewed periodically as the content of the dataset changes.

Now let us look at the data in the column "Level Info." Looking at the View in the fifth row (View 4) View we see [0, 0, 2/0, 0, 1, 0, 2, 1, 0/0, 2/0, 3/0]. This notation indicates the aggregation level for each dimension of the View in the order in which the dimensions appear in the outline. Dimensions marked with the #/# notation are for dimensions with multiple hierarchies, with the first number representing the aggregation level and the second number representing the hierarchy to which the aggregation level refers (again, in the order in which they appear in the outline and starting at 0). Note that this notation is only based on the physical outline order. If the second hierarchy (that is numbered as hierarchy 1) were to have the longest bitmap and, therefore, be deemed the primary hierarchy, it would, in this notation, remain numbered as 1. The bitmap and any single View can refer to only one hierarchy per dimension at a time. This view, at its lowest level, has records with the following members:

- [Measures]: All stored, nonformula level-0
- [Years]: All stored, nonformula level-0
- [Time]: [1st Half] and [2nd Half] ONLY
- [Transaction Type]: All stored level-0
- [Payment Type]: Dimension Top Level
- [Promotions]: All stored, nonformula level-0
- [Age]: Top Level ONLY
- [Income Level]: Top Level ONLY
- [Products]: All stored level-0
- [Stores]: [Brick & Mortar] AND [Online] ONLY
- [Geography]: [Central], [Mid West], [North East], [South], [South West] and [West] ONLY

Note: The bitmap found in this View would allow retrieval by upper-level members of the same hierarchy as those shown above (e.g., [MDX] in the Time dimension), but the lower-level members could not be queried from this View (e.g., [Jan], [Feb] … in the Time dimension).

Let us look at a fairly important observation we can make in View 4. Notice, in particular, the aggregation level for [Time]. It is at level-2, which includes the upper-level members [1st Half] and [2nd Half]. How often do your users really report at the half level? In fact, 8 of the 26 Views are Half views that exist to speed up reporting at the Half level (all have been marked with an asterisk). This would seem to be a good candidate for a hint, such as "Never aggregate to intermediate levels."

Now, let us consider View 4 for the dimension [Products]. If you remember from Figure 7.6, there were two hierarchies [High End Merchandise] that contained two shared members and one unique unshared member ingloriously named [Stored member] and the incorrectly named hierarchy [All Merchandise] (incorrectly named because it lacks the [Stored member]). This extra member can be found in the hierarchy 0 bitmap even though it is not in the primary hierarchy. An extra bit from the formula log(Count(hierarchies)) was added when this situation was detected. Nevertheless, this view could not be used to report a roll-up of [High End Merchandise] directly because there is no bit pattern that uniquely identifies the three members of that hierarchy ([HDTV], [Flat Panel] and [Stored member]).

ASO must do one of two things if it is to use this View (or the level-0 View for that matter) to roll-up [High End Merchandise]. It either must translate the query (by looking at the outline) to a bitmap mask that matches [Stored member] and [HDTV] and [Flat Panel] in one query or alternatively must translate the bitmap found on the view for this dimension (0/0) to one that has the hierarchy information queried (0/1). My guess (based on watching file I/O in resource monitor) is that it does the latter, using data that is stored in the file ess001.dat in the metadata subdirectory of appname/dbname (as opposed to the data file ess001.dat in the default subdirectory). In any case, this would not be a costly operation once the row had been brought into memory.

In contrast, let us look at [Stores]. As we know, [Stores] has two attribute dimensions that function as alternate hierarchies [Store Manager] and [Square Footage]. An inspection of the detail in the outline reveals that every [Store] has a [Store Manager], so [Store Manager] is an implied share of [Store] and even though the View we are looking at has *no information in the bitmap* about store managers individually, a query of the top-level member [Store Manager] could be answered directly without either of the two types of translations mentioned above; it is really a query of its implied share "parent" [Stores]. Suppose a query for a specific store manager was made? There is no possible translation of the bitmap in View 4 that could answer that question. The association of store manager to store was done at level-0 in the [Store] hierarchy. This view only has data about the composites found in [Brick & Mortar] and [Online]. The association is lost within this view.

An even more curious observation can be made about the attribute [Square Footage]. Inspection of the detail in the outline reveals that [Online] stores never have a [Square Footage] attribute, only level-0 descendants of [Brick & Mortar] stores have a [Square Footage] association. Nevertheless, we cannot query any [Square Footage] information from this View 4 *even for those stores that are descendants of [Brick & Mortar]*. The coincidental fact that only descendants of [Brick & Mortar] have [Square Footage] is just that, a coincidence. Even though we know all [Brick & Mortar] descendant stores have a [Square Footage] association in View 4, we have no idea of which stores have what association.

7.5.3 Aggregate View: What Is "Query Cost"

Let us return for a moment to the eight Views for the Half level mentioned above for View 4. Admittedly, when you look at the sizes of these eight views, they are relatively small, but if they are rarely used, why build them and why are they so high on the list of Views to be built? The answer is because they have a high Query Cost.

No definition of how Query Cost is calculated can be found in the documentation. Some indication of the calculation in the Query Cost column (as seen in the wizard dialog in Figure 7.10) can be found in the DBAG. The following is reprinted with permission from Oracle Corporation, *Oracle Essbase Administrators Guide Release 11.1.2.1* (Oracle Press, 1996, 2011) Chap. 64, p. 993):

> **The Relative "Query Cost" performance improvement**
>
> The Query Cost number that is displayed by each aggregate view in the list projects an average retrieval time for retrieving values from the associated aggregate view. The default view selection estimates the cost as the average of all possible queries.

When using query tracking, the estimated cost is the average for all tracked queries. The cost number for a specific aggregate view can be different in different selection lists; for example, aggregate view 0, 0, 1/0, 2/0, 0 can show a different query cost in the default selection list than it would show in a selection that includes tracked queries in the analysis.

To compute the percentage improvement, divide the query cost value for the aggregate view into the query cost value shown for storing only level 0 input cells.

But, wait, if the column measures cost, then why does it select those views with the *highest* cost first? Some have suggested that this column reflects the cost of *building* the View. Based on the DBAG definition, this is clearly not the case. In fact, this column appears to be poorly named. What is actually measured here is the Utility of the View as a function of the view size. All views are a fraction of the size of the level-0 View. With two views of equal size, the one that could be used to answer more of the possible query "questions" will be more useful and have the higher "cost" as shown in the wizard. The use of query tracking takes this concept one step farther and assigns a higher utility or "cost" to those views that, based on past experience, will be queried more often.

7.5.4 So What Is Aggregated and How Is It Used?

Which brings us to repeat a comment made earlier: Aggregations are like "stepping stones," different ones can be used to cross the river without getting your feet wet (i.e., querying the input-level data). Now, if you supply a query "hint" in your outline so that [1st Half] and [2nd Half] are not aggregated, does that mean any query at the Half level will not be able to take advantage of aggregations? No. It could use a View that was Aggregated at the Quarters. In fact, the situation is even better than that. A query can be run against any View whose aggregation level on each dimension is less than or equal to the aggregation level of the query (for the same hierarchy). You do not have to Aggregate all dimensions. I summarize this in a rule:

> R12: A query will be run against the smallest View whose aggregation level on each dimension is less than or equal to the aggregation level of the query (for the same hierarchy), so you do not have to create Aggregated Views on all dimensions.

The process of building an Aggregated View is itself a query. We can evaluate the queries needed to build the Views in Figure 7.10 against the queries above it. Take a look at View 18 (on the 19th row). Using the rule above, of course, it can be calculated from View 0, the level-0 View, but it also can be calculated from View 4. Looking further, we find it also can be calculated from Views 6, 8, 10, and, 15. The column *Database Size in Mb* is cumulative. The size of any single view can be calculated by subtracting the Database Size of the row immediately above. When we do, we see sizes for Views 0, 4, 6, 8, 10, and 15 of 6.53125, .041871, 1.524792, .428817, .373747, and 6.25567 Mb, respectively. With these six views to choose from, we might as well run our query against the smallest, which would be View 4.

Returning to the eight Views for [1st Half] and [2nd Half], we see by looking in the third column that these are Views 4, 5, 6, 7, 13, 18, 20, and 23. Notice that View 18 is based on one of its fellow [1st Half] and [2nd Half] views, View 4. Suppose we eliminated View

4 and 6, the two [1st Half] and [2nd Half] Views, then which could be used to compute View 18? Of the four remaining Views in the list enumerated in the paragraph above, View 10 is the smallest. It should be noted that View 15 at .373747 Mb is almost nine times larger than View 4. If the [1st Half] and [2nd Half] are queried 1/9 or less as often, it probably pays not to create the "Half" views. Note that View 10 is a View at the "Qtr" level.

Because a query that would have run against View 18 still can be run from another Aggregated View that is not at level-2 (the Half level), it still can perform well. You do not always need the most optimal View.

The goal is always the smallest total size of *meaningful* aggregations. Aggregated Views should not be created just because they are small; their resource impact is cumulative and can be nontrivial. Only create Aggregations that will aid in querying or calculation.

Okay, let us suppose that we decided to eliminate all of the 8 "Half" views. My first inclination was to go to the Design Wizard and uncheck each of the eight (4, 5, 6, 7, 13, 18, 20, and 23). When I uncheck View 4, the wizard unchecks all higher views 5–25 automatically. This is because the cost column was derived for each view assuming that the prior views had already been built. The wizard does not check to see which of the specific higher views is dependent on View 4; it assumes they all are and unchecks them. The wizard does not want to go to the trouble of evaluating dependency by executing Rule R12.

Other than by adding hints in the outline, how would we eliminate a specific View or set of Views? We first need to understand the structure of the .csc file.

I want to complete a comment made above about the small size of the ASOsamp cube with the dataset delivered in the file dataload.txt (after all, how many people worry about performance on a 6-Mb cube?). In comparison, consider the following Design Aggregation run on ASOsamp with a much larger dataset (Figure 7.11).

The 11.896 Gb of the cube with all of its 35 Aggregated Views is only 16.5% larger than the level-0 View. The aggregated cube in Figure 7.10 was 558% larger than its level-0 View. The outlines are identical, so the actual data really does matter a great deal. Notice Views 15 and 25 (the 16th and the 26th) seen in Figure 7.10, each of which were over 95% of the input-level View, are no longer called for by the wizard in Figure 7.11 because it found better things to do with your time and memory.

7.5.5 Design Aggregation CSC File

Let us briefly look at how the data in the Aggregation Wizard is represented in the Aggregation in the CSC file. At first glance, the content of Figure 7.12 looks quite different from the GUI Representation seen in Figure 7.10. File that can be run using MaxL:

Figure 7.12 corresponds to Figure 7.10. The first number (in the medium oval), 26, is the number of Views contained within the script, including the level-0 view, which must be included. The second number (4142187940) is an Outline ID that is tied to the OTL (Outline) file to which this script pertains. Certain types of edits of an OTL file will cause a restructure of the outline that could result in changes to the Bitmap, which would invalidate this script. I refer you to Tim German's presentation (*Essbase ASO: Optimizing Aggregations)* referenced earlier.

These two descriptive members are followed by pairs of numbers for each View. The first pair (in the small circle) is always for the level-0 View and will always be 0 and 1, the View ID followed by the View ID size as a percentage of the size of the level-0 View (100% for the first pair). This continues for the remaining pairs, each of which corresponds to the remaining Views. The View ID, the first half of each pair, is a shorthand reference to the [0, 0, 2/0, 0, 1, 0, 2, 1, 0/0, 2/0, 3/0] notation seen in the wizard.

Select	Level Info	Database S...	Query Cost
☑	[0, 0, 0/0, 0, 0, 0, 0, 0, 0/0, 0/0, 0/0]	10204.156	3.487965776811378E8
☑	[0, 0, 0/0, 0, 0, 1, 2, 1, 4/0, 2/0, 2/0]	10204.171	2.5992902578696972E8
☑	[0, 0, 0/0, 1, 1, 1, 2, 1, 0/0, 2/0, 2/0]	10204.197	4449120.64368667
☑	[0, 0, 2/0, 1, 0, 0, 1, 1, 0/0, 2/0, 0/0]	10204.725	3216893.209120389
☑	[0, 0, 1/0, 0, 1, 1, 1, 0, 0/0, 2/0, 0/0]	10205.681	2529095.4743196107
☑	[0, 0, 1/0, 0, 0, 1, 2, 1, 3/0, 0/0, 0/0]	10207.434	2137625.434468617
☑	[0, 0, 2/0, 0, 1, 1, 1, 1, 0/0, 0/0, 0/0]	10212.454	1705656.6939164046
☑	[0, 0, 2/0, 0, 0, 0, 1, 1, 4/0, 0/0, 0/0]	10217.003	1590479.3294428007
☑	[0, 0, 0/0, 0, 0, 0, 0, 1, 3/0, 2/0, 0/0]	10221.06	1410353.873632136
☑	[0, 0, 1/0, 0, 0, 0, 2, 0, 0/0, 2/0, 0/0]	10227.8	1210704.947809894
☑	[0, 0, 1/0, 1, 1, 1, 2, 0, 0/0, 0/0, 0/0]	10234.539	1066100.864876101
☑	[0, 0, 1/0, 0, 0, 1, 0, 1, 0/0, 2/0, 0/0]	10236.465	938472.49157699
☑	[0, 0, 1/0, 1, 0, 1, 1, 1, 0/0, 0/0, 0/0]	10251.813	836495.2754439785
☑	[0, 0, 1/0, 0, 1, 0, 2, 1, 0/0, 0/0, 0/0]	10271.157	723609.1213925092
☑	[0, 0, 2/0, 1, 1, 1, 0, 0, 0/0, 0/0, 2/0]	10288.112	658831.7050742193
☑	[0, 0, 0/0, 1, 0, 1, 1, 0, 1/0, 1/0, 0/0]	10308.781	613430.9312002733
☑	[0, 0, 0/0, 0, 0, 1, 2, 1, 0/0, 0/0, 0/0]	10374.889	530150.4805658102
☑	[0, 0, 2/0, 0, 1, 0, 1, 0, 3/0, 0/0, 0/0]	10402.054	479644.8254508798
☑	[0, 0, 3/0, 1, 1, 0, 0, 1, 0/0, 0/0, 0/0]	10415.667	442045.18261627597
☑	[0, 0, 2/0, 1, 0, 1, 0, 0, 3/0, 0/0, 0/0]	10435.36	411962.0209303453
☑	[0, 0, 2/0, 0, 0, 0, 0, 0, 0/0, 2/0, 0/0]	10478.63	359318.4423710668
☑	[0, 0, 0/0, 0, 1, 0, 1, 0, 0/0, 2/0, 0/0]	10496.426	329422.10021566687
☑	[0, 0, 3/0, 0, 0, 1, 2, 0, 0/0, 0/0, 0/0]	10520.952	295866.48695298634
☑	[0, 0, 1/0, 1, 0, 0, 1, 1, 0/0, 0/0, 2/0]	10572.16	266139.954031597
☑	[0, 0, 1/0, 0, 1, 1, 1, 0, 0/0, 0/0, 0/0]	10683.654	234507.0450331463
☑	[0, 0, 2/0, 1, 0, 0, 2, 0, 0/0, 0/0, 0/0]	10823.181	206992.500084904
☑	[0, 0, 0/0, 0, 1, 0, 1, 1, 3/0, 0/0, 0/0]	10850.336	194823.01118374555
☑	[0, 0, 1/0, 0, 0, 1, 0, 1, 1/0, 0/0, 2/0]	10889.286	180817.89117039947
☑	[0, 0, 2/0, 0, 0, 0, 1, 1, 0/0, 0/0, 0/0]	11102.688	157715.4528722849
☑	[0, 0, 0/0, 1, 1, 1, 0, 1, 0/0, 0/0, 0/0]	11145.963	147764.1082157052
☑	[0, 0, 1/0, 0, 0, 0, 0, 1, 4/0, 0/0, 0/0]	11184.436	139494.655248038
☑	[0, 0, 0/0, 1, 0, 0, 0, 0, 0/0, 2/0, 0/0]	11304.492	126582.65404573943
☑	[0, 0, 0/0, 1, 1, 1, 2, 0, 0/0, 0/0, 0/0]	11329.016	121532.00724769995
☑	[0, 0, 0/0, 0, 0, 1, 1, 0, 4/0, 0/0, 0/0]	11379.774	115405.38297656925
☑	[0, 0, 1/0, 1, 1, 0, 1, 0, 0/0, 0/0, 0/0]	11593.116	106316.87253871745
☑	[0, 0, 3/0, 0, 0, 1, 0, 1, 0/0, 0/0, 0/0]	11636.381	99922.41514327354
☑	[0, 0, 0/0, 0, 1, 0, 1, 1, 0/0, 0/0, 2/0]	11784.97	93273.0816529286
☑	[0, 0, 3/0, 0, 0, 1, 1, 0, 0/0, 0/0, 0/0]	11896.385	88343.76381583398

Figure 7.11 ASOsamp Design Aggregation using 1,026,432,000 cells and all recommended views. (From Oracle Essbase Administration Services. With permission.)

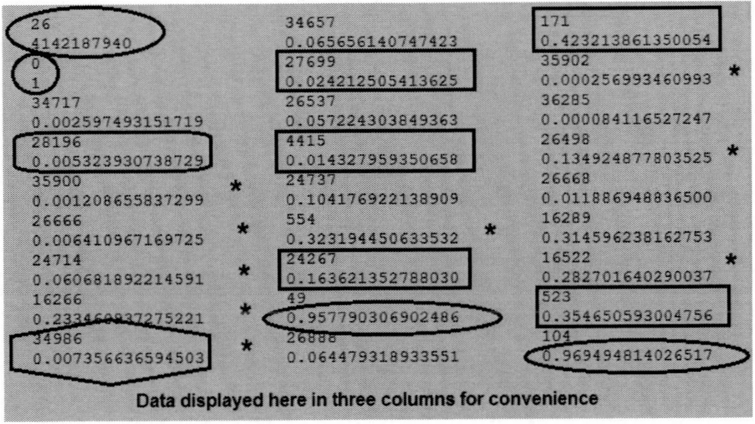

Figure 7.12 ASOsamp CSC file Design Aggregation using dataload.txt and all recommended views. (From Oracle Essbase Administration Services. With permission.)

It is important to realize that the percentage size relative to the level-0 View will change depending on the distribution of your data, even though the View definition does not change. The wizard bases its analysis on ASOSAMPLESIZEPERCENT configuration setting. The default value for this setting is whatever percent equals 1,000,000 cells. So, with a large cube, running the wizard multiple times will yield varying results based on where the random sampling done by the wizard falls.

The DBAG warns that editing of this file is unsupported. How could we edit to eliminate the eight "Half" views (marked with asterisks in Figure 7.10 and Figure 7.12)? We could simply let the Design Aggregation Wizard create and save this CSC file without materializing the views. We then could edit out the appropriate pairs of rows (which appear in the order they were in, in the wizard). The DBAG actually does not say that the editing of this file is totally unsupported; it says that editing without knowing the estimated percentage View size is unsupported. We have the View size calculated by the wizard for the remaining rows, so it should be fine.

The remaining question is: Have the relative costs of our remaining Views changed as a result of the deletions? To answer this we would have to go through the full set of Rule R12 analysis to ensure that none of our remaining views were dependent on one of the views we have eliminated. I have gone through that process and at least for the 25 Aggregated Views dataset in the small Figure 7.10 dataset, there is no such dependency. I have not analyzed the 35 Aggregated Views in Figure 7.11 for the effect of elimination of the (coincidentally) eight "Half" views presented there by the wizard. I will leave that as an exercise for you, the reader.

What would the cost be, however, if we had eliminated a dependent View/row of one of the remaining Views/rows? The time to compute that View would increase.

This section started out with my declaration that "a detailed discussion of aggregations ..." is beyond the scope of this chapter. Nevertheless, a chapter entitled "How ASO Works and How to Design for Performance" warrants a few remarks about aggregations.

By now you are wondering, if he said he was going to include only a "few" comments on Aggregation, what would "not a few" have looked like? Well, I hope it has been interesting and informative.

7.6 DESIGN ALTERNATIVES AND THEIR COSTS

In Section 7.4.3 (Primary Lessons from the Bitmap), I implicitly defined cost as the increase in the number of bits in the bitmap attached to each input-level cell. The rules derived there were those where the balance would not have been affected by other types of cost. In this section, we will look at design alternatives and possibly some new rules where these other costs should be considered.

7.6.1 Other Types of Cost

First of all, increases in the bitmap to accommodate more opportunities that take advantage of Stored hierarchies and consolidations have very little cost. Given the requirement to round the key-length up to the nearest 64-bit boundary, the odds are that there already are unused bits and, therefore, there will be no cost because the size of the database will not increase. Some people have asked whether this would increase the time required to compute Aggregated Views. This should not be an issue. More opportunities to aggregate do not mean that more aggregation is required. Instead, by limiting the Aggregated Views, the same time can be spent in materializing more useful Aggregated Views.

Other types of cost include:

- Fact data Enrichment: When an Attribute dimension must be converted to a standard dimension, thus requiring the addition of the former Attribute data to the fact data in a preload step.
- Fact data Additions: Sometimes it makes sense to precalculate and load upper-level data (7.6.2.1) or convert "Balance data" to "Flow Data" (7.6.2.4).
- Metadata Enrichment: To support Compound Attributes (7.6.2.5) or "Natural Sign" processing (7.6.2.1).

While these costs involve development effort for your external processes, these are one-time costs. Similarly, the cost of executing the newly developed process is a one-time-per-load cost and does not pose any repetitive penalty on query performance.

7.6.2 Alternative Design Options: Designing to Maximize Use of Stored Hierarchies

7.6.2.1 Time Spans (YTD, QTD) Using Stored Hierarchies TimeSpans can be written in MDX or constructed using Stored hierarchies. By now, you will be able to guess which approach I recommend.

The MTD hierarchy remains unchanged. Two new Stored hierarchies are added: [Internal Calculation YTDs] and [Internal Calculation QTDs]. They are named this way to discourage users from opening them (although that will not hurt) because they do not have the familiar look of the YTD and QTD hierarchies that appear below them, which look as they did in the original ASOsamp (Figure 7.13).

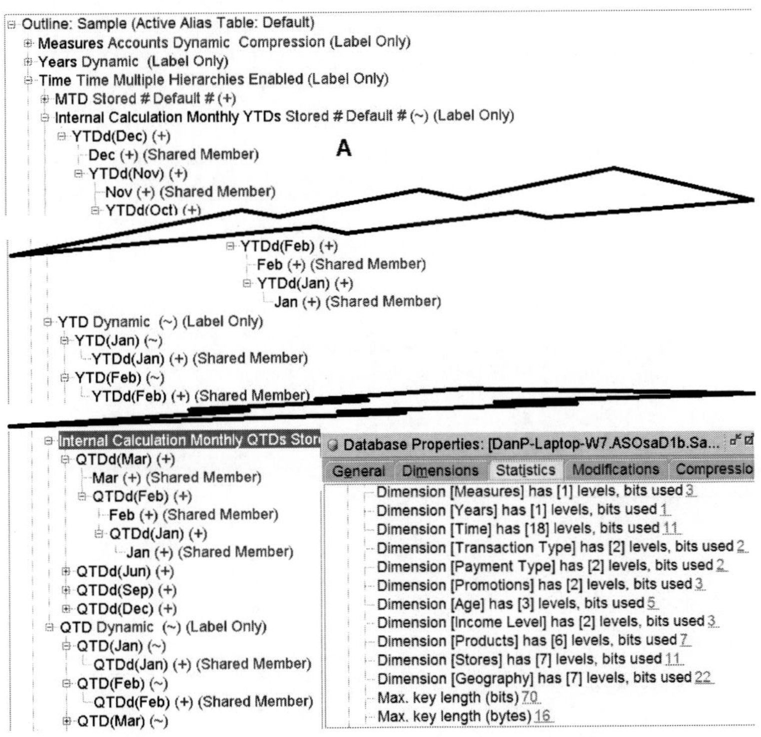

Figure 7.13 Alternative YTD and QTD design for ASOsamp. (From Oracle Essbase Administration Services. With permission.)

The [Internal Calculation YTDs] hierarchy builds [YTDd(Dec)] from the sum of [Dec] and [YTDd(Nov)]; this is in turn built from the sum of [Nov] and [YTDd(Oct)], continuing down until you get to [YTDd(Jan)], which is an Implied Share and, therefore, de facto alias of [Jan]. The quarters are built up in a similar fashion, but go down only three levels. This is known as a "Stacked" hierarchy (it has the look of being recursive, but it is not truly recursive).

The YTD and QTD Dynamic hierarchies are used so that a user does not have to drill down five levels from YTDd(Dec) through YTDd(Nov), etc., to get to YTDd(Jun). They are organized with a flat hierarchy of the familiar names from ASOsamp YTD(Jan), YTD(Feb), etc., and have a single Implied Share member below them with the name from the stacked hierarchy YTDd(Jan), YTDd(Feb), etc. This technique does not even require any actual Dynamic calculation because it simply leverages Implied Sharing and there is no need to be concerned with Solve Orders. Notice that if a member formula had been used instead of setting YTD(Jan) = YTDd(Jan), there would have been Dynamic calculation.

The cost of this redesign is to increase the bitmap for the [Time] dimension from 4 to 11 bits. In this particular case, it is an unfortunate occurrence because the pre-redesign bitmap was at 63 bits, and these changes resulted in the bitmap exceeding the 64-bit boundary and, thus, 8 bytes of bitmap on every record in the data database. If you are in this unusual case where the change forces you over a 64-bit boundary, you will have to decide by testing if this change results in a net performance increase for your cube. You should remember that the natural increase (as the business finds more things to track) in the number of members defined in the cube will probably cause this jump in the bitmap length. At 63 bits, it was probably going to happen soon anyway.

You might be ready to object that your user wants a separate TimeSpan dimension (they do not want [JunYTD] but ([Jun], [YTD]). Stored consolidations work *only* within one dimension. How can you make it work across two? The answer is: Do not try; do it in one dimension and make it look like two (Figure 7.14).

Here the Implied Share hierarchies YTD and QTD are removed (remember, they are included in the outline only for user convenience anyway), but the Stacked hierarchies [Internal Calculation YTDs] and [Internal Calculation QTDs] remain. An additional dimension, [TimeSpan], is added with the Dynamic members [YTD], [QTD], and [Period]. [Period] means for the time period itself as queried in the Time dimension

```
Outline Editor: [DanP-Laptop-W7.ASOsaD1c.Sample]
Outline | Properties | Query Hints | Text List Manager | Modifications
Outline: Sample (Active Alias Table: Default)
  Measures Accounts Dynamic  Compression (Label Only)
  Years Dynamic  (Label Only)
  Time Time Multiple Hierarchies Enabled (Label Only)
    Full Year Stored # Default # (+)
      1st Half (+)
        Qtr1 (+)
        Qtr2 (+)
      2nd Half (+)
    Internal Calculation Monthly YTDs Stored # Default # (~) (Label Only)
    Internal Calculation Monthly QTDs Stored # Default # (~) (Label Only)
  TimeSpan Dynamic
    Per (+) /* Data Loaded Here */
    QTD (+) [5: ( StrToMbr ( Concat( "QTDd(",[Time].CurrentMember.Member_Name,")") ), [Per] )]
    YTD (+) [5: ( StrToMbr ( Concat( "YTDd(",[Time].CurrentMember.Member_Name,")") ), [Per] )]
```

Figure 7.14 Alternative YTD and QTD design for ASOsamp using a TimeSpan dimension. (From Oracle Essbase Administration Services. With permission.)

([Jun], (Period]) as opposed to [Jun], [YTD]). All data is stored in [Period] (which is the only stored, nonformula member in this dimension). Then MDX formulas for [YTD] and [QTD] redirect queries made against ([Jun], [YTD]) to ([YTDd(Jun)], [Period]) using concatenation functions. (*Note:* Only the new [TimeSpan] dimension has been shown in Figure 7.14.)

There is one issue with these formulas as written. There is no MDX that translates queries for ([YTD], [Qtr3]), and the other upper-level members of the [Full Year] hierarchy. What should [YTD] be for [Qtr3] be? It is clear, if [Qtr3] is in the past, but suppose we are part way through it, say [Jul]? You might want it to be equivalent to ([YTD], [Jul]) not only for the current year, but also for prior years for variance analysis (otherwise you would be comparing a one-month value to a three-month value). I have found that different organizations have different conventions. Assuming you have a substitution variable that indicates the most recent closed month and the current year, it would be simple to add special code for upper-level members of the [Time] dimension code to redirect, for example, ([Qtr3], [YTD]) to ([YTDd(Sep)], [Period]) assuming that [Sep] for the queried year was closed. If [Sep] was not yet closed, the code could redirect to [YTDd(Jul)] or [YTDd(Aug)] or, if none were closed, it could simply provide a value of #Missing. This also would be a good place to code a special case providing a value of #Missing for February 29th on nonleap years.

Finally, this technique becomes enormously successful when used in a cube with daily time periods, as in Figure 7.15. (*Note:* The daily cubes shown below have [TimeSpan] members similar to those shown in the figures above; the MDX is not shown here due to space constraints.)

There is one problem with the cube in Figure 7.15. The cube still works, but when we look at the Statistics Tab in Database Properties (see left side of Figure 7.16), we see that the number of bits for the [Time] dimension that increased from 4 (Figure 7.5) to 11 (Figure 7.13) in the monthly cube, now go to 37 in the daily cube (see left side of Figure 7.16). That does not seem like a bad deal. A little over 3 times as many bits in exchange for a cube with room for 30 times as much detail.

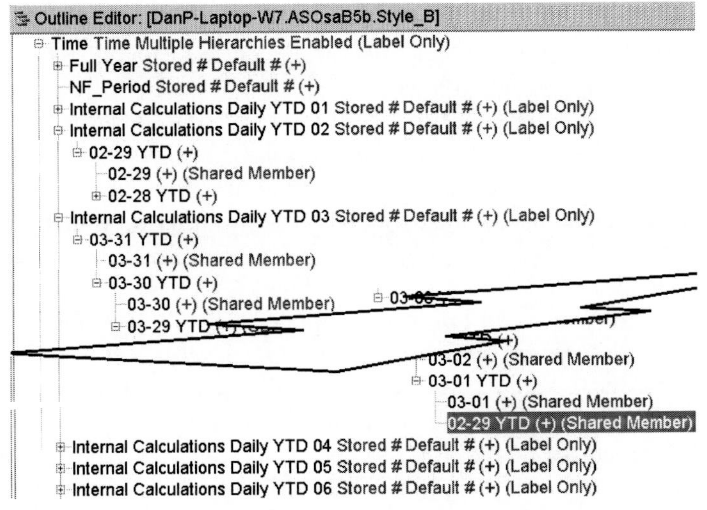

Figure 7.15 ASOsamp with Daily time periods. (From Oracle Essbase Administration Services. With permission.)

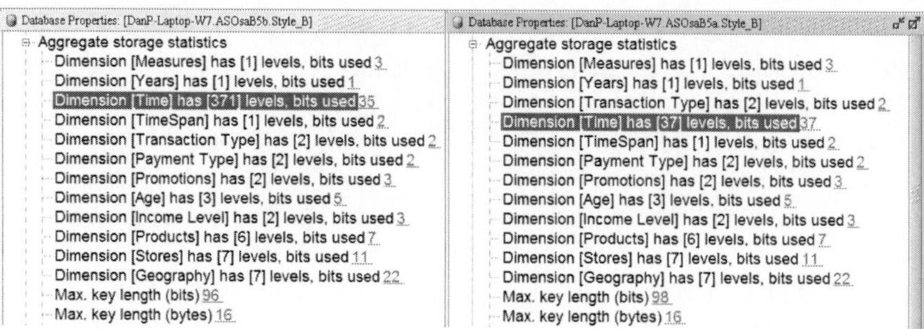

Figure 7.16 Database Properties–Statistics for cubes in Figure 7.13 (left) and Figure 7.15 (right). (From Oracle Essbase Administration Services. With permission.)

However, the number of levels for the [Time] dimension have risen from 4 (Figure 7.5) to 18 (Figure 7.13) in the monthly cube, and now balloons up to 371 in the daily cube (see left side of Figure 7.16). There was a hard limit of 2**52 Views (as described in Section 7.4.3.2) for a cube, and that calculation was based on the number of levels per dimension. We are in no danger on this cube, but it points out something else: Even though we did not build a Stacked dimension 366 members high going from Jan 1 to Dec 31st, it calculated as if it were. Because each stacked month is in a separate alternate Stored hierarchy, there has to be an Aggregate view for each of the 12 YTD months to make this cube really perform for any of the 366 days of the year. One might think that the aggregation engine could build all 12 Views in a single pass of the input-level, but this does not seem to be the case. While Aggregated Views can be built from earlier Aggregated Views, my observations of the Resource monitor seem to indicate that each View is built separately. Therefore, this design, while better than an all-MDX design, might not be optimal.

7.6.2.2 Upper-Level Data Loads The key thing to understand is that even though ASO is great at aggregation, sometimes it might pay to do some of the work for it in advance. Try loading the data for the prior month-end YTD total as a precalculated value. This can be done with a special month-end process or accomplished by always loading each day to both the daily and the full-month members. This process can be accomplished easily in one pass with a simple Load rule and, given the capabilities of the load buffer and slices, would have negligible additional cost. Finally, with version 11.1.2.1 of Essbase, we have one additional option: Running a calculation script to Aggregate the prior month-end members and the daily members for the most recent month into a full-month member. Both the use of a calculation script and the "double loading" method have the additional advantage of ensuring that the monthly total and the daily detail tie. A separate full-month process could have a bug generating different results than the sum of the daily loads.

But wait, I thought you could not load to upper-levels in an ASO cube? Yes, that is true, but nothing prevents you from having an upper-level-in-name-only member, one that is actually at level-0. You can see how this could be done in Figure 7.17, where the bottom of each monthly stack has been changed to have a separate level-0 End-of-the-Prior-Month-YTD member named [01 YTD], [02 YTD], etc. There still will be the [BOY YTD] member for the prior-year-ending YTD, which will be at the bottom of the [Jan] stack. By doing this and not linking the monthly stacks, the number of levels decreases to a much more palatable 37 (see the right side of Figure 7.16).

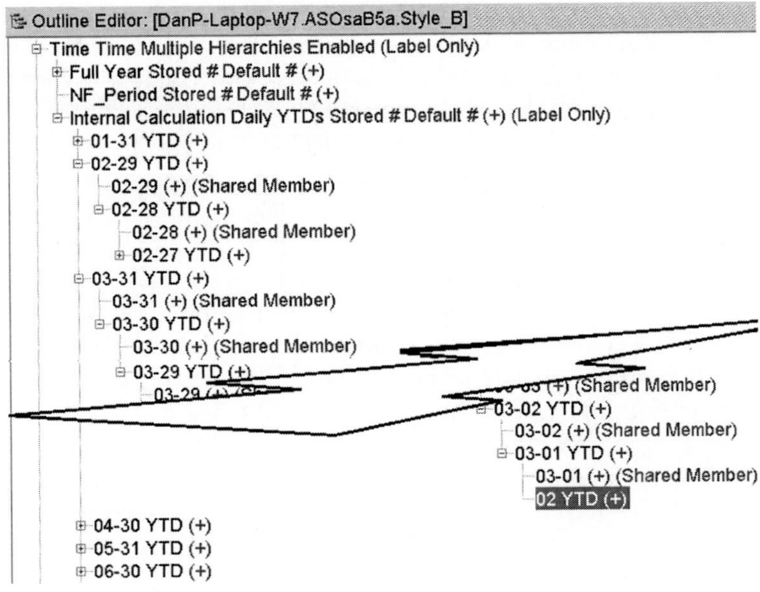

Figure 7.17 ASOsamp with Daily time periods, with Upper-level data loaded. (From Oracle Essbase Administration Services. With permission.)

Note that we have included a not strictly required [12 YTD] member. By adding this last member, we can build in some additional performance improvements. With a bit of extra code added to the YTD and QTD formulas, we can redirect queries to last-day-of-the-month dates, such as 06-30 and 08-31 to the YTD members. Why would we want to do this? Because the last days of the month are usually the most frequently queried and, frankly, the other days of the month are rarely queried past month end. Thus, if we write a little bit of code, we are already into dynamic MDX for the concatenation anyway. We can now afford to include a Hint in the outline instructing ASO not to consider intermediate levels of aggregation on the YTD stacks, knowing that it will only have to go to the level-0 View (in the [Time] dimension) if mid-month data is needed.

We could even modify the whole procedure to use a generic daily stack and a separate monthly dimension. This would not decrease the number of levels, but it might make some developers happier because they do not have to set up the 12 monthly stacks. But, that is a one-time cost. In any case, I would advise you to use either the solution in Figure 7.17 or this last solution with a separate [Year], [Month], and [Time] dimensions to avoid having 371 levels.

7.6.2.3 Loading Data with the "Natural Sign" Loading Data with the "Natural Sign" is one of the simplest and most powerful changes you can make to your cube design. As you know, Stored Consolidation can only be additive. Accounting applications often have very large "Accounts" dimensions, and users usually want to see positive balances even for those accounts, such as Revenues and Liabilities, that are maintained in most accounting systems with negative values. This type of data storage (with Revenues and Liabilities normally having negative values) is known as "Natural Sign" recordkeeping.

If the data for these negative values is instead converted to the positive values preferred by the users for reporting, then the outline will require negative consolidation at various points (Sales: Total expenses) and you will not be able to take advantage of Stored consolidation. The design alternative being suggested here is to load the data with the "Natural Sign" and let the data "make the decision" of when to add and when to subtract.

Of course, your users still do not want to see negative numbers when they look at expenses. The answer is to flip the sign dynamically after the Stored consolidation is completed. This is best done by attaching one or more UDAs to those accounts with negative Natural Signs. This information will be available from your accounting system. As an added benefit, you will be able to take advantage of this information when designing in-cube variance calculations, ensuring that an increase in expenses is reflected as a negative impact. The dynamic flipping of the sign based on the UDAs is best accomplished using MDX in your smallest dimension—the one with the fewest Stored values.

An Analysis dimension, such as [Time Span], is ideal for this purpose. The normal [TimeSpan] dimension would be as shown in Figure 7.14 [TimeSpan]. The same dimension with Natural Sign Processing is shown in Figure 7.18.

The reason to use the smallest dimension is that the equations and extra members shown in Figure 7.18 will have to be repeated for each Stored member in the dimension. For example, if instead of [TimeSpan] the [Scenario] dimension was used, it would require the types of additions for both [Actual] and [Plan].

One issue with this approach is that while the accounting system will be able to supply you with the Expense/Liability for the UDAs of the level-0 members, it might not maintain them for the upper-level accounts. In this case, you will have to write SQL to determine which upper-level accounts require the sign-flipping UDAs. Any upper-level that is homogeneously made up of accounts with the Expense/Liability tag should itself get that tag. The problem arises for the nonhomogeneous accounts, such as [Net Income]. One solution is to create an exception table in which your users can indicate whether these accounts should be flipped. However, to minimize maintenance I suggest implementing the following rule in your SQL for a default setting for the nonhomogeneous: Set the UDA to the value given to the first-born level-0 descendant. This solution will, based on my experience, generate the correct answer in over 99% of cases. This is because people generally design hierarchies to show positive values first and offsetting negative values farther down.

The most common place where this rule will fail is on Cash Flow hierarchies. In that case, you will have to use an exception table.

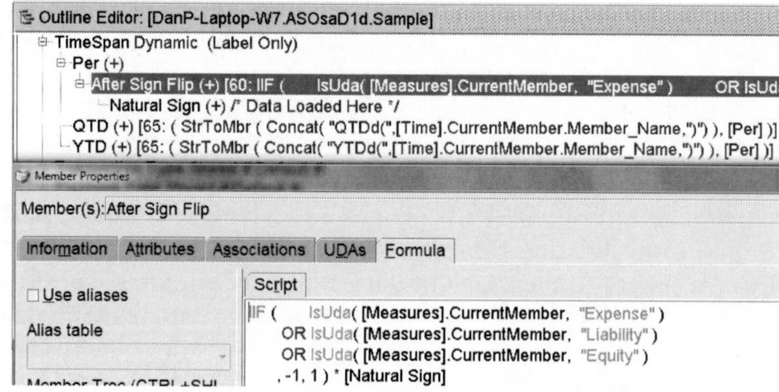

Figure 7.18 Natural Sign Processing. (From Oracle Essbase Administration Services. With permission.)

7.6.2.4 Loading "Balance Data" or "Flow Data" As we have seen, ASO cubes are highly sensitive to the number of input-level data cells in the database. Therefore, it makes sense to minimize this number, assuming no data is lost and no excessive penalties are incurred in recreating the lost data. Many cubes contain "Balance" type data, which has a balance at a point-in-time rather than over a period of time (referred to as transactional or "Flow" data). Accounting balance sheet data is the primary example. Many other cubes contain balance data in the form of readings, such as temperature or odometer, etc.

Frequently, the balances or readings do not change in every time period in your cube. Not every balance sheet account reflects activity every day or month. Certainly, there are some of them that do, but you will find that the overwhelming majority do not. This is also true of many types of "reading" data. If you store the actual balance or reading, you will be adding a data cell every time period whether the data has changed or not. Instead, create a "Beginning of Year" (BOY) value as a new stored member in your time hierarchy. Load the changes (if any) into the monthly members. Now balance sheet balances will be reconstructed in your YTD members (balance sheet data without the YTD Time Span will be perfect for Cash Flow statements). Transactional or flow data will always have a beginning balance of zero. In my experience, this technique has reduced the number of input cells by as much as 95%.

There are two basic techniques for this load. The simplest is to extract the data as monthly changes instead of as balances. If it is not possible to change the input, there is a second technique: Load each month twice. First, load it in its normal location (BOY, Jan, Feb, etc.). For example, let us say we are loading [Jun] now; the next month, before you load the new data, load the prior month with its sign reversed. Thus, in June you would load ([May] times -1) into [Jun] followed by the normal monthly load for [Jun]. Of course, the second loading of the May data into [Jun] should only be done for those accounts that are Balance type accounts.

This means that you will have to add a UDA indicating Balance type accounts. In fact, if you also are adding UDAs for flipping of the Natural Sign, you can combine your efforts. Instead of creating UDAs that say simply "Flip" or "NoFlip" as required in the previous section, create more meaningful UDAs (they were probably in your accounting system anyway), such as "asset, liability, equity, income, and expense" and then code your sign-flip logic to look for multiple UDAs with an OR function, as in Figure 7.19.

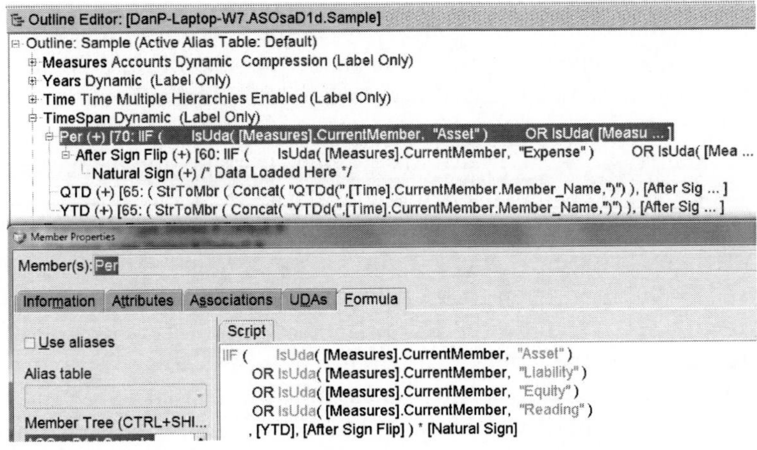

Figure 7.19 Flow Data Processing. (From Oracle Essbase Administration Services. With permission.)

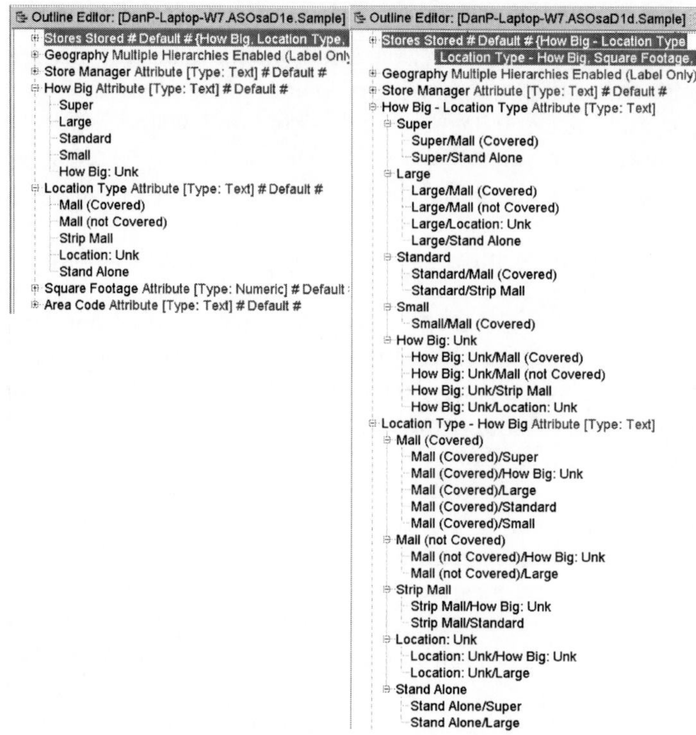

Figure 7.20 ASOsamp with two new noncompound attributes (left) and compound attributes (right). (From Oracle Essbase Administration Services. With permission.)

7.6.2.5 Compound Attributes Previously (near the end of Section 7.4.3.2), the issue of query performance degradation due to queries against multiple attribute dimensions was introduced. One possible solution is to convert one of the Attribute dimensions to a Stored dimension. This, of course, means that your users will always have to include that dimension on their spreadsheets, and the former Attribute association will have to be made on every data record at load time instead of through metadata when the outline is built.

The alternative, that of manually compounding the attributes into a single attribute dimension, should be considered. To demonstrate this approach, ASOsamp has been modified on the left side of Figure 7.20 with two newly added attributes of the [Stores] dimension: [How Big] and [Location Type]. Querying against these two attributes presents the performance problems I have discussed. The right side of Figure 7.20 shows these two attributes combined into a compound attribute.

Obviously, this could be a maintenance nightmare with larger, frequently changing Attributes. However, there is the advantage that "illegal" combinations are not offered to the user when they create queries. Only those combinations that you have explicitly set up can be queried by the user. This would be a definite advantage in the case of larger, more generic attributes. For instance, an auto manufacturer could have [Make] and [Color] as attributes, but ensure that while the user could query for ([Pink], [Cadillac]), nobody would waste their time with a query for ([Pink], [Corvette]). Okay, maybe there are some pink Corvettes out there, but you get the idea.

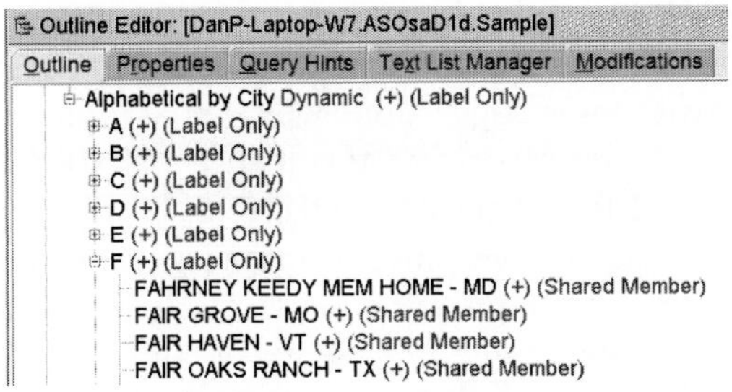

Outline Editor: [DanP-Laptop-W7.ASOsaD1d.Sample]
Outline Properties Query Hints Text List Manager Modifications
Alphabetical by City Dynamic (+) (Label Only)
A (+) (Label Only)
B (+) (Label Only)
C (+) (Label Only)
D (+) (Label Only)
E (+) (Label Only)
F (+) (Label Only)
FAHRNEY KEEDY MEM HOME - MD (+) (Shared Member)
FAIR GROVE - MO (+) (Shared Member)
FAIR HAVEN - VT (+) (Shared Member)
FAIR OAKS RANCH - TX (+) (Shared Member)

Figure 7.21 A dictionary hierarchy for Geography in ASOsamp. (From Oracle Essbase Administration Services. With permission.)

7.6.2.6 "Dictionary" Hierarchies Sometimes your users want to see all of the members alphabetically or maybe alphabetically by description, or even sorted by some other method. While it would seem the job of your query system to do this, there is little cost to adding a Dynamic hierarchy with just this kind of arrangement. The only cost will be to the size of the outline page file. If you use label-only headings, you will be ensured that there is no inadvertent cost of rolling up members when someone tries to drill down on what really should be an information-only hierarchy. See Figure 7.21 for a cube with a dictionary hierarchy for the cities in the [Geography] dimension.

7.7 TIPS TO IMPROVE DATA LOADING AND AGGREGATION PERFORMANCE

The two best and simplest ways to increase load performance are dealt with in the *Essbase Technical Reference Manual.* They include:

1. Use parallel load streams
2. Increase the settings for DLTHREADSPREPARE and DLTHREADSWRITE

This will increase performance, but you still will be limited by the bandwidth of your computer's I/O connections and/or of the I/O device itself. At some point, the people who manage your network or SAN (storage area network) may start to complain about your use of resources. It can be expensive or impossible to increase the I/O throughput, but relatively speaking, with today's computers, it is not difficult to add processing power. Therefore, the answer is once more to maximize the use of:

Pop's Rule: "Computers do arithmetic very fast, but they don't like to run errands."

Use operating system level compression on your input files to reduce the amount of data that has to be pushed through the limited bandwidth. You also can speed up Aggregation and even the initial loading of your cubes into memory (after system restarts, for instance) by compressing the .dat files that house your loaded data. Essentially, you are just implementing the ASO equivalent of BSO compression. When doing so, it is important to not set compression on the file objects themselves, but on the subdirectories in which they will be created. Otherwise, you will lose the setting whenever you clear the data and reload. It is important to remember to set it on both the "default" directory and on any other tablespaces not in your home APP directory, *including the TEMP* tablespace.

It may seem counterintuitive to add unnecessary CPU (central processing unit) load for compressing and uncompressing of files, but the increased effective bandwidth is well worth the cost. I know that these suggestions will work—if you are not already maxed out on CPU (and cannot buy more). In fact, if you have already added parallel loads and increased DLTHREADSPREPARE and DLTHREADSWRITE, you might try reducing them to give you the CPU headroom to employ compression. It is certainly worth testing.

A final cautionary note regarding testing, particularly of Loading and Aggregation: Most operating systems today use file I/O memory mapping, which allows files once accessed to be accessed a second time or by another parallel process more quickly. If you are working in Windows and watching the resource monitor, this is what is happening when you watch the "Free" memory being eaten up by the "Standby" memory (see the histogram at the bottom of the Memory tab). This effect is found with both the input files on a data load and the .dat files on aggregation and queries. Assuming that no other processes are reading the same files (such as two cubes loading the same data), then simply stopping and starting the application will give you a common basis for comparison when testing the effects of different member formulae or different ASO cache sizes, or of different compression settings on input or .dat files.

7.8 A FINAL WORD ABOUT RULE R1, ASO CACHE, AND MEMORY

For you who are still concerned about my rule R1:

> R1: The Input-level and Aggregation-data for all loaded ASO cubes should fit into memory (or it ain't really ASO).

I hope you have used some of the rules and techniques in this chapter to make your cube smaller and faster. If you still do not have enough memory, the real answer is to get more. Assuming that is not possible, what are the implications and the options? First of all, you are going to have to live with some suboptimal performance, limited by the speed of your I/O. Let us look at the options.

7.8.1 Aggregation

We know that there is improvement from creating Aggregated Views, but that in some cases (multiple attribute queries) the level-0 View will be required. Sometimes you simply need all of the detail in that view. Frequently, however, there is one dimension that is the main culprit. It has many members and a high degree of cardinality, meaning that the data is spread widely across the members. With luck, your attributes are not tied to this dimension or tied to upper-level members in that dimension. With a little more luck, the detail in this dimension is not frequently needed. Then you can materialize a View that consolidates this dimension to the top level or, at least, to the level where the attributes are associated. You must review the suggested aggregations to make sure you do not start pushing even this new View out of memory.

7.8.2 ASO Cache

The memory dedicated to the ASO cache for each cube is reserved for that cube and even if no user is querying it, the memory is reserved. That is not to say it might not be paged out, but you might be better served by minimizing the cache. In particular, the larger ASO cache settings are only needed during original data loads (slice loading generally does not involve a large enough dataset to require changing the ASO cache) and, to a lesser extent, aggregation. The TEMP tablespace is used when ASO cache is not available. Therefore, make sure your TEMP tablespace is on a separate disk drive from your main tablespaces. *If there is an SSD drive available, it will be best used for the TEMP tablespace.* Finally, if you have a number of cubes running simultaneously, you might want to test taking a portion of your limited RAM and configuring it as a RAM drive. It should be listed first in your TEMP tablespace list for each cube. This will work to some extent as a shared ASO cache. Nevertheless, you will have to test.

7.8.3 Memory

The final word on memory really is: **Get more.**

If you are far from fitting your cubes into memory, you might do well to investigate adding extra SAN or channel adapters to increase the speed with which you can get data to and from your disk drives. If your CPUs are not at 100% utilization, you should test system level compression of the MAIN and TEMP tablespaces, as suggested in the previous section.

Other than that, your next dollars are probably best spent on memory.

7.9 SUMMARY

Dynamic MDX—Where Is It Okay?
Stored Hierarchy or Stored Members
Where Did I Load That Data?
Solve-Order: Now What?
Who Is on First? What Is on Second?

The answer is to think about your code in terms of Translation and Redirection. Sure, some of your MDX will have to be actual calculations; after all, you cannot compute ratios with Stored consolidations. Other than these cases, you should have to write relatively little MDX in your cube. Or, at least, only a few long chunks of complex MDX on very few members. By thinking in terms of Translation and Redirection of the type shown for YTD, you impart a kind of Object orientation to your cube. Once you write a piece of MDX (and document it then and there with comments), you should be able to forget about it. Additionally, consider writing comments on those members that are the targets of your MDX. It is important to identify members as unused directly by the users and which pieces of MDX will redirect where.

Also, organize your dynamic consolidations and MDX by Solve-Order groups starting from the highest dynamic Solve-Order. Remember that while the lowest Solve-Order is *computed* first, then the next lowest, etc., the query engine resolves or interprets the *highest* Solve-Order first. These are the Solve-Order ranges that I generally use to help Organize my cube's calculations:

- 200–225: Variances
- 150–175: Interdimensional calculations
- 100–125: Intradimensional calculations
- 85–90: XREFs (if you really must use these performance killers)
- 50–75: Translation/Redirection

Solve-Order Range 50–75: Translation/Redirection is used when you absolutely, positively insist on writing MDX, make your life easy; write it using the natural, untranslated ntuple at the highest level of the Solve-Order group that makes sense. In other words, if you are using the [Time Span] or Natural Sign or the "Flow Data" techniques introduced above, use the normal member names you expect your users to use in their queries. Let the MDX you wrote to translate these to, for example, JanYTD and do not worry about the few processing cycles you could have saved. Then you can let your carefully organized hierarchy of Solve-Order groups translate it into the actual structure of your cube. The performance impact of your MDX will not be high as long as you do not reference something with a higher Solve-Order than that of the member to which you are attaching the MDX.

In conclusion, let ASO be ASO, use Stored hierarchies wherever possible, and, finally, Stop writing code: Nobody will think less of you.

7.10 AFTERWARD AND CAVEAT TO THE READER

As many people have noted, there is little written about the Black Box that is the internal workings of Essbase ASO. What I have included within this chapter is from neither any secret documents nor any extensive discussions with the development team. It is based on my own analysis of the documentation that is available and training in computational theory remembered from many years ago in engineering school and other work I have done since then. While I have not reverse engineered code to verify the mechanisms I have described, I have tested the implications of my "gedanken" (thought) experiments in real code.

Readers are cautioned to test and verify for themselves these rules and to realize that the results I have presented are limited by my skills in formulating test scenarios.

Readers are also encouraged to challenge these rules and invited to communicate with me via LinkedIn regarding any test results or conditions that seem to point out anomalies.

8

DEEP INSIDE THE ESSBASE JAVA API

Tim Tow

CONTENTS

8.1 INTRODUCTION

One of the key differences between an application and a platform is the presence of an application programming interface, or API. The Essbase platform was created from the ground up on a robust API, and, in fact, nearly all functionality in the Essbase product is also available to developers through the API. This is important as it allows developers to tailor Essbase applications in nearly infinite ways to meet their business requirements. It also allows Essbase to be used in ways above and beyond the vision of the Essbase product team.

This chapter assumes you are not yet familiar with Java, so it will introduce you to some of the terminology and organization techniques used in Java. Once you know a little about the terminology of Java, we can introduce you to the objects you will encounter when writing code with the Essbase Java API. After you are familiar with the objects, you will be introduced to some of the techniques you can use to connect to Essbase, query data from the database, and query members from the Essbase outline. Along the way, you may learn a bit about how Essbase works under-the-covers.

Essbase has featured an API since it was introduced in the early 1990s. In the beginning, the API was available for both the C and the Visual Basic programming languages. These APIs, particularly the Visual Basic API, were extremely popular and were used by many companies to tailor how their users worked with Essbase. But, due to the ever-changing nature of technology, another API was soon introduced that would eventually become the lead API for Essbase development: the Essbase Java API.

The Java programming language was introduced in 1995 as a general purpose, multithreaded, object-oriented language. Java is well suited to the new generation of Web-based applications that were gaining popularity at the time. The Essbase Java API was introduced to a select set of Essbase partners in the summer of 1998 and was first delivered as part of the Essbase Enterprise product in Essbase 6.5. It was designed as a server-based API and ran inside a Java application server as its container. The initial version supported a subset of Essbase functionality suited for writing custom user interfaces.

Over the next several years, the Essbase Java API underwent very little change, although the container name changed twice. In Essbase version 7X, the container for the Java Essbase API was named Essbase Deployment Services (EDS). In Essbase 9.0 through 9.2, the container was named Essbase High Availability Services (AHAS). Change finally came to the Essbase Java API in version 9.3 when the container name changed once again to Analytic Provider Services (APS) to reflect the merging of the Java API and the Smart View provider containers. Additionally, the necessity of a container disappeared in version 9.3 with the introduction of *embedded mode* connections that enable Java applications to connect directly to the Essbase database.

Shortly after the introduction of Essbase 9.3, Oracle acquired Hyperion Solutions, which was a very important development for the future of the Essbase Java API. The Oracle Fusion strategy focuses on acquiring best-of-breed technologies and weaving them together into a new set of integrated applications designed to work together and written on a common Java platform. Essbase is one of the key technologies central to Oracle Fusion, and as Fusion depends on the Java platform, the Essbase Java API also has become a key Fusion technology. In addition to embedded mode connections, the functionality of the Java API has been expanded as well to include nearly all functionality available in the original Essbase API for C. This trend appears to be accelerating as Oracle integrates Essbase deeper into its stack, and, at some point in the near future, it may be the lead API where new Essbase innovations first appear.

In addition to writing custom applications, an API is useful for developers who want a deeper understanding of how Essbase works. This is because applications are comprised of low-level operations that must be executed to accomplish a task. The process of writing code at this level has the natural side effect of exposing the developer to the order, or sequence, in which subtasks must be completed. Many of the features exposed to developers are completely hidden to the casual user, and, thus, developers gain insights not available to normal users.

Java is an object-oriented language, so unlike the Essbase C and Visual Basic APIs, the Essbase Java API is object-oriented. In the next section, we will explore the object model of the Essbase Java API and introduce the concept of task sequences.

8.2 ESSBASE JAVA API OBJECT MODEL

The most important part of writing code in any object-oriented language is to understand the object model. An object model defines the components that can be programmed and the actions that can be performed on those components. Although it sounds complicated, it really is not. The objects that comprise the Essbase Java API object model are the objects most Essbase professionals work with every day in EAS (Essbase Administrative Services) or MaxL, the only difference being that they use a funny Java naming convention. In this section, you will learn about these objects and how they are organized, but first we will discuss some basic Java terminology that will be used throughout the chapter.

Java code is organized into files called *classes*. A *class* contains the definition, or blueprint, for an object. An object is defined by describing its attributes, describing what it can do and describing what happens to it. An attribute used to describe an object is called a *property*. A property describes a single aspect of an object, and an object may have many properties that describe it. To use a real-world example, a planet may be described, in part, by its color, how many moons it has, and whether it has life on it. In object-oriented terms, you could say a planet object has *color, moonCount,* and *hasLife* properties. Objects can often do things, or have actions that they can take. In object-oriented terms, an action is called a *method*. For example, a planet may have a *rotate* method. Objects also may have things that happen to them. In programming terminology, the things that can happen to an object are called *events*. For example, a planet may have a *dayOccurred* event.

A class is a definition of an object, but it is not considered an object. In essence, it is the pattern from which an object is created. An object created from the pattern is called an object *instance*. An instance can store properties that describe the object. An example of an instance of a planet object is Earth. This instance, Earth, has a *color* property of blue, a *moonCount* property of 1, and a *hasLife* property of True. One or more instances of a class, grouped together, are referred to as a *collection* of objects. Using our planet example, you could say that our solar system is a collection of planets.

In Java, related classes are organized into directory hierarchies where the directories are named based on the functionality provided by the classes they contain. The directory hierarchies are called *packages*. Related packages, in turn, are grouped together for deployment in *jar* files. A jar file is a self-contained collection of classes compressed into a single file that, internally, maintains its package hierarchy. In other words, it is a glorified *zip* file.

Now that we have learned how Java code is organized and distributed, let us turn our attention to how Java classes are organized in the Essbase Java API. The Java API is organized into six major packages. The packages, along with their functionality, are displayed in Table 8.1.

Classes from these packages are split between two different jar files for deployment. The "ess_japi.jar" file contains classes required for the client portion of the API, while the "ess_es_server.jar" file contains classes required by the server components of the API.

The Essbase packages contain two distinct types of classes: interfaces and concrete classes. An interface class is a special type of class that contains only the property and method definitions and is used to define a public programming interface. A concrete class, on the other hand, is a class that can be instantiated and, in the case of the Essbase Java API, often *implements* an interface. Interfaces provide a consistent contract between an API and its consumers. Interfaces also provide freedom for the implementers of an API to implement functionality as needed, while maintaining a consistent external interface. Though it is possible to write code against the concrete Essbase classes,

Table 8.1 Java API Packages

Package	Description
com.essbase.api.base	The base package contains basic objects used by all Essbase packages.
com.essbase.api.dataquery	The dataquery package contains objects for querying data from Essbase using the query-by-example grid API or MDX.
com.essbase.api.datasource	The datasource package contains objects related to the Essbase server, application, cube and security.
com.essbase.api.domain	The domain package contains objects related to the APS server including information on clusters and Essbase servers configured in APS.
com.essbase.api.metadata	The metadata package contains objects defining Essbase outlines, dimensions, members and other related items.
com.essbase.api.session	The session package contains objects used to create an Essbase Java API instance.

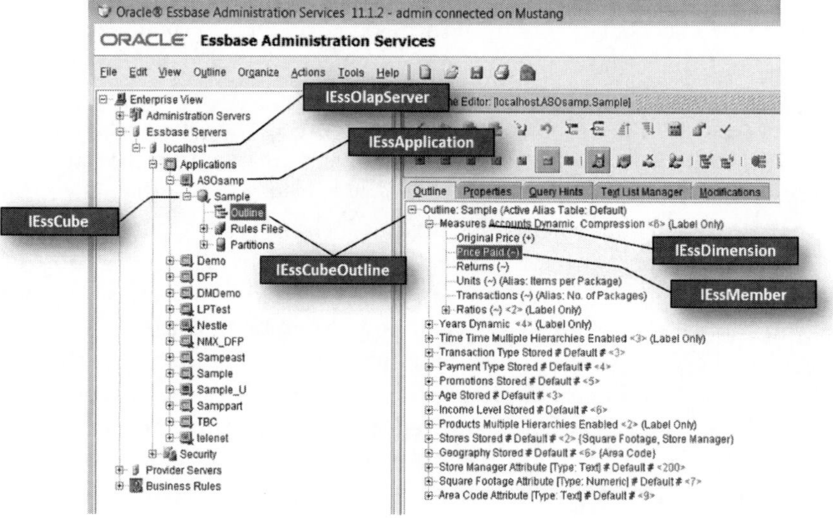

Figure 8.1 Essbase application and outline classes. (From Oracle Essbase Administration Services. With permission.)

it is strongly recommended that you write your code against the documented interface classes.

So far, we have discussed a bunch of technical terms, but have not really talked about anything that sounds like Essbase. Thankfully, the Essbase classes are named in accordance with the same terminology that Essbase developers use every day. The primary difference is that the Java classes that developers use are interface classes and, so, by Java convention, are named starting with the letter "I." For example, when you write Java code to do something with an Essbase server, you will write code against the *IEssOlapServer* interface. It is actually easy to determine which classes to use when you relate them to the objects you see in the Essbase Administrative Services (EAS) console as shown in Figure 8.1.

The *IEssOlapServer* object represents, naturally, an Essbase server. In EAS, you can perform certain operations on an Essbase server. For example, you can connect to an

Essbase server, look at existing applications, create new applications, look at a list of existing users and create new users, among other operations. Likewise, the *IEssOlapServer* interface includes *connect*, *getApplications*, *createApplication*, *getOlapUsers*, and *createOlapUser* methods to perform these operations.

Note: Naming conventions in Java typically use camel casing where the first letter of the first word in a method name is in lower case, but the first letter of subsequent words in the method name use an initial capital letter.

Much like Essbase itself, the objects in the API have a hierarchy. An Essbase server can have multiple Essbase applications. In the Java API, you could say that the *IEssOlapServer.getApplications* method returns the collection of *IEssOlapApplication* objects, or Essbase applications, on the server. In other words, there is a one-to-many relationship between the server and the application. Further, you also could say the *IEssOlapServer* is the parent object of each *IEssOlapApplication*. There are a number of things you can do with Essbase applications in EAS. Applications can be started, they can be stopped, and you can look at the existing databases in the application, or even create a new database within an application. The *IEssOlapApplication interface*, likewise, includes *start*, *stop*, *getCubes*, and *createCube* methods to perform these operations.

The *IEssCube* interface represents an Essbase database or cube. There are many things you can do with an Essbase cube and, thus, the *IEssCube* interface contains many methods. The methods of the *IEssCube* interface include methods to load data, calculate the database, read the dimensions and members of the database, create and open the database outline for editing, create and manipulate new files, such as Calc Scripts, and obtain the objects used to define and execute a data query.

The *IEssCubeOutline* interface has methods for querying and manipulating the dimensions and members in the outline, verifying changes to an outline, saving the outline, and restructuring the cube. There is a one-to-one relationship between the *IEssCube* and the *IEssCubeOutline* objects. An *IEssCubeOutline* instance is obtained using the *IEssCube.openOutline* method.

An Essbase outline must contain two or more dimensions. Likewise, the *IEssCubeOutline* interface contains a *getDimensions* method that returns a collection of *IEssDimension* objects. The *IEssDimension* interface contains methods to do things you would typically do with dimensions, including reading and changing the dense/sparse storage options and reading or modifying level and generation names. It also has a method, *getDimensionRootMember*, which returns the *IEssMember* object that represents the dimension member.

Essbase members are represented in the API in the *IEssMember* interface. This interface has methods to get or set the value of every property of a member including its name, description, formatting string, formula, aliases, attributes, and child members.

The objects discussed so far are very intuitive to people who work with Essbase on a regular basis. There are a number of other objects that are not so obvious, despite the fact that Essbase users may have been working with them, albeit indirectly, for years. The reason that these objects are not well known is that they are used primarily for querying data from the database and as such are not represented in the EAS interface. They do, however, manifest themselves "under-the-covers" in the classic Essbase Excel® add-in. You can see these objects when you preview data for a database in EAS (Figure 8.2).

The *IEssCubeView* object is a container object for all of the Essbase operations, and an *IEssCubeView* instance is obtained from the *IEssCube*. If you think about it, it makes

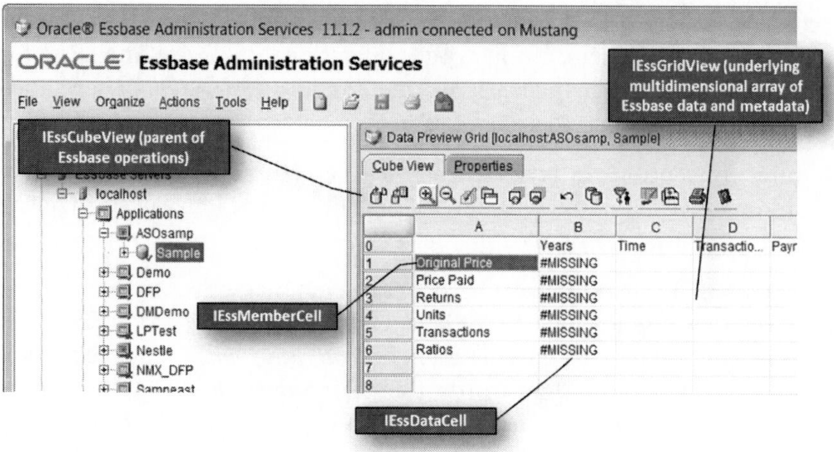

Figure 8.2 Essbase data classes. (From Oracle Essbase Administration Services. With permission.)

sense that an Essbase operation applies to an Essbase database. The standard Essbase operations also are represented as objects in the Java API. For example, the *IEssCubeView* interface contains a *createIEssOpRetrieve* method that returns, naturally, an instance of the *IEssOpRetrieve* object. The *IEssOpRetrieve* instance is then passed as an argument to the *IEssCubeView.performOperation.*

When you first consider the idea that Essbase operations are represented as objects, it may seem counterintuitive. Once you start looking at the interface definitions for the Essbase operations, the reason that Essbase operations are considered objects starts to make sense. Many Essbase operations require a number of optional parameters for execution, and wrapping these parameters into an object is an elegant solution for passing those parameters. For example, the Essbase Zoom In operation requires one or more member cells to be selected for the zoom operation to work properly. If you think about how the Zoom In operation works in the classic Essbase Excel add-in, it makes sense that you cannot Zoom In if you have not selected a member.

In addition to containing the operation objects, the *IEssCubeView* object is also the container object for Essbase query options. The *IEssCubeView* includes methods for controlling options including the zoom level, the alias table, whether member names or alias names are displayed, and whether zoom operations suppress missing rows. The method names for these options are intuitive, and for the options mentioned above, the corresponding methods are named *setDrillLevel, setAliasTable, setAliasNames,* and *setSuppressMissing.*

When most Essbase users think about Essbase operations, such as Retrieve and Zoom In, they think of those operations as occurring in the context of an Excel spreadsheet. In the Java API, there is not an Excel spreadsheet to provide the member grid for the operation. Instead of a spreadsheet, the Java API uses the *IEssGridView* interface to provide the member grid. An instance of an *IEssGridView* is obtained from the *IEssCubeView* instance using the *IEssCubeView.getGridView* method. An *IEssGridView* instance is a multidimensional array of information used both to form the member layout for an operation and to return values after the operation is performed. It is easy to visualize the data that is returned from a retrieve operation in the classic Excel add-in. The *IEssGridView* object is, in many ways, a virtual representation of this data, but it has many additional layers as well. There is a layer that identifies the type of data in the cell, a layer that identifies attributes for a cell, a layer that returns information about the text measure, also known as smart lists, if applicable, and a layer that returns formatted cells values. You also can write values to these layers and, in the case of a query, you *must* write values to the grid using the *IEssGridView.setValue* method.

The final two interfaces, *IEssMemberCell* and *IEssDataCell*, refer to the information returned from an Essbase query. These two object types identify, as their names imply, a cell or cells that contain either an Essbase member or a number returned from Essbase. The *IEssMemberCell* interface contains properties that read the dimension number and attributes of the cell. Have you ever wondered how the classic Essbase Excel add-in and Smart View determine the formats used to create Styles? Both of those products use attributes to determine the appropriate format to apply to the cell.

The *IEssDataCell* interface includes methods for both reading and writing the value of the cell. Other methods can tell you if the data cell is read-only, read-write, or if the user has no access. Data cells are also the attachment point in Essbase for Linked Reporting Objects (LROs), and naturally, the *IEssDataCell* interface has methods for determining if the cell has associated LROs, determining what type of LROs are associated with the cell, as well as adding and removing LROs from the cell. Another useful method of this interface returns the members represented by the data cell.

Now that you have been introduced to some of the common objects that are used when programming in the Essbase Java API, let us talk a little about the order in which some of these objects may be used when writing code. When you write Java applications, or write code in any language for that matter, you are specifying the actions you want the computer to perform. Imagine for a minute that you want to write a program that instructs your friend to go to the store and get a gallon of milk. You may think to yourself that it should be an easy task because the store is less than a block away on the left-hand side of the road. However, if you were programming a robot to get you a gallon of milk, you would need to give it very explicit instructions. If the robot were sitting when it started, you would have to program instructions including how to stand up, which way to turn, how to walk, how to open the door, etc. As you can easily see, the program may get quite detailed and require that instructions be executed in a certain order for the program to complete successfully. In the Essbase Java API, the order in which operations much be completed is called the *Task Sequence.*

There are a number of operations in Essbase where the task sequence is very important. There are other places where the task sequence is not important at all. One of the challenges when writing code in the Essbase Java API is to understand when there is an important task sequence and when an operation does not require a specific sequence. Ideally, you could look up the task sequence for any operation in the documentation, but unfortunately, the API documentation does not contain task sequence information. The Essbase Java API does ship with a number of sample programs, however, and these are probably the best place to find the proper task sequences for the most common Essbase operations. The sample code files are located in the following directory:

```
%EPMHOME%\common\EssbaseJavaAPI\11.1.2.0\samples\japi.
```

What do you do if there is not sample code that shows the task sequence? In that case, all you can do is perform the operation and visually observe what happens. Though this approach is not always helpful, at times it can help you understand the operations that

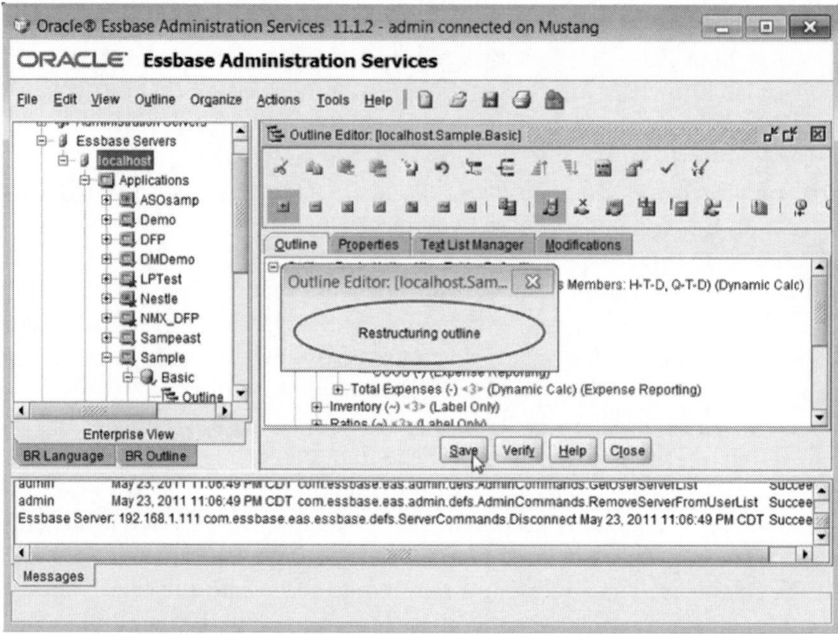

Figure 8.3 Database restructure. (From Oracle Essbase Administration Services. With permission.)

happen under the covers. For example, when you modify and save an outline in EAS, you can see the various steps that EAS performs as it verifies and saves the outline and then restructures the database (Figure 8.3).

When working with the Java API, there are times where there is neither sample code nor a way to visually observe the operation. In those cases, the only way to find the proper task sequence is by trial and error or by contacting Oracle Support.

Now that you know a bit more about the objects inside the Java API and have been introduced to the concept of a task sequence, we can start working with some actual Java code. In the next section, you will learn how to connect to an Essbase server and access a specific database.

8.3 ESSBASE CONNECTIONS

If you think about accomplishing a given task in Smart View, the first thing you do is connect to a specific Essbase database. In other words, the first *operation* in your Smart View *task sequence* is to connect to the database. Likewise, when you are working with the Java API, the first thing in your task sequence is to connect to the database.

In reality, the process of connecting to a database has its own task sequence, as there are a number of steps that must be taken to create the connection to a specific database. Generally, the steps required to connect to a database include:

- Initialize the API
- Create an *IEssOlapServer* object for the desired server
- Connect to the server
- Get a reference to the specified application and cube
- Set the cube active on the connection

Let us look at the code for these steps and then discuss each line. Here is the code to begin the connection to the Sample.Basic database on the Mustang server:

```
// initialize the JAPI
IEssbase essbase = IEssbase.Home.create(IEssbase.JAPI_VERSION);
```

The *IEssbase.Home* object exists solely for initializing an instance of the Java API. You must also tell the API which version of the API you are writing your code against, although frankly, in over 10 years of writing code with the Java API, I have never used anything other than the *IEssbase.JAPI_VERSION* constant to specify the version. The *IEssbase* object that is returned provides the context from which you can sign on to Essbase.

Note: Comments in Java are specified using two slash characters (//). I recommend that you comment your code such that someone who is not a programmer can read the comments and understand what the code is doing. Even if you do not comment extensively, be sure to write comments when you choose a certain method or algorithm from several alternatives, so that you can later remember why you decided on a particular alternative.

```
// connect to the server
IEssOlapServer server = essbase.signOn("timt", "essbase", false,
                        null, "embedded", "mustang");
```

The *IEssbase* interface contains eight methods named *signOn* where each method has different arguments and return different types of objects. In Java, when you have the same method name with different arguments or return values, the different methods are called *overloads*. In this case, I chose an overload that takes six arguments and returns an instance of on *IEssOlapServer* that has been connected to the server. The six arguments of this overload are the *username, password, passwordIsToken, userNameAs, providerUrl,* and *olapServerName*. Three of the argument names are self-explanatory, but the other three arguments are not. The *passwordIsToken* argument is used to indicate that the password field contains a single-sign-on (SSO) token instead of a password, while the *userNameAs* argument allows an administrator to impersonate another user. While these two arguments may be quite useful in certain circumstances, the *providerUrl* argument is always important, as it indicates the location of the APS server to use for the connection or, alternately, that you want to use a direct, "embedded mode," connection to Essbase and bypass the need for an APS server. In the example above, the *signOn* method will use an embedded connection to the "mustang" server for user "timt" who uses the (very insecure) password "essbase."

```
// get the cube
IEssCube cube = server.getApplication("sample").getCube("basic");
```

Once you are connected to the server, you can access the applications and databases for which you have permission. Unlike the classic Essbase add-in or Smart View, however, there is not a nice dialog that pops up for you to make a selection. Rather, you have to know the names of the application and database you want to access. The *IEssOlapServer* contains a collection of applications, and you can return a specific application by name using the *getApplication* method. Likewise, the *IEssOlapApplication* instance returned by the *getApplication* method contains a collection of databases. The *IEssOlapApplication.getCube* method returns a specific *IEssCube* object by name.

```
// set the cube active
cube.setActive();
```

Many operations in Essbase require that a database be set active. In fact, you may have noticed numerous messages in your Essbase.log file similar to this log entry.

```
[Sun Dec 11 21:59:54 2011]Local/ESSBASE0///4728/Info(1051009)
Setting application Sample active for user [timt]
```

The Classic Add-in, Smart View, and your custom Java API code will add similar messages to the log when you set the cube active.

There are a couple of other considerations you need to make when you write Java API code against Essbase. First, you must either explicitly handle any exceptions that may occur in the code or you must explicitly flag your code such that any procedure that calls your code is forced to handle the exception. In the Java API, any Essbase exception is raised within an *EssException* object instance. To handle the *EssException* in your code, use a normal Java try/catch block.

The other thing you must consider is cleaning up connections that you make to Essbase. In other words, if you connect to an Essbase database, you must disconnect when you are done so that your application does not leave hanging connections. The most obvious thing to do is to simply disconnect your Essbase connection as the last line in your application. That strategy is fine as long as you code executes normally, but what happens if there is an exception? If you simply have the code to disconnect from Essbase as the last line in your program, there is no guarantee that that line will execute. In fact, if an exception occurs, then it is unlikely that the last line of your program will execute. How do you guarantee the disconnect code executes? Simple. The try/catch/finally block can provide this functionality for you. The try/catch/finally block is used to execute code and catch specified exceptions. Regardless of the code path taken, be it normal completion or an exception, the finally block executes, so it is a great place to put your cleanup code. Do not forget, however, to protect your disconnection code from exceptions. Here is a general pattern you can use with Essbase:

```
IEssbase essbase = null;
IEssOlapServer server = null;
try {
     // initialize the JAPI
     essbase = IEssbase.Home.create(IEssbase.JAPI_VERSION);
     // connect to the server
     server = essbase.signOn("timt", "essbase", false, null,
               "embedded", "mustang");
     ...
} catch (EssException e) {
     // very simplistic exception handling
     e.printStackTrace(System.out);
} finally {
     // cleanup here
     try {
          if (server != null && server.isConnected())
```

```
                // disconnect from the server
                server.disconnect();
            if (essbase != null && essbase.isSignedOn())
                // mark the IEssbase object as signed off
                essbase.signOff();
        } catch (EssException e) {
            // again, simplistic exception handling
            e.printStackTrace(System.out);
        }
}
```

So far in this chapter, we have discussed some of the Essbase objects available in the Java API and have learned how to use those objects to connect to an Essbase database. In the next section, we will discuss how to retrieve data from Essbase.

8.4 RETRIEVING DATA FROM ESSBASE

The primary reason for anyone to use Essbase is to store data that users can later retrieve into their spreadsheets. For nearly every Essbase user, this seems to be a fairly easy task. Using Smart View, they can connect to the database of their choice, double-click on the worksheet, and have that worksheet populated by Essbase data. Users with Essbase experience may be able to lay out their own Essbase reports by typing Essbase member names into the worksheet. This query-by-example methodology is unique to Essbase and uses a subsection of the API commonly known as the "Grid API." The Grid API is an integral part of the Java API. You can think of the grid used in the Java API as an invisible worksheet. The grid used in Java API is provided by an instance of the *IEssGridView* interface. One of the main differences is that, instead of typing members into the worksheet, you will use Java methods to place the member values in the appropriate cells of the grid.

The standard tasks required to return data from Essbase using the Java API include:

- Obtain a connection to the desired Essbase cube.
- Open an instance of an *IEssCubeView* object from the cube.
- Get the *IEssGridView* instance associated with the given *IEssCubeView* instance.
- Set the values of cells to the desired member names using the standard Essbase layout rules.
- Set the desired Essbase options on the *IEssCubeView*.
- Create an instance of an *IEssOperation* object.
- Set any property values required by the operation.
- Perform the operation on the *IEssCubeView*.
- Read the data placed into the *IEssGridView* by the Essbase operation.

It seems like there are many steps required just to do a simple retrieve, but it really is not too bad once you start writing the code, so let us just dive in and get started. As we already covered connecting to Essbase in the last section, let us start by opening an instance of the cubeview object.

```
// get the cubeview
IEssCubeView cv = cube.openCubeView("default");
```

The cubeview instance is returned by the *openCubeView* method, which has a single argument to pass the cubeview name. The name appears to serve as a unique identifier for the cubeview, but, actually, it appears to have no purpose in Essbase 11.1.1.4 and 11.1.2 and higher. In those versions of Essbase, the Java API was changed to allow a single simultaneous operation. That change is enforced via an exception that is thrown if there is an attempt to create a second cubeview while the first cubeview is still open.

The cubeview is also the container for Essbase options that affect the Essbase operations. The *IEssCubeView* interface contains a number of methods used to set the Essbase options. You will find most of the method names familiar as they have counterparts in the Options dialogs of the classic Excel add-in and Smart View.

```
// set some options
cv.setAliasNames(true);
cv.setSuppressMissing(true);

// properties don't take effect until updated
cv.updatePropertyValues();
```

You must call the *updatePropertyValues* method for the options to take effect. This is because the properties are not automatically pushed into the internal API structures in order to optimize performance. You may update Essbase options anywhere in the task sequence prior to performing a given Essbase operation.

The next task in the sequence is to get the *IEssGridView* instance from the *IEssCubeView* instance. The gridview object must be initialized before use in order to set its size. The reason for this is that the grid size is not predetermined. The internal structures used to store information inside the grid require an allocation of memory. As the developer, you are in the unique position to know how large you need the grid to be. Because you know the size, you can set the grid size based on your needs, minimizing unnecessary and time-consuming memory allocations. There are certain operations, such as the Zoom In operation, that may increase the size of the grid. When you are sizing the grid before an operation, you do not have to consider the postoperation size of the grid. The Essbase server will resize the grid automatically during the operation.

```
// get the gridview from the cubeview
IEssGridView gv = cv.getGridView();
// set the size
gv.setSize(3, 5);
```

The internal grid is a zero-based, multidimensional array. The *setValue* method is used to place values into the cells. There are different overloads for placing member names and data into the cells. In all of the overloads, the first two arguments are the zero-based row and column sizes. The third argument is either a Java String data type for member names or a Java double data type to represent Essbase data.

```
// layout the members to retrieve
gv.setValue(0, 1, "Actual");
gv.setValue(0, 2, "New York");
gv.setValue(0, 3, "Sales");
gv.setValue(1, 1, "Qtr1");
gv.setValue(1, 2, "Qtr2");
gv.setValue(1, 3, "Qtr3");
gv.setValue(1, 4, "Qtr4");
gv.setValue(2, 0, "Product");
```

All Essbase operations are implemented in the Java API as a subclass of the *IEssOperation* class. Instances of the operations are created by the cubeview object using the common Factory Method pattern to simplify the object creation. The operation object is then passed as an argument to the cubeview's *performOperation* method for execution.

```
// create the operation
IEssOpRetrieve retrieve = cv.createIEssOpRetrieve();
// perform the operation
cv.performOperation(retrieve);
```

Once the operation is complete, you need to read the results on a cell-by-cell basis. Most algorithms for reading the grid use a nested loop algorithm that loops through each column of each row and processes the data in each cell. What you do with the data from the cells is your business, but most commonly the data may be written to a file, written to an HTML file, or formatted for use in a spreadsheet.

```
// now read the results
// loop the rows
for (int row = 0; row < gv.getCountRows(); row++) {
     // loop the columns in the row
     for (int col = 0; col < gv.getCountColumns(); col++) {
          // print the values tab delimited
          System.out.print(gv.getValue(row, col));

          // print a tab character between cells
          System.out.print("\t");
     }
     // print a newline character between rows
     System.out.print("\n");
}
```

There are a few things to note about this example. First, when looping through the rows and columns of the internal grid, make sure to read the grid size from the *IEssGridView.getCountRows* and *IEssGridView.getCountColumns* methods. During Essbase operations, such as Zoom In, it is fairly obvious that the grid metrics will change. The grid metrics can change, though, even in the case of a simple retrieve. For example, when you change the *IEssCubeView.setUseBothForRowDimensions* property from false to true, the grid will grow by at least one column to accommodate both the member name and alias in separate columns. Retrieve operations with suppress missing turned on also will frequently change the grid size. Further, for optimization in a production application, you would normally set up the loops with variables that store the row count and column counts, as accessing the *IEssGridView.getCountRows* and *IEssGridView.getCountColumns* methods during each loop incurs unnecessary overhead.

In this simple example, the algorithm is getting the string representation of the value of the cell. The output from this operation looks much like a retrieval using Smart View.

```
               Actual          New York        Sales
               Qtr1            Qtr2            Qtr3            Qtr4
Product        7705.0          9085.0          9325.0          8583.0
```

There is much more information that can be obtained from the gridview. For example, instead of using the *IEssGridView.getValue* method, if you use the *IEssGridView.getCellType* method, the output looks like this:

Text	Member	Member	Member	Text
Text	Member	Member	Member	Member
Member	Data	Data	Data	Data

In other words, in addition to providing just the member names and data values in the cells, the Java API also can tell you if a given cell contains a member, data, or if it is text. Technically, the *IEssGridView.getCellType* method returns an *IEssCell.EEssCellType* object that has both cell type names, as shown above, and an integer value. The integer value is useful in Java for conditionally executing code using a switch statement, which, in Java versions prior to version 7, requires an integer for condition evaluation. If you change the *IEssGridView.getValue* method to instead call the *IEssGridView.getCellType.intValue* method, the output changes once again to show the integer representations of the cell types.

2	0	0	0	2
2	0	0	0	0
0	1	1	1	1

Integer values like these are normally supported by constants whose names are indicative of the type. The values of the cell types are shown in Table 8.2.

If you are using the integer values in your code, you should not. Instead, always use the named constants both to clarify the meaning of your code and to assure that any future changes to the values will be automatically detected by your code.

Another interesting piece of information you can get from the grid is the cell content type. The *IEssGridView.getCellContentType* method returns an integer which corresponds to the following constant values (Table 8.3).

If you change the code to print the value of *IEssGridView.getCellContentType* instead of the value of *IEssGridView.getValue*, the output changes once again.

4	10	10	10	4
4	10	10	10	10
10	3	3	3	3

Up to this point in our look at the Java API, you could easily see how the API related to what you are able to see in the classic Excel and Smart View add-ins. This is the first place where you can see a real difference between the level of information available

Table 8.2 Cell Type Named Constants

IEssCell.EEssCellType Constant	Value
MEMBER_INT_VALUE	0
DATA_INT_VALUE	1
TEXT_INT_VALUE	2
MEMBERwKEY_INT_VALUE	3

Table 8.3 Cell Content Type Constants

IEssGridView Constant	Value
CELL_CONTENT_TYPE_STRING	1
CELL_CONTENT_TYPE_DOUBLE	3
CELL_CONTENT_TYPE_BLANK	4
CELL_CONTENT_TYPE_ERROR	6
CELL_CONTENT_TYPE_MISSING	7
CELL_CONTENT_TYPE_ZERO	8
CELL_CONTENT_TYPE_NOACCESS	9
CELL_CONTENT_TYPE_MEMBER	10
CELL_CONTENT_TYPE_MEMBEREX	19
CELL_CONTENT_TYPE_STRINGEX	18
CELL_CONTENT_TYPE_STRINGEXwFORMULA	20
CELL_CONTENT_TYPE_FORMULAEX	21
CELL_CONTENT_TYPE_HYBRID_MEMBER	22
CELL_CONTENT_TYPE_MEMBERwKEY	23
CELL_CONTENT_TYPE_FORMULA	11
CELL_CONTENT_TYPE_ZEROwFORMULA	12
CELL_CONTENT_TYPE_DOUBLEwFORMULA	13
CELL_CONTENT_TYPE_BLANKwFORMULA	14
CELL_CONTENT_TYPE_STRINGwFORMULA	15
CELL_CONTENT_TYPE_MISSINGwFORMULA	16
CELL_CONTENT_TYPE_NOACCESSwFORMULA	17
CELL_CONTENT_TYPE_SMARTLIST	24
CELL_CONTENT_TYPE_DATE	25
CELL_CONTENT_TYPE_MEANINGLESS	26

from the add-ins and the information available to you as a developer. Some of the more interesting values in this list include the values for missing and no access cells and the value for smart lists. Smart list data cells are cells that contain a text measure. Smart list data cells also have an associated smart list name which can be obtained using the *IEssCubeView.getSmartListName* method.

The *IEssGridView.getCell* method returns an *IEssCell* instance. If the cell type indicates that the cell contains a member, the *IEssCell* can be cast to a more specific *IEssMemberCell* object, and if the cell type indicates that the cell is data, it can be cast to a more specific *IEssDataCell* object. As mentioned earlier, there are numerous properties on these interfaces that provide the information used by Excel to apply formatting styles. If the cell returned by the *getCell* method is a member cell, you can determine the dimension number of the member it contains. To do so, modify the sample code with the following changes:

```
// get the cell object
IEssCell cell = gv.getCell(row, col);

// if it is a member
if (cell.getCellType().equals(IEssCell.EEssCellType.MEMBER)) {
    // cast to a member cell and print the dimension number
```

```
    IEssMemberCell memberCell = (IEssMemberCell)cell;

    System.out.print(memberCell.getDimensionNumber());
}
```

The result is a grid of dimension numbers in cells that contain Essbase members.

	5	4	2	
	1	1	1	1
3				

Likewise, you can cast data cells to an *IEssDataCell* object and get information about the cell. For example, you can tell if a data value is read-only or read-write using this object. To do so, modify the sample code with the following changes:

```
// get the cell object
IEssCell cell = gv.getCell(row, col);

// if it is a data cell
if (cell.getCellType().equals(IEssCell.EEssCellType.DATA)) {
    // cast to a data cell and print the access mode
    IEssDataCell dataCell = (IEssDataCell)cell;

    System.out.print(dataCell.getAccessMode());
} else if (cell.getCellType().equals(IEssCell.EEssCellType.MEMBER)) {
    // just print the member name
    System.out.print(cell.getValue());
}
```

Here are the results of this code.

```
            Actual      New York     Sales
            Qtr1        Qtr2         Qtr3         Qtr4
Product     Read only   Read only    Read only    Read only
```

The dimension number of member cells and access mode of data cells are just two of a number of attributes available for each cell type. The attribute methods available for the two cell types are shown in Table 8.4.

It would seem that storing each of these attributes for each cell in a large retrieve would incur a large amount of memory usage. Under the covers, however, memory usage is minimized because all of these attributes are stored in a single integer. This is possible using a technique called bitmasking. Bitmasking uses each bit, or a series of bits, in the binary representation of a number to pack different pieces of information. If we update our code example once again, we can look at an example of how this works with attributes in the Java API. Let us change the output line again to write the attributes.

```
// get the cell object
IEssCell cell = gv.getCell(row, col);

// if it is a data cell
```

Table 8.4 Attribute Methods

Member Cells	Data Cells
getDimensionNumber	getAccessMode
isDimensionTop	isCellNoteLinked
isDrillThrough	isDrillThrough
isDynCalc	isObjectsLinked
isExpShare	isPartitionLinked
isImpShare	isURLDrillThrough
isLabelOnly	isUrlLinked
isNeverShare	isWinAppLinked
isNonUnique	
isStoreData	
isZoominable	

```
if (cell.getCellType().equals(IEssCell.EEssCellType.DATA)) {
    // print data cell attribute value
    System.out.print(gv.getDataCellAttributes(row, col));
} else if (cell.getCellType().equals(IEssCell.EEssCellType.MEMBER)) {
    // print member cell attribute value
    System.out.print(gv.getMemberCellAttributes(row, col));
}
```

The attribute numbers are below. One thing that is immediately apparent is that cells containing members generally have a large attribute number. The reason for the large number is that member cell attribute numbers use the first five bits to store the dimension number.

```
           536870928   402653200   134217744
           134         134         134         134
268435475  1           1           1           1
```

You can use bitwise math to convert the attribute number back to an attribute value understandable by humans. For example, the algorithm for converting the attribute number to the dimension number for a member cells is:

1 + (attribute number & 0xF8000000) / 134217728 (or 2^{27})

This is not the kind of math that most of us are used to on a daily basis, but when you use the Java API, it is useful to know that the attribute numbers are there in case you need to package or store the attributes for a large number of cells.

You are probably starting to see that there is quite a bit more to Essbase than just the data that you commonly see on a worksheet. The fact that there is more information available is exactly what makes the Java API so powerful. It allows you, as a developer, to leverage this information to better serve your customers.

So far in this section, you saw that there are a number of tasks that need to be performed before an operation can be completed. Once these basic tasks are completed, however, you can perform multiple operations using the same objects. To continue with our example, we could now use the objects in place to complete a Zoom In operation. The Zoom In operation is a good example of an operation object that requires additional information to complete successfully. If you think about how you do a Zoom In operation in the Excel add-ins, you have to first select one or more members on which you wish the Zoom In to occur. In the Java API, you will write code to select the member cells. First, you will need to create an *IEssOpZoomIn* operation object.

```
// do another operation on the same grid
IEssOpZoomIn zoomIn = cv.createIEssOpZoomIn();
```

Once you have the object, you can add a single cell to the selection using the *IEssOpZoomIn.addCell* method or add a range of cells using the *IEssOpZoomIn.addRange* method. In our example, we will simply select the cell that currently contains the member name "Product."

```
// tell Essbase which cell or cells to zoom
zoomIn.addCell(2, 0);
```

Now that a cell has been selected for the zoom operation, you can perform the operation.

```
// perform the zoom
cv.performOperation(zoomIn);
```

The Zoom In operation occurs on the existing grid and results in the following output.

```
            Actual      New York    Sales
            Qtr1        Qtr2        Qtr3        Qtr4
Colas       1998.0      2358.0      2612.0      1972.0
Root Beer   1778.0      1989.0      1879.0      2293.0
Cream Soda  2033.0      2543.0      2421.0      2308.0
Fruit Soda  1896.0      2195.0      2413.0      2010.0
```

Now that we have discussed the tasks necessary to perform retrieval operations from the cube, let us take a look at how to send data back to the Essbase database.

8.5 SENDING DATA TO ESSBASE

The task sequence necessary to send data to the Essbase database is only slightly different than the tasks required for a retrieve operation. The good news, if you have used the classic Excel add-in, is that you are probably already familiar with the primary difference between retrieve and send operations. In the Classic Add-in, updating the Essbase database is often referred to as *lock and send*. As the name implies, you must first lock the cells before you send data to the database. There are other considerations that must be made when updating Essbase databases. First, you must consider whether the cells you intend to update are actually writable. There are a number of reasons that cells may be read-only. First, the user's security may not allow writing back to a member combination. The member combination also may contain a dynamically calculated member that is not writable. If the database is an ASO (aggregate storage option) database, the member combination must contain only level-0 members. Another consideration is whether the database is a BSO (block storage option) or an ASO database, as BSO databases require a lock, but ASO databases will throw an exception if you try to execute a lock. Finally, Essbase gives you no error message if a given cell cannot be written. As long as you are aware of these items, writing code to update an Essbase database is fairly easy. For our example, we will continue our code sample after the Zoom In operation from the previous section.

The first thing we will do is reset the grid in order to clear the contents and prepare the grid for our update. To clear the internal grid, simply call the *IEssGridView.setSize* method and set the size of the grid to zero rows by zero columns.

```
// clear the grid
gv.setSize(0, 0);
```

Next, let us resize the grid to the new required size and fill it with the members we wish to update.

```
// resize for the update
gv.setSize(5, 5);

// layout the members to retrieve
gv.setValue(0, 1, "Budget");
gv.setValue(0, 2, "New York");
gv.setValue(0, 3, "Sales");
gv.setValue(1, 1, "Jan");
gv.setValue(1, 2, "Feb");
gv.setValue(1, 3, "Mar");
gv.setValue(1, 4, "Qtr1");
gv.setValue(2, 0, "Cola");
gv.setValue(3, 0, "Diet Cola");
gv.setValue(4, 0, "Colas");

// remove suppress missing for this example
cv.setSuppressMissing(false);
cv.updatePropertyValues();

// now redo the retrieve
cv.performOperation(retrieve);
```

Let us see what the data looks like before the update.

```
              Budget      New York    Sales
              Jan         Feb         Mar         Qtr1
Cola          640.0       610.0       640.0       1890.0
Diet Cola     #Missing    #Missing    #Missing    #Missing
Colas         640.0       610.0       640.0       1890.0
```

The process of updating the values in the grid is straightforward, as you use the same *IEssGridView.setValue* method used to set the members into the grid.

```
// now add values to the grid for cola and diet cola
// for all three months and the quarter
```

```
gv.setValue(2, 1, 100);
gv.setValue(2, 2, 100);
gv.setValue(2, 3, 100);
gv.setValue(2, 4, 100);
gv.setValue(3, 1, 100);
gv.setValue(3, 2, 100);
gv.setValue(3, 3, 100);
gv.setValue(3, 4, 100);
gv.setValue(4, 1, 100);
gv.setValue(4, 2, 100);
gv.setValue(4, 3, 100);
gv.setValue(4, 4, 100);
```

The creation of the operation is very straightforward, but locking the data cells for update does give us some things to think about. When you lock data cells, Essbase will place an exclusive write lock on data blocks where the data for the given data cells are located. There are two ways to lock blocks in the Essbase Java API. First, you can explicitly lock the blocks with the *IEssOpLock* operation, call the *IEssOpUpdate* operation to write the data, and then unlock the blocks using an *IEssOpUnlock* operation. Alternatively, you can use the *IEssOpUpdate.setPreviousLockRequired* method to direct the *IEssOpUpdate* operation to automatically lock and unlock the cells. If the value passed to *setPreviousLockRequired* is false or, in other words, if the cells have not been previously locked by an *IEssOpLock* operation, the *IEssOpUpdate* operation will automatically lock the cells before the update and then unlock the cells after the update is complete. Here is the code to update the cells.

```
// create the operation
IEssOpUpdate update = cv.createIEssOpUpdate();

// mark it as locked
update.setPreviousLockRequired(false);
// perform the operation
cv.performOperation(update);
```

If you are working with an ASO database, the process is a little different. ASO databases do not store their data in blocks, thus, there is no way to lock the blocks for update. When writing to an ASO database, you must pass a Boolean value of *true* to the *setPreviousLockRequired* method and not call *IEssOpLock* or *IEssOpUnlock*. In fact, if you call the methods to lock or unlock data blocks on an ASO database, the Essbase API will throw an *EssException*.

Once the update is complete, we can retrieve the cells back from the database. In this example, we are reusing the same retrieve object used previously. This is an important point because it demonstrates that you can use the same *IEssOperation* object for multiple operations.

```
// now redo the retrieve
cv.performOperation(retrieve);
```

The gridview now contains the following data.

```
                Budget          New York        Sales
                Jan             Feb             Mar             Qtr1
Cola            100.0           100.0           100.0           300.0
Diet Cola       100.0           100.0           100.0           300.0
Colas           100.0           100.0           100.0           300.0
```

There are a couple of points to examine in this grid. First, our code wrote the value 100 into the Qtrl column for both Cola and Diet Cola, but the value shown in the cell is 300. How can that be? The reason Qtrl does not contain 100 is that the Qtrl member is marked as a dynamically calculated member in the outline and, as such, the block does not store this number. Further, as the number was dynamically calculated when it was retrieved, it automatically reflects the sum of its children as it was defined in the Essbase outline. If you were to look at *IEssDataCell.getAccessMode* for the cells in the Qtrl column, you would see that the cells in that column are marked as read-only.

Also, if you look at the total row for Colas, you will notice that it still has the value of 100 that the code posted into that row. Despite the fact that it is a parent, the Colas member is not marked as a dynamic calculation member. In order to see the Colas value property calculated, you must execute a Calc Script. Of course, the Java API can calculate Essbase, so let us take a look at calculations in the next section.

8.6 CALCULATING ESSBASE DATABASES

One of the most powerful facets of Essbase is its ability to calculate data, and the calculations used by companies can take many forms. They can be simple calculations of the entire Essbase outline, aggregations of small slices of the database or top-down allocation calculations. In any case, most users who execute calculations in Essbase perform those executions via a prewritten Calc Script. The Java API supports these types of calculations and, additionally, allows you to specify and execute calculation scripts on-the-fly. In this section, we will take a brief tour of the calculation functionality in the Essbase API.

Essbase calculations are performed on a single database and, as you will remember, a database is represented in the Essbase Java API in an *IEssCube* object. The *IEssCube.calculate* method has three different overloads that provide the ability to execute the default calculation, execute a calculation from a server-based Calc Script file or create and execute a calculation script on the fly. The simplest overload is the overload that executes the default calc. To execute the default calc, simply call the calculate method with no arguments.

```
// execute the default calc
cube.calculate();
```

The second overload lets you execute a server-based Calc Script or, alternatively, check the syntax of a Calc Script. This overload has 2 arguments, a flag to indicate that the calculation operation should only check the syntax and a string containing the name of the Calc Script on the server. For example, if you wanted to check the syntax of a Calc Script file named CalcProd that is located on your server, you would call the following methods.

```
// check the syntax of CalcProd.csc
cube.calculate(true, "CalcProd");
```

In the code example above, the *IEssCube.calculate* method has a void return type. In other words, it does not have a return code, so how would you know if the CalcProd.csc file has a syntax error? If there is a syntax error, the method will throw an EssException. This is a very common pattern in Java and in the Essbase Java API.

Another common pattern in the Essbase Java API is the presence of method overloads that have the same number and type of arguments, but are in a different order. This is exactly the case with the overload that allows you to specify a Calc Script to be executed on-the-fly, which also takes a string and a Boolean as arguments. In this case, however, the string argument is the first argument in the list and represents the text of the Calc Script that will be sent to the server. The second argument is a Boolean flag that indicates whether the method should merely perform a syntax check on the script text. For this example, let us consider our previous code sample where we updated some Essbase data. In that last example, we saw that the Colas member was not calculated after the update, so this is a perfect example of a situation where you may want to write a custom calculation to aggregate a slice of the database. The Calc Script to aggregate a small slice of the database may appear as below:

```
FIX(BUDGET, "New York", Sales)
        AGG(Product);
ENDFIX;
```

In most cases, you would want to build the script above in code. The most efficient way to incrementally build a string in Java utilizes the *StringBuilder* class. The *StringBuilder* stores characters in an array in memory. The *StringBuilder.toString* method returns the contents of:

```
StringBuilder as a Java String object.
// create a stringbuilder
StringBuilder calc = new StringBuilder(1024);

// add the lines of the script
calc.append("FIX(BUDGET, \"New York\", Sales)\n");
calc.append("AGG(Product);\n");
calc.append("ENDFIX;");

// execute the calc
cube.calculate(calc.toString(), false);
```

If we retrieve the data once more, we will see that now the total for Colas is now correctly aggregated.

```
               Budget         New York        Sales
               Jan            Feb             Mar           Qtr1
Cola           100.0          100.0           100.0         300.0
Diet Cola      100.0          100.0           100.0         300.0
Colas          200.0          200.0           200.0         600.0
```

In this chapter, we have discussed how to connect to Essbase, get access to an individual cube and then read and write data to it. There are a number of other things you will need to do in order to create a complete application, and quite often those things revolve around Essbase members. Next, let us turn our attention to the different ways that you can get member information via the Java API.

8.7 MEMBER INFORMATION

It may be needless to say, but Essbase members play a pivotal role in every Essbase application. After all, the very structure of the database is determined by the members it contains. Essbase members also are highly configurable because they have many properties that determine how the data is physically stored within the database, how users interact with the database, or even how the Essbase members interact with each other inside the database. Due to the important role that members play, all Essbase APIs over the history of the product have featured the ability to query, and even manipulate, the members. With each major new version of Essbase, new features have been added that affect members and that affects how you can work with them. This section will help you understand the different methodologies you can use to get information about Essbase members, the benefits and costs of each methodology, and the pitfalls you may encounter.

There are a couple of primary ways to work with Essbase member information. The first methodology we are going to discuss is an object-based methodology that provides a fully qualified member object in the form of the *IEssMember* interface. The *IEssMember* interface makes it fairly easy to examine different properties of a member. Further, you can create new members and modify the Essbase database outline using the *IEssMember* interface. The downside of using IEssMember objects is that they are fairly heavy objects, so they generally have increased memory and processing requirements, particularly in large outlines. The other downside is that there are a number of ways to obtain an *IEssMember* object, but not all *IEssMember* objects are created equal. Depending on how you get the *IEssMember* object, certain properties may not be available and will actually throw an exception if you try to access them. We will discuss several methods of obtaining members, the problems you may encounter with each and strategies for getting the information you need.

The second methodology we will discuss uses an outline member query that returns a delimited string containing just the member information you request. The benefit of this technique is that it is blazingly fast. On the downside, only certain properties are available using this technique, and it is poorly documented. This technique also requires some string manipulation for processing the results.

As with everything in the Java API, it will be easier to understand these points after you have see some of the code examples. Let us start by looking at Essbase member objects.

8.7.1 Accessing Essbase Member Information via IEssMember Objects

The most common way to get information about Essbase members via the Essbase Java API is to get an *IEssMember* object. An *IEssMember* object contains all of the properties and settings that Essbase administrators are used to seeing in the EAS Member Properties dialog box. These properties include the name, consolidation and data storage properties, along with the aliases, attributes, and user-defined attributes (UDAs).

Once you have an *IEssMember object*, it is very easy to call a method to get the member property you want, keeping in mind that not all *IEssMember* objects completely describe the object (Figure 8.4). In this section, we will use the following method call to print out some of the member properties. If the property is not available, it will print the exception message returned by the Java API.

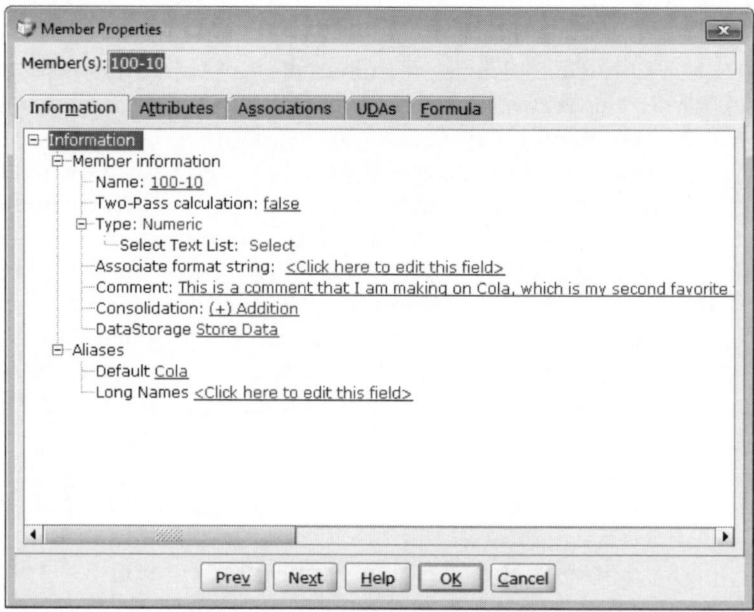

Figure 8.4 Member properties. (From Oracle Essbase Administration Services. With permission.)

```
// print member information
private static void printMember(String desc, IEssMember member) {
   try {
        System.out.println("\n=== " + desc + " ===");
        System.out.print("Name: ");
        System.out.println(member.getName());
        System.out.print("Level: ");
        System.out.println(member.getLevelNumber());
        System.out.print("Related Members-Parent: ");
        System.out.println(member.getRelatedMemberNames()[0]);
   } catch (EssException e) {
        System.out.println("Error: " + e.getMessage());
   }
}
```

Now let us take a look at some of the different methods for getting an *IEssMember* object and discuss the pros and cons of each method. In the examples, we will use the Product dimension of the Sample Basic database, specifically the Colas member and its descendants. In Table 8.5 are the member names, aliases, and level numbers for the members we will see in the examples.

8.7.2 Getting IEssMember Objects Using IEssCube.getMember

The most straightforward way to get an *IEssMember* object is to request it by name using the *IEssCube.getMember* method. If we continue using the code sample from earlier in the chapter, the code to get the member is quite simple.

```
// get the member object
IEssMember member = cube.getMember("100-10");
```

Table 8.5 Product Dimension Member, Alias, and Level

Member	Alias	Level
Product	Product	2
100	Colas	1
100–10	Cola	0
100–20	Diet Cola	0
100–30	Caffeine Free Cola	0

The output from this call is as follows.

```
===  IEssCube.getMember  ===
Name: Cola
Level: 0
Related Members-Parent: Error: Cannot perform operation. The cube
outline is not open. This operation is not allowed on member objects
obtained using IEssCube.getMember and is allowed only on member
objects obtained using open outline or member selection sequence.
```

The *IEssCube.getMember* method is very easy to use, but it is easy to see its drawbacks. The first drawback is that *IEssMember* objects obtained using this technique can return only a few properties. The available properties, which are documented in the *IEssCube.getMember* documentation, include the name, level, generation, consolidation type, dimension name, dimension number, parent member name, first child member name, previous and next sibling names, member number, and a flag that indicates if the member is a dimension root member. As you can see, any attempt to call an unsupported method throws an exception.

Another drawback is that the *IEssCube.getMember* method only returns base members and will never return a shared member. In most cases, this is not a problem. However, if you are writing an application that needs to get information about all of the members in the outline hierarchy and you have shared members, this method is a poor choice. One of the most efficient algorithms for getting information from a tree structure, like an Essbase outline, is called a preordered walk algorithm. This algorithm walks down the tree structure using the information about the parent, the first child, and the next sibling nodes (or *members*) in the tree. If you use *IEssCube.getMember* in your code, however, you will never get accurate parent or sibling information when you encounter a shared member because the call to the *getMember* method will return the base member and not the shared member instance. As a result, your code will enter an infinite loop and run until you terminate the program execution.

In addition to the shared member problem, there is another problem with this technique. The documentation for this method is inconsistent in that it states that the first child member name and sibling information are available in *IEssMember* objects returned via *getMember*. However, the documentation for *IEssMember* shows that the *getFirstChildMemberName*, *getPreviousSiblingMemberName*, and *getNextSiblingMemberName* methods have been marked as *deprecated*. A deprecated method is a method that has been officially marked by the authors to be avoided as it may later be removed. The *IEssMember* object does have a new method, *getRelatedMembers*, which is intended to return this information. Unfortunately, the new *getRelatedMembers* method is not supported with *IEssCube.getMember*.

Finally, you can pass an alias name from any alias table as the argument to *IEssCube.getMember* and the method will successfully return the correct member. However, calls to *IEssMember.getName* on the instance returned will not return the member name, but rather will return the alias name passed as the argument.

```
// get the member object using the alias
member = cube.getMember("Cola");
```

Depending on how you intend to use the information from the object, this behavior could cause you to get incorrect information. Here are the results from getting an *IEssMember* using the alias. Note how the name property should contain the member name, 100-10. Instead, the method call returned the alias used to query for the member.

```
===  IEssCube.getMember  ===
Name: Cola
Level: 0
Related Members-Parent: Error: Cannot perform operation. The cube
outline is not open. This operation is not allowed on member objects
obtained using IEssCube.getMember and is allowed only on member
objects obtained using open outline or member selection sequence.
```

8.7.3 Getting IEssMember Objects Using IEssCubeOutline.findMember

Partially described *IEssMember* objects are a problem in the Java API, but there are reasons that they exist. Partially-described *IEssMember* objects were originally designed to allow access to some member information while maintaining a relatively low amount of processing overhead. You can get a fully described *IEssMember* from the Java API as well, but not directly from the *IEssCube* object. Instead, you must get the member from the Essbase outline, which is represented in the Java API by the *IEssCubeOutline* class. You can get the *IEssCubeOutline* instance using the *IEssCube.openOutline* method.

```
// open the outline
IEssCubeOutline outline = cube.openOutline();
```

Have you ever opened a large outline in EAS and then left to get coffee while EAS spent several minutes completing the process? Essentially, this is the same thing the line above is doing, which is the cause of the increased overhead level, and perhaps slow performance, that you may see using *IEssCubeOutline.findMember.* The good news is that once you have opened the outline, you can query as many members as you like and you will get fully described *IEssMember* objects. Here is a simple example.

```
// get the member object from the outline
member = outline.findMember("100-10");
```

Here is the output. Notice that this version of the *IEssMember* object does not throw an exception when accessing the *getRelatedMembers* method.

```
=== IEssCubeOutline.findMember ===
Name: 100-10
Level: 0
Related Members-Parent: 100
```

Unfortunately, unlike *IEssCube.getMember*, it does not work with alias names. *IEssCubeOutline.findMember* requires a member name and will throw an exception if you pass an alias. If you substitute the alias name "Cola" for the member name in this example, the *IEssCubeOutline.findMember* throws the following exception.

```
Cannot find member. Object not found.
```

In addition, as the *IEssCubeOutline.findMember* method performs a lookup by member name, it also cannot return shared members.

When working with Essbase, it is often the case that you need information about multiple related members. So far in our examples, we have been looking at methods that return information about a single member. We will next turn our attention to methods that can return multiple members based on their relationship to a given member.

8.7.4 Getting IEssMember Objects Using IEssMemberSelection.executeQuery

Member selection is such an important part of working with Essbase that there is an interface specifically designed to query member information, the *IEssMemberSelection* interface. This interface has six overloads of the *executeQuery* method that provide robust options for selecting sets of members. The different overloads allow flexibility in how you can select the members, and they fall into three general categories. First, you can simply specify a member name, as in the earlier methods. Second, you can specify member selection rules using query type and query option arguments. Finally, you can specify member selection rules using the same member specification syntax used for Calc Scripts. The first option is very similar in usefulness to the other techniques discussed previously. Each of the last two options provides the ability to select members quite differently, but the task sequence you follow is the same, regardless of the *executeQuery* overload that you use. The task sequence includes the following tasks.

- Open a member selection object
- Execute the query
- Get the members into an iterator
- Loop the iterator to process the members
- Close the member selection object

The first of the *executeQuery* overloads uses a number of method arguments to determine the set of members to return. The selection may be based on the member relationship to a base member, may be based on level or generation number, may be a search that finds members based on an exact match, or may be a wildcard search. Other arguments provide the ability to search based on the member name only, on the alias name only, or on a combination of both member names and aliases and may be limited to a specified dimension. This technique also provides the ability for *cursoring*, or returning only a part of the query results at a time. Let us take a look at a simple example.

The first task to complete when using the *IEssMemberSelection* interface is to obtain an instance of *IEssMemberSelection*. This is quite easy using the *IEssCube.openMemberSelection* method.

```
// open a member selection
IEssMemberSelection selection = cube.openMemberSelection("default");
```

The *openMemberSelection* method requires you to pass a name argument. The argument has no special requirements and is not required to be unique. When you use a member selection object, however, it is a requirement that you subsequently call the *IEssMemberSelection.close* method when you are done using it. If you fail to call the close method, the result will be orphaned connections on your Essbase server. To prevent orphaned connections, use a try/catch/finally block to close the selection if necessary. You will need to declare the *IEssMemberSelection* object outside of your try/catch/finally block in order for the variable to be in scope in the finally block.

```
IEssMemberSelection selection;

try {
     // open the member selection
     selection = cube.openMemberSelection("default");

     // do some work here
} catch (EssException e) {
     // process your exception here
} finally {
     // if the member selection object has been created
     if (selection != null) {
         // close the member selection to prevent hanging connections
         selection.close();
     }
}
```

Here is a query that returns the children of the Colas member. The first argument, "Colas," is the base member to use for the query. The second argument, *IEssMemberSelection.QUERY_TYPE_CHILDREN*, specifies that the query should return members based on a relationship to the base member, which, in this case, is the children. The third argument allows you to specify certain options, such as returning only a count of the members and whether or not to return relational members when accessing a hybrid analysis database; in our example, we will not specify any options. This argument uses an integer type so you must pass a numeric zero to specify no options. The fourth argument, "Product," limits the search for the base member to the Product dimension. The fifth and sixth arguments are used to specify additional options for certain query types. The last two arguments are cursoring options and, in this case, specify that the query should return members starting with the first member in the query and return the first 1000 members. These options are extremely useful if you have a large outline, as you can use them to reduce the number of members in memory.

```
// execute the query
selection.executeQuery("Colas",
                  IEssMemberSelection.QUERY_TYPE_CHILDREN,
                  0,
                  "Product", null, null, 0, 1000);
```

Once the query has been executed, you must grab the members to process. The *IEssMemberSelection.getMembers* returns an *IEssIterator* that gives you access to each member.

```
// return the members
IEssIterator members = selection.getMembers();

// loop the members and print
for (int i = 0; i < members.getCount(); i++) {
     // get the member
     member = (IEssMember)members.getAt(i);

     // print it
     printMember("IEssMemberSelection.executeQuery-" + i, member);
}
```

The *IEssIterator.getAt* method returns a generic object that you must cast to an *IEssMember* before use. Further, if you run *executeQuery* multiple times, you must fetch all of the member objects returned for one *executeQuery* before calling *executeQuery* a second time. The results from this execute query are below.

```
=== IEssMemberSelection.executeQuery-0 ===
Name: 100-10
Level: 0
Parent: 100
Related Members-Parent: Error: Cannot get related member names.
Essbase Error(1013384): Unknown Error: Not a valid entry

=== IEssMemberSelection.executeQuery-1 ===
Name: 100-20
Level: 0
Parent: 100
Related Members-Parent: Error: Cannot get related member names.
Essbase Error(1013384): Unknown Error: Not a valid entry

=== IEssMemberSelection.executeQuery-2 ===
Name: 100-30
Level: 0
Parent: 100
Related Members-Parent: Error: Cannot get related member names.
Essbase Error(1013384): Unknown Error: Not a valid entry
```

There are a couple of things to note from these results. First, you can easily see from the exception raised by the *getRelatedMembers* method that the *IEssMember* objects are partially described objects. Also, you should note that the base member is not returned, so if you need information about that member, you may need to do a separate query. As this query returns members based on a relationship, any shared members that are returned ***should*** show the proper parent member. Here is an example of this overload that returns the children of Diet.

```
// execute the query on a parent of shared members
selection.executeQuery("Diet", EssMemberSelection.QUERY_TYPE_
CHILDREN,
                       0, "Product", null, null, 0, 1000);
```

As we are querying for the children of Diet, it seems that the objects returned by this query should have *Diet* as the parent. However, it appears that this overload does not properly return shared members.

```
Name: 100-20
Parent: 100

Name: 200-20
Parent: 200

Name: 300-30
Parent: 300
```

If you need accurate information about shared members, you cannot rely on this overload, but there are plenty of other reasons to use it. For example, this *executeQuery* overload can be used to perform searches and wildcard searches based on the member name or alias. Here is an example of a wildcard search.

```
// do a wildcard search
selection.executeQuery(null,
                 IEssMemberSelection.QUERY_TYPE_WILDSEARCH,
                 IEssMemberSelection.QUERY_OPTION_MEMBERSANDALIASES,
                 null, "Co*", null);
```

When you are using *executeQuery* to do searches, the first argument is ignored. The second argument, in this case, is the numeric constant that specifies that the query should do a wildcard search of the outline. The third argument, *IEssMemberSelection.QUERY_OPTION_MEMBERSANDALIASES*, specifies that the query should look for the base member name both in members and in alias tables. The fourth argument specifies the dimension to which the search should be limited, and if the argument is null as in our example, all dimensions will be searched. The fifth argument specifies the search string for the member. If you are doing a wildcard search, you must specify an asterisk character at the end of the string. The final argument can be optionally used to limit the search to a specified alias table. Note that this example uses the overload that does not provide member cursoring.

Below are the summarized results of this query. Notice how this returns members from four dimensions including the hidden Attribute Calculations dimension. That is because we did not limit the search to a single dimension.

```
Name: COGS
Name: Connecticut
Name: Colorado
Name: Count
Name: 100-10
Name: 100
```

Another thing you should note about the wildcard search is that the asterisk wildcard character works only at the end of the search string. What that means is that the APIs do not support full-text matching or, in other words, using a wildcard character anywhere in the search string. If you use an asterisk wildcard character anywhere except as the last character, the API will truncate the characters after the asterisk before performing the query. As a result, the search will not return the set of members that you expect. In fact, if you use an asterisk as the first character in the search string, the search will return all members in the specified dimension, and if you do not specify a dimension, the search will return all members in the outline.

These few examples of the *executeQuery* overload show only a small bit of the functionality available in this overload. Other query functionalities include the ability to query members based on a named level or generation, user-defined attributes, attribute dimensions, dynamic time series, and varying attributes. This overload, however, has a fairly large number of options that can make it complex to use. On the other hand, most Essbase professionals have worked with Essbase calculation scripts during their career, and the Essbase Calc Script language features a robust set of member set functions. We will next look at an overload of *executeQuery* that leverages the Calc Script member set functions.

The Calc Script member set functions provide the most flexible way to specify member sets available in the Essbase API. There are at least 45 different functions that you can use to create member sets and you can nest the functions to provide more control over the members in your set. Here is an example of this *executeQuery* overload.

```
// execute the query
selection.executeQuery(
"<OutputType Binary <SelectMbrInfo ( MemberName, ParentMemberName )",
"@ICHILD(Colas)");
```

There are a couple of things to note about the arguments for this overload. The first argument specifies the property values that will be available in the partially described *IEssMember* object that is returned. Keep in mind, however, that if you call methods on the partially described *IEssMember* object, it will not throw an exception, but it may return incorrect information. Below are selected fields from *IEssMember* objects created from this query. Can you spot the incorrect information in the list below?

```
Name: 100-10
Level: 0
Parent: 100
Name: 100-20
Level: 0
Parent: 100

Name: 100-30
Level: 0
Parent: 100
Name: 100
Level: 0
Parent: Product
```

If you noticed that the level for member name 100 is incorrectly reported as level-0, you are correct. As the *executeQuery* method in this example did not specify that the level number should be returned, then the value reported is the default value for an integer field in Java which is, of course, zero.

The member set functions can be extremely useful, but they may not work in exactly the same way as they work in the calculation engine. For example, the @Merge member set function will merge lists, but it does not appear to return a unique list of members as stated in the documentation. Consider the following example adapted from the @MERGE documentation in the Essbase Technical Reference.

```
// use member set overload
selection.executeQuery(
"<OutputType Binary <SelectMbrInfo ( MemberName, ParentMemberName )",
"@MERGE(@CHILD(Colas), @CHILD(\"Diet Drinks\"))");
```

According to the documentation, the member name returns Cola, Diet Cola, Caffeine Free Cola, Diet Root Beer, and Diet Cream Soda. The documentation also notes that Diet Cola appears only once in the merged list even though it is a child of both Colas and Diet. When @MERGE is used with *executeQuery*, the Diet Cola member is returned twice, which is contrary to the documented behavior.

```
Name: 100-10
Parent: 100

Name: 100-20
Parent: 100

Name: 100-30
Parent: 100

Name: 100-20
Parent: Diet

Name: 200-20
Parent: Diet

Name: 300-30
Parent: Diet
```

8.7.5 Getting IEssMember Objects Using IEssCubeOutline.executeQuery

Finally, there are two overloads of *IEssCubeOutline.executeQuery* that we need to discuss briefly. The reason this conversation will be brief is that both overloads of *IEssCubeOutline.executeQuery* appear to be broken in Essbase 11.1.2. Regardless of the arguments you use to open the outline or the arguments used in the *executeQuery* call itself, this method throws the following exception.

```
Error: Cannot query members by name. Essbase Error(1060000):
Invalid outline handle passed to ESSOTL function
EssOtlQueryMembersByName
```

This method seems promising as it should return fully described objects. However, given the fact that it does not appear to work, I would not recommend spending any time on this method until it is fixed.

In this section, we have seen how useful the *IEssMember* object can be and have discussed numerous ways to obtain an *IEssMember* object. Additionally, we discussed many of the limitations of *IEssMember* objects that are dependent on the method by which it was obtained. After this discussion, you may be thinking that the Essbase Java APIs for working with members are unnecessarily complicated (or even a jumbled mess). You are probably right. That being said, if you exercise care, use sufficient test cases and follow good rules of thumb, you can get a wide variety of useful information from the APIs. In summary, the rules of thumb to use when using *IEssMember* objects include:

- *IEssMember* objects opened from an *IEssCubeOutline* are fully described objects and all member properties are available, but you incur the overhead of opening an *IEssCubeOutline* object. *IEssMember* objects obtained from other sources are partially described and, therefore, not all member properties are available.
- Working with shared members can be problematic and requires special care to assure the *IEssMember* object returns the appropriate parent and sibling information.
- Cursoring is useful when working with large outlines, but it is only available using a single *executeQuery* overload.
- Member set functions are useful for specifying members, but you must test the functions to assure the member sets return the correct members.

Next, let us discuss the second major methodology for getting member information, the member query.

8.8 GETTING MEMBER INFORMATION USING MEMBER QUERIES

The final method we will examine for getting member information, *IEssCube.queryMembers*, is also the fastest method for getting member information. In fact, this method can be up to 20 times faster than getting member information via an *IEssMember* object. There are, however, some downsides to this approach. First, not all member properties can be obtained using this method. Additionally, the member information is returned in a string that must be parsed to get the individual properties and the documentation for this method is poor. Unless you are manipulating members in an Essbase outline, which requires working with an *IEssMember* object, this method is probably the best choice for most applications. In this section, we will see an example of the method call and will discuss how to parse the information. We will also explore the available query options, but first let us look at a very simple example. This is the simplest form of a query you can run with this method.

```
// query members from the cube
String results = cube.queryMembers("Colas");
```

What this query will return is a list of the member names that are tab-delimited (as indicated by the escape sequence "\t" in the output):

```
100-10\t100-20\t100-30\t100
```

Note that the query returns the children of Colas by default. What this means is that you cannot return information about a single member with this method unless the member is level-0 (or, in other words, has no children). The return value is in the form of a single string, so you must parse the string using Java string manipulation methods. For this example, you can easily parse the information using the Java split method:

```
// split the results on the tab character
String[] memberArray = results.split("\t");
// loop the array elements
for (String name : memberArray) {
     // print the name
     System.out.println("Name: " + name);
}
```

This parsing routine simply prints the name to the command line.

```
Name: 100-10
Name: 100-20
Name: 100-30
Name: 100
```

This example shows the results of a very simple query, but the query language has a number of options for specifying the members to be returned, how they are sorted and formatted, and for specifying different properties you can return using this method. Let us next look at the options available for specifying members. Here is an example of a query that specifies the members based on a relationship.

```
// query members from the cube
results = cube.queryMembers("<DESCENDANTSOF Product");
```

When you run this query and parse the results, you get the all of the members in the Product dimension.

```
Name: 100-10
Name: 100-20
Name: 100-30
Name: 100
Name: 200-10
Name: 200-20
Name: 200-30
Name: 200-40
Name: 200
Name: 300-10
Name: 300-20
Name: 300-30
Name: 300
Name: 400-10
Name: 400-20
Name: 400-30
Name: 400
Name: 100-20
Name: 200-20
Name: 300-30
Name: Diet
Name: Product
```

The documented commands you can use for specifying relationships include the following:

```
<CHILDRENOF
<ALLINSAMEDIM
<DIMTOP
<OFSAMEGENERATION
<ONSAMELEVELAS
<ANCESTORSOF
<PARENTOF
<DESCENDANTSOF
```

```
<ALLSIBLINGSOF
<LSIBLINGOF
```

This member information method is unique in that you can specify the order in which the members are sorted before they are returned. In the above example, you see the default sort order, which is the natural order. This is the same order in which you see member names when zooming in with the Excel add-ins. If you would like to see the members in outline order with parents before children, you can use the <SORTNONE command in the query.

```
// query members from the cube
results = cube.queryMembers("<DESCENDANTSOF Product <SORTNONE");
```

This query produces the following output that is sorted, of course, in outline order.

```
Name: Product
Name: 100
Name: 100-10
Name: 100-20
Name: 100-30
Name: 200
Name: 200-10
Name: 200-20
Name: 200-30
Name: 200-40
Name: 300
Name: 300-10
Name: 300-20
Name: 300-30
Name: 400
Name: 400-10
Name: 400-20
Name: 400-30
Name: Diet
Name: 100-20
Name: 200-20
Name: 300-30
```

The documented options for sorting members include the following commands.

```
<SORTASCENDING
<SORTDESCENDING
<SORTNONE
<SORTMBRNAMES
<SORTALTNAMES
<SORTMBRNUMBERS
<SORTDIMNUMBERS
<SORTLEVELNUMBERS
<SORTGENERATION
```

Finally, you can return a number of properties of a member using the <FORMAT command in the query. Here is an example that returns member name, alias and level number of the children of Product.

```
// query members from the cube
results = cube.queryMembers("<CHILDRENOF Product <SORTNONE
                          <FORMAT {MBRNAMES ALTNAMES
                          LEVELNUMBERS}");
```

Note: There is one unusual behavior with the <FORMAT command that you need to be aware of. The <FORMAT command and the opening curly bracket ({) must be separated by a space. If you fail to separate these items by a space, the first property you specify inside the curly brackets will not be returned.

This query returns the following tab-delimited string.

```
Product\t\t2\t100\tColas\t1\t200\tRoot Beer\t1\t300\tCream Soda\t1\
t400\tFruit Soda\t1\tDiet\tDiet Drinks\t1
```

Though you can parse multiple members that are tab-delimited, there is a better way. You can specify different delimiters for the members and for the properties. If we make a minor modification to the query, we can return each member on its own line.

```
// query members from the cube
results = cube.queryMembers("<NEWLINESEPARATED
                          <CHILDRENOF Product
                          <SORTNONE
                          <FORMAT {ALTNAMES MBRNAMES
                          LEVELNUMBERS}");
```

The output looks a bit different. The \n is the Java escape sequence for a newline character.

```
Product\t\t2\n
100\tColas\t1\n
200\tRoot Beer\t1\n
300\tCream Soda\t1\n
400\tFruit Soda\t1\n
Diet\tDiet Drinks\t1\n
```

If you change the delimiters, you also need to change the parsing routines. You can use an algorithm that first splits the string on the newline character to return an array of member lines, and then split each line on the tab character to parse the properties. Here is the earlier parsing example rewritten to use a double loop.

```
// split into lines using the newline character
memberArray = results.split("\n");

// loop the array elements
for (String name : memberArray) {
    // split the properties on the tab character
    String[] properties = name.split("\t");

    // print the properties
    System.out.println("Name: " + properties[0]
                 + " | Alias: " + properties[1]
                 + " | Level: " + properties[2]);
}
```

This parsing routine produces the following output:

```
Name: Product | Alias: | Level: 2
Name: 100 | Alias: Colas | Level: 1
Name: 200 | Alias: Root Beer | Level: 1
Name: 300 | Alias: Cream Soda | Level: 1
Name: 400 | Alias: Fruit Soda | Level: 1
Name: Diet | Alias: Diet Drinks | Level: 1
```

Although this query method does not return all member properties, the properties it does return are very useful. Here is a list of the documented properties that this method returns.

```
MBRNAMES
ALTNAMES
MBRNUMBERS
DIMNUMBERS
LEVELNUMBERS
GENERATIONS
CALCSTRINGS
UCALCS
ATTRIBUTES
```

The ATTRIBUTES property returns a tab-separated list of attribute names for the member. Additionally, there are at least three undocumented properties that you can use with this method. The DIMTYPES and STATUSES properties, though undocumented, are in the code sample provided in the documentation. In order to support outlines with duplicate members, the MBRID property was also added.

We have discussed a lot in this section and, as you can see, there are a number of ways to get Essbase member information. Each method has its advantages and disadvantages, but with this knowledge you will know the options available to you when you need to access member information with the APIs.

8.9 SUMMARY

We have explored a number of concepts in this chapter, but we have just touched on a small number of the numerous classes in the Essbase Java API. These classes provide an almost unlimited amount of functionality that you can use to create your own custom applications. Hopefully, you can use the Java API to save yourself time and to save your company money.

9

SYSTEM AUTOMATION THE GROOVY WAY

Joe Aultman

CONTENTS

9.1 THE IMPORTANCE OF BEING AUTOMATED

There are many noble goals an Essbase professional aims to achieve: designing an elegant set of dimensions, discovering the most efficient outline order and dense/sparse settings, filling the cubes with flawless data. The lion's share of most project time is usually dedicated to these goals. Often overlooked, however, is the essential art of system automation.

A well-designed database that requires a high degree of manual interaction, whether that be to update the outline, to import and export data, or to run and verify calc scripts, is still incomplete. Manual processes tend to degrade in quality over time as they become rote, boring maintenance steps. Quality suffers and documentation is not kept up to date. Worst of all, knowledge of those processes and how they get done (indeed of their very existence) may live only in the head of a single person. This is why no cube is complete until it is highly automated, and neither is a developer until automation techniques are mastered.

Most Essbase administrators have set up automation on their databases in one form or another. After all, getting up at 3 a.m. to load data, update outlines, or run backups can get old really fast. Yet, these things must be done, and most of the time they need to be done at inconvenient times, are repeated annoyingly often, and involve tedious procedures. So, while automation is clearly an essential administrative function, this fundamental discipline has seen very little standardization across the industry. No one seems to do things the same as anyone else. It is a little odd that this area does not get more attention. You might not find a single ASO cube at some companies, while others are devoid of attribute dimensions, alternate hierarchies, or some other Essbase feature. Automation, on the other hand, is practically, virtually, essentially everywhere. It is time to shine the spotlight on this neglected corner of the Essbase world.

This chapter is an introduction to the best available automation methods for Essbase. It takes us beyond the common methods found in the wild by exploring a programming language called Groovy and how it relates to Java. Groovy leverages the Java API (application programming interface) and easily performs tasks that otherwise would be quite difficult. I will introduce new ideas that were almost inconceivable with older techniques. In short, with Groovy I will display a new state-of-the-art in Essbase automation.

9.2 THE AUTOMATION LANDSCAPE

We define our goal as being able to script maintenance-type interactions with Essbase in the most powerful way possible, without making them too hard to develop. In a scripting language, free-form code is written to take step-by-step actions toward completing a task. This is opposed to application languages, which tend to be more structured or object-oriented. Scripts are typically run (or at least appear to run) by reading through and interpreting the source code at runtime. Application code, on the other hand, is explicitly compiled into executable programs.

Groovy lives in a hazy borderland between these programming modes, providing the ease-of-use features of scripting coupled with the power and structure of application programming. This position makes it a strong candidate to be the automation technology of choice for Essbase administrators. Before we launch into adopting a new automation method, however, perhaps we should take a step back and re-evaluate the most commonly used existing methods. Let's review them and see if Groovy automation is worth examining as a better way for you and your organization.

MaxL is the dominant method for issuing programmatic commands to Essbase. It is fairly comprehensive in functionality, and its documentation is pretty complete. Between the two command languages, MaxL is clearly the better choice. ESSCMD is older, more cryptic, harder to write, harder to read, less complete, less well documented, and does not support ASO (aggregate storage option). Hyperion invested heavily in creating MaxL, and Oracle has moved it forward with each release of Essbase. A problem with the language, however, is its inability to robustly handle error conditions. There is no significant method of branching, either, so the only real way to check and react to varying conditions is to embed commands in a script of another type.

The Windows® command interpreter, PowerShell™, the various UNIX™ shells, etc., can make calls to multiple MaxL scripts and check for error code conditions after each script. This allows a certain level of flow control if several workarounds are put in place. Because MaxL normally returns only its success or failure, a series of custom return codes must be created, maintained, checked for line-by-line in the MaxL code, and returned to the calling code. Furthermore, the output from MaxL commands is in the form of strings that are formatted for human visual consumption, which makes them hard to process in code. This output is typically spooled to a file on the operating system, read back into the host script, and parsed. This is all really clunky and is not resilient to change. A more flexible and powerful solution is called for.

Using Perl and MaxL together offers a key advantage over most other scripting solutions. A module for Perl ships with Essbase and is part of every installation. This module allows programmers to make MaxL calls directly against Essbase and easily receive back both the return code and the command output. However, the output still comes back as one long string, and still must be parsed carefully to get any meaning out of it. While this is not too hard, it is subject to changes in format from release to release, and still this solution has other, more significant disadvantages. The MaxL module is built for Perl 5 and has to be compiled from source, using the right brand and version of C compiler, which varies depending on how Perl was obtained. This can be a very difficult task for some, and it must be repeated with every new release of Essbase. A very similar module was released by a third party, this one for the Python language, that did not have this cumbersome compilation requirement, but we do not feel it should be considered seriously as an option. It is not maintained, distributed, or supported by Oracle, so there is no guarantee that it will be compatible with later releases of Essbase. We, therefore, will stick with Perl as the sole option for employing this scripting technique.

Once the technical hurdles have been cleared so that using Perl and MaxL together is even possible, we need to deal with certain issues involving the language itself. Perl is considered by many to be a difficult language to learn and understand. In fact, it is referred to by some as a "write-only" language because it can be so difficult to read someone else's code, or even one's own code a few weeks after writing it. These accusations can be exaggerated, but they contain truth. Generally speaking, it is easier with Perl to write unreadable and unmaintainable code than it is with rival languages. It is also generally harder for a novice to learn enough about Perl even to understand well-written code that a veteran would easily grasp.

While Perl 5 is stable, it has not changed much over the past 10 or 15 years. Other scripting languages have come out that share Perl's power, among them JavaScript, Ruby, Python, and the subject of this chapter, Groovy. These languages add newer, more modern features and capabilities while avoiding Perl's sometimes cryptic and often confusing syntax. (As it so happens, Groovy also offers a few key features that make it a perfect choice for creating Essbase scripting solutions. More on those in a bit.)

Some readers may feel Perl is getting a bit of unfair treatment here, and, truth be told, they may have a case. The purpose of this chapter is, after all, to promote Groovy as a superior alternative, so it stands to reason Perl would get beat up on a little along the way. In the interest of fairness, it seems appropriate to set the record straight about what we are really saying about Perl. Perl is fun and powerful and weird and byzantine and old and cool. Given the shortcomings listed above, it is not recommended as a language to learn starting from square one in order to accomplish our Essbase scripting goals. There is a better way. However, if an organization has thoroughly addressed each of these shortcomings, has the right programmers on hand, and also knows how to leverage Java objects within their chosen language (as we will be doing in this chapter), then Perl plus MaxL plus the Essbase Java API would be a powerful, capable solution, which may be a good choice for that organization. The rest of us will be best served by looking to something more appropriate.

One final automation option we need to look at is direct API development. Essbase has a few APIs: one for C, one for Visual Basic, and one for Java. We are going to dismiss the first two out of hand as inappropriate for our purposes. C itself and the C API are too hard to work with for scripting. Pointers, preprocessors, and explicit memory management are not for us. The Visual Basic API works only with VB6, which is long dead. It can still be used inside of Microsoft Office Visual Basic for Applications modules, but that is not appropriate for daily automation work.

We are left, then, with Java. This comes with its own set of problems and advantages. While compiling the interface module is not needed, compiling everything else is. Java is not a scripting language, and so building full programs—executable classes, main methods and all—is required in order to do anything. This is not what we have in mind. On the other hand, the Java API is the most viable API option, and there are dozens, perhaps hundreds of Java programmers for every Perl programmer in the world. This means hiring, succession, and learning curve issues are greatly reduced. The Java option warrants a closer look.

This option has been around for quite some time, yet has not seen widespread adoption by the Essbase community. This is for good reason. For routine daily maintenance tasks, it takes too much work. Many discussions between Essbase developers about cool and useful things we could do with Essbase have ended with the words: "It would take an API app for that." The perception has been that the gap between regular scripting and full Java development is too wide, and that is a pretty valid point of view. Programming in Java is serious programming. It takes a lot just to get off the ground. There is a need for "scaffolding" in many places, which are the bits of code that need to be in place before we can write the interesting parts. Energy has to be expended considering the exact type of every variable and object, informing the compiler about all these types, and managing conversions between them. Not many have been willing to brave these waters just to better manage their nightly batch processes.

Having looked at all our options, we still do not have the right solution. We have established that nothing short of API development can give us the abilities we need for the highest level of Essbase automation, yet for most of us, this seems a bridge too far. We need a solution that makes the plunge into API development much less scary. We need something that can leverage Java, its abundance of available libraries, its army of programmers, and its ubiquity while loosening its syntax requirements, changing its inability to run as a scripting language, and altering its static typing system.

Groovy is the answer to these needs. This chapter showcases the Groovy language as the best choice for automating an Essbase environment. It would be impossible to teach the whole language here, so we will have to narrowly focus on its power, flexibility, ease of use, and integration with Java. In particular, we want to show how it both is and is not the same as Java development, how it takes Java and makes it more expressive, powerful, easy, and fun. The idea is to get you excited, get you convinced, get you started, and then get you out in the world learning the language in full. Our approach will be to show you the language in action first, then explain what we have shown you. With that in mind, we will build a functional program that executes commands against Essbase, then step back a bit for a broader view of Groovy, its place in the world, and the features it offers us as Essbase developers. After that, we will go over several examples of how to do common automation tasks.

This chapter is meant to offer a streamlined path to JAPI development, which is appropriate for the automation tasks that tie our Essbase environments together. Nothing here should be taken to contradict or detract from the previous chapter. There, the focus is on detailed information about the JAPI, demonstrated with pure, unpretentious Java. Here, we simplify and smooth over the JAPI as much as we can with fancy-pants Groovy. While much of our focus is on Groovy's advantages over Java, Groovy's intent is explicitly to be very Java-friendly. We, therefore, house no ill will toward Java.

9.3 HOW TO MAKE AN OUTLINE EXTRACTOR IN SEVEN EASY STEPS

Because example can often be the most powerful way to learn, let's dive straight into some serious code and showcase the power of the scripting solution we have chosen. We will start at square one and, layering in standard Groovy features and Java API calls, very quickly we will create a solution to a common need that faces Essbase administrators everywhere. I do expect the reader to have a certain familiarity with programming concepts like variables and methods, but knowledge of any particular language is not assumed. Hopefully, each step will be small enough that the code and concepts introduced along the way will come in easily digestible chunks, so that by the end, every reader will be able to at least roughly understand what is going on in the final program. This example, I think, is pretty impressive. With barely 30 lines of code, we will have an outline extractor that walks through an application and outputs the outlines of all of its databases in XML format. With that bold promise, let's get down to business.

9.3.1 Step One: Saying Hello

First, we will need to know how to produce any kind of output, so we will write the traditional first program we always write when we start out with a new language. This is the entire program:

```
println 'Hello, World!'
```

Those who know Java will be impressed with the simplicity here. We have created no classes and no main method. Groovy allows us to get right down to business and does that overhead work for us at runtime. This allows us to focus on the code that does the stuff we want done.

Groovy is an extension of Java that removes many of the more tedious elements of Java programming while remaining highly compatible with Java's native syntax. When used for scripting, the Groovy runtime identifies the code to be executed, wraps it with a main method and a class declaration, compiles it, executes it, then deletes the files created during the process. All of this happens automatically behind the scenes, which allows a Groovy developer to concentrate on coding, working, and thinking as if the program runs directly from its source code.

9.3.2 Step Two: Iteration

Now that we can create output, we are going to need to know how to iterate through a set of data, in other words, to step through it element by element. Essbase's Sample application has three databases, and we want to run the same code against all of them. For now, so we can concentrate just on the iteration part, we will hard code their names and, changing our initial script a bit, say hello to the databases in turn.

```
['Basic', 'Interntl', 'Xchgrate'].each { println "Hello,
Sample.${it}!" }
```

This produces:

```
Hello, Sample.Basic!
Hello, Sample.Interntl!
Hello, Sample.Xchgrate!
```

Java programmers, and even a few Perl jockeys, will really start to sit up and take notice here. We have declared no looping variable and used no "for"-type statement to get the looping done. Groovy has allowed us to write a block of code called a closure (the part between the curly braces) and run it against "each" of the items found in our hard-coded "list." No muss, no fuss. Just efficient, workman-like code.

Groovy's iterators, such as each, provide to their closures a variable called it which has a different value for each iteration of the code. In some cases, a different name for this variable is useful, or more than one variable is needed. These needs are easily met with named parameter lists.

Groovy allows the quoting of strings with single or double quotation marks. When using double quotes, the string can be turned into a GString (seriously!) with the $ symbol and a reference to a variable, an expression, or a call to something that returns a value. The value of the $ expression is substituted into the string at runtime.

9.3.3 Step Three: Connecting to Essbase and Retrieving Databases

We are now ready to start using Java API calls to actually retrieve the list of databases from Sample itself. We will add a couple of lines of code above our loop to make the connection and a couple more below to tear it down cleanly. Then we will be able to loop on a real thing retrieved from Essbase.

```
import com.essbase.api.session.IEssbase
essHome = IEssbase.Home.create(IEssbase.JAPI_VERSION)
essSvr = essHome.signOn('user', 'pass', false, null,
  'http://aps_server:13080/aps/JAPI', 'ess_server')
essSvr.getApplication('Sample').cubes.all.each { println it.name }
essSvr.disconnect()
essHome.signOff()
```

This produces:

```
Basic
Xchgrate
Interntl
```

At this point, Java developers who have worked with the JAPI may begin snapping their pencils in surprise. Interacting with Essbase, in particular looping over JAPI collections, is not supposed to be this easy, but Groovy makes it so. First off, getApplication returns an object of type IEssOlapApplication, which does not even have a cubes property, it has a getCubes method. Further, getCubes returns an IEssIterator, which does not have an all property, either; similarly, it has a getAll method. Yet, we seem to be using these properties. Groovy has automatically added them to the objects based on finding the native methods and seeing that they match a certain pattern. Using these properties makes our code very expressive and powerful, but also very readable. Now, of course we did not have to use the cubes and all properties. Calls to the native methods would have been fine.

Another item to note is how we use the return value of the all property, or the getAll method that it aliases. The return value is documented as a plain Java array, which has no built-in iteration methods. Groovy, however, automatically adds its powerful iterators to every array it finds, allowing us to proceed directly from the all property to an each method, and our looping construct is built in a single line. This is much clearer and easier than what the JAPI natively allows. This can be seen by comparing what we have written above to the sample Java code that is provided with the API.

Groovy makes working with existing Java classes easier by inspecting them and adding enhancements. Any method with the form getSomething() or setSomething(value) can be called as if they are properties of the class by removing the 'get' or 'set' from the beginning and changing the initial capital letter of what remains to lower case. Java collection classes also automatically receive Groovy's powerful iteration methods, such as each, any, and find.

9.3.4 Step Four: Retrieving Dimensions

Now that we are getting Sample and a list of its databases from Essbase, let's go one step farther and get the dimensions from the databases. All we have to do is expand the body of the closure that we are running against every cube. Now it will list not only the name of the cube, but also the names of its dimensions.

```
import com.essbase.api.session.IEssbase
essHome = IEssbase.Home.create(IEssbase.JAPI_VERSION)
essSvr = essHome.signOn('user', 'pass', false, null,
  'http://aps_server:13080/aps/JAPI', 'ess_server')
essSvr.getApplication('Sample').cubes.all.each { essCube ->
    println essCube.name + ':'
    essCube.dimensions.all.each { println it.name }
    essCube.clearActive()
}
essSvr.disconnect()
essHome.signOff()
```

This produces (edited for brevity):

```
Basic:
Year
```

```
Measures
Product
Market
...
```

Here we have a loop within a loop, so we have started using named parameter lists (the part between the opening curly brace and the arrow) in our closure definitions instead of the default every time. This is really helpful when a closure's code gets complex enough to contain additional closures. It is still okay to use it within the innermost closure, but we are better off using named parameters in the outer closures. Some may prefer to eliminate it entirely when working with nested closures.

Another thing to note is the clearActive call that we have added. We did not need this before, but now that we are digging around inside the cube objects we are retrieving, the Java API is calling an implicit setActive on the cube for us (thanks, JAPI), and we will get an error if we try to move on and access another cube unless we release the one that has been set as active.

9.3.5 Step Five: Retrieving Members

We are getting close to our planned outline extractor. The next step is to dive deeper into our dimensions and pull out the members. There is a close relationship between a "dimension" and the root member of that dimension. For now we will use this knowledge and pass the name of each dimension on to the code we have outputting member names. Because the number of levels can vary throughout an outline, our method of nesting loops ever deeper will not work this time. We will have to extract the code that processes members so that it can make calls back to itself.

```
import com.essbase.api.session.IEssbase

doMbrThing = { essCube, mbrName ->
      if (mbrName.size() == 0 ) return
      essMbr = essCube.getMember(mbrName)
      println '--' * essMbr.generationNumber + essMbr.name
      doMbrThing(essCube, essMbr.firstChildMemberName)
      if (!essMbr.isDimensionRootMember()) doMbrThing(essCube,
         essMbr.nextSiblingMemberName)
}

essHome = IEssbase.Home.create(IEssbase.JAPI_VERSION)
essSvr = essHome.signOn('user', 'pass', false, null,
  'http://aps_server:13080/aps/JAPI', 'ess_server')
essSvr.getApplication('Sample').cubes.all.each { essCube ->
    println "\n${essCube.name}\n${'-' * essCube.name.size()}"
    essCube.dimensions.all.each { doMbrThing(essCube, it.name) }
    essCube.clearActive()
}
essSvr.disconnect()
essHome.signOff()
```

This produces:

```
Basic
-----
--Year
```

```
----Qtr1
------Jan
------Feb
...
```

We have created a member processor by assigning a closure to be the value of a variable. We can think of this as giving the closure a name. The important concept to understand is that when we do this, we are then able to pass the closure around like a piece of data. We also can do the thing we are doing here and use the variable to call the closure like a function. We could have defined a regular old Java function here, but closures have a bit more flexibility, and this is after all a chapter about Groovy.

In the above code, the member processor outputs information on the member passed to it, then calls itself twice, the first time passing the member's first child and the second time passing its next sibling. This effectively executes a depth-first walk of the outline hierarchy. Beyond this recursion (code that calls itself), there is not much new in this step. One thing of note is the little trick we are pulling to give the output an outline-like structure by prepending dashes based on the member's generation.

Groovy's operator overloading feature allows for many interesting additions to Java's standard behavior. For instance, with Strings, 'Essbrase' - 'r' results in 'Essbase', 'x' * 5 is 'xxxxx', and 'ab' << 'cd' is 'abcd'. In addition Groovy adds a number of methods to strings, such as padLeft, padRight, and center, several direct type conversions, richer regular expression support, and useful iterators like eachLine and findAll.

9.3.6 Step Six: XML Output

We have now reached the point of turning our output into XML format. With Groovy's builder concept, specifically its MarkupBuilder object, this is an easy task. We replace the println calls with calls into a builder. Builders are designed to perform a special behavior when methods are called on them that do not actually exist within the builder object. A MarkupBuilder knows how to turn such an arbitrary method call into an XML tag. It uses a data map to assign attributes to the tag and a closure to assign the body. This is probably better understood after looking at some code.

```
import com.essbase.api.session.IEssbase

doMbrThing = { essCube, mbrName ->
    if (mbrName.size() == 0 ) return
    essMbr = essCube.getMember(mbrName)
    xml.member(name:essMbr.name) {
        doMbrThing(essCube, essMbr.firstChildMemberName)
    }
    doMbrThing(essCube, essMbr.nextSiblingMemberName)
}

writer = new StringWriter()
xml = new groovy.xml.MarkupBuilder(writer)
essHome = IEssbase.Home.create(IEssbase.JAPI_VERSION)
essSvr = essHome.signOn('user', 'pass', false, null,
  'http://aps_server:13080/aps/JAPI', 'ess_server')
essApp = essSvr.getApplication('Sample')
xml.application(name: essApp.name) {
    essApp.cubes.all.each { essCube ->
        xml.cube(name: essCube.name) {
```

```
            essCube.dimensions.all.each { doMbrThing(essCube,
            it.name) }
        }
        essCube.clearActive()
    }
}
essSvr.disconnect()
essHome.signOff()
println writer.toString()
```

This produces:

```
<application name='Sample'>
  <cube name='Basic'>
    <member name='Year'>
      <member name='Qtr1'>
        <member name='Jan' />
        <member name='Feb' />
...
```

At this point, developers coming to Groovy from other languages may have inky mouths from biting straight through their pens. How can outputting XML be that easy? With Groovy, it just is. Every call into the builder is saying, "Make a tag here, and here is what it should look like." The builder calls are nested in the code loops, so we can see the structure of the intended XML mirrored in the structure of the code that produces it.

9.3.7 Step Seven: More Details in the XML

Currently, we are only outputting member names. One last change we will want to make here is to output more details. Unfortunately, as you will have learned in the previous chapter, not all instances of IEssMember are built the same, and, in our case, we cannot even get an alias from the member objects we have created. Such is the case with members retrieved through the IEssCube.getMember method. In order to get the details we want, we will open the outline of each database and use that as the source of our member objects. This will slow the code down, but we are scripting here, and speed is less of a concern.

```
import com.essbase.api.session.Iessbase

doMbrThing = { essOtl, mbrName ->
    if (mbrName.size() == 0 ) return
    essMbr = essOtl.findMember(mbrName)
    xml.member(name:essMbr.name, alias:essMbr.getAlias(null),
    consolidation:essMbr.consolidationType.toString()[0],
    storage:essMbr.shareOption, twopass:essMbr.
    twoPassCalculationMember, formula:essMbr.formula) {
        doMbrThing(essOtl, essMbr.firstChildMemberName)
    }
    doMbrThing(essOtl, essMbr.nextSiblingMemberName)
}

writer = new StringWriter()
xml = new groovy.xml.MarkupBuilder(writer)
essHome = IEssbase.Home.create(IEssbase.JAPI_VERSION)
```

```
essSvr = essHome.signOn('user', 'pass', false, null,
  'http://aps_server:13080/aps/JAPI', 'ess_server')
essApp = essSvr.getApplication('Sample')
xml.application(name: essApp.name) {
    essApp.cubes.all.each { essCube ->
        essOtl = essCube.openOutline()
        xml.cube(name: essCube.name) {
            essOtl.dimensions.all.each { essDim ->
                essMbr = essOtl.findMember(essDim.name)
                xml.dimension(density: essMbr.dimensionStorageType,
                category: essDim.category, name: essMbr.name,
                alias: essMbr.getAlias(null), storage: essMbr.
                shareOption, twopass: essMbr.
                twoPassCalculationMember, formula: essMbr.formula)
                {
                    doMbrThing(essOtl, essMbr.firstChildMemberName)
                }
            }
        }
        essOtl.close()
        essCube.clearActive()
    }
}
essSvr.disconnect()
essHome.signOff()
println writer.toString()
```

This produces:

```
<application name='Sample'>
  <cube name='Basic'>
    <dimension density='Dense' category='Time' name='Year' alias=''
    storage='Dynamic calc (no store)' twopass='false' formula=''>
      <member name='Qtr1' alias='' consolidation='+'
      storage='Dynamic calc (no store)' twopass='false' formula=''>
        <member name='Jan' alias='' consolidation='+'
        storage='Store data' twopass='false' formula='' />
        <member name='Feb' alias='' consolidation='+'
        storage='Store data' twopass='false' formula='' />
...
```

Now, instead of passing a cube object around, we open its outline and pass that object around. Since dimension objects have "how you got it" limitations similar to member objects, we pull both of these object types from the outline. We also have separated dimension processing from member processing so that we can get 'dimension' and 'member' XML tags where appropriate. The attributes that apply to dimension tags are different from the ones that apply to member tags. Now the member processor is no longer doing double duty, so its use is more intuitive.

Our outline extractor is pretty far along now, but this is as far as we will take it. This code is for demonstration purposes only. The firstChildMemberName and nextSibling-MemberName methods work for us here, but are actually deprecated, and this extraction technique would not perform well if run against larger and more complex outlines. This extractor is a fun toy, but real outlines are big, hairy beasts. We would require something more heavy-duty to take one on.

Introducing Groovy by building this script right off the bat was perhaps a bit of a drink from the fire hose, but hopefully no one's head is spinning too much. We used a lot of Groovy's features to very quickly create a prototype outline extractor using very little code. We built tight, nested loops to step through the outlines, created JAPI objects along the way, and extracted the information we need from them. An exciting thing to see is how much the code is able to concentrate on the work that needs to be done and not the "scaffolding" that needs to be in place in order for the work to be done. We spent little energy creating temporary variables to loop on or in setting up those loops. We did not define any classes. We leveraged methods and properties that Groovy adds to Java objects. The result is a program that is remarkably dense, yet readable.

Developing with Groovy in this way can be a rather enjoyable activity because the language takes care of so many of the less interesting operations for us. It is accessible to newcomers and immediately useable by Java programmers. This example illustrates Groovy's power and ease of use, and paves the way for the next section, where we will look more closely at this language and its features.

9.4 GROOVY THINGS ABOUT GROOVY: A DEEPER LOOK AT THE LANGUAGE

Groovy (http://groovy.codehaus.org/) is a standard (JSR 241) language created by seasoned Java developers who saw features in other languages like Python, Ruby, and Smalltalk, and wanted to bring those features into the Java world. At the same time, they wanted to maintain a high level of friendliness to Java itself. To accomplish these goals, they adopted a syntax that aligns very closely with Java. In fact, most of the time, Java code can be cut and pasted into a Groovy program and executed without modification. Objects from the Java Runtime Environment (JRE) or any third-party classes can be created and used in Groovy with absolute ease. For that matter, integration in the other direction is just as simple. Classes written in Groovy can be precompiled and used in Java as easily as any Java class.

In addition to this high level of language compatibility, Groovy also offers many extra features that are not available in pure Java, such as:

- Ability to use for scripting or for fully structured application programming
- Choice to execute code directly from source or to compile
- Dynamic typing (optional type declarations)
- Anonymous code blocks/code as data (closures)
- Relaxed syntax requirements (optional returns, semicolons, and parentheses)
- Ease of use for collection types beyond simple arrays (lists, maps, ranges)
- Treatment of everything as an object (no division of types into primitives and references)
- Automatic accessor and mutator methods (getters and setters) on class instance fields
- Enhanced value substitution within strings (GStrings)
- Integration of regular expressions

These features add up to make Groovy a fun and productive language to work with, yet it is up to the individual developer how much to use these features. Experienced Java programmers may start off writing Groovy code with a familiar Java-like style and migrate over time to more idiomatic Groovy. Others may jump right in and start writing Groovy-style right away.

While a complete exploration of the language is beyond the scope of this book, it will serve our purposes to take a closer look at the features listed above and see how they make our jobs easier.

9.4.1 Writing Scripts or Full-Blown Programs

Groovy is not strictly a scripting language. It is a full Java-like application programming language that can also be applied effectively for scripting. This is good news for us as Essbase administrators. We can stay within the same language for both disciplines. Most of us just want to make our backups, dimension builds, data loads, and such better. We can use Groovy for powerful, flexible scripts that leverage the JAPI for automation requirements we cannot otherwise meet. Some of us are application and Web developers with larger, more robust programs in mind. Why go anywhere else? With the full power of Java behind it, plus its tools for building user interfaces more easily, Groovy offers the opportunity to write complete applications in the same language as our automation scripts.

9.4.2 Running from Script or Compiling

Groovy can be, and very often is, launched from source code. This is especially true in scripting scenarios. The developer simply writes code, runs it, modifies it, and runs it again. The launcher program does a fair bit of invisible magic behind the scenes to augment, compile, and execute the code. This is all hidden from the developer, who only sees how easy it is to get the script running.

There is another option available to the developer, however, and that is compiling Groovy source into executable classes. Groovy comes with its own compiler, groovyc, which works basically the same as Java's javac. It turns Groovy scripts into class files that can be launched with the native Java launcher (java). The only wrinkle is that Groovy 'jar' files need to be included in Java's class path, either on the command line or through an environment variable. This example shows how to write, compile, and run a program from a Windows command prompt. For simplicity, it is assumed the current directory is the Groovy 'lib' directory.

```
> echo println 'Hello World' > hw.groovy
> groovyc hw.groovy
> java -cp ".;.\groovy-xxx.jar;.\asm-3.2.jar" hw
```

Normally, we would use the run-from-source option for running our nightly backups, hourly data loads, and such, but the compile-to-classes option adds some interesting possibilities. It may be a path to overcome resistance from server admins who do not wish to install full Java and Groovy development kits on production servers. (These are required for the run-from-source model.) An Essbase server will have a Java runtime environment installed, so deploying compiled executables should not be problematic. Additionally, precompiling the scripts for deployment could be considered an extra layer of obfuscation to help keep user names and passwords away from prying eyes, though additional steps should certainly be taken, and these strings should never be written into the scripts themselves. Also, binary distributions can mitigate a potential problem where scripts can get out of sync between environments if they are modified directly in production instead of having changes written and tested in development first. This is no substitute for genuine version control and change management, but it could be helpful.

9.4.3 Dynamic Typing

Groovy, along with most scripting languages, is in the large family of languages that are known as dynamically typed. The definition of the term is somewhat complex, and not everyone agrees on it, so we will focus on the most important aspect of its meaning to us. Dynamic typing means that we do not have to declare the type of every variable in our source code. In Groovy, we do not have to type int i; to declare the variable i. We can type def i and later assign a value of any type to it without worrying that the compiler will complain. In scripts, we do not even have to use the keyword def. We can just assign a value to a new variable and keep on moving. We also can leave out type declarations from the parameters in function and closure definitions.

The sample code in this chapter takes advantage of these options extensively. They are very helpful when writing simple programs that can be understood at a glance, when objects are very short-lived, or when declaring their types does not really add any additional meaning to the program. The more complex a program is, and the more it does with a given object, the more static typing (explicitly declaring the types of variables and parameters) is called for. It is also very useful when working in an integrated development environment (IDE), such as IntelliJ IDEA, to use static typing more often, as the IDE is better able to do code-completion assistance and other magic tricks. Finally, static typing allows the compiler to catch some type compatibility errors that otherwise would only be caught at runtime. Ultimately, the individual developer will find the right mix of dynamic and static typing that works best. The important thing to us is that the choice is available.

9.4.4 Closures

Groovy features the ability to define blocks of code that can be thought of as living pieces of the program: as functions and as data. They are called closures. A closure can be assigned as a value to a variable and then called through the variable name. Closures can also be passed as parameters to methods, either in the form of variables or as closure literals defined in place. The following snippet does the same thing in two equivalent ways (recall that the name 'it' is the default name given to the parameter when a closure only has one):

```
//method one
testArr = [1, 3, 5, 7, 4, 2, 3, 8, 5]
println testArr.findAll{ it % 2 == 0 } //mod operator (the
remainder after dividing)

//method two
isEven = {
    if ( it % 2 == 0 ) {
        return true
    } else {
    return false
      }
}

println testArr.findAll{ isEven(it) }
```

The result is that [4, 2, 8] is printed both times. It is very common to use closures defined in place with iterator methods like the findAll we see in line three above, but it can be very powerful to define the closure elsewhere and pass in a reference to it. Consider the possibility of adding this:

```
isOdd = {
       return !isEven(it) //negation operator (returns the opposite
       Boolean value)
}

// I've decided I want to look for odds instead of evens.
isWhatIWant = isOdd

println testArr.findAll{ isWhatIWant(it) }
```

This prints [1, 3, 5, 7, 3, 5]. By having a variable to represent the work we want to do and setting it to refer to whichever closure we want to run, we have gained the ability to decide at runtime which block of code we want off the iterator to run for us. This is very powerful. Our code not only can decide what to do for itself (which we may be used to), but also, by passing closures, it can designate what should be done in other areas of the program (which we may not be so used to). Another very nice feature that closures allow is the ability to ease resource management. Worrying about opening and closing files, network connections, and such things is one of the more tedious, error-prone aspects of programming. These things should not be left up to us every time we want to work with a system resource. We may fail to implement correct exception handling or just plain forget to tidy up after ourselves. Closures provide an excellent way to avoid this. Whenever a resource needs to be opened at the beginning of an operation and cleaned up afterward, a method, such as the withReader method that Groovy adds to File objects, can take care of the housekeeping for us. We pass in a closure to that method, which opens the resource, executes the code in the closure, then closes the resource again. We get to concentrate on the important parts of the program.

In the end, closures are one of the most important features that make Groovy what it is. They provide the exceptional expressive capability that makes this solution so accessible for Essbase administrators to use. They are perhaps the grooviest part of Groovy.

9.4.5 Relaxed Syntax

Part of the Groovy philosophy is that the language should try to maximize both readability and expressiveness. The first of those terms, *readability*, is easy to understand, but *expressiveness* may not be as clear. Expressiveness means the ability to do more work with less code. It means saying more while writing less. A language, such as APL, may be highly expressive, but very difficult to read without expertise in that language. Groovy attempts to allow very expressive code that can still make a good bit of sense to a wide audience.

At times, certain syntax requirements can harm both readability and expressiveness. With that in mind, its creators gave Groovy a more relaxed syntax than Java. In particular, these three elements were made optional:

- Explicit return statements
- Semicolons at the ends of lines
- Parentheses around the parameters in method calls

Groovy's dynamic nature, its ability to execute code passed in as a command line argument, the presence of closures , and its general "less is more" approach to syntax are all factors in allowing us this syntactic freedom. However, the biggest driver is ease of use, both in writing and reading code. Consider this line:

```
[6, 3, 4, 8, 2, 7].findAll{ it % 2 == 0 }.each{ println it }
```

We are back to finding the even numbers in an array, this time printing 6, 4, 8, and 2 on separate lines. There is a decent amount of work happening here. There are two method calls and two closures. One of the closures returns a value. Still, it is pretty easy to see what is going on, and there is little to no clutter. Compare that to this line, which is what the above would look like if the three optional elements were required instead:

```
[6, 3, 4, 8, 2, 7].findAll( { return it % 2 == 0; } ).each( {
println(it); } );
```

We have added 15 characters, plus whitespace to say the same thing, and significantly reduced the ease both of writing and of reading the code. Because a big part of the beauty of Groovy code is the ability to say and do more things, in a readable manner, in fewer lines, it is clear to see what a big payoff we get from having these pieces of syntax optional.

There are some costs to having these looser syntax requirements, which should be understood. An important one is that having optional semicolons means that whitespace (line breaks at least) matter in a Groovy program, as can be seen in this example:

```
adderFunc = {
  i = 1
  + 2
}
```

If a line of code can be interpreted to end at a line break, it will be. That means i will be assigned a value of 1, and then a 2 will be returned. In order to add 1 and 2, the developer will need to keep the formula on one line, move the plus sign to the end of the previous line, or surround the formula with parentheses.

Missing returns can sometimes cause methods and closures to return unexpected values or lead the developer to forget that something is being returned at all. When methods are defined using the def keyword instead of void or an explicit type, we may not notice a problem with the value returned. It is usually better, if a method returns a value, to declare what type it is.

Missing parentheses may cause compiler errors that do not seem to be warranted. The official wording is that for method calls, the parentheses can be omitted "if there is at least one parameter and there is no ambiguity." In reality, ambiguities can be subtle. In practice, array and map literals as parameters are often the culprits. In particular, for complicated reasons, parentheses are necessary when the first argument to a method starts with a square bracket. If the developer remembers to favor readability when deciding whether to use method call parentheses, these subtle ambiguities will mostly be avoided.

9.4.6 Enhanced Collection Classes

Java provides arrays at the language level and has a rich set of collections available through its library. Groovy adds lists, maps, and ranges to the language-level mix, making them easy to define and work with.

A list is very similar to an array, but more flexible. For example, it will automatically expand its size when a value is assigned to it at an out-of-range index position. Groovy will prefer to make lists over arrays, but arrays are still easily created. Both types can be defined with square bracket literals, such as [1, 2, 3].

A map is like a list in which every element is referred to by a name instead of a position. Groovy has native support for maps, which can be used to build key-value tables. They can be defined with literals like [one: 1, two: 2, three: 3].

A range is like a shorthand way to define a list of elements. Anything that can be considered to have sequential values can be defined with a range. That said, it is usually integers that are used for ranges, in definitions like 1..10, which results in a list of the values 1 through 10. They can go backward like in 10..1 or use negative numbers like in –3..3.

All of these collection types can be used to define objects anonymously for immediate use. This is extremely useful because we often do not need or want to go through the trouble of creating a collection, giving it a name, populating it, using it, then getting rid of it. We can get right down to work, as in:

```
['stoneless cherry', 'boneless chicken', 'endless story'].each {
giveMyLove( it ) }
```

Here we have created a list and passed it directly to the each method, which will run the closure against its elements, in turn. With luck, we will fare better than the guitar player in Animal House who sang of doing the same things.

We can define maps in place when doing method calls, and this allows us to have named (rather than positional) parameter lists. For this usage, we also can leave off the square brackets.

```
greasedLighting = new Car(automatic: true, systematic: true, hydro-
matic: true)
```

Range literals make it very easy to loop on integers.

```
(5..1).each { print "${it}..."; sleep 1000; } // slowly prints
5...4...3...2...1...

println "Blastoff!!"
```

Groovy provides several useful built-in iterators for all collections. Among them are:

- each: Execute a closure against every element of the collection
- [1, 2, 3, 4].each{println it} // prints each element on a new line
- collect: Execute a closure against every element of the collection and gather the return values of each into a new collection
- [1, 2, 3, 4].collect{ it * –1 } // returns [–1, –2, –3, –4]
- find: locate and return the first element of the collection that makes a closure return a value of true
- [1, 2, 3, 4].find{ it > 2 } // returns 3, the first value > 2

- findAll: Gather all of the elements of the collection that make a closure return a value of true, and return them in a new collection
- [1, 2, 3, 4].findAll{ it > 2 } // returns [3, 4], all values that are > 2
- every: Execute a closure against every element of the collection and return a true if the closure returns a true every time[1, 2, 3, 4].every{ it > 2 } // returns false (some values are <= 2)
- any: Execute a closure against elements of the collection, and check if any one of them is found that makes the closure return a true
- [1, 2, 3, 4].any{ it > 2 } // returns true (at least one value is > 2)

These methods, enabled by closures, are found throughout Groovy code and are prime contributors to the expressiveness, power, and readability the language offers.

9.4.7 *Everything Is an Object*

In Groovy, every value, every variable, every parameter, every everything is an object. This contrasts with Java where some things are objects (reference types) and some are simply values (primitive types). With only one kind of thing available, we do not have to spend any energy thinking about which thing is which. We are free to think of everything the same way. This leads to some very interesting constructions like calling methods on integers.

```
3.times{ println 'Location! ' } // prints Location! Location!
Location!
2.step(10, 2) { println it + ' is even' } // steps from 2 to 10
(exclusive) by 2s
cutoffDate = 6.months.ago // creates a Date object using today's
date, minus 6 months
```

The important thing to remember about this feature is that Groovy handles all conversions automatically. The source code may appear to have primitive types, but they are always created as objects when the code runs. When Groovy has to interact with Java objects, quite often those objects expect to receive primitive types as parameters. The change happens automatically. Primitives go out where needed, and primitives coming in from Java are immediately changed into objects. This is called automatic "boxing" and "unboxing." In effect, it means there is no need for us to think about it.

9.4.8 *Automatic Getters and Setters*

As mentioned in a sidebar in Section 9.3.3, Groovy looks through objects as they are created, finds methods that match certain patterns, and automatically sets up access to them through a property-like syntax. The reverse is also true. Groovy makes creating custom classes much easier by automatically creating "getter" and "setter" functions. The following code calls these methods in both ways.

```
class EssDB {
      String name                // class fields, for which automatic
      String application         // getters and setters are created
}
db = new EssDB()
```

```
db.setApplication( "Sample")    // calls the automatic setter
db.name = "Basic"               // also calls the automatic setter
println db.application + '.'
  + db.getName()                // both call the automatic getter
```

These features make it easier to work with classes created by others and to create new custom classes. As a side note, these features also make it simple to build and work with Java "beans," although that subject is outside the scope of this chapter. The main thing to know is that Groovy lets you work with objects and their properties the way you want to.

9.4.9 GStrings

Another feature mentioned in a previous sidebar (Section 9.3.2) is GStrings. They are a way to build strings out of different values and literals at runtime.

```
funFact = "My favorite Essbase database is ${db.application}.${db.
          name}."
println funFact // prints My favorite Essbase database is Sample.
                   Basic.
```

This convenience feature makes string construction much easier to write and to read. Most particularly, it relieves the burden of having to add spaces at the beginning or end of the string snippets that are being added together.

It is important to understand that GStrings are not like functions. They do not change once they have been evaluated, as demonstrated below.

```
timeStamp = "It is now ${new Date()}"
println timestamp  // prints the current time, down to the second
sleep(10000)       // waits 10 seconds
println timeStamp  // prints the same time as before, down to the
                      second

2.times {
       println "It is now ${new Date()}" // prints a different time
                                            each iteration
       sleep(10000)
}
```

In the first part, the GString is not re-evaluated. It is just reprinted. In the second part, the GString is re-evaluated because the closure is executed two separate times.

9.4.10 Regular Expressions

Java provides a library that allows very nifty and powerful pattern-based searching and matching for strings. Groovy integrates this library at the language level. The technology is called "regular expressions," and it is provided by the package java.util.regex. Regular expressions ("regexes") provide an extremely versatile method for defining and looking for potentially complex patterns of characters within strings. This is an exceedingly common programming task, and once regexes are learned, many developers find them indispensable. We can use them to verify properly formatted email addresses, work intelligently with phone numbers in varied input formats, split names up into their different parts, and pretty much work with anything that involves looking through, processing, or modifying strings of even the slightest complexity. Regular expressions allow us to do these things without engineering custom code on a case-by-case basis. We identify the patterns we are dealing with and let the regex engine do the hard work.

Even a minor exploration of regexes is more than we can cover in this book. There are, in fact, entire books devoted to the subject. All we can offer is a little teaser. This program uses two regular expression substitutions. The first is simple. It replaces spaces in the book title with underscores. The second moves the author's last name to the end and removes the comma.

```
class Book {String title; String author;}
book = new Book(title: "Ender's Game", author: "Card, Orson Scott")
underscoredName = book.title.replaceAll(/ /,'_')
firstNameFirst = book.author.replaceAll(/^([^,]+),\s+(.+)$/,'$2
                 $1')
println "My favorite book is _${underscoredName}_ by ${first
        NameFirst}."
```

The result is: My favorite book is _Ender's_Game_ by Orson Scott Card.

In addition to this Java-style usage, Groovy provides special regex operators.

```
if (testString =~ /\d+/) {println "Match!"} // works if the string
                                               has any numbers
if (testString ==~ /\d+/) {println "Match!"}// works if the string
                                               is all digits
```

Regexes are a rich subject that reward exploration. They are featured in many languages, libraries, and tools, so they can be a valuable part of any developer's toolkit.

9.4.11 Random Acts of Grooviness

Space demands that we wrap up our discussion of the language itself pretty soon now, so we will hit upon a few more subjects here rapid fire. In other words, many more things are awesome about Groovy, and here are the highlights:

Groovy truth—It is acceptable to use any object, variable, value, etc. anywhere that a Boolean expression is expected. Empty collections, zero-length strings, nulls, the number 0, and things like that are interpreted as false. Pretty much everything else evaluates to true. Use this feature with caution, and remember to favor readability.

Safe dereferencing—There are times in our programming lives when we are not sure if one of our object variables has a value, or if one of its methods could return a null. At these times, we might write something like:

```
if ( obj != null && obj.property == whatever ) { do_something(); }
```

This keeps us from encountering a null pointer exception (NPE) for trying to access property when obj is null. In Groovy, we can use a special operator together with Groovy truth to write instead:if (obj?.property == whatever) { do_something(); }This is especially helpful when we need to go more than one property (or method) deep and be careful of NPEs all along the way.

Optional exception handling—In Java, there are some exceptions that must be checked when calling a method, and code must be written to handle them. From one perspective, this is perfectly reasonable. These "checked" exceptions represent potentially serious problems for which we should have plans in place. From another perspective, it is a waste of energy to force the programmer to check for an exception that, through some means, can be assured never to happen. Taking this second view, Groovy does not enforce these required exception handling rules. All exceptions are treated as "unchecked," meaning it is up to the developer to decide whether to write handling code for them. This way, when exception handling is found in Groovy code, we can be sure it is there by choice.

Multiline strings—Groovy allows a "triple-quote" string literal that makes creating formatted multiline strings easier. These strings, sometimes called "heredocs," treat line breaks literally and do not need to be assembled from smaller strings.

```
thesisTitle = """\
      Dr. Groovy
      or: How I Learned to Stop Worrying
       and Love the Closure """
```

The backslash on the first line convinces Groovy to ignore the line break that immediately follows, so that the first line of our string can start at the left margin, just like the rest of the lines.

Currying—Groovy provides a method to permanently lock down the values of one or more closure arguments. For example:

```
defragDb = { app, db -> code_that_defrags_a_database() } // takes 2
parameters
defragSampleDb = defragDb.curry('Sample')
['Basic', 'Interntl', 'Xchgrate'].each { defragSampleDb(it) }
//takes only one
```

This is a concept taken from "functional" programming, where generic functions are frequently defined, with more specific ones being derived from them in the manner as above. The term *currying* is named for Haskell Curry, an important figure in the functional programming world.

This concludes our whirlwind tour of Groovy. While we were not able to go very deeply into each feature, we hope we have provided a nice jump start for the aspiring Groovy developer. We hope, at least, that we have provided enough information for the rest of the chapter to make some sense.

9.5 WHAT'S COOKIN'? GROOVY RECIPES FOR THE BUSY DEVELOPER

What follows are several scripts that represent the minimum amount of code necessary to get a number of different jobs done. For production code, it would be better to lace them with try/catch/finally blocks as described in the previous chapter. Most of the snippets are fully functional programs, except that the correct strings for your environment may need to be filled in where appropriate.

9.5.1 Clearing and Loading Data

Our first recipe shows how to load data into Sample.Basic from data files that Oracle provides. It also clears existing data from the database. We demonstrate how we could load from a relational repository if only Sample.Basic had one. The method calls we use for loading are named beginDataLoad, but the way we use them, it really means "do" the load. That means we do not need to call endDataLoad. The last two parameters of each call are a Boolean to indicate whether to "abort on error" and an integer indicating the load buffer id. We use 0 for the buffer id, which is always ignored for BSO (block storage option) anyway, and enables us to load to ASO with no additional complexity. It is possible to set up and use more complex load buffers manually, but we do not cover that here.

```
import com.essbase.api.session.IEssbase
import com.essbase.api.datasource.IEssOlapFileObject
essHome = IEssbase.Home.create(IEssbase.JAPI_VERSION)
essSvr = essHome.signOn( 'user', 'pass', false, null, 'embedded',
        'ess_server')
essCube = essSvr.getApplication('Sample').getCube('Basic')
essCube.clearAllData()
essCube.beginDataload('Data', IEssOlapFileObject.TYPE_RULES, 'Data.
xls', IEssOlapFileObject.TYPE_EXCEL, false, 0) // load from file
(Excel)
essCube.clearAllData()
essCube.beginDataload(null, IEssOlapFileObject.TYPE_RULES,
'Calcdat.txt', IEssOlapFileObject.TYPE_TEXT, false, 0) // load from
file (txt, no Load rule)
essCube.beginDataload('loadSql', IEssOlapFileObject.TYPE_RULES,
'sqlUser', 'sqlPass', false, 0) // load from relational
essCube.clearActive(); essSvr.disconnect(); essHome.signOff();
```

Note that the cleanup code is consolidated on the last line to save space. Normally, we would not do that. We would use the cleanup code specified in this section's final recipe.

9.5.2 Running a Calc Script

The next step after loading data is often to calc the database, so we do that now. There are three ways to execute a calc script in the IEssCube interface, and we demonstrate all of them. The Chapter 8 (Deep Inside the Essbase Java API) contains detailed information about these methods. Note that we have to assume that Sample.Basic has a calc script called Rollup.csc.

```
import com.essbase.api.session.IEssbase
essHome = IEssbase.Home.create(IEssbase.JAPI_VERSION)
essSvr = essHome.signOn( 'user', 'pass', false, null, 'embedded',
        'ess_server')
essCube = essSvr.getApplication('Sample').getCube('Basic')
essCube.calculate('CALC ALL;', false) // execute from a string
essCube.calculate(false, 'Rollup')    // execute from a file (leave
off '.csc')
essCube.calculate()                   // execute the cube's default
calc
essCube.clearActive(); essSvr.disconnect(); essHome.signOff();
```

The "execute from a string" method suggests interesting possibilities: building scripts on the fly, passing in parameters, or doing custom token substitution.

9.5.3 Selecting Members

Several methods of retrieving member information are detailed in the previous chapter. Here we demonstrate using the one that allows us to get a list of members using our familiar calc script member set functions. We retrieve and print the level-0 descendants of the "East" member in Sample.Basic.

```
import com.essbase.api.session.IEssbase
essHome = IEssbase.Home.create(IEssbase.JAPI_VERSION)
essSvr = essHome.signOn('user', 'pass', false, null, 'embedded',
        'ess_server')
essCube = essSvr.getApplication('Sample').getCube('Basic')
mbrSel = essCube.openMemberSelection('default')
mbrSel.executeQuery('<OutputType Binary <SelectMbrInfo
(MemberName)', '@RELATIVE("East", 0)')
mbrs = []
mbrSel.members.all.each { mbrs << it.name } // append to list
println mbrs
mbrSel.close() // must be closed or we get orphaned connections
essCube.clearActive(); essSvr.disconnect(); essHome.signOff();
```

In this query, we only ask that the IEssMember objects we get from Essbase have one piece of data in them (MemberName). There are over 30 other items to choose from, such as MemberAliasName, ChildrenCount, and UDAList. We can put as many of these as we need in the query, separated by commas.

9.5.4 Processing an Export File

This recipe piggy-backs on the previous one, referencing the member list retrieved there while processing a data file. The Calcdat.txt data file we loaded to Sample.Basic in recipe 9.5.1 is in the same format as an Essbase export file, if the "column format" option were not selected when the data was exported. Here, we assume that we want to reload only some of the data in the file. Suppose the database has undergone extensive updates during the day, and the manager for all of "East" wants to go back to the day's starting point. The format of the file makes this a little difficult. Data lines do not have a member of the "Market" dimension in them. Rather, Essbase applies the data to the "Market" member most recently mentioned on a previous line. We can use this knowledge of the file format to figure out which data lines we need. The following code is meant to be pasted in a script immediately below the code in the previous recipe.

```
inf = new File ("Calcdat.txt")                  // input file
outf = new File ("Calcdat_Filtered.txt")     // output file
outf.delete() // make sure output file is empty
inf.withReader { outf.append it.readLine() + '\n' } // copy 1st
line from inf to outf
copying = false // flag indicating whether we are currently copying
lines
inf.eachLine { line ->
  if (line[1] =~ /\d/) { //quick way to i.d. Product/Market lines
    copying = (mbrs =~ line.tokenize('"')[2]) as Boolean //decide
whether to turn on the flag
  }
  if (copying) outf.append line + '\n' // copy line to outf
}
```

Both the withReader and eachLine methods used here feature Groovy's automatic resource management. They create file readers for us and, more importantly, guarantee they also will clean them up before returning.

The =~ found on two lines is a regular expression operator (see Section 9.4.10). We use it to search within strings. We identify lines that have a "Product" member and a "Market" member by checking if their second character is a digit (\d). When we find one of those lines, we split it apart at the double-quotes, pull out the "Market" member, and check to see if it is in the list of members we care about. The matcher object returned by the =~ operator converts directly to a Boolean value indicating whether there is or is not a match, and, thus, whether we should begin copying lines from file to file.

9.5.5 Sorting an Outline and Querying Attributes

Sorting the members of an outline is a common need. Usually, this means doing it alphabetically or numerically by the member name, but what about other ways? What about sorting an employee dimension where names are the aliases and the member names are ID numbers? What if we want to sort our sales departments by their revenue dollars? It could happen. In this recipe, we run queries against Sample.Basic to sort its Market dimension. We sort by population size (descending), and members with identical populations are placed in alphabetical order. This is a two-in-one demonstration because we have not as yet seen how to access member attributes.

```
import com.essbase.api.session.IEssbase
import com.essbase.api.datasource.IEssCube.EEssRestructureOption

essHome = IEssbase.Home.create(IEssbase.JAPI_VERSION)
essSvr = essHome.signOn('user', 'pass', false, null, 'embedded',
        'ess_server')
essCube = essSvr.getApplication('Sample').getCube('Basic')
mbrSel = essCube.openMemberSelection('default')
// selecting members with calc script member set functions
mbrSel.executeQuery('<OutputType Binary <SelectMbrInfo (MemberName,
MemberAliasName)', '@DESCENDANTS("Market")')
mbrs = []
mbrSel.members.all.each {
      def attrs = essCube.getAssociatedAttributes(it.name,
                  'Population')
       mbrs << [(it.name), (attrs ? (attrs[0][3] + 'f').toFloat() :
       0)]
}
mbrs = mbrs.sort{it[0]}.reverse().sort{it[1]} // sorting three ways
at once
mbrSel.close()
mbrSel = null

essOtl = essCube.openOutline(false, true, true)
// use 'collect' to make a simpler collection from the old then
iterate on that
mbrs.collect {it[0]}.each { mbrName ->
      essMbr = essOtl.findMember(mbrName)
      essPrnt = essOtl.findMember(essMbr.getParentMemberName())
      essOtl.moveMember(essMbr, essPrnt, null)
}
```

```
essOtl.save(EEssRestructureOption.KEEP_ALL_DATA)

essOtl.close(); essCube.clearActive(); essSvr.disconnect(); ess-
Home.signOff();
```

The sort method we use here is a very powerful collection method. The collection can contain anything (here our collection is an array of arrays). The sort method executes a closure against each element of the collection, and whatever value the closure returns is used to determine the sort order. We sort the same array twice using different closures. We also use the reverse collection method to coax our array into the order we need. The way we use moveMember places the member as the first child beneath the parent member, so we move the ones we want to end up higher in the outline after the ones we want to end up lower in the outline (see recipe 9.5.8 for a similar technique).

9.5.6 Querying Data and Balancing against a Data Repository

At the end of data load script, it is nice to know that all the data is loaded and rolled up properly. One way we can do this is by running and parsing Report Scripts. With the JAPI, we can just query the data directly. We can script user operations like zoom and pivot, then pull data out of the resulting grid. We can use Groovy's SQL (structured query language) package to easily query data in a source repository for comparison. Again, pretending that Sample.Basic has a relational data source, we will make sure that source and Essbase agree on the sales dollars at the product family level.

```
import com.essbase.api.session.IEssbase
import groovy.sql.Sql
sqlVals = [:] //empty map
sql = Sql.newInstance("jdbc:sqlserver://sqlServerName;databaseName=
                      dbName", 'sqlUser', 'sqlPass', "com.
                      microsoft.sqlserver.jdbc.SQLServerDriver")
sql.eachRow("SELECT Prod_Fam, SUM(Sales) FROM TBC_Data GROUP BY
Prod_Fam") { record ->
 sqlVals[record[0]] = record[1] // add map entries (key=Prod_Fam,
 value=Sales)
}
essHome = IEssbase.Home.create(IEssbase.JAPI_VERSION)
essSvr = essHome.signOn('user', 'pass', false, null, 'embedded',
         'ess_server')
essCube = essSvr.getApplication('Sample').getCube('Basic')
cv = essCube.openCubeView('default')
grid = cv.getGridView()
grid.setSize(2, 5) // 2 rows, 5 columns
grid.setValue(0, 1, "Actual"); grid.setValue(0, 2, "Sales"); grid.
setValue(0, 3, "Market"); grid.setValue(0, 4, "Year"); //col hdrs
grid.setValue(1, 0, "Product") //row hdr
opZoom = cv.createIEssOpZoomIn()
opZoom.addCell(1, 0) // add "Year" cell to zoom operation
cv.performOperation(opZoom)
essVals = [:] // empty map
(1..<grid.countRows).each{
    essVals[grid.getStringValue(it,0)] = grid.getDoubleValue(it,1)
//add map entries
}
```

```
grid = null; cv?.close(); cv = null;
essCube.clearActive(); essSvr.disconnect(); essHome.signOff();
allmatch = true
sqlVals.each{ key, val ->
    println "${key}: ${val} vs. ${essVals[key]} match:
            ${val==essVals[key]}"
    if (val != essVals[key]) { allmatch = false }
}
System.exit(allmatch ? 0 : 1)
```

This script builds two maps with identical keys and verifies they have identical values. Actually, essVals has an extra entry ("Diet"), but we do not test this shared member. We let sqlVals drive the comparison loop, and that member is not in there.

Since the SQL query part is made up, the only way to get this code to run is to comment out that section and add the line below, which populates the map with the correct values.

```
sqlVals = ['100':106134 ,'200':109086, '300':101405, '400':84230]
```

The 1..<grid.countRows we use to loop on the grid rows is a special "exclusive" syntax for ranges, which stops just short of executing on the upper bound (see Section 9.4.6).

The allmatch ? 0 : 1 construction is using the common C-style ternary operator. If the first segment evaluates to true, then the middle segment is returned, otherwise the last segment is returned.

We end the script by exiting with a numeric code: 0 is good, 1 is bad. This is in anticipation of the next recipe.

9.5.7 Calling Other Scripts

We may write some very useful utility scripts that we want to use from within our other scripts. We need to know how to launch external scripts and get information back from them. There are a number of ways. We demonstrate three ways to call the script defined in the previous recipe, assuming it has been saved to a file named QueryData.groovy. The first way uses an execute method that Groovy adds to String objects:

```
proc = "groovy QueryData.groovy".execute()
inStr = proc.in.text //the text _out_ of the child process comes
        _in_ to us
errStr = proc.err.text //a separate stream of error text
//bothStr = proc.text //combined in & err: have to use EITHER this
OR the lines above
sts = proc.exitValue()
if (sts) {println "Oh, No! Sample.Basic is out of balance!"}
else {println "WOO HOO!"}
```

Now. we see why we put in the System.exit call above. We can access that exit code from other scripts using this technique.

Another technique uses the AntBuilder class. Ant is a Java-based tool that uses XML configuration files to run complex build processes for applications. Among the many tasks it can do, such as compile, copy, and test files, is the ability to run programs. Groovy ships with Ant included plus a builder for XML structures that Ant can process.

```
ant = new AntBuilder()
ant.exec(executable:"groovy", outputproperty:"cmdOut",
resultproperty:"cmdExit", errorproperty:"cmdErr") {
    arg(value:"QueryData")
}
sts = ant.project.properties.cmdExit as Integer
```

Here we have accessed the exit status in a different way. We also capture the output and error streams from the executed script. The Ant exec task is very flexible, allowing fine control of the arguments to the child process and the environment in which it runs. We use an AntBuilder to set those up with code, in a manner similar to using the MarkupBuilder in our outline extractor demonstration.

A third technique to execute an external script illustrates a way to actually share variables among the calling and called scripts through a Binding. This technique does not use the exit code from the called script. In fact, the called script runs in the same process as the calling script, so a System.exit call will end both scripts. The following code only works if the exit line is commented out of QueryData.groovy.

```
gse = new GroovyScriptEngine('.')
bnd = new Binding()
gse.run('QueryData.groovy', bnd)
ret = bnd.getVariable('allmatch')
sts = ret ? 0 : 1
```

Through the binding, we can peek into the called script and access its variables. We pull back allmatch and use its value instead of an exit code to determine success or failure. This brings up an important point: Any script variable that is not originally declared with a type or the "def" keyword is included in that script's binding, making it global within its own script and available to outside scripts. Production scripts should use def frequently to introduce untyped variables that are not needed by external scripts. Large scripts should likewise use def to avoid variable name conflicts in the global scope.

9.5.8 Adding Members to an Outline

In this recipe, we imagine an outline with a unified time dimension, having years, quarters, months, and weeks all in the same dimension. Weeks are organized in a 4-5-4 fiscal calendar configuration. We have the associated year appended to the names of lower-level members (like "Q1 FY12") to keep names unique in the dimension. There are aliases at various levels in the default table and an extra alias table ("Close Dates") for week-level members, which stores Friday's date for that week. At year end, we need to add 52 (sometimes 53) weeks, 12 months, 4 quarters, and 1 year member to the outline to make room for the coming year's data. We need to assign aliases in both tables. We could manage (with a few spreadsheets, text files, and Load rules) to avoid doing all of that manually, but it would still feel like work. This code adds the members and aliases directly to the outline.

```
import com.essbase.api.session.IEssbase
import com.essbase.api.datasource.IEssCube.EEssRestructureOption
import groovy.time.TimeCategory

essHome = IEssbase.Home.create(IEssbase.JAPI_VERSION)
```

```
essSvr = essHome.signOn('user', 'pass', false, null, 'embedded',
        'ess_server')
essCube = essSvr.getApplication('GL').getCube('GL')

essOtl = essCube.openOutline(false, true, false)
essCalMbr = essOtl.findMember('Calendar')
essYrMbr = essCalMbr.createChildMember('FY13', essOtl.
          findMember('FY12'))
essYrMbr.setAlias(null, '2013')
essYrMbr.updatePropertyValues()

wkOfYr = 52
aliasDate = new Date('12/27/2013') // the last Friday of the fiscal
year

(4..1).each { qtrNum -> // Q4 to Q1
    essQtrMbr = essYrMbr.createChildMember("Q${qtrNum} FY13")
    (3..1).each { mthNum -> // 3 mths per qtr
        mth = new Date("${(qtrNum-1)*3 + mthNum}/1/2012").
              format('MMM')
        essMthMbr = essQtrMbr.createChildMember("${mth} FY13")
        (5..1).each { wkNum -> // up to 5 wks in a month
            if (wkNum < 5 || mthNum == 2) { //5 wks in the qtr's
            2nd mth
                essWkMbr = essMthMbr.createChildMember("Week${wkO
                fYr--} FY13")
                essWkMbr.setAlias(null, "${mth}Wk${wkNum} FY13")
                essWkMbr.setAlias("Close Dates", aliasDate.
                format("'d'MM/dd/yy"))
                essWkMbr.updatePropertyValues()
                essWkMbr = null
                use (TimeCategory) { aliasDate -= 7.days } //roll
                back the calendar
            }
        }
        essMthMbr = null
    }
    essQtrMbr = null
}
essYrMbr = null
essCalMbr = null

essOtl.save(EEssRestructureOption.KEEP_ALL_DATA)
essOtl.close(); essCube.clearActive(); essSvr.disconnect();
essHome.signOff();
```

We create the members in reverse. We start with Q4, December, and week 52 and work backward through time. This is because, by default, createChildMember adds the new member as the first child of the parent. Rolling with that, we add the members in an order that keeps us from having to sort the outline later.

9.5.9 Unlocking Objects

Often, when applications crash, are not exited properly by the user, or time out, they may fail to clean up their operations and release the locks they have on server files.

In this recipe, we loop through all the databases on a server and check for locks on the types of files that most commonly need to have locks on them cleared.

```
import com.essbase.api.session.IEssbase

essHome = IEssbase.Home.create(IEssbase.JAPI_VERSION)
essSvr = essHome.signOn('user', 'pass', false, null, 'embedded',
'ess_server')
essSvr.applications.all.each { essApp ->
    essApp.cubes.all.each { essCube ->
        com.essbase.api.datasource.IEssOlapFileObject.with { //
        'with' saves typing!
            [TYPE_OUTLINE, TYPE_CALCSCRIPT, TYPE_PARTITION, TYPE_
            REPORT, TYPE_RULES]
        }.each { fileType ->
                essCube.getOlapFileObjects(fileType).all.each {
                fileObj ->
                    if (fileObj.isLocked()) {
                         essCube.unlockOlapFileObject(fileType,
                         fileObj.name)
                         println "Unlocked ${essApp.
                         name}.${essCube.name}.${fileObj.name}!"
                    }
            }
        }
        essCube.clearActive()
    }
}
essSvr.disconnect(); essHome.signOff();
```

9.5.10 Executing a MaxL Command

Many developers are familiar with a battery of MaxL commands and may be thinking as they read these recipes about MaxL commands that do the same things. We can leverage that knowledge to run MaxL commands from inside our scripts, going back and forth between full JAPI programming and MaxL as it suits us. This recipe demonstrates two methods of doing this. The first is applicable only to the latest versions of Essbase.

```
import com.essbase.api.session.IEssbase

essHome = IEssbase.Home.create(IEssbase.JAPI_VERSION)
essSvr = essHome.signOn('user', 'pass', false, null, 'embedded',
         'ess_server')
essMaxL = essSvr.openMaxLSession("default") // 11.1.2.x feature
essMaxL.execute("alter system load application Sample;")
essMaxL.execute("alter application Sample load database Basic;")
essMaxL.execute("alter database Sample.Basic reset data;")
essMaxL.execute("""import database Sample.Basic data from data_file
                  'Path\\To\\Calcdat.txt' on error abort;""")

messages = essMaxL.messages.each {
    println it //print the results of each command
}

essMaxL.close(); essSvr.disconnect(); essHome.signOff();
```

The second technique is needed for older Essbase versions. It uses an AntBuilder to call the essmsh executable and run individual commands via the -i command line option.

```
String mshExec(String command, List args) {
    def ant = new AntBuilder()
    ant.exec(executable: "essmsh",
            inputstring: command,
            outputproperty: "cmdOut", // standard output
            errorproperty: "cmdErr", // error output
            resultproperty: "cmdExit") { // result code
        arg(line: "-l user pass") // the first arg set is essmsh
        arguments
        arg(line: "-s ess_server") // the second set is more essmsh
        arguments
        arg(value: "-i") // the third argument is the "read from
        input" flag
        args.each { a -> // for all the command line arguments
             arg(value: a) // add each one to the arguments for the
             called script
        }
    }
    def sts = ant.project.properties.cmdExit
    if (sts.toInteger() != 0) {
        println ant.project.properties.cmdErr
        throw new Exception("MaxL script failed with status code
                               ${sts}!")
    }
    return ant.project.properties.cmdOut
}

List parseMaxLDisplayX(String MaxLOut) {
    lines = MaxLOut.tokenize('\n')
    rulerLine = lines.findIndexOf{it =~ /^\+-+/}
    colWidth = (lines[rulerLine] =~ /^(\+-+)/)[0][1].size()
    lineWidth = lines[rulerLine].size()
    listOfMaps = []
    i = 1
    while (lines[rulerLine + i].size() == lineWidth) {
        values = [:]
        ((colWidth + 1)..lineWidth).step(colWidth) {
            values[lines[rulerLine - 1][(it - 20)..<it].trim()] =
            lines[rulerLine + i][(it - 20)..<it].trim()
        }
        listOfMaps << values
        i++
    }
    return listOfMaps
}

MaxLOut = mshExec('display database Sample.Basic;',[]) // single
item displayeparseMaxLDisplayX(MaxLOut).each{ println "Sample.Basic
has a data cache of ${it.data_cache_size} bytes!" }
```

```
MaxLOut = mshExec('display database $1.$2;', ['Sample','Basic']) //
passing in args
parseMaxLDisplayX(MaxLOut).each{ println "Sample.Basic has ${it.
number_dimensions} dimensions!" }

MaxLOut = mshExec('display application all;',[]) // multi-item
display
parseMaxLDisplayX(MaxLOut).each{ println "${it.application} has
${it.number_of_databases} database(s)!" }
```

Included here is a function that parses the output from MaxL "display" commands and returns a list of maps. Each map in the list contains key-value pairs drawn from the text table embedded in MaxL's output string. The parsing function is useful for either technique of running MaxL commands.

9.5.11 Using Command Line Arguments and Config File Settings

Many of our scripts will benefit from the ability to accept settings from the outside world, whether through command line arguments or by loading settings from files. We can generalize script to do both of these things. It seems reasonable to accept command line arguments for the server, user, password, application, database, and calc script. It also makes sense only to enable server, user, and password to come from a file. Groovy provides classes named CliBuilder and ConfigSlurper, which make these tasks easy. This recipe shows how to use them to load settings for the script and, while we are at it, we will let the script accept a list of multiple calc scripts to be run on the same database.

First, we need to place the following code in a file called essConfig.groovy.

```
essUser='user'
essPass='pass'
environments {
  prod {
    essSvrName='prod_ess_server'
  }
  dev {
    essSvrName='dev_ess_server'
  }
}
```

This config file has a nested, tree-like structure. The section at the top contains default values while the lower section defines values that apply to specific "environments." This way, we can have multiple possible configurations defined in one file. Config files can be much more complex than this one. They can be nested more deeply and can even return objects instead of just simple values.

The following code sets up a command line interface and accesses the config settings from the file above to be able to run any calc script on any database.

```
import com.essbase.api.session.IEssbase

def cs = new ConfigSlurper('dev').parse(new File('essConfig.
        groovy').toURL())
```

```
def cl = new CliBuilder(usage: 'groovy runCalc [options] script-
         Name...',
        header: '(Options a & d required)',
        stopAtNonOption: false); assert cl.stopAtNonOption == false
        // stop on parse errors

cl.u(args: 1, longOpt: 'username', 'Essbase user name')
cl.p(args: 1, longOpt: 'password', 'Essbase password')
cl.s(args: 1, longOpt: 'server', 'Essbase server')
cl.a(required: true, args: 1, longOpt: 'application', 'Essbase
application')
cl.d(required: true, args: 1, longOpt: 'database', 'Essbase
database')

def opt = cl.parse(args) // process command line arguments
if (!opt) { return }     // if parsing failed, opt is null.
end script
if (opt.arguments().size() < 1) { //also need a standalone
argument
    println 'error: missing scriptName'
    cl.usage()
    return
}

svr = opt.s ?: cs.essSvr         // command line
user = opt.u ?: cs.essUser       // args override
pass = opt.p ?: cs.essPass       // config settings

essHome = IEssbase.Home.create(IEssbase.JAPI_VERSION)
essSvr = essHome.signOn(user, pass, false, null, 'embedded', svr)
essCube = essSvr.getApplication(opt.a).getCube(opt.d)
opt.arguments().each{
    essCube.calculate(false, it-'.csc') // removes .csc if present
    println "$user ran $opt.a.$opt.d.${opt.arguments()[0]}
    successfully on $svr!"
}
essCube.clearActive(); essSvr.disconnect(); essHome.signOff();
```

This code will execute a calc script if we save it to runcalc.groovy and run it like this:

```
>groovy runcalc -a Sample -d Basic Rollup.csc
```

The CliBuilder has set up five options, to which we can refer by short names (prepended by one dash) or long names (prepended by two dashes). Two of the options are required, as is at least one calc script name as a freestanding argument. If we make a mistake, we are presented with usage details:

```
usage: groovy runCalc [options] scriptName...
(Options a & d required)
 -a,--application <arg>   Essbase application
 -d,--database <arg>      Essbase database
 -p,--password <arg>      Essbase password
 -s,--server <arg>        Essbase server
 -u,--username <arg>      Essbase user name
```

The ConfigSlurper is configured to load some settings as default values and other settings from the "dev" section of the config file. We would only need to change 'dev' to 'prod' when setting up the slurper to load the other settings instead.

When a setting, such as server, is provided both through the config file and the command line, the command line setting takes precedence. We implement this feature using the ?: operator, also known as the "Elvis" operator (tilt your head to the left). This operator is often used to provide default values. If the expression on the left has meaning and could be useful, then it will evaluate to a Groovy true value (see Section 9.4.11) and be used, otherwise, it must be something like a null or an empty string, so the value on the right is used instead. In our case, when the option is not provided on the command line, its value is a null, so the config file setting is used.

9.5.12 Logging

We have written our scripts in this chapter to blast through their jobs without leaving much of a trace. When we put code into production, we will want to add logging capabilities. There are many logging methods available. This recipe demonstrates logging with the java.util.logging package. This package is powerful enough to set up a network of different Logger objects. Loggers are automatically placed in parent/child relationships determined by their dot-separated names. Logging calls of different severity levels are made against these objects. Each logger has a severity threshold, and if the log event's level matches (or exceeds) this value, the logger passes the event on to its collection of one or more Handler objects. Handlers check their own severity thresholds, apply formatting to log messages, and forward them to various targets, such as files, sockets, consoles, and memory buffers. Thus, a single log event can be sent to multiple places in multiple formats.

```
import java.util.logging.*
log = Logger.getLogger("")
log.handlers.each{ println "${it.class}: ${it.level}"}
log.level = Level.ALL
fh = new FileHandler("essScripts.log")
fh.level = Level.FINE
fh.formatter = new SimpleFormatter()
log.addHandler(fh)
fh2 = new FileHandler("everything.log", true)
fh2.level = Level.ALL
log.addHandler(fh2)

log.finest("Could I _BE_ any more fine?!")
log.finer("I'm the judge here, and I say that's gonna cost ya.")
log.fine("I'm a logging event, and I'm fine with that.")
log.config("I am configuring this application.")
log.info("Pardon me, user, here's a little FYI.")
log.warning("Something happened you might want to know about.")
log.severe("Captain, there's a problem with the warp core!")
```

This code is simple enough to use the nameless "root logger" instead of making a child logger. We demonstrate that the root logger automatically has an associated ConsoleHandler with a severity threshold of INFO. We set up the first file handler with a different Formatter than the default XMLFormatter and have it overwrite its target file if it already exists. The second file handler gets a different threshold, keeps the default formatter, and appends to an existing file. When we run this code, we get different sets of events, in different formats, written to the console and the two different files.

9.5.13 Installing Groovy

After all of this, we hope there are some readers who are eager to install Groovy and begin scripting with it. There are only a few steps.

(1) **Install a Java Development Kit (JDK)**—If needed, JDKs are available for download from Oracle. Either the Standard Edition (SE) or the Enterprise Edition (EE) will do. EE is a superset of SE, with libraries and tools for developing large scale, distributed applications. Which to get depends on what the developer is planning to do.

(2) **Set JAVA_HOME**—Setting this environment variable on the development machine helps Groovy find the Java installation. It should point to the root directory of the JDK, which contains 'bin', 'jre', and 'lib' directories.

(3) **Install Groovy**—The binary distribution at http://groovy.codehaus.org should work fine. The Windows installer adds the Groovy bin directory to the PATH variable, '.groovy' to the PATHEXT variable, and creates a GROOVY_HOME variable, provided steps one and two above have been done. Anyone installing in other ways will have to do those things manually.

(4) **Verify installation**—First, we enter this command to check if the system can find the groovy executable.

```
>groovy --version
```

This should output a version string from groovy, proving that it is there. Now we can test a small inline program, which will be compiled and run.

```
>groovy -e "println 'Hello, World!'"
```

This should print Hello, World! to the console.

(5) **Put the JAPI directory in CLASSPATH**—This is a semicolon delimited environment variable that lets Groovy and Java know where to look for .class and .jar files that are needed at runtime. We need to create it or modify it to include the JAPI jars. This example refers to all the .jar files in the directory by using a wildcard character.

```
C:\Hyperion\products\Essbase\EssbaseClient\JavaAPI\lib\*;
```

(6) **Create a utility library**—The need arises from time to time in programming Groovy and Java to incorporate third-party libraries into our programs. To incorporate extra .jar files, we can create a directory and add it to the class path variable described in step five. Adding CLASSPATH entries like the following, in the order shown, first lets us find all standalone .class and .groovy files, then all .jar files in the directory.

```
C:\MyCompany\Batch\lib; C:\MyCompany\Batch\lib\*
```

We can put an uncompiled file named 'MyClass.groovy' containing the code for a class named 'MyClass' into this directory and instantiate that class from other scripts

(7) **Find log4j and add it to the utility library**—The Essbase JAPI has a third-part dependency as described in step 6. It does its logging with a package called 'log4j' and

cannot run in embedded mode without a log4j .jar file in the class path. We need to find one and copy it to the utility library. There should be one or more in the Oracle EPM directory structure (perhaps in 'common/loggers'). If there is more than one, take the one with the highest version number.

(8) **Test a JAPI program**—Run the following script to prove that everything is working.

```
import com.essbase.api.session.IEssbase
essHome = IEssbase.Home.create(IEssbase.JAPI_VERSION)
println 'JAPI found.'
essSvr = essHome.signOn('user', 'pass', false, null, 'embedded',
         'ess_server')
println 'Embedded mode enabled.'
essSvr.disconnect(); essHome.signOff();
println 'Congratulations, you are ready to start getting Groovy
with Essbase!'
```

(9) **(Optional) Explore IDE integration**—While it is not necessary to code Groovy in an IDE, they can offer significant advantages such as code completion and syntax highlighting. However, it may be best to concentrate on learning the language first, creating files with a familiar editor. Once a developer is comfortable with that technique, it may then be time to move on to an IDE.

There are two prominent IDEs with strong Groovy support: Eclipse and IntelliJ IDEA. Eclipse's support is provided through an installable plug-in, and IDEA's is included in the product installation. I will not pick a side here. They are both fine IDEs.

9.5.14 Setting Up and Tearing Down Essbase Objects

The code in this chapter takes a pretty quick-and-dirty approach to creating and disposing of objects from the Essbase JAPI. This is a necessary approach to get as much information onto the page as possible. In production code, it will be better to be a little more disciplined and careful with our objects. We want to make sure we are not leaving open connections and locked resources on the Essbase server. The previous chapter demonstrates using try/catch/finally blocks to ensure this. The Table 9.1 illustrates common ways of creating several of the most common JAPI objects and the code that should be run to clean them up.

9.6 WRAPPING IT UP

No harried developer is going to drop everything and start learning a new language or technology because a book says they should. There had better be a good reason. We feel there are many excellent reasons to adopt Groovy as an automation tool for Essbase environments. Because there is so little startup work, it can be approached incrementally. Developers can learn bit by bit, accomplishing new and robust automation tasks each step along the way. Small scripts can be added as new steps to existing batches, or Groovy can become the muscle and bone of the entire automation solution. Because it integrates so tightly with Java and eases interactions with the Essbase Java API so much, we do not need to shy away from JAPI programming. Instead, we can write ever more elegant, powerful, and efficient scripts that make our automations sing. We can call the tune and have Essbase dance to it.

Table 9.1 JAPI Object Creation

Class/Interface	Operation	Code
IEssbase	Setup	`IEssbase.Home.create(IEssbase.JAPI_VERSION)`

	Teardown	`if (essHome?.isSignedOn()) {`
		`  essHome.signOff()`
		`}`
		`essHome = null`

IEssOlapServer	Setup	`essSvr = essHome.signOn(userId, password, false, null, apsUrl, essSvr)` `essSvr = essHome.signOn(userId, password, false, null, 'Embedded', essSvr)`

	Teardown	`if (essSvr?.isConnected()) {`
		`  essSvr.disconnect()`
		`}`
		`essSvr = null`

IEssOlapApplication	Setup	`essApp = essSvr.getApplication(app)`
	Teardown	`essApp = null`
IEssCube	Setup	`essCube = essApp.getCube(cube)`
	Teardown	`essCube?.clearActive() essCube = null`
IEssCubeOutline	Setup	`essOtl = essCube.openOutline(readOnly, lock, keepTrans)`

	Teardown	`essOtl?.cube?.with {`
		`  if`
		`(getOlapFileObject(IEssOlapFileObject.TYPE_OUTLINE, essCube.name).isLocked()) {`
		`unlockOlapFileObject(IEssOlapFileObject.TYPE_OUTLINE, essCube.name)`
		`  }`
		` }`
		` if (essOtl?.isOpen())  {`
		`essOtl.close()`
		` }`
		` essOtl = null`

IEssMemberSelection	Setup	`essMbrSel = essCube.openMemberSelection('default')`
	Teardown	`essMbrSel.close()` `essMbrSel = null`
IEssAttributeQuery	Setup	`essAttrQry = essMbrSel.createAttributeQuery()`
	Teardown	`essAttrQry = null`
IEssCubeView	Setup	`essCubeView = essCube.openCubeView('default')`
	Teardown	`essCubeView?.close()` `essCubeView = null`
IEssGridView	Setup	`essGridView = essCubeView.getGridView()`
	Teardown	`essGridView = null`

Groovy was created to give Java features that it did not have. It was given the power to run as scripts. It takes many of the hard parts of programming and makes them go away. It holds a chair and a whip up to unruly Java libraries and makes them more docile. They were not thinking of us in the Essbase world when they created all this, but it is hard to imagine their work could have resulted in a better match for us. I hope you will learn to use Groovy, that it will be fun, and that it will help you be a better developer. I hope it will make you happy.

10

ADVANCED SMART VIEW

Robb Salzman

CONTENTS

10.1 INTRODUCTION

There is no question about it, finance and accounting people love Excel®. Given Excel's usefulness and pervasiveness in the enterprise, there are few who do not use Excel. With its evolved flexibility, power, and potential, Excel has made its way into almost every modern office. In the early days of Essbase, Arbor Software recognized the importance of Excel and used it as the standard interface to their new OLAP (online analytical processing) database. When Arbor Software subsequently merged with Hyperion to form Hyperion Solutions, the technological direction was toward the Web interfaces driven by Java on the server. However, many users found the spreadsheet interface much better for their needs and the response from Hyperion Solutions was the Smart View add-in for Excel. Smart View added new capabilities so it could talk to other data sources. After the Oracle acquisition of Hyperion Solutions, Smart View has continued to improve, which validates Excel as the favorite interface for business users.

This chapter discusses the programmatic and reporting side of this capability, starting with considerations for efficient Essbase reporting to get that extra margin of performance from interactive use and then diving deep into the programming power of Excel. Follow along and explore how to take your reporting beyond the out-of-the-box capabilities and make the marriage of Essbase and Excel complete.

10.1.1 Overview

Why "programmatic and reporting" and not "reporting and programmatic"? The whole point of retrieving Essbase data in Excel is reporting, right? Given the advanced nature of this book, the assumption is you already have a background in creating reports in Excel and now want a better understanding of how those spreadsheet queries really work. Once those underpinnings are dealt with, the bulk of this chapter is designed to introduce you to the Smart View VBA (Visual Basic for Applications) functions and their capabilities.

This chapter is written for Excel users who want to leverage that tool to extend and automate Essbase reports. Whether you have a minimal amount of VBA experience, are capable of creating and editing Excel macros, or are a seasoned programmer, this chapter is for you. In addition to automating and expanding the reporting and analysis of Essbase in Excel, we also will take a look at how Excel and Essbase interact. Understanding this interaction is key to building efficient, high performance solutions.

10.1.1.1 Retrieving Data Efficiently To create efficient Essbase reports within Excel, it is important to construct your spreadsheets correctly. Reports and data input sheets can be tuned and optimized to run very efficiently using a few easy to implement rules. This chapter will review and apply these rules and discuss creating efficient, dynamic Essbase spreadsheets.

10.1.1.2 Code Theory and Examples Finally, we dive into automation. My hope is the chapter that follows will greatly smooth out the learning and implementation curve allowing you to quickly impress your boss and win the favor of your co-workers with the cool solutions you build with Excel Smart View automation. Automation is the path to making a user's life much easier. Smart View and Excel have well-evolved user interfaces. However, they also provide API (application programming interface)-based VBA functions. The VBA functions provide you with a means of extending the Smart View functionality. With these functions, you can automate and customize Smart View functionality to fit the way your users prefer to use Excel. This chapter will address the more common automation and customization requests and discuss how they are implemented, complete with code you can use to help you get started.

10.2 A WORD OR TWO ABOUT THE CLASSIC ADD-IN

When Smart View was originally released in System 9, it was missing many key capabilities present in the Essbase add-in. (Prior to System 9, there were multiple Hyperion Excel add-ins, each addressing their own tool; System 9's Smart View was the first unified Excel client.) For many, it was a step backwards. In the following years, the Smart View team at Oracle made it their quest to satisfy both Microsoft® Office users and Essbase Excel Add-In users through what they called "parity," or matched capabilities of both tools. As of the writing of this book, the 11.1.2.1.102 patch release of Smart View (and the 11.1.2.1.103 release that patches the patch) achieves, mostly, that parity. By function, here are the features that bring the Classic Add-In's functionality to Smart View:

- Member name and alias on the same row.
- Cell formula preservation.
- Formula fill/stretch, e.g., if a cell corresponding to a parent has a formula, and the user drills down, the resulting new rows created by the children also will have that formula with the correct cell references.
- Options that can be set specific to a sheet within a workbook.
- Enhanced zoom (ad hoc) options.
- Range-based operations, e.g., select a group of cells and retrieve or submit only those cells.
- Linked Reporting Objects.
- A host of new VBA functions, described for you in this chapter.

For many years, the Essbase Classic Add-In was the data analyst's main tool for interacting with Essbase via Excel. Unfortunately, this add-in did not have the ability to communicate with the relational repositories associated with Hyperion Planning and HFM (Hyperion Financial Management). The Classic Add-In connected directly to Essbase, and only Essbase. Oracle recognized this limitation and sought to provide a common add-in across the entire suite of Hyperion products. In addition, this new add-in needed to work with more than just Excel. Smart View was the answer. This chapter will focus on using Smart View as your reporting and analysis tool for Essbase using Excel.

10.3 TUNE YOUR REPORTS, CREATE EFFICIENT SMART VIEW SPREADSHEETS

10.3.1 Hardware: It's Your Laptop

The first thing to understand about Smart View performance is that it is, in large part, a function of the machine you are currently using, the network you are attached to, and Excel itself. We will assume that you are not the company IT (Information Technology) hardware purchaser who can order for himself (and keep) the most powerful laptop that is offered. Unless you are that lucky soul, like the rest of us, you are using technology that was "adequate" several years ago. Excel handles some things well and some things not so well. In terms of performance boundaries, Smart View and Excel are fairly congruent. What improves performance in Excel usually also improves performance in

Smart View. The Smart View developers were keen to recognize the importance of this and the synergy that results.

Like the speedometer in your car, both Excel and Smart View "advertise" an optimistic row limit capability. This number is merely a concept and, again like your car, neither is really capable of functioning with that many rows nor should you try. Excel and Smart View both prefer data that is organized into a smaller number of columns and a larger number of rows. Typically this means periods and maybe a couple of scenarios in the columns, the rest in the rows. Shortly, we will explore the tuning implications of these properties and more. This chapter assumes you are experienced with Excel and have an understanding of efficient use of Excel's formula and calculation capabilities. If not, consider brushing up before proceeding.

Because much of the rendering done by Smart View happens in Excel, much of the performance tuning can be done here as well. This is great news because now you can take performance into your own hands instead of calling the network engineer and hearing "it's not my fault; the networks look fine from here."

10.3.2 How Smart View Is Architected; What Are All Those URLs?

Smart View is a middleman service that operates in a client–server fashion. The Smart View server is a Web service that passes information back and forth from itself to Excel (your laptop) via Web service calls, which in simple terms are XML strings. This means that each of those URLs you configured in Smart View is a Web service URL.

The Smart View server, which is called Analytic Provider Services (APS), is the server that runs the Web service. APS communicates with the Essbase server in an Essbase-native format using the Essbase Java API. The server then converts the results from Essbase into XML and passes the XML back to the waiting Smart View client. The Smart View client is responsible for reading the XML returned from the server and rendering the results in Excel as your data and metadata.

10.3.3 Spreadsheet Efficiency Meets Essbase

The implication of this is that not only is your hardware important, but how you construct your reports and worksheets is equally if not more important for maximum retrieval speed. Two key components come into play here: (1) the size of the data set (XML) being requested from, or sent to, the Smart View server, and (2) the configuration of the query that Smart View uses against Essbase. In other words, if you create a huge spreadsheet that has an inefficient arrangement of dimensions, the resulting XML string passed over the network and parsed at each end will be huge and the Essbase query executed on the server will run very slowly. By creating smaller, efficient sheets, you can dramatically increase the performance of Smart View all by yourself.

10.3.4 How Many Cells?

Sometimes people like to create a report that is 17 columns (months, quarters, total year) or more across and with many rows. If this report has 200 rows, then it also has 3400 cells. While that is not a huge number to Essbase, it is significant. Limit the number of cells and you are almost guaranteed to have snappy spreadsheets.

10.3.5 Dimension Arrangement for Efficient Spreadsheets

Efficient spreadsheets are a simple matter if you follow a few rules. The reason for this is the layout of the sheet is reflected by the construction of the query to Essbase. Essbase likes things in a certain order to allow it to perform best. Violate that order and things slow down, as you will see below.

A report in Smart View can be thought of as having four axes: point of view (POV), Page, Row, and Column. While POV and Page may seem very similar, and they are, there is an important distinction. POV members are single members that are off-grid, e.g., the member Actual. Page dimension members are also single member selections, but within a set of members, e.g., Jan is selected in the set of 12 months Jan through Dec. If more than one member of a dimension is on-grid, it is either a Row or Column dimension. A large number of choices in the Page will negatively affect performance.

For block storage option (BSO) databases, a report or spreadsheet with dense dimensions in both the Rows and Columns will retrieve much faster than one with sparse dimensions on the Rows and Columns. The implication of this is, while designing your reports and worksheets, try to keep the Row and Column dimension choices limited to dense dimensions as much as is practical.

10.3.6 Attributes, DTS, and Dynamically Calculated Members

The impact of attributes and dynamically calculated members on reports are covered at length in this book (see Chapter 4, BSO Will Never Die and Here Is Why, and Chapter 7, How ASO Works and How to Design for Performance). From a query perspective, it is important to know that any member that is dynamically calculated during a retrieve will negatively impact retrieve performance. In the BSO architecture, the main culprits in this performance consideration are Attribute Dimensions, Dynamically Calculated Members, and DTS (Dynamic Time Series) members. ASO doesn't have the block concept, but its dynamic nature means that queries to nonaggregated views, formulas, and attribute combinations may be similarly slow. Clearly you cannot create spreadsheets with only precalculated members, but if you keep in mind the performance impact these members have, you will be able to manage your design with an eye on performance.

10.3.7 Use "Navigate Without Data" to Improve Performance during Development

Navigate Without Data does exactly what it says, it allows Smart View to retrieve metadata without the corresponding data. This can be useful when creating expensive queries. Perhaps the most helpful aspect of the Navigate Without Data option setting is its ability to greatly enhance performance. When a sheet's members are programmatically manipulated more than once, such as moving a member from the POV to the grid then pivoting the grid, it is a good practice to enable Navigate Without Data during the sheet manipulations. Enabling this setting allows the sheet to refresh several times very quickly because only metadata is queried.

10.3.8 Compression

Network performance of Smart View can be enhanced using compression. Smart View providers use a compression scheme called GZIP. Because the communication between the client and the server is primarily alphanumeric text, using GZIP compression greatly increases efficiency.

To get an idea just how efficient GZIP compression is, simply use your favorite zip utility to zip a fairly large data load file. In most cases, the compressed file will be 80% smaller than the nonzipped version. You can expect similar results and similar reductions in network bandwidth requirements when you use Smart View compression.

Smart View APS compression is disabled by default. If you think your network is the culprit in poor retrieval performance, test to see if the overhead of performing and compression and decompression actually speeds retrieves.

To enable compression in APS, you will have to *disable* the disabling of compression. Locate the **essbase.properties** file and add or edit the following setting to equal false:

```
smartview.webservice.gzip.compression.disable=false
```

You must restart the APS service to have compression take effect.

10.4 EXCEL AUTOMATION

You have now reached the true core of this chapter: Smart View and Smart View VBA functions. We also will use a few Excel API and forms capabilities toward the end. I like to think the primary purpose of automating Smart View is to make the user's life easier. However, things can be done as well to limit what a user can do—making an administrator's life easier.

10.4.1 VBA: Traditional Automation

This automation discussion will use VBA as the primary language to implement the discussed functionality. The nice thing about VBA is it comes with its own development environment, the Visual Basic Editor (VBE), and you don't need to be a rocket scientist to work with it. Here are a few tips for effective use of VBA in an Excel workbook:

- Use forms for complicated user inputs.
- Use Collections to work with many objects at once.
- Use the Err object to create an effective error handling strategy.
- Store things you want to remember and retrieve between sessions in the registry by using the functions GetSetting and SetSetting.
- Keep your functions and subs small and specific to one task. This makes debugging and code reuse much easier.
- Even though you can theoretically put everything you code into a single module, the best practice is to create many modules with each module named to indicate the set of functionalities it provides to keep things organized.

If these concepts are a bit unfamiliar to you, pay close attention to the comments in the example code where these concepts will be explained in more detail.

10.4.2 Smart View VBA Functions Refresher and Newer Features

People often call the Smart View VBA functions the "Smart View API." This is not necessarily wrong because the functions are used to program Smart View. However, the Smart View documentation only refers to them as the VBA functions. For the sake of consistency, I will discuss all programmatic Smart View functionality in terms of the VBA functions.

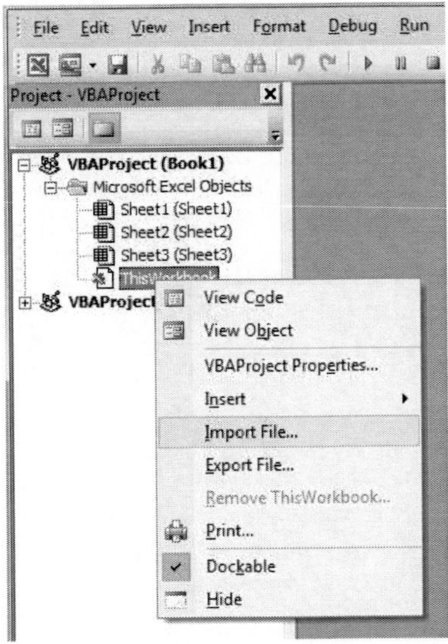

Figure 10.1 Importing the SmartView.bas.

To implement the VBA functions in Excel, first import the SmartView.bas file into your workbook via the VBE. To import the SmartView.bas file, right click on your project in the Project pane, then select Import File and browse to your local machine's install directory of Smart View (Figure 10.1). This directory is usually found at C:\Oracle\Smart View\Bin.

If this is the first time you have used the VBA environment to program with Smart View, you will likely need to add a reference to HsAddin.dll, found in the same directory as SmartView.bas. To add a reference to HsAddin.dll, select Tools, References, then select Browse and navigate to the Smart View directory, then select HsAddin.dll, as shown in Figure 10.2.

Now that the SmartView.bas module is present, you automatically have declarations necessary for all the Smart View VBA functions to work.

Tip: To figure out how to code a complicated bit of functionality in Excel, use the Record Macro function to "record" yourself manually performing that task. Excel will create the code for you.

Newer features in the Smart View VBA functions are a valuable set of enhancements. A few new functions are highlighted in Table 10.1.

10.4.3 Setting and Managing Options

The Smart View VBA functions provide a set of functions that allow you to manage Smart View user options. Three main functions include:

1. HypSetOption
2. HypSetSheetOption
3. HypSetGlobalOption

HypSetSheetOption is specific to the currently active sheet. The sheet name parameter is unused by Smart View. Table 10.2 provides some clarification and

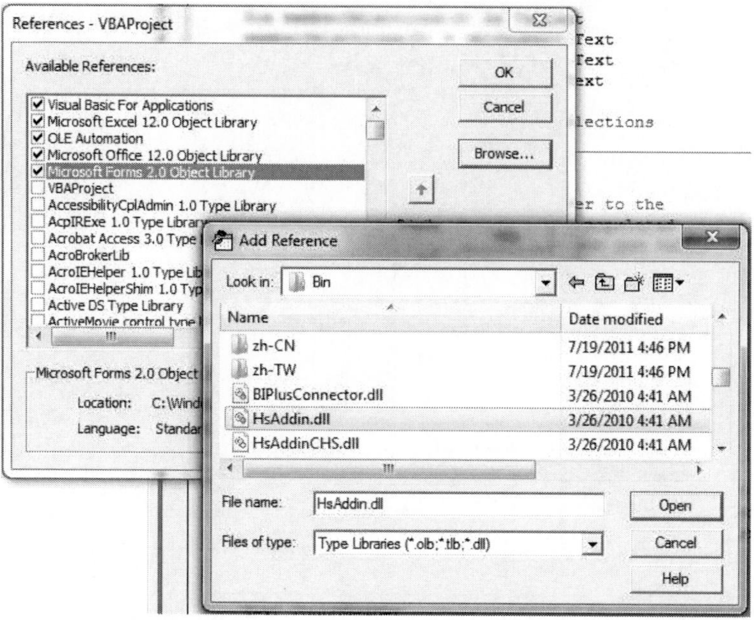

Figure 10.2 Adding a reference to HsAddin.dll.

examples of some of the more complicated options that can be managed by HypSetSheetOption.

HypSetOption allows you to set a default set of options that can be overridden by HypSetSheetOption, or by HypSetOption itself. HypSetOption is easier to use in multiple sheet workbooks because it doesn't require you to activate each sheet for which you wish to set options.

HypSetGlobalOption provides access to global properties like the verbosity of logging, whether or not to use Excel formatting, and navigating without data.

10.4.4 Connecting, Logging In, and Refreshing Forms

Automating the connection and login process is one of the best ways to enhance the user experience in Excel. By preparing and automating connections ahead of time, you can simplify and unify your users' experience. A simple login dialog can be creating using standard Excel VBA forms.

Why would you want to create your own login dialog? Maybe you only need the out of the box functionality provided by Smart View; however, if that were the case you probably wouldn't be reading this section. Providing your own login dialog box allows some additional flexibility and capability. For example, you can create your own look and feel, use particular fonts, company logos, and add special instructions in a custom login dialog. A custom login dialog also provides the ability to capture things, such as the user name or any other information you want the user to provide.

10.4.4.1 Connecting and Logging In Below is an example of code used to create connections and login to Essbase. The error handling used here is explained in Section 10.4.13 (Error Handling).

Table 10.1 Newer VBA Functions

Function	Description
HypAddLRO HypDeleteLROs HypDeleteAllLROs HypListLRO HypRetrieveLRO HypUpdateLRO	Linked Reporting Objects are a useful addition to Reports. The ability to programmatically manage LROs adds a new dimension of functionality for user and admins. These functions allow you to add custom forms, buttons, etc., for making LRO use by your user easy and intuitive.
HypSetOption HypGetOption	These two little gems greatly simplify the management of Smart View options. With these you can set default options, and options that are specific to a particular sheet. A great way to use these is to set a company standard for Smart View options (which reduces frivolous calls for help). Store each of the settings in a table, and then have your Smart View application look up and set these before your user starts work as in the example below.

```
Sub svEnforceEnterpriseSettings()
    Dim cn As New Connection
    Dim rs As Recordset
    Dim svRetVal As Long

    With cn
        .ConnectionString = "driver={SQL Server};" & _
        "server=MyServer;uid=sa;pwd=pwd;database=MySmartViewDB"
        .ConnectionTimeout = 30
        .Open
    End With
    strQuery = "SELECT * FROM MySVSettings"
    Set rs = cn.Execute(strQuery)
    Do While Not rs.EOF
        svRetVal = hypSetOption(rs.Fields("SETTING_NAME"),
rs.Fields("SETTING_VALUE"), "MySvSheet")
        rs.MoveNext
    Loop
    rs.Close
    cn.Close
End Sub
```

Function	Description
HypGetMemberInformation HypMenuVMemberInformation	If you've ever wanted to extract outline or dimension information, or place account, period, or entity property information on a report next to the member, this is your function. This little powerhouse provides access to 39 different member properties. Look for the table "Constants for Member Information" in the Smart View User's Guide. If you want to skip having to loop over the collection of Member property constants and just want a dialog with everything already there, the second function on the left will do just that.
HypGetDrillThoughReports HypExecuteDrillThroughReport	Your imagination should be swirling by now. The first function on the left gets a list of drill through reports. Just use the one below it to execute the chosen report. With these two functions, you can create a dialog that contains a dropdown for the list of drill through reports available on the current sheet, and button to execute that report.

(*Continued*)

Table 10.1 (*Continued*) Newer VBA Functions

Function	Description
HypGetNameRangeList HypRetrieveNameRange	Named ranges are one of the best features of Excel when it comes to automation. These two new functions programmatically extend the named range capability to Smart View. The new functionality allows Smart View to work with multiple retrieve ranges on a single worksheet. Because Smart View now allows you to retrieve a range on the sheet, you can select the desired named range programmatically and refresh its data. Here is an example that submits data, calculates a Calc Script, retrieves a named range, runs a second Calc Script, and then retrieves the corresponding named range.

```
Sub runForecasts()
    'using Smart View to refresh named ranges in Excel
    Dim svRetVal As Long
    Dim isWaitForCalcToComplete As Boolean

    isWaitForCalcToComplete = True
    svRetVal = HypSubmitData()
    svRetVal = HypExecuteCalcScript(Empty, "CurrFcst",
isWaitForCalcToComplete)
    svRetVal = HypRetrieveNameRange(Empty, Range("ShortRangeFCST"))
    svRetVal = HypExecuteCalcScript(Empty, "LongFcst",
isWaitForCalcToComplete)
    svRetVal = HypRetrieveNameRange(Empty, Range("LongRangeFCST"))
End Sub
```

Function	Description
HypShowPOV	If the POV toolbar has ever caused you headaches, this function is your pain relief. To hide the POV toolbar, call HypShowPOV(false). To show the POV toolbar, call HypShowPOV(true).

```
Sub SVconnect(sUser, sPassword, sApp, sDb, sUrl, sServer, Optional
sSheet)
    Dim svRetVal As Long
    Dim isCreatedConnection As Boolean
    Dim isConnected As Boolean
    Dim sProvider
    Dim sConnName

    If IsMissing(sSheet) Then sSheet = DEFAULT_SHEETNAME
    sConnName = sApp & "." & sDb
    sProvider = HYP_ANALYTIC_SERVICES
    isCreatedConnection = HypConnectionExists(sConnName)
    If (isSVError(svRetVal)) Then
       Call handleSVError(svRetVal, "HypConnectionExists",
       "SVconnect")
       Exit Sub
    End If

    If Not isCreatedConnection Then
        svRetVal = HypCreateConnection(sSheet, sUser, sPassword,
        sProvider, sUrl, sServer, sApp, sDb, sConnName, "")
```

Table 10.2 HypSetSheetOption Options

Option	Option Name	Description	Example
1	Zoom Level	During a "drill" operation, such as double clicking on a member, sets the effect the operation will have.	If set to (1) all levels, a zoom operation will return all ancestors and descendants of the currently selected member. If set to (2) bottom level, a zoom operation will return all the base level (level-0) members that descend from the zoomed member.
2	Include Selection	When you zoom on a member, this option will determine if the member is to remain on the sheet along with the returned set of members.	If Zoom Level (above) is (2) a zoom operation will return the member you zoomed on and its base level descendants. If you Keep Only on a cell within a selection of cells, the rest of the grid will remain and the cells in the selection will all be removed except the cell on which keep only was performed.
3	Within Selection	This setting will restrict zoom, keep only, and remove only operations to the currently selected cells, leaving unselected cells unchanged.	When zooming, with zoom level set to bottom level, only the selected members will actually zoom to the base level descendants with this option enabled
4	Remove Unselected	With this option enabled, a zoom operation will be performed on the selected cells per the within selection setting and remove all the unselected cells and their corresponding data from the sheet	With (1) Zoom Level set to Base Level, (2) Include Selection set to true, and (3) within selection set true and (4) remove unselected set true, if the first three members on a report at selected and in that selection the second member is right clicked and zoom in is chosen, the report will clear except for the first three rows and all the base level members of the members in the first three rows will be added.

Data from Oracle Hyperion Smart View for Office, Fusion Edition Release 1.11.1 copyright 2004, 2008, Oracle.

```
        If (isSVError(svRetVal)) Then
            Call handleSVError(svRetVal, "HypCreateConnection",
            "SVconnect")
            Exit Sub
        End If
    End If

    isConnected = (HypConnected(sSheet) = HYPERION_IS_CONNECTED)

    If isConnected Then
        SVDisconnect sSheet
    End If
    svRetVal = HypConnect(sSheet, sUser, sPassword, sConnName)
    If (isSVError(svRetVal)) Then
        Call handleSVError(svRetVal, "HypConnect", "SVconnect")
```

```
        Exit Sub
    End If
    svRetVal = HypSetActiveConnection(sConnName)
    If (isSVError(svRetVal)) Then
        Call handleSVError(svRetVal, "HypSetActiveConnection",
        "SVconnect")
        Exit Sub
    End If
End Sub
```

Having login information will allow you to do things like looking something up about a user in a custom SQL (Structured Query Language) table, track and store things about your users, and provide single sign on capability to other applications from which you may want to present data alongside the Smart View data.

10.4.4.2 Refreshing Sheets If you have gone through the trouble to create a custom login, automated retrievals also are likely part of your report functionality. Refreshing multiple sheets used to be a tedious task involving looping over all the sheets in a workbook, and then doing the same in other workbooks, verifying each connection, and then refreshing each in turn. This has all changed with the addition of this VBA function: HypRetrieveAllWorkbooks. This function will save a huge amount of time in your coding by allowing you to refresh all worksheets currently open in Excel.

10.4.5 Cascading Reports

Cascading reports are a new feature to Smart View and provide a significant level of convenience. A cascading report is one that starts with a base report that, for instance, has the Period dimension in the POV. By selecting several members of the Period dimension, the report can be cascaded by those selections. This means that a new worksheet will be created for each selected Period and the rest of the report's layout will flow to that sheet, only the Period will be different. Each new spreadsheet will be named for the member to which it cascades.

In Figure 10.3, our initial report has been cascaded by period (month).

10.4.6 Linking Smart View Functionality to Common Form Elements

This section will provide a few quick examples for linking Smart View functionality to common Excel form elements, such as text boxes, drop down lists, and buttons. Because

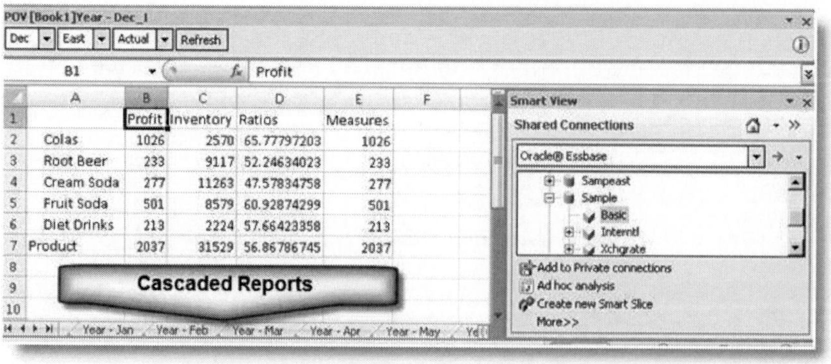

Figure 10.3 Reports cascaded by period.

many of the form elements share similar coding needs, the goal here is to provide a few templates that you can use to create your applications.

10.4.7 Managing Combo Edits

Consider a planning and budgeting cube. Using this cube, among other things, we budget product revenues. Our example company has products in a dimension called "Segments," channels for peddling those products in a dimension called, you guessed it, Channel, and an Entity dimension containing various business units by geographical unit (Figure 10.4).

Although it isn't visible from Figure 10.4, we know from a business perspective that:

- Only some entities can sell through some channels.
- Only certain products are sold through each channel.

Thus, the relationship of valid data intersections may be represented as: Segment -> Channel -> Entities: A given product only has valid data intersections for *x* list of channels, which are only valid for *y* list of entities. This relationship is commonly called a sparse interdimensional relationship.

In Figure 10.5, we see that, for instance, the only valid places to plan operating revenue for Latin America is in the Government channel for all products, and EMEA sells neither Audio Systems nor Televisions, but has some data in all Channels. At this point, you may realize the challenge here. How do you prevent planners from placing data into intersections that are invalid? If you do not enforce some of these restrictions, planners will inevitably enter data into the wrong combination. Trying to find this misplaced data later is not easy and can eat up an administrator's time.

10.4.8 Creating a Combo Edits Lookup Table for Valid Sparse Combinations

Several proven methods exist in Essbase to handle this situation, each with its drawbacks usually involving added dimensions and members, and extra maintenance.

```
- Entity Country <3> (Never Share)
  - TotalGeography (+) <5> (Alias: Total Geography) (UDAS: USD) /* Total Geography */
    + E01 (+) <4> (Alias: North America) (UDAS: USD) /* North America */
    + E02 (+) <6> (Alias: Latin America) (UDAS: USD) /* Latin America */
    + E03 (+) <4> (Alias: EMEA) (UDAS: EUR) /* EMEA */
    + E04 (+) <9> (Alias: APAC) (UDAS: USD) /* APAC */
      E05 (+) (Alias: Corporate HQ) (UDAS: USD) /* Corporate HQ */
  + Function (~) <4> (UDAS: USD)
    No Entity (~) (UDAS: USD)
- Segments <1> (Never Share)
  - Total (+) <2>
    - AllSegments (+) <2> (Alias: All Segments) /* All Segments */
      - Seg01 (+) <4> (Alias: Electronics) /* Electronics */
        + AS (+) <2> (Alias: Audio Systems) /* Audio Systems */
        + DV (+) <4> (Alias: Digital Video) /* Digital Video */
        + TV (+) <3> (Alias: Televisions) /* Televisions */
        + VC (+) <2> (Alias: VCRs) /* VCRs */
      + Seg02 (+) <3> (Alias: Services) /* Services */
      NoSegment (+) (Alias: No Segment) (Never Share)
- Channels <2> (Never Share)
  - All Channels (+) <3>
      Distribution (+)
      Government (+)
      Education (+)
    No Channel (+)
```

Figure 10.4 Sparse interdimensional relationships.

	A	B	C	D	E	F	G
1			North America	Latin America	EMEA	APAC	Corporate HQ
2			Operating Revenue	Operating Revenue	Operating Revenue	Operating Revenue	Operating Revenue
3	Audio Systems	Distribution	89998246.19			34775884.63	
4	Audio Systems	Education	63103663.68				
5	Digital Video	Distribution			73818785.58	30325474.52	
6	Digital Video	Education			51759184.98		
7	Televisions	Government		7799329.14			
8	Televisions	Education					
9	VCRs	Government		4626337.23			
10	Install	Distribution	45358822.99			17354324.72	
11	Install	Government		5606146.65			
12	Install	Education			37204427.81		
13	Service Contracts	Distribution	30134335.23			11314284.32	
14	Service Contracts	Government		3724468.39			
15	Service Contracts	Education			24716926.66		
16	Repair	Distribution	32859897.65			14086306.81	
17	Repair	Government		4061335.66			
18	Repair	Education			26952500.32		
19							

Figure 10.5 Sparse relationships of products to channel to entity.

	A	B	C
1	Audio Systems	Distribution	North America
2	Audio Systems	Distribution	APAC
3	Audio Systems	Education	North America
4	Digital Video	Distribution	EMEA
5	Digital Video	Distribution	APAC
6	Digital Video	Education	EMEA
7	Televisions	Government	Latin America
8	VCRs	Government	Latin America
9	Install	Distribution	North America
10	Install	Distribution	APAC
11	Install	Government	Latin America
12	Install	Education	EMEA
13	Service Contracts	Distribution	North America
14	Service Contracts	Distribution	APAC
15	Service Contracts	Government	Latin America
16	Service Contracts	Education	EMEA
17	Repair	Distribution	North America
18	Repair	Distribution	APAC
19	Repair	Government	Latin America
20	Repair	Education	EMEA

Figure 10.6 Combo edits lookup table.

For situations where a combination of METAREAD and ANDs in Essbase filter security cannot be applied, such as in Essbase databases generated by Hyperion Planning, a code-based solution is necessary. One solution is a combo edits lookup or a set of valid data-dependent lists that drive the contents of dropdown selections to assure that only valid selections may be made. For the sake of simplicity, we will use a simple spreadsheet lookup. A combo edits lookup is simply a table that lists all the valid combinations of several sparsely related dimensions. In this case, our sparsely related dimensions are Segment, Channel, and Entity. Given your understanding of a spreadsheet lookup after this exercise, you should easily make the intuitive leap to using an SQL table for the lookup.

A lookup table for this application may look something like what is shown in Figure 10.6.

The following Excel VBA macro can be used to generate the lookup shown above.

```
Public Sub genComboEditsLookup()
    Dim cellCount As Integer
    Dim cellValue As String
    Dim cell As Range
    Dim arrValidEnt() As String
```

```
    Dim arrValidChn() As String
    Dim arrValidSeg() As String
    ReDim Preserve arrValidEnt(100)
    ReDim Preserve arrValidChn(100)
    ReDim Preserve arrValidSeg(100)

    Sheets("Sheet1").Activate
    cellCount = 0
    With Sheets("Sheet1")
        ' We created a named range called "data"
        For Each cell In Range("data")
            'Make sure the cell has text, otherwise don't add it
            If Len(cell.Value) > 0 Then
                ' cellCount keeps track of how many lookups we've
                ' added to the collections
                cellCount = cellCount + 1
                ' rather than redim the array every time,
                ' we redim it in increments of 100 to improve
                performance
                If (cellCount Mod 100 = 0) Then
                    ReDim Preserve arrValidEnt(cellCount + 100)
                    ReDim Preserve arrValidChn(cellCount + 100)
                    ReDim Preserve arrValidSeg(cellCount + 100)
                End If
                ' add the member of each dimension to its collection
                ' (The corresponding subscript of each collection
                ' represents one valid combination of the sparse
                members)
                arrValidEnt(cellCount - 1) = Cells(1, cell.Column).
                Value
                arrValidChn(cellCount - 1) = Cells(cell.row, 2).
                Value
                arrValidSeg(cellCount - 1) = Cells(cell.row, 1).
                Value
            End If
        Next cell
    End With
    ' Activate a different (blank) sheet to layout the collections
    ' We'll use this data for lookups later on. We name the ranges
    to
    ' make the lookup code we'll write later easier to read.
    Sheets("Sheet2").Activate
    With Application.WorksheetFunction
        Range("a1:a" & cellCount).Value = .Transpose(arrValidSeg)
        Range("a1:a" & cellCount).Name = "Segment"
        Range("b1:b" & cellCount).Value = .Transpose(arrValidChn)
        Range("b1:b" & cellCount).Name = "Channel"
        Range("c1:c" & cellCount).Value = .Transpose(arrValidEnt)
        Range("c1:c" & cellCount).Name = "Entity"
      End With
End Sub
```

Programmatically, we can manage the POV selections on our worksheet by using choices made by the user from a dropdown selection box. In this case, each dropdown box choice drives what selections appear in the next dropdown. For instance, if the user chooses "Audio Systems" from the Segment dropdown, the Channel dropdown would be populated based on a lookup to the table where our valid sparse interdimensional relationships are stored (Figure 10.6): "Distribution," "Government," "Education." If the user then selects "Government" from the Channel dropdown, the Entities dropdown would be limited to "North America" and "Latin America" based on the Segment -> Channel -> Entities interdimensional relationship established for this worksheet.

Here's how to look up a list of members in one dimension that correspond to the member selected in another dimension:

```
Sub lookupDimMemberList(memberNm As String, _
                memberDim As String, _
                lookupDim As String, _
                lookupDimMemberList As Collection)
    Dim cell As Range
    Dim lookupMatch As String

    For Each cell In Range(memberDim)
        ' Does the current row contain our member?
        If Range(memberDim).Cells(cell.row).Value = memberNm Then
            ' If so, then our lookup is in the same row in the
            ' lookupDim range
            lookupMatch = Range(lookupDim).Cells(cell.row).Value
            'we only want unique members
            On Error Resume Next
                lookupDimMemberList.Add lookupMatch, lookupMatch
            On Error GoTo 0
        End If
    Next cell
End Sub
```

Simply put, the lookup table of valid member combinations provides a list of what members may be loaded in a dropdown based on the selection in another dropdown using the preceding method.

10.4.9 Adding the Combo Boxes

Let's put this together with some custom POV dropdown selections. On the Developer ribbon, click Insert, ActiveX Controls, Combo Box. Use the cross cursor to "draw" the Combo Box near the top of your spreadsheet. In the range names dropdown, change the name to "cboSegment" (Figure 10.7).

Now do the same thing for the "cboChannel" and "cboEntity" Combo Boxes (Figure 10.8).

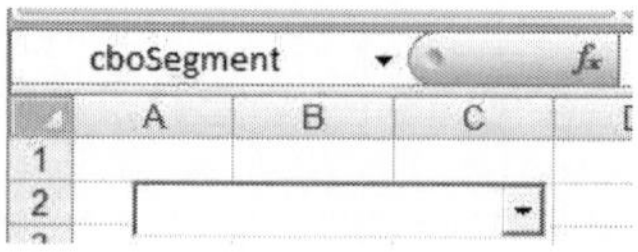

Figure 10.7 cboSegment Combo Box.

Figure 10.8 cboSegment, cboChannel, cboEntity.

10.4.10 Adding the Initialization Code

In the VB code, double click "ThisWorkbook," then click the dropdown on the left and select "Workbook." This will insert the Workbook_Open() method.

Add the call to InitCombo to the method. Then, below the Workbook_Open method, add the following code to initialize the first Combo Box.

```
Private Sub InitCombo()
    Dim segmentRange As Range
    Dim cell As Range
    Dim col As New Collection
    Dim item As Variant

    Sheet3.cboSegment.Clear
    Set segmentRange = Range("Segment")
    For Each cell In segmentRange.Cells
        On Error Resume Next
            col.Add cell.Value, cell.Value
        On Error GoTo 0
    Next cell
    For Each item In col
        Sheet3.cboSegment.AddItem item
    Next item
End Sub
```

This will initialize the Segment Combo Box with a unique list of Segment members based on the segment range in our lookup.

10.4.11 Adding Events to Drive the Combo Boxes

The following will demonstrate how to add events to the cboSegment and cboChannel Combo Boxes. This is the "magic" behind managing the user so that he only chooses valid combinations of members for data entry. When a combo box selection is changed, the Change event for that control fires. We will implement this event to do the lookup and load the next Combo Box with only members that are valid with the current selection. In other words, if a user chooses the VCRs segment, only the Government member will be available as a choice in the cboChannel Combo Box.

To add an event to the Combo Box, double click on the ThisWorkbook object listed under "Microsoft Excel Objects" in the VBA editor, This opens the module for ThisWorkbook, which is where we will add our events (Figure 10.9).

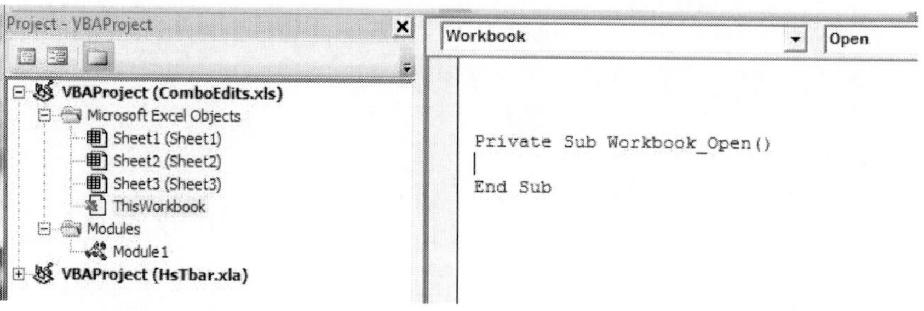

Figure 10.9 ThisWorkbook.

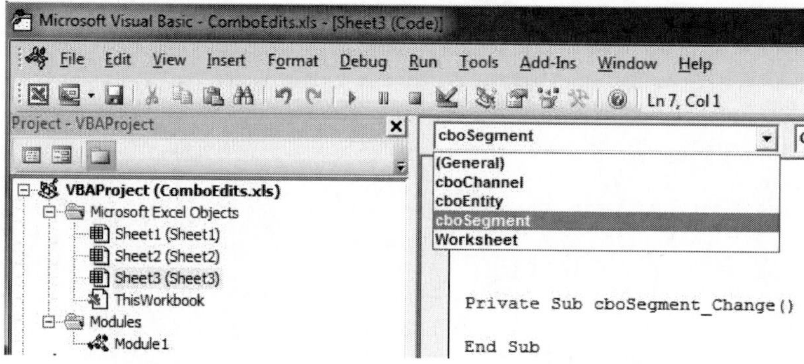

Figure 10.10 Adding the change event.

Adding the event method template code is as simple as clicking the left dropdown above the code and selecting cboSegment. This will immediately add the _Change event (Figure 10.10).

```
Private Sub cboSegment_Change()
    'we pass this empty collection over to the
    'lookUpDimMemberList method to be populated
    'with a list of Channel members that are valid
    'with the currently selected Segment.
    Dim lookupMatches As New Collection
    Dim selectDimensionName As String
    Dim lookupDimensionName As String
    Dim selectedMember As String

    selectedMember = cboSegment.Text
    selectDimensionName = "Segment"
    lookupDimensionName = "Channel"
    cboChannel.Clear

    'use our previously coded method to get lookup the member(s)
    that
    'are valid with the currently selected Segment member.
    lookupDimMemberList selectedMember, selectDimensionName,
    lookupDimensionName, lookupMatches
    Dim foundMember As Variant
```

```
    For Each foundMember In lookupMatches
        cboChannel.AddItem foundMember
    Next foundMember
End Sub

Private Sub cboChannel_Change()
    'we pass this empty collection over to the
    'lookUpDimMemberList method to be populated
    'with a list of Entity members that are valid with the
    'currently selected Channel.
    Dim lookupMatches As New Collection
    Dim selectDimensionName As String
    Dim lookupDimensionName As String
    Dim selectedMember As String
     selectedMember = cboChannel.Text
     selectDimensionName = "Channel"
     lookupDimensionName = "Entity"
     cboEntity.Clear

     'use our previously coded method to get lookup the Entity
     member(s) that
     'are valid with the currently selected Channel member.
     lookupDimMemberList selectedMember, selectDimensionName,
     lookupDimensionName, lookupMatches
     Dim foundMember As Variant
     For Each foundMember In lookupMatches
         cboEntity.AddItem foundMember
     Next foundMember
End Sub
```

If you implemented the code correctly here, you should be able to test the Combo Box selections and find that our company only sells Televisions to Latin American Governments and only sells Audio Systems to Schools in North America and EMEA.

10.4.12 Next Steps

By now the ideas for putting this logic to good use should start to flow. The custom Combo Boxes for Segment, Channel, and Entity are meant to be used as POV member selections in a Smart View data entry sheet. By adding the Smart View call HypSetPOV to your Combo Box events, you tie the selections of the Combo Boxes directly to the POV of the sheet. Here is how it should look in the cboEntity_Change() event:

```
Private Sub cboEntity_Change()
    If Len(cboChannel.Text) > 0 And Len(cboEntity.Text) > 0 Then
        svSetPOV
    End If
End Sub
```

In Module1, the method svSetPOV() should contain:

```
Public Sub svSetPOV()
    Dim svRetVal As Long

    Sheet1.Activate
```

```
    With Sheet3
        svRetVal = HypSetPOV(Empty, "Segments#" & .cboSegment.Text)
        svRetVal = HypSetPOV(Empty, "Channels#" & .cboChannel.Text)
        svRetVal = HypSetPOV(Empty, "Entity#" & .cboEntity.Text)
    End With
    MsgBox svRetVal
End Sub
```

10.4.13 Error Handling

One of the things you can count on in VBA is errors. The Smart View VBA functions provide an error code to help diagnose problems. The problem is that an error number is not very informative. Every Smart View VBA project will benefit from having some form of error handling and interpretation. Doing this will greatly improve development progress and at the same time reduce stress. The following is an example of catching and interpreting errors in a Smart View VBA project:

```
Function s_SVGetErrorMsg(lErrorCode As Long, sSvFunc As String,
sXlFunc As String) As String
    Dim sErrorMsg As String
' note: the list of errors here is not complete. The idea is to
convery
' to you the concept and let you code the rest on your own.
    Select Case lErrorCode
        Case 0
             sErrorMsg = "Function ran successfully"
        Case -1
             sErrorMsg = "Valid return value, True"
        Case -2
             sErrorMsg = "Termination error"
        Case -3
             sErrorMsg = "Initialization error"
        Case -4
             sErrorMsg = "Spreadsheet is not yet connected to the
                          server"
        Case -6
             sErrorMsg = "Not used"
        Case -7
             sErrorMsg = "Spreadsheet has become unstable"
        Case -8
             sErrorMsg = "No Undo information exists"
        Case Else
             sErrorMsg = "Unspecified Error: " & CStr(lErrorCode)
    End Select
    s_SVGetErrorMsg = "SmartView error: " & sErrorMsg & " " &
    sXlFunc & " " & sSvFunc & " " & lErrorCode
End Function
Sub handleSVError(lErrorCode As Long, sSvFunc As String, sXlFunc As
String)
    Exit Sub
    'If (ThisWorkbook.isDebug) Then MsgBox s_SVGetErrorMsg
    (lErrorCode, sSvFunc, sXlFunc)
End Sub
```

```
Function isSVError(lErrCode As Long) As Boolean
    Dim res As Boolean

    res = False
    If Not (lErrCode = 0) Then res = True
    isSVError = res
End Function
```

10.5 AFTERTHOUGHTS

For those who can provide solutions outside of the normal range, people who enjoy making the square peg fit into the round hole, requirements can creep like a heavy fog. Gathering requirements for a solution that transcends normal functionality must be an iterative process. What users ask for and what they really want are often two very different things. With this in mind, while it might be tempting to quickly code what is being asked for merely to show it can be done, it is preferable to take the time to verify and validate the requirements through mockup and dialog. You may be surprised how different the user requirements really are compared to what you initially thought they would be.

Much of the discussion and instruction in this chapter centers on automating Smart View and manipulating it programmatically with the Smart View VBA functions. Many solutions have been created using these processes, techniques, and tools. However, one thing to keep in mind with regard to Excel and its programmatic capabilities—less is more. Code written in VBA is really script, and usually inefficient script. Not much can be done specifically within the VBA environment to optimize this. Therefore, the reader should strive to keep it simple.

11

HOW TO SUCCESSFULLY MANAGE AN ESSBASE SYSTEM

Natalie Delemar and David Anderson

CONTENTS

11.1 WHO ARE YOU?

You were brought in to save the day. You were hired as the savior of their EPM (Enterprise Performance Management)/BI (Business Intelligence)/Analytics/Reporting or the whatever internal abbreviation your company uses for Essbase. You probably were not there when they selected it, bought it, nor even when they implemented it, but you are now responsible for it. It is clear to anyone with a resting pulse that the existing system is nowhere near its potential. You have a ton of ideas on how to improve it, but you have been bogged down with the day-to-day maintenance issues. Then the moment you were praying for comes. Management approves a project to enhance or expand the functionality of the system—you have an opportunity. This is not an opportunity for failure. This is an opportunity to make things right, solve world hunger and poverty, well, maybe not *that*. This is an opportunity to really make an impact at your organization, improve the ROI (return on investment) of the system, and make you and Essbase shine. These moments are rare and should not be squandered.

Though your title does not say it, you are your company's internal Essbase consultant. Internal consultants serve internal clients as trusted advisors and:

- Assist their clients with solving problems and resolving business issues
- Help implement solutions that are strategic to the organization
- Assist their clients in achieving effectiveness, profitability, or increased performance
- Bring a specialized expertise in a specific discipline, such as Human Resources (HR), Training, Information Technology (IT), Business Intelligence, Finance, etc.
- Act as change agents for their organization and help implement change initiatives

Impressive, is it not? It does fit your job description. Internal consultants are similar to external consultants in that they need to have strong consulting skills, such as technical expertise, project management skills, and business acumen, and the additional advantage/burden of knowing the company's systems and culture from the inside.

You are the linchpin to this Essbase project's success because only you know Essbase and your business. You uniquely have the ability and opportunity to bring tremendous value to your organization.

11.2 PURPOSE

This chapter was written to give you, the Internal Essbase Consultant/Hyperion manager/Essbase administrator/technical lead or whatever you are called, the key considerations in successfully managing an Essbase project whether staffed internally, externally, or in combination. We will focus on the areas that are unique to you as an administrator. In this chapter, we will review your preproject tasks, take you through whether you should go it alone or take on a partner and then discuss selecting and managing a consulting partner, managing expectations, and managing your project. Finally, we will examine postproject tasks. Though this will be from the administrator's perspective, it should be interesting and instructive reading for anyone involved in Essbase projects.

11.3 SETTING THE STAGE FOR AN ESSBASE PROJECT

11.3.1 Why Are You Doing This?

While the purpose of any new Essbase project will vary due to the nature of your organization and the business involved in a given project, the goal is almost always to use the analytic power of Essbase to replace an overly manual, burdensome process that prevents analysts from doing true analysis because so much time is spent on gathering data. In simple words, you must identify a pain point within your organization that is best and most easily fixed by Essbase.

11.3.2 Making Your Case

It is fairly easy to identify the potential pain points in your organization, such as a customer profitability analysis, that takes days to synthesize. The beauty of Essbase shines through by being able to demonstrate not only significant reductions in the time to produce the data, but also in the provision of additional business value in the form of new analyses. To best display this value and, subsequently, achieve buy in, a project's purpose needs to be understood by both the business and your management team. A project that aligns itself with the companies' goals and strategic initiatives will have a greater chance of success in receiving funding. Many of us have had the distinct pleasure of being part of the IT budget process during a number of planning cycles. In any given year, by the end of a long arduous process of negotiating with the CIO, CFO, and CEO, the projects that are not on the floor are those that are strategic to the organization and that will add to the bottom line.

Another way to garner support for your Essbase-based project is to demonstrate how quickly Essbase can go to market especially when compared to relationally based solutions. Once Essbase has been stood up in an organization, you quickly can spin off new cubes that provide new analyses. Often, the business never even thought what you are providing was possible or they were told by IT that development would take months or years. This is the magic of Essbase. Use it to your benefit to sell your project.

11.3.3 Essbase Dream Team

Implementing that revenue-generating Essbase project at your company is a team effort that includes you, the Essbase administrator, possibly an external consulting company, a project sponsor, subject matter experts (SMEs), and, of course, the wide audience of end users. All of these players must combine together as a team both during the implementation and after the Essbase system has gone live. While you might have thought of the external consultants (if any) and the internal Essbase administrator as the key players in the success or failure of an Essbase project, their participation alone is not nearly sufficient for project success. A large Essbase project cannot begin without high tier stakeholders who enable projects by securing financing, an IT department that enables Essbase to talk to source systems, SMEs who will help translate the business's needs to Essbase, and, of course, a legion of happy day-to-day users who will continually emphasize how Essbase has made their life easier and the business more profitable. You must identify these players before the Essbase project begins so that you can start the project with everyone ready to give all of their effort. The following sections address the various stakeholders involved in an Essbase project from a role perspective.

11.3.3.1 Just Who Is the Essbase Administrator? Hopefully, it is you. If this question cannot be answered easily, beware; this is a sign of danger because it is vital to know who performs the most basic Essbase tasks. If there is not an Essbase administrator at your company and you are responsible for Essbase, why do you not have that title? If you are Essbase's owner and truly are not the Essbase administrator, you have a problem in that the title refers to a hybrid skill set that is a marriage of business functions and all of the technical skills relevant to Essbase. This straddling of the business and the IT world is vital to Essbase's success. It is essential because you are best suited to understand how the business works and, simultaneously, how Essbase interfaces with, reports on, and analyzes said business. What makes Essbase different from other more mainstream technologies is that its analytical nature requires a more balanced understanding than just simple transactional or even reporting systems. Essbase, properly implemented and managed, can be that annoying monitor that goes beep in a hospital room, showing the managers exactly what is happening to their business. This breadth and depth of technical knowledge will not be found on the business side; technology is magic to them. And, it is not available in the IT department; for goodness sakes, it is just a database, what is the big deal? Only a person who walks both sides of the street can match the business requirements to Essbase's considerable abilities.

11.3.3.2 Project Sponsor, aka Daddy Warbucks The role of a project sponsor is easy to identify; he is the person with the big picture of the project in mind and the purse strings to match. A project sponsor typically manages the project budget as well as providing guidance on project direction and major issues. Your project sponsor should be your knight in shining armor and act as your project's protector and champion when roadblocks to your project occur. He should be an evangelist for your project and help garner executive buy-in and generate excitement among the participants. The project sponsor also has the responsibility of holding the project manager and team members accountable for meeting objectives and deliverables. If team members are not delivering, putting you in an awkward position, you should feel free to address it and expect it to be handled by your project sponsor. Alternatively, you may be in a situation depending on the size of the project and your organization, where your project has very little involvement from the project sponsor except for authorizing the project. While this is not the ideal position for a sponsor, unfortunately, it is a common management model. Many of us have personally known plenty of administrators who have delivered quality projects without the benefit of an invested project sponsor. In those situations, typically you are delivering a business unit-level solution and you have a user community that is actively involved and invested in the project. Even when the sponsor is not actively involved, it is in your best interest to cultivate a relationship and build rapport with your project sponsor. You will need him or her to have your back if things do not proceed exactly as planned.

11.3.3.3 The Unloved IT Department Oracle's acquisition of Hyperion has had a positive impact on the perception of Essbase by IT departments. Traditionally, IT wanted nothing to do with Essbase because it came from a vendor who traditionally sold to the CFO (instead of the CIO). To make matters worse, it was not a relational tool. Essbase still is not relational, but Oracle's brand is as mainstream as it gets, and that has added an air of normality to the product. Now that the era of hostile resistance has passed, the IT department's participation in an Essbase project may range from a throwback "we will run it on our servers if we must" to full formal project management, hardware and infrastructure support, automated task scheduling, backup and disaster recovery, and extracting data from source systems. Where IT falls on this continuum is, unfortunately, not up to you, but instead is the result of negotiation between the project sponsor and the head of IT. An effective way of knowing where that line materializes is through the use of a roles and responsibilities matrix (RACI: responsible, accountable, consulted, and informed) so that you can clearly outline the typical responsibilities and the roles required to support them. It becomes tangible to both IT and the business at that point when you have specific responsibilities outlined, such as "Restarting EPM (Enterprise Performance Management) services" or "Updating scripts." Be aware of the politics that might be involved with IT, the business, and Essbase, and be prepared to work around them if necessary.

11.3.3.4 Subject Matter Experts (SMEs) There is no way to work around business experts. Either they are with you and, together, you can vanquish any organizational issue, or they can severely hamper your project. SMEs translate the company's business process into business and functional requirements, and while they might not write code, they should understand how data is sourced, the Essbase database design, and formulas and calculations. There may be one or many SMEs, depending on the size and scope of your project.

11.3.3.5 Unloved and Underappreciated Users It is easy to get caught up in the project implementation and, ultimately, forget who it is for—the users. The end users, not the project sponsor, are the ones that truly understand the day-to-day challenges that you are trying to address with Essbase. Though end users do not like to get inundated with technical jargon, they can be your biggest asset as they are the ones who need the system to do their jobs and rely on the system to make them more productive. You should solicit suggestions from end users; it is up to you to engage them from the start of the project to get their buy-in and participation. Involve a few user representatives from the different user communities that will utilize the new system throughout the project especially in requirements building and testing.

11.3.3.6 Ideal Dream Team As we conclude the discussion of our dream team, in an ideal world where resources are not a constraint, your company should invest in creating a dream team that would have:

- A consulting company that has the right skills, people, and price to help see your Essbase project through.
- An Essbase administrator who can bridge the knowledge gaps between IT, the business, and Essbase.

- A project sponsor who is deeply involved and invested in the project's success, using all of his considerable organizational clout as needed.
- A project manager who is engaged and knows common project management tools and techniques.
- An IT department that is amenable to bring Essbase into its quiver of tools, and that is ready to support the project.
- One or more SMEs who will actively engage to assist with business requirements.
- And, finally, enthusiastic users who are more than mere Essbase consumers, but instead are active participants in the development and refinement of the system.

Does this list resemble your company's Essbase project environment? Where it does not, you need to review why your company is not able to assemble a project team that looks like this and fix it. Essbase projects are difficult enough without adding the complication of missing key players.

11.3.4 Source Data (or, At Least I Think That Is Where This Report Came From)

You have received your mandate. You have obtained your project sponsor and your cast of characters are all lined up. But, stop for a moment. Before you get too excited, how is your data? Unless your project is not requiring any new sources or if data will be completely supplied by user input, bad source data can bring your project to a screeching halt and often after you have spent an exorbitant amount of money.

The issue of bad source data is magnified with Essbase because, unlike SQL (structured query language) data repositories that can bury bad hierarchies or incorrect data assumptions in the data not selected, the inherent dimensionality of Essbase assumes that every hierarchy and data element must be correct because it is exposed. Who wants a system that is reporting erroneous data? Implementation of any business intelligence tool will expose and highlight your bad data. Many companies "mask" bad data by reporting with Excel® and other end-user applications. These tools often allow users to fix data in their reports; consequently, they are not forced to be disciplined about data quality. It is up to you as the Essbase administrator to make sure that your IT department provides good data; if they do not, it is still your responsibility, but the job just got harder. Chapter 2 of this book, Slay Bad Data in Essbase, gives both an overview and a concrete method to fix bad data in Essbase. This section will only review at a high level the various data source models and offer strategies to deal with the issues that often are seen in these data sources.

11.3.4.1 Data Warehouse An enterprise data warehouse is, because of its validated data and metadata, relational schema designed for retrieval, and data definitions, the most desirable source for Essbase data. While there is no guarantee that the data you need for your Essbase implementation is there or that it is stored at the right level, because of the data investment the business has already made in the warehouse, there is a very good chance what you need is there. Make the corporate warehouse your first and preferred stop for data and, remember, warehouses are relationally based and that means you can use SQL to extract, transform, and load into Essbase.

11.3.4.2 Data Mart The problem with data warehouses is that they were in all probability never designed for Essbase. Sometimes this does not matter and the fact data and metadata that you need can be quickly accessed through traditional Essbase data and dimension SQL Load rules or via Essbase Studio or its predecessor, Essbase Integration Services. Often, the atomic level of the data is simply too low and the effort to aggregate the data before it gets to Essbase is beyond an Essbase implementer's capabilities. Another concern is that the definitions that made sense when the warehouse was defined are simply not correct for your Essbase application, or worse yet, the data you need is not there at all. This is where a data mart can be handy as a source of preaggregated fact data, calculated measures, and alternate hierarchies.

There are dangers inherent in the data mart approach around resources, data quality, and internal political considerations. If the data mart is more than a simplified and focused access point to the data warehouse, the effort to extract, transform, and load data from source systems into the data mart can be just as complex as a true data warehouse, albeit, at a smaller scale. Can your project timeline support a 30-day data mart build before you start pointing Essbase at the data? Data warehouses are enterprise-wide constructs that have had exhaustive review by IT and the business. Data marts seldom undergo this same scrutiny and review. How are you going to guarantee that the Essbase data mart is as good? Who is going to do that? How will it fit into the timeline? Lastly, IT departments get all of the blame when systems report bad data. The enterprise data warehouse was designed to mitigate that situation and, therefore, will cast a jaundiced eye over additional data sources. You, your project sponsor, and the SMEs are going to have to work in concert to convince the business that this additional source of data is vital. Armed with a truly valid reason, you should get the buy-in needed from IT.

11.3.4.3 Source Systems Sometimes all of the skillfully crafted arguments in support of the need for a data warehouse (or data mart) will not suffice. For whatever reason, be it organizational, technological, or schedule-based, neither a data warehouse nor data mart exists for your Essbase project. The source system, whether it is an ERP (Enterprise Resource Planning) system, product sales data system, or inventory control system, will be the direct source of your data and metadata. This is not an impossible situation; after all, a data warehouse or mart would have to go to the source systems. There are, however, numerous challenges that now arise:

- How do I get data out of the system? SQL? Flat files?
- What does the metadata look like? Can I transform it to make it work in Essbase?
- How do I validate the data after a custom multistep extraction and transformation process?

These are just a sample of what must be carefully considered.

The procedure for getting data out of a source system varies based on product age and platform. Generally, older mainframe and minisystems do not have a relational interface to the outside world and extracts will be in the form of flat files. You or your IT department will need to build ETL (extract, transfer, and load) processes to get that data from whatever the source computer is to your Essbase server and then perform whatever additional transformations are required before you load the data into Essbase. Although you may not have thought that the Essbase administrator job description included data integration, you are about to find out how flexible your skill set really is. SQL is your friend in this case because an intermediate SQL data store is a good place to park data. IT departments are familiar with automating loading file extracts to relational data stores, and once loaded, custom SQL queries will allow you to transform the data as needed.

If you do not have a data warehouse or mart for fact data or a corporate metadata manager (you really do live under an unlucky star, do not you?), you must build the hierarchy yourself. In some ways, metadata is trickier than fact data because that is at the leaf level while the hierarchies must be constructed from a supporting structure that may not exist. With luck, most of your hierarchies can be lifted straight from the source application. The tricky bit is what to do when the hierarchy Essbase needs are nowhere to be found. Do not build and maintain that hierarchy in Essbase alone. Essbase databases can become corrupt. They can get deleted (with intention or sometimes without). They can get modified by someone who should not have administrator rights to Essbase. You need a good hierarchy source outside of Essbase—parent/child SQL tables often work well. The additional effort to build that metadata store will be worthwhile in the end. Many customers have invested in Oracle's DRM (Data Relationship Management) product to alleviate the burden of metadata management. Depending on the size of your organization, number of dimensions and members, frequency of updates and complexity, purchasing a metadata management tool you should explore within your organization. These tools require significant financial resources to implement, but once in place, they can be a lifesaver.

Data validation against a source system is the same process as when going against a proven data warehouse or data mart. Extract subtotals where applicable from the source and compare them to Essbase. If the data is right, their variance will be zero. If there is a variance, start back tracking. Again, Chapter 2 will give you the technique to do this technical validation.

Ensuring data quality all comes back to you, the Essbase administrator. Data that mathematically agrees with its source is valid as far as Essbase and the source are concerned, but that technical approach does not address all data quality issues. If the source definition is bad, even within a warehouse, then Essbase will reflect bad data that deviates even farther from the truth because of its aggregated nature.

11.3.5 You Are Super Glue

The only comprehensive and ultimately correct way to solve issues, be they data quality, calculations, or reports is to have a detailed understanding of the business processes, learn and document how data is compiled, and then translate that combination of business and technology to Essbase. This is too low level and technical for the project sponsor and external consultants do not know your business well enough. IT is only interested in the nuts and bolts of the system, and the SMEs understand the business but not IT. The end users are not involved, interested, or available to help resolve data issues. That leaves you: the Essbase administrator. You are the glue that joins your company's business to the analytic functionality of Essbase. No other player in your organization will have this combination of skills and perspective. See, you are special. You knew it all along; you just did not know how very special and unique you really are.

11.3.6 Training Thyself

Now that you know how special you are, you need to retain that uniqueness by ensuring that your Essbase skills are keeping pace with the needs of your organization. Yes, even though Essbase constantly has new releases that are supposed to be really great, for the average client-based Essbase team member, the two new calculation functions for BSO (block storage option) and the latest and greatest enhancements to ASO (aggregate storage option) do not exactly have us doing cartwheels. What is the practical difference from a business perspective if users are still interfacing with the same applications/cubes via the same old methods? That being said, there are justifiable reasons for acquiring training for yourself. Though, on-the-job training is best, project implementation should not be the first time you are exposed to a particular functionality or tool that will be utilized during your project.

If you are anything like me or most of my fellow Essbase administrator friends who did not come from the consulting world, you taught yourself Essbase. Yes, you might have gone to a boot camp to give yourself a kick start, but after that, you were reading the DBAG (Database Administrator's Guide) like it was your new religion and blowing things up in development to see if and how they worked. We might have graduated from the DBAG, but there are a plethora of resources available to you to self train: Google, Oracle Technology Network (OTN), Network 54, and other Essbase Expert blogs. A number of the authors in this book have blogs that can be a great starting point to learning about a new feature or Essbase-related technology. The user communities on the OTN and Network 54 message boards can be quite helpful and they typically are quicker to respond than Oracle support. For situations where you need to get new employees cross-trained in Essbase administration, Oracle University, 1230 LAP, MTG Resources, and many other third-party groups offer formal classes. If you do need formal training, be prepared to convince your sponsor and/or management. These classes can be somewhat costly.

11.4 GO IT ALONE? OR NOT?

Once the decision to develop a new Essbase application has been made, whether as a brand new installation or an extension of an existing system, the decision whether to bring in external resources has to be made. Both the purely internal and externally supplemented approaches are valid. Which approach is right for you depends on internal skills, resource availability, and timing.

11.4.1 Can We Do This on Our Own?

The decision to execute a development project internally should be made carefully and deliberately. Depending on your organization, management may expect you to deliver internally on all of your projects. On the other end of the spectrum are companies that call consultants for everything and anything outside of day-to-day administrative tasks. They often seem to have consultants perpetually. Regardless of where your company falls on the spectrum, I would encourage you to evaluate whether going internally works for you and to be honest with your management team on your assessment. You should consider three factors when deciding to execute a project externally: bandwidth, technical expertise, and innovation.

11.4.1.1 Bandwidth Do you and other team members have the bandwidth to undertake such a project? Are you and your team constantly putting out production fires that take up all of your time? A serious consideration for engaging outside resources for certain projects is bandwidth. Are you responsible for production processes and development processes without the time or bodies to complete either in a reasonable timeframe? If you are one of the fortunate administrators who is in an organization that has separate Essbase production and development teams at your disposal, good for you. This makes your job on delivering on projects much easier, but the only way to know for sure if you have the bandwidth is to estimate work effort. Map out a high level project and assign man-hours to the deliverables. If you are not able to come up with an estimate on the work effort, this is another indication you might need to engage a partner.

11.4.1.2 Technical Expertise Are there large knowledge gaps of the technology by internal resources that could jeopardize the project? Will it take too long to get up to speed on these technologies that are needed to implement the solution? Are you confident you can select the right tools, i.e., DRM, ODI (Oracle Data Integrator), Studio, or EPMA (Enterprise Performance Management Architect) for your project? If you are not familiar with the aforementioned, you might need a partner to navigate the myriad of Essbase tools by Oracle and third parties that might benefit your organization.

11.4.1.3 Innovation Do people in your company challenge the status quo? Your company may have the age-old disease of: "We always do things this way." And, may not be equipped with the resources to think innovatively and, dare I say, the mother of all clichés: "out of the box." Even if you have solid technical resources with the bandwidth, you might need a consulting company for help with best practices and designing the right solution. You may be a technically strong administrator, but it requires a different skill set to design an Essbase solution. Are you or someone in your organization competent enough to architect the right solution?

In doing this assessment, be honest with regard to your own weaknesses as well as those of your company. If you struggle with too many areas, then there is probably a need for concern with regards to an Essbase project's success and, thus, it may be best to engage outside resources.

11.4.2 Going Outside

You have come to the realization that you do not have the bandwidth, the expertise, or the time to staff your project internally. Does management agree? If yes, you are golden. If not, have you clearly communicated the potential risk of failure to your sponsor and management team? A large sign with the word DANGER in flashing lights and sirens should make it clear. Were you completely honest with them on the capabilities of the internal resources (including yourself) or did you shoot yourself in the foot and tell them that you are all-knowing and all-capable? Resist the need to continue the perception of you being superhuman. Agreeing to participate to that extent in something that is outside of your capabilities will either severely impact your quality of life or even worse, jeopardize your career. Do not do this to yourself! Look at the importance of this technology from a strategic perspective and effectively communicate the risks to organization if the project fails. Make sure it is understood that it is not just outright failure that has impacts, but they also exist if the project does not meet its objectives or it does not get completed in the necessary time frame. If the project is a "nice to have," then maybe it is not the end of the world. If your project is strategic to your organization and there are eyes of people with the letter "C" in their title who are watching it closely, do not do this alone. Go and find yourself a partner; run from that project as fast as can.

11.4.2.1 Selecting the Right Partner If your company has made the decision to go outside for Essbase help, the next step is to select a suitable partner. Project and internal company requirements drive the kind of consulting company that ultimately gets hired.

It may be a large or small company specializing in Essbase or it might be just a generalist vendor. Companies, like individuals, are not all things to all men, so you must carefully consider the strengths and weaknesses of each type of partner.

11.4.2.1.1 What Every Partner Must Have It seems obvious that the partner you are hiring must know Essbase. This expertise requirement needs to be stated up front, and repeatedly, during your search and evaluation. Without it, only a measure of good luck will ensure that your project actually finishes successfully. Do not trust fate, and do not be shy when asking; the consulting company must have resources that can handle the technical challenges that an Essbase implementation brings. Do not be shy about requesting résumés. If you have read through some of the other chapters in this book, you will understand that the world of Essbase is quite broad and the amount of required knowledge is correspondingly high. Good consultants will not know absolutely everything there is to know about Essbase (and will not claim that they do), but they must have the knowledge to know how and where to look it up and the ability to apply what they discover.

Additionally, when you are interviewing potential partners, make sure that their Essbase consultants can do more than just Essbase. Some of the necessary skills include: scripting, SQL, project management (even if just working as a member of a team), general Oracle EPM product knowledge, and a modicum of infrastructure expertise. A consultant who possesses all five of those skills and Essbase is a single billable unit; do not get yourself and your company into the position of hiring six resources where one decent consultant would suffice.

Finally, do your due diligence. Research the firm's reputation and make sure to ask for references. Check them out!

11.4.2.2 Gotchas Be sure that the resource you interviewed is literally the person who will be on the project or is representative of the caliber of Essbase consultant you will get. What you do not want is to interview a "ringer," i.e., the partner's sole Essbase hero and then end up with something much less. There is nothing wrong in talking to star power to give you a feel for the best the consulting company has to offer, but realism has to temper this exchange. Ask specifically for representative consultants, not the Oracle ace, unless he/she will be on your project. To be fair to the consulting company, it is almost impossible, particularly when the selection process and the actual implementation are months apart, to get the consultants in October who were presented in April. Consulting income is tied to billable hours and, when consultants are on the bench, they are a dead loss to their employer; they are going to get placed as soon as possible. It is up to you to research the partner and make sure that they can backfill with similar quality consultants. Then make your decisions quickly, or learn to accept equivalent substitutes.

What you never want to do is to end up being a school for consultants. It is imperative that the Essbase consultant can hit the ground running and learn whatever particular minor technology he needs, as required. You do not need to engage the guy who does not know a dense block from his elbow or his aggregate view from his you-know-what. You are paying for expertise and should get the same. If you are not getting the expertise you expected, raise the issue with your engagement manager and, if you do not get satisfaction, bounce him and maybe the partner out the door.

A last suggestion for everyone's sanity. Make sure that you hire the right resources for the project. Hyperion consultants designing a data warehouse are not a pretty sight and will end in tragedy. Even within the Oracle EPM product line, an HFM (Hyperion Financial Management) consultant is not likely to do a good job as an Essbase developer and vice versa. The EPM product line has become vast and specialties have developed out of necessity. Planning and Essbase, for instance, are not synonymous. These are sophisticated products and the expertise is similarly specialized.

11.4.2.3 A Taxonomy of Consulting Companies When Caesar uttered, "All Gaul is divided into three parts," he could very well have been defining Essbase consulting vendors. (Okay, maybe not, but three categories do make sense and, besides, you will now be able to pick the right consulting company all thanks to this one chapter; talk about value.) Consulting vendors can be divided into three ranks: large full-service vendors, midsized regional players, and boutique (Oracle EPM-only) consulting companies. The breadth of company size is terrific, from global behemoths with tens of thousands of employees to boutique groups of less than 20 consultants. Add to that the fourth resource group: independent consultants. As the relative strengths and weaknesses of each type of consulting group are discussed, compare what they offer (and sometimes do not) with what your company needs for Essbase to succeed.

When you go big, you get the whole package: A sophisticated client management experience, business advisory, big name consultants, access to all the technical resources the vendor has to offer, and maybe a passel of extremely smart college graduates. Not all of the larger vendors work like this, particularly with regards to recent graduates, but you are buying expertise and scope that can implement practically any product. Process reengineering as part of the preproject? Is Essbase part of a global project with multiple international simultaneous implementations? Do you need someone to interface back to a GL (General Ledger) package last actively sold in 1983? Do you want the slickest documentation, the most masterful status reports? There is no question that a large consulting vendor can do the work, the question is: Is this overkill for your project? Only you can answer that question in your own project scope definition. Also, do not assume a big vendor has the technological depth you require for your project. Due diligence on their consultants should be completed regardless of the type of vendor you select.

Perhaps the size of your project is smaller; maybe it is just an Essbase implementation across your company and its subsidiaries or even just a single application. Regional and boutique vendors play within that space, although the smaller vendors may have difficulty backfilling if resources roll off the project. Regardless, at this point, you are looking for a vendor that is interested in growing with your company. As a rule (and, yes, there are certainly exceptions), smaller vendors are going to charge lower rates for equal and sometimes better resources. However, particularly in the boutique vendors, these companies are not going to be able to rapidly add resources, move outside of their expertise, or travel all over the world at the drop of a hat. Moreover, you are getting less professional management—small vendors simply do not have the base that the larger multinationals do. It is not that smaller vendors do not have excellent project managers, consultants, and status reports. It is simply a matter that within a given vendor, there are fewer resources and the ones you get may not be the best. So, if you ask to replace them, there is no depth to the services bench.

Lastly, we come to the smallest of all consulting entities: the independent consultant. Often, these are senior consultants, talented and skilled in their craft. One big advantage of the independent is that you are never shown one resume and then get someone else. Top that with the fact that they are usually available at a very reasonable price. Additionally, they have the skill set needed to run a business, get placed without the benefit of a dedicated sales group, and keep up to date with the ever-expanding world of Essbase. Independents tend to be highly motivated professionals. However, the resource constraints that hold true for the medium size to boutique vendors are even more restrictive for the individual. If you hired a turkey, there is no salvaging the relationship, out he goes. Both the boutique vendors and the independents can be found in all kinds of projects both on their own and as subcontracted resources on a Big Four (Oracle Consulting Services, Ernst & Young, Deloitte, and IBM/PWC) project. Large vendors do not always have the answers, the industry is small, and the resources limited, so do not be shocked when you see an independent consultant working under the name of another company.

11.4.2.4 How Do You Choose? As with any purchase, you have to look beyond the hype. There are several avenues to help you make your decision:

- The Oracle Partner Network (OPN) lists and classifies consulting vendors by specialty and OPN level.
- The Oracle Development Tools User Group (ODTUG) KScope conference is the preeminent global Oracle EPM conference. Attend it to see the consulting presenters in action; even if you cannot go, download the presentations from their Technical Reference section in the areas in which you are interested. It can be an illuminating way to see if technical depth is really there. The URL is http://www.odtug.com and downloads are free.
- Regional seminars, whether sponsored by ODTUG, the Oracle Applications User Group, or a local consulting company.

Unless you have a truly massive global project where only the largest vendors make sense, it really is a question of balancing your limited resources (time to manage the project, money to pay the rates) with what the consulting companies offer. Keep in mind the above dictums, but always from the perspective of what a particular project is trying to accomplish. You might be pleasantly surprised with what you end up with.

11.4.3 Request for Proposal

A request for proposal (RFP) is a formal document that is used by companies when they need outside services, such as software or consulting services. In the context of this book, the request is more likely to be services than software. Writing the effective proposal is a balancing act. On one hand, the author wants to obtain enough detailed feedback so as to be comfortable with a vendor. On the other hand, the request should not be so detailed that it cannot be responded to in a reasonable time. There are many key points to remember in the proposal creation process.

11.4.3.1 Get the Right People Involved Before arriving at a solution, it is important to understand the problem. To completely understand the problem, it is important to involve the necessary resources. For an EPM system, that would include the project sponsor, IT, the pertinent departmental representatives, subject matter experts, and end users.

11.4.3.2 Define the New System Requirements Define the requirements in as much detail as possible. Distinguish between the must have features and those that are not that critical. Describe the business problem the system will address. A typical description might be: Actual sales data will be loaded weekly; the budget cycle will start in August; there will be multiple iterations; forecasts will be created in March, June and September.

Other topics may include:

- Define complex calculations.
- Research and document inbound and outbound data sources.
- Gather sample reports and input information for replacement systems.
- Define the number of users.
- Establish the project budget.
- Define the projected start and end dates.

Occasionally companies do not know what their requirements are or are unfamiliar with the software. In cases like this, consider hiring a consultant to develop the requirement documentation. The danger of this approach that needs to be acknowledged is the unscrupulous consultant might structure the requirement in his/her favor.

11.4.3.3 Identify the Recipients for the RFP EPM consulting vendors come in all sizes and skill levels, as was previously discussed. There are advantages to each. Consider issuing the RFP to a minimum of five consulting vendors including, where practical, independents. Use this opportunity to get familiar with the vendors. Short preliminary meeting with the vendors can also be used to discuss the project goals and obtain suggestions. The final RFP list of three to four vendors can be gleaned from these meetings.

11.4.3.4 Create the RFP A strong RFP should contain these components:

- Cover letter
- Table of Contents
- Introduction
- Company background
- Executive summary
- Objective of the proposal
- State the project requirements
- Company resources (including team that developed the requirement as well as personnel for the project)
- Timelines
- Selection criteria
- Qualifications and references
- The vendor should provide details with regard to:
    - Description of their development process
    - Definition of project stages
    - How milestones are determined
    - Maintenance of quality control
    - Types of testing
    - The proposed team and their qualifications
    - Proposed schedule
    - Costs and details
    - Terms and conditions

11.5 MANAGING YOUR PARTNER

Face it. it is much easier to manage a good consulting company than a bad one. Making sure you select the right one from the start will make the job of managing your partner significantly easier. After you have selected the right partner, your goal should be to effectively manage the consulting company to fully leverage its skills for the duration of the project and to also develop a strategic, long-term partnership. Finding a trustworthy partner that you can use for multiple projects will save you time, money, and stress. It is much easier to work with a partner that is proven than to take the time to locate a new one. Who wants to go through the selection process over and over and over again? Not I and neither do you.

11.5.1 Communication Is Key

It takes effort to have a successful working relationship with your partner; you have to actively manage the relationship. And, what is the foundation of a good relationship? It's COMMUNICATION. If you could only take away one piece of advice from this section on managing your partner, it should be to communicate early and clearly on your expectations of them. Do not assume or leave anything to chance. The more detailed information you give them from the start, the better the chance they have of meeting your project's goals.

In addition to your expectations, be clear on your project's objectives, success criteria, budget, resources, and timeline. The project charter contains the majority of this information and, though it will be covered more in depth later in the chapter, it is important to note that you should share it with your partner as soon as possible. They should provide feedback on the charter especially if any part of their Statement of Work (SOW) conflicts with it. Any conflicts will need to be resolved to move forward with the project. Be open and frank on any requirements you have for who they staff on your project. If you have specific requirements around skill set, technologies, years of experience, or location (i.e., if they are local or will need to travel to your site), those should be shared early, verbally, and in writing.

11.5.1.1 Handling Issues Issues within the project and with your partner should be addressed as they happen without delay. Do not risk the chance of an issue snowballing by waiting needlessly. They work for you and you should feel comfortable in communicating any concerns you have as they arise. Your partner should have a standard protocol for escalating issues and communicating concerns. Once the issue has been communicated, they should come back to you with a response in a reasonable amount of time and with a solution to resolve the issue or to prevent the issue from reoccurring.

What do you do when you have a "what have I (or my management team) done by hiring these yahoos" realization half way into the project? You have followed protocol, escalated the issue or issues, met with their management, met with your management team, and the issues still remain. Depending on how severe the problem, you may want to consider firing your partner. Obviously, this decision cannot be taken lightly and has to be done with the realization that your project will most certainly not meet its deadline and be over budget. However, if their performance is subpar and the solution is half-baked, what difference does it make anyway? There are consulting companies who claim that a large portion of their business is cleaning up other consulting companies' messes. Find one of them or review the "selecting a partner" section of this chapter again.

11.5.2 What They Should Provide You

The primary deliverable from your consulting partner is an Essbase system that works to your company's specifications. It is easy to make that statement, but quite a bit harder to actually deliver on it. Fear not, there are a series of basic project management tasks and documents that will define your company's needs, exactly what is expected of all of the project participants, and when, how, and by who project components are delivered. Your partner is responsible for and, therefore, should provide you with the following artifacts:

- Statement of Work
- Project Plan
- Design Documents
- System Documents
- Training Plan and Documents
- Status Reports

Though partners can provide the following documents, its best that you take the lead and they assist you with creating or refining the:

- Project Charter (discussed later in the chapter)
- Requirements Document

11.5.2.1 Statement of Work (SOW) The first document a consulting company must produce is a SOW that describes at a high level the what, how, and when of the Essbase project. The SOW is also the consulting company's proposal in response to your company's RFP and, in addition, a SOW often stands in as the contract and, thus, is the controlling document for all disputes. If you do accept a consulting company's bid, carefully review the SOW to ensure that it is satisfactory or negotiate necessary changes before it is signed.

While the SOW is a high-level document, the project plan is the mechanism that maps the SOW's milestones and deliverables against specific tasks and resources. Who manages the plan is dependent on the particulars of your organization and the project, but unless the consultants are there as staff augmentation, they are the practice experts and they should produce a plan. There are several common project planning pitfalls that are to be avoided to deliver Essbase on time while meeting budget. No one purposely creates a plan doomed to fail, but circumstances and resource pressure can make good plans go bad quickly. The following are points to consider in the development and management of the project plan:

1. Do not overload resources to make the plan hit a deadline. If a task takes 40 hours, is scheduled over 5 calendar days, and for internal reasons you need it to happen in 2 calendar days, making a resource work 20 hours per day is not a practical way to meet the date. Allocate additional resources to the task or reschedule the start dates to meet the date.
2. The consulting company will have a template plan that will typically be modified to suit your project. As that modification occurs, there may be conflicts between the efforts required to complete the tasks as defined in the SOW with the resources available. Upon examination, if a task truly does take longer than anticipated, pretending that it will not just means that the plan has an even more tenuous relationship with reality than plans usually do. Both the consulting

vendor and you, the client's representative, need to acknowledge reality. This will result in either allocating more money for the necessary resources or negotiating removing something from the plan and re-allocating those resources.
3. For whatever reason, the project is behind schedule. The drop-dead date has not changed. The easy way to make the remaining tasks within the timeframe is to state that, despite previously agreed upon durations, the tasks will now face 50% less time. If the estimates of task duration were good, how will these tasks be accomplished in less time? Everyone already knows the answer; those tasks will not magically complete in less time. Once again, you must either negotiate a compromise on deliverables or allocate more money to bring in more project resources.

11.5.3 Business Requirements Document

A Business Requirements Document (BRD) is a document used in a project to define in detail what needs to be done in the solution to meet the project objectives. Though clients tend to want to shun the responsibility of creating the BRD and pass it to the consultants, it should be created and owned by you. It details the features and functionality within the proposed solution. More likely than not, your organization has a BRD template. This does not mean that it is any good or that it will meet the needs of your project and facilitate your getting solid requirements. Because business users will need to sign off on it, the BRD has to be written in such a way that the business users who do not have technical knowledge can easily understand it. It is important to keep the BRD free of too much techno speak. The building of the BRD should be a collaborative effort between you, the users, and the stakeholders.

The key components of an Essbase project's BRD:

- Functional requirements
- Data requirements
- Data-cleansing requirements (if known by the time the BRD is constructed)
- Reporting requirements
- Performance ranges
- Security
- Availability of application

Investing the time to create a thorough and complete BRD saves time and money. Much like the project charter keeps the project manager on task throughout the project and answers the various questions that develop over time, the BRD does the same for the development team. With a proper BRD, the development team will have 90% of their business questions answered before they even start the project work. With a robust BRD, the Technical Design Document (TDD) creation can begin immediately.

11.5.3.1 Technical Design Document The TDD is supplied by your partner. While you will still rely on the project plan for task identification and time duration, you must marry those up against the Essbase project's design document to determine if the project plan comprehensively addresses all of the project deliverables. This discussion is predicated on traditional waterfall methodology. Given the more mainstream approach, a TDD should identify:

- Application goals and objectives
- Reporting requirements

- Proposed dimensionality
- Data sources and elements
- Extract, transform, and loading processes both into and out of Essbase
- Automation requirements
- Security model
- Calculation requirements
- Input form requirements
- Supporting technology used for the solution, e.g., Studio, ODI, Dodeca, etc.

11.5.3.2 Status Reports Any consulting company worth their weight should provide timely, periodic status reports. Do not allow the Status Reports to be your only form of communication with your partner. Insist on periodic reviews of actual deliverables even if they are in development. Sit down and spend some time each week face-to-face.

11.5.3.3 Expertise and Knowledge Transfer You hired consultants, not contractors. This is important because, just like this book, consultants tell you *why* they do a task in a particular way. In this spirit, do not be afraid to ask the consultant for his professional opinion on your project's team composition, communications plan, resources, project plan, and any other questions you may have. They have watched this before, made the mistakes, and are not anxious to repeat the experience. This is all part of the knowledge transfer that was part of your RFP.

Knowledge transfer should happen throughout the project. As the consultants are designing, building, and testing, you and your team should be learning. Do not wait until the solution is delivered, and pour over the system documentation. Unless your system is extremely simple, system documentation cannot substitute for learning during the project. Knowledge transfer should be planned and deliberate. Good consultants should be able to explain why and how they are doing something without excessive jargon and without giving you the run-around. Delaying knowledge transfer can lead to unnecessary expense by keeping consultants onsite longer than needed as a security blanket and can generate vendor dependence.

11.5.3.4 System Documentation System documentation can be a bit of a sham if not handled in a focused manner. Forests have been sacrificed to the idea of voluminous documentation that rarely is read if ever. You need to define what system documents must show and keep that list short. Once documentation is provided, a commitment should be made and a plan developed to keep it current. Documentation should include:

- A complete listing of data and metadata elements
- Descriptions of what code routines do, where, and *why* (once armed with this information, a dissection of each code block is not necessary)
- Data flow diagrams
- Description of forms
- Description of calculations and business rules
- The automation schedule
- The automation scripts
- Security

11.5.3.5 Training Plan and Documents In contrast to system documentation, training documents will be read en masse when the system is implemented and singly or in groups on an ongoing basis as users adopt the system. At a minimum, training documents must include:

- A description of data and metadata sources (for background and in simple business terms)
- A calculation overview (in business terms, do not show MDX (multidimensional expressions) statements if written in MDX, provide the information in plain English)
- Dimensionality
- Connection, retrieve, and submit (if it is a write-back implementation) instructions
- Reports: Their description and how to access
- Security model

11.5.4 Success or Failure Is Your Responsibility

In the end, consultants work at your company's bidding. The consultants are looking for you to be the day-to-day agent of the business's requirements. Ensure that the consultants are implementing the right solution to your pain point by requiring the documents and advice detailed above. If you define your requirements explicitly, review documentation closely, and actively participate in the management of the plan, we will not need to wish you luck. You will have made your own.

11.6 MANAGING EXPECTATIONS

It is a term we often hear when having to deliver services to our internal customers. "We need to manage the clients' expectations." But, what does that really mean? Expectations are your customers' perceptions of how the system needs to perform and provide value. These expectations can ultimately define your success or failure within the organization and because of their enormous impact on you and your career, expectations cannot be left to chance and need to be managed. It is imperative that you understand and moreover meet or even exceed these expectations to be successful. It is a common mistake to "assume" you know what your customers are thinking. You do not.

Having a clear understanding of your clients' expectations of you and the system is key to project success. Listen to their story and hear what they are really saying. Their expectations can be unrealistic, like pie in the sky or castles in the air. Your job is to bring them back down to Earth, but gently. This deflation of dreams can be mitigated if frank discussions are had up front about what is expected. It is as literal (and simple) as asking, "What are your expectations of the system?" Sometimes they will tell you; sometimes you will have to pull it out of them.

Their expectations can be influenced by a number of factors including you, your peers, your predecessor, and your manager; their prior experience at different organizations; their perceived knowledge; and a whole host of other factors. It is impossible to control or cover these influences. What you can do is understand why they have these expectations. Once understood, you can bring them back to reality to define more realistic opportunities by educating them about the greatness and limitations of Essbase, communicating often during the process, and explaining why. Do this as early as possible in the project because expectations become more solidified the longer they are not addressed. The act of expectation setting should be a give and take discussion until both parties are reasonably satisfied. Do not forget that expectations can change over time, therefore, you should monitor them periodically to ensure you and your customers are on the same page.

11.6.1 Service Level Agreement

The Service Level Agreement (SLA) formalizes some of these expectations. An SLA is a formal contract that sets expectations, priorities, and clarifies responsibilities, in measurable terms, between you and your customers by setting the criteria and standard for service. The SLA may include things like:

- What percentage of the time services will be available
- What times the system is down for maintenance
- Number of users that can be served simultaneously
- Specific performance benchmarks to which actual performance will be periodically compared like retrieval times and calculation times
- Turnaround times for processing security requests
- Turnaround times for creation of new report
- Turnaround times for changes to a report
- Turnaround times for hierarchy changes
- Data is refresh frequency from source systems

When negotiating SLAs, consider what you can control versus what you cannot. If you are using shared resources, it can be difficult and dangerous to commit to definite performance metrics. Be open and honest on what you can commit to and what you cannot. If you are creating an ad hoc environment, frame your commitment carefully. Because you cannot control what will be queried, it will be difficult to guarantee specific performance SLAs. We told you that clients can be unrealistic, but guess what? You can be as well. In other words, do yourself a favor, do not over commit.

An SLA can be as detailed as you and your customer believe it needs to be to properly address expectations. The SLA should be treated as a living document that can and should be refined and amended as needed. The management aspect of the SLA should not be overlooked and the following also should be defined in the document:

- How will service effectiveness be tracked?
- How will information about service effectiveness be reported and addressed?
- How will service-related disagreements be resolved?
- How will the parties review and revise the agreement?

It also is important to have SLAs with IT. The same principle applies where it should be mutually agreed upon. SLAs with IT are extremely important because they will affect fulfilling your customer SLAs. These SLAs typically revolve around delivery of data through ETL, up-time of shared platforms, and maintenance windows.

11.7 MANAGING THE PROJECT

You have completed your preproject tasks and you have selected a partner and/or built your internal team. Now, the real fun begins: managing the project. Many Hyperion managers and Essbase Developers hate project management. Project management is not fun; some would even call it boring. It is often a necessary evil so that you can successfully make Essbase do things that cause everyone to "ooh" and "ahh" at what is being built. Unfortunately, the cool stuff is only part of the job. Our role as an internal consultant encompasses much more than our technical expertise and requires us to take on roles, such as change management and project management. Who wants to do that? I am not going to try to convince you this is a fantastic part of your job or that it is easy. It is not. But, as was said before, its successful execution means that you actually get to build that "oh, so wonderful Essbase application that my company can never live without" and it does not necessarily have to be painful. Given how much you are impacted by the successful delivery of a project, you need to be good at project management even if you do not like it. Hopefully, the next few sections will give you the tools needed for a strong foundation on managing your Essbase project. Even if you are not the official project manager, it is important for you to understand the principles of effective project management.

11.7.1 If You Fail to Plan, You Are Planning to Fail

The common theme that can be stated regarding any company's decision to implement an Essbase solution is that effective project management and project planning techniques are vital to achieve success. How the project will be managed cannot be an afterthought and, no, not just anybody in the organization can do it despite what your management says. Regardless of what you may have heard from your manager, a formal plan to manage the project is not and should not be optional. I am not implying you have to have a PMP (Project Management Professional) certification, but you do have to have the time and a solid understanding of project management techniques to ensure that the schedule, resources, cost, scope, and quality of the project are properly managed.

There are a few basic items you should always know about the project you are managing. This information will help you steer the project away from failure and will be a huge force in ensuring its success. The success factors are discussed next.

11.7.2 Baseline Definitions

Baseline definitions include:

- Project objectives are well defined and documented.
- Project requirements are well defined and documented.
- Project roles and responsibilities are clearly defined, and accepted by all parties involved.
- Project baseline (cost and time) is known.

11.7.3 Active Management

Active management is essential to success. You or the project manager:

- Are able to describe how much work has been completed to date on the project, how much remaining work there is to complete on the project, and if there is a variance (includes scope, schedule and costs).
- Are able to describe known issues and risks facing the project and what the plans are for resolution or mitigation.

11.7.4 The Project Charter

The project charter, a document created by the company that defines the objectives and scope of the project that is signed by key stakeholders authorizing the project, acts as a mechanism to describe the four baseline definitions described previously.

It must identify the reasons for undertaking the project along with its constraints, risks, assumptions, benefits, budget, major deliverables and milestones, out of scope work, sponsor and stakeholders, and how the project is executed.

11.7.4.1 Why a Project Charter Why should you have a project charter? The project charter is your target and your license for the project. The project charter is used to document agreed upon objectives, authorize the project, and to manage scope. It provides a reference document to make sure everyone is on the same page farther down the road during the project. Think of it as your measuring stick that you can use to beat people up with later. Having a clear idea of the purpose of the project and the desired outcome is an important success factor in your project.

11.7.4.2 Ownership Though the components of the charter have input from many stakeholders, it is owned by the project sponsor. When the finance manager says you need to add this functionality to the system and it is not in scope then—BAM! You whip out the project charter. It is not bulletproof, but can be invaluable in preventing you from "harming" someone at your organization. And, that alone makes it worth its weight in gold.

11.7.5 What You Need to Know

Here are some practical questions that will assist you in constructing a well-defined project charter document. The answers to the questions in Table 11.1 are not required for a successful, solid charter, but will give you a great starting point.

Each of these areas within the charter is important in their own right, but a few of the areas need further analysis and discussion. These areas are roles, scope, milestones, risks, change control, project governance, and the communication plan.

11.7.5.1 Roles While the definition of roles is essential, understand that one person may play multiple roles in the project. In some projects, the team may not be large enough to have a different person for each role. The important thing to remember is that each "function" needs to be identified as the responsibility of someone, even if they are not called by that role.

- Project Sponsor: Individual who acquires project funding and provides support and tactical guidance to the project manager.
- Project Manager (PM): Individual who manages the project to achieve project objectives.
- Project Management Team: Individuals who participate in project management activities.
- Project Team: Individuals who perform activities and tasks defined for the project in support of project objectives.
- Stakeholder Group: Individuals or groups who represent the vested interest of their group on a project.
- Project Steering Group: Provides guidance and decisions regarding project direction and changes affecting project outcomes, which includes resolution of escalated issues, risks and conflicts. Depending on the size of the organization, this might be the project sponsor.
- Project Change Control Board: Has decision-making authority on resolution of major impact Project Change Requests. Depending on the organization, this might be the project steering group.

Table 11.1 Key Questions to Create a Charter Document

Project Charter Section	Questions to Ask	Did We Do It (Y/N)?
Project Purpose/Goal/ Objectives	Why are we undertaking this project? What is the project's purpose? What are the main objectives of this project? What business issue are we addressing with this project? What business problem are we solving? Are the goals SMART: specific, measurable, achievable, relevant, and time-lined?	
Scope	Exactly, what is in scope for this project? What is out of scope? What is the required functionality of the system? What are the nice to haves that can be addressed later?	
Anticipated Benefits	What will we gain by undertaking this project? What are the tangible qualitative and quantitative benefits to the organization? What are the intangible benefits to the organization? How will these be measured throughout the project?	
Roles and Responsibilities/Staffing	Who are the key stakeholders that can both positively and negatively affect the project? What are their roles? Who are the internal resources that will be dedicated to this project? Will they be part-time or full-time? How many hours can they dedicate to this project? Who is responsible for what? Are these clearly defined? Is the project complex where a responsibility assignment matrix (RACI) is needed? Who are in the following standard roles and groups for the project: executive sponsor, project manager, steering committee, project management team, project team, change control board?	
Milestones	What are the major deliverables for this project?	
Estimated Project Schedule	When does the solution have to be completed? What is the timeline for the major milestones?	
Assumptions/ Dependencies	What key assumptions are being made that may impact the ability to execute the project as planned? Are there assumptions that are being made in relation to staff, cost, time, or resources? Is this projected dependent on the outcome of another project or other projects?	
Risks	What are the risks associated with this project? What are the levels of the risk: high, medium, low? What obstacles are present that can potentially affect the success of the project? What are the response plans for mitigation of risks?	
Success Criteria	What constitutes that this project is a success? How is this measured?	
Change Control	How will changes to the charter and/or the project plan be managed? Who has the authority to approve changes?	

(Continued)

Table 11.1 (*Continued*) Key Questions to Create a Charter Document

Project Charter Section	Questions to Ask	Did We Do It (Y/N)?
Project Governance	Who has the authority to approve changes in scope (inclusive of time or cost)? Who is responsible for issue and risk management? How will risks and issues escalate if they remain unresolved?	
Communication Plan	What is the communication plan for project? How should communications between stakeholders be performed?	
Financial Targets	What is the overall budget for this project?	

11.7.6 Scope

Scope is typically defined in your project charter and your business requirements document. Your project charter is your high-level overview of the scope, and your business requirements document help define the detailed scope. Cleary defined scope will save you from the hell of a never-ending project and from the *evil of scope creep*. The importance of a well-defined scope cannot be stressed enough because, without it, your Essbase project will grow until it cannot be done on time or within budget. It is human nature to want more, and a clear scope definition is essential to curb this inclination and achieve success. It needs to be written in such a way that it will be absolutely clear if extra work is added later in the project. If I could put it in flashing lights for you in this book, believe me I would. The scope statement has two components: the deliverables and the boundaries. It is very common to see the deliverables within a scope statement defined in terms of functionality, i.e., system will support alternate hierarchies, system will calculate these metrics, etc. With Essbase projects, it is important also to define scope in terms of boundaries: What specific data elements and their sources will be included? Not defining this aspect can add significant time and effort that may not be readily apparent.

11.7.7 Milestones

Key points along the project plan are often referred to as milestones. The main objective of establishing milestones is to provide a measurement of the project's progress and success, and to allow early re-assessment of the ability to meet essential timelines. This measurement not only assists you in determining the project status, but also provides critical management-level information for assessing the successful completion of the project.

You can take a couple of approaches to creating the project milestones. For an Essbase project, a suitable approach is to organize milestones around functional components. As you review the deliverables and activities in the project plan, identify milestones based on the completion or start of a group of related activities that are designed to deliver a portion of functionality.

11.7.8 Communication Plan

A well-planned project has a well-planned communication strategy. A regular communication schedule will help to ensure that everyone remains engaged and informed throughout the project. The communications plan will identify information you will need to communicate to project stakeholders and also gather information that you will require inwardly from project stakeholders. The communication plan also defines:

- The recipient
- The delivery method
- The content
- The frequency

Just like in a strong marriage, communication is one of the pillars of a good project. The information in Table 11.2 is an example of a basic communication matrix.

A more complex matrix might have additional information, such as who is delivering and developing the communication vehicle and what inputs are needed to produce the communication. It also might have distribution information for the assumption logs, issues logs, and updated project plans.

The communication plan should include as well a listing of all the communication vehicles and what they provide. Table 11.3 provides a sample of communication vehicles.

11.7.9 Project Governance

Project governance is the structure within which project decisions are made and, therefore, is closely tied to Roles and Responsibilities and the Communication Plan. It describes the necessary processes and controls that are required for a project to be successful. The communication plan addresses how these parties should interchange information. As previously mentioned, the project steering group provides guidance and decisions regarding project direction and changes affecting project outcomes that may include resolution of escalated issues, risks and conflicts.

11.7.10 Risks

Project risks are circumstances or events that exist outside of the control of the project team and will have an adverse impact on the project if they occur. In other words, an issue is a current problem that must be dealt with. A risk is a potential future problem that has not yet occurred. All projects contain some risk. Risk may be impossible to completely eliminate, but it can be anticipated and managed, thereby reducing the probability that they will occur and minimizing their impact if they do. Risks that have a medium-to-high probability of occurring with a high negative impact should be documented and tracked. For each risk listed, identify activities to perform to eliminate or mitigate the risk. As changes to a given risk occur, they should be logged in the Risk, Assumptions, Issues, and Dependencies log as noted in the next section.

11.7.11 Change and Change Control

You must plan and expect change during a project. Implementations are unpredictable events. Accept that plans will change and you will need to change as required while holding on to your original goals. Planning is a continuous cycle; the more you learn about a project, the more accurate the scope, time and cost planning for the project becomes. There are updates to work that need to be replanned, risks that need to be managed, and changes that need to be analyzed and incorporated into a project plan, if approved.

Changes must be logged and reviewed/approved by a Change Control Board and tracked in project meetings. The log should cover the following information: Change number, Change date, Change description, Status (approved, not approved or deferred), Current status or Resolution, and Closed date.

Table 11.2 Basic Communication Matrix Example

Communication Vehicle	Who/Target	Purpose	When/Frequency	Type/Method
Project kickoff	All stakeholders	Communicate plans and stakeholder roles/responsibilities Encourage communication among stakeholders	At or near project start date	Meeting
Status reports	All stakeholders and project office	Update stakeholders on progress of the project	Regularly scheduled Monthly is recommended for large/midsize projects	Email
Status meetings	Entire project team	To review detailed plans (tasks, assignments, and action items)	Regularly scheduled Weekly is recommended for entire team	Meeting
Weekly executive status and report	Project advisory group and project manager	Update project steering on status and discuss critical issues; work through issues and change requests here before escalating to the Sponsor(s)	Regularly scheduled	Meeting/Email
Executive sponsor meetings	Executive sponsor(s) and project manager	Update sponsor(s) on status and discuss critical issues; seek approval for changes to project plan	Not regularly scheduled As needed when issues cannot be resolved or changes need to be made to project plan	Meeting

Table 11.3 Communication Vehicle List

Communication Vehicle	Description
Status Reports	This report will present the past week's activity and the planned activity for the current week.
Weekly Executive Status Report	This report will summarize the current project status for each key area of the project.
Issues Log	All issues that have been submitted via an Issue Submission Form on or before the close of business the previous Friday will be included in the Issue Log for review.
Scope Change Request Log	All changes in scope requested on or before the close of business the previous Friday will be included in the Scope Change Log for Review.
Weekly Status Meetings	To review detailed plans (tasks, assignments, and action items). Updates to all existing Issues and Scope Change requests are due at the Weekly Meeting. Any Issue or Scope Change request that has gone unresolved for more than two weeks will be elevated to the Executive Steering Committee for resolution.

11.7.12 Project Execution and Monitoring

During execution of the project, you and/or the PM should be doing the following:

- Report on the progress of the project.
- Meet with stakeholders to keep them informed about the project and its progress.
- Ensure project is on track and in control as planned in the project management plan and project baseline.
- Identify possible changes to the project.
- Assess proposed changes to the project.
- Identify corrective actions.
- Identify areas for improvement and recognize items that went well, documenting these as lessons learned and taking any corrective actions if necessary (this should be performed throughout the project and not only at the end).

Monitoring the project's progress against plan is critical so that the health of the project can be accurately assessed and reported. Proper monitoring will address the last two success factors in managing your project: how much work has been completed and describe known issues and risks facing the project. Progress should be analyzed and monitored considering all aspects of the project's scope, timeline, financials, resources, risk, quality, and communications. Once the project has begun, monitoring becomes a continuous cycle of work, progress measurement, status reporting, corrective action, and more work.

11.7.12.1 Status Reporting Project Status reporting provides information to help ensure projects are delivered on time and on budget with the specified quality. Project status reports should seek to:

- Provide an early warning system to team members that allow them to adjust their work effort accordingly.
- Provide information to help ensure projects are delivered on time and on budget with the specified quality.
- Provide an assessment of program and project performance on an ongoing basis relative to plans, objectives, staffing, and life balancing.

- Foster the identification of corrective strategies to deal with issues identified during the assessment which, if left unchecked, could undermine the likelihood of success.
- Help project teams anticipate and minimize the occurrence of any situation that reduces project value.

Project Status Reports should contain the following items (see Figure 11.1 and Figure 11.2 for samples):

Project Status Report

Project STATUS OVERVIEW						
Project Name				Where are we?		Notes
				Performance to Budget Cost	GREEN	
Project Manager				Performance to Plan	YELLOW	
Executive Sponsor				Project Risks	GREEN	
Planned Start Date		Actual Start Date		Issue Resolution	RED	
Planned End Date		Forecast End Date		Dependencies	GREEN	

BUDGET STATUS OVERVIEW	Project Budget
Planned Spend to Date	
Actual Spend to Date	
Variance	
Status Indicator	GREEN
Comments	

* *Green – On track, Yellow – Issues being managed, Red – Requires attention*

8

Figure 11.1 Status Report template.

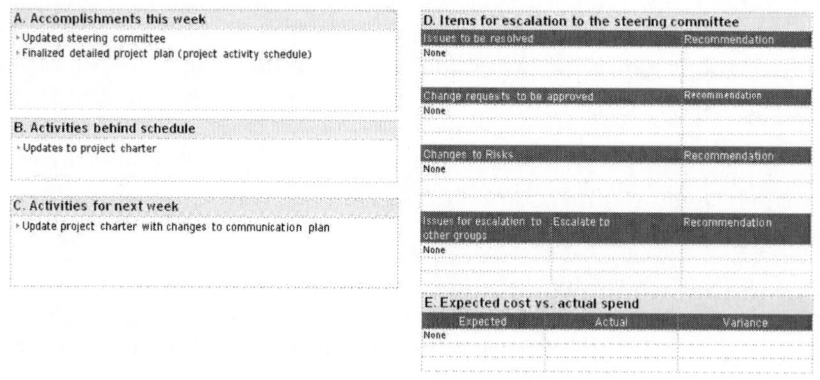
Status Report Page 2

As of [date]

A. Accomplishments this week
- Updated steering committee
- Finalized detailed project plan (project activity schedule)

B. Activities behind schedule
- Updates to project charter

C. Activities for next week
- Update project charter with changes to communication plan

D. Items for escalation to the steering committee

Issues to be resolved	Recommendation
None	

Change requests to be approved	Recommendation
None	

Changes to Risks	Recommendation
None	

Issues for escalation to other groups	Escalate to	Recommendation
None		

E. Expected cost vs. actual spend

Expected	Actual	Variance
None		

Figure 11.2 Status Report template (page 2).

- Project Health: Summary of the project's health status (e.g., Cost, Schedule, Scope, Resource); this is derived from the individual status reports submitted by the team members to the team lead or project manager.
- Project Progress Assessments: Narrative overview of project status including accomplishments, future plans, and barriers to completion (e.g., the Executive Summary).
- Issues: Summary of any issues that have been identified, are open, have been resolved, or have been rejected.
- Risks: Summary of any risks pertaining to the project(s).
- Change Requests: Summary of any change requests that have been identified, have been resolved or have been rejected.
- Deliverables: Summary of any deliverables that have been created, completed, or removed from the scope of the project.
- Milestones: Summary of any progress milestones, such as milestones description, milestone status, milestone due date, and milestones estimate to complete.
- Project Metrics: Summary of any progress metrics, such as earned value, SPI, CPI, and projected completion date, and effort specific metrics, such as hours per program, lines of code, system down time, and fatal errors on development projects (as applicable).
- Expense to budget report and graph with stoplight features:
  - Green is used when the project or key area is on track and in control
  - Yellow is used when the project or key area is not on track but in control
  - Red is used when the project or key area is not on track and not in control

11.7.12.2 Risks, Assumptions, Issues, and Dependencies (RAID) Log It is standard fare to keep an issues log during a project. The RAID log might seem like overkill in a small project, but it is one of the key tools in managing critical issues. A RAID log records the decisions made on the project, serves as a good reference when future decisions are being considered, and is a source of information when the project is reviewed. Typically, issues arise in one or more of the following areas: budget, schedule, resources, or quality of work. In the RAID log (Figure 11.3), every issue must be dated, described, and assigned to a person who has the responsibility for its resolution. At the end of the

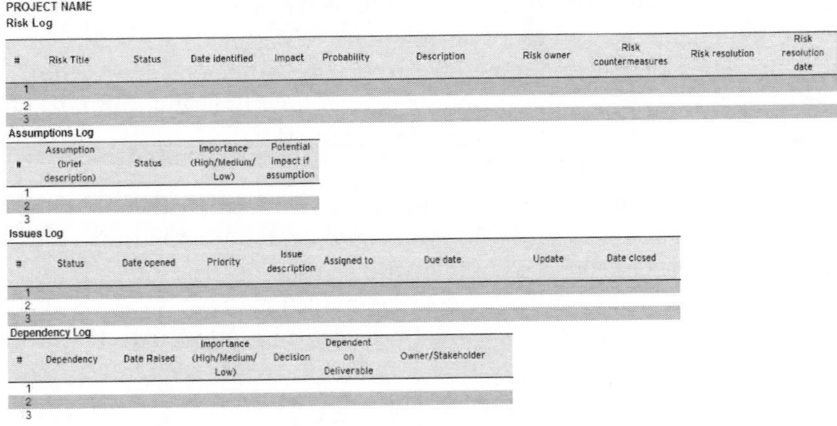
PROJECT NAME

Risk Log

#	Risk Title	Status	Date identified	Impact	Probability	Description	Risk owner	Risk countermeasures	Risk resolution	Risk resolution date
1										
2										
3										

Assumptions Log

#	Assumption (brief description)	Status	Importance (High/Medium/ Low)	Potential impact if assumption
1				
2				
3				

Issues Log

#	Status	Date opened	Priority	Issue description	Assigned to	Due date	Update	Date closed
1								
2								
3								

Dependency Log

#	Dependency	Date Raised	Importance (High/Medium/ Low)	Decision	Dependent on Deliverable	Owner/Stakeholder
1						
2						
3						

Figure 11.3 Sample RAID log.

project, all issues must have a resolution, even if that resolution is punted to a future phase. Some issues are minor and can be resolved without impact on the project. Other issues can turn into risks or change requests and have to be dealt with accordingly. Therefore, managing issues includes understanding the impact of an issue and change control.

11.7.13 Avoid Skimping on These Areas

11.7.13.1 System Testing and User Acceptance Testing System Testing and User Acceptance Testing (UAT) phases typically involve:

- Formal test plan
- Unit tests (Does it work?)
- Integration tests (Does the new system work with what is already there?)
- Performance tests
- Quality Assurance tests
- User Acceptance tests (Does the application work?)

Formal testing is often honored more in the breach than in the observance. There is often a strong temptation to skip on this step for time, resource, or budgetary reasons. Do not do it. Painful experience has revealed that 100-hour work weeks on your "go live" week to work on fixes or (worse yet) users throwing their hands up and saying that they give up because it just doesn't work can be the results of inadequate testing. Do not willingly incite customer mutiny. This would be a bad thing.

11.7.13.2 Training How will the lack of training or improper training hurt? A common angst will be annoying user calls regarding things that seem so obvious to you and could have been addressed with good training. During training, make sure that special care is taken to educate SMEs over and above the standard user. They will pass the word, and they will be able to take care of a lot of the questions and traffic that would otherwise come your way.

11.7.13.3 Documentation Will you regret not doing this? Yes, you will. It will be late at night and something looks wrong with one of the loads and, instead of focusing on the real issue, you get stuck for two hours trying to figure how or why the Load rules were written the way they were. Great care should be taken to document Load rules and Dimensional build rules as well as all calculations. What made sense at the time you were doing the development (for some obscure reason you came across in discovery) will be far from your memory three months later. You will need a reminder, and that reminder is a thorough and complete set of documentation.

11.7.13.4 Automation Are you really trying to kill yourself with boredom doing a series of clicks to load and calc data when you could be doing something entirely more productive? There is absolutely no point in owning a state-of-the-art OLAP (online analytical processing) tool that you then have to manually handle every input and extract. A great deal of the system processes should be able to be automated. If you find that you are doing an excessive amount of things manually, reach back to your consulting partner for suggestions. Often, they may end up leaving before this step is complete and sometimes before it is even started. Reach back to them if you need ideas on how this should work.

11.7.13.5 Backup/Recovery Skimp on it and you will SEVERELY pay for this later if, heaven forbid, a user runs a clear script by accident or a freak storm hits your data center. Believe me on this subject even if you disregard the rest of this chapter. Oracle produces a backup guide—get it, read it, understand it, and backup those databases, BSO and ASO. Supporting files and data sources would probably be a good idea as well. Backup and recovery is covered in Chapter 1 (Building the Foundation: Essbase Infrastructure). Check it out for some great information around this topic.

11.7.14 Who Is the PM?

It might be very tempting to cede project manager duties to your partner. Don't do it. If you want them to be a note taker, then have at it. They can take notes. Outside of that, you or someone in your organization needs to handle the project manager duties of monitoring the project deliverables, milestones, resources, timeframes, risks, issues, budget, and dependencies, along with keeping the project on track. Remember, no matter how conscientious your partner is, you are one of a long stream of clients; if this one goes south, he or she will just go on to the next one. In contrast, this is your job, your project, and your potential state of unemployment. Who is more committed? Observe the consultants, learn from them where possible, ask for their advice, but *you* be in control as this project's success or failure will directly impact you.

11.7.15 Tips for a Successful Project (Besides Everything I Already Told You)

Here are some practical tips for a winning project:

- Keep your business users involved and engaged to garner enthusiasm and buy-in.
- Do not simply replace a report with a solution, look to add value.
- Allow for some change to business requirements (*This Is Not The Same As A Change In Scope*).
- Have business users build reports. This engages them directly and a business user not being able to build a report because data elements are missing from a design is courting disaster.

11.7.16 Why Do Projects Fail?

And, now the top 11 reasons Essbase projects (or any project for that matter) fail. Yes, another flashing lights moment.

1. Lack of management commitment
2. Lack of business/user participation and buy-in
3. Imposed, unrealistic schedule
4. Unrealistic scope for the schedule
5. Unrealistic budget
6. Unrealistic expectations
7. Untrained or unavailable staff
8. Constantly changing business requirements
9. Ineffective project management
10. Scope creep
11. Bad source data

Are any of these a surprise? They should not be and the information in the preceding pages in this chapter should have mitigated any of these from happening to you.

11.7.16.1 A Special Note about Lack of Business/User Participation and Buy-in Lack of business user participation and buy-in leads to low user adoption. This is a fate that has been suffered by many an organization and can turn the Essbase system you slaved over into shelf-ware. Why does this seem to happen frequently? We mentioned earlier in the chapter the need to have end users involved throughout the project. It is critical to having a strong user adoption. Also, management needs to stress the importance of the new system. Management needs to be clear that the new system is not optional and needs to be utilized. A strong message from the right executive can make a world of difference. And, finally, turn the old system off. Shut it down. Burn it down. Do whatever is necessary to keep users from logging into the old system. Users tend to be technologically lazy and if given a choice would prefer to perform 50 steps over and over versus using 1% of their brain power to learn the 10 steps in the new system.

11.8 POST GO-LIVE TASKS AND CONSIDERATIONS

11.8.1 Lessons Learned

Lessons learned are an effective way of getting quality feedback to improve your performance on future phases and future projects. A good practice is to have the PM participate as a member of the project team when conducting lessons learned sessions. Ask someone who did not manage the project to facilitate and run the session so that the team members feel open about providing honest feedback about the project's successes and challenges. There may be some temptation to politically spin the results. Be the first to lay bare your soul. Confession is good and this will engender an atmosphere of frankness and honesty.

The following questions should be asked in each of the following areas: project management, risk management, scope control, issue resolution, communication, and team dynamics:

- What worked well and why?
- What did not work well and why?
- What could be done better next time?
- What did we miss doing that we should have done?

From the lessons learned, you should be able to walk away with:

- What went well that should be replicated?
- What should be added?
- What should be avoided?
- What should be improved?

This is also a good time to note functionality or data that did not make it into the project. Should there be a Phase II?

11.8.2 End User Training

It is easy to overlook on-going training. Toward the end of a project, mass training is rolled out to prepare users for the new system before go-live. But what happens after go-live? Three months later? Or even a year later? Users will leave, new employees will be hired, and colleagues will change roles. If there is not a training plan for post go-live, you will either spend a lot of time doing one-on-one training sessions or troubleshooting user errors and fielding annoying questions that you really do not have time to answer. When developing your training, do yourself a favor and plan for the future.

11.8.3 Troubleshooting

So, where do you go for help if you need it when the DBAG has failed you yet again? You have a myriad of resources at your fingertips including some you might not have even known were available to you:

- If you suspect a bug, release notes for later versions
- Network 54
- OTN
- Blogs
- Knowledge base on Oracle Support Web site
- My handy-dandy network of fellow Essbase developers and Admins
- My consulting partner (this goes to the top of the list if I am still under a support agreement with them)
- Open an Oracle Support ticket

11.9 IT IS ALL ABOUT YOU

Managing and working with any Essbase development project can be the most rewarding aspect of your job. The fulfillment that development projects provide causes the dealing with production issues, doing performance tuning, or performing day-to-day administrative tasks to pale in comparison. Development projects break up the monotony of being an administrator and keep things exciting while giving you opportunities to grow technically and be innovative, all while furthering your career.

We hope this chapter has given you some new insights into taking your career above and beyond mere administrative tasks. When these career development opportunities arise (and they will), grasp these tools and use them to significantly increase your success.

POSTSCRIPT

Did you really read this book all the way through and finally arrive here? You are one patient and thorough geek. Or are you the nonsequential sort who drinks way too much coffee and are thus reading this last bit out of order? No matter. If you read even one chapter, I will wager that at least a few new ideas and techniques came your way. The authors of this book certainly learned a lot in the writing, and we are ostensibly all experts.

Will *Developing Essbase Applications: Advanced Techniques for Finance and IT Professionals* be the only advanced Essbase book there will ever be? I hope not for two reasons: length and diversity. Each topic could have been a book in its own right and you are reading (or have read, depending on your character) what we could fit into a chapter. Additionally, while I would back my coauthors against all comers, we do not have a lock on all Essbase knowledge. There are bound to be differing opinions and approaches to good Essbase practices.

Happily, there are other venues for spreading and learning knowledge. You have likely seen many of the writers of this book on Essbase message boards, blogs, and conferences where we spread the magic of Essbase. That desire to share knowledge is what led to this book. I encourage you to harness your own enthusiasm and answer that question, create the new must-read blog, and present what you know to the world.

The physicist Richard Feynman wrote, "I was born not knowing and have had only a little time to change that here and there." I hope this book helped you a little with knowing more about Essbase.

INDEX

J

K

L

N

O

Q

R